MICHIGAN:

CHAMPIONS OF THE WEST

BRUCE MADEJ
WITH

ROB TOONKEL
MIKE PEARSON
—AND—
GREG KINNEY

SPORTS PUBLISHING
A DIVISION OF SAGAMORE PUBLISHING
Champaign, Illinois

Book layout: Susan M. McKinney, Jennifer L. Polson and Anne E. Kolodziej
Editor: Susan M. McKinney
Interior design: Deborah M. Bellaire

Library of Congress Number: 97-61764
ISBN: 1-57167-115-3

We have made every effort to trace the ownership of copyrighted photos. If we have failed to give adequate credit, we will be pleased to make changes in future printings.

Printed in the United States.

If you play or follow sports, for the sake of sports alone, not money or fame, one can truly learn the joys of life through sport. I dedicate this book to those who allowed me to remain a kid at heart and follow sports since I was a pre-school child to this very day.

To my mother, Sally, and father, Bill, my brother, Richard, and my Uncle Louis for putting up with me in my early years. To the joys of my life — my three boys—Mike, John and Billy and my wife, Suzette; these are my "Champions" who make the important "Moments" I will forever cherish. — *Bruce Madej*

To my parents and family: the definition of creators. To Tom, Nico, Bob, Joel, Gary, Barb and Jeff: the definition of builders. To Amy, Andy, Anne, Avi, Lanya, Sara and Sue: the definition of support. And to the University of Michigan: the definition of success. — *Rob Toonkel*

To my wife, Laura, and my children—Tony, Tom, Paige and Parker—God's special gifts to me. — *Mike Pearson*

To my sisters and brothers spread across the country, and now across the ocean, who are becoming Michigan fans despite themselves. — *Greg Kinney*

SPECIAL THANKS TO THE FOLLOWING FOR THEIR SUPPORT OF UNIVERSITY OF MICHIGAN ATHLETICS.

Chelsea Office Supply
Keep up the tradition, Go Blue!

Cueter Chrysler Plymouth Jeep Eagle
Where the Pride is Inside

University Bank ▪ Ann Arbor 313-741-5858
Your Local Community Bank

Northwest Airlines 1-800-225-2525
Some People Just Know How to Fly

Law Offices of Richard B. Oole ▪ Grand Rapids ▪ 616-361-2619
21 Years of Serving Clients in Michigan and Florida

Michigan Brush Mfg. Co., Inc.
1-800-MI-BRUSH

Michigan Trenching Service
Rob Lyons

NBD Bank
May the Excellence of Academics & Athletics Continue!

Don & Judy Rumelhart
Best of luck with your continued success! Go Wolverines!

CONTENTS

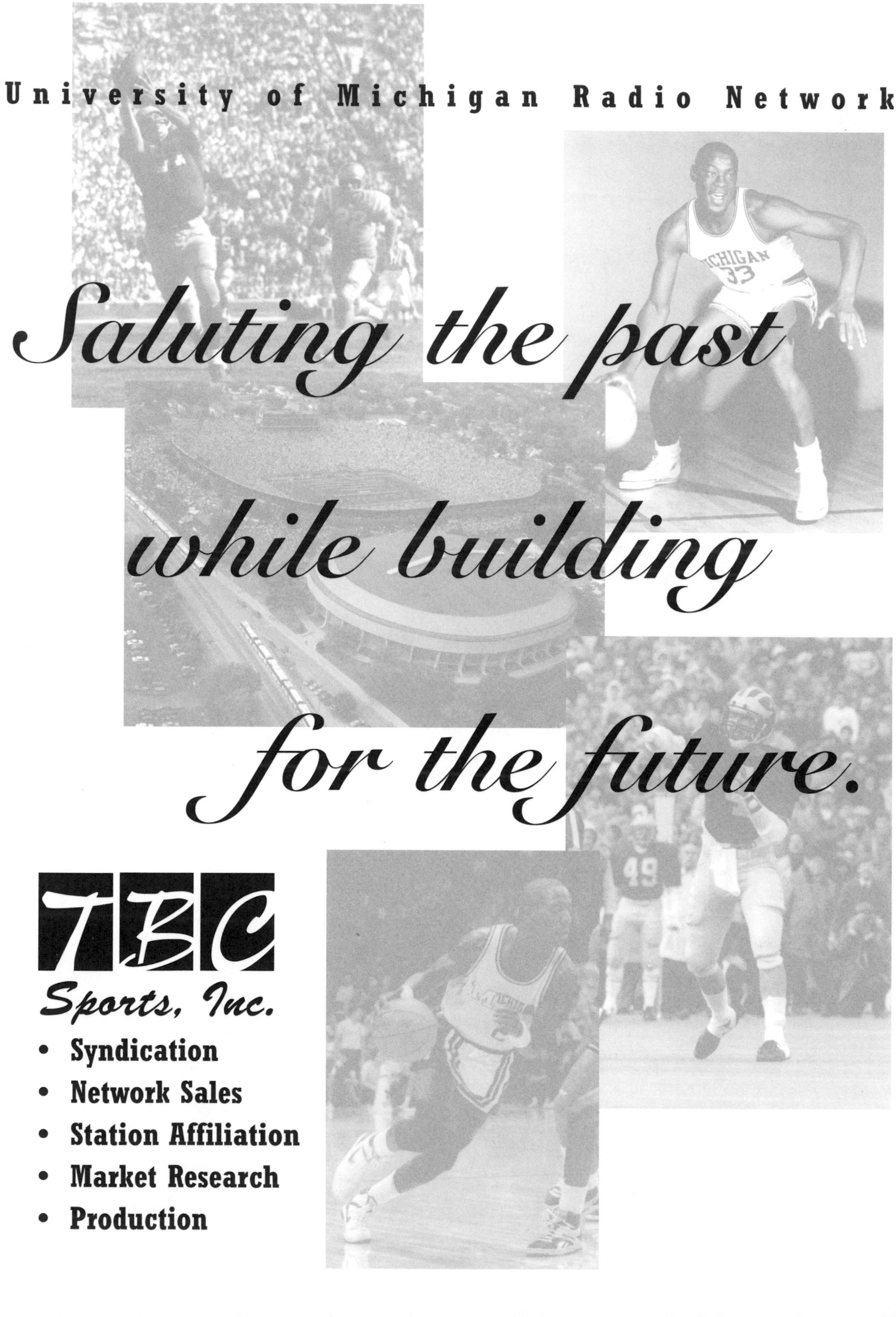
University of Michigan Radio Network
MICHIGAN 33
Saluting the past
while building
for the future.
49
TBC
Sports, Inc.
• Syndication
• Network Sales
• Station Affiliation
• Market Research
• Production

Acknowledgments

While *Michigan: Champions of the West* chronicles University of Michigan athletics, it surely does not mention all the greats who played, coached and still staff one of the great athletic departments in collegiate sport. I, too, cannot truly acknowledge everyone who has played a part in this book.

Rob Toonkel and Mike Pearson played extremely special roles. For without the support of these two co-authors, this book would have been a figment of my imagination for many years to come. Rob is one of the brightest young men I have had the opportunity to work alongside, while Mike has not only helped me with this book, but he has also been a great sounding board, discussing the benefits and pratfalls of the business of Media/Sports Information.

Greg Kinney of the U-M Bentley Historical Library also deserves special credit. Greg not only was a co-author writing the Michigan Lore, he also has done an amazing job working with our Media Relations Department as we archive Michigan sports for generations to come.

Then there are the many people who have played a role in helping record and promote the great tradition we have in Ann Arbor. Jim Schneider, Amy Carlton, BJ Sohn, Barb Cossman, Brian Fishman and newcomer Dave Ablauf are doing their part right now to make sure their sports get the proper support and attention. Also thanks to Jay Levin and all the former members of the Michigan Media Relations staff who have assisted me throughout the years.

Of course, the two major players who have the hardest job of keeping track of all of my staff and what is going on are Tara Preston and Sue Vershum. They are the first line of contact with the public and the media.

I'd also like to thank the many photographers I have worked with through the years who have really built our photo files — Bob Kalmbach, Per Kjeldsen, Barry Rankin and Duane Black, just to name a few.

Thanks also to those who really helped me enter and then grow in the profession—Will Snyder, Wayne DeNeff, Will and Pat Perry, Jim Vruggink, Keith Molin and my bosses Joe Roberson, Jack Weidenbach, Bo Schembechler and Don Canham.

And a special acknowledgment to the coaches and student-athletes I have worked with at Michigan, and those came before them. This is why all Michigan athletes are truly "Champions of the West."

—Bruce Madej

Weber's Inn
ANN ARBOR

Weber's Restaurant and Inn have been a part of Ann Arbor and the University of Michigan since 1937. Coaches, news media, sports heroes and alumni make Weber's a part of their Ann Arbor visits.

Weber's Restaurant has been at its location of Jackson Avenue at I-94 since 1962. In 1970 Herman Weber opened the Weber's Inn addition to complement his famous restaurant.

Now football weekends are a tradition for thousands of fans who stay at the hotel, enjoy the pre-game brunch and then take the local shuttle bus directly to the game avoiding the parking problems.

Weber's Inn and Restaurant is independently owned and operated by the Weber Family. They salute the University of Michigan's athletic program and are proud to be associated with it. Weber's Inn has hosted the University of Michigan's "M-Club" weekly Sports Luncheons since the early 1970s. Coaches from all intercollegiate sports regularly update the club members at these Monday luncheons.

Weber's Restaurant & Inn
3050 Jackson Avenue
Ann Arbor, Michigan 48103
I-94 at exit 172
(734) 769-2500

September, 1997

To become the Director of Athletics at the University of Michigan is truly a dream come true for anyone wishing to be a part of intercollegiate athletics. When you read this book, *Michigan: Champions of the West*, you'll understand why I'm excited to return to Ann Arbor and play an important role in keeping our great tradition alive.

Tom Goss, football player.

Everyone talks about the Michigan tradition. This book explains why it started and by whom it was started.

I, too, was a student-athlete at Michigan, playing football under then head coach Bump Elliott. I remember a muddy Saturday afternoon in 1968 when my teammate, Ron Johnson, set a Michigan record, running for 347 yards against Wisconsin in Michigan Stadium. And I also remember lining up opposite Dan Dierdorf in practice. In those days, he was one hard-hitting offensive lineman.

I have fond remembrances of coming to Michigan and watching Cazzie Russell contribute some of the most memorable moments I have ever seen on the hardwood. I also remember football teammate Dave Porter who also excelled on the wrestling mat, and Don Canham, who in those days was our track coach.

Great moments, created by great athletes, create our great memories, and, in turn, sustain Michigan's great tradition. While we talk about our great tradition, it is our current set of student-athletes, coaches and staff who will be put to the test. Integrity has been our mainstay and integrity is what we must build upon to continue this tradition into the next millennium.

I'm ready for the test as we work to continue making Michigan the Champions of the West.

Tom Goss

TOM GOSS
Director of Athletics
University of Michigan

Tom Goss, University of Michigan Athletic Director.

America's Time Capsule

July 7, 1896: The city of Chicago hosted the Democratic National Convention, nominating William Jennings Bryan as its candidate.

October 1, 1896: The Federal Post Office established rural free delivery.

November 3, 1896: William McKinley won the U.S. presidency in a landslide.

March 17, 1897: Bob Fitzsimmons defeated "Gentleman Jim" Corbett for the world heavyweight boxing title.

April 19, 1897: John McDermott won the first Boston Marathon in a time of two hours, 55 minutes, and 10 seconds.

University Lore

THE *MICHIGANENSIAN* made its debut in April of 1897 and has remained ever since the official student yearbook. The *Ensian* was the result of the consolidation of the *Palladium*, the *Castallian*, and *Res Gestae* which had originally been published by the secret societies, the independent students and the law students respectively. The first *Ensian* included only a few photographs but had most of the features of the modern yearbook plus numerous student poems and essays and reflections on college life.

Michigan Moment

BIRTH OF THE BIG TEN

On January 11, 1896, Purdue president James Smart met with six other university presidents at Chicago's Auditorium to discuss regulation and control of intercollegiate athletics. In that first meeting, which was attended by the presidents of the University of Chicago, University of Illinois, Lake Forest University, University of Minnesota, Northwestern University, Purdue University, and the University of Wisconsin, the administrators approved 12 rules that would be debated and revised over time. Their first action was to restrict collegiate athletes to full-time students who were not delinquent in their studies. Less than a month later, on February 8, the faculty representatives of those schools reconvened at Chicago's Palmer House, but the University of Michigan had replaced Lake Forest at the meeting. The seven men, including U-M faculty representative Dr. Joseph Nancrede, then established the "Intercollegiate Conference of Faculty Representatives", later referred to as the "Western Conference" or "Big Ten". Indiana and Iowa became the eighth and ninth Conference members in 1899. In 1901, the first Conference-sponsored championship was held, in outdoor track and field. At Marshall Field in Chicago, Michigan emerged the winner from a field of nine teams. Michigan withdrew in January 1908 in response to retroactive provisions of some of the new eligibility rules, but returned in 1917 to a Conference that had grown with the addition of Ohio State in 1912. The Conference would remain unchanged until Chicago withdrew in 1946, due to its inability to "provide reasonable competition." Three years later, in 1949, Michigan State gained Big Ten membership. The latest addition to the Big Ten occurred in 1990, when Penn State was brought on as the Conference's 11th member. Beginning in 1981-82, women became an integral part of the Conference, as championships in women's sports were sponsored for the first time.

Chicago's Palmer House gave birth to the Big Ten Conference.

CHAMPION OF THE WEST

GUSTAVE FERBERT

Known to his intimate friends as "Dutch", Gustave H. Ferbert was a legendary character in the early days of University of Michigan athletics. Ferbert was a brilliant star of the 1893, '94, '95 and '96 football squads, playing quarterback and right halfback. The Wolverines compiled an impressive 33-6-1 record during those four seasons, outscoring their foes by an average of 26 to five. Upon Ferbert's graduation in 1896, Athletic Director Charles Baird named the 22-year-old to replace William Ward as Michigan's head football coach. Success came immediately to Ferbert in 1897, as the Wolverines rolled to a 6-1-1 overall record, with a scoreless tie coming at the hands of Ohio Wesleyan and its young coach, Fielding Yost. Four years later, Yost would come to Ann Arbor as Michigan's coach. Ferbert's best Wolverine team was the '98 squad, which was unbeaten in 10 games and won the school's first-ever Big Ten football championship. In Ferbert's final season as coach in 1899, U-M won eight of 10 contests, giving "Dutch" a three-season record of 24-3-1. After giving up coaching, Ferbert journeyed to Alaska to seek his fortune in mining. In 1902, he ventured into the depths of the Klondike and was out of contact for more than a year. Feared dead, Ferbert emerged from the Seward Peninsula a millionaire, thanks to the success of his claims. He retired from active mining in 1928, but continued in that field as an advisor until his death in Cleveland, Ohio in January of 1943 at the age of 69.

another CHAMPION OF THE WEST

EDWIN DENBY

He won but a single varsity letter during his athletic career at the University of Michigan, but Edwin Denby made a much greater contribution later in life through public service to his country. A native of Evansville, Indiana, Denby was a center on Coach William McCauley's outstanding 1895 football squad, which compiled an 8-1 record and outscored its opponents by a count of 266-14. Denby's father, Charles, served as an excellent example to young Edwin, acting as the United States' longtime minister to China. The younger Denby, an 1896 graduate of the U-M law school, was a serviceman on the Navy's U.S.S. Yosemite during the Spanish-American war. Following his discharge as a war hero, Denby then entered the political arena, serving the State of Michigan legislature and the U.S. House of Representatives. In 1921, he was appointed Secretary of the Navy by President Warren Harding. Denby resigned the secretaryship three years later in order to relieve President Harding from the embarrassment caused by his controversial role in the Teapot Dome scandal. Following his resignation from the cabinet, Denby returned to Detroit and entered a career in banking and industrial law. Soon after, the city selected him as chairman of a $5 million building program campaign of the Y.M.C.A. Denby died 10 days shy of his 59th birthday on February 8, 1929.

Maize Blue Item

The first Michigan football game played indoors occurred on Thanksgiving Day, 1896, as the Wolverines battled the University of Chicago at the Chicago Coliseum. Unfortunately, Coach Amos Alonzo Stagg's Maroons prevailed over Michigan, 7-6, in the final game of the inaugural year of the Western Intercollegiate Conference, denying Michigan the league championship.

M List

All-Time Big Ten Championships Won (as of July 1997)

	Men's	Women's	Total
Michigan	250	31	281
Illinois	193	15	208
Ohio State	116	31	147
Indiana	117	26	143
Wisconsin	111	30	141
Minnesota	106	7	113
Iowa	69	20	89
Chicago	72	0	72
Michigan State	53	6	59
Purdue	50	7	57
Northwestern	37	15	52
Penn State	3	6	9

1897-98

America's Time Capsule

July 2, 1897: A coal miners' strike put 75,000 men out of work in Pennsylvania, Ohio, and West Virginia.

September 21, 1897: In response to a letter from young Virginia O'Hanlon, a *New York Sun* editorial declared, "Yes, Virginia, there is a Santa Claus."

February 15, 1898: An explosion destroyed the battleship Maine, as 260 crew members perished.

April 24, 1898: The United States declared war on Spain, and the Spanish-American War began.

June 1, 1898: Congress passed the Erdman Arbitration Act, making government mediation in railroad disputes legitimate.

University Lore

Impromptu student bands had appeared at football games in the 1880s, but the U-M's famed Marching Band traces it origins to the student-organized ensemble that accompanied the football team to Detroit for the 1897 Minnesota game. The Student Athletic Association raised money to buy the band uniforms. The band did not receive official recognition or support from the university until 1914 when an allotment of "$25 per member for a 30 member band" was provided by the Board of Regents.

Michigan Moment

GREATEST HOMECOMING GAMES

Since the tradition began at the University of Michigan in 1897, the Homecoming football game has been a very special event at the Ann Arbor campus. Here are some of U-M's greatest Homecoming highlights:

•1907—Pennsylvania 7, Michigan 0—In Michigan's first season outside of the Big Ten, these two powerhouses played a grueling contest. The Quakers scored in the first half on an onside kick. Michigan apparently scored in the second half, but the play was called back due to the fact that on the forward pass, the ball had not gone five yards outside of the point where the ball was put in play.

•1910—Michigan 6, Minnesota 0—In front of 18,000 fans, Coach Fielding Yost's Wolverines stunned the eventual Big Ten champion Golden Gophers, handing Minnesota its only loss in seven contests and the only time that season that a team had scored against the Gophers.

Photo: Michiganensian

Alumni team that played in the first homecoming game.

•1945—Michigan 7, Ohio State 3—In a battle for second place in the Big Ten, Michigan's Henry Fonde ran the ball in from the one-yard line with less than seven minutes left. Ohio State, which had taken the lead on a 17-yard field goal in the third quarter, outgained the Wolverines on the ground and in total offense. The win was a payback for Michigan, which had lost the 1944 contest between the two teams in the waning minutes of the game.

•1979—Michigan 27, Indiana 21—With six seconds to play and the ball on Indiana's 45-yard line, it looked as though Michigan would manage only a tie. However, Anthony Carter turned a simple pass play over the middle into a game-winning touchdown, breaking two tackles and sprinting into the end zone as the clock expired.

•1983—Michigan 16, Iowa 13—Michigan, 6-0, used two Bob Bergeron field goals to forge a 6-0 lead, but its margin was cut in half when Iowa's Tom Nichol booted a 56-yard field goal. With 1:30 left in the game and the score tied at 13-13, U-M drove 43 yards from their own 29-yard line. Just 12 seconds remained when Bergeron split the uprights from 45 yards out.

CHAMPIONSHIP *Moment*

MICHIGAN STARTS HOMECOMING TRADITION

The Homecoming tradition started at Michigan in 1897, under the name The Alumni Game. Designed to attract the attention of Michigan's numerous alumni to the school's fledgling athletic program, the game featured the Michigan football squad against a team of Michigan alumni. The game also was designed to foster alumni relations, encourage college spirit and generate interest in the University of Michigan. The Homecoming game featured Michigan against an alumni team from 1897-99. In 1900, pressure from U-M alumni to see a real college opponent led to the Homecoming game being scheduled against Purdue, a game that Michigan won, 11-6. Except for 1906, Michigan has played another college team ever since.

CHAMPION OF THE WEST

CHARLES BAIRD

Charles Baird arrived in Ann Arbor in 1890, and enrolled in the law department. Elected as the freshman athletic representative of the library department in 1891, Baird won a letter on Michigan's 1892 football team. Elected manager in the spring of 1893, he held that position for the 1893 through 1895 seasons. An 1895 graduate of the University of Michigan, Baird returned in 1898 as the Graduate Manager of Athletics, Michigan's first athletic director. The athletic department was $3,000 in debt when Baird took office, but he paid off the debt by the end of 1899, repairing the department's credit. Baird was responsible for improving the campus' athletic fields and for the construction of Ferry Field to replace an outdated Regents Field. He made the Michigan Athletic Department one of the best in the Midwest and a place other universities attempted to emulate. After his resignation in 1908, Baird continued to offer advice to benefit the Wolverines. He later donated the carillon bells that would be heard daily on the Ann Arbor campus. Baird died of a heart attack in 1944 in Kansas City, Missouri.

Maize & Blue Item

The University of Michigan band made its first appearance on campus in the Fall of 1897. A few minutes before each football game, any persons who were in possession of musical instruments were encouraged to gather at the Engineering building. During the band's first several years, U-M students and the Ann Arbor Chamber of Commerce provided the organization with its only financial support. However, in 1926 the U-M's Board of Regents began to set aside 50 cents of each student's tuition to help support the musicians.

M List: Homecoming Facts for Michigan's 100 Homecoming Games

- Overall Record: 74-24-2
- Non-Exhibition Record: 72-23-0
- Number of games vs. Big Ten teams: 80
- Number of games held in October: 64
- Earliest Homecoming: September 27, 1986, vs. Florida State
- Latest Homecoming: November 27, 1902, vs. Minnesota
- Opponent Most Often Faced: Minnesota, 30 times
- Homecoming Shutouts: 24 for, 6 against
- Most Points Scored in a Homecoming Game: 75, vs. Wisconsin, 1905
- Longest Winning Streak: 22 games, 1968-89

America's Time Capsule

August 1, 1898: The United States estimated that 4,200 servicemen fighting in Cuba suffered from yellow fever or typhoid.

November 8, 1898: Rough Rider Teddy Roosevelt was elected governor of New York.

December 10, 1898: A peace treaty was signed in Paris by the United States and Spain, ending the Spanish-American War.

February 14, 1899: Congress approved the use of voting machines for federal elections.

June 9, 1899: Jim Jeffries knocked out Bob Fitzsimmons for the world heavyweight boxing title.

University Lore

At least 125 U-M students enlisted in the military when the war with Spain began in 1898. Most served in the 33rd or 34th Michigan Infantry in the Cuban campaign. Others served with the Michigan Naval Reserve on the cruiser Yosemite. Faculty who served included Drs. Victor Vaughan and Charles Nancrede, who treated the wounded from the battle of Santiago, and Dean Mortimer Cooley, chief engineer of the Yosemite. A total of 576 Michigan men served during the war; five died in combat and nine succumbed to disease.

Michigan Moment

MICHIGAN CLAIMS FIRST CONFERENCE CROWN

On November 24, 1898, the Universities of Michigan and Chicago lined up in the Windy City for the two teams' traditional season-ending game. The annual battle between these two squads had been the Thanksgiving Day season finale for five seasons, but had taken on much importance in the last two years. In both 1896 and 1897, Chicago had denied the Wolverines a share of the Western Conference Championship by defeating Michigan, 7-6 and 21-12. While both of these previous games were played inside the Chicago Coliseum, today's contest would be played outside in near-freezing temperatures. The winner would be awarded the Conference championship. Weighing in at an average of 190 pounds, Chicago was the heaviest team in college football history. Chicago held an 11-5 lead late in the game, but All-America center William Cunningham kept the Wolverines within striking distance. With less than two minutes left, a rarely used substitute named Charles Widman was given the ball and scampered 65 yards down the field for the Michigan touchdown and an 11-11 tie. William Caley kicked the successful point after for a 12-11 edge. The Wolverines preserved the win and claimed their first Conference championship. Widman's run would be forever immortalized, as it was this dash that moved Louis Elbel to write "The Victors," long considered one of the nation's top marching songs.

An artist's conception of action between Michigan and Chicago in 1898.

CHAMPIONSHIP *Moment*

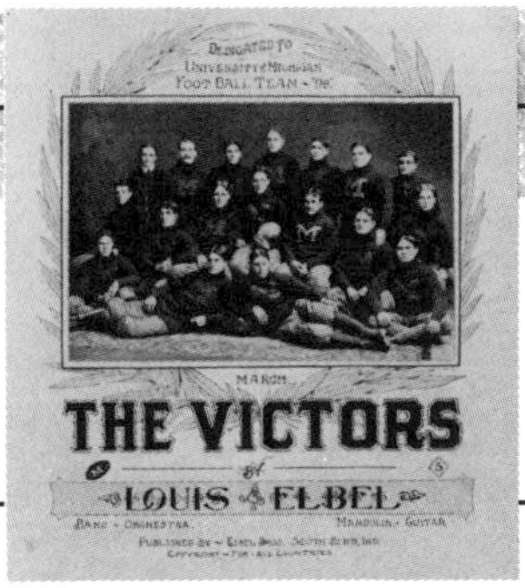

The following are Louis Elbel's lyrics to the world's most famous fight song:

Now for a cheer they are here, triumphant!
Here they come with banners flying,
In stalwart step they're nighing,
With shouts of vict'ry crying,
We hurrah, hurrah, we greet you now, Hail!

Far we their praises sing
For the glory and fame they've bro't us
Loud let the bells them ring
For here they come with banners flying
Far we their praises tell
For the glory and fame they've bro't us
Loud let the bells them ring
For here they come with banners flying
Here they come, Hurrah!

Hail! to the victors valiant
Hail! to the conqu'ring heroes
Hail! Hail! to Michigan, the leaders and best
Hail! to the victors valiant
Hail! to the conqu'ring heroes
Hail! Hail! to Michigan,
the champions of the West!

We cheer them again
We cheer and cheer again
For Michigan, we cheer for Michigan
We cheer with might and main
We cheer, cheer, cheer
With might and main we cheer!

Hail! to the victors valiant
Hail! to the conqu'ring heroes
Hail! Hail! to Michigan,
the champions of the West!

CHAMPION OF THE WEST

LOUIS ELBEL

One of the 1,400 fans in attendance at Marshall Field in Chicago was a man by the name of Louis Elbel. A junior at the University of Michigan, Elbel had come south to see Michigan's 1896 and 1897 contests with Chicago, only to return home disappointed. A member of the Michigan track team, Elbel was also active in music at the University. By Elbel's own account, he was one of the most enthusiastic and loyal supporters of the football team, leading him to wear a badge proclaiming him as "Cheer Leader". On the street after the Wolverines' victory over Chicago, several hundred Michigan fans celebrated, assisted by the band. On the walk back to his sister's house, young Louis realized that his University did not have an appropriate celebration song. As the words and melody of "The Victors" refrain came to him, he wrote his thoughts down on paper, then polished his inspiration the following night on the piano at his house in South Bend. Louis was satisfied just writing the song, but his brother, who was in the music business, suggested that it be printed. The printed copies were received by Elbel in early April, 1899. On the eighth of April, John Philip Sousa and his band came to University Hall for a scheduled concert, and Louis courageously approached the famed musician to inquire if Sousa's band would consider playing "The Victors". The great band leader took Elbel's song and gave the debut performance in front of a packed house. Two nights later, "The Victors" was performed by the U-M orchestra. It was at that performance where the words were sung for the first time in public, by members of the orchestra and of the Glee Club.

Maize & Blue Item

On May 30, 1899, Coach C.F. Watkins' Michigan baseball team defeated Wisconsin, 6-1, and claimed the University's first Conference championship in that sport. Neil Snow, a U-M freshman who would later gain fame as a football player, was one of the stars of the Wolverine "9." Michigan lost its first Conference game at the hands of Wisconsin, but lost only one of its last six league games, finishing with a .714 winning percentage, just ahead of runner-up Illinois.

M List: Michigan's Athletic Directors

1898-1908	Charles Baird
1908-1921	Philip Bartelme
1921-1940	Fielding Yost
1941-1968	Herbert "Fritz" Crisler
1968-1988	Donald Canham
1988-1990	Glenn "Bo" Schembechler
1990-1994	Jack Weidenbach
1994-1997	Joe Roberson
1997-	Tom Goss

M 1899-1900

America's Time Capsule

October 14, 1899: William McKinley became the first President to ride in an automobile.

November 21, 1899: Vice President Garret Hobart died. New York Governor Theodore Roosevelt was nominated as Hobart's replacement. Roosevelt first declined the nomination, but later relented at the Republican National Convention.

March 14, 1900: Congress standardized the gold dollar as the unit of monetary value in the United States.

May 14, 1900: Carrie Nation began her anti-liquor campaign.

July 4, 1900: The Democratic Party nominated William Jennings Bryan of Nebraska as its presidential candidate.

University Lore

Charles Horton Cooley, (U-M Ph. D., 1894), instructor of political economy, was named assistant professor of sociology and taught the university's first course in the subject in 1899. Cooley, the son of famed Law School professor and State Supreme Court Justice Thomas McIntyre Cooley, would go on to become one of the seminal theorists in the young discipline. His books on social organization and culture became classics and are still assigned in university courses.

Michigan Moment

KEENE FITZPATRICK REJOINS "M" TRACK SQUAD

Nearly a century ago, a mustachioed man named Keene Fitzpatrick labored devotedly at the University of Michigan, in the giant shadow cast by Fielding Yost. A native of Natick, Massachusetts, Fitzpatrick first came to Ann Arbor in 1894 as an instructor at U-M's gymnasium, eventually taking over duties as Michigan's trainer, track coach and assistant football coach. He returned to the East for a couple of years, joining Mike Murphy's training staff at Yale. However, when Charles Baird began his duties as Michigan's Director of Athletics in 1898, Fitzpatrick was persuaded to return to Ann Arbor, where he'd stay for 13 highly productive years. While he was officially listed as the school's track coach and trainer, Fitzpatrick also served as Yost's "right arm" with the U-M football staff. But it was "Fitz's" expertise on the cinder track that gained him his greatest acclaim. At the second modern Olympiad in Paris, France in 1900, Fitzpatrick accompanied four Wolverine competitors to the Games: silver medal hurdler Jack McLean; pole vaulter Charles Dvorak; middle distance runner Howard Hayes, and sprinter Clark Leiblee. Among Fitzpatrick's star performers at the next two respective Olympiads in St. Louis and London were gold-medal sprinter Archie Hahn, hurdler and weight man John Garrels, and weight medalist Ralph Rose. Fitzpatrick moved from Michigan to Princeton University following the 1909-10 season, and remained at the New Jersey campus as coach of the track team and trainer of the football squad until his retirement in 1932. At the 1935 presentation at the Michigan Union, Baird said, "I often think that if I were to be asked to produce a live, flesh-and-blood speciman of the perfect gentleman, I would unhesitantly select Keene Fitzpatrick. He was indeed a supercoach." On May 22, 1949, at the age of 79 years, Fitzpatrick died at his home in Princeton, New Jersey.

CHAMPION OF THE WEST

WILLIAM CUNNINGHAM

The University of Michigan has had several firsts during its storied football history. Among its notable achievements were becoming the first university outside of the East to be declared national champion and the first Big Ten university to play in the Rose Bowl. William Cunningham is also the answer to a Michigan trivia question. Of the more than 100 football players who've won All-America honors at the U-M, the hefty lineman was the very first Wolverine to earn that distinction. A four-year letter winner from 1896-99, Cunningham's Michigan squads won the 1898 Big Ten title and combined for a cumulative record of 33-4-1. His all-star selection by Caspar Whitney may have been cemented by a recommendation from Chicago coach Amos Alonzo Stagg whose team was defeated by Cunningham and his Michigan teammates. In fact, it was that contest that inspired songwriter Louis Elbel to write *The Victors*, one of the greatest college fight songs. After leaving football, Cunningham traveled to China as a medical missionary, staying there from 1904 to 1925. He returned that year to the United States and practiced medicine in Oklahoma and Ohio. Cunningham died in 1957 at the age of 84.

another CHAMPION OF THE WEST

THOMAS TRUEBLOOD

One of the most fascinating success stories in University of Michigan athletic history belongs to Thomas Trueblood. A former U-M faculty tennis champion, he took up the game of golf at the age of 40 because his doctor told him that "tennis was too strenuous." Trueblood began a 67-year affiliation with the University in 1884. He founded the U-M Department of Speech in 1892, the first such unit at any major university in the country. In 1901, just five years after taking up the game, Trueblood organized the first Michigan golf team. Twenty years later, golf became a varsity sport at the U-M in 1921, with Trueblood named as the school's first official coach. During Trueblood's 15 "official" seasons as coach, the Wolverines earned five Big Ten titles (1932, '33, '34, '35, '36) and were the runner-up eight times. Retired as professor emeritus of speech by the University when he reach the age of 70 in 1926, Trueblood turned his full attention to coaching. During his last 10 seasons, from 1927-36, Michigan golf teams never finished lower than second in Conference championship competition. He coached many stars, led by 1932 NCAA champion John Fischer and 1936 NCAA titlist Chuck Kocsis. On June 4, 1951, at the age of 95, Trueblood died in Bradenton, Florida.

Maize & Blue Item

Howard W. Hayes, one of Michigan's all-time greats in track and field, served as captain of the Wolverines and became a school record holder in the half-mile run. Hayes, who distinguished himself as a 1900 Olympic silver medal winner in that event, also earned acclaim later in his professional career as a Municipal Court judge in Chicago. He committed suicide in 1937 at the age of 59.

M List

Original Cost of Some of U-M'S Athletic Facilities

Building (Current name if different)	Cost	Built
Ferry Field House (Marie Hartwig Bldg.)	$30,000	1911
Yost Fieldhouse (Yost Ice Arena)	$ 563,168	1923
Intramural Building	$ 743,000	1928
Matt Mann Pool (Cliff Keen Arena)	$ 828,000	1956
Michigan Stadium	$ 950,000	1927
Track and Tennis Building	$ 1,000,000	1974
Oosterbaan Fieldhouse	$ 1,600,000	1980
Varsity Tennis Complex	$ 5,000,000	1997
Special Events Arena (Crisler Arena)	$ 7,200,000	1967
Donald B. Canham Natatorium	$ 8,500,000	1989

1900-01

America's Time Capsule

September 8, 1900: A hurricane ravaged Galveston, Texas, killing 6,000 people and causing property damages of $20 million.

November 6, 1900: William McKinney won the presidency for a second term.

January 10, 1901: A well near Beaumont, Texas, brought in oil, the first evidence of oil from that region.

March 3, 1901: The United States Steel Corporation was incorporated in New Jersey.

June 15, 1901: Willie Anderson won the U.S. Open golf tournament.

University Lore

The Research Club was organized in 1900 with Dr. Victor Vaughan as president. Membership was restricted to distinguished senior scholars elected by the current members. A Junior Research Club was formed in 1902 for younger faculty. Both clubs explicitly denied membership to women, which led to the formation of the Women's Research Club. In 1926 the Research Club's Executive Committee was charged with selecting the annual Henry Russell Lecturer, the university's most prestigious faculty honor.

Michigan Moment

MICHIGAN VICTORIOUS IN THE FIRST-EVER BIG TEN TRACK MEET

Though several schools had been competing in Western Conference track meets for a few years, the first Conference sponsored championship meet was held in the spring of 1901. Coming off a half-point win in 1900, the Michigan contingent prepared for a close contest. Instead, the Wolverines raced, jumped and threw to a sizeable victory over its conference opponents. Archie Hahn and Clark Leiblee finished one-two in the 100-yard dash, the future Olympian finishing in 10 seconds flat. Howard Hayes was a double winner for the Maize and Blue, winning the 880-yard run and finishing first as part of Michigan's champion relay team. Freshman Nelson Kellogg pulled the upset of the day, breaking up an expected 1-2-3 finish by Wisconsin in the two-mile by winning in 10 minutes, 9.4 seconds. Three other Michigan entrants took top honors, Bruce Shorts in the hammer throw, Charles Dvorak in the pole vault and John Robinson in the shot put. The victories, combined with a host of second- and third-place finishes, put Michigan on top of the pack. Coach Keene Fitzpatrick's men would stay atop the conference standings for the next four seasons.

Champion sprinter Howard Hayes

CHAMPION OF THE WEST

LANGDON "BIFF" LEA

As the sixth man ever to coach U-M's football squad and the third Princeton graduate to lead the Wolverines, "Biff" Lea's career in Ann Arbor was brief and relatively unspectacular. While his 7-2-1 record in 1900 was respectable, perhaps his greatest contribution to the U-M was to quietly set the table for his successor, Fielding Yost, and Yost's mighty "Point-a-Minute" squads. Lea established a set of strict rules for his players. One such stipulation was, "The word 'Can't' is not in the football vocabulary. Any man feeling that way about any part of the game in detail is not wanted on the field. (We want) only those who say 'I will' with teeth together and who never stop fighting." Lea returned to his alma mater after just one season at Michigan. As a player at Princeton, Lea was spectacular, earning All-America honors as a tackle in 1893, '94 and '95. Several years later, he was inducted into the College Football Hall of Fame.

another CHAMPION OF THE WEST

JOHN McLEAN

Perhaps the most famous Wolverine athlete from tiny Menominee, Michigan, was Olympic medalist John McLean. His fame came from his performance at the 1900 Olympic Games in Paris, France, where he became one of the first Michigan athletes to win an Olympic medal, a silver in the high hurdles. McLean, a four-time track and field letterman at the U-M, might also have won a medal in the broad jump event, but he refused to compete in the Sunday finals due to religious reasons. McLean also participated in the 800-meter run and and low hurdles at the Paris games. The speedy halfback also starred for coach Gustave Ferbert's Wolverine football team in 1898 and '99. Michigan's '98 squad compiled a perfect 10-0 record en route to the school's first-ever Big Ten Conference championship. Following his athletic career, McLean served on the faculty of Knox College in Galesburg, Illinois and was also an investment banker. He died on June 4, 1955, at the age of 77.

Maize & Blue Item

The University of Michigan's Athletic Association recognized very early the importance of bringing high school athletes to its campus. The A.A.'s Interscholastic Department began at the turn of the century after observing the successful results of similar programs at many of the large Eastern colleges. High school athletes in track and field and football were the first to make their debuts at the Ann Arbor campus in the quest for state championships.

M List: Differences Between College Football, Then and Now

- The playing field was 110 yards long (until 1912).
- Touchdowns were worth five points (until 1912).
- Field goals were worth five points (until 1904), four points from 1904-09.
- Forward passes were not allowed (until 1906).
- One forward pass was allowed if the ball went five yards to left or right of center. If neither team touched the ball, it went to the opponent (until 1910).
- Teams had three downs to make five yards.
- The scoring team received the ensuing kickoff.

1901-02

America's Time Capsule

September 6, 1901: President McKinley was shot as he attended a reception in Buffalo, N.Y. He died of his wounds eight days later.

September 14, 1901: Forty-two-year-old Theodore Roosevelt took the presidential oath of office.

October 16, 1901: In one of his first controversial moves as president, Theodore Roosevelt invited black leader Booker T. Washington to the White House. The South was incensed and reacted with violence against blacks.

May 12, 1902: Nearly 140,000 United Mine Workers went on strike.

May 20, 1902: Four years after the end of the Spanish-American War, Cuban independence was achieved.

University Lore

THE UNIVERSITY OF MICHIGAN
ARTES · SCIENTIA · VERITAS
1817 ™

With the first issue of the *Michigan Law Review* in June 1902, Michigan joined Harvard, Yale and Columbia as publishers of law reviews. The idea for the review apparently originated with G. C. Ohlinger, a junior in the Law Department, who presented his plan to a faculty committee in September 1901. Originally published monthly during the school year, the *Review* aimed to be scholarly "but not so academic as to be out of touch with the profession." Prof. Floyd Mechem served as managing editor with the assistance of 10 student editors.

Michigan Moment

MICHIGAN DEFEATS STANFORD IN THE FIRST ROSE BOWL

For several years, a polo match had been one of the "highlights" of the annual Tournament of Roses festivities. However, in 1901, the tournament of Roses committee decided to switch to a football match-up between undefeated Michigan and Pacific Coast champion Stanford to liven up the New Year's Day event. Ironically, just one year before, rookie Michigan coach Fielding Yost had been the head man of the Indians, but he was forced to seek other employment due to Stanford's institution of a rule that allowed only SU graduates to coach its teams. Few of the 8,000 fans who were in the stands on that 85-degree afternoon gave Michigan much of a chance against the powerful Stanford team. Touchdowns by Neil Snow and Curtis Redden helped put Michigan out in front by a 17-0 count at halftime. The Wolverines dominated the second half, as Stanford was barely able to touch the ball while Michigan scored on nearly every posession. Snow scored four rushing touchdowns in the second half alone. After A.E. Herrnstein dashed 22 yards into the end zone to make the score 49-0 in favor of Michigan, Stanford coach Ralph Fisher pleaded with Yost to call off the game eight minutes early. The punishing Wolverine attack had whittled the Indians to less than the mandatory 11 players. Despite the fact that the game brought in a profit of more than $3,000, the Tournament of Roses committee felt that a game with such a lopsided score would not be a good draw in the future. A chariot race replaced the game the following year, and it wasn't until 1916 that a football game was again part of the festivities.

First Tournament of Roses game, Michigan versus Stanford.

CHAMPION OF THE WEST

NEIL SNOW

It was the noted Walter Camp who said of Michigan's Neil Snow, "No college ever developed a better all-around athlete." As a 10-letter winner in football, track and baseball, it is difficult to argue with Camp's appraisal of the Detroit star. Snow was Michigan's second All-American, earning national accolades as a senior end on the 1901 national championship squad. On February 17, 1960, nearly 59 years after he'd last played, Snow was inducted into the College Football Hall of Fame. He was awarded two monograms in track, highlighted by his Big Ten high jump title in 1902. In addition to his duties on the cinders, Snow's talents were shared during the spring by the Wolverine baseball team. From 1899-1902, Snow and the Michigan "9" captured two Big Ten titles. Following his stellar career as as athlete, Snow was much sought after as a coach, turning down many lucrative offers from high schools and colleges to enter a business career. He was president, treasurer and general manager of the Detroit Twist Drill Company at the time of his death in 1914 at the age of 34.

another CHAMPION OF THE WEST

HARRISON "BOSS" WEEKS

Five brothers from Allegan, Michigan played football for the Wolverines, but second-oldest Harrison Weeks was undeniably the "Boss" of the quintet. Three of the brothers were varsity letter winners, including oldest brother Alanson who played halfback on the unbeaten 1898 squad. However, it was Harrison who led Coach Fielding Yost's powerful "Point-a-Minute" teams at quarterback in 1901 and '02. The role of quarterback then was quite different from modern times, as Boss's job was to direct strategy and call defensive signals. Once on the field, the quarterback was clearly in charge, and there was no communication with the bench. During Weeks' two seasons with the Wolverines, Michigan's football squad averaged more than 54 points per game and yielded a total of just 12 points in 22 games! So proficient was Boss Weeks as a player, that three decades after he played, Yost called him the greatest field general he had ever coached. Despite being a finely tuned athlete, Weeks succumbed to diphtheria in 1906 at the tender age of 27.

Maize & Blue Item

How dominating was the 1901 Michigan football squad? Football historians can readily recite U-M' s 11-0 record and amazing 550-0 scoring margin. Obscured, however, is that few of the 11 games ever made it through the regulation 70 minutes. The 128-0 disposing of Buffalo was done in just 55 minutes, while the 50-0 destruction of Albion and 57-0 beating of Case were mercifully called after just 40 minutes. The farthest any opponent went into Michigan territory occured when Northwestern made it to the 35-yard line. In fact, four of U-M's 11 opponents never had the ball on Michigan's side of the field.

M List: Statistics of the First Rose Bowl

Michigan		Stanford
27	First Downs	5
90	Rushing Attempts	24
527	Net Rushing Yards	67
21/38.9	Punts/Avg.	16/34.9
1	Fumbles	9

Michigan's Leading Rushers

	Yds	TD
Willie Heston	170	0
Neil Snow	107	5
A.E. Herrnstein	97	1

1902-03

America's Time Capsule

November 4, 1902: In congressional elections, the Republicans maintained their Senate majority over Democrats, 57-33.

December 17, 1902: The first radio message was transmitted across the Atlantic.

January 22, 1903: A 99-year lease was signed by the United States and Columbia giving America sovereignty over a canal zone in Panama.

July 4, 1903: President Roosevelt sent a message around the world and back in 12 minutes through use of the first Pacific communications cable.

August 8, 1903: Great Britain defeated the United States to capture tennis' Davis Cup.

University Lore

The country's first formal courses in actuarial theory were taught by the Mathematics Department in 1902. Prof. James Glover offered instruction in "The Mathematics of Insurance and Statistics" and "The Theory of Insurance and Annuities." The purpose of the courses was not to train students for a particular profession but to teach "the principles underlying all commercial transactions." Glover became chairman of the Mathematics Department in 1926 and was named the Edward Olney Professor of Mathematics in 1934.

Michigan Moment

U-M's "POINT-A-MINUTE" TEAM KEEPS ROLLING

Following the incredible 1901 campaign, the Wolverine football team suffered no letdown in 1902. Michigan retained most of its starters from the previous season, captained by quarterback Harrison (Boss) Weeks. Willie Heston ran for three touchdowns in the season opener, a 68-0 shutout of Albion. The unlikely happened a week later when Case actually scored a touchdown against Michigan, the first points yielded by the Wolverines since 1900. Michigan would take out its frustration of being score upon the following week when it man-handled rival Michigan Agricultural College, 119-0, behind a team-record seven TDs by Al Herrnstein. Indiana (60-0) and Notre Dame (23-0) followed M.A.C. as shutout victims in the next two games. Six thousand fans came out to Regents Field on October 25 to see Michigan dismantle Ohio State, 86-0. Heston netted 217 yards on just 11 carries as the previously undefeated Buckeyes suffered their worst defeat ever. More than three times as many fans were in the stands at Chicago for Michigan's closest game in two seasons, a 6-0 victory over Wisconsin. Michigan's offensive juggernaut revved up again in early November, scoring a 107-0 victory over Iowa at Ann Arbor, then followed up that performance on November 15 with a 21-0 defeat of Chicago. Michigan ended its second straight undefeated season with a 63-0 rout of Oberlin and a hard-fought 23-6 win over Minnesota on Thanksgiving. The Wolverines accumulated a total of 644 points for the season, a records that stands today, while allowing just 12 total points in 11 games. They coasted to a second straight Conference title and national championship. Heston scored 15 touchdowns on the year, but placed a distant second to Herrnstein who finished with a team-record 26 in his final season.

CHAMPION OF THE WEST

ARCHIE HAHN

Archibald "Archie" Hahn was a colossal force on the track for the University of Michigan. The native of Dodgeville, Wisconsin, was a four-time letter winner, and one of only a few Big Ten athletes whose team captured four consecutive Conference titles. Hahn captured Conference 100-yard dash crowns in 1901 and '02, and a 220-yard dash title in 1903, but his best performances were saved for the 1904 Olympic Games in St. Louis. In Hahn's first event as an Olympian, the 60-meter run, he equalled a world record with a time of 7.2 seconds. Two days later at 200 meters, Hahn again won easily, finishing in an Olympic record time of :21.6, a mark that would stand until the 1932 games in Los Angeles when it was shattered by another "M" man, Eddie Tolan. Hahn captured a third gold medal three days later in the 100 dash. At the 1906 Olympic games in Athens, Hahn would again stand on the top step of the victory stand, capturing a gold medal in the 100-meter dash. Among the many stops in his career, he served as Steve Farrell's assistant track coach at Michigan and as a football trainer under Fielding Yost. In the mid 1920s, Hahn joined his former coach, Keene Fitzpatrick, at Princeton and remained there several years before becoming head coach at the University of Virginia. In 1955, three years after he retired from Virginia, Hahn died of a heart ailment at the age of 74.

another CHAMPION OF THE WEST

CHARLES DVORAK

Michigan's honors list in the pole vault event includes many great names: James Booker in the 1920s, Eeles Landstrom during the decade of the 1950s, and Jim Stokes in the 1970s. But the forerunner of all of those legends, Charles Dvorak, mastered the field event in its infantile stages. From 1900 through 1904, no one was more adept at pole vaulting than Dvorak. He claimed individual Conference titles in both 1901 and 1903, leaping well over 11 feet both times, and was a key member of four consecutive Big Ten team titlists (1901-04). Perhaps Dvorak's greatest accomplishments came as an Olympian, where he earned two medals. His silver medal in 1900 at Paris came when pole vaulting was still categorized as a "special" event. Four years later in St. Louis, Dvorak's vault of 11'5 3/4" captured the gold medal. He went on to coach track at the University of Idaho in 1908 and remained there until moving to Seattle in 1937 where he served the next 15 years as a high school coach. Dvorak died at the age of 91 in 1969.

Maize & Blue Item

Michigan's track and field squad edged host Chicago, 49-40, on a cold and rainy day to win its third consecutive Western Conference title. The Wolverines trailed early by a count of 19-8, but a record-setting pole vault of 11'9" by Charles Dvorak, a convincing victory by sprinter Archie Hahn in the 220-dash and a win by M.A. "Mother" Hall in the 880-yard run triggered the wave of Michigan momentum for Coach Keene Fitzpatrick's squad.

M List: Football Dominance

During the 1902 season, Michigan's football squad scored a team record 644 points, including four victories by margins of 86 points or more. Here are a few other dominating performances by the Wolverines on the gridiron:

- 1904 Michigan 130, West Virginia 0 — Michigan scored more than two and half points per minute in this 50-minute contest.
- 1947 Michigan 69, Pittsburgh 0 — Though the first period was scoreless, Michigan tallied no less than three touchdowns in each of the last three quarters.
- 1969 Michigan 51, Iowa 6 — Michigan rolled to the best offensive performance in Big Ten history at the time, gaining 673 yards, including 524 on the ground.
- 1971 Michigan 56, Virginia 0 — Michigan erupted for 35 first half points en route to an eight-touchdown thrashing of the Cavaliers.
- 1975 Michigan 69, Northwestern 0 — Michigan ran for a Big Ten record-tying 573 yards in posting its greatest margin of victory in 28 years.

MICHIGAN MOMENT

America's Time Capsule

October 13, 1903: The Boston Red Sox defeated the Pittsburgh Pirates in baseball's first World Series.

December 17, 1903: Orville and Wilbur Wright made their first successful flight in a crude flying machine at Kitty Hawk, North Carolina.

January 4, 1904: The Supreme Court ruled that Puerto Ricans are not aliens and must not be refused admission into the United States.

June 1, 1904: President Theodore Roosevelt was nominated as the Republican candidate at the national convention in Chicago.

July 6, 1904: The Democrats convened in St. Louis to nominate Alton Parker for president.

University Lore

Wilfred Bryon Shaw received his B.A. degree in 1904 and was immediately named general secretary of the Alumni Association and managing editor of the Michigan Alumnus, beginning nearly 50 years of service to the university's alumni. He established the Michigan Alumnus Quarterly Review and initiated the Alumni University program. In 1929 Shaw was appointed Director of Alumni Relations, a post he held until his retirement in 1950. Shaw edited the massive Encyclopedic Survey of the University, but is probably best known today for his many fine etchings of campus scenes.

THE BATTLE FOR THE LITTLE BROWN JUG

The date was October 31, 1903. Fielding Yost brought his Michigan football team into Minneapolis on a 29-game winning streak, not having allowed a single point during the entire 1903 campaign. Minnesota would surely be a formidible opponent, entering the game with a 10-0 record—38-3-4 over the last four years—and having allowed just six points during 1903. Michigan's rivalry with the Golden Gophers was of such competitive proportions that Yost sent his trainer, Keene Fitzpatrick, to a local hardware store to purchase a five-gallon jug, for the purpose of preserving his team's water supply. The game proved to be a fierce battle, with neither team crossing the goal line during the first half. Michigan started the second half by driving the ball 74 yards, climaxing the possession with a one-yard touchdown plunge by Willie Heston. The extra point made the score 6-0. It stayed that way until just two minutes remained in the game, when Minnesota took advantage of a fumbled U-M punt and methodically drove the ball 45 yards for the Gophers' only TD of the day. The successful point after was added, and Minnesota had tied the game at 6-6. At that moment, the 20,000 fans in attendance stormed the field in celebration of the Gophers' magnificent accomplishment. With a mass of humanity engulfing the field and darkness setting in, officials ended the game and the 6-6 tie went into the books. In their hurry to leave the field before the fans overtook it, Michigan left its 35-cent water jug behind. The following morning, Minnesota custodian Oscar Munson carried the jug into Athletic Director L.J. Cooke's office, and it was kept as a memento of the Gophers' monumental accomplishment. When Yost sent a letter requesting the return of his jug, Cooke wrote back, "If you want it, you'll have to win it." Due to the brutality and savagery of the 1903 game, the two teams didn't meet again until 1909, when Michigan did indeed win back the jug.

CHAMPION OF THE WEST

RALPH ROSE

In an era when the largest athletes weighed less than 200 pounds, 6-foot-6, 235-pound Ralph Rose was considered Goliathan. Though the Michigan track and field letterman officially competed in Ann Arbor for only one year (1904), he concluded that season by winning both the shot put and discus events at the Big Ten meet in Chicago. A few weeks later at the 1904 Olympic games in St. Louis, Rose put on a dazzling performance, winning a gold medal in the shot put (a world-record toss of 48′7″), a silver medal in the discus (128′10 1/2″) and a bronze medal in the hammer throw (150′). In his final event of the 1904 games, Rose finished sixth in the 56-pound throw. He sparkled again at the 1908 Olympics in London, winning his second gold medal in the shot put with a toss of 46′7″. Over the next two years, Rose broke his own shot put record three more times, including a toss of 51 feet, a mark that wouldn't be topped for nearly two decades. Rose competed in the 1912 summer games in Stockholm, Sweden, at the age of 28. Entered in the shot put, Rose threw the weight just over 50 feet. His feat held up until the final round, when fellow American Patrick McDonald bested it, leaving Rose with the silver medal. The 1912 Olympics marked the only time the "combined" shot put event was held, where the competitor threw the weight with both his left and right hands. Rose's combined total of 90 feet, 10-1/2 inches was enough to best McDonald and deliver Rose's third gold. The six-time medal winner passed away from tuberculosis on October 16, 1913, at the young age of 29.

another CHAMPION OF THE WEST

HENRY SCHULTE

Though he gained his greatest fame as a track and field coach, Henry "Indian" Schulte never officially competed on the cinder track at Michigan's Ferry Field during his distiguished career as a Wolverine athlete. As a guard for Coach Fielding Yost's outstanding 1903, '04 and '05 squads, Schulte toiled in the pits, opening holes for All-America running back Willie Heston. After brief coaching stops at State Normal Universities in Michigan and Missouri, his first major assignment was in his home state at the University of Missouri from 1914-19. Schulte guided the Tigers to three championships in track and field before being lured to the University of Nebraska. During his 20 seasons in Lincoln, the Cornhuskers became a powerhouse in track, claiming 15 conference titles. Schulte's skill in developing athletes was recognized in 1928 when, in charge of decathlon performers, he was a member of the American Olympic Staff at Amsterdam. Following a long illness, he died in 1944 at the age of 65.

Maize Blue Item

In the 14 years between 1892 and 1905, there was no bigger rivalry in midwestern college football than that between Michigan and Chicago. In the later years, this game had even more of an aura as Fielding Yost paced the sidelines across from Amos Alonzo Stagg. Between 1896 and 1905, the game affected the conference championship eight times, including five occurences where the teams dueled for the title between themselves.

M List — Best of Michigan's Brown Jug Games

1910	Michigan 6, Minnesota 0 — Michigan's shutout victory in the season finale vs. the Gophers preserves its unbeaten record (3-0-3).
1926	Michigan 7, Minnesota 6 — The Wolverines win, despite the fact that the Gophers held a more than substantial edge in first downs (18-2), rushing yards (307-23) and total offense (322-44).
1949	Michigan 14, Minnesota 7 — Michigan (2-2) snaps the Golden Gophers' eight-game winning streak behind the performance of halfback Charles Ortmann. Ortmann accounted for 207 of the team's 228 offensive yards.
1975	Michigan 28, Minnesota 21 — Gordon Bell's second touchdown run of the day with 6:56 left in the game finally subdued the Gophers. Bell finished with 172 of Michigan's 345 yards rushing.
1994	Michigan 38, Minnesota 22 — In a quarterback duel between Michigan's Todd Collins and Minnesota's Tim Schade, Michigan came back from a 15-7 deficit to post a 16-point win. While Collins' 352 yards passing was a school record, Schade finished with 394 yards through the air, the best performance ever at Michigan Stadium.

MICHIGAN MOMENT

America's Time Capsule

October 8, 1904: Automobile racing as an organized sport began with the Vanderbilt Club race on Long Island, New York.

October 27, 1904: The first section of New York City's subway system was opened to the public.

November 8, 1904: Theodore Roosevelt was reelected president of the United States, defeating Alton Parker by nearly two million votes.

April 17, 1905: The Supreme Court found a New York state law that limited maximum hours for workers unconstitutional, ruling that such a law interfered with the right to free contract.

May 5, 1905: Boston's Cy Young threw baseball's first-ever perfect game, retiring 27 consecutive Philadelphia Athletic batters.

University Lore

The West Engineering Building was completed in September 1904, behind schedule and over budget. Final cost of the 94,318 square-foot Mason-and-Kahn-designed building was $275,000 plus $25,000 for equipment. It included extensive lab areas and a ship tank for the naval architecture program. Known as the New Engineering Building until 1923 when East Engineering was completed, West Engineering was officially renamed West Hall in 1996 following the College of Engineering's move to North Campus. It now houses several LS&A programs and the School of Information.

HESTON VS. ECKERSALL

Two of the greatest players who ever wore football cleats faced off against each other at old Ferry Field on November 12, 1904. Willie Heston, Michigan's 180-pound senior All-American, was absolutely burly when compared to Chicago's Walter Eckersall, a frail-looking 145-pound sophomore quarterback. While their size may have differed, their contributions to intercollegiate football history made them both giants of the game. The contest versus Chicago was to be Heston's final game for the Maize and Blue, ending a career that had seen him score more touchdowns (80) and gain more ground than any other two players combined. Coach Amos Alonzo Stagg's Maroons knew their only chance to keep Michigan from a fourth consecutive Western championship lay in bottling up Heston. Knowing that Stagg would make Heston a marked man, U-M coach Fielding Yost devised a plan to throw off his wily counterpart. In previous games, Heston had almost always tucked the ball under his right arm and angled to the right side. On this day, however, Heston streaked equally effectively to the left side and scored a pair of touchdowns in the process. Eckersall enjoyed moments of brilliance, too, though more so as a punter and tackler. On one play, Eckersall hit Heston and made him fumble, scooping up the loose ball and streaking 40 yards for a touchdown. In the end, however, it was the Wolverines who prevailed, winning by a score of 22-12. The great Michigan juggernaut, which had compiled a perfect 10-0 record and a season scoring margin of 567-22, needed everything it could muster to beat the scrawny kid from Chicago.

Michigan halfback Tom Hammond sprints around end for a big gainer.

CHAMPIONSHIP *Moment*

Michigan's "Point-a-Minute" teams of the early 1900s established many records that are unthinkable today. In compiling a 55-1-1 record from 1901-05, Yost's men had two separate winning streaks of 29 and 26 games. The Wolverines always left the home crowd happy, going a perfect 44-0 in Ann Arbor during that span. While the offense scored in triple digits three times and broke the 70-point barrier on 10 other occasions, these same men allowed more than six points on defense only once. Of the 57 games played during this era, Michigan shut out the opposition 50 times. Here is a year-by-year synopsis of the Wolverines' dominance:

Year	W	L	T	PF	PA
1901	11	0	0	550	0
1902	11	0	0	644	12
1903	11	0	1	565	6
1904	10	0	0	567	22
1905	12	1	0	495	2
Totals	**55**	**1**	**1**	**2821**	**42**

CHAMPION OF THE WEST

WILLIE HESTON

William Martin Heston was born September 9, 1878 in Galesburg, Illinois. Soon after Willie turned 16, his family headed to the West Coast, where he flourished academically and athletically. Heston initially attended college at San Jose Normal in California, playing at one point for Fielding Yost. Soon after Yost's move to Michigan, Heston followed his tracks to Ann Arbor. Heston eventually rewrote the U-M record book, scoring 72 touchdowns, gaining more than 5,000 yards, and averaging better than eight yards per carry, all in just 36 games. From 1901-04, Heston's Michigan teams went 43-0-1 and won four national championships. His 170 yards rushing in the 1902 Rose Bowl was a standard that stood for 57 years. Named an All-American in 1903 and 1904, Heston has been enshrined in numerous Halls of Fame. After coaching stints at Drake and North Carolina State, Heston began practicing law in 1908. Heston branched out into real estate for a short time before becoming an assistant prosecuting attorney in Detroit in 1911. Five years later, he was elected to the bench and served seven years as a judge. Heston started a cemetery near Flat Rock, Michigan, where he served as the manager for 17 years. He died on his birthday in 1963, in Traverse City.

Maize & Blue Item

The folks at "Michigan Replay" do a masterful job each Sunday morning of showing Wolverine fans game action of the previous Saturday, but they'll never produce anything as historical as B.G. Smith did on November 12, 1904. Hired by Ann Arbor's Temple Theater to film the Michigan-Chicago game, Smith used about 700 feet of film at a cost of $350 to record U-M's 22-12 victory over Chicago. Said Smith, superintendent of the film department of the American Kinetograph Company of Orange, New Jersey, "This is the first time that pictures of a football game were ever taken."

M List

Top Scoring Efforts by Michigan Men's Teams

Sport	Points	Opponent	Year
Football	130	West Virginia	1904
	128	Buffalo	1901
Hockey	21	Ohio State	1964
	17	Michigan State	1950
Men's Basketball	128	Purdue	1966
	127	Iowa	1990
Baseball (since 1946)	27	Georgia Tech	1995
	26	Detroit	1946
Wrestling	50	Morgan State	1988
	47	Central Michigan	1983

MICHIGAN MOMENT

America's Time Capsule

September 22, 1905: Willie Anderson won his third consecutive U.S. Open golf tournament championship.

October 14, 1905: The New York Giants defeated the Philadelphia Athletics to win baseball's second World Series.

February 23, 1906: Tommy Burns won the world heavyweight boxing title.

April 7, 1906: The first successful transatlantic wireless transmission was made from New York City to a receiving station in Ireland.

April 18, 1906: A massive earthquake rocked San Francisco, as some people were killed and more than 500,000 others were left homeless.

University Lore

The Women's Athletic Association sponsored its first competitions in basketball, baseball and tennis in the fall of 1905. Organized the previous spring, the WAA aimed "to promote athletic activities by and to foster a comprehensive recreational program for the women of the University of Michigan." The WAA eventually sponsored inter-class, intramural and club competition in more than twenty sports as well as recreational activities such as horseback riding. "Telegraphic" intercollegiate contests were held in archery, track and other sports. The WAA disbanded in 1970.

FERRY FIELD MAKES ITS DEBUT

Regents Field had sufficed as a permanent home field close to campus, but was hardly large enough for the crowds that the Michigan Wolverines were attracting. A long-term solution became easier when in 1902, Detroit native Dexter M. Ferry donated 21 acres of land to the University, stretching from South State Street to the railroad tracks. This donation united the land comprising the athletic campus of the University of Michigan. In honor of this gift, the University Regents renamed Regents Field as Ferry Field. Knowing that it was imperative to accommodate more fans, the Regents approved the construction of a new football field. The new complex was to continue under the name Ferry Field and would be located closer to campus at the site where the Michigan outdoor track now lies. But while the name stayed the same, much else about the new field was different. Unlike the old field, which was home to the football, baseball and track teams, the grass on Ferry Field was for football use only. Michigan built separate practice fields so that use of Ferry Field could be restricted to game days only. In addition, Ferry Field had the capacity to seat 18,000 fans, more than 20 times larger than the capacity of the former home. To facilitate media coverage, Ferry Field also offered a press box on the Hoover Street side; that was later demolished to accomodate the construction of the Intramural Sports Building. The final game on Regents Field was played on November 25, 1905 as Michigan won its 26th consecutive game by dismantling Oberlin, 75-0. The victory boosted Michigan's all-time record at Regents Field to an astonishing 87-2-3, a winning percentage of .962.

Photo: Michigan Union

Ferry Field, 1907 Penn State game.

CHAMPIONSHIP *Moment*

MICHIGAN'S IMCOMPARABLE ERA ENDS

The day dawned clear and cold at the University of Chicago's Marshall Field on Thanksgiving Day, 1905. The undefeated Maroons were faced with the challenge of playing Michigan, the greatest collection of gridiron strength ever assembled. The teams battled to a scoreless tie until just four-and-a-half minutes remained. At that point, Maroon All-American Walter Eckersall boomed a 70-yard punt into the Michigan end zone. Unadvisedly, a U-M substitute halfback named Denny Clark fielded the punt near the end line and started to run upfield. He was hit by UC captain Maurice Catlin before he could escape the end zone and was thrown for a safety. That two-point play was all Chicago needed, and Michigan's incomparable era was ended. Afterwards, some newspapers placed blame for the loss squarely upon Clark. "It may be said, and said truthfully," one writer sermonized, "that Clark of Michigan defeated his own eleven." After the game, Clark despondently moaned that "...I shall kill myself because I am in disgrace." Twenty-seven years later, in 1932, Clark shot himself through the heart. In a suicide note to his wife, he reportedly expressed the hope that his "final play" would be of some benefit in atoning for his error at Marshall Field.

CHAMPION OF THE WEST

TOM HAMMOND

To say that Tom Hammond was versatile would be a mammoth understatement. From 1903-05, the Ann Arbor star played no less than five different positions for Coach Fielding Yost's Michigan football team. Known primarily as a blocking back for the famed "Point-a-Minute" teams, Hammond saw action at right end, fullback, right tackle, right halfback and left halfback. Although Hammond labored in the shadows of more famous Wolverine teammates such as Willie Heston and Germany Schultz, Yost was well aware of his hometown star's significant contributions. During Hammond's three letter-winning seasons, Michigan outscored its opponents by an amazing 1,627 to 30 margin. In his three years with the team, Hammond and the Wolverines were 33-1-1, claiming two national championships and two conference titles. A 2-0 defeat at the hands of Chicago in Hammond's final game at Michigan turned out to be the only loss he ever suffered. Following his playing days, Hammond rose to the rank of major general for the U.S. Army. He died in Chicago in 1950 at the age of 66.

Maize & Blue Item

On April 29, 1906, Michigan track and field's four-mile relay team of James Maloney, Horace Ramey, Harry Coe and Floyd Rowe broke the world record (18:10.4) for that event at the Penn Relays. The first three Wolverine runners each had almost identical mile times of 4:32, while anchor-man Rowe cruised in with a clocking of 4:35, nearly 150 yards ahead of the anchor man for second-place Yale.

M *List*

Wolverines' Current Homes

Sport	Venue	Since
Football	Michigan Stadium	1927
Basketball	Crisler Arena	1967
Hockey	Yost Arena	1973
Baseball	Fisher Stadium	1923
Field Hockey	Phyllis Ocker Field	1995
Soccer	Michigan Soccer Field	1995
Wrestling	Cliff Keen Arena	1989
Gymnastics	Cliff Keen Arena	1989
Volleyball	Cliff Keen Arena	1989
Tennis	Varsity Tennis Center	1997
Golf	Michigan Golf Course	1931
Swimming	Canham Natatorium	1989
Softball	Alumni Field (Varsity Diamond)	1982
Track	Ferry Field/Indoor Track Building	1927/1974

1906-07

America's Time Capsule

October 14, 1906: The Chicago White Sox beat the Chicago Cubs to win the third World Series.

November 9, 1906: Theodore Roosevelt became the first President to travel abroad, journeying to Panama to inspect the progress on the Panama Canal.

December 24, 1906: Reginald Fessenden made the first known radio broadcast of voice and music from his Branch Rock, Massachusetts experiment station.

February 20, 1907: President Roosevelt signed the Immigration Act of 1907, restricting immigration by Japanese laborers.

March 21, 1907: U.S. Marines were sent to Honduras to quell a political disturbance.

University Lore

THE UNIVERSITY OF MICHIGAN · ARTES · SCIENTIA · VERITAS · 1817 ™

With the appointment of Prof. Emil Lorch, formal instruction in architecture was resumed after a 26-year lapse. Twenty-two students enrolled in Lorch's initial class in the Fall of 1906. Established as a sub-department of the Department of Engineering with Lorch as the chair, architecture gained a measure of independence in 1913 and became a separate college in 1931. The noted Chicago architect William Le Baron Jenny had commuted to Ann Arbor to teach architecture from 1876 to 1880.

Michigan Moment

MICHIGAN LEAVES THE CONFERENCE

College football seemed out of control. Brutality in the game had increased steadily since the beginning of the 20th century, and consequently, 18 players had died in the past two years. President Theodore Roosevelt threatened to abolish the sport with a national order, but Michigan President James Angell called for a meeting of the Western Conference Presidents to work out the problems at the regional level. During a series of meetings in 1906 and 1907, the Conference members suggested eight guidelines to govern the game. Among the suggestions were a reduction in players' eligibility to three years, trimming the season back to a maximum of five games per season, the elimination of pre-season practice, and severe restrictions on coaches, including one that would force the highly popular Fielding Yost to leave U-M. When the proposal was brought back to Ann Arbor, the community unanimously opposed it. In light of Yost's six-year record of 59-2-1, few were willing to lose such a great coach. When the Conference leaders reconvened in 1907, Angell presented Michigan's opposing views. With the support of several other Western Conference schools, all of Michigan's desires were approved, except for the removal of the retroactive clause of the three-year rule. Despite Angell's insistence, he returned to Ann Arbor without the main sticking point resolved. Faced with giving in and facing a bleak season or dropping out of the Big Ten, Michigan chose the latter on January 14, 1908. The University remained a college football independent for 10 seasons, until resuming Conference membership in November of 1917.

Photo: Walter Graham Scrapbook

U-M's football lineup for 1906.

CHAMPION OF THE WEST

HORACE PRETTYMAN

During his distinguished career as a University of Michigan athlete and as a businessman in the Ann Arbor community, Horace Prettyman made several notable contributions. His fame as a collegian came on the football field where he earned a record seven varsity letters from 1882-90. Three times—1884, '85 and '86—Prettyman served as the Wolverine captain, a record that still stands today. He was perhaps better known later in life as the proprietor of the Campus Club, alias Prettyman's Boarding House. Sixteen students were taken in as roomers at a cost of $1.50 per week. Board at "Prett's" cost $2.50 per week, and it was estimated that Mr. and Mrs. Prettyman served an estimated one million meals to tens of thousands of students, including numerous Wolverine athletes. When the University purchased the facility from Prettyman in 1914, he turned his attention to eventually becoming the principal owner and president of the Ann Arbor Press and president of the White Swan Laundry and the Wolverine Power Company. He died in 1945 at the age of 87.

another CHAMPION OF THE WEST

JOHN GARRELS

One of Michigan's greatest two-sport stars was John Garrels, a two-year letter winner in football and a four-year star in track and field. He gained the most fame as a record-breaking hurdler from 1904-07, earning four Big Ten individual titles, one at 120 yards and three more at 220 yards. At the 1908 Olympic Games in London, Garrels claimed a silver medal in the 110-meter hurdles (:15.7) and, oddly enough, a bronze medal in the shot put (43'3"). As an end for Coach Fielding Yost's gridiron squad from 1905-06, Garrels endured defeats only twice in 18 games. Born in Bay City, he attended schools in both that city and in Detroit. Garrels was graduated in 1907 with a chemical engineering degree, and served as as technical director for Wyandotte Chemicals Corp. for 27 years. He succumbed to heart disease in 1956 at the age of 70.

Maize & Blue Item

On October 27, 1906, Michigan's football team took on Illinois at Ferry Field and swamped the Illini, 28-9. The game marked the only Conference contest U-M would play in 1906, tying for the Big Ten title with a 1-0 record. It would be the last time Michigan would play a Big Ten game until November 24, 1917. The Wolverines would withdraw from the Conference, holding a 30-6-1 football record over league foes since 1896.

M List

Michigan has 23 former players and five former coachers enshrined in the College Football Hall of Fame. A list of the men who played prior to 1940 for the Wolverines includes the following:

Al Benbrook	1908-1910
Benny Friedman	1924-1926
Tom Harmon	1938-1940
Willie Heston	1901-1904
Harry Kipke	1921-1923
John Maulbetsch	1914-1916
Harry Newman	1930-1932
Bennie Oosterbaan	1925-1927
Germany Schulz	1904-1905,1907-1908
Neil Snow	1898-1901
Ernie Vick	1918-1921
Bob Westfall	1939-1941
Francis "Whitey" Wistert	1931-1933

America's Time Capsule

September 12, 1907: The Lusitania, the world's largest steamship, completed its maiden voyage between Ireland and New York.

October 12, 1907: The Chicago Cubs swept the World Series from the Detroit Tigers.

November 16, 1907: Oklahoma became the 46th state.

December 6, 1907: Three hundred sixty-one miners were killed in a West Virginia coal mine explosion.

May 10, 1908: Mother's Day was first celebrated.

University Lore

"Michigenda," the first production of the all-male Michigan Union Opera was greeted with great ovations according to the *Michigan Daily*. Set in the magical kingdom of Michigenda, in which there were no professors, the student written and produced musical comedy drew thunderous applause for clever satires on well-known professors and student life. It also netted $2,000 for the Union building fund. The Opera's productions became a campus staple and many popular Michigan songs had their origin in Opera productions. In 1956 the Opera was transformed into MUSKET (Michigan Union Show Ko-Eds Too).

Michigan Moment

"M" GRIDDERS SCRAMBLE TO FILL SCHEDULE

Now an "ex-member" of the Western Conference, Michigan was forced to look far and wide for athletic competition. Michigan had to plan the bulk of its schedule by itself and what resulted turned out positively. The Brown Jug battle with Minnesota was continued until 1910, and Michigan was able to play Ohio State until the Buckeyes joined the Conference in 1912. Intrastate rival Michigan State could be counted on for a football game per year, and local schools Case and Mt. Union planned contests with Michigan. But when it became obvious that a seven-game schedule could not be filled locally, Michigan forged bonds with other teams around the nation. A series with Vanderbilt that had begun in 1905 was continued, and rivalries were instituted with Cornell, Pennsylvania and Syracuse. Games with these teams soon became fierce rivalries, as Michigan played no less than two games with these squads every year between 1906-1917. The baseball team dealt with the open schedule in a similar manner. Forced with the prospect of losing 60 percent of its games off the 1905 schedule, the team soon began a practice of going on a tour of the South in the early part of the season. This five-to-10 game stretch typically included opponents such as Kentucky, Tennessee, Alabama, and Vanderbilt. So succesful was this venture that Michigan maintained the practice of a Southern tour many years after the Wolverines rejoined the Big Ten.

U-M Coach Dan McGugin (hands on hips) at a Wolverines versus Vanderbilt football game.

CHAMPIONSHIP *Moment*

TRADITIONAL BLOCK "M" DISPLAYED FIRST IN 1907

The origin of the block "M", the formation of which has become a tradition at Michigan's home football games, dates back to 1907. The large block "M" was formed in the cheering sections by 750 yellow and 1,250 blue banners, sold to spectators at the cost of 25 cents each. Said the *Michigan Daily* in its November 17, 1907 edition, "Probably no more beautiful feature was ever seen at a football game than the block "M" section. At a signal from the yellmaster, the black mass of humanity on the bleacher suddenly became transformed, as though by a magic touch, into a gigantic "M" outlined against a background of blue."

CHAMPION OF THE WEST

DAN McGUGIN

Dan McGugin was a favorite of Michigan coaching legend Fielding Yost. Not only did McGugin star at guard for Yost during his playing days for the "Point-a-Minute" Michigan teams of 1901 and '02, McGugin ended up marrying his coach's sister and asking Yost to serve as the best man in his wedding. One of the lightest men on the team, McGugin's speed and quickness more than made up for his lack of bulk. Following his playing days, McGugin served as Yost's assistant in 1903, then got the head coaching job at Vanderbilt. For the next 31 years, the "Colonel"dominated Southern football, compiling a record of 197-55-19 as the Commodores' leader. One of his proudest accomplishments was in holding Michigan to a 0-0 tie in 1922 when that team was coach by his old mentor and brother-in-law. McGugin later became athletic director at Vanderbilt. He died following a heart attack in 1936 at the age of 56.

Maize & Blue Item

From 1893 through 1907, beating a Michigan football team on its home field was akin to the infrequent appearance of Haley's Comet. The Wolverines' record during their 14-year home unbeaten streak was an unbelievable 92-0-3. However, on November 16, 1907, Michigan's home-field dominance came to a crashing halt, losing 6-0 to a talented Pennsylvania squad.

M List

Several of Michigan's M-men took their expertise to other schools after their playing time at Michigan has ended. In all, 52 Wolverine football players have served as head coach of 59 different schools in 33 states. Here's a list of some of the former U-M players who have gone on to coach at Big Ten and other major schools.

Dave Allerdice	Texas
Stanley Borleske	North Dakota State
William Edmunds	West Virginia, Washington University, Vermont
Pete Elliott	Nebraska, California, Illinois, Miami (Florida)
Forest Evashevski	Hamilton, Washington State, Iowa
A.E. Herrnstein	Purdue, Ohio State
Frank Longman	Arkansas, Wooster (Ohio), Notre Dame
John Maultbesch	Oklahoma, A&M, Marshall
Dan McGugin	Vanderbilt
Henry Schulte	Eastern Michigan, Missouri, Nebraska
Fred Trosko	Eastern Michigan

1908-09

America's Time Capsule

October 1, 1908: The Model T was introduced by Henry Ford.

November 3, 1908: William Howard Taft was elected president of the United States.

April 6, 1909: Robert Peary reached the North Pole.

July 12, 1909: Congress proposed an amendment to authorize a national income tax.

July 27, 1909: Orville Wright set a flight-duration record of just more than one hour.

University Lore

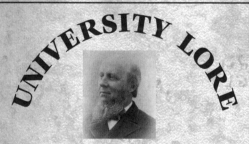

In February of 1909, 80-year-old President James B. Angell submitted his resignation to the Regents, to take effect in June. Angell's 38-year tenure was the longest of any U-M president. A charismatic, persuasive and paternal figure, he was known to generations of students as "Prexy Angell." Enrollment had grown from 1,100 to over 5,000, too large for a successor to impress a personal stamp on the campus in the way Angell had. The Regents granted Angell the title of emeritus president, a $4,000 pension and permission to keep living in the President's House.

Michigan Moment

MICHIGAN CAGERS MAKE THEIR DEBUT

Without a conference to play in, a modern facility to use and few fans to attend games, Michigan launched its first varsity basketball team in 1909. However, those three factors would combine to suspend basketball as a varsity sport at U-M for nine years following the opening season. There were no stars, though one member of the team, Gregory Peck, Sr., would eventually sire a silver screen celebrity. J. Paul Wilson, captain of those original Michigan cagers, recalled Coach George McNeal's squad in a 1970s article. "In the fall of 1908," Wilson said, "the first varsity basketball team was organized without much enthusiasm on the part of the athletic department. The 'powers-that-be' would much rather have had us go out for the track team. It was quite hard to get organized as only two of us had played together." While Michigan claimed just one victory (over Oberlin) in its five-game schedule of 1909, the team was competitive, losing a pair of hard-fought contests to both Ohio State and Michigan State. Besides Wilson and Peck, other members of first Wolverine basketball team included Harry Farquhar, Frank West, James Raiss, Griff Hayes and Charles "Chick" Lathers.

Photo: Michiganensian

Michigan's first U-M basketball team.

CHAMPIONSHIP *Moment*

"M" WOMEN GAIN THEIR OWN ATHLETIC FIELD

The first athletic field exclusively devoted to University of Michigan female students was purchased in 1909. Mrs. William Hussey, first President of the Woman's League, oversaw the acquisition of a six-and-a-half-acre tract of land, known previously as "Sleepy Hollow." It was located adjacent to the Observatory Building on the northeast campus. Previous to this, tennis was the only outdoor sport available for coed participation. Now they had available space for a hockey field, an archery range, and various other outdoor venues. Said the 1909 *Michiganensian* of the new field, "Huge oaks and high ground form effective screens, and the women are thus assured of seclusion. There will be room for picturesque picnic grounds where the girls may gather, and the whole tract will be open for the use of all University women."

CHAMPION OF THE WEST

ADOLPH "GERMANY" SCHULZ

It wasn't until Germany Schulz's legendary football career had ended that he heard any form of praise from his coach, Fielding Yost. "No one ever lived who could equal Schulz in the line," said Yost. "On defense, once he put his hand on a runner, it was all over. On offense, he could open holes no ball carrier could miss." The word "durable" described Schulz to a tee, as the 6-2, 245-pounder missed only 10 minutes of competition during his four seasons at Michigan. From 1904-08, anchored by Schulz, Wolverine football teams won 32 games, lost four and tied one. As an offensive center, Schulz was credited with an innovation that is now standard in the game, the spiral pass from center. The son of a Fort Wayne, Indiana doctor, he hardened himself for the football season by working in steel mills. After graduation from U-M, Schulz coached at his alma mater, Wisconsin, Kansas State, Tulane and Detroit. He left the coaching field in 1922 to enter the insurance business. Just two weeks before his death in 1951 at the age of 67, Schulz was honored by the Associated Press with his selection to the all-time All-America team.

Maize & Blue Item

Dr. George A. "Doc" May was one of the campus's most familiar faces his 41-years of service to the University of Michigan. He joined the athletic staff of Michigan in 1901. Thousands of men passed through Doc May's compulsory physical education classes or worked under him during his lengthy stint as Director of Waterman Gymnasium and as gymnastics coach. He also attained national fame as a track starter.

M List: Michigan's Baseball Team

Michigan's 1909 baseball team compiled a record of 18-3-1, good for a .841 winning percentage. However, the past of Michigan baseball is so storied, that winning percentage is no better than ninth among Michigan's all-time winningest teams (min. 15 games):

Season	W	L	T	Pct.
1945	20	1	0	.952
1918	16	1	0	.941
1946	18	3	0	.857
1895	19	3	1	.848
1983	50	9	0	.847
1985	55	10	0	.846
1923	22	4	0	.846
1905	16	3	0	.842
1909	18	3	1	.841
1921	21	4	0	.840

1909-10

America's Time Capsule

October 16, 1909: The Pittsburgh Pirates defeated the Detroit Tigers in the sixth World Series.

February 6, 1910: The Boy Scouts of America organization was chartered by Chicago publisher William Boyce.

March 16, 1910: Auto racer Barney Oldfield set a land-speed record of 133 miles per hour.

June 19, 1910: Spokane, Washington became the first city to celebrate Father's Day.

July 4, 1910: Jack Johnson successfully defended his world heavyweight boxing championship against Jim Jeffries.

University Lore

The idea of a memorial building dedicated to University men who had fallen in the Civil War was first proposed in 1864. It finally came to fruition in 1910 with the opening of the Alumni Memorial Building. The classical style building designed by architects Donaldson and Meier cost $195,855.29. The Memorial building housed the Alumni Association, but its main purpose was to serve as the University's art museum. The opening exhibit was from Charles Freer's collection of American and Oriental art, now in the Freer Gallery in Washington, D.C.

Michigan Moment

MICHIGAN UPSETS PENN

For three years running, the University of Pennsylvania football team had ruined undefeated seasons for the Michigan Wolverines. A 6-0 loss in the season finale of 1907 was particularly painful to U-M coach Fielding Yost, as that defeat ended a 95-game home unbeaten streak. Penn's 29-0 victory in 1908 was equally demoralizing to Yost's troops. On November 13, 1909, in Philadelphia, Michigan players decided that it was time for the worm to turn. It just so happened that on the day of the game, the U.S. Battleship Michigan was docked at the nearby League Island Navy Yard, with the entire crew of 400 in attendance at the game cheering on the Wolverines. Before the game, each bluejacket marched onto Franklin Field carrying a Maize and Blue flag and broke into a cheer for their adopted football team:

Photo: Walter Graham Scrapbook

Dave Allerdice

> "Wow! Wow! Wow! We're here now.
> Two stack, twin screw, battleship queen.
> Michigan! Michigan! Football team!

The Wolverines then began to dismantle their hosts' game plan. Perhaps the key play in Michigan's 12-6 victory that day was a fake field goal by Captain Dave Allerdice, who got off a beautiful pass that set up the day's first score and shift the momentum into U-M's favor. Afterward, Allerdice credited the crew of the U.S. Michigan as the real key to victory. "Every one of the fellows seemed to feel," said Allerdice, "that it was a personal obligation, not only to win for Michigan, but also for the men who had taken so much pains to fix up this ceremony for us."

CHAMPION OF THE WEST

STAN WELLS

One of Michigan's most spectacular football players of 1909, '10 and '11 won All-Western honors as a tackle and an end, but was strangely enough the school's first forward passer of note. In an era when the pass was considered risky, Stan Wells threw the pigskin with unusual accuracy. In U-M's famous 6-0 victory over Minnesota in 1910, Wells twice connected with Stan Borleske on long passes, then carried the ball over himself for the winning touchdown. A native of Ohio, Wells began an administrative career with first the Detroit Steel Products Company, then the Life and Casualty Insurance Company in Nashville, Tennessee. While living in Nashville, he officiated football games in the Southern and Southeastern Conferences from 1928 to 1940. Wells died of a heart attack in 1967 at the age of 78.

another CHAMPION OF THE WEST

JOSEPH HORNER

Michigan's first great shot putter was Joseph Horner, a letter winner for the Wolverine track and field squad from 1909-11. A native of Grand Rapids, Horner gained fame as a youth in western Michigan in 1905 when he established a shotput record at Central High School that would stand for 32 years. Upon his graduation, he began rewriting the record book at Michigan as well. Horner's 48'8" toss in 1911 set a world's indoor mark that also lasted until 1937. To his feats with the shot put and discus, he added the unique ability, usually denied a weight man, of being one of the best intercollegiate sprinters, hurdlers and vaulters of his day. Horner was a candidate for the United States Olympic team in 1912, a year after his graduation from the U-M, but gave up sports competition to go to work for the *Saginaw News*. Following service in World War I as a navy pilot, Horner joined the *Press-Gazette* newspaper in Green Bay, Wisconsin. He worked his way up the ladder to vice president and general manager of that paper. Horner died in 1960 at the age of 72 after undergoing brain surgery.

Maize & Blue Item

For 41 years, nearly everything associated with physical education at the U-M went through George "Doc" May. The native of Philadelphia came to Ann Arbor from Yale in 1901 with a goal of using his medical degree to become an eye, ear and throat specialist. Instead, May soon became the director of gymnastic classes, adding athletics to the lives of many students in the form of fencing, boxing and calisthenics. May died in 1948 at the age of 75.

M List: Michigan as a Streakbreaker

Team	Sport	Type	Year
Pennsylvania	Football	24-game unbeaten streak	1909
Vanderbilt	Football	21-game unbeaten streak	1923
Indiana	Wrestling	35-1 in the last five years	1937
Indiana	Swimming	47-meet win streak	1965
Ohio State	Football	22-game win streak	1969
Penn State	Wrestling	38-match unbeaten streak	1973
Iowa	Wrestling	99-match Big Ten win streak	1989
Rutgers	Basketball	31-game win streak	1976
Indiana	Basketball	50-game home-win streak	1995
Duke	Basketball	103-1 at home vs. non-conference opp.	1996

MICHIGAN MOMENT

America's Time Capsule

November 8, 1910: In congressional elections, the Democratic party took control of Congress for the first time in 16 years.

November 14, 1910: The first successful attempt of a naval aircraft launching from the deck of a warship was made off the cruiser Birmingham.

March 25, 1911: One hundred forty-six persons perished in a New York City industrial fire.

May 11, 1911: The Supreme Court ordered Standard Oil dissolved because it violated the antitrust law.

May 30, 1911: Ray Harroun won the first Indianapolis 500 automobile race.

UNIVERSITY LORE

In August of 1909, Harry Burns Hutchins, Dean of the Law Department, was named interim President for one year to succeed President Angell. After several candidates, including Woodrow Wilson, declined to accept the presidency, the Regents decided to make Hutchins President for a three-year term. Following some stormy negotiations with Regent Chase Osborn, Hutchins accepted a five-year appointment. At the end of his term the Regents asked him to continue in office and Hutchins served until 1920.

WOLVERINE GRIDDERS DEFEAT GOPHERS

Despite Michigan's absence from the Big Ten Conference, the Wolverines were able to maintain their football series with Minnesota. Coach Henry Williams' unbeaten and unscored-upon Golden Gophers carried a perfect 6-0 record into their 1910 game at Ferry Field. A rather impotent offense had held Coach Fielding Yost's squad to an unusual record of 2-0-3. The game was a brutal one, nearly approaching the ferocity of the 1903 battle. Though the first three periods were scoreless, there were a few scoring opportunities. In addition to missing a field goal from inside U-M's 10-yard line, Minnesota also had a touchdown called back following a blocked punt. When the fourth quarter began, Michigan found itself in possession of the ball at the Gopher nine-yard line. However, the Minnesota defense did not allow any further penetration, and U-M's field-goal attempt sailed wide. Michigan's final possession would start on its own 47-yard line with less than five minutes remaining. In an attempt to gain some much-needed yardage, Yost called upon the rarely used forward pass. Stanley Borleske caught Stan Wells' first pass and advanced to the Gopher 30-yard line. On the following play, Yost called again for Wells to pass, and this time Borleske's grab had the ball first-and-goal at the three-yard line. Two plays later, Wells plunged over for a touchdown and Michigan took a 6-0 lead. Minnesota took the ensuing kickoff and moved methodically down the field, but time ran out before the Gophers could score. The game would mark the last between Michigan and Minnesota until 1919, as the Conference barred any members from playing the Wolverines.

A triumphant Fielding Yost with the Little Brown Jug.

CHAMPION OF THE WEST

AL BENBROOK

Hall of Famer Al Benbrook was one of college football's great running guards. Instead of having his all-star lineman dig into the turf on every play, Michigan coach Fielding Yost used Benbrook's quickness to pioneer the style of pulling out of the line to lead the interference on the offense. And, on defense, Benbrook was one of the first guards to pull out of his position and back up the line. Walter Eckersall, longtime football authority, rated Benbrook the greatest guard of all time—placing him above Yale's legendary "Pudge" Heffelfinger. Selected to the National Football Foundation College Football Hall of Fame in 1991, Benbrook won All-America acclaim in both 1909 and '10, becoming the first Michigan guard to earn national honors. He also competed in track and field for the Wolverines. Following his graduation from the U-M, Benbrook served in World War I with a machine gun battalion, then returned to the states to a successful career manufacturing office furniture. He died on August 16, 1943, just eight days short of his 56th birthday.

another CHAMPION OF THE WEST

VICTOR PATTENGILL

Reared in the shadows of rival Michigan Agricultural College, Lansing's Vic Pattengill was one the University of Michigan's most vocal supporters. Twice elected president of the "M" Club, in 1919 and again in 1932, Pattengill was a letter-winning halfback and end for Coach Fielding Yost's football team. The two squads for which he lettered (1909 and '10) compiled a combined record of 9-1-3. Returning to Lansing after his graduation from the U-M in 1912, Pattengill served as football coach of the city's high school without remuneration. The son of Lansing's superintendent of schools and namesake of Pattengill Junior High School, Vic made his mark in real estate. Although only 54, Pattengill fell ill in 1941 and never recovered, dying two years later.

Maize & Blue Item

A man's admiration for his brother was the inspiration for Michigan's famed marching song, "Varsity". During the Wolverines' game against undefeated Minnesota in 1910, Fred Lawton watched older brother George help lead Michigan to a 6-0 upset victory. A year later, on October 6, 1911, Lawton's famed lyrics and Earl "Monk" Moore's music were first sung by U-M students. Eighty-five years later, "Varsity" remains as one of the University's most famous songs.

M List: Notable Michigan Unbeaten Streaks

Games	Type	Sport	Years
55	Unbeaten	Football	1901-05
47	Winning	Tennis	1954-58
45	Winning	Men's Gymnastics	1968-72
41	Winning	Men's Swimming	1984-89
36	Winning	Women's Swimming	1986-90
34	Winning	Wrestling	1962-65
27	Winning	Baseball	1945-46
26	Winning	Women's Gymnastics	1994-95
23	Unbeaten	Ice Hockey	1996
22	Winning	Softball	1993
17	Winning	Women's Tennis	1975-76
17	Winning	Men's Basketball	1984-85

1911-12

America's Time Capsule

October 26, 1911: The American League's Philadelphia Athletics defeated the New York Giants to win the World Series.

February 14, 1912: Arizona was admitted to the union as the 48th U.S. state.

April 15, 1912: About 1,500 persons were killed when the British liner Titanic struck an iceberg and sank off the coast of Newfoundland.

April 20, 1912: The Detroit Tigers defeated Cleveland, 6-5, in 11 innings in the Navin Field dedication game

July 22, 1912: The Olympic Games came to a close in Stockholm, Sweden. Among the American gold-medal winners was decathlete Jim Thorpe.

University Lore

After years of discussion and some faculty opposition, the Regents, in December 1911, authorized the establishment of an independent Graduate Department. Graduate study had been administered by the Graduate Council, a part the College of LS&A. Karl Eugen Guthe was named the first Dean of the Graduate Department. With the aid of a distinguished executive committee, Guthe did much to raise the quality and scope of graduate work before his premature death in 1915. He was succeeded as dean by Prof. Alfred Lloyd.

Michigan Moment

MICHIGAN ATHLETES SHINE AT 1912 OLYMPIC GAMES

The 1912 Summer Olympics in Stockholm, Sweden are probably best remembered by historians as the games in which a 24-year-old American Indian athlete named Jim Thorpe made his mark. Thorpe captured the two-most demanding events in track and field—the pentathlon and the decathlon. "You sir," said the Swede's King Gustav to Thorpe at the victory stand, "are the greatest athlete in the world." To which Thorpe is said to have replied, "Thanks, King." A trio of University of Michigan athletes also represented the United States and each of the three made a wonderful showing. Ralph Craig, the amateur record-setting sprinter, proved himself to be the fastest man in the world at 100 meters, despite an unnerving seven false starts. In one of those, Craig sprinted the entire distance before being called back. He later won a second gold medal in the 200-meter dash. A second Michigan man, Ralph Rose, placed his name in the Olympic record book by winning an event no longer competed. Throwing the shot put once with his left hand and once with his right hand, Rose's cumulative total of 90'10 1/2" earned him a gold medal. He also won a silver in the single-hand shot shot competition. Carroll Huff, former Michigan track and field captain, merited a place in the 400-meter finals, but finished fifth in a time of :49.5 behind Olympic record-setting Charlie Reidpath of the United States.

Photo: U-M Athletic Dept.

Carroll Haff, U-M track, 1911-13, Olympian 1912

CHAMPION OF THE WEST

RALPH CRAIG

Twenty-three-year-old Ralph Craig, a native of Detroit, was the favorite to win the 100-meter dash at the 1912 Summer Olympics in Stockholm, Sweden. A member of Michigan's track and field squad from 1909-11, Craig excelled at the sprints, having equalled the world record at 220 yards both in 1910 and 1912. At the 1912 Olympic Games, the competitors in the 100-meter race were an anxious lot, false-starting seven times. On the eighth try, the start went smoothly, and Craig ran neck-and-neck in a tightly bunched group. Finally, at the 60-meter mark, Craig ignited the after-burners to take first place by two feet in a time of :10.8, leading a 1-2-3 USA finish. In the 200-meter race, Craig also won the gold medal, finishing in a time of :21.7, the best Olympic clocking since fellow "M" man Archie Hahn ran a :21.6 in 1904. Craig left Stockholm with a pair of gold medals, joining Hahn as the Olympics' only two 100 and 200 victors. Craig's Olympic experience did not end in Stockholm, for in 1948, at the age of 59, Ralph Craig was the captain of, and an alternate on, the U.S. Yachting Team at the summer games in London. The 36 years between games marked the longest span ever between two Olympics by any American athlete. Retiring as an industrial engineer, Craig died at the age of 83 in 1972 at his summer home on Lake George in New York.

another CHAMPION OF THE WEST

JIMMY CRAIG

Though Jimmy Craig was an outstanding athlete for the University of Michigan from 1911-13, his feats sometimes tended to fall in the shadow of his older brother, Ralph, a two-time Olympic champion. But Jimmy's football coach, Fielding Yost, held a special fondness for the younger Craig. "Jimmy's combative spirit was as great as that of any man I ever knew," said Yost. "He thrived on defeat; he was at his best when the going was the hardest. Jimmy reached the heights when Michigan was behind." Craig was noted chiefly as a ball carrier. His last-minute, game-winning run against Minnesota is perhaps his most famous moment. On defense, Craig consistently showed his ability to diagnose the opponents' plays. Said Yost, "He always seemed to know beforehand what the opposing team intended to do." Michigan's record during the All-American's career was a sparking 16-4-2 in 22 games, a span which saw the Wolverines outscore their foes by a difference of 300 points, 424 to 124. Craig died in January of 1990.

Maize & Blue Item

Michigan started fast in its 1911 battle against powerful Pennsylvania, taking a 6-0 lead. Penn held a 9-6 advantage late in the game, when Yost dug into his bag of tricks for a final play. Upon the snap of the ball, U-M captain Fred Conklin appeared to be smothered by Penn defenders on an end run. However, the ball shot out of the scrum and straight into the hands of U-M's Jimmy Craig who ran 35 yards for the winning TD.

M List: All-Time Big Ten Football Standings (as Big Ten members)

Team	Wins	Losses	Ties	Pct.
Penn State	25	7	0	.7813
Michigan	390	149	18	.7163
Ohio State	374	141	24	.7161
Michigan State	183	134	9	.5752
Chicago	120	99	14	.5451
Minnesota	284	285	28	.4992
Illinois	295	302	31	.4944
Purdue	253	300	31	.4598
Wisconsin	257	317	41	.4512
Iowa	231	296	25	.4411
Northwestern	204	391	21	.3482
Indiana	168	363	24	.3243

1912-13

America's Time Capsule

October 14, 1912: Presidential candidate Theodore Roosevelt was shot in an assassination attempt in Milwaukee, Wisconsin.

October 16, 1912: The Boston Red Sox won the ninth annual baseball World Series over the New York Giants.

November 5, 1912: Democrat Woodrow Wilson won the U.S. presidency in a landslide victory.

May 31, 1913: The Seventeenth Amendment, providing for the popular election of U.S. senators, went into effect.

July 28, 1913: The U.S. won the Davis Cup challenge for the first time in 11 years.

University Lore

The Athletic Administration Building, or "Club House" as it was known, became the center of campus athletics in 1912. The Tudor style building at the east end of Ferry Field included locker room facilities, offices and a large lecture room. The Administration Building was extensively remodeled in 1926 after Yost Field House opened. It has been renamed the Marie D. Hartwig building for the first Director of Women's Athletics and now houses the Ticket Office, Sports Information Office and the Athletic Alumni and Development Offices.

Michigan Moment

MICHIGAN "9" DOMINATES COMPETITION

Photo: U-M Athletic Dept.

George Sisler

Branch Rickey's four seasons as head coach of the Michigan baseball team concluded in 1913 on a high note. While his overall record of 1910, '11 and '12 was a respectable 47-28-3, it wasn't nearly as glittery as the 21-4-1 record his Wolverines accumulated in 1913. It was the first time in history that a Michigan baseball team won 20 games or more. During Rickey's sparkling major league career as a baseball administrator, his most famous player, of course, was Jackie Robinson. However, the "Mahatma" also had a pretty good player at Michigan in future Hall of Famer George Sisler. The square-jawed sophomore was listed as a pitcher for Rickey's 1913 varsity squad, but, though individual statistics aren't available, he likely also starred as a hitter. Other standouts for the '13 Wolverines included centerfielder and team captain Joe Bell, shortstop Roy Baker, first baseman Miller Pontius, infielder Perry Howard, pitcher Roy Baribeau, second basemen Ed McQueen and Scott Dunagan, catchers Russ Baer and Goodloe Rogers, and left fielder Frank Sheehy. Rickey's charges began their season winning 16 of their first 19 games. The Wolverines were particularly successful on their home field, winning 12 of 14 contests. Rickey left his post as U-M's coach after the season to finish his law degree, and was replaced by Carl Lundgren.

CHAMPIONSHIP *Moment*

THE INTRAMURAL SPORTS PROGRAM

The University of Michigan's intramural sports program had its inception in 1912, becoming one of the first educational institutions to have an organized program with a director. In fact, the word "intramural" was coined by former U-M faculty member A.S. Whitney. Its derivation is from the Latin meaning "within the walls." Floyd Rowe became the program's first director in 1913, overseeing a total of 2,058 participants. Eleven years later in 1924, participation exceeded 10,000. Elmer Mitchell and Earl Riskey were two of the program's most influential directors. U-M's Intramural Sports Building, located on Ferry Field and bordering on Hoover Street, opened in 1928. It was the first structure of its kind in the country to be used primarily for intramural activities.

CHAMPION OF THE WEST

BRANCH RICKEY

Branch Rickey, a 1967 inductee into Cooperstown's Baseball Hall of Fame, began his storied career at the University of Michigan in 1909. While U-M's law school was Rickey's first priority, his hobby—baseball—ultimately brought him his greatest acclaim. During his four years as the Wolverines' skipper, 1910-13, Michigan baseball teams won nearly 70 percent of their games. His most famous player at the U-M was future Hall of Famer George Sisler. Born in Stockdale, Ohio, in 1881, Rickey broke into baseball as a catcher with the St. Louis Browns in 1905 and completed his playing career with the New York Yankees in 1907. His springboard to fame was with St. Louis, where he raised the Cardinals from rags to World Series riches through his expert supervision of the Redbirds' farm system. Following several championship years with the Cardinals, Rickey gave up his general manager's post to become president of the Brooklyn Dodgers. It was the Brooklyn team built on his formula of "youth and speed" that won four pennants. Rickey broke the major leagues' unwritten color barrier in 1947 by bringing Jackie Robinson into the bigs. The "Mahatma" died in December of 1965 after lingering 26 days in a coma.

Maize & Blue Item

Carroll "Hap" Haff, who completed his outstanding career in 1913, was one of three Michigan track and field athletes who participated in the 1912 Summer Olympics. His specialties were middle-distance races, and his quarter-mile record remained unbroken for nearly two decades. Following his athletic career, Haff served as a Wall Street broker for 25 years. He died in 1947 at the age of 55.

M List: U-M Baseball Players Who Have Received the Big Ten Conference Medal of Honor

1925	William Giles	1951	Leo Koceski
1929	Ernest McCoy	1955	Daniel Cline
1937	John Gee	1970	Mark Henry
1939	Leo Beebe	1976	Dick Walterhouse
1941	Forest Evashevski	1980	George Foussaines
1946	Bliss Bowman Jr.	1982	Jim Pacoriek
1947	Paul White	1985	Ken Hayward
1948	Jack Weisenburger	1986	Casey Close

1913-14

MICHIGAN MOMENT

CHAMPIONS OF THE WEST TRIUMPH OVER EAST

In a Phoenix-like fashion, Michigan's football team rose from the ashes of a disastrous mid-season defeat to finish the schedule in a burst of glory. Following U-M's shutout victories against over-matched Case and Mt. Union, cross-state rival Michigan Agricultural College came to Ann Arbor to face the team they had never beaten. Perhaps, Michigan was a bit overconfident, remembering the 55-7 lashing it had applied to the Aggies the year before. Whatever the reason, M.A.C. triumphed on this day, 12-7. Only the psychological genius of Fielding Yost could have lifted the Michigan troops from the depths of despair, and for the next four games, the Wolverines were their old, dominating selves. The turning-point game came October 25th at Vanderbilt, where U-M dominated its host, 33-2. Then came a three-game slate against foes from the East: Syracuse, Cornell and Pennsylvania. Boosting Michigan's talent level on November 1 was the return of academically sidelined all-star Jimmy Craig to the lineup. Unleashed for the first time, the speedy All-America halfback proceeded to run through the SU's defense, leading U-M to a 43-7 victory. A trip to Cornell was next for the Wolverines. Though U-M struggled a bit, it still managed to shut out the Big Red, 17-0. Now came Michigan's season finale versus Pennsylvania. Penn had beaten U-M, 27-21, in Philadelphia in 1912, so Yost's players appeared especially determined. Michigan scored all its points in the first half, then counted upon its defense—headed by Captain George Paterson, Miller Pontius and Jim Raynsford—to withstand Penn's challenges. The Wolverines won, 13-0, winding up the season with a respectable 6-1 record.

Photo: U-M Athletic Dept.

James Craig

America's Time Capsule

October 11, 1913: The Philadelphia Athletics defeated the New York Giants to capture the 10th annual World Series.

December 23, 1913: President Woodrow Wilson reformed the American banking system by establishing the Federal Reserve System.

April 22, 1914: Mexico severed diplomatic relations with the United States.

May 7, 1914: A congressional resolution established the second Sunday in May to be celebrated as Mother's Day.

August 15, 1914: Australia defeated the United States to win the Davis Cup tennis challenge.

UNIVERSITY LORE

When the students returned in the fall of 1913, they assembled in a magnificent new auditorium that would quickly gain fame as one of the world's great concert halls. The Albert Kahn-designed Hill Auditorium seated 4,200 and the huge stage had a seating capacity of 300. Cost of the fully equipped building was $347,000. The remarkable acoustics were the work of Kahn's chief engineer John Hoyt (U-M '91) and consulting engineer Hugh Tallant. It is named for former regent Arthur S. Hill who willed the university $200,000 to replace the inadequate auditorium in University Hall.

CHAMPION OF THE WEST

GEORGE SISLER

The baseball career of Michigan legend George Sisler paralleled that of Babe Ruth in many ways. Like the Bambino, he debuted in the majors as a left-handed pitcher. Like Ruth, Sisler's hitting was too phenomenal to be restricted to the pitcher's mound. And like the Sultan of Swat, he was a charter member of Cooperstown's Hall of Fame. During Sisler's three-year stay in Ann Arbor, from 1913-15, he and the Wolverines won 76 percent of their games. As a pitcher, Sisler's fastball had great velocity and his curveball darted away from his opponents' bats. He followed his former coach Branch Rickey to the majors, debuting with Rickey's St. Louis Browns mere days after leaving Ann Arbor. Sisler began his 16-year career in the majors as a pitcher, but it soon became unthinkable not to have his bat in the lineup every day. In the field, his speed and gracefulness made him a wizard with the first baseman's mitt. Sisler's career batting average of .340 included six seasons with more than 200 hits. His record 257 hits in 1920 included 49 doubles, 18 triples and 19 home runs. Sisler's MVP year in 1922 was highlighted by a 41-game hitting streak and a lofty .420 average. After retiring as a player following the 1930 season, Sisler operated printing and sporting goods companies in St. Louis. Rickey recalled him to baseball in the 1940s as a scout and special hitting instructor at Brooklyn and Pittsburgh. Sisler died in 1973 at the age of 80.

another CHAMPION OF THE WEST

PHILLIP BARTELME

Phillip Bartelme, who arguably was one of the University of Michigan's most influential athletic figures of the early 20th century, labored in virtual obscurity as leader of the Wolverine program from 1909-21. The reason U-M's second director of athletics is easily forgotten was that he was succeeded by the immortal Fielding Yost. Yet, consider these three significant accomplishments by Bartelme. First, he brought the sports of basketball, hockey and swimming to varsity status. Secondly, he oversaw the construction of the Athletic Administration Building and the concrete bleachers at old Ferry Field. Thirdly, he was responsible for hiring the first full-time director of Intramural sports at the University. Following his 13 years at Michigan, Bartelme entered professional baseball as president of the Syracuse, N.Y. club. Later, he served as assistant business manager of the St. Louis Cardinals and as president of Sacramento's minor league club. Bartelme died in 1954 at the age of 78.

Maize & Blue Item

Led by the sensational George Sisler, Michigan's baseball team posted a 7-1 record on its season-opening Southern jaunt. Back in Ann Arbor, the Wolverines began a streak of 47 consecutive shutout innings, where they outscored the opponents 60-0 and allowed just 11 hits. Though they would surrender runs to Syracuse in a 4-2 victory, two more shutouts would follow and U-M would stretch its winning streak to 14 games, en route to posting a 22-6 season mark.

M List: Michigan's Football Opponents

Between 1907 and 1916, Michigan needed non-conference games to fill its schedule. Teams Michigan has played the most, currently in the Big Ten and outside the conference:

Conference Teams	Games	Non-Conference	Games
Ohio State	93	Case	27
Michigan State	89	Notre Dame	26
Minnesota	87	Pennsylvania	21
Illinois	82	Navy	18
Northwestern	59	Cornell	18

1914-15

America's Time Capsule

October 13, 1914: The National League's Boston Braves completed their sweep of the Philadelphia Athletics to win baseball's World Series.

January 25, 1915: Alexander Graham Bell placed the first successful transcontinental telephone call from New York City to San Francisco.

February 8, 1915: D.W. Griffith's famous motion picture, "Birth of a Nation," opened in Los Angeles.

April 5, 1915: Jess Willard defeated Jack Johnson in 23 rounds to win the world heavyweight boxing title.

May 7, 1915: A German submarine sank the British steamship Lusitania and nearly 1,200 drowned.

University Lore

As part of a broader effort to improve academic standards that began with the adoption of the letter grade system in 1912, the faculty, in 1914, recommended a new nomenclature for the divisions of the University. Those which granted initial degrees were to be called colleges; those which gave professional degrees were to be termed schools. The Regents adopted the proposal in January 1915. Thus, it became proper to speak of the Medical School and the College of Engineering. Sub-divisions of Schools and Colleges were termed Departments.

Michigan Moment

SISLER TWO-HITS THE AGGIES

The batting prowess of George Sisler's major league career is well documented: an all-time record 257 hits in 1920, a single-season best average of .420, and a lifetime average of .340. However, many are surprised to learn of Sisler's mastery as a moundsman. One of his greatest collegiate pitching performances at the University of Michigan came on May 28, 1915, against a talented Michigan Agricultural College squad. The Aggies had handed the Wolverines a 3-1 defeat six games earlier. A number of big league scouts were on hand this day, and Sisler gave them plenty to talk about. In his nine innings of work, the senior southpaw limited M.A.C. to just two hits, while striking out 10 Aggie batters. His performance came on the heels of a brilliant 2-0 masterpiece he had spun against Cornell. As a batter, Sisler scored enough runs—three—to singlehandedly whip M.A.C., cracking out four hits in five at bats, including a pair of triples. And, if that wasn't enough, he also stole two bases and had five fielding assists, including one that started a double play. Now, you've already been told about his wizardry as a batter in the majors, but how did he do as a pitcher? Well, in his very first big league pitching appearance, Sisler out-dueled the immortal Walter Johnson, beating the "Big Train", 2-1. His career record as a pitcher was just under .500 at five wins and six losses, and his earned-run average was an impressive 2.35. But, when you could hit like George Sisler . . . well, it was almost criminal to waste him on the mound!

Photo: U-M Athletic Dept.

George Sisler

CHAMPIONSHIP *Moment*

WATERMAN GYM

Built to provide an indoor area for male students to participate in athletics, Waterman Gym enclosed a 150'x90' area in which basketball and other indoor sports could be played. Named after Joshua Waterman, who donated $20,000 in 1891 for such a purpose, the facility offered a 14-laps-to-the-mile track in its balcony. Though construction was delayed two years becuase of poor economic conditions, the "modern" building was completed in 1894. Though it served the needs of the university well in its early days, by the mid-1910s, Waterman Gym had become hopelessly out of date. Many campaigns were taken up to fix the dilapidated facility, but nothing was done until a $68,000 massive renovation in 1916. This upgrade added 48 feet to each end of the gym and replaced the ancient shower facilities in the basement. The improved building now contained areas for wreslting, boxing and badminton as well as a golf range in the basement. Lit during the daytime by a 195-foot skylight, the Waterman Gym was torn down in 1977 to make room for the U-M Chemistry Building.

CHAMPION OF THE WEST

JOHN MAULBETSCH

When you wear a nickname like "The German Bullet," you better be good! And, fortunately for John Maulbetsch, he lived up to his nickname. Although his playing weight was never more than 155 pounds, Maulbetsch's peculiar running style was very effective. Maulbetsch earned his greatest acclaim in a 1914 game against Pennsylvania, after which the legendary Walter Camp exclaimed, "If anyone tells you the East plays the best brand of football, Maulbetsch shot that theory full of holes." Michigan's ninth All-American grew up in Ann Arbor and played fullback on the 1908 and '09 Ann Arbor High teams which won consecutive state championships. Following one year at Adrian College, Maulbetsch enrolled at the University of Michigan and won varsity letters in 1914, '15 and '16. Upon graduation, he began a coaching career, serving as head coach at Phillips University, except for a tour of duty with the U.S. Navy in 1918. Maulbetsch then coached at Oklahoma A&M from 1921-29 and at Marshall College in Huntington, West Virginia in 1930. For the four years prior to his death in 1950, Maulbetsch operated an automobile dealership.

Maize & Blue Item

Harold Smith, Michigan's 1915 track and field captain, may have had a common name, but he was an uncommonly great dash man for the Wolverines. His highlight of the '15 season came at the annual Eastern Intercollegiate meet at Franklin Field in Philadelphia. Pitted among the best collegiate sprinters in the country, Smith placed first in both the 100- and 220-yard dashes, earning him honors as the top individual performer of the meet.

M *List*: The Growth of Michigan's Offensive Line

Weighing in at an average of 193 pounds, Michigan's starting offensive line in 1914 may have been powerful enough in its day to enable the Wolverines to go 6-3, but would be overmatched by today's standards.

Year	Avg. Height	Avg. Weight
1901	5'11"	184
1914	5'10"	193
1918	5'10"	177
1922	5'11"	183
1936	5'11"	189
1951	6'0"	191
1966	6'1"	224
1981	6'5"	257
1996	6'5"	291

1915-16

America's Time Capsule

October 13, 1915: The Boston Red Sox won the World Series from the Philadelphia Phillies.

December 10, 1915: The millionth Model T rolled off Ford's assembly line in Detroit.

March 9, 1916: Legendary Mexican bandit "Pancho" Villa led 1,500 guerillas across the border, killing 17 Americans in New Mexico.

June 30, 1916: Charles Evans won the U.S. Open golf tournament.

August 4, 1916: The United States purchased the Virgin Islands from Denmark for $25 million.

University Lore

The University's first dormitories for women, Helen Newberry Residence Hall and the Martha Cook Building, opened in 1915. The children of Helen Handy Newberry donated $75,000 to the Student Christian Association for a residence hall to be built next to Newberry Hall (now the Kelsey Museum). The SCA then deeded Helen Newberry Residence Hall to the University. The Martha Cook Building, located on S. State across from the President's House, was the gift of William Cook.

Michigan Moment

MICHIGAN-PENN BATTLE TO 0-0 TIE

Cedric "Pat" Smith

Michigan's football squadron boarded the train to Philadelphia losers of three straight games, including a 24-0 blanking at the hands of Michigan Agricultural College. There was little the team could do to salvage such a disappointing campaign, but a win at Franklin Field would certainly ease the pain. Pennsylvania, like Michigan, was suffering through a three-game losing streak, a skein that had evaporated the Quakers'national championship aspirations. Nevertheless, Penn came into the game a slight favorite. The game ended with Penn in possession of the ball on the Michigan 22-yard line, but that distance had been familiar for the Quakers during the game. Three times the home team missed field goals that would have erased the zero from its side of the scoreboard. The Wolverines' Laurence Roehm also kept the Quakers off the board with an interception in the end zone in the second quarter. U-M standouts John Maulbetsch and Cedric Smith were held for just short gains by the Penn defense. Michigan did have one chance to score, but it was snuffed out as the holder was tackled on the fake of an attempted 26-yard field goal. The 0-0 tie was Michigan's first since the Wolverines left the same field with a scoreless deadlock in 1910. Despite coming back without a win for the fourth consecutive week, the Wolverines did experience something special, a return trip on a train with "record-breaking speed". The newest piece of technology was able to cover the 114-mile distance between St. Thomas and Niagara Falls in just 90 minutes and arrived in Ann Arbor one hour ahead of schedule.

CHAMPIONSHIP Moment

TWO-MILE RELAY TEAM SETS WORLD RECORD

The 1916 team was, by all accounts, the greatest track and field yet assembled at the University of Michigan. Coach Steve Farrell had a scattering of veterans which included America's best collegiate sprinter, a star miler and a versatile relay team. The biggest dual meet of the year was a 71-50 victory over Stanford at Ferry Field. Among the five events in which records were broken that day were the mile, the low and high hurdles, the 220-yard dash, and the 880-yard run. The record breaker in the 880 was Joe Ufer, the father of legendary Michigan broadcaster Bob Ufer. Another highlight of the indoor season was the two-mile relay team's world-record-setting performance against Cornell. The quartet of H.L. Carroll, Ufer, Howard Donnelly and George Murphy lowered the indoor mark of 7:56.6 which was established in 1906 by the Irish-American Athletic Club of New York City.

CHAMPION OF THE WEST

STEVE FARRELL

Steve Farrell, coach of U-M's track and field squad from 1912-30, won ten Big Ten team championships during his reign in Ann Arbor. Born in 1865 at Rockville, Connecticut, he was a star quarter- and half-miler as a youngster. He regularly ran on the pro circuit which included stops in Boston, New York, Philadelphia, Buffalo and Chicago. Farrell later joined the Barnum and Bailey circus, at which he was featured nightly in a race against a horse. Farrell's pals of boyhood days included Keene Fitzpatrick, Pooch Donovan, Piper Donovan, Johnny Mack and Mike Murphy, all of whom eventually became famous track coaches. Farrell's first coaching jobs were at Maine, for seven years, and at Ohio State, for three seasons. He began his stint at Michigan in 1913, also doubling as Fielding Yost's football trainer. Among the track and field stars Farrell developed were Olympic champions Ralph Craig, DeHart Hubbard and Eddie Tolan, plus Olympic medalists Carl Johnson and James Booker. When Michigan rejoined the Big Ten Conference in 1918, Farrell's troops immediately rose to the top of the standings, sweeping indoor and outdoor championships in both '18, '19, '23 and '25. After Farrell retired, he took up the game of golf. Ironically, it was at the first tee of the University golf course where he suffered a fatal heart attack in 1933 at the age of 67.

Maize & Blue Item

The *Michigan Alumnus*, in its December issue, revealed that the 1915 University of Michigan football team was invited to play the University of California in the 1916 Rose Bowl game. However, U-M's Senate Council vetoed the trip, saying "On the grounds that such a game, not under collegiate auspices and held primarily for exhibition purposes, would not be for the best interest of athletics, the Council at its meeting on November 9 decided not to allow the Varsity football team to play at Pasadena on New Year's Day." As substitutes for Michigan and Cal, Washington State beat Brown, 14-0.

M List: Michigan's Head Athletic Trainers (since 1912)

1912-15	Steven Farrell
1916-17	Harry Tutthill
1918	Dr. George May
1919	Information not available
1920-22	Archie Hahn
1923-29	Charles Hoyt
1930-47	Ray Roberts
1947-68	Jim Hunt
1968-79	Lindsay McLean
1980-90	Russ Miller
1991-present	Paul Schmidt

1916-17

America's Time Capsule

September 30, 1916: The New York Giants' 26-game winning streak, baseball's longest ever, was halted by the Boston Braves.

November 7, 1916: Woodrow Wilson was reelected president of the United States.

February 3, 1917: The United States severed diplomatic relations with Germany due to increased submarine warfare.

March 2, 1917: The Jones Act made Puerto Rico a U.S. territory.

April 2, 1917: President Wilson requested a declaration of war against Germany.

University Lore

In 1910 President Hutchins wrote "the saloon problem here is one of the most difficult problems with which the university authorities have to deal." In 1916, Michigan was voting on a state prohibition amendment. William Jennings Bryan drew 5,000 to a prohibition rally at Weinberg's Coliseum on South 5th St. The next night there was a sizable student presence at preacher Billy Sunday's revival style rally. A straw poll among students showed a 2,879 to 429 margin in favor of prohibition.

Michigan Moment

MICHIGAN SPRING SPORTS SEASON CANCELLED

On April 4, 1917, Athletic Director Philip Bartelme announced that Michigan's entire slate of spring sports would be cancelled because of World War I. This action, which was taken to allow for military training for the athletes and the student body on athletic facilities, was followed nationwide over the next few weeks. Before the end of April, Harvard, Yale, Princeton, Cornell, Columbia, Pennsylvania, Dartmouth and Iowa suspended all of their athletic programs to allow for military training. There was much negative sentiment towards this ruling, especially by those who felt that athletic competition kept young men in shape for possible military service. Others noted that the military academies at West Point and Annapolis had not forsaken their athletic programs during the beginning of the overseas conflict (although Navy did eventually cancel its spring sports). Though there was early talk of the possibility of the 1917 football schedule being cancelled, such a move was not necessary and Michigan and many other schools reinstated their athletic programs in the fall.

Photo: U-M Athletic Dept.

U-M Athletic Director Philip Bartelme

CHAMPION OF THE WEST

RALPH AIGLER

Among the 140 men and women who have served at Big Ten institutions as faculty representatives, no one comes close to the University of Michigan's Ralph Aigler in terms of longevity. Only one other individual—Ohio State's Thomas French from 1912-44—approaches Professor Aigler's 39-year regime in Ann Arbor. But, more than simply just years of service, Ralph Aigler's contributions as faculty rep from 1917-1955 were marked by tremendous accomplishment. At the top of his achievements was his leadership in bring Michigan back into Conference membership. The school had quit the league in a huff in 1908. Aigler also had great influencing in wooing Fritz Crisler away from Princeton in 1938 to become the Wolverine football coach. A member of the U-M law school faculty for 47 years, Aigler also had a hand in the planning and construction of many of the school's athletic facilities. Aigler served as chairman of the athletic board during the building of Yost Fieldhouse, the golf course, the women's pool and the Intramural building. He also helped draft the Big Ten's original five-year pact with the Rose Bowl in 1946. Aigler retired in 1953 and died 11 years later in Tucson, Arizona.

another CHAMPION OF THE WEST

CEDRIC "PAT" SMITH

The first fullback to gain All-America status at the University of Michigan was Cedric "Pat" Smith. Following in the footsteps of great Michigan running backs like Willie Heston and Jimmy Craig, Smith earned a varsity letter for the Wolverines in 1915 and '16. Following his junior season in which he had been elected to become captain, Smith instead chose to join the Naval Reserve, even before the United States formally declared war. His coach, Fielding Yost, had great praise for his star fullback. "Pat was a brilliant player ... fast, brainy and an excellent punter and passer," said Yost. "I would call him an all-around star. He was unfortunate in being injured on a number of occasions, but the following Saturday he was usually ready to put on another stellar performance." Smith also excelled as a member of U-M's track and field squad in 1916, '17 and '19, winning the Big Ten shot put title that final year. The Bay City native then participated in George Halas' fledgling American Professional Football Association for four seasons with the Buffalo All-Americans. He was the league's third-leading scorer as a rookie. Smith died in 1969 at the age of 74.

Maize & Blue Item

The sports of soccer, bowling and rifle began a short-lived existence as varsity sports at Michigan during the 1916-17 athletic season. Of the three sports, bowling and rifle had the most success, and both squads were captained by Wilbur Schoepfle. On the lanes, the Wolverine keglers defeated all of their opponents during the regular season, but lost a roll-off for the championship of the West to Illinois.

M List — Important Big Ten Historical Dates

January 11, 1895 - Plans for an organization for controlling athletics were established
February 8, 1896 - Seven schools became inaugural members of the Conference
December 1, 1899 - Iowa and Indiana became members of the Conference
June 1, 1901 - First Conference championship meet (track and field) held in Chicago
January 14, 1908 - Michigan withdrew from the Conference
April 6, 1912 - Ohio State was admitted to membership
November 20, 1917 - Michigan rejoined the Big Ten
March 8, 1946 - Chicago withdrew from the Conference
May 20, 1949 - Michigan State was admitted in the Big Ten
August 15, 1981 - Nine Conference schools affiliated their women's programs with the Big Ten
October 16, 1981 - First women's championship (Field Hockey) held at Iowa
June 4, 1990 - Penn State became the 11th member of the Conference

1917-18

America's Time Capsule

October 15, 1917: The Chicago White Sox defeated the New York Giants to win the World Series.

November 3, 1917: U.S. forces engaged in their first World War I battle in Europe.

December 18, 1917: The U.S. Constitution's 18th amendment was passed, outlawing the manufacture and sale of alcoholic liquors.

May 15, 1918: Airmail service began between New York City and Washington, D.C.

June 25, 1918: American forces halted the Germans in the Battle of Belleau Wood in France.

University Lore

THE UNIVERSITY OF MICHIGAN ARTES SCIENTIA VERITAS 1817 ™

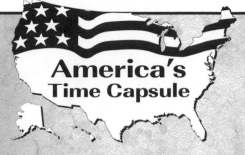

One campus landmark came down to make room for another in the summer of 1917. The Old University Library, with its twin towers, university clock, and curving red brick wall, had been a focal point of campus since 1883. The building had been declared unsafe in 1915 and by July 14, 1917 only the gutted clock tower and the fire proof stack addition remained. The stack was incorporated into the new General Library ("The Grad") which was completed in 1920 at a cost of nearly $650,000.

Michigan Moment

MICHIGAN REJOINS THE BIG TEN CONFERENCE

It was on a train headed toward Ithaca, New York in the Fall of 1916 that University of Michigan athletic director Phil Bartelme got the ball rolling. "I am getting tired of begging for games to fill out our schedules," Bartelme told U-M faculty representative Ralph Aigler. "I believe the thing to do is to get back to our own group and that means rejoining the Conference." The following spring, Aigler presented a lengthy report to the Board of Regents which concluded with a resolution that said in part, "...it is the sense of this Board that steps be taken to resume membership in the Western Intercollegiate Conference." As a result, U-M's Senate Council took power over the Athletic Board of Control, opening the door for reapplication of Conference membership. On November 20, 1917, after nine years of exile, Michigan was once again part of the nation's most dominant conference. Since that day, nearly 80 years ago, the Wolverines have reigned as champions on a regular basis. In men's competition, Michigan has won 250 team titles, including 51 championships in track and field, 36 in baseball, 31 in football, 30 in swimming and 12 each in basketball, gymnastics and golf. Since women's athletics became part of the Big Ten in 1981, Wolverine swimmers have claimed 11 titles, more than any other squad. Gymnastics ranks second with seven championships, softball is third with four, cross country has three titles, and track has two crowns.

CHAMPION OF THE WEST

FRANK CULVER

The 1980s tandem of Kurt Becker and Stefan Humphries is generally regarded as one of the greatest pairs of guards that intercollegiate football has ever known. But, nearly 70 years before Becker and Humphries wore the Maize and Blue for Bo Schembechler, Coach Fielding Yost's guard combo of Frank Culver and Ernest "Aqua" Allmendinger were held in equal esteem. Michigan's all-star fullback Cedric "Pat" Smith was the beneficiary of the roadblocks set by fellow All-Americans Culver and Allmendinger. A versatile 195 pounder, Culver earned national honors his sophomore season for the 8-2 Wolverines. He and many of his teammates then entered World War I service in 1918, before returning to campus for the 1919 campaign. Culver, a native of Detroit, graduated from U-M's law school and enjoyed a distinguished career in the Motor City as an attorney and chief assistant prosecutor. He died in the courtroom in 1956 at the age of 57.

another CHAMPION OF THE WEST

ERNEST ALLMENDINGER

A native son of Ann Arbor, Ernest Allmendinger spent much of his life around the vibrant city from his birth on August 25, 1890. Given the name "Aqua" because of his days as a waterboy for the railroad building crews, he played right guard and right tackle at Ann Arbor High School, where his team lost one game in three seasons. While earning a forestry degree at U-M, he played three seasons under coach Fielding Yost. With Allmendinger helping to anchor a strong line, Michigan compiled a record of 16-4-2 between 1911-13. Following graduation, Allmendinger split his time seasonally. He spent his summers working in western forests and his autumns as an assistant football coach at U-M. When the U.S. entered World War I, Allmendinger enlisted in the service. While in training, he also played football for the Camp Sheridan team and was named to Walter Camp's All-America service team in 1917. He rose to the rank of captain in 1919 before the war's end in 1919. Beginning in 1921, "Aqua" spent 34 years with the Washtenaw Road Commission and later worked for the Huron-Clinton Metropolitan Authority. He died on May 7, 1973 at the age of 82.

Maize & Blue Item

Now that Michigan could find some quality opposition with its return to the Big Ten, the University revived its varsity basketball program. Under Coach Elmer Mitchell, the team won four of its first five games, all non-conference contests. However, the more experienced Big Ten teams were too much for U-M to handle and it suffered through an 0-10 Conference season. Michigan was led by James McClintock's 108 points.

M List — Facts About Michigan's Conference Medal of Honor Winners

Since Michigan first awarded a Big Ten Conference Medal of Honor award, 93 athletes have been given this prestigious honor. Since 1982, an award has been made to both a male and female athlete. Here are some interesting facts about U-M honorees:

First recipient:	Alan Boyd, 1918
First woman recipient:	Diane Dietz, 1982
Men's sports:	Football, 36; Track, 12; Basketball, 9; Swimming, 8
Women's sports:	Track 6, Volleyball 3, Gymnastics, Tennis, Swimming, 2
Only athlete named twice:	Paul White, 1944 and 1947
1997 recipients:	Jason Botterill and Shareen Luze

1918-19

America's Time Capsule

September 11, 1918: The Chicago Cubs lost the World Series to the Boston Red Sox.

November 9, 1918: Kaiser Wilhelm II of Germany abdicated.

November 11, 1918: World War I ended on the 11th hour of the 11th day of the 11th month.

June 11, 1919: Walter Hagen won the U.S. Open golf tournament.

July 4, 1919: Jack Dempsey won the world heavyweight boxing title with a technical knockout against the defending champion, Jess Willard.

University Lore

In the Fall of 1918, the U.S. War Department established a Students' Army Training Corps on campus. The 2,700 students who enrolled in SATC were issued arms and uniforms and received privates' pay. Another 600 students joined the Students' Naval Training Corps. Neither the campus SATC nor SNTC saw actions as units. Fifty-seven SATC and one SNTC students died on campus during the influenza epidemic. A total of 12,601 Michigan students, alumni, and faculty saw service during the war and 243 lost their lives.

Michigan Moment

MICHIGAN CELEBRATES BIG TEN RETURN WITH FIVE TITLES

Michigan resumed membership in the Big Ten during the 1918-19 season, marking the first full year since 1906-07 that the Wolverines were involved in Conference play. The 10-year hiatus had little effect on U-M teams, as they collected five Conference titles, including championships in football, baseball, indoor and outdoor track, and tennis. The football team's 14-0 victory over Ohio State in the season finale gave the Wolverines their first undefeated and untied campaign since 1904, enabling them to claim the mythical national championship as well. On the diamond, Michigan's baseball team shut out half of its opponents in a 14-game schedule. A 3-2 loss to Notre Dame was the only setback of the season for the Maize and Blue as they rolled to a 13-1 record overall. U-M's 9-0 Conference mark was only the second perfect record in Western Conference history and the first since 1910. The indoor track team won its second-ever title with a narrow win at the Conference meet in Evanston, Illinois. Carl Johnson won two sprint events and the high jump, as Michigan beat out second-place Chicago by just two points, the closest margin in the short history of indoor track championships. Johnson starred again at the 1919 outdoor track championships in Chicago, winning four events. Cedric Smith placed first in the hammer throw and Joseph Baker captured the shot put event as Michigan easily held off Chicago to win its seventh Conference outdoor title. In only its second season of Conference competition, the U-M tennis team collected its first league title. Walter Wesbrook won the Conference singles championship and teamed up with Nicholas Bartz to claim first place in doubles as well.

Michigan's 1918 football team.

CHAMPION OF THE WEST

FRANK STEKETEE

Though he won All-America honors with Coach Fielding Yost's football squad as a fullback, some of Frank Steketee's greatest moments came as a punter and placekicker. As a result of his prodigious field goals, "Stek" is given credit for Michigan victories over Syracuse, Illinois and Minnesota. In that game against the Orangemen, he intercepted a pass, ran for a touchdown and kicked three field goals. Steketee also once booted a record 100-yard punt. A letter winner in 1918, '20 and '21, the son of prominent Grand Rapids businessman Jacob Steketee became the first Michigan man to be chosen an All-American during his initial season of competition. The freshman rule was relaxed in 1918 because of World War I. Steketee served in the Naval Reserves in 1919 during the first war and also was an Army serviceman in World War II. At the time of his death in 1951 at the age of 51, he was an account examiner in the finance division of the Michigan State Highway Department.

another CHAMPION OF THE WEST

CARL JOHNSON

From 1918 through 1920, Carl Johnson was as dominant a performer as any in University of Michigan track and field history. During those three letter-winning seasons, Johnson won an impressive 16 individual Big Ten titles, including three as a sprinter, seven as a hurdler, three as a high jumper and three as a long jumper. His greatest track feats were recorded during his junior year at the Big Ten outdoor meet. He took four firsts, winning the high hurdles in :15.4, the low hurdles in :25.0, the high jump at 6'2 1/4", and the broad jump with a leap of 24'1". Johnson's latter two efforts were both records and accomplished, amazingly, within a period of about 60 seconds. His senior outdoor season was hampered by a back injury. Johnson earned a spot on the 1920 U.S. Olympic team, placing second in the long jump at the games in Antwerp. Although a native of Ann Arbor, he moved with his parents to Spokane, Washington. Forming a one-man track team at Lewis & Clarke High School, Johnson's accomplishments alone won second place at the 1915 National Interscholastic meet in Chicago. Besides being a sports star, he also was a campus leader at U-M, serving as president of the University's Student Council. During his post-athletic career, Johnson enjoyed great success in the investment business. He died in 1932 at the age of 34, a victim of peritonitis, induced by acute appendicitis.

Maize & Blue Item

Michigan's first full football season back in the Big Ten Conference was marred by an American health tragedy. An outbreak of influenza that had started in Fort Riley, Kansas gripped the world, killing several hundreds of thousands of United States citizens. With the disease spreading rampantly, U.S. Surgeon General Rupert Blue asked that public gatherings be banned. From mid-October through early November, 1918, Michigan's planned contests with Camp Custer, Michigan State and Northwestern were all cancelled, with only the Michigan State contest eventually being made up.

M List

From 1892 to 1918, the Michigan football team compiled a 195-36-11 and finished with a winning record each season. The 1996 Michigan football team finished the regular season 8-4, the 29th consecutive regular season that Michigan finished with a winning record. A list of the teams with the most consecutive winning regular seasons follows.

School	Seasons	Years
Notre Dame	42	1889-1932 (No teams in 1890,1891)
Alabama	38	1911-1950 (No teams in 1918,1943)
Nebraska	35	1962-Present
Oklahoma	29	1966-1994
Michigan	29	1968-Present
Virginia	28	1888-1915
Michigan	27	1892-1918

Additionally, Michigan finished with a 5-3 record in the Big Ten in 1996, the 29th straight season that Michigan had a winning conference record. This 29-season streak is the longest in Big Ten history. The previous record was 20 straight seasons, by Ohio State from 1967-1986.

MICHIGAN MOMENT

America's Time Capsule

September 26, 1919: President Woodrow Wilson suffered a stroke during a national tour.

October 9, 1919: The Chicago White Sox lost the World Series to the Cincinnati Reds.

April 20, 1920: The Olympic Games began in Antwerp, Belgium.

July 3, 1920: Bill Tilden won the men's singles title at the Wimbledon tennis championship.

July 5, 1920: Governor James Cox of Ohio became the Democrat's presidential nominee.

University Lore

The Michigan Union was organized in 1904, the first student union in the nation, and almost immediately a fund-raising for a Union Clubhouse began. In 1907, a house on State Street was purchased as a temporary clubhouse. Plans for a new building were unveiled in 1910 by architects Allen and Irving Pond (Pond may be best known for scoring U-M's first intercollegiate touchdown in 1879). Ground was finally broken in 1917, but World War I delayed completion until 1920. One of the first acts of the new Union's directors was to formally bar women from using the front door, a practice enforced until 1954.

WOLVERINES WIN THIRD-CONSECUTIVE BASEBALL TITLE

The Michigan baseball team, coached expertly by Carl Lundgren, made a shambles of the Big Ten race for the third consecutive season in 1920. Directly on the heels of respective 9-1 and 9-0 records in 1918 and '19, the 1920 Wolverines rolled to a 9-1 mark in Conference play. Captain Vernon "Slicker" Parks was easily the season's individual star. Only once, in the final Illinois game, was the standout pitcher knocked out of the box. He typically limited opponents to no more than four or five hits. Eddie Ruzicka was U-M's No. 2 hurler, and pitched a no-hitter versus Western Michigan. Right fielder Jack Perrin and shortstop Mike Knode shared batting honors for the Wolverines. Michigan went undefeated through its first seven Conference games before being tripped up by Illinois. An 8-4 victory over Wisconsin gave Michigan its final one-game margin over 8-2 Ohio State. U-M's overall record of 17-6-1 featured a nine-game winning streak. Somewhat surprisingly, Coach Lundgren moved from Ann Arbor following the 1920 season to accept a similar post at the University of Illinois, his alma mater. Though Lundgren's departure left some long faces, his successor, Ray Fisher, ultimately turned those frowns into smiles.

Photo: U-M Athletic Dept.

Baseball coach Carl Lundgren

CHAMPION OF THE WEST

WALTER WESBROOK

Michigan tennis great Walter Wesbrook was once asked to reveal his greatest single thrill in collegiate athletics. Was it, perhaps, when he became the first Michigan player to win the Big Ten singles championship? Would it be when he and Nick Bartz became the first Wolverines to claim a Conference doubles crown? Or was it the day that he extended tennis immortal Bill Tilden to a fifth set before losing the National Clay Court Singles Championship? Instead, he enjoyed telling about the indoor track and field meet at Champaign, Illinois in 1921 when he became pole vault champion of the Illinois Relays. In fact, Wesbrook's love for track nearly kept him from making his greatest contribution to Michigan athletics history. He seriously considered forsaking tennis in order to travel with the 1919 Wolverine track team to the Eastern Intercollegiate meet in Boston. At the last minute, Wesbrook decided to stick with tennis. It was a wise decision, for he would go on to win Big Ten singles titles in both 1919 and '20, and become only the second Conference athlete to win a pair of championships. A ruptured appendix kept the left-hander from winning a third straight title in 1921. After college, he turned to teaching the game in California and did so until his retirement.

another CHAMPION OF THE WEST

ERNIE VICK

Following in the footsteps of previous All-America centers like William Cunningham and Germany Schulz, Henry "Ernie" Vick enjoyed an outstanding career under Coach Fielding Yost. Much smaller than his predecessors, the 1921 All-American excelled as a blocker and tackler. He also gained acclaim as a center passer. Said Yost, "Ernie was the most accurate passer who ever put the ball in play. Under pressure, he was dependable at all times. Anybody can stand up while the sun shines, but it takes a real player like Ernie to stand up during the storm." On the baseball field, Vick helped the Wolverines to a cumulative two-year overall record of 42 victories against only 10 losses. Before the much-publicized Bo Jackson and Deion Sanders, there was Ernie Vick. The Toledo, Ohio native played professionally on the gridiron from 1925 through '28 with the Detroit Lions and the Chicago Bears. As a major league baseball player, Vick performed from 1922-26 with the St. Louis Cardinals. Following his days as a pro, he worked as a manufacturer's representative and also served as a Big Ten official in both football and baseball, retiring in 1952. Vick died in 1980 at the age of 80.

Maize Blue Item

Angus "Gus" Goetz had a busy schedule during his four-year career with the Michigan football team. Not only was he the first man in modern history to twice be chosen as captain of the Wolverine gridders (1919 and '20), Goetz is probably the only one to spend three of his four seasons as a student in U-M's medical school.

M List

In 1920, Michigan hosted its first ever Conference championship, the Big Ten Outdoor Track and Field meet. Since then, Michigan has gone on to host 76 more Conference championships. Here are the meets most frequently held in Ann Arbor :

Sport	Championships Hosted	Last
Men's Outdoor Track	10	1988
Men's Swimming	9	1996
Men's Gymnastics	9	1987
Men's Golf	8	1994
Wrestling	8	1988
Baseball	7	1997
Men's Cross Country	5	1985
Men's Indoor Track	3	1994
Men's Tennis	3	1981
Women's Gymnastics	3	1993
Softball	3	1996

America's Time Capsule

September 28, 1920: Eight members of the Chicago White Sox were indicted on charges of having taken bribes to throw the 1919 World Series.

November 2, 1920: Warren Harding was elected U.S. president by a landslide margin.

November 2, 1920: Radio station KDKA in Pittsburgh broadcast the results of the presidential election, the first time that happened.

June 29, 1921: Elizabeth Ryan and Bill Tilden claimed Wimbledon tennis titles.

July 2, 1921: Jack Dempsey successfully defended his heavyweight boxing title against Georges Carpentier.

University Lore

On July 1, 1920, Marion Leroy Burton, president of the University of Minnesota, became Michigan's fifth president. Tall, red-headed, with a commanding presence and a persuasive voice, he could captivate students and legislators alike. His talent for organization and vision of an expanding university exactly fit the needs and spirit of the post-war age. His tenure was tragically short, however, as he died in February 1925 following a heart attack. He had doubled the University's annual income and secured more than $10 million in appropriations and $2 million in gifts for new buildings.

Michigan Moment

MICHIGAN CAGERS CLAIM FIRST TITLE

Coach E.J. Mather's 1920-21 Wolverine basketball team didn't have a fancy monicker such as the "Fab 5"; but, if they did, a nickname like the "Lonesome 5" would have been a perfect fit. You see, on most occasions, Mather only played five men during the course of a game. In fact, that's exactly what happened the night of March 7, 1921, when Michigan's basketball claimed its very first Big Ten championship. U-M blazed off to a perfect 8-0 mark and spirits were high. But then, three Conference games later, it found itself buried in the basement of the standings at 0-3. U-M managed to win its next two games, but a second loss to Wisconsin again pushed them into the second division. Suddenly, Mather regained his magic touch, a pair of non-Conference victories over rival M.A.C., and consecutive wins over Purdue, Illinois, Purdue again, and Ohio State. The season finale came at Urbana where U-M was pitted against league-leading Illinois. Michigan's starting lineup featured Art Karpus and Bill Miller at the forwards, Bob Dunne at center, and Jack Williams and Bud Rea in the backcourt. The same iron-man five would leave the floor at the finish of the 40-minute game. Other than an 18-18 tie at one point in the second half, U-M maintained its lead, eventually winning, 28-26. Miller, with 12 points, and Dunne, with eight, led the team in scoring. It was later revealed that Karpus sustained a broken nose during the rough and tumble first half and that Williams, Michigan's ace rebounder, had suffered all day from an acute pain around his appendix. However, a share of the Big Ten crown, Michigan's first ever, made its pain considerably more bearable.

Photo: Michiganensian

The U-M's 1920-21 basketball team

CHAMPIONSHIP *Moment*

WOLVERINE '9' WINS MARATHON

Though Ray Fisher's Michigan baseball squad played the equivalent of two games on May 30, 1921, it was given credit for only one victory. Before a vocal crowd of 2,500 fans, the Wolverines and the Wisconsin Badgers matched up for a marathon 18-inning game, won finally by Michigan, 9-8, on A.J. Karpus' run-scoring single. The thriller was marked by both good and sloppy baseball and by a controversial call. With the Badgers leading, 5-4, in the bottom of the ninth and one out, Michigan's Jack Perrin laced a line drive over first base. The ball ultimately came to rest out of bounds behind the right-field scoreboard. As Perrin slid toward home, so too came a perfect relay throw and Perrin was called out. Fisher at once raced onto the field and reminded the umpire of a Conference rule under which a ball, landing in fair territory and rolling out of sight of the umpire, was to be ruled an automatic home run. The umpire reversed his decision and the Wisconsin team descended en masse on him. After leaving the field for 15 minutes, they finally reappeared, having decided to finish the game under protest. Wisconsin took leads in both the 15th and 16th innings, but both times Michigan tied the contest. Finally, thanks to the heroics of Karpus in the 18th inning, the Wolverines were able to walk off the field victorious.

CHAMPION OF THE WEST

ED MATHER

Edwin J. Mather will be remembered in Michigan athletic lore as the man who put basketball on the map at the Ann Arbor campus. Hired by U-M athletic director Phil Bartelme, Mather came to the Wolverines after a successful coaching stint at Kalamazoo and Lake Forest. In four of his five seasons at K-College, he led the Hornets to four M.I.A.A. basketball titles. Ironically, Mather's Michigan debut in 1919 came against Kalamazoo, and the Wolverine "5" defeated the defending M.I.A.A. champs, 22-12. In 1920-21, Michigan rose to the top of the Big Ten standings for the very first time, recording an 18-4 overall mark. The Wolverines also won back-to-back championships under Mather in 1925-26 and '26-27. "The Skipper", as he was affectionately known to his players, accumulated a career record of 108 victories against only 53 defeats in nine total seasons at Michigan. Mather died August 26, 1928, at the age of 41 following a long illness.

Maize & Blue Item

More than 200 Wolverines have gone on to play professional football, but the very first was Eddie Usher in 1921. A three-time letter winner as a back and end in 1918, '20 and 21, the Toledo, Ohio native first saw action with the Buffalo All-Americans. Usher also later played pro football for the Rock Island Independents, the Green Bay Packers and the Detroit Tigers before retiring in 1925.

M List: Selected Michigan Players in the NHL

Player	Yrs. at 'M'	Yrs. in NHL	Team(s)
Red Berenson	1960-62	1962-78	Mtl, NYR, St.L, Det.
Murray Eaves	1979-80	1980-90	Wpg, Det
Gregory Fox	1973-76	1977-85	Atl, Chi, Pitt
Patrick Hughes	1974-76	1978-87	Mtl, Pit, Edm, Buf, St.L, Hfd
Jeff Norton	1985-87		NYI, SJ, St.L
Myles O'Connor	1986-89		
David Oliver	1991-94		Edm
David Richter	1979-82	1982-90	Min, Phi, Van, St.L
David Shand	1974	1976-85	Atl, Tor, Wash
Chris Tamer	1990-93		Pit

America's Time Capsule

September 8, 1921: Margaret Forman of Washington,D.C. won the title of the first Miss America.

November 11, 1921: The "Unknown Soldier" of World War I was buried at Arlington National Cemetery.

February 21, 1922: An explosion of the airship Roma killed 34 of its 45-man crew.

May 30, 1922: The Lincoln Memorial, designed by Henry Bacon, was dedicated in Washington, D.C.

July 15, 1922: Gene Sarazen won the U.S. Open golf tournament.

University Lore

The School of Education was established as an independent unit in May 1921 by action of the Regent's and began offering classes in the Fall term of 1921. Prof. Allen S. Whitney was appointed the first dean. Teacher education at the university began in 1879 with creation of the chair of the Science and Art of Teaching in the Department of LS&A. The School of Education was first located in Tappan Hall, but moved to offices in the new University Elementary School in 1930.

Michigan Moment

SWIMMING, WRESTLING AND GOLF MAKE VARSITY DEBUT

The sports of swimming, wrestling and golf made their varsity debuts at the University of Michigan during the 1921-22 season. Since those teams were initiated more than seven decades ago, the trio has accounted for an incredible 53 Big Ten team championships. The first Wolverine swimmers, coached by J. Jerome, lost their only meet of the '21-22 campaign, a 48-20 defeat at the hands of the Erie YMCA. Michigan's great tradition in swimming really began upon the arrival of Matt Mann in 1925, whose teams from 1925-54 won 13 national titles and 16 Big Ten team crowns. The '21-22 Michigan wrestlers were coached by Clifford Thorne of Detroit. Captained by C.P. Haller, the Wolverine grapplers registered a respectable 3-1 mark that first season, beating Detroit Junior College, the Detroit YMCA, and Michigan Agricultural College. Their lone loss was a two-point defeat at the hands of M.A.C., 20-18. The stars of the team included Haller at heavyweight, G.L. DeFoe at featherweight, E.W. Gilliard at lightweight, E.M. Clifford at welterweight, and M.R. Smith at light heavyweight. Like the swimming program, Michigan's wrestlers have great tradition, having claimed 11 Big Ten team titles. The Wolverine golf squad, in its first year of competition, won four of its five Conference matches and placed second at the Conference meet in Chicago. Captain John Winters, a spectacular driver, was one of five men on the first team who were awarded varsity letters. Professor Thomas Trueblood, who organized the first informal campus team in 1901, was the head coach of the inaugural Wolverine linksmen. Since that time, the U-M golfers have earned a dozen Big Ten team titles.

Photo: Alumni Association

Golf coach Thomas Trueblood

CHAMPIONSHIP *Moment*

YOST HIRED AS MICHIGAN'S ATHLETIC DIRECTOR

Fielding Yost's 25-year career as head coach of the University of Michigan football team is well documented. His "Point-a-Minute" teams of the turn of the century played 56 consecutive games without a loss, earning four straight mythical national championships. But what about Yost the athletic director? That portion of his legendary career often is overshadowed by his success on the gridiron. Named to the A.D. post in 1921, Yost accepted only the highest personal, academic and athletic standards, while spreading that ideal to the facilities which support Michigan's athletic pursuits. Yost conceived and engineered today's modern athletic campus, including the construction of Michigan Stadium, the university's 18-hole golf course, the nation's first Intramural Sports Building, and the nation's first multi-purpose field house—now known as Yost Ice Arena. Among the coaches he hired from 1921-41 were baseball's Ray Fisher, basketball's Bennie Oosterbaan, football's Harry Kipke and Fritz Crisler, golf's Thomas Trueblood, swimming's Matt Mann and wrestling's Cliff Keen.

CHAMPION OF THE WEST

PAUL GOEBEL

The University of Michigan has had a proud record of producing scholar-athletes, those men and women who have succeeded in life beyond their activities on the athletic fields. Among those near the top of the list is Grand Rapids athlete/politician Paul Goebel. A three-time letter winner in football from 1920-22, Goebel enjoyed a highly successful senior campaign. Not only was he chosen as team captain of the 1922 squad, he also was selected to the All-America team as an end and earned the Big Ten Conference Medal of Honor for proficiency in academics and athletics. Goebel played football for four more seasons, playing professionally with the Columbus Tigers, the Chicago Bears and the New York Yankees. Beyond his pro career, his participation in football continued for nearly 30 years as a Big Ten official until 1953. Goebel was a master politician, serving his hometown as mayor from 1950-58. He represented the United States on goodwill tours to Germany and the Middle East, and in 1953, he was made an "Officer in the House of Orange Nassau" by Queen Juliana of The Netherlands. Goebel also was a Regent for his alma mater, a member of the State of Michigan Higher Education Assistance Authority, and as Chairman of the State of Michigan Board of Ethics. His loyalty to the U-M was underlined by his service as Director of the National Alumni Association, President of the Grand Rapids alumni group, and President of the Varsity "M" Club. Inducted into U-M's Hall of Honor in 1981, Goebel died in 1988 at the age of 86.

Maize & Blue Item

Senior Howard Hoffman was the star of the University of Michigan's track and field squad of the early 1920s. A three-time letter winner from 1920-22, his speciality was the javelin toss. Hoffman was the Big Ten champion in both 1920 and '21 in that event, but his biggest claim to fame was in becoming the first Wolverine track athlete to win an NCAA individual title, that coming during his senior season.

M List

When Each Men's Sport Started at U-M (First Year of Varsity Status)

Baseball	1866
Football	1879
Men's Track	1893
Men's Tennis	1893
Men's Basketball	1909
Men's Cross Country	1919
Men's Swimming	1921
Wrestling	1921
Hockey	1923
Men's Golf	1922
Men's Gymnastics	1930

MICHIGAN MOMENT

America's Time Capsule

October 4, 1922: Famed sportswriter Grantland Rice reported the first radio play-by-play coverage of the World Series.

October 8, 1922: John McGraw's New York Giants won their second consecutive World Series title against the New York Yankees.

March 13, 1923: Motion pictures with sound were first demonstrated in New York City.

July 15, 1923: Golf amateur "Bobby" Jones won the U.S. Open.

August 2, 1923: President Warren Harding died of an embolism while recovering from an attack of ptomaine poisoning.

UNIVERSITY LORE

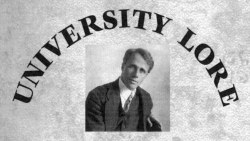

Robert Frost's year as the university's first poet in residence was such a success that he was invited to return for the 1922-23 academic year. President Burton had established the Fellowship in Creative Art to bring an artist to campus for a year. They were not to teach, but work at their art and be available for discussion with groups or individual students. Frost always treasured the years he spent on campus and returned to Ann Arbor on several occasions. He gave one of his last public readings at Hill Auditorium in April 1962.

WOLVERINE ATHLETES ROLL TO SIX TITLES

Michigan was a force with which to be reckoned during the 1922-23 school year. While no other school was winning more than two Big Ten titles, U-M brought home half a dozen, four of these outright. Led by Harry Kipke, the Michigan football team shut out its first five opponents and rolled to a 6-0-1 record. Along with claiming Michigan's first Big Ten title and undefeated season since 1918, the Wolverine squad shared national championship honors with Pittsburgh. The U-M cross country team won its first ever Conference championship at Lafayette, Indiana. Egbert Isbell, who would later win the two-mile run at the Big Ten indoor and outdoor track meets, was the champion, finishing in 26:33. After placing second in the Big Ten for two straight seasons, the Wolverine baseball squad rolled to a 10-0 Conference record and a 22-4 overall mark. At the 1923 Big Ten indoor track and field meet in Chicago, Michigan blew away the competition, more than doubling the score of second-place Illinois. Charles Reinke won his first of what would be three championships in the 880-yard run, while five other Wolverines had first-place finishes to bring the indoor track title back to Ann Arbor for the first time since 1919. U-M took the 1923 Big Ten outdoor track title by the slimmest of margins, holding off Illinois by one-half of a point. Seven Michigan athletes won individual titles, including William DeHart Hubbard and James Brooker, who later would travel to the Paris Olympics in 1924 and return with medals. At the Big Ten tennis championships in Chicago, Charles Merkel became the second Michigan player to win the Big Ten singles championship. His victory led U-M to a share of the Conference crown in tennis. The six championships in one season by one school was a Big Ten record which would stand until Michigan won eight titles during the 1943-44 campaign.

The Michigan baseball team in 1923.

CHAMPIONSHIP *Moment*

DEDICATION GAME OF OHIO STADIUM

Michigan dominated its football series with Ohio State from 1897 through 1918, posting a nearly perfect 13-0-2 record through the first 15 meetings. The Buckeyes finally got in the victory column in 1919, and continued that success in both 1920 and '21. The 1922 meeting between Michigan and Ohio State was a milestone game, marking the first contest ever between the two schools at OSU's new 66,000-seat stadium, the largest in the Midwest. Though the horseshoe-shaped structure had already been the site for two Buckeye contests, OSU saved its dedication game for Michigan. An overflow crowd filled Ohio Stadium on October 21, anticipating a fourth-consecutive Buckeye victory over the Wolverines. However, despite the vocal support from OSU's enthusiastic throng, Michigan controlled the game from start to finish. The Wolverines jumped out to a 3-0 lead on Paul Goebel's field goal from the 11-yard line. From then on, the game belonged to All-America halfback Harry Kipke. His first of two touchdowns came in the second quarter on a 25-yard run around right end. Kipke scored again in the third period on a 35-yard pass play, then sewed up the 19-0 Michigan victory with a 38-yard field goal in the final quarter.

CHAMPION OF THE WEST

WILLIAM DeHART HUBBARD

He's the answer to a great trivia question: Who was the first African-American athlete to win an individual gold medal at the Olympics? Twelve years before Jesse Owen's monumental performance in Berlin came Michigan's William DeHart Hubbard. Hubbard's leap of 24-feet-5-inches at the 1924 games in Paris easily outdistanced the competition and earned him a place of honor in Olympic history. From 1923-25, there was no better athlete on the University of Michigan campus than Hubbard. The track and field star from Cincinnati, Ohio set U-M standards that would stand for several years. Eight times Hubbard won Big Ten titles and four times he captured NCAA individual championships. As a sprinter in 1925, he tied the world indoor record in the 60-yard dash (:06.2) and tied the world outdoor standard in the 100-yard dash (:09.6). As a broad jumper, Hubbard established the world mark at the 1925 NCAA meet (25'10 7/8"). The greatest of his collegiate performances came on June 13, 1925, in Chicago when he won the aforementioned broad jump *and* earned the 100-yard dash title in a meet record time of :09.8. A long-time employee for the Parks and Recreation Department in Cincinnati, he died in 1976. Hubbard was inducted posthumously into the U-M Hall of Honor in 1979 and into the Ohio Track and Field Hall of Fame in 1985.

Maize & Blue Item

In 1923, the Michigan baseball team became only the second Big Ten squad in the last 13 seasons to post an undefeated Big Ten record. Coach Ray Fisher's Wolverines clinched its seventh Conference championship on May 28 at Columbus with a 5-2 victory over eventual runnerup Ohio State. Future major leaguers Pete Appleton, a pitcher, and Jack Blott, a catcher, plus all-around star Harry Kipke were Michigan's stars that season.

M List: Michigan Indoor/ Outdoor Track and Field Title Sweeps

With 26 indoor and 30 outdoor Big Ten track and field titles, Michigan leads all Conference schools in first-place finishes. Seventeen times, Michigan has swept both titles in the same season. A list of those years and the track coach appears below:

Years	Coach
1918, '19, '23, '25	Stephen Farrell
1935, '37, '38, '39	Charles Hoyt
1940, '43, '44	Kenneth Doherty
1955, '56, 61	Don Canham
1976, '78, 82	Jack Harvey

Note: The Michigan women have swept both titles once, in 1994, under the leadership of James Henry.

1923-24

America's Time Capsule

September 14, 1923: Jack Dempsey retained his heavyweight boxing crown with a second-round knockout of Luis Angel Firpo, the "Wild Bull of the Pampas."

October 15, 1923: The Yankees won the World Series over the Giants in an all-New York City showdown.

January 25, 1924: The first Winter Olympics were held in Chamonix, France, as the Americans finished fourth in the unofficial team standings.

June 30, 1924: The Teapot Dome oil leasing scandal indicted several oil company presidents on charges of bribery and conspiracy to defraud the United States.

July 21, 1924: Life sentences were given to Nathan Leopold and Richard Loeb for the highly publicized murder of Bobby Franks.

University Lore

The William L. Clements Library was dedicated in 1923. The Italian Renaissance style building was designed by Albert Kahn to house the collection that William Clements ('89) had donated to the university. A Bay City, Michigan, industrialist and university regent, Clements began collecting books in the 1890s and gradually assembled one of the world's great collections on the European discovery and settlement of the new world. After parting with his books, Clements began purchasing historical manuscripts for the library, with a focus on British manuscripts relating to the American Revolution.

Michigan Moment

THE BATTLE OF ROCKWELL'S RUN

The football game in Madison, Wisconsin matched the hometown Badgers against the undefeated but injury-riddled Michigan Wolverines. Three of Coach Fielding Yost's stars sat injured on the sidelines. While the absence of U-M quarterback Charlie Uteritz, guard Harold Steele and tackle Ed VanDervoort certainly hindered Michigan's chance to stay unbeaten, Yost's troops took a further blow in the game itself when All-America center Jack Blott broke his leg. Midway through the second quarter, with Wisconsin leading, 3-0, the Wolverine defense forced the Badgers to punt from their own 24-yard line. The UW kicker arched a 40-yard punt toward substitute quarterback Tod Rockwell, who probably wouldn't even have been on the field if Uteritz hadn't been injured the week before. Rockwell fielded the punt and started around his left flank. After advancing the ball about 15 yards, three Badger defenders converged on him. One spun him around and a second buffeted Rockwell to his knees, but Rockwell didn't stop, eventually sprinting into the end zone. Instantly, the Badger supporters sent a chorus of boos toward referee Walter Eckersall, who had ruled that the ball was never grounded. The last play of the game, a 50-yard desperation pass by the Badgers, was too much for the UW faithful. What appeared to be an incomplete pass was actually completed and if it hadn't been for the heads-up play of U-M's Butch Slaughter who came across the field to tackle the Wisconsin man sprinting toward the Michigan end zone, the Badgers would have won, 9-6. As the final gun went off, referee Eckersall, pursued by several thousand fans, was hustled off the field by policemen. The controversial 6-3 victory ultimately allowed Michigan to tie Illinois for the 1923 Big Ten title.

Photo: Michiganensian

Tod Rockwell

CHAMPIONSHIP *Moment*

THE DEDICATION OF YOST FIELD HOUSE

Yost Field House, a structure that was once the world's first and finest of its kind, was dedicated on November 15, 1923. In his speech that day, Regent James Murfin said, "This splendid building is unique. It is a realization of a dream many have had. Its accomplishment at this time is due in no small measure to the long head and stout heart of a Michigan institution sometimes called 'Hurry Up.' A future period will more accurately gauge the value of his services and the influence of his character upon the men and women of Michigan. Nor is this the time perhaps to do more than remark in passing they have been magnificent and are being appreciated more and more every day by those who observe and know this splendid man—Fielding H. Yost." The building served as the home for, amongst many others, Michigan's basketball, hockey, track and wrestling teams. In 1996, the University began a $5.5 million renovation of the structure that today is known as Yost Ice Arena.

CHAMPION OF THE WEST

JACK BLOTT

Jack Blott's contributions to the University of Michigan as an athlete, as a coach, and as a staff member earned him a special place in Wolverine athletic lore. An all-star center for the football team, he also played catcher for the baseball squad during 1922-24. Blott's greatest fame at Michigan probably came on the gridiron in 1923 where Walter Camp selected him to his All-America team because of his all-around play. On the baseball diamond, he captained the Wolverines his senior year, leading them to a co-championship with Ohio State. Altogether, Blott played for four Big Ten championship teams at Michigan. Following his graduation, he spent one year in the major leagues with the Cincinnati Reds. Blott began a 23-year football coaching career at Michigan in 1924, helping develop such Wolverine stars as Maynard Morris, Chuck Bernard, Otto Pommerening and Francis Wistert. He was named head football coach at Wesleyan (Connecticut) University in 1934, then returned in 1940 to join Detroit's Ford Motor Company. Blott rejoined the Michigan staff in 1946 when Fritz Crisler selected him as line coach, retiring from that position 12 years later. He then served as manager of the U-M ice rink and the golf service building until his death in 1963 at the age of 61.

Maize & Blue Item

America's premier athlete of the 1924 Summer Olympic Games in Paris may have been swimming star Johnny Weissmuller, but the athlete who perhaps set the greatest milestone was Michigan's William DeHart Hubbard. Hubbard's effort of 24-feet-5-inches in track and field's long jump event was six inches better than fellow American and world record holder Edward Gourdin, becoming the first African-American athlete to win an individual gold medal.

M List — Longest Tenure Among U-M Assistant Football Coaches

Assistant FB Coaches	Years	Dates
Jerry Hanlon	23	1969-91
Cliff Keen	23	1926-30, 32, 34-36, 41, 46-58
Tirrel Burton	22	1970-91
Jack Blott	20	1926-33, 46-58
Gary Moeller	18	1969-76, 80-89
Lloyd Carr	15	1980-94
Ray Fisher	15	1921-28, 30, 33-35, 43-45
Don Dufek	12	1954-65
Robert Holloway	12	1954-65

America's Time Capsule

October 10, 1924: The Washington Senators, led by pitcher Walter Johnson, defeated the New York Giants, four games to three, in the World Series.

November 4, 1924: Calvin Coolidge was re-elected president of the United States, defeating Democrat John Davis.

January 5, 1925: Mrs. William B. Ross was inaugurated governor of Wyoming, becoming the first woman governor in U.S. history.

July 21, 1925: Tennessee teacher John Scopes was convicted for teaching the theory of evolution to his students.

August 24, 1925: Helen Wills and Bill Tilden successfully defended their singles titles at the U.S. Lawn Tennis championships.

University Lore

The University Hospital Building, "Old Main" to later generations, was completed in the summer of 1925. The original appropriation for the hospital was made in 1917 but World War I delayed groundbreaking until 1919. Funding shortfalls halted construction for a time in 1922-23. Albert Kahn's double-Y design, with patient wards in each arm of the Y, had 434,445 square feet of floor space and 755 beds. Construction costs totaled $3,395, 961.87, over $400,000 of which was for equipment. "Old Main" was demolished in 1989 to make way for a new hospital.

Michigan Moment

WOLVERINES DEDICATE TWO MORE STADIA

Game action at Illinois, circa 1924.

Michigan's football team had become a popular opponent for schools that were dedicating new football stadia. The 1922 season featured two of these games, as the Wolverines participated in the celebration of facilities at both Vanderbilt and Ohio State. In 1924, Michigan's football schedule feature two more dedication games, back-to-back contests with Michigan Agricultural College (Michigan State) and Illinois. On October 11th, Michigan travelled north and west to East Lansing to crack the champagne on M.A.C.'s 14,000-seat Macklin Field. To this point, the Aggies had managed just two wins against the Wolverines in 18 tries. Michigan had won the last eight games between the intrastate rivals, by a lopsided margin of 248-6. However, the proud home squad refused to give an inch on this special day. After three-and-one-half quarters, the teams remained deadlocked at 0-0. As the game wound down to the final moments, it seemed apparent that M.A.C. would emerge with a shocking tie. But Michigan had other ideas. On the M.A.C. 33-yard line, U-M quarterback Fred Parker launched a pass to team captain Herb Steger, who grabbed the ball and burst into the end zone for the game-winning score. A week later Michigan headed to Champaign for the dedication game of the University of Illinois' Memorial Stadium. Historians, of course, refer to this as the Red Grange game. The "Galloping Ghost" singlehandedly defeated Michigan, scoring four touchdowns in the opening 12 minutes on runs of 95,67,56 and 44 yards. Despite trailing 27-0, the Michigan men refused to stop fighting and actually outscored the Fighting Illini the rest of the game. However, seven of the points came with Illinois' No. 77 on the bench in the second quarter. Grange returned in the third quarter to throw for one touchdown and run for another, making the final score 39-14.

CHAMPIONSHIP *Moment*

U-M'S JABLONSKI AND ILLINOIS' KINDERMAN HOOK UP IN MOUND DUEL

On May 2, 1925, the University of Michigan's Ferry Field was the scene of one of the greatest pitching duels in Big Ten baseball history. Together, the Wolverines' Peter Jablonski and Illinois ace Bill Kinderman allowed but four total hits during a nine-inning classic. Michigan's only threat was in the fourth inning when it loaded the bases, but failed to score. The game remained scoreless until the fateful sixth inning when UI's Jerome Jordan led off by hitting a slow roller toward the mound. Jablonski couldn't field it in time and made the mistake of throwing wildly to first anyway; it was ruled a hit and an error. Another U-M throwing miscue followed that and Illinois had scratched out what turned out to be the only run of the contest. Despite Jablonski's one-hitter, the Illini won by a score of 1-0. Whatever happened to "Jabby" Jablonski? Well, he ultimately became a major league pitcher, but you probably won't find his name in any baseball encyclopedia. He played in the big leagues for 18 seasons under the name of "Pete Appleton", posting a career record of 57-66 in 341 lifetime games.

CHAMPION OF THE WEST

PHIL NORTHROP

One of Michigan's greatest "triple threats" in the sport of track and field was 1920s star Phil Northrop. A letter winner from 1925-27, the Motor City native was a major contributor in the long jump, javelin and pole vault, setting records in the latter two events. Though Northrop was an understudy to the legendary DeHart Hubbard in the long jump as a sophomore, he ultimately posted a near-record leap of 24 feet. He won the Big Ten title in the pole vault his junior year, catapulting himself over the bar at a height of 13-feet-plus. It was the javelin event where Northrop won his greatest acclaim, winning Conference titles in both 1925 and '26. His record throw of 207 feet stood as the Big Ten standard for 10 years. With Northrop as the leading point scorer, Coach Steve Farrell's Michigan track teams won the Conference indoor title in 1925 and the outdoor crown in 1925 and '26. Two other other times, the Wolverines were runners-up in the Big Ten standings. Northrop was graduated from the U-M School of Dentistry in 1928 and received his M.S. in Oral Surgery in 1931. He served on the University's faculty from 1935-63 and died at 59, just two months after leaving the U-M to devote more time to his private practice.

Announcing Michigan's football victory over Wisconsin in 1924, the very first radio broadcast in the Midwest, were WWJ Radio's Ty Tyson and Doc Holland. Due to the fans' response, Fielding Yost took immediate action to make U-M the first school in the nation to regularly air its football games.

M List: Michigan Athletes Who Have Earned Nine or More Letters (1866-1960)

Pete Elliott	12	1946-49	FB,MBK,Golf
Neil Snow	10	1899-1902	FB,BB,Trk
Robert Dunne	9	1919-22	FB,MBK,Trk
Harry Kipke	9	1922-24	FB,MBK,BB
Bennie Oosterbaan	9	1926-28	FB,MBK,BB
Norman Daniels	9	1930-32	FB,MBK,BB
Russell Oliver	9	1933-35	FB,MBK,BB
Dan Smick	9	1937-39	FB,MBK,BB
Don Lund	9	1943-45	FB,MBK,BB
Bob Wiese	9	1943-45,47	FB,MBK,BB
Ron Kramer	9	1955-57	FB,MBK,Trk

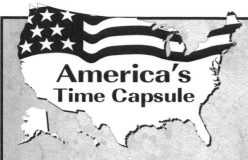

America's Time Capsule

September 3, 1925: The U.S. Army dirigible Shenandoah was wrecked in a storm near Ava, Ohio, killing 14 people.

October 15, 1925: Baseball's World Series was won by the Pittsburgh Pirates in seven games over the Washington Senators.

March 7, 1926: The American Telephone and Telegraph Company successfully demonstrated the first transatlantic radiotelephone conversation between New York City and London.

May 9, 1926: Rear Admiral Richard Byrd made the first successful flight over the North Pole.

August 6, 1926: Nineteen-year-old Gertrude Ederle of New York City became the first woman to swim the English Channel.

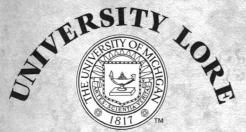

University Lore

Following President Burton's death, Alfred Lloyd, Dean of the Graduate School, was named interim President. Thirty-six-year-old Clarence Cook Little, then president of the University of Maine, was named president in September 1925. A cancer researcher with outspoken views on educational reform, Little proposed establishing a "University College" in which all students would be enrolled for their first two years. The faculty and deans were generally skeptical of the plan, leading to strained relations with Little, who lacked Burton's tact and political skills. Little resigned as president in June 1929.

Michigan Moment

YOST BRIDLES THE GALLOPING GHOST

The objective for Michigan's football team on October 24, 1925, at Illinois' Memorial Stadium could easily be summed up in one seven-letter word—R-E-V-E-N-G-E. Just one year before, Coach George Little's Wolverines had been humiliated by the Illini and their junior halfback, Harold "Red" Grange. So embarrassed was U-M athletic director Fielding Yost by Michigan's performance that day, he decided to abandon his seat in the stands and return as head coach, a post he had held for 23 spectacular years. For 12 months, Yost schemed how to bridle Illinois' Galloping Ghost. He replaced Michigan's unsuccessful six-man line of 1924 with a seven-man front and a diamond-shaped secondary. Legendary Illini coach Bob Zuppke tried to counter the wily Yost by shifting Grange from his customary halfback post to quarterback. At last, it was game day. A steady rain throughout the night had turned the Memorial Stadium field into a muddy quagmire. Twenty-five times the Wheaton Iceman carried the ball, and 25 times Michigan sent a shudder through the sellout crowd as Grange was jolted to the turf by bone-crushing tackles. The final statistics showed No. 77 with a meager net total of 55 yards, less than a fifth of what he had accumulated the year before. Among Yost's defensive stars that day were sophomore Bennie Oosterbaan and senior captain Bob Brown. The only score of the game came just before the first half ended when Michigan's little Benny Friedman converted a 25-yard field goal. Though the final margin was just 3-0, that didn't matter to Yost. The burden he carried for more than a year had finally been lifted from his shoulders.

Michigan's 1925 football squad.

CHAMPIONSHIP *Moment*

YOST RETURNS TO COACH FOOTBALL TEAM

Fielding Yost's return to coaching togs in 1925 was hardly a surprise to his cohorts in the University of Michigan's athletic department. His self-imposed sabbatical from the gridiron in 1924 proved to be unbearable. So with coach George Little's departure to Wisconsin as coach and athletic director, Yost eagerly reassumed the Wolverine football helm. Joining Yost's 1925 U-M varsity was a brilliant group of sophomores, including future All-American Bennie Oosterbaan. The '25 season started exceptionally well, as Michigan posted consecutive shutouts versus Michigan State, Indiana, Wisconsin, Illinois and Navy. Then, on November 7, the Wolverines traveled to rainy Chicago to play underrated Northwestern. Several inches of water covered the Soldier Field turf and the game became a punting duel. A fumble on one of those punts, which resulted in a Wildcat field goal, ultimately cost Michigan the game. U-M rebounded from the defeat with shutout victories over Ohio State and Minnesota, boosting its season scoring totals to 227 points against just three. However, those three points probably cost the Wolverines a national title. Despite the disappointment, Yost would call the 1925 Michigan squad "the finest I ever coached."

CHAMPION OF THE WEST

BENNY FRIEDMAN

Benny Friedman enjoyed a career that took him around the country and around the globe. Born March 18, 1905, the former Cleveland Glenville High School enjoyed a tenure as Michigan's quarterback that would see him start all 16 of the Wolverines' games over the next two seasons. Part of the famed Benny to Bennie combination which featured him and offensive end Oosterbaan, Friedman threw 25 touchdown passes during his career. However, things didn't always come easy for Friedman, who rose from a role with the "scrubs" as a sophomore in 1924 to a starting role his junior year. Friedman also was the kicker for the Wolverines, booting the field goal that beat Illinois in 1925 and converting the extra point that defeated Minnesota in 1926. Chosen as Big Ten MVP in 1926, Friedman became the first Wolverine quarterback to be named All-American. Following graduation, Friedman played professionally for four NFL teams, leading the pro ranks in passing rating and completion percentage with the Brooklyn Dodgers in 1933. After coaching the City College of New York from 1934 to 1941, Friedman served in the Navy for four years during World War II. He returned to the mainland to take positions as athletic director and head football coach at Brandeis University in 1949, a role he served until 1962 when he became owner and director of a private camp in Maine. A member of the Michigan Hall of Honor, Michigan Jewish Hall of Fame and College Football Hall of Fame, Friedman died in 1982.

Maize & Blue Item

At the national collegiate track and field meet in Chicago, Michigan's all-star tandem of Harry Hawkins and Phil Northrop became NCAA individual champions. Hawkins' effort of 148-feet-0 1/4-inches made him the first Wolverine hammer thrower ever to win an NCAA title, while Northrop's javelin toss of 200-feet-10-inches enabled him to successfully defend his NCAA title in that event.

M List: Michigan's Sports Information Directors

Phil Pack	1925-38
William Reed	1938-39
Fred DeLano	1940-44
Les Etter	1944-68
Will Perry	1968-80
John Humenik	1980-82
Bruce Madej	1982-Present

1926-27

America's Time Capsule

November 18, 1926: The Detroit Cougars played their first NHL game, in which they dropped a 2-0 decision to the Boston Bruins.

September 23, 1926: Challenger Gene Tunney defeated boxing champ Jack Dempsey in a ten-round heavyweight title fight in Philadelphia.

April 7, 1927: Television was demonstrated for the first time in New York City, as Secretary of Commerce Herbert Hoover was seen and heard from his office in Washington, D.C.

May 20, 1927: Aviator Charles Lindbergh took off from Long Island, New York for Paris, France, in his monoplane, The Spirit of St. Louis. He successfully landed 33 1/2 hours later.

August 2, 1927: President Calvin Coolidge declined renomination for a second term.

University Lore

Three academic programs were expanded in 1926-27. Library Science, previously taught only in the summer session, was made a department of College of LS&A. The Department of Forestry was elevated to the School of Forestry and Conservation under Dean Samuel Trask Dana. The private University School of Music, under the direction of Earl V. Moore, became officially affiliated with the university. It would become the University of Michigan School of Music in 1946.

Michigan Moment

YOST CONCLUDES HIS COACHING CAREER

Perhaps the only person who knew that the 1926 season would be Fielding Yost's last was Yost himself. Now, at age 55, he recognized that his double duty as football coach and athletic director was probably too much for one man to handle. As the '26 campaign began, Michigan once again was the prohibitive favorite to win a second consecutive Big Ten title. Yost build his team around All-Americans Benny Friedman and Bennie Oosterbaan, collegiate football's best quarterback-end tandem. Friedman, who would play every minute of every game in 1926, and Oosterbaan again made a wonderful combination as Michigan won its first four games by a margin of 130-6. In game five, the Wolverines dropped a 10-0 decision to Navy in front of 80,000 fans at Baltimore, but would return home the following week to beat Wisconsin 37-0. Michigan next headed to Columbus to face Ohio State, a team that had lost four straight to the Wolverines. The home crowd went wild as OSU jumped out to a 10-0 edge, but Friedman, Oosterbaan and Co. mounted a comeback in the second half and pulled off a 17-16 win. To clinch a tie for the Big Ten title with Northwestern, Michigan would need to subdue one more opponent, the Minnesota Golden Gophers. In the second of two Brown Jug Battles in 1926, the Wolverines travelled to Minneapolis. When the game ended, Minnesota had won the statistical battle, claiming more first downs, 18-2, and more total yards, 322-44. Yet, because Oosterbaan was able to return a fumble 60 yards for a touchdown, it was Michigan who left with a 7-6 victory. The triumph allowed Yost to leave the coaching position the same way he came in at Michigan, a four-time Conference winner. Nine months later, Yost officially announced his retirement as Michigan's coach, turning his attention towards building the finest athletic complex in the nation.

CHAMPIONSHIP *Moment*

"M" SWIMMERS RACE TO CONFERENCE TITLE

Michigan coach Matt Mann didn't mince any words when it came to evaluating his 1927 Wolverine swimming team. "The University of Michigan swimming team of 1926-27," he said, "is the greatest team ever organized by any college." Though there were no national meets held in those days, it's difficult to argue otherwise. Led by Captain Paul Samson, a record-breaking freestyler, Michigan lapped its competition at the '27 Big Ten meet in Champaign, Ill. Mann's Wolverine swimmers broke six records to outdistance runner-up Minnesota by 16 points and claim their very first Conference championship. Samson was clearly collegiate swimming's most spectacular individual performer, breaking national records at 40, 220 and 440 yards. Teammate Richard Spindle also set a national record in the 150-yard backstroke event. Besides Samson and Spindle, another Michigan swimmer who won Big Ten individual championships was Carl Darnall, in the 50- and 100-yard freestyle.

CHAMPION OF THE WEST

FIELDING YOST

No coach, in any sport, enjoyed a better debut than Michigan's Fielding Yost . . . and it was one that lasted five years! From 1901-05, Michigan's football record under Yost was 51-1-1, as the "Point a Minute" Wolverines outscored their opponents by an amazing margin of 2,821 points to just 42. Ironically, Michigan can thank a fellow Big Ten institution for ultimately allowing Yost to wind his way to Ann Arbor. After brief stints at Ohio Wesleyan, Nebraska, and Kansas, Yost went to Champaign to talk to University of Illinois athletic director George Huff about his job opening for a football coach. The Illini A.D. informed Yost that the job had already been filled, and the young West Virginian headed to California to coach Stanford. After just one season on the West Coast, Yost began to make his way back east. At this same time, U-M athletic director Charles Baird was looking for a coach for his school's football team. He called upon Huff, his old friend at Illinois, and was forwarded Yost's name. Thus, the Yost-Michigan tandem came to be. It was a marriage that would remain for the next 40 years and bring Michigan to the forefront of collegiate sports. Yost served 25 years as the football coach of the Wolverines, winning 10 Conference titles, six national championships and 165 games. But Yost was more than just a football coach. He served as Michigan's athletic director from 1921-1941 and his "athletics for all" philosophy transformed U-M's athletic campus into what it is today.

Maize & Blue Item

On December 8, 1925, Fielding Yost told the public of U-M's 1926 football schedule. The slate of games contained one shocking aspect, Michigan would play Minnesota twice—once in Ann Arbor and once in Minneapolis. The football coach explained that when he offered the date of October 16 to other teams he was turned down in his attempt to land one more home game. Yost proposed a home-and-home series and thus created the only such occurrence on the U-M football schedule.

M List

Fielding Yost's Greatest Michigan Teams

Year	Record	Conf Place	Notes
1901	11-0-0	1st	Rose Bowl, National Champs
1902	11-0-0	1st	National Champions
1903	11-0-1	1st	National Champions
1904	10-0-0	1st	National Champions
1906	4-1-0	1st	
1918	5-0-0	1st	National Champions
1922	6-0-1	1st	
1923	8-0-0	1st	National Champions
1925	7-1-0	1st	
1926	7-1-0	1st	

1927-28

America's Time Capsule

September 30, 1927: Babe Ruth slugged his record-setting 60th home run for the New York Yankees.

October 6, 1927: The world's first talking motion picture—The Jazz Singer—using the sound-on-film process was released.

November 13, 1927: The Holland Tunnel, America's first underwater tunnel, was opened to traffic, linking New Jersey with Manhattan.

May 25, 1928: Amelia Earhart became the first woman to fly an airplane across the Atlantic.

July 30, 1928: George Eastman demonstrated the world's first color motion pictures at Rochester, New York.

University Lore

The Intra-Mural Sports Building, the first university facility in the country devoted to intra-mural recreation, opened in 1928. Part of the package proposed by the Day Committee that included Michigan Stadium, Palmer Field, tennis courts and the university golf course, the I-M Building was central to the university's program of "Athletics for All." The 415-by-110-foot steel arch structure included four basketball courts, 18 handball and 13 squash courts, a special area for boxing and wrestling, a pool and 4,000 lockers.

Michigan Moment

THE CONSTRUCTION OF MICHIGAN STADIUM

Interest in college football boomed during the "Roaring 20s." Among Big Ten institutions alone, six new campus stadiums were constructed. At the University of Michigan, athletic director Fielding Yost sought a facility that would seat an unheard of 100,000-plus. However, because of the recent expansion of Ferry Field, U-M Regents were reticent to approve Yost's request. Finally, on April 22, 1926, as a result of Yost's dogged perseverance, the Regents approved the new stadium. The structure was to be built upon a plot the University had purchased in 1925, land that at one time had been home to a barn, a strawberry patch and an underground spring. The high water table led to nearly three-quarters of the stadium being built below ground level. After much debate, the Regents and Yost reached an agreement that the stadium would seat 72,000, with ultimate plans of expansion to its current capacity. The construction was financed by the sale of 3,000 $500 bonds, entitling each bondholder to buy season tickets for every season from 1927 until the bonds would be retired in 1936. Due to the Great Depression, however, not a penny was paid on these bonds between 1931 and 1936, and they were not completely retired until October 15, 1947. Fashioned after the Yale Bowl, 440 tons of reinforcing steel and 31,000 square feet of wire mesh went into the building of the 44-section, 72-row, 72,000-seat stadium. The structure was erected at a cost of $950,000. As the stadium neared its completion, Yost requested and was granted an additional 10,000 temporary seats for the concourse at the top of the stadium. On October 1, 1927—one day after Babe Ruth had slugged his historic 60th home run for the New York Yankees—Michigan Stadium opened at the corner of Main Street and Stadium Boulevard. Its capacity of 84,401 made it the largest college-owned stadium in the nation.

CHAMPIONSHIP *Moment*

MICHIGAN DEDICATES ITS NEW STADIUM

Three weeks after the first game at Michigan Stadium—October 22, 1927—the Wolverines faced Ohio State in the stadium's dedication game. The Buckeyes were looking to avenge a game five years earlier, when U-M spoiled the dedication of Ohio Stadium with a 19-0 victory. A capacity crowd of 84,401 was on hand to see Coach Tad Wieman's team attempt to win its sixth consecutive game over OSU. By the end of the game, the fans would need to remember only two names: Bennie Oosterbaan and Louis Gilbert. The tandem accounted for all of Michigan's 21 points, with Oosterbaan throwing touchdown passes of 25, 38 and 23 yards to Gilbert. It was Gilbert who also added all three extra points. As Michigan Stadium was dedicated with the resounding 21-0 victory, the Buckeyes left with only nightmares of the two seniors who had singlehandedly destroyed them.

CHAMPION OF THE WEST

BENNIE OOSTERBAAN

As a Wolverine athlete, Benjamin Gaylord Oosterbaan was an icon of greatness and dedication. Three times an All-American in football, twice an All-American in basketball, and twice an All-Conference player in baseball, Oosterbaan was Michigan's greatest all-time all-around performer. He was a key member of six different teams that won Big Ten titles. As an end on the football team in 1925, Bennie led the Big Ten in touchdowns. In 1928 as a basketball player, Oosterbaan led the Big Ten in scoring, then turned his attention to baseball, where he finished as the Conference's leading hitter. Offered professional contracts in both baseball and football, Oosterbaan turned them down to stay at Michigan. He served as an assistant football coach for 20 years, and, from 1939-46, was head coach of the Wolverine cagers. When Fritz Crisler stepped down in 1947, Bennie was named U-M's head football coach. In his first season, the '48 Michigan football team went 9-0, won the Big Ten, and claimed the national championship. Oosterbaan became the only coach in NCAA football history to win the national championship his first year. In 11 years as football coach, he recorded a record of 63-33-4, including a victory in the 1951 Rose Bowl. His teams won three Conference titles and finished in the top 20 in the polls seven times. Oosterbaan is enshrined in the National Football Hall of Fame, the Michigan Sports Hall of Fame, and U-M's Hall of Honor. His number 47 was the first Wolverine football jersey retired.

Maize & Blue Item

Michigan's first national champion wrestler, Ed "Don" George, starred for the Wolverines in the late 1920s. The 1929 Big Ten heavyweight champ was an Olympic finalist the year before at the games in Amsterdam, losing a disputed decision. He wrestled on the professional circuit following his graduation, gaining international acclaim. George was inducted into Michigan's Hall of Honor in 1981.

M List

Michigan Stadium Construction Trivia

- The number of tons of reinforcing steel used in the construction was estimated at 440 (880,000 pounds).
- The 31,000 square feet of wire mesh used in building the stadium could, at that time, imprison all the inmates of Sing Sing, and the federal prisons of Atlanta and Leavenworth.
- *Nature Magazine* estimated that it would take 14,000 woodchucks, working eight-hour days, 11 1/2 months to move an amount of dirt equal to the 240,000 square yards that were excavated out of the Michigan Stadium site before the cement was poured.
- 45,000,000 words were typed before the stadium was even authorized, and 4,500 yards of type were devoted to the construction process. Of these 4,500 yards of type, 3,000 were made up of adjectives.

1928-29

America's Time Capsule

October 9, 1928: The St. Louis Cardinals were swept in four straight games by the New York Yankees at the World Series.

November 6, 1928: In a landslide Republican victory, Herbert Hoover defeated Alfred Smith for the presidency of the United States.

February 14, 1929: The mass murder known as the St. Valentine's Day Massacre took place on Chicago's North Side.

May 16, 1929: "Wings" was selected as the best picture at the first Academy Awards.

June 30, 1929: Bobby Jones won the U.S. Open golf tournament over runner-up Al Espinosa.

University Lore

The Michigan League opened in May 1929, two years after Dr. Eliza Mosher, the first Dean of Women, turned the ceremonial first shovel of dirt. The Women's League, founded in 1890, began a million dollar fund raising campaign in 1921 for construction of a social center for women students. The building designed by Allen and Irving Pond, who had also designed the Michigan Union, included spacious lounges, meeting and reception rooms, dining areas and living quarters as well as the Lydia Mendelssohn Theater.

Michigan Moment

WOLVERINE VICTORY OVER HOOSIERS LEADS TO BIG TEN TITLE

Michigan's wrestling team accomplished several feats during its 1928-29 season. Not only did Coach Cliff Keen's Wolverines claim the Big Ten team championship and place second in the NCAA meet to Oklahoma State, individually, they boasted a pair of all-stars in 175-pounder Carl Dougovito and heavyweight Ed George, both of whom claimed Big Ten titles. But despite all of those milestones, it was a dual meet against Indiana on March 2, 1929, that may have generated the most excitement of the season. Unlike today, when the Big Ten championship is decided at one big meet, the format was different in 1929. The Conference was divided into Eastern and Western divisions for wrestling, and a winner was chosen for each section on the basis of performance in dual meets. Then, the two division leaders would meet for the title. U-M's battle against the once-tied but otherwise undefeated Hoosiers turned out to be the most closely contested meet Ann Arbor had yet seen. IU needed a clear-cut victory over Michigan in able to lock horns with perennial champ Illinois, but the undefeated Wolverines would be able to advance with either a win or a tie. Indiana didn't waste any time, jumping off to a 3-0 lead after the initial bout. Victories by U-M's Bud Hewitt, Red Elliott and Otto Kelly gave the Wolverines a 9-3 advantage, but IU rallied with wins in the next three matches to take a 14-9 lead. Now, only the heavyweight event remained, and that meant that Michigan's Ed George would need a pin to gain five points and tie the score. The big Wolverine displayed his superiority quickly by gaining control of his opponent's legs in the first few seconds. George carefully worked himself into position for a cradle hold and ultimately a pin, knotting the final team score at 14-14 and assuring Michigan of a third consecutive Eastern Division title. From there, the Wolverines went on to defeat Illinois for Michigan's first Big Ten team championship.

Michigan's Ed George

CHAMPIONSHIP *Moment*

THE EVOLUTION OF FOOTBALL UNIFORMS AT MICHIGAN

1879	White canvas with blue stockings and a belt
1890s	Blue jerseys
1915	Gold numbers added to the back jerseys
1928	Yellow jersey with blue numbers (vs. Navy)
1938	Winged helmet design
1949	White jersey with blue numbers (beginning of different jerseys for road games)
1959	White numbers on sides of helmets
1968	Last year of numbers on helmets
1968	Block 'M' on sleeve of jersey (only year)
1969	Numbers on sleeve of jersey
1974-75	White pants worn on the road
1976	Sleeve striping moved and numbers placed on shoulders.
1976	Orange Bowl—names added to road jerseys
1980	Names added to back of jerseys
1997	Yellow trim around blue
Current	(Home) Blue jersey, yellow lettering, maize pants
Current	(Away) White jersey, blue lettering, maize pants

CHAMPION OF THE WEST

BILL ORWIG

One of the University of Michigan's early basketball stars was 1920s standout James W. "Bill" Orwig. Raised in Toledo, Ohio, where he won letters in football, basketball, baseball and swimming at Scott High School, Orwig traveled up the road to Ann Arbor to compete collegiately. As an undergraduate for the Wolverine basketball squad, he lettered in 1928, '29 and '30 as a guard, helping Michigan win its third Big Ten title in four years his junior season. He also lettered in football for U-M. Orwig received his B.S. degree from Michigan in 1930 and then started his coaching career at Benton Harbor High School as football and basketball mentor. In 1936, he returned to Toledo to coach both sports at Libbey High, earning his greatest success on the gridiron with three state football championships and six city basketball crowns. After service in World War II, Orwig became head football, basketball and track coach at the Univeristy of Toledo in 1946. He returned to Michigan in 1948 to serve as an assistant coach on Bennie Oosterbaan's football staff, helping direct the Wolverine gridders to four Big Ten titles. In 1954, Orwig turned his attentions to a career in athletic administration, being named athletic director at the University of Nebraska. Seven years later, he assumed similar duties at Indiana, serving in that capacity for 15 years until his retirement in 1975. Orwig hired coaches Bob Knight, John Pont and Sam Bell during his service at IU, and Hoosier athletic teams accounted for 36 Big Ten championships. He died in 1994 at the age of 87.

Maize & Blue Item

Originally constructed as a roller skating rink and amusement center, the Sports Coliseum was purchased by U-M in 1925. It became Michigan's first indoor ice complex, a facility the ice hockey team desperately needed. In 1929, the building was improved with its own artificial ice plant, and Michigan became the first school in the nation to provide an artificial ice surface for use by students and a hockey team.

M List: Michigan's Big Ten Basketball Championships

Year	Overall Record	Conference Record
1920-21	18-4	8-4
1925-26	12-5	8-4
1926-27	14-3	10-2
1928-29	13-3	10-2
1947-48	16-6	10-2
1963-64	23-5	11-3
1964-65	24-4	13-1
1965-66	18-8	11-3
1973-74	22-5	12-2
1976-77	26-4	16-2
1984-85	26-4	16-2
1985-86	28-5	14-4

1929-30

America's Time Capsule

October 29, 1929: A record 16.41 million shares were traded for whatever they would bring, signaling the beginning of the American Depression.

November 29, 1929: Lt. Commander Richard E. Byrd completed the first flight over the South Pole.

March 13, 1930: The planet Pluto was identified from an observatory in Flagstaff, Arizona.

June 7, 1930: Gallant Fox captured horse racing's Triple Crown with a victory at the Belmont Stakes.

June 12, 1930: Germany's Max Schmelling defeated Jack Sharkey to win the world heavyweight boxing championship.

University Lore

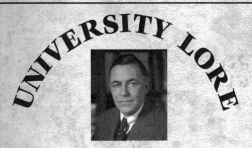

Just weeks before the stock market crash of 1929, Alexander Grant Ruthven was named the university's seventh president. He had received his Ph.D. in Zoology from Michigan in 1906 and immediately became an instructor in the department and curator, later director, of the University Museum. He restructured the university's administration in a more corporate style and allowed for a greater role in governance by deans and faculty. Ruthven retired as president in 1951.

Michigan Moment

MICHIGAN TRACK TEAM WINS OUTDOOR TITLE

Stephen Farrell's coaching career at the University of Michigan had a happy ending as the Wolverines defeated three-time defending champion Illinois to win the 1930 Big Ten outdoor track and field championship. U-M defeated the Fighting Illini by six-and-a-half points at the meet in Evanston, Illinois to claim the program's 11th Conference title. Two Wolverines claimed individual first-place honors, including John Campbell in the hammer throw and Booker Brooks in the discus. Eddie Tolan notched two second-place finishes as a junior, coming in behind an Ohio State counterpart in the 100- and 220-yard dash events. The eventual Olympian finished second on the team in points earned behind Brooks who also was the runner-up in the shot put. Despite the heroics of those two, the title was still up for grabs entering the final event, the one-mile relay. There, the quartet of Dalton Seymour, Ralph Mueller, Ed Russell and Dan Seymour took top honors to give Farrell a perfect going-away gift.

Discus champion Booker Brooks

CHAMPIONSHIP *Moment*

CHAMPIONS OF THE WEST *AND* THE EAST

Michigan's baseball team successfully captured the title of "Champions of the West" against their Big Ten foes during the spring of 1929, winning seven of nine Conference games to finish a half-game in front of Iowa. But the season didn't stop there, as Coach Ray Fisher's Michigan "9" were invited to try their hand against competition from Japan in a 12-game summer tour of the Orient. U-M's invitation to travel to the Far East came as the result of a two-game spring exhibition series in Ann Arbor when the Wolverines had hosted the University of Meiji. The Michigan men left July 29 and "trained" their way through South Dakota, Washington, British Columbia and Hawaii, playing 10 games in 16 days. The Japanese people rolled out the red carpet for the boys from Michigan when they arrived on August 29, being feted from one end of the island to the other. Michigan started out strong, defeating Meiji twice. The Wolverines then ran up against their stiffest competition at Waseda University, losing the opener by a score of 4-2. That would prove to be the last time Michigan tasted defeat on its trip as it posted an impressive 8-0-1 mark the rest of the way, finishing the tour at 10-1-1. It was the best record an American university had compiled in Japan since 1914.

CHAMPION OF THE WEST

JAMES KELLY

An Indiana product by birth, James Kelly moved to Ann Arbor to attend the University of Michigan and stayed in the area for the remainder of his life. As a Wolverine, Kelly made his impact as a wrestler, becoming Michigan's first ever NCAA wrestling champion. As a junior in 1929, Kelly was a part of Michigan's Big Ten champion and runner-up NCAA team. He finished with a 2-1 record in the conference championship and then wrestled his way to a second place finish in the nation at 145 pounds. Kelly bulked up to the 155-pound weight class for his senior year, helping U-M to a 7-1 record and another Big Ten Conference title. Kelly won the Big Ten individual crown in 1930. Though Michigan finished fifth nationally, Kelly compiled a 4-0 record in the NCAA tournament, becoming the first Wolverine wrestler to claim national honors. Following his graduation from Michigan's Law School, Kelly practiced as an attorney in the Ann Arbor area for over 50 years. The World War II Navy veteran died in December of 1984 at the age of 77.

Maize & Blue Item

Earl Riskey did almost everything during his 40-year affiliation with U-M's Intramural department. The man who served as a coach, administrator, teacher, official, participant and spectator was known worldwide as the inventor of the paddleball. He gained more notoriety in 1934 when he played 32 different sports in a 16-hour span.

M List: U-M Wrestling's Individual NCAA Champions

Wrestler	Weight	Year(s)
James Kelly	155	1930
Carl Dougovito	175	1932
Harold Nichols	145	1939
Donald Nichols	175	1940
William Courtright	155	1946
Jack Barden	191	1963
James Kamman	152	1967
David Porter	Hwt.	1966, 68
Jarrett Hubbard	150	1973, 74
Mark Churella	150, 167	1977, 78, 79
Novard Nalen	130	1953, 54
Kirk Trost	Hwt.	1980

1930-31

America's Time Capsule

September 27, 1930: Bobby Jones became the first player to capture golf's Grand Slam when he won the U.S. Amateur tournament.

December 11, 1930: The powerful Bank of the United States closed in New York City, due to the deepening economic crisis.

January 7, 1931: The President's Emergency Committee for Unemployment Relief announced that between four and five million Americans were out of work.

March 3, 1931: President Herbert Hoover signed a congressional act making "The Star Spangled Banner" the USA's national anthem.

May 1, 1931: The Empire State Building, the world's tallest building, opened in New York City.

University Lore

Alice Crocker Lloyd assumed the office of Dean of Women on July 1, 1930. Lloyd received her BA degree at Michigan in 1916, taught school for a time, completed nursing training and served as a social worker. Dean Lloyd's devotion to the interests and welfare of women students made her a much-loved figure on campus and a national leader in women's education. During her 20-year tenure, the Michigan League's programs blossomed and five women's dorms were built, the largest of which was later named for her.

Michigan Moment

SWIMMING TEAM CAPTURES FIRST OF FIVE CONSECUTIVE BIG TEN TITLES

The most dominant team in any Big Ten sport from 1927 through the mid 1940s, Coach Matt Mann's Michigan swimming and diving squad had one of its greatest seasons during the 1930-31 campaign. Thanks to four individual titles and two relay crowns, the Wolverine swimmers piled up 57 out of a possible 117 points at the 1931 Conference Championship meet in Ann Arbor on March 13. U-M's 37-point margin of victory over runners-up Northwestern and Iowa was the most lopsided win in the first 21 years of the Big Ten meet and stood as the standard for another 20 years. Six new records were established, including four by sensational sophomore John Schmieler, who claimed individual championships in both the 220-yard freestyle (2:22.2) and the 200-yard breaststroke (a record 2:31.4). Other Michigan titlists included Fred Fenske in the 50-yard freestyle (:25.0) and Frank Kennedy in the 440-yard freestyle (a record 5:06.4). Victorious Michigan relay squads included the 400-yard freestyle unit of Dan Marcus, Ivan Smith, Bob Klintworth and Bob Ladd (a record 3:44.2), and the 300-yard medley foursome, anchored by Kennedy (a record 3:12.6). Besides its six firsts, Michigan's perfectly balanced team posted four second-place finishes, three thirds and two fourths in the nine events. Michigan's aquatic team added the national collegiate swimming championship to its long list of conquests on March 28, paced by Schmieler who scored a first in the 200 breaststroke.

Photo: U-M Athletic Dept.

John Schmieler

CHAMPIONSHIP *Moment*

UNIVERSITY GOLF COURSE OPENS

The University of Michigan Golf Course opened in 1931, becoming just the fourth 18-hole course to be located on a college campus. As it had in many other areas, Michigan initially moved into the golf course business early, in 1892, when two Scottish professors urged the University to lay out a six-hole course. That course, the Ann Arbor Golf and Outing Club, became the very first venue of its kind in the state of Michigan. About 25 years later, U-M athletic director Fielding Yost decided that a more formidable course was needed, so he enlisted the services of Dr. Alister MacKenzie to design the current U-M layout. Among the courses already on the Scotsman's impressive resume were the Augusta National in Georgia and Cypress Point in Pebble Beach, California, Michigan's new course took about two years to construct and cost $365,000. The initial U-M greens fees in 1931 were just 50 cents per round for students and faculty and only $1 for alumni.

CHAMPION OF THE WEST

CARL DOUGOVITO

If the University of Michigan ever selects its all-time wrestling squad, the name Carl Dougovito would likely be one of the selections on the all-star ballot. At the time, just the second individual among 17 Wolverine grapplers who have claimed NCAA championships, Dougovito was an awesome performer. He wrestled in the 175-pound classification his sophomore and junior seasons, placing at the national runner-up both years to Oklahoma State star Conrad Caldwell. Dougovito stepped down to 158 pounds as a senior and won the NCAA crown, joining former teammate James "Otto" Kelly as the only Wolverines to achieve that feat. On the Big Ten level, Dougovito claimed his first individual Conference title in 1929 (175 pounds), leading Michigan to its first-ever team championship. He repeated as Conference champ in 1931 (165 pounds) for Coach Cliff Keen and placed second in '32 (165 pounds), marking his only loss in Big Ten tournament action. Following his senior season, Dougovito was selected to compete for the United States Olympic team as a welterweight.

Maize & Blue Item

The sport of men's gymnastics made its varsity debut on the U-M campus January 30, 1931. Coach Wilbur West's squad started off strong in that inaugural meet against rival Ohio State, winning in succession the horizontal bar, pommel horse and rings events. However, OSU responded with victories in the last three events to give them the final 931-874 triumph. Six weeks later at the Conference meet, Michigan placed fifth among eight teams.

M List

Football Letter Winner Contributors

Between 1879 and 1995, 761 of Michigan's 1,672 football letter winners came from the state of Michigan. Here's a list of the most popular hometowns of those "Wolverine Staters."

Detroit	157
Ann Arbor	72
Grand Rapids	34
Flint	32
Saginaw	22
Bay City	18
Muskegon Heights	13
Muskegon	12
Ypsilanti	11
Royal Oak	11
Jackson	11
Dearborn	10
Trenton	10

America's Time Capsule

October 25, 1931: The George Washington Bridge, connecting Manhattan with New Jersey across the Hudson River, was opened to traffic.

March 1, 1932: Charles A. Lindbergh, Jr., 20-month-old son of the famous aviator, was kidnapped from his home at Hopewell, New Jersey.

May 2, 1932: Pearl Buck's *The Good Earth* was awarded a Pulitzer prize in the category of fiction.

July 2, 1932: Franklin Roosevelt accepted the Democratic party's nomination for president, and announced the "new deal."

August 14, 1932: The United States won the unofficial team championship at the Summer Olympic games in Los Angeles by claiming the last of its 16 gold medals.

University Lore

The McMath-Hulbert Observatory, located at Lake Angelus near Pontiac, was donated to the University in January 1932. Constructed by three amateur astronomers, Robert R. McMath, Francis McMath and Judge Henry Hulbert, it included unique mechanical devices which made it possible to record the movement of celestial bodies with a motion picture camera. Francis McMath and U-M professors later designed other devices to improve the Observatory's capabilities, among them the spectroheliokinematograph to record changes in the solar surface.

Michigan Moment

"M" FOOTBALL TEAM DOUBLES UP

After owning an average home attendance of 59,564 in Michigan Stadium's inaugural season, gate receipts slumped to an average of 43,650 per home game in 1928. In an attempt to boost attendance while keeping the season at the same length, the Michigan football squad tried a new feature in 1929. The season opener would be a doubleheader at home, featuring games against Albion and Mount Union. Though the attendance was relatively poor, the Wolverines won both games.

Photo: U-M Athletic Dept.

Michigan's 1931 football team.

As the beginning of the 1930 season neared, and extra revenue was necessary due to the Great Depression, Michigan scheduled another doubleheader. On September 27, Michigan shut out Denison, 33-0, and Eastern Michigan, 7-0, in front of only 12,760 fans. The vast amount of empty seats would become commonplace at Michigan home games, though the Wolverines won the Big Ten crown and finished undefeated. For seven home games, Michigan drew just over 247,000 fans, for an average of only 35,308 a game, a drop of over 25 percent. The Wolverines swept their third straight doubleheader to begin the 1931 season. Central State Teachers College and Michigan Normal were the victims of Michigan's 27-0 and 34-0 wins. Only 13,169 seats were sold for this two-game set. In a campaign that saw Michigan finish 7-1-1 at the end of the scheduled season, Michigan Stadium reached half of its capacity for just one game (Ohio State). With revenue falling far short of expectations, the Big Ten Conference added an extra week of games onto the end of the season. The added week did little for Michigan's monetary situation, as only 9,190 turned out to see the Wolverines beat Wisconsin, 16-0. However, in another "added" game in Chicago, Purdue beat Northwestern 7-0 in front of 40,000. Purdue's win left the Wildcats, Boilermakers and Wolverines tied atop the conference at 5-1, allowing Michigan its 13th Big Ten title.

CHAMPIONSHIP *Moment*

"M" SWIMMERS DUNK BIG TEN COMPETITION

Matt Mann's tankmen had captured national championships in 1927, 1928 and 1931, but a fourth crown in six years would not come easy. At the Intramural Building Pool on the U-M campus, Michigan found itself trailing Stanford with just three events remaining. Dick Degener started the Wolverine climb with a second-place finish in the diving event, missing first place by just 3.84 points. Degener's second-place finish was respectable, but the Wolverines could ill afford to take anything but top honors in the meet's final two events. In the 220-yard freestyle, Michigan was represented by Johnny Schmieler, who had set the record in the 200-yard breaststroke a day earlier. The junior had significant competition in Rutgers' Walter Spence, who finished first in the 100-yard freestyle earlier in the meet. True to form, Spence led after 100 yards, but Schmeiler rallied to take the lead at the last turn and come in with a record time of 2:15.4. The uphill fight was not over. The 300-yard medley relay was still to be conquered. Michigan led off with Taylor Drysdale, who had already won the 150-yard backstroke title. Louis Lemak followed Drysdale in the water as Michigan and Northwestern stood neck in neck. Bob Ladd swam the final leg for the Wolverines, and used a spectacular finish to barely beat out the Wildcat trio. The new record time of 3:08.6 allowed the Wolverines to conquer the Indians, 34-31, extending the Mann dynasty.

CHAMPION OF THE WEST

EDDIE TOLAN

Eddie Tolan was a native of Denver, Colorado, and the king of U.S. sprinting from 1929-31. On May 25, 1929, "The Midnight Express" was the first man in the world to be officially credited with a time of 9.5 seconds for 100 yards. As a member of the Michigan track team, Tolan won races at the Big Ten meet four times, including two wins in the 100-yard dash. Tolan further entrenched himself as the best sprinter in the land with a win in the 200 at the 1931 NCAA meet. By 1932, Tolan dropped to the second best in the land. The new title holder was Marquette's George Metcalfe, a man who went undefeated during the 1932 season. In the Olympic trials at 100 meters, Metcalfe beat Tolan and although both were headed to the Summer Games in Los Angeles, Metcalfe was the heavy favorite. When the 100-meter preliminary heats were run, Tolan notched his first win over his rival, setting an Olympic-record of 10.4. When the final came, Tolan grabbed the lead at 40 meters, but Metcalfe drew even with him and the two finished in a dead heat. Many had no idea who won, and in prior Olympic games, a controversy may have resulted. However, these games featured the first use of a photo-finish camera. Judges spent hours viewing films, determining that Tolan had crossed the finish line first by one inch, in an Olympic record 10.3 seconds. To stake Michigan's claim as the only university to have three double-event gold medalists in the sprints, Tolan would still have to win the 200-meter event. Victory would not come easy, as Archie Hahn's 28-year-old Olympic record was bettered four times in the prelims. Meanwhile, Eddie just qualified for the final by barely finishing third in the last heat. When the pressure of the final was on, Tolan performed beautifully. He surged ahead at the 150-meter mark, then was able to withstand a brief stumble toward the finish for an Olympic-record 21.2 seconds. Tolan's finish led a medal sweep by the Americans in the event.

Maize & Blue Item

Michigan had maintained a golf team since 1922 under the tutelage of Tom Trueblood, but it took until 1932 to grab a Big Ten title. A sophomore from Cincinnati, John Fischer, led the Wolverines to the crown by carding a 303 at the four rounds in Minneapolis, Minnesota. The four Wolverine golfers finished with a 1248, beating runner-up Minnesota by 24 strokes and ending of a five-year string of second-place finishes for U-M.

M List

Gold and Maize and Blue

In the 1932 Los Angeles Olympics, Eddie Tolan won the 14th gold medal by a Michigan athlete in track and field. Here's a list of track and field medal winners:

Athlete	Year	Event (s)
Archie Hahn	1904	60-meter dash, 100-meter dash, 200-meter dash
Charles Dvorak	1904	Pole vault
Ralph Rose	1904	Shot put
Fred Schule	1904	110-meter hurdles
Archie Hahn	1906	100-meter dash
Ralph Rose	1908	Shot put
Ralph Craig	1912	100-meter dash, 200-meter dash
Ralph Rose	1912	Shot put combined
William DeHart Hubbard	1924	Long jump
Eddie Tolan	1932	100-meter dash, 200-meter dash

1932-33

America's Time Capsule

October 2, 1932: The Chicago Cubs were swept in four straight games by the New York Yankees at the 29th annual World Series.

November 8, 1932: In a landslide victory over Herbert Hoover, Franklin Roosevelt was elected president of the United States.

March13, 1933: United States banks began to reopen across the country, following a prolonged depression.

May 27, 1933: Chicago's Century of Progress Exposition began, in honor of that city's centennial celebration.

July 6, 1933: Babe Ruth hit a home run at major league baseball's first all-star game, as the American League defeated the National League, 4-2, at Chicago's Comiskey Park.

University Lore

Niels Bohr ("The Foundations of Quantum Mechanics") and Enrico Fermi ("Structure of the Atomic Nucleus") were the featured lecturers at the University's 1933 Summer Symposia on Theoretical Physics. Initiated in 1923 as two special lectures, the Symposia annually drew some of the world's leading theoretical physicists to campus. U-M professors David Dennison, George Uhlenbeck, and Otto Laporte were also frequent instructors. Before the Symposia ended in 1941, future Nobel prize winners Hans Bethe, Werner Heisenberg, J. Robert Oppenheimer, and Edwin O. Lawrence were among the guest lecturers.

Michigan Moment

WOLVERINE FOOTBALL TEAM WEARS NATIONAL CROWN

U-M's 1932-33 football team.

In Harry Kipke's first two years at the helm of the Michigan football team, the Wolverines rolled to a 16-1-2 record, earning the conference title each year. The 1932 season looked to be a continuation of this success, featuring senior quarterback Harry Newman, center Charles Bernard and end Ted Petoskey. Michigan started off the year by blasting Michigan State, 26-0, in what was supposed to be a close game. While Michigan's tally raised eyebrows, the shutout itself was not surprising, given that the two teams had battled to scoreless deadlocks each of the previous two years. The Wolverines then bowled over Northwestern, 15-6. The Wildcats, who had tied the Wolverines for the Big Ten title in both 1930 and 1931 were done in by several fumbles and two touchdowns by Stanley Fay.

U-M then gained revenge upon Ohio State, who had served as the only blemish on Michigan's record since 1930. Despite being held to just 48 yards rushing in Columbus, the Wolverines used two Newman touchdown passes to grab a 14-0 win. After suppressing Illinois, 32-0, Michigan allowed only its second touchdown of the year in a game against Princeton. In a cold, wet Michigan Stadium the Tigers held a 7-2 halftime lead, but Petoskey's runs and Newman's passes brought the Wolverines back for a 14-7 victory. As the race for the Big Ten title intensified, Michigan picked off five Hoosier passes in a 7-0 win at Indiana, then used a 77-yard touchdown run by Newman to post a 12-0 victory against Chicago. In the season finale at Minnesota, the Wolverines knew they would need a victory to keep their Conference title string alive. The Gopher defense stopped the Michigan ground game all afternoon, but the Wolverines' defense was just as effective at halting the Minnesota passing attack. In the second quarter, Michigan recovered a fumble at the Minnesota 24-yard line and drove to the 15-yard line, where Newman launched a kick that just cleared the right upright. Though Michigan would gain just 48 yards in the game, the field goal was all that was necessary for a 3-0 win. The 8-0 Wolverines were named national champions in several listings following the season.

CHAMPIONSHIP *Moment*

"M" ICERS DEFEAT WISCONSIN

Michigan's hockey team looked to the weekend series with Wisconsin as an all-or-nothing affair. Two wins would leave U-M in the thick of the Western Conference title hunt, while a pair of losses would place the Wolverines among the also-rans. Coming to the Coliseum straight off the train trip from Madison, the Badgers were in no shape to play a hockey game Friday night. Michigan blitzed the visitors, 8-1, behind captain Emmie Reid's four goals, but Saturday night's affair would not be so simple. A rested and ready Wisconsin team took the ice for the second game intent on revenge. Fans began entering the arena over an hour before the game began, and they were treated to an awesome display of hockey once the puck dropped. For 14 minutes the teams battled without a goal until U-M's Keith Crossman beat Jack Greeley to give Michigan a 1-0 lead. The Wolverines lost Reid to injury in the second period, but kept Wisconsin off the scoreboard until the Badgers tied the game 2:35 into the final period. The teams were still locked in the 1-1 tie when Michigan's George David picked up a penalty with five minutes left. No sooner did David return than defenseman Neil Gabler drew a two-minute sentence. Gabler, who had previously lettered in 1926 and 1927, was led to the box as Michigan's chances for victory looked dim. The Wolverines successfully played defense until less than a minute remained in the game. As Gabler was being let out of the box, a U-M player check sent the loose puck his way. Gabler only had time to take a single shot. Greeley, who had made 38 saves to this point, succeeded in blocking it. However, the momentous blast had enough resiliency to dribble across the line, and Michigan grabbed an improbable 2-1 victory from an even more improbable player.

CHAMPION OF THE WEST

HARRY NEWMAN

In Harry Newman's three-year Michigan career, the Wolverines lost a grand total of one game. While leading Michigan to 24 victories, three Big Ten titles and a national championship, Newman made the people of Ann Arbor realize that the glory days of Michigan football were not only in the past. The native of Detroit was plagued by an ankle injury in 1931, playing only three games. After the 1931 campaign, Newman considered quitting college football altogether. But if his junior year could be described as disappointing, Newman's senior year could only be summed up as successful. He started every one of U-M's games at quarterback and the Wolverines won all of their eight contests in 1932. Newman established career highs in attempts, completions, yards and touchdowns as a quarterback. However, Newman truly starred as a return man. Four weeks after returning a kick 73 yards against Illinois, Harry Newman ran a Chicago punt back 77 yards for a touchdown in a close game versus Chicago. Following the 1932 season, Harry Newman was named Michigan's MVP, paving the way for the *Chicago Tribune* to name him as the most valuable player in the Big Ten. He also was named the winner of the Douglas Fairbanks Trophy, given to the best college football player in the nation. Harry played for the New York Giants in 1933, becoming an All-NFL player in his rookie season. He led the NFL in pass completions, passing yards and passing touchdowns in 1933, and in least interception percentage in 1934. He closed out his professional career with the Giants in 1935. Harry Newman is a member of the National Football Foundation Hall of Fame.

Maize & Blue Item

Using wins by Willis Ward in both the 100-yard dash and high jump, Michigan posted 60.5 points in taking the Big Ten outdoor track crown back to Ann Arbor for the second straight year. In Evanston, Illinois, the Conference lowered prices, invited bands and "olympiad-ized" the meet to try to renew interest in the sport. Though the Wolverines picked up just Ward's first two places, the team grabbed enough second, third and fourth places to score the most points in nine years.

M List

Michigan Football and the NFL

Here is a list of Michigan best "offensive" players who went on to star in the NFL:

Player, Position	Years at 'M'	Years in NFL	Team(s)
Terry Barr, FL/DB/HB	1954-56	1957-65	Detroit
Anthony Carter, WR	1979-82	1985-95	Minnesota, Detroit
Dan Dierdorf, OT/OG	1968-70	1971-83	St. Louis
Jim Harbaugh, QB	1983-86	1987-96	Chicago, Indianapolis
Desmond Howard, WR	1989-91	1922-96	Washington, Jacksonville, Green Bay
Mike Kenn, OT	1975-77	1978-94	Atlanta
Ron Kramer, TE	1954-56	1957-67	Green Bay, Detroit
Jim Mandich, TE	1967-69	1970-78	Miami, Pittsburgh
Reggie McKenzie, OG	1968-71	1972-84	Buffalo, Seattle
John Morrow, C/OG	1953-55	1956-66	L.A. Rams, Cleveland
Bubba Paris, OT	1978-81	1982-91	San Francisco, Detroit, Indianapolis

1933-34

MICHIGAN MOMENT

NATIONAL CHAMPIONS AGAIN

With nine of the starters from the 1932 squad returning, great things were expected from Harry Kipke's 1933 Michigan football team. The team could not do much better than the undefeated Big Ten title and National Championship season of the year before, but anything less would only qualify as disappointing. With that tall order, the Wolverines fulfilled it to the letter. They stormed through the 1933 season shutting out five opponents and allowing the other three six points each. Entering the season, U-M was forced to find a way around the loss of Harry Newman at quarterback. Placing team captain Stanley Fay at the position was one solution, but the best option was simply to run the ball more. Using backs Herman Everhardus and John Regeczi, the Wolverines outrushed six of their eight opponents. Michigan opened the season with a 20-6 win over Michigan State. Though no Michigan quarterback completed any of the three passes attempted, the defense limited the Spartans to 88 yards on the ground. The following week, Regeczi had 101 yards rushing and Everhardus added 94 as Michigan mangled Cornell, 40-0. The Big Red were outgained in total offense 421-91 and reached the first-down marker just twice. The Wolverine juggernaut rolled over Ohio State, 13-0, and Chicago, 28-0, before beating Illinois by the slimmest of margins, 7-6. Michigan neutralized Iowa, 10-6, as Everhardus rushed for 84 yards. The annual Brown Jug game turned into a grueling contest with the Conference title on the line. The Golden Gophers limited Michigan to 61 total yards and zero complete passes, but could not score themselves, and the game ended in a 0-0 deadlock. For the season finale, Michigan headed to the state of Illinois for the third time in 1933 this time, to face Northwestern. NU held the Wolverines to a season-low 37 yards rushing but threw six interceptions to thwart their chances of an upset bid. Michigan's 13-0 win gave it a fourth straight Conference title and second straight National Championship. Following the season, Ted Petoskey, Charles Bernard and Francis Wistert were All-Americans.

Photo: Michiganensian

U-M's Everhardus scored his second touchdown versus Chicago in the 1933 game.

America's Time Capsule

December 5, 1933: Prohibition in the United States was repealed when Congress adopted the 21st Ammendment.

December 17, 1933: The Chicago Bears defeated the New York Giants, 23-21, winning the first National Football League championship playoff.

May 23, 1934: Dr. Wallace Carothers of the DuPont Laboratories first developed a synthetic fiber called nylon.

June 14, 1934: Max Baer scored a technical knockout over Primo Carnera to win the world heavyweight boxing championship.

July 22, 1934: John Dillinger, America's public enemy number one, was shot and killed in Chicago by FBI agents.

UNIVERSITY LORE

With the opening of Hutchins Hall in Fall 1933, the Law Quad was completed at a total cost of $4.79 million. William W. Cook ('80, '81), a successful, if controversial, Wall Street lawyer, had funded construction of the Lawyers' Club, which was completed in 1924. The John P. Cook Dormitory followed in 1930 and the William W. Cook Legal Research Building in 1931. Designed by Starret Brothers of New York in Tudor Gothic style, the Quad was supposed to resemble the colleges of Oxford and Cambridge and the Inns of Court in London.

CHAMPION OF THE WEST

HARRY KIPKE

At just 5 feet, 9 inches tall and 155 pounds, Lansing native Harry Kipke was one of Michigan's smallest players. Despite his size, Kipke would eventually win nine letters in football, baseball and basketball. As a halfback and punter on the football team, Kipke was one of the main reasons that Michigan attained a record of 19-1-2 between 1921 and 1923. He was named an All-American in 1922, when he single-handedly destroyed Ohio State in the dedication game of Ohio Stadium. Besides scoring two touchdowns in Michigan's 19-0 win, Kipke punted 11 times in the game, including two that went into the endzone and nine others that went out of bounds inside the Buckeye 8-yard line. Afterwards, legendary sportswriter Walter Camp proclaimed Kipke as the greatest punter in football history." During Kipke's three years on the basketball team, Michigan won 36 times and lost only 15, while his baseball teams would win two Big Ten titles in going 56-13. Still, football was his first love, and soon after graduation, he began a coaching career that would take him to Michigan State and ultimately back to his alma mater. Kipke took over the head coaching reins of the Wolverines in 1929, and from 1930-33, there was no better team in the nation. Over those four years, Kipke's squads posted a combined 31-1-3, winning four Big Ten titles and claiming two national championships. Kipke stayed on as coach until 1937, posting a 46-26-4 record in his nine-year stint. Despite entering the Navy in 1942 and later serving as president of the Coca-Cola Bottling Company of Chicago, Kipke stayed involved with the Maize and Blue. He was a regent for eight years and remained strong in the alumni association for several decades.

another CHAMPION OF THE WEST

CHARLES HOYT

Charles Hoyt and the track were one and inseparable from his high school days in Iowa through his college days and professional career. As an undergraduate at Grinnell College, Hoyt was an interscholastic champion in both the 100-yard and 220-yard dash. Hoyt graduated in 1917 and saw brief war action in the Navy, before returning to his alma mater as an assistant coach. After one year as coach and Athletic Director in Sioux City, Iowa, Hoyt came to Michigan as a football trainer and assistant track coach under Steve Farrell in 1923. When Farrell retired in 1930, Hoyt assumed the top track position. Idolized in the eyes of his athletes and well regarded professionally, Hoyt continued the dynasty of Michigan track. Between 1930 and 1939, Hoyt's indoor and outdoor track squads claimed 14 of a possible 20 conference titles, including six straight indoor crowns from 1934-39. He tutored such individual stars as Eddie Tolan, Sam Stoller and William Watson over his 10-year head coaching stint at Michigan. In that time, Hoyt's teams lost just four dual meets. He resigned from his Michigan post in March 1939 to head to Yale as the head track coach.

Maize & Blue Item

Sixty-five thousand fans flowed into Michigan Stadium to see undefeated Minnesota play undefeated Michigan on a November day. The Golden Gophers, 3-0-3 on the season, had been Michigan's toughest competition in its 16-game winning and 20-game unbeaten streak. The contest was a Brown Jug classic, as they battled to a 0-0 tie on a damp field. Defense was king as the teams combined for 34 punts and zero passing yards. Michigan got no closer than the Minnesota 30-yard line throughout the game, while the only Gopher threat was a 25-yard field goal that was wide.

M List

Football's 0-0 Ties

In the 117-year history of Michigan football, the Wolverines have played to a 0-0 tie 12 times. A list of those scoreless games appears below:

vs.	Toronto, 1879
vs.	Ohio Wesleyan, 1897
vs.	Ohio State, 1900
at	Michigan State, 1908
at	Pennsylvania, 1910
at	Pennsylvania, 1915
at	Vanderbilt, 1922
vs.	Iowa, 1929
vs.	Michigan State, 1930
vs.	Michigan State, 1931
vs.	Minnesota, 1933
vs.	Northwestern, 1938

1934-35

America's Time Capsule

September 23, 1934: The Detroit Lions defeated the San Francisco Giants at the University of Detroit Stadium. It was the first game in the franchise's history.

October 9, 1934: Dizzy Dean and the St. Louis Cardinals won the World Series over the Detroit Tigers.

December 9, 1934: The Chicago Bears lost the NFL championship game to the New York Giants, 30-13.

May 24, 1935: More than 20,000 fans at Cincinnati's Crosley Field watched their Reds beat the Philadelphia Phillies in baseball's first-ever night game.

August 14, 1935: President Roosevelt signed the Social Security Act, establishing payment of benefits to senior citizens.

University Lore

Enrollment increased slightly following four years of decline, but the effects of the great Depression were still being felt. State funding had declined by nearly one third from three years earlier. Faculty and staff salaries were cut, and 65 teaching positions were eliminated. During the course of the decade, a number of the New Deal's "alphabet agencies" appeared on campus. The FERA and NYA provided work for students on a variety of projects. The CWA, PWA, and WPA supported construction of dormitories and the Health Service Building. The Extension Service offered courses in CCC camps.

Michigan Moment

"M" GOLFERS WIN NCAA TITLE

In 1934, the Wolverines had become the first non-Eastern school to capture an NCAA golf championship. At the Congressional Country Club in Washington D.C., Michigan looked to stretch the eastern drought to two years. Loaded with two of the best collegiate golfers in the nation, John Fischer and Chuck Kocsis, U-M held high hopes of defending its title. Fischer and Kocsis had led the way through the Big Ten match, the former breaking the Conference record with a 281 and the latter carding a 284. Michigan blasted the old Conference record by 57 strokes, finishing with an 1,163 to second place Northwestern's 1,223. It was the fourth straight Conference title annexed by the Michigan golf team under head coach Tom Trueblood. Represented by Fischer, Kocsis, Woodrow Malloy, Dana Seeley and Lawrence David, Michigan faced up against contenders Oklahoma, Stanford, Texas, Princeton, Notre Dame, Yale and Georgia Tech. Malloy carded a 72 on the first day, tying him for the top spot, and continued his lead with a 76 on day two. Malloy, Kocsis and Lewis Johnson of South Carolina tied for medalist honors at 148. There would be no tie for the team title, however, as Michigan scored a 606 for the 36-hole team tournament, earning the championship.

Photo: U-M Athletic Dept.

Michigan's 1934 golf team.

CHAMPIONSHIP *Moment*

MICHIGAN'S TEAM EFFORT OVER-SHADOWED BY OWENS

At Ann Arbor's Ferry Field, Jesse Owens made headlines around the world by setting three world records and tying another at the 1935 Big Ten outdoor track championship. But while the Buckeye great grabbed individual honors, it was the home team that took home the aggregate trophy, albeit by a very slim margin. While Owens was setting a record so unbelievable in the long jump that it had to measured three times, Wolverines Willis Ward and Sam Stoller finished second and fourth, respectively. Stoller had just come off a third-place finish in the 100-yard dash, finishing behind Owens, but picking up points for Michigan nonetheless. With one event left, Ward had picked up the only individual title for the Maize and Blue, finishing in a tie with Illinois' Robert Reigal in the high jump. Eighteen Michigan men scored in the first 14 events, but Ohio State held a 43-1/2-43 lead with the mile relay remaining. In the final event, the Michigan contingent of Fred Stiles, Frank Aikens, Harvey Patton and Stan Birleson came across the line in a Conference record 3:15.2 to keep the team title in Ann Arbor. In all, seven Conference records were broken at the meet, highlighted by Owens' runs and jumps. In this case, however, Michigan proved that depth is more powerful than any individual.

CHAMPION OF THE WEST

GERALD FORD

Leslie Lynch King was born in relatively plain settings in Omaha, Nebraska on July 14, 1913. His parents soon divorced, then his mother moved to Grand Rapids and married a man named Gerald R. Ford. The son was formally adopted and renamed for his stepfather. Young Gerald was athletic, playing on the Grand Rapids South High School football, basketball and track teams. The captain of the football team his senior year and the owner of good grades in school, Gerald was offered a $100 scholarship to play football at the University of Michigan, which he gladly accepted. A center, Ford was a substitute behind All-American Charles Bernard on Michigan's National Championship squads of 1932 and 1933. Following the graduation of Bernard, Ford started at center for all of Michigan's games during his senior season. At the end of the season, Ford was honored with the team's Most Valuable Player award. Ford graduated with a B.A. in 1935, and wished to attend law school, but money was a problem. Ford got a job as assistant football coach at Yale, attending law school in the offseason. After obtaining his degree in January 1941, Ford returned to Grand Rapids to practice. His first job was short lived, as World War II broke out and Ford entered the Navy. After serving in the Pacific and reaching the post of lieutenant commander, Ford returned to Michigan in 1946. In 1948, Ford ran for Congress and was elected. He would serve 13 terms in the House of Representatives, rising in power to serve on the Warren Commission and become house minority leader in 1965. Ford held hopes to become Speaker of the House, but with Republicans in the minority, was not able to realize his dream. That desire was soon shelved when he was asked by Richard Nixon to be his vice-president soon after the resignation of Spiro Agnew. Ford accepted the position, rising to the office of the president when Nixon resigned on August 9, 1974. He quickly succeeded in stabilizing a country rocked by political turmoil.

America's Time Capsule

April 11, 1936: The Detroit Red Wings won their first Stanley Cup against Toronto, three games to one.

September 8, 1935: Powerful Louisiana politician Huey Long was assassinated in the corridor of the state capitol in Baton Rouge.

October 7, 1935: The Chicago Cubs lost baseball's World Series to the Detroit Tigers, four games to two.

November 9, 1935: The Committee for Industrial Organization (CIO) was established by John L. Lewis.

August 16, 1936: The Summer Olympic Games, featuring American track star Jesse Owens, ended in Berlin, Germany.

University Lore

The University Musical Society's 43rd May Festival marked the beginning of a long relationship with the Philadelphia Symphony Orchestra. Leopold Stokowski directed the Orchestra and featured artists included Lily Pons and Ephrem Zimbalist. Eugene Ormandy would bring the Orchestra to Hill Auditorium the next year and for forty-three years following. Founded in 1894 by professor Albert A. Stanley, the May Festival brought many of the world's great musical artists to Ann Arbor until financial considerations brought the series to an end in 1995.

Michigan Moment

BASEBALL ENJOYS BANNER YEAR

After recording five Big Ten titles in Ray Fisher's first nine years as coach, Michigan had gone titleless since 1929. With a mixture of experienced and novice players, the Wolverines opened up the Big Ten portion of the schedule, scoring six third-inning runs to beat Ohio State, 12-9. Behind strong pitching by senior Berger Larson, Johnny Gee and Herman Fishman, Michigan raced off to a 5-0 conference mark. Both U-M and Iowa stood atop the standings with 8-1 records with a series slated between them for June 2-3. Before the matchup to decide the Conference title could take place, Michigan had some non-conference business to take care of. The 12-3 Michigan State Spartans arrived in Ann Arbor for the mythical state championship. Larson struck out 11 Spartans and allowed just five hits in the 2-1 Michigan win in the first game, while the Wolverines scored all their runs in the final two innings to win the second tilt, 5-2. Rain canceled the first of the two big Iowa games, the seventh cancellation of the season. When the second game was played, Larson stuck out 13 Hawkeyes as U-M pulled out an 8-6 victory. Two Iowa errors in the bottom of the eighth led to the winning margin for the Wolverines. Michigan's 9-1 Big Ten mark brought the Conference crown back to Ann Arbor. Pitching was key for the Wolverines as Fishman finished the season 8-0 with 44 strikeouts and just 15 walks in 70 innings. His 0.86 earned run average was a Conference record that would stand for 15 years. Syracuse native Gee finished 5-0, while Larson was named the Conference MVP with a 7-2 record and 83 strikeouts in 72 innings. Offensively, sophomore shortstop Steve Uricek led U-M with a .385 batting average, 35 hits and five triples.

Photo: U-M Athletic Dept.

U-M pitcher Berger Larson

CHAMPION OF THE WEST

CHUCK KOCSIS

Michigan's golf team had put together a dynasty between 1932-36, winning five Big Ten titles and two national championships. John Fischer had been the fuel for this fire between 1932-34, but it was Chuck Kocsis who kept the Wolverines rolling into the mid-1930s. Kocsis had already built up an impressive resume before his days at U-M, edging Tommy Armour by a stroke to claim the 1930 Michigan Open championship. The Detroit native made an immediate impact at Michigan, where he won individual medalist honors at the Big Ten Championship in 1934 with his four-round total of 283. He followed this performance with a runner-up finish at the NCAA championship in Cleveland, Ohio. As a senior in 1936, Kocsis once again claimed the Western Conference title, which he had given up to teammate Fischer in 1935. His first round of 65 led to a medal-winning total of 286. At the NCAA championship, Kocsis claimed the individual title he had finished just short of two years earlier.

another CHAMPION OF THE WEST

THOMAS TRUEBLOOD

For more than fifty years of his career, Thomas Trueblood had a profound effect upon both Michigan academics and athletics. Trueblood's legacy, however, has continued on long since his death in 1951 at the age of 95. He arrived in Ann Arbor in 1884, offering to teach speech to University students. This unheard-of course was greeted with such skepticism by the university that it gave him a room, but no salary, basing his earnings on the tuition he made from students who took his course. Trueblood's speech classes became so popular that the first speech department in the nation was instituted at Michigan in 1918. Besides speech, Trueblood had another love—golf. He learned the game in 1896, and began teaching it to interested Wolverines in 1901. Few people in the United States knew of the game's existence in this era, but Trueblood managed to maintain an informal team of golfers for athletic play. In 1922, the sport was recognized by the university, and Trueblood was named the head coach. His teams won four straight Big Ten titles from 1932-35 and captured the national championship in both 1934 and 1935. Trueblood tutored such Michigan stars as Chuck Kocsis and John Fischer before retiring after the 1935 season at the age of 79. Trueblood left not only a career mark of 54-8-2 on the links, he was the designer of the "locomotive yell," still used at football games by alumni cheerleaders.

Maize & Blue Item

American Olympic coach Lawson Robertson originally planned for his 1936 4x100 meter relay unit to include U-M sprinter Sam Stoller, Marty Glickman, Frank Wykoff, Foy Draper, and *not* superstar Jesse Owens so that other individuals could participate in the Games. At the last minute, Robertson removed Stoller and Glickman from the race in favor of Owens and Ralph Metcalfe. Improving the team's speed was his reasoning.

M List

On February 19, 1936, the Michigan hockey team took on St. Thomas University and set some records that continue to survive today. The 12-5 final score marked the first time the Wolverines had broken the 10 goal barrier as a team, and the first and only time a Michigan player has broken the same mark. Left wing Gib James finished the contest with 10 goals and one assist to set a Wolverine record, while fellow linesman Vic Heyliger picked up eight assists to set another individual high.

The following are the times, scorer and assists for each of the 12 Wolverine goals that evening:
First Period: James (David) 9:55; James (Heyliger) 10:40
Second Period: James (Heyliger) 2:28; James 7:25; James (Heyliger) 15:45; James (Heyliger) 18:08; James (Heyliger) 19:50
Third Period: James (Heyliger) 1:30; Fabello (James, Heyliger) 2:30; James (Heyliger) 11:40; David 13:50; James (Radford) 15:05

MICHIGAN MOMENT

America's Time Capsule

November 3, 1936: Franklin Roosevelt was elected president of the United States in a crushing victory over Republican Alf Landon.

May 6, 1937: The dirigible Hindenburg burst into flames at Lakehurst, N.J., marking the virtual end of lighter-than-air transportation.

May 12, 1937: Americans listened to the coronation of King George IV of England in radio's first worldwide broadcast.

June 5, 1937: Jockey Charles Kurtsinger rode War Admiral to victory at the Belmont Stakes, thus winning horse racing's triple crown.

June 22, 1937: Joe Louis knocked out Jim Braddock to capture the heavyweight boxing title in a match held at Chicago.

University Lore

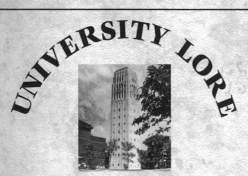

Burton Tower, U-M's most famous landmark, was dedicated in December, 1936. Beginning in 1919, several proposals for a campanile to replace the clock and bells of the Old Library were offered, but none came to fruition. In 1935, former Athletic Director Charles Baird's gift of a 55-bell carillon revived plans for a tower. Albert Kahn's design of reinforced concrete walls with limestone facing is 41 feet 7 inches square at the base and 212 feet high. The cost of the memorial to President Burton was $243,664.21.

HEYLIGER-WILKINSON SHOWDOWN HIGHLIGHTS HOCKEY SEASON

Michigan's Vic Heyliger

The Michigan Coliseum was packed with fans on the weekend of January 15-16, 1937 as 1,500 people turned out to see Michigan's Vic Heyliger take on Minnesota's "Bud" Wilkinson in the battle of Western Conference stars. The Gophers took the opening contest as Wilkinson, who would eventually become a legendary football coach at Oklahoma, turned aside 32 Michigan shots in a 3-0 victory. The teams played a scoreless first period before Minnesota lit the lamp twice in the second. Heyliger was stopped no less than three times on open breakaways by the Minnesota netminder and suffered a cut on his head when clipped in the second period. Early in the third period, Heyliger suffered a charley horse, but continued to play. Michigan goalie Bill Wood stopped 21 Gopher shots in the loss. The following evening, Minnesota looked to sweep the weekend, but the Wolverines would have none of it. Six times in the first period, Michigan shots found the back of the net, behind the same goaltender who had blanked U-M the previous night. Johnny Fabello, who had spent up until noon Friday at University Health Services with a head cold, opened the scoring just 2:25 into the game. Heyliger then converted the next three goals, picking up the hat trick on a penalty shot just 11 minutes into the game. Gib James scored the last four goals for Michigan, adding two in the first period and one each in the second and third stanzas. James and Heyliger both finished with five-point performances in the 8-1 blasting of Minnesota. Wood stopped 40 Gopher shots to hand the visitors their first loss of the season.

CHAMPIONSHIP *Moment*

GEE WHIZ!

Up until May 25, 1937, there was very little Johnny A. Gee Jr. had not accomplished. A three-year starter for the Wolverine basketball team, the 6-9 center had averaged 5.5 points per game over 52 contests. Named the captain of the 1937 team, the Syracuse, New York, native led Michigan to a 16-4 record his senior season, an eight-win improvement over his sophomore year. On the diamond, Gee was also a force to be reckoned with. He had been part of the 1936 Big Ten Championship team which finished 20-5. Gee had recently been honored as a Conference Medal of Honor winner for his excellent marks in both academics and athletics. Despite his lengthy list of accomplishments beforehand, Gee waited until the next-to-last start of his career to get one more thing done—toss a no-hitter. Taking the mound on the road against Hillsdale, Gee needed a ground out to escape a first inning jam, as he walked two batters. After that point, the lefthander would issue just one free pass while mowing down 12 Chargers. Gee got all the offensive help he needed in the sixth as Michigan scored three times. Steve Uricek's double scored Leo Beebe and Pete Lisagor, and Uricek came in to score when the ball got past the left fielder. After pitching the first no-hitter in Michigan baseball history since 1915, Gee finished his career with a 21-strikeout, two-hitter against Toledo the following week. Following graduation, Gee went to have an eight-year career in major league baseball with the Pittsburgh Pirates and New York Giants.

CHAMPION OF THE WEST

BILL WATSON

Originally, Bill Watson's goal was to be a boxing star, and therefore the young man took up track to get in shape. At the high school level, the Saginaw native broke school records in the high jump, shot put and discus, then made an assault upon the state record books. By the time Watson came to the University of Michigan in 1935, he had climbed out of the ring and began his ascent into the Big Ten track record books. An admirer of Willis Ward and track coach Charles Hoyt, Watson came to U-M to follow in their footsteps. In his career, Watson did more than follow behind such great leaders, he ran side-by-side with them. Rain could not stop Watson at the 1937 Big Ten Track Championship in Ann Arbor. The sophomore blew away the field in the long jump, shot put and discus, giving credit to his new nickname as "the one-man track team." His three top finishes helped Michigan to capture the team crown. Winning the long jump, shot put and discus would become second nature to Watson, who swept all three events again in both 1938 and 1939. Each year he shattered more records in helping Michigan to the team title. In his six seasons with the indoor and outdoor track teams, Watson won 12 individual titles as the Wolverines emerged victorious each time. Although his dreams of making the 1940 Olympics were destroyed when the games were canceled, Watson served as secretary to heavyweight champion Joe Louis following his graduation from U-M. He later went on to serve in the Detroit Police Force, before passing away in 1973.

Maize & Blue Item

Following a week of exams, the swim team took a car trip east to tangle with the New York Athletic Club and Colgate University. Not only had the Wolverines lost four straight to the NYAC, no team had beaten this aggregation since 1904. Having fallen just short, 43-41, in 1936, Michigan came out tough, winning six of the nine events. Frank Barnard won both the 220- and 440-yard freestyle as Michigan convincingly ended the 33-year winning streak of the NYAC, 47-28.

M List

Olympian Swimming Standouts

After winning the silver medal in three-meter diving at the 1932 Olympics, Michigan's Dick Degener came back to take the gold at the 1936 games. Since then, eight other former Wolverines have claimed gold medals in Olympic swimming and diving:

Swimmer	Year (s)	Event
Dick Degener	1936	Three-meter diving
John Davies	1952	200 breaststroke
Robert Webster	1960, 1964	10-meter diving
Carl Robie	1968	200 butterfly
Micki King	1972	Three-meter diving
Phil Boggs	1976	Three-meter diving
Brent Lang	1988	400 free relay
Mike Barrowman	1992	200 breaststroke
Tom Dolan	1996	400 individual medley

MICHIGAN MOMENT

MICHIGAN SWIMMERS TAKE TROPHY AGAIN

For the first time in five years, the top spot in the national swimming meet was going to be competitive, and all eyes were upon Ohio State and Harvard as they looked to dethrone four-time defending champion Michigan. Just a few weeks earlier, the Buckeyes had knocked Michigan from the pinnacle of the Big Ten, and looked to do the same at the national meet in New Brunswick, New Jersey. Captain Ed Kirar started Michigan on the right track by tying a meet record in 50-yard freestyle with a time of 23.0 seconds. Michigan failed to pick up another first place finish on Friday, but Tom Haynie, the defending champion at 220-yard freestyle grabbed second place, and the 300-yard medley relay team came in third. The Wolverines found themselves in second place, trailing the Buckeyes by two points and leading the third-place Crimson by four. Kirar began the second and final day of competition with his second crown of the meet, taking the 100-yard freestyle title in 52.7 seconds. Ohio State led 39-36 entering the final event, the 400-yard freestyle relay. If the Wolverines were to garner a fifth straight national championship, Michigan would have to win the event, while the Buckeyes could do no better than third. Waldemar Tomski swam the first leg for Michigan, gaining a slight lead on his Buckeye opponent. Ed Hutchens' portion left the teams in a dead heat, while Haynie's efforts, though excellent, did little to break the deadlock. For the final four laps, Kirar took the helm. With one length to go, Ohio State's Bill Neunzig had the lead. Splashing furiously, Kirar came in to touch the wall first, and when he looked to other lanes, saw the unbelievable. Charles Hutter, the Harvard entrant, had narrowly beaten out Neunzig. The combination of unlikely events placed the trophy once again in Wolverine hands, by the slimmest of margins, 46-45.

Ed Kirar

America's Time Capsule

December 12, 1937: The Chicago Bears lost the NFL championship game to the Washington Redskins, 28-21.

April 10, 1938: The German army occupied and annexed Austria.

May 2, 1938: Thornton Wilder's "Our Town" won a Pulitzer prize for drama.

June 25, 1938: President Franklin Roosevelt signed the Wage and Hours Act, raising the minimum wage for workers engaged in interstate commerce from 25 cents to 40 cents per hour.

July 1, 1938: Don Budge and Helen Wills Moody captured Wimbledon tennis titles.

UNIVERSITY LORE

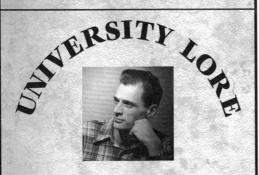

The reasonable tuition and the lure of a Hopwood Award brought a young, working-class Brooklynite to Ann Arbor in 1934. Four years later, Arthur Miller had won two Hopwood's for drama and shared the Theater Guild National Award. Considered by many to be the nation's greatest playwright, Miller's breakthrough came in 1947 with "All My Sons," followed by the Pulitzer Prize winning "Death of a Salesman" in 1949. His own experiences with the McCarthy investigations provided the subtext for "The Crucible."

CHAMPIONSHIP *Moment*

"M" GRAPPLERS STAR IN 1937

Despite finishing second in the 1937 Big Ten Championship and coming into the 1938 postseason with a 7-1 dual meet record, Michigan's wrestling team was not highly touted amongst its Western foes. In the 14th year of the Cliff Keen era, Michigan's mighty had taken a back seat to defending champion Illinois and favorite Indiana, who had scalded the Wolverines in the opening dual meet of the season. In Evanston, Illinois, senior co-captain Johnny Spiecher knocked off two- time defending champion Robert Myers of Indiana in the first round, en route to winning the individual championship at 118 pounds. Junior Harland Danner also collected personal honors, winning at 155 pounds, a feat he would repeat in 1940. Sophomore Don Nichols would work his way up the ladder at 175 pounds, claiming the title with a defeat of Illinois' Chuck Mutter. As a senior, Nichols would once again stand on top of the Big Ten at 175. Along with the titlists, other Wolverines grabbed points here and there that clinched the 28-25 win over second place Indiana. Senior co-captain Earl Thomas made it to the semi-finals at 135 pounds, and Harold Nichols reached the semi-finals in the 145-pound weight class. Nichols would move up to top Conference honors in 1939.

CHAMPION OF THE WEST

JOHN TOWNSEND

Considered by many as the greatest basketball player in Michigan's early years, John Townsend was known as "the Houdini of the Hardwood." Coming to Michigan from Indianapolis' Arsena Technical High School, the 6'4", 200-pound Townsend did not limit his talents to the basketball floor. While earning high marks in the classroom, Townsend was also a shot putter and discus thrower for the 1937 and 1938 Big Ten outdoor track champions. But on the basketball court, Townsend was simply amazing. The leading scorer on the team each of his three years, he was also known for his passing ability to sizeable teammates James Rae (6'5") and John Gee (6'9"). In 1937, he rang up 123 Conference points, placing him second amongst the Big Ten leaders. As a captain his senior year, he averaged 11.3 points per game, accounting for nearly a third of the team's average scoring output. He was named All-Conference all three seasons and an All-American in 1938. Following his graduation in 1938, Townsend returned to Indianapolis and went on to practice law with his brother Earl, who had been a letter winner on the 1936 team. Both Townsends served as Big Ten basketball officials from 1940-47. Inducted into the Michigan Hall of Honor in 1980, Townsend is retired from the practice of law.

Maize & Blue Item

Charles Hoyt's indoor track squad had taken the Big Ten title every year since 1934, and the 1938 meet in Chicago looked to be no different. The Michigan men would earn top honors in just two events, but picked up enough second, third and fourth places to grab the crown for the fifth straight year. Elmer Gedeon's top spot in the 70-yard high hurdles and William Watson's first-place finish in the shot put comprised Michigan's individual champions in the meet.

M List

Michigan Track and Field Champions

Seven Michigan track and field athletes have won two NCAA individual titles.

Name	Year(s)	Events
DeHart Hubbard	1923,25	Long jump, 100-meter dash
Phillip Northrup	1925,26	Javelin throw, pole vault
Ross Hume	1944,45	1,500-meter dash, 800-meter dash
Charles Fonville	1947,48	Shot put
Don McEwen	1950,51	Two-mile run
John Scherer	1988,89	10,000-meter run, 5,000-meter run
Kevin Sullivan	1995	Mile run, 1,500-meter run

1938-39

MICHIGAN MOMENT

CRISLER INTRODUCES "WINGED HELMET"

Michigan took the field in 1938 with a new coach, Herbert "Fritz" Crisler, to improve on 1937's mediocre 4-4 record. Another noticeable change in the Wolverines was a new helmet that the team donned. Instead of the plain black helmet that Michigan players had been wearing, this headgear had a yellow "winged" design on what was otherwise blue. This unique idea belonged to the new coach. The main reason for the change was the simple choice to spruce up what had otherwise been boring. At this time, most college uniforms were dark in color, and when combined with the black helmets that most teams wore, the shadowed figures on the field resembled a funeral procession. The reason that is given much more credit than Crisler meant it to is that the special helmet allowed quarterbacks to distinguish their receivers downfield. Crisler's color choice for the helmet was obvious. Michigan's graduating class of 1867 had voted to make maize and blue the official school colors, representing the colors of corn and sky. The uniforms worn by Crisler's teams were the same as they had been in the past, blue jerseys with gold numerals, which were added in 1915. Michigan had switched to this color scheme early on in the school's football history, after wearing jerseys consisting of white, close- fitting canvas, with blue stockings and a belt for the Wolverines' first game against Racine in 1879. The only change in the typical blue uniforms before 1949 came in 1928. As Michigan planned to play Navy in Baltimore, the Midshipmen refused to wear any other color than their traditional blue. Therefore, Michigan came out in bright yellow jerseys with blue numerals. The team was said to look like canaries, and the uniforms were put away after the 6-6 tie. In 1949, when playing Northwestern, Michigan wore white away jerseys for the first time. Currently, the Michigan home uniforms consist of blue jerseys with yellow lettering and maize pants. On the road, Michigan wears white jerseys with blue lettering and maize pants. From 1959 to 1968, Michigan players had white numbers on the sides of their helmets. Also in 1968, Michigan added a block "M" on the sleeves of its jerseys. This "M" was replaced by numerals on the shirt sleeves for Bo Schembechler's first season in 1969. In 1974-75, the Wolverines tried wearing white pants for road games. The most recent change in the Michigan uniforms occurred in 1980, when the players' names were added to the back of the jerseys.

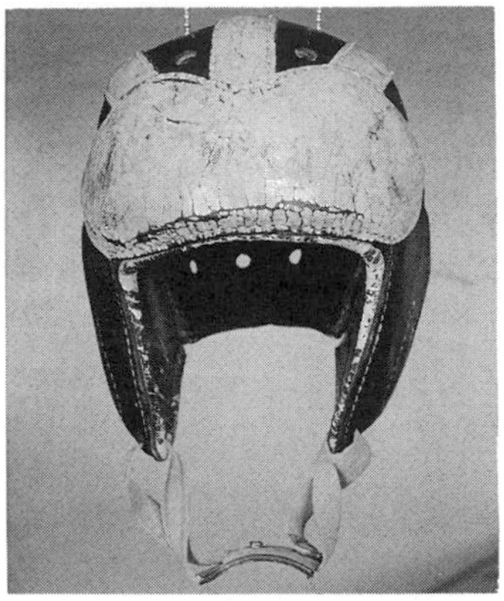

America's Time Capsule

October 9, 1938: The New York Yankees defeated the Chicago Cubs in four straight games for the World Series title.

October 30, 1938: American radio listeners panicked as Orson Welles staged his play "War of the Worlds." They mistook the realistically performed news reports as an actual invasion from Mars.

May 10, 1939: Following 109 years of division, the Methodist Church was reunified.

June 12, 1939: Byron Nelson captured the U.S. Open golf tournament championship.

June 28, 1939: The Pan American Airways airliner "Dixie Clipper" began regular transatlantic passenger service.

UNIVERSITY LORE

The Horace H. Rackham School of Graduate Studies Building was dedicated in June of 1938. Designed by the firm of Smith, Hinchman and Grylls, the building measures 196 by 250 feet with a total floor area of 155,410 square feet, including a 1,200-seat auditorium and 250-seat amphitheater. It is constructed of Indiana limestone on a granite base. The cost of the building, including equipment, was $2.5 million. Funding came from a $10 million bequest to the Graduate School from the Horace H. and Mary A. Rackham Fund.

CHAMPIONSHIP *Moment*

MANN OVERBOARD

In 1937, it had been a blowout, in 1938, a close call. No one was quite sure what to expect at the 1939 NCAA swimming championship in Ann Arbor, but one thing was for certain, Matt Mann's Wolverines and Mike Peppe's Buckeyes would be in quest of the title. The six events held on the first day left a close battle in the race for the crown. Michigan took a 34-30 lead in a day that featured many unexpected occurrences. After Ohio's Curly Stanhope won the 1500-meter race, Michigan's Charley Barker upset teammate Walt Tomski in the 50-yard freestyle. Tomski, the defending NCAA champion, who tied the NCAA mark in this event in the preliminaries, came in second behind the sophomore Barker. Tom Haynie was Michigan's other winner on the opening day, taking top honors in the 220-yard freestyle. Using its prowess in the freestyle, Michigan streaked to its sixth straight national title (third NCAA). Haynie closed out his Michigan career with a victory in the 440-yard freestyle, coming in ahead of teammate James Welsh. Barker tied for the title in the 100-yard freestyle, coming in a 52.9 seconds along with Paul Wolf of USC. The deadlock marked the first ever tie in the history of the NCAA event. Michigan's 400-yard freestyle relay team of Barker, Edward Hutchens, Haynie and Tomski finished the evening by shaving one-tenth of a second off the existing pool record in winning the event. With 47 of its points coming in freestyle events, the Wolverines held off the Buckeyes, 65-58, and continued the annual tradition of giving Matt Mann a post-event toss in the pool.

CHAMPION OF THE WEST

"FRITZ" CRISLER

Young Herbert "Fritz" Crisler's career-long love affair with athletics prospered during his under graduate career at the University of Chicago, where he earned nine letters in basketball, baseball and football, playing the latter sport under the legendary Amos Alonzo Stagg. He also starred in the classroom, receiving the prestigious Big Ten Conference Medal of Honor and graduating with honors in 1922. At that point, Crisler became Stagg's assistant and remained there until 1930. After that, he filled football head coaching duties at Minnesota (10-7-1) and Princeton (35-9-1). The Conference title won by U-M in 1943 was its first in 10 years, and the No. 3 final ranking equalled the school's best ever. Crisler lifted Michigan to the top spot in 1947, as the Wolverines finished a perfect 10-0 and shut out Southern California in the Rose Bowl. Crisler was named Coach of the Year for the '47 season, and U-M was named the best team in the country by The Associated Press. He handed over the head coaching position to his assistant, Bennie Oosterbaan, in 1948, but continued as U-M's Athletic Director, a post he had assumed in 1941 when Yost retired. As A.D., Crisler enlarged Michigan Stadium twice, pushing it over the 100,000 capacity mark, and was responsible for the building of the basketball arena which now bears his name. A College Football Hall of Fame inductee in 1954, Crisler retired in 1968, but remained in Ann Arbor, where he died in 1982.

Maize & Blue Item

Following Franklin Cappon's departure for a football and basketball coaching job at Princeton, the Board in Control of Athletics was forced to look for a new cage coach. They didn't need to look far. Assistant coach and former basketball and football All-American Bennie Oosterbaan was promoted on March 9, 1938. Oosterbaan would compile five winning seasons in eight campaigns at the helm.

M List

NCAA Meets in Ann Arbor

In 1939, Michigan hosted the NCAA swimming championships for the first time. The NCAA would come back to swim in Ann Arbor three more times between 1939-58. A list of NCAA championship events Michigan has hosted:

Sport	Years
Golf	1947
Gymnastics (Men's)	1951, 1971
Swimming (Men's)	1939, 1945, 1948, 1958
Swimming (Women's)	1996
Track (Men's Outdoor)	1954
Wrestling	1934

1939-40

America's Time Capsule

September 3, 1939: The nations of France and Great Britain declared war on Germany, while President Roosevelt said that the United States would remain neutral.

December 10, 1939: The Green Bay Packers defeated the New York Giants, 27-0, to win the NFL championship.

May 3, 1940: "I am an American Day" was proclaimed by an Act of Congress.

May 6, 1940: John Steinbeck won a Pulitzer prize for his book *The Grapes of Wrath*.

May 15, 1940: The first successful helicopter flight in the United States took place.

University Lore

The University of Michigan · Artes · Scientia · Veritas · 1817 ™

The West Quadrangle men's dormitory opened in the Fall of 1939, even though the dining rooms were not completed and some of the furnishings had not arrived. The seven new houses of West Quad, plus the Allen-Rumsey House, completed in 1937, were home to 932 students, mostly freshmen. Total cost of the Quadrangle exceeded $1,836,400, of which $940,000 came from the New Deal's Public Works Administration.

Michigan Moment

WOLVERINE GRIDDERS BLAST CHICAGO

Michigan's football team had started out the 1939 season 2-0, and was looking for its first perfect record after three games since the Big Ten championship season of 1933. The Wolverines would earn that win by handing the University of Chicago the worst defeat in its history, an 85-0 shellacking in Chicago. U-M scored every which way, with Tom Harmon running for two touchdowns, passing for two more, and adding a field goal and three extra points. Before the first quarter ended, Bob Zimmerman, Hercules Renda and Bob Czak all had touchdown runs to raise the score to 21-0. The Wolverines accounted for 34 points in the second quarter, with Harmon opening up the scoring with a 57-yard touchdown run. Harmon passed to quarterback Forest Evashevski for another score, and after Fred Trosko ran the ball in, he threw a scoring pass to Bob Westfall for his second touchdown pass. Dave Strong accounted for the last of Michigan's 55 points in the half with a 57-yard touchdown run, matching Harmon's earlier figure. Chicago's best ball movement of the game occurred in the second quarter when the Maroons managed to reach the visitor's 40-yard line, only to turn the ball over on downs. Using third stringers after the intermission, the Wolverines notched six points in the third quarter. The starters returned in the final period to sew up the rout. Harmon made the score 64-0 when he split the uprights from the 12-yard line, and Westfall soon followed with a 23-yard scoring run. Harmon, who finished with 127 rushing yards on the day, scored his final points on a 41-yard run. Dave Nelson finally closed out the Wolverine scoring with a 55-yard punt return. In scoring the most points in a game by a Wolverine team since 1904, U-M amassed 417 rushing yards to Chicago's 90. Chicago turned the ball over eight times during the game, while Michigan never lost the ball. Chicago would withdraw its football team from the Big Ten following the season and the 85-0 game would be the last played in this once vicious rivalry.

Photo: Michiganensian

Paul Kromer on a touchdown run in the U-M versus Chicago game in 1939.

CHAMPIONSHIP *Moment*

THE HARMON-KINNICK SHOWDOWN

It was a game pitting the best players in the Big Ten and the nation against one another. Halfback Tom Harmon of Michigan and quarterback Nile Kinnick of Iowa looked to be the highlights of what was to be a great football game. Kinnick drew first blood as the senior quarterback connected with Floyd Dean on a 70-yard touchdown pass in the first quarter. Iowa had a 7-0 lead as Kinnick added the extra point. The All-American would never score another point on the Wolverines. After punting on the ensuing possession, Michigan recovered the ball when Kinnick fumbled. Harmon took advantage of the miscue, converting a touchdown five plays later when he burst over the end line from one yard out. Iowa responded with a long drive, but Harmon picked off a Kinnick pass in the end zone to quell the rally. Harmon added a two-yard run for a touchdown and a 13-7 lead in the second quarter, then extended it to 20-7 before the half. Joe Savilla blocked a Kinnick punt and the Wolverines took over on the 37-yard line. Harmon took just two plays to score his third touchdown, going in from the eight-yard line to further the Michigan advantage. Despite scoring all of Michigan's total up to that point, the Gary, Indiana, native was saving the best for last. In the third quarter, Harmon picked off a Kinnick pass at the Michigan five-yard line and dashed down the right sideline for a 95-yard touchdown. He then converted the extra point to make the score Harmon 27, Iowa 7. The junior compiled 146 of Michigan's 170 yards on the day. The game marked Iowa's only loss of the year as the Hawkeyes finished 6-1-1 and ranked eighth in the nation. Kinnick was named the winner of the Heisman Trophy, beating out Harmon, who finished second.

CHAMPION OF THE WEST

DICK WAKEFIELD

Dick Wakefield was born in Chicago in 1921 as the son of former major league player Howard Wakefield. In his first year of eligibility, Wakefield led the Wolverines to their first Big Ten baseball crown since 1936. Known for his power, Wakefield slammed nine home runs and batted .368 during the 1941 season, several of them memorable for the long distances they traveled. After helping Michigan to a 24-8 overall mark in his only season, he signed with the Detroit Tigers for $52,000. Wakefield progressed quickly through the minor leagues, earning Most Valuable Player honors in the Texas League in 1942. Called up to the pros in 1943, Wakefield immediately made an impact, finishing second in the American League batting race with a .316 average. He improved on that the following season, topping the circuit with a .355 mark. After having his career paused by military service, he was traded from the Tigers to the Yankees in 1949. He briefly saw action with the Yankees and New York Giants before retiring in 1952. After his baseball career was over, Wakefield worked in taxes, bankruptcy courts and the steel industry. He died in Michigan in 1985 at the age of 64.

Maize & Blue Item

At the 1940 NCAA Swimming meet in New Haven, Connecticut, sophomore John Gillis swam on the world record-setting 400-yard medley relay team enabling Michigan to capture its fourth straight title. Entering the final event trailing Ohio State, the foursome of Gillis, Edward Hutchens, Charles Barker, and John Sharemet swam the race in 3:31, chopping six-tenths of a second off the existing mark. In November 1940, Gillis announced that he was giving up swimming for his first love— hockey. Gillis, who claimed, "Hockey is a lot more fun," played two seasons for the hockey squad, lettering in both years.

M List: Michigan Men Who Went On to the Broadcast Booth

- Tom Harmon
- Lary Sorenson
- Tim McCormick
- John Wangler
- Jim Brandstatter
- Steve Grote
- Ron Kramer
- Rick Bay
- Don Lund
- Dan Dierdorf
- Bob Ufer
- Dennis Franklin
- Neal Morton

1940-41

America's Time Capsule

September 16, 1940: Congress passed the Selective Service Act, requiring all men between the ages of 20 and 36 to register for the armed services.

November 5, 1940: Franklin Roosevelt defeated Republican Wendell Willkie for a second term as president.

December 8, 1940: The Chicago Bears beat the Washington Redskins, 73-0, in the NFL championship game.

June 22, 1941: Germany invaded the U.S.S.R.

July 17, 1941: Joe DiMaggio's incredible baseball hitting streak of 56 consecutive games was ended by the Cleveland Indians.

University Lore

As the war in Europe expanded, the students and faculty debated the merits of pacifism, neutrality and intervention. The Michigan Anti-War Committee brought Montana Senator Burton K. Wheeler and socialist Norman Thomas to campus for peace rallies while the American Student Defense League collected 1,000 signatures in support of the lend-lease program. In the fall of 1940 President Ruthven appointed a committee on National Defense. A year later it was replaced by the University War Board.

Michigan Moment

MICHIGAN FOOTBALL TEAM FLIES OVER CAL

To open the 1940 football season, the Michigan Wolverines planned an unheard of venture. The California Golden Bears were the first scheduled opponent, and by playing their first game at Berkeley, Michigan would use the newest mode of travel, the airplane. As the Wolverines prepared to become the first college team to fly cross-country to a game, all athletes under 21 were required to get their parents' permission. When it came time to board the plane, no one was left behind, and the team boarded United Airlines DC-3's to San Francisco, with stops in Des Moines, Denver and Salt Lake City. The final stop on the two-day trip, Salt Lake City, was provided to allow the Wolverines a day of practice in between. A crowd of 35,401 turned out to see the September 28, 1940 battle between the 1938 Pac-Ten Champion Golden Bears and the Wolverines. Michigan back Tom Harmon celebrated his 21st birthday by running roughshod over Cal. In fact, the closest the Bears got to the Michigan end zone was midfield. Harmon took the opening kickoff at his own 6-yard line and weaved his way down the field on a 94-yard return to give Michigan a 7-0 lead. The second quarter featured Harmon's second return for a touchdown, a punt which he took on his own 28-yard line and ran back all the way. He continued his unbelievable performance before on the next drive. Following a California punt which put the ball inside U-M's 20-yard line, Michigan prepared to start its next drive from the 14. Quarterback Forest Evashevski handed the ball to Harmon, who took it and 12 men (see item) to make the score 21-0 with an 86-yard run. Michigan refused to let up in the second half. Cliff Wise ended a 52-yard drive with a touchdown run in the third quarter, and Harmon opened up the scoring in the final period with an eight yard touchdown run. Michigan's final points came from the hands of Harmon, who tossed the ball five yards to David Nelson for the last score of the 41-0 win. In Michigan's first game against a West Coast opponent since the Rose Bowl win of 1902, Michigan outgained California 351-32 on the ground and 407-56 overall. California managed just three first downs, while Michigan made 23. With his eye-catching performance, Harmon began his campaign for the Heisman Trophy.

Members of U-M's football team prepare for their first flight.

CHAMPIONSHIP *Moment*

MICHIGAN TENNIS TEAM CAPTURES BIG TEN CROWN

Since 1934, when a point system was instituted to determine the Big Ten tennis champion, Northwestern and Chicago had taken the crown each season. Since 1936, the two teams had finished 1-2 each year. Nothing different was expected in 1941 outside of the possibility of adding Michigan to the mix. The Wolverines had posted a 17-3 record during the season and led by coach LeRoy Weir, looked to make some noise in Chicago. In a first day of competition full of upsets, Michigan pulled off the most noteworthy headline. The duo of Gerry Schaflander and Tom Gamon knocked off the undefeated Minnesota tandem of Mike Lieberman and Ken Silgen to highlight a first day of competition where Michigan advanced three singles and two doubles netters. Michigan was not as lucky the second day, seeing the elimination of Captain Jim Tobin in singles and the combinations of Tobin and Alfred Hammett and Schaflander and Gamon. However, Gamon and Alden Johnson stayed alive in the singles bracket. Gamon's victory over Chicago's Ralph Johansen and Johnson's 6-0, 6-0 shutout of Minnesota's Ken Silgen gave the Wolverines 16 points for the meet. With Northwestern and Chicago topping out at 12 points apiece, the Wolverines were awarded their first conference tennis crown since 1923.

CHAMPION OF THE WEST

TOM HARMON

Tom Harmon arrived in Ann Arbor in 1938, the same time as Fritz Crisler. Though both would become synonymous with Michigan football history, Crisler was the man on the sidelines. Once the game began, Harmon, a Gary, Indiana native, was the man who grabbed all the attention. In just three years, Harmon rewrote the record books at Michigan, the Big Ten, and the NCAA and forced people to forget about the lean Wolverine seasons of the mid-1930s. Harmon was a workhorse, playing all 60 minutes of the game eight times in his career. Though he carried the ball only 77 times his sophomore season, he gained nearly 400 yards, and threw for another 310 as a quarterback. Great things were expected out of the young man in 1939, and Tom would not disappoint. Though Harmon's statistics (884 yards rushing, 488 yards passing, 102 points) enabled him to lead the Big Ten in both total offense and scoring, his 1939 season may best be remembered by two games. His besting of Nile Kinnick of Iowa and Frank Reagan of Pennsylvania are forever marked as two of the best individual battles in college football. Harmon was named Michigan's MVP and an All-American, but when the 1939 Heisman Trophy balloting was tallied, Harmon finished second to Kinnick. However, when the following season came to a close, there would be no doubt. Harmon simply blew away the competition in 1940, finishing as the Big Ten leader in total offense and scoring for the second straight season. The 1940 season also marked the second season in a row where Tom lead the nation in all-purpose yards and points per game. Harmon ran for 852 yards in 1940, an amount that would bring his career total to 2,134, and a figure that would not be topped until 1942. He scored 16 touchdowns and 117 points in his senior season, and finished his career as the NCAA leader in points per game. As a passer, he established career highs in completions, yards and touchdowns. As he left the field at his final game, the crowd gave him a standing ovation. Ironically, this game was not in Ann Arbor, but in Columbus, Ohio, where the Wolverines had just handed the Buckeyes their worst loss in 35 years, 40-0. Harmon was simply unstoppable in the game, rushing for 149 and passing for 148 more. The senior also did all of Michigan's punting in the game, averaging 50 yards. When the postseason honors were announced, Harmon was an All-American, the Chicago Tribune Big Ten MVP, the winner of the Maxwell Award, the AP Male Athlete of the Year, and capped it all off by winning the Heisman Trophy with the most votes of any recipient until 1951. The Chicago Bears selected Harmon as the number one pick in the 1941 NFL draft, but World War II broke out and Tom entered the Air Force. In rising to the post of captain, Harmon was shot down twice and presumed dead, only to walk back to safety. Awarded the Purple Heart and Silver Star, Harmon returned to the states to play two years with the Los Angeles Rams. After his playing days were over, Harmon pioneered a path for future athletes by switching to the broadcast booth. Harmon died in 1990.

Tom Harmon: An Original Superstar

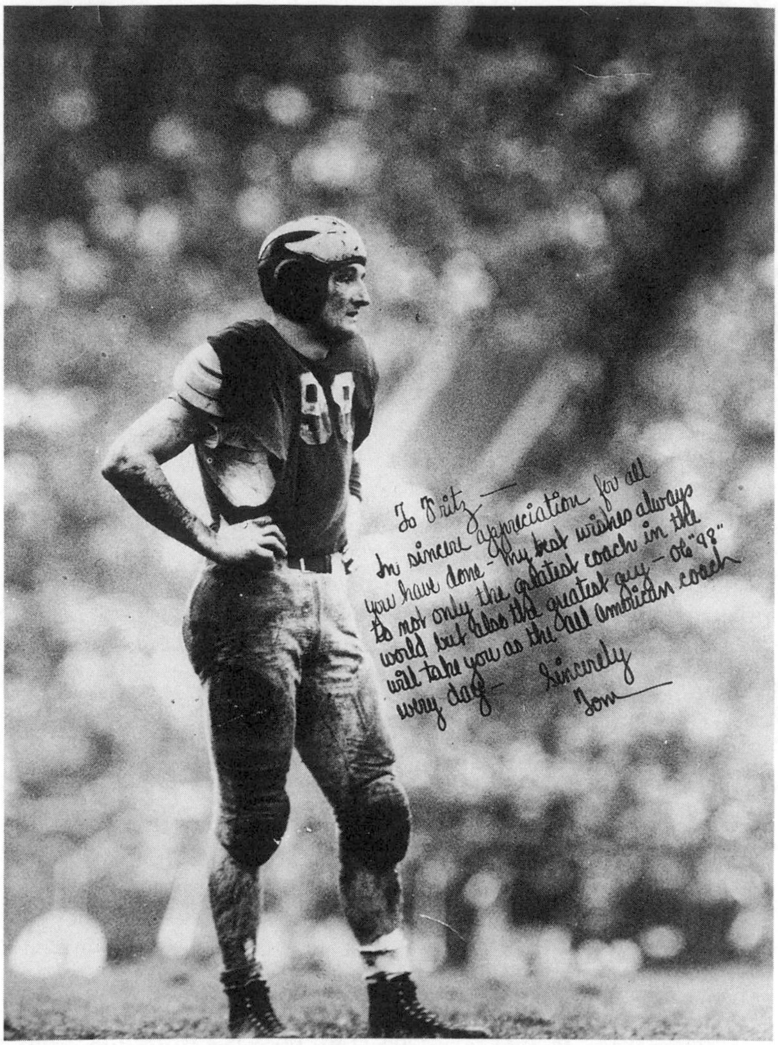

By his inscription on this photo, it's obvious that Tom Harmon admired Fritz Crisler, his coach at the University of Michigan.

Maize Blue Item

In Berkeley, California, the sight of Tom Harmon streaking down the sideline was nothing unusual. After all, the senior halfback had already beaten the Golden Bears for a 95-yard touchdown run and 70-yard punt return. But as Harmon broke into the clear on a run which began on the Michigan 14-yard line, an unusual occurrence began to unfold. Out of the stands jumped a crazed Cal fan, who began to run Harmon down. At the two-yard line, Harmon caused the would-be tackler to miss as the standout scored his fourth touchdown of the day.

Tom Harmon's elusive running style helped him win the 1940 Heisman Trophy.

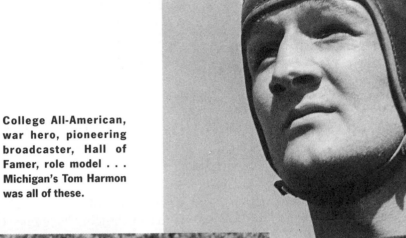

College All-American, war hero, pioneering broadcaster, Hall of Famer, role model . . . Michigan's Tom Harmon was all of these.

Harmon heads for the end zone after picking off a pass from Iowa's legendary Nile Kinnick.

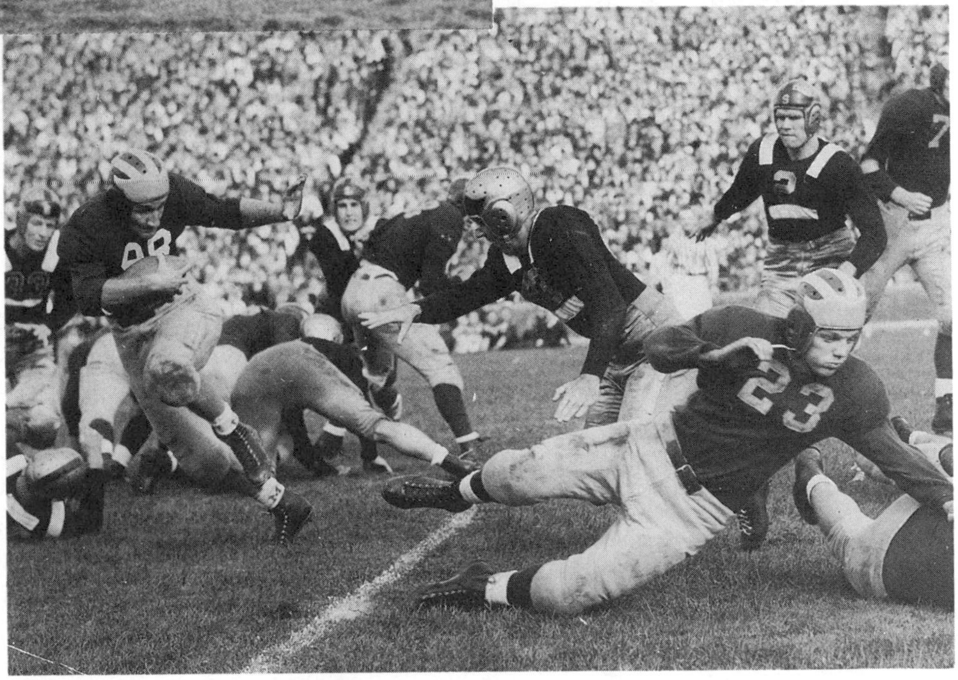

Fellow running back Dave Nelson (23) throws a block to help spring Harmon for a long gainer.

1941-42

America's Time Capsule

December 7, 1941: About 3,000 Americans lost their lives when the Japanese attacked Pearl Harbor, Hawaii.

December 11, 1941: Germany and Italy declared war against the United States.

December 21, 1941: The Chicago Bears won the NFL championship, defeating the New York Giants, 37-9.

January 9, 1942: Joe Louis successfully defended his world heavyweight boxing title for the 20th time, knocking out Max Baer in the first round.

April 18, 1942: American bombers, under the command of Maj. Gen. James Doolittle, conducted a successful air raid on Tokyo.

University Lore

The School of Public Health was established in 1941 with Dr. Henry Vaughan as dean. The Rockefeller and Kellogg Foundations provided funds for a building and equipment. Initially the school had three departments: Public Health Practice, Epidemiology and Environmental Health. Departments of Tropical Diseases and Public Health Statistics were soon added. The School's mission was both to train students for public health careers and conduct advanced research. The School immediately contributed to the war effort by developing an influenza vaccine and conducting research on a quinine substitute.

Michigan Moment

MICHIGAN SWIMS TO FOURTH STRAIGHT TITLE

It was assumed that Michigan would have little trouble swimming to its fourth straight Conference crown at the 1942 Big Ten Championship at the Intramural Building Pool. The closest competition for Michigan was expected to be Ohio State, whom the Wolverines had already beaten twice. Surprise was the word of day one, however, as OSU posed a significant threat with 13 men placed in the finals, slightly ahead of Michigan's 12.

Jim Skinner

Michigan's 300-yard medley relay team began the meet with a first-place finish, followed by Jack Patten's victory in the 220-yard freestyle. However, the Buckeyes kept pace, winning the low-board diving and 150-yard backstroke. The Wolverines were paced by second-place finishes by William Burton (50-yard and 100-yard freestyle), and Dick Riedl (150-yard backstroke). Jim Skinner earned the top spot in the 200-yard breaststroke, but the Buckeyes' Jack Ryan won the 440-yard freestyle to tie the score at 44-44. One event remained, pitting the 400-yard freestyle relay teams of Ohio State and Michigan against one another for the Conference crown. U-M's quartet of Burton, Bob West, Lou Kivi, and Gus Sharemet had recorded a mark three seconds below the Conference standard earlier in the season. In front of the home crowd, Burton got off to a lead in his leg as the Buckeyes languished in third place. West and Kivi kept the Wolverines in a close race as Ohio State began its fight to the finish. In the final 100 yards, Sharemet held off both Iowa and Ohio State to take the event and the meet by a final margin of 54-50.

CHAMPIONSHIP *Moment*

WOLVERINE "9" WINS AGAIN

As the war raged in Europe in 1942, opposing teams of the Michigan baseball squad had little peace either. The 1941 Wolverines had earned the Big Ten title and were favored to do so again this season. After returning from a brief southern trip, U-M beat Western Michigan, 5-3, thanks to an eighth-inning grand slam off the bat of Bud Chamberlain. The Wolverines began whipping teams, scoring double figures in three of their next four games. This included a 13-1 pounding of Purdue where Chamberlain hit another grand slam, highlighting an 11-run first inning. The Wolverines closed out a seven-game winning streak with a 3-2 win over Notre Dame. Though U-M got just two hits, the Wolverines took advantage of the strong pitching of Mickey Fishman and 11 walks courtesy of the Irish. After dropping three of its next four contests, the Michigan team returned to glory as Fishman shut down Northwestern, 9-0. The junior spun a one hitter, allowing only a single with two outs in the ninth inning. Seven errors doomed the team in a 5-1 loss to Eastern Michigan, but the Wolverines rebounded to win four straight Conference contests including a 16-1 scalding of Chicago. A sweep of the Maroons left Michigan in need of just one more Conference win to deliver a second straight title. Delayed by an 11-inning, 3-2 loss to Ohio State on May 29, Michigan repelled the Buckeyes the following afternoon as Bill Cartmill and Chamberlain went a combined 7-for-8. The 7-1 victory allowed U-M to bring its 14th Big Ten baseball title back to Ann Arbor.

CHAMPION OF THE WEST

BOB WESTFALL

After graduating from Ann Arbor High School in 1938, Robert Westfall did not travel far to continue his education. At the University of Michigan, Westfall immediately established himself as another of Michigan's great backs. Despite being overshadowed by Tom Harmon and Forest Evashevski in his three-year career, Westfall carved out a career unparalleled by few others in Michigan history. Standing at just five feet, seven inches, Westfall's stature might have been deceiving, but his speed surely was not. As a member of the Harmon-laden backfield in 1939, Bob finished second on the team in rushing with 368 yards. During Harmon's Heisman campaign of 1940, Westfall gained 808 yards on the ground, just short of Harmon's 852. It was Westfall, not Harmon, who led the Big Ten in Conference rushing yards that season. Westfall closed out his career in 1941 by rushing for a team-high 688 yards and earning both All-Big Ten and All-American honors. After placing eighth in the Heisman Trophy voting, he played in three collegiate All-Star games in 1942. After a short stint of military service, Westfall played professionally with the Detroit Lions from 1944-47, and finished his degree in June 1945. He served as secretary-treasurer of the Adrian Salvage Company from 1948 to 1953 before becoming president of the Adrian Steel Company, a position he held for more than 15 years.

Maize & Blue Item

When Big Ten powers Illinois and Northwestern shot themselves out of the Big Ten Golf tournament in 1942, the field was wide open for the taking. Thus, Michigan seized control of the opportunity and won its first championship since 1936 by a margin of three strokes over second-place Ohio State. The Wolverines were led by Ben Smith, who finished second overall by carding a 303. Captain John Leidy came in fifth with a 307 as Michigan began a string of three consecutive Conference golf crowns.

M List

Michigan's 30 National Championships

Sport	Titles	Years
Baseball	2	1953, 62
Men's Basketball	1	1989
Men's Golf	2	1934, 35
Men's Gymnastics	2	1963, 70
Ice Hockey	8	1948, 51, 52, 53, 55, 56, 64, 96
Men's Swimming and Diving	11	1937, 38, 39, 40, 41, 48, 57, 58, 59, 61, 95
Men's Tennis	1	1957
Men's Track	1	1923
Men's Trampoline	2	1969, 70

Note: Michigan won unofficial swimming and diving championships in 1927, 28, 31, 32, 34, 35, 36. Football national championship seasons (not recognized by NCAA) are: 1901, 02, 03, 04, 18, 23, 32, 33, 47, 48.

1942-43

America's Time Capsule

December 1, 1942: Nationwide gasoline rationing went into effect.

December 13, 1942: The Chicago Bears were defeated in the NFL championship game by the Washington Redskins, 14-6.

May 1, 1943: Count Fleet, with jockey Johnny Longden, won the 69th annual Kentucky Derby.

May 5, 1943: Postmaster Frank Walker inaugurated a postal-zone numbering system to speed up mail delivery.

July 19, 1943: More than 500 Allied planes bombed Rome.

University Lore

The campus changed dramatically as the university joined the war effort. The Army's Judge Advocate General School took over the Law Quad. The Japanese Language School opened in January. The Engineering College provided advanced instruction to the Army. The Navy's Post-Graduate Naval Architecture Group moved to campus and the first installment of Navy V-12 seamen turned West Quad into "The Ship." Over 12,000 military personnel received training on campus between 1942 and 1945.

Michigan Moment

WOLVERINES AND FIGHTING IRISH FACE OFF

Michigan had taught Notre Dame how to play American football during a series of three games in 1887 and 1888. After the two teams went their separate ways for a decade, they would meet back on the gridiron six times in 12 years beginning in 1898. Notre Dame had managed to break the Michigan winning streak with an 11-3 victory in 1909, and the two teams looked forward to playing again in the 1910 season. However, in the week prior to that 1910 contest, the two teams could not iron out their differences over the eligibility of some of Michigan's players. Consequently, the game was canceled, and future matchups were avoided. It was not until 1942 that Notre Dame and Michigan played again. It was to be a battle between the third and fifth best teams in the nation from 1941. The Fighting Irish would score first, taking a 7-0 lead on a seven-yard pass from future Heisman Trophy winner Angelo Bertelli. Michigan would tie the score on George Ceithaml's 1-yard touchdown run, and then take the lead when Don Robinson scored on a fake field goal. Notre Dame blocked Jim Brieske's attempted extra point, and the Wolverine edge was 13-7. Notre Dame got the score back when it capitalized on a fumbled punt and took the ball on a 12-yard drive to take a 14-13 edge into halftime. The Wolverines would put the game away with a third-quarter lesson in scoring touchdowns. Paul White ended a 58-yard, second-half opening drive with a two-yard plunge that put Michigan up, 20-14. Bob Kolesar recovered the ball when Notre Dame fumbled on the ensuing kickoff. Seven plays later, Tom Kuzma was standing in the end zone following a three-yard run, and it was 26-14. Later in the third quarter, White picked off a pass deep in Irish territory and Michigan needed to go only 24 yards for its fifth touchdown of the day, this one coming on a 1-yard run by Kuzma. A fourth-quarter touchdown by Notre Dame would round out the scoring and leave the final margin at 32-20.

Photo: U-M Athletic Dept.

Creighton Miller scores for Notre Dame in the U-M battle.

CHAMPIONSHIP *Moment*

MICHIGAN WAR HEROES

Dozens of Michigan football players went off to serve in World War II, but it was those who made the loudest noise on the field who also made headlines during the war. On April 15, 1943, the war department reported that Tom Harmon was shot down over Latin America and had not been heard from since April 8. Given up by many as lost to the sea, wild animals or starvation, Harmon was reported alive and well on April 17. With no water, little food and only a small jungle kit to survive in the swampy area, Harmon managed to survive seven days by drinking from swamps and eating chocolate. After a week of walking, an action helped by his years of football, Harmon came upon a hut in the small town of Parimaribo, Dutch Guiana. There, the natives listened to his plight and took him to the local Air Force Base and back to safety. Harmon immediately rejoined the service, and was again listed as missing in action on November 4, 1943 when his plane disappeared over China during a dive-bombing attack. On November 30, 1943, cheers once again replaced tears as he was reported safe after being rescued by Chinese Allies. On February 13, 1945, a plane carrying Sergeant Bob Chappuis was shot down in Northern Italy, but the Michigan athlete parachuted to safety. He and his mate made it to a local cabin, and from there were transferred from village to village as the war dragged on. Chappuis and his partner made it to the town of Asola, where they stayed for the remainder of the war.

CHAMPION OF THE WEST

BOB UFER

Though Bob Ufer began his Michigan athletic career as a freshman football player in 1939, he soon turned to the track for his athletic exploits. Four years later, Pennsylvania native had set eight U-M records and the world mark in the 440-yard dash before his graduation in 1943. Ufer then traded in his spikes for a place where tenure never runs out, the broadcast booth. From 1945 when he first entered the WPAG broadcast booth to the 1981 Iowa contest when he retired, Ufer described 362 consecutive games in memorable fashion. His passion and enthusiasm for the game, combined with legendary sayings made him the "Voice of Michigan Football." Famous for his colorful descriptions entitled "Uferisms", Ufer had the ability to inflict life into the simple games and make the unbelievable seem ever more so. Ufer sucumbed to prostate cancer on October 26, 1981, but not before touching the hearts of nearly every Michigan football fan with a rousing display of spirit at halftime of the 1981 Iowa game. A bronze plaque has been placed just outside the entrance of the Michigan press box to enshrine the man who will forever be part of "Meechigan" history.

Maize & Blue Item

Julius Franks joined the Michigan football team in 1941, earning high marks at the guard position. In 1942, there were few in the game who played harder than the Hamtramck All-American. Soon after playing in the college all-star game in 1942, Franks became ill with tuberculosis and was soon involved in the battle for his life. After months in the hospital, Franks emerged a champion yet again, and completed his degree in dentistry in 1947.

M List: Michigan-Notre Dame Thrillers

Michigan and Notre Dame are notorious for coming down to the final minutes to decide their football contests. Here is a list of Michigan-Notre Dame games that have been decided in the final stanza:

Year	Winner, score	Time Remaining When Go-ahead Score Made
1994	Michigan, 26-24	0:02
1980	Notre Dame, 29-27	0:04
1988	Notre Dame, 19-17	1:13
1990	Notre Dame, 28-24	1:40
1992	Tie, 17-17	5:28
1978	Michigan, 28-14	14:55

1943-44

America's Time Capsule

December 24, 1943: General Dwight D. Eisenhower was appointed Supreme Commander of Allied forces for the Europeon invasion.

December 26, 1943: Coach George Halas' Chicago Bears won the NFL title by defeating the Washington Redskins, 41-21.

March 6, 1944: U.S. pilots dropped 2,000 tons of bombs on Berlin.

June 6, 1944: More than 4,000 ships, 3,000 planes and 4,000,000 Allied troops began the Normandy invasion.

August 25, 1944: Paris was liberated as the Germans surrendered to the French.

University Lore

Thomas E. Dewey, (BA '23) won the Republican nomination for President, the first U-M grad to head a major party ticket. A stalwart of the Varsity Glee Club and Michigan Union Operas, Dewey considered a career in music, but opted for law school at Columbia. He gained fame as special prosecutor in organized crime cases in the 1930s and was twice elected governor of New York. Dewey lost the 1944 election to Franklin Roosevelt, but was nominated again in 1948. Declared a certain winner by the pollsters, he lost again as Harry Truman staged a dramatic comeback.

Michigan Moment

WORLD WAR II AND MICHIGAN ATHLETICS

With the onset of World War II, the rosters of college teams were pulled apart by the call for young men to serve. The Big Ten had already relaxed some Conference rules, allowing some Service teams to schedule games with Conference teams and raising the limit on games from nine to ten. However, as U.S. involvement increased, the Conference was forced to remove restrictions on freshmen in 1943, then waived all eligibility rules for students in the Armed Forces who were receiving instruction at member schools. As it became apparent that the more liberal rules would still not provide enough athletes for competition, the Big Ten waived all the eligibility rules, except that the student had to be regularly enrolled and could not receive compensation for his athletic participation.

Elroy Hirsch

Despite the most valiant of attempts, the war had an effect throughout the Big Ten. No Conference gymnastics meet was held between 1943-46, and the Conference golf championships were shortened to 36 holes in 1944 and 1945. The war wreaked havoc with Michigan's football roster. Though Michigan lost eventual All-Americans Bob Chappuis and Elmer Madar for the 1943-45 seasons and would not see Bump Elliott until 1946, the Wolverines did gain some players from other schools. Bill Daley, a Golden Gopher from 1940-42, played for Michigan while a Marine Corps Trainee in 1943. Daley finished the year with 817 yards rushing, the fourth-best total in the nation and deserving of the All-American honors he received. Elroy Hirsch came over from Wisconsin to play four sports at Michigan and lead the Wolverine football team in touchdowns scored, yards passing and punt returns. Though the musical roster may have been tough on fans, it did not hinder the Wolverines' success, as Michigan went 23-6 between 1942-44.

CHAMPION OF THE WEST

ROSS AND BOB HUME

Twins Ross (left) and Bob Hume hailed from Canonburg, Pennsylvania, and they were inseparable in every way, including the finish line. After spending the 1940-41 academic year at a Pittsburgh prep school, the brothers arrived in Ann Arbor in the fall of 1941. Immediately part of the freshman track team, they easily made the varsity as soon as they became eligible in 1942. At first the two ran separate events, but by the 1944 season, the two were running together...all the way. It soon became practice for the brothers to come across the finish line holding hands so as to create a tie. At the 1944 outdoor championship in Champaign, they did so in the mile race, while Ross also won the two-mile and Bob finished second at 880 yards and third in the two mile. The pair repeated their feat at the 1944 NCAA championship, coming across together in the one mile race in 4:16.6. They finished ahead of their closest competition by more than 100 yards. In total, the twins would tie for the top spot 11 times in their careers, including the 1945 Big Ten indoor and outdoor mile races. They would separately collect the title at the 1945 NCAA meet that year, Ross in the 800-meter race and Bob in the 1500-meter race. In the six Big Ten track championships the brothers participated in, Michigan won five of them. Both graduated from the U-M in 1945 and attended Medical School at Michigan. Bob became a doctor in 1948, eventually settling in Kalamazoo and practicing there, while Ross also joined the medical profession.

another CHAMPION OF THE WEST

ELROY HIRSCH

Born in Wausau, Wisconsin in 1923, Elroy Hirsch became an outstanding athlete in high school. Attending the University of Wisconsin in 1941, he earned All-America accolades at halfback for the Badgers. His efforts led UW to an 8-1 record and a number three national ranking. However, in 1942, Hirsch's V-12 Marine Corps training unit was assigned to the University of Michigan, and it was then that "Crazylegs" became a part of U-M history. While the program stuffed three semesters of work into one academic year, Hirsch found enough time to play four sports, becoming the only athlete in modern Michigan history to do so. In 1943, the transfer led the Wolverine football team in passing, punt returns and scoring, while placing fourth in rushing. Hirsch also did some punting for U-M, booting a 76-yard kick against Northwestern. Michigan compiled a record of 8-1 in Hirsch's only season, while Wisconsin slumped to 1-9. Hirsch decided to take a shot at making the basketball team, if only for the fact that he wanted to go on the team trip to Madison to visit his future wife. As a center, he soon acquired the starting job, posting a 7.3 scoring average for the season. While he was playing basketball, Hirsch also kept in shape by running with the indoor track team, picking up his third varsity letter and finishing third in the long jump at the 1944 indoor championship. When he took the mound for the baseball squad, Hirsch posted a sparkling 6-0 record, which included a one-hitter over Ohio State. With his help, the Wolverines earned Conference crowns in football, baseball and track. Following service in the Marine Corps, Hirsch returned to Wisconsin. He went on to play nine years in the NFL, setting a reception record in 1951. In nine years as a pro, Hirsch caught 343 balls for 6,299 yards and 54 touchdowns. He became general manager of the Rams in 1960, until serving as Wisconsin's athletic director from 1969-87.

Maize & Blue Item

Though it would go nearly unnoticed with war raging in Europe, Michigan destroyed the rest of the Big Nine during the 1943-44 school year. Of the 10 championships competed by the Conference, the Wolverines won eight: golf, indoor track, outdoor track, baseball, swimming, wrestling, football and tennis. As U-M did not have a cross country team, the eight titles in nine sports remains a Big Ten record never to be matched.

M List

The eight titles Michigan won in 1943-44 is the most ever captured by the school during a single season. Here are the University's best seasons:

Most Men's Big Ten Championships in One Season

Year	Titles	Men's Sports
1943-44	8	Football, Baseball, Track (In+Out), Tennis, Swimming, Wrestling, Golf
1922-23	6	FB, Baseball, Track (In+Out), Cross Country, Tennis
1960-61	6	Baseball, Gymnastics, Track (In+Out), Tennis, Hockey

Most Women's Big Ten Championships in One Season

Year	Titles	Women's Sports
1992-93	5	Cross Country, Gymnastics, Out. Track, Softball, Swimming
1993-94	5	Cross Country, Gymnastics, Track (In+Out), Swimming
1994-95	4	Cross Country, Gymnastics, Softball, Swimming
1991-92	3	Gymnastics, Softball, Swimming

1944-45

MICHIGAN MOMENT

America's Time Capsule

October 9, 1944: The St. Louis Cardinals beat the St. Louis Browns, four games to two, in the 41st World Series.

November 7, 1944: Franklin Roosevelt was reelected president of the United States for a record fourth term. He died five months later—April 12, 1945—at the age of 63, and was succeeded by Harry Truman.

December 16, 1944: The last major German offensive of World War II—the Battle of the Bulge—began.

May 8, 1945: The Germans unconditionally surrendered, ending the European phase of World War II.

August 6, 1945: The city of Hiroshima, Japan was destroyed by the first atomic bomb to be used in war. Nine days later, the Japanese surrendered to the Allies.

University Lore

Ruth Buchanan, an employee of the Museum, was one of many staff members who responded to the flood of V-mail from U-M alumni in the military. Buchanan sent over 17,000 letters and 57,000 copies of the *Michigan Daily* to servicemen and women around the world. For her morale boosting work she was awarded the nations's Emblem of Honor Pin. More than 32,000 alumni served in the military during the war and at least 500 University men and women died serving their country.

WOLVERINES NIP ILLINI FOR TRACK TITLE

The dynasty seemed to be at its end. Michigan had taken two straight Big Ten indoor track titles and seven of the last nine, but the Wolverines could be looked at as no better than co-favorites in Chicago in 1945. Illinois packed a powerful team, a group that handed the Wolverines a 58-46 defeat in dual meet action at Champaign just a week earlier. Michigan still had the best long distance runners, and it proved so by delivering the first five men to cross the finish line in the mile run. Brothers Ross and Bob Hume crossed the line in a tie for first as Michigan took the top five spots for the first and only time in any event in the history of the conference. In the two mile run, Michigan swept the top three spots, led by Ross Hume. A top-four sweep was made impossible when Bob Hume had to quit due to cramping. Though a Michigan athlete did not take first place in the half mile, Wolverines filled spots 2-5, including fifth place Archie Parsons, who finished just inches ahead of an Illinois runner. Having won two events, Michigan would not win another in the entire championship. Illinois, on the other hand, would take home seven individual titles. But while the Wolverines were not on top, they were consistently in the top five, as 18 men scored points for the maize and blue. This list included Julian Witherspoon, who came in second in the 60-yard dash, and Dick Forrestel, who was runner-up in the 440-yard dash. When the final totals were calculated, Illinois finished with 54-1/10 points, exactly one point behind U-M's 55-1/10 point tally.

U-M's 1944-45 track team.

CHAMPIONSHIP *Moment*

WEIR PACES "M" TENNIS SQUAD TO BIG TEN CROWN

After collecting the Big Ten title in 1944, Michigan's men's tennis team rolled through the 1945 campaign without a hitch. As the team went through the slate undefeated at 9-0, U-M lost only nine individual matches all year, while winning 70. There was still some unfinished business to be taken care of in Evanston. Though Michigan would rack up just three individual titles at the Conference Championship, it was enough to hold off Ohio State and the remainder of the field. Alden Johnson and Dave Post won Michigan's only tandem title, coming through in the third division of doubles. Johnson was also victorious in the singles competition, as was Jack Hersh. Despite being put in early trouble when Wolverine ace Roger Lewis was eliminated in the first round, Michigan finished with 18 points to Ohio State's 12-1/2. The Conference title was the third in five years for Coach LeRoy Weir, who had compiled a 47-10 record over that span. Weir would retire after the 1946 season with a career mark of 102-36.

CHAMPION OF THE WEST

DON LUND

Only nine men in history have earned nine or more athletic letters at the University of Michigan, and only one of them also played professional baseball and later coached U-M to a national championship. Detroit native Don Lund is that one unique individual, and from 1942-45, he displayed his athletic abilities on U-M's football, basketball and baseball teams. As a fullback and punter on the football team, Lund helped lead the Wolverines to the 1943 Big Ten championship. He was a two-year starter at guard for Michigan's cagers before serving as centerfielder for the baseball outfit in the spring. It was on the diamond where Lund would make his major league mark, playing seven years with the Detroit Tigers, St. Louis Browns and Brooklyn Dodgers. After his career ended in 1954, he served as a scout and a coach for the Tigers. Lund was the choice to replace Ray Fisher when the legend retired as Michigan baseball coach in 1959, leading the Wolverines to the Big Ten title in 1961 and to the College World Series crown in 1962. Lund later served his alma mater as an athletic administrator.

Maize & Blue Item

The Michigan football team played its first game under the lights on September 23, 1944. Playing at Marquette, Michigan was held scoreless in the first half for the first time since 1942, but used two second-half scores to win as the defense pitched a shutout. Wolverine back Bob Nussbaumer ran for 117 yards in the 14-0 victory.

M List

U-M Night Football

The Michigan football team has played 19 night games since playing its first in the 1944 season. Michigan night games, by site:

Site, City	(Opponent)	# of times
Metrodome, Minneapolis, MN	(Minnesota)	5
Notre Dame Stadium, South Bend, IN	(Notre Dame)	3
Jack Murphy Stadium, San Diego, CA	(Colorado State+BYU)	2
Alumni Stadium, Chesnut Hill, MA	(Boston Coll.)	1
Camp Randall Stadium, Madison, WI	(Wisconsin)	1
Rose Bowl, Pasadena, CA	(UCLA)	1
Gator Bowl, Jacksonville, FL	(North Carolina)	1
Astrodome, Houston, TX	(UCLA)	1
Orange Bowl, Miami, FL	(Oklahoma)	1
Superdome, New Orleans, LA	(Auburn)	1
Alamodome, San Antonio, TX	(Texas A&M)	1
Marquette Stadium, Milwaukee, WI	(Marquette)	1

America's Time Capsule

September 2, 1945: Japan signed the formal document of surrender aboard the U.S.S. Missouri in Tokyo Bay.

October 10, 1945: The Chicago Cubs lost the World Series to the Detroit Tigers, four games to three.

February 15, 1946: Scientists developed the world's first electronic digital computer in Philadelphia.

July 4, 1946: Pres. Harry Truman proclaimed Philippine independence.

August 25, 1946: Ben Hogan won the PGA golf tournament.

University Lore

Fall enrollment reached 12,000 and jumped another 2,500 in winter term as a rush of returning veterans boosted enrollment to an all-time high and changed the student population dramatically. Not only were the 6,500 veterans older than the rest of the student body, one-third were married. The University built temporary housing on campus and leased the Willow Run apartments Henry Ford had built for bomber plant workers. Enrollment peaked at 20,000 students in 1948, 11,000 of whom were veterans.

Michigan Moment

MICHIGAN BATTLES ARMY JUGGERNAUT

The end of World War II saw an army squad conquering on both sides of the Atlantic. The version on U.S. soil was proving their might on the football field. Led by All-Americans Glenn Davis and Doc Blanchard, the Cadets had won 11 straight games and captured the 1944 national championship. On a cloudy afternoon in Yankee Stadium, 62,878 came out to see Army take on Michigan. After a scoreless first period, Michigan made it to the Army 10-yard line before being set back with a holding penalty. Michigan surrendered the ball on the Cadet 33, and Army marched 67 yards to take a 7-0 lead. Less than two minutes later, Blanchard showed his power, breaking a 68-yard run for a touchdown and a 14-0 lead.

Despite the two touchdown disadvantage, Michigan did not give up. The Wolverines took the second-half kickoff and went 75 yards in 10 plays to score on a 33-yard pass from Walt Teninga to Art Renner. The close score and the seemingly endless determination of the Michigan players put fear into the throngs of Army supporters. Michigan kept up the pressure when Army attempted to answer U-M's touchdown. The Cadets came within three yards of the Michigan end zone before being driven back and ultimately fumbling on the 26-yard line. However, Michigan would fumble the ball right back and Army would score a touchdown on the last play of the third quarter. In the final period, Davis would run the ball around left end 70 yards for Army's fourth score of the day. Despite being outgained in total yards 446-237, Michigan had forced the Cadets to respect the younger, smaller team. The Wolverines' one fault would have been not being able to contain Blanchard and Davis, who recorded 370 of Army's 380 rushing yards.When it was all over, Army had preserved its number-one ranking with a 28-7 win, yet had a new respect for the team from the Midwest.

Photo: Michiganensian

The Army's Doc Blanchard on the loose in a 1945 game versus the Wolverines.

CHAMPION OF THE WEST

MATT MANN

Born in Yorkshire, England, in 1884, Matt Mann would spend much of his life associated with the sport of swimming on both sides of the Atlantic. At the age of nine, Mann won the boys' swimming championship of England. At 21, he came to Canada and then to the United States, settling in Buffalo where he set national "Y" records for the 100-yard and 220-yard freestyle. Mann moved to Massachusetts, then to New York City and finally to the Detroit Athletic Club in 1919. Here, he coached over a dozen swimmers who would go on to the Olympics. In 1925, he was brought to the University of Michigan as head swim coach and thus embarked on a 29-year legacy of national success. Among Mann's startling statistics are 16 conference titles, 13 national crowns and a dual meet record of 202-25-3. Under his tenure, Michigan turned out more Olympian swimmers than any other college or University in the United States. He was named the coach of the 1952 United States Olympic swimming team, which captured four of the six swimming gold medals awarded. Ironically, one event the U.S. team did not capture was the 200-meter breaststroke, won by U-M swimmer but Australian competitor John Davies. Mann was forced to retire due to University age rules in 1954, but went on to coach at Oklahoma, where he raised the program to the NCAA's top 10 during his tenure. He died in December 1962.

another CHAMPION OF THE WEST

WILLIAM COURTRIGHT

William Courtright showed so much potential on the mats in 1943 that coach Cliff Keen named the sophomore the team captain. However, the honor was reassigned when Courtright went to serve his country in WWII. In Europe, Courtright fought in Northern France and Germany, earning corporal stripes with General Patton's third Army. When the war was over, Courtright returned to Michigan and the world of wrestling, garnering the captain status he left in 1943. Though he started the season struggling at 165 pounds, he excelled once he dropped to the 155-pound weight class. He underlined his comeback season with a 6-1 record in dual meets, leading up to a Big Ten title. At the Big Ten Championship, Courtright set a Conference record by recording four falls in a combined time of 9:30. He pinned Minnesota's Kramer in 2:50 to pick up the title. Moving to NCAA forum, Courtright decisioned Jack St. Clair of Oklahoma A&M by a 4-3 margin to crown his season with a national title. Returning for his senior season with the designation of captain once again, Courtright suffered a knee injury in a dual meet with Illinois. His determination to continue would pay off at the 1947 Big Ten meet, where he scored a 9-1 decision over Ken Marlin of Illinois to claim his second Big Ten title. He managed to advance to the NCAA finals before bowing out to Gale Mikles of Michigan State.

Maize & Blue Item

Fritz Crisler knew his young crew was no match for the 1945 Army team. Using the liberal substitution rules put in place due to the war, Crisler drew up two teams, one for offense and one for defense. It was the first ever use of the two-platoon system, a method designed to rest the players, and an idea that flustered both sportswriters and the Army team alike. Though U-M would lose 28-7 to the eventual national champions, the game marked Army's smallest margin of victory during the season.

M List: Milestone Games

On September. 22, 1945, Michigan faced Indiana for the Wolverines' 500th football game. The Wolverines lost this contest, 13-7, in front of 27,000 fans in Ann Arbor. Following is a list of all of Michigan's milestone games:

#	Date	Opponent	Site	Result	Score
1	March 30, 1879	Racine	A	W	1-0
100	November 6, 1897	Purdue	H	W	34-4
200	November 2, 1907	Vanderbilt	H	W	8-0
250	October 24, 1914	Syracuse	A	L	6-20
300	October 1, 1921	Mt. Union	H	W	44-0
400	October 21, 1933	Ohio State	H	W	13-0
500	September 22, 1945	Indiana	H	L	7-13
600	November 19, 1955	Ohio State	H	L	0-17
700	November 5, 1966	Illinois	H	L	21-28
750	October 23, 1971	Minnesota	A	W	35-7
800	January 1, 1976	Oklahoma	Miami, Fla.	L	6-14
900	September. 29, 1984	Indiana	A	W	14-6
1000	October 24, 1992	Minnesota	H	W	63-13

America's Time Capsule

October 16, 1946: Gordie Howe played his first NHL game for the Detroit Red Wings.

December 15, 1946: Coach George Halas' Chicago Bears won the NFL championship, beating the New York Giants, 24-14.

April 11, 1947: Jackie Robinson made his debut with the Brooklyn Dodgers as major league baseball's first black player.

April 16, 1947: Some 500 persons died in a ship explosion at Texas City, Texas.

June 23, 1947: Despite President Truman's veto, the controversial Taft-Hartley Labor Act was passed by Congress.

University Lore

In February 1947, the University paid the federal government $1 for Willow Run Airport. The 1,917-acre site was constructed in 1941 for the B24 Liberators produced at the adjoining bomber plant. The University leased the terminal and hangar facilities to a consortium of seven airlines, reserving 500 acres and several buildings for its own use. Aeronautical engineering and other labs were set up at Willow Run, which became the site for many classified research projects. In 1972 the University divested the Willow Run labs to the non-profit Environmental Research Institute.

Michigan Moment

MICHIGAN GOLFERS CONTINUE DOMINANCE

Facing a nine-stroke deficit behind leader Purdue halfway through the Big Ten golf championship at West Lafayette, Indiana, the Wolverines decided to make a run for a second straight Conference golf title. Despite also trailing Ohio State by six strokes, the Wolverines hung tough in the third round, taking a three-stroke lead. On a course where par was only attained twice during the tournament, the golfers held strong to capture the title by five strokes over the Buckeyes. Ed Schalon tied for medalist honors by shooting a 297, followed by Jon Jenswold's 309 and Dave Barclay's 311. Following the comeback performance, the Wolverines returned home to take on the nation at the NCAA championship, which had been awarded to the Michigan Golf Course. At the team competition, Michigan finished fifth, led by Bill Courtright's 151 and Schalon's 153. Barclay finished third on the team with a 157, but the Rockford, Illinois native may have been saving up for the individual tournament, played in match play following the team competition. While his teammates and rivals went down one-by-one, Barclay advanced through the ranks during the eight-day event. Facing LSU's Jack Coyle in the final round, Barclay and his opponent stood tied through 27 holes of the 36-hole match. In an drama-packed final nine, Barclay grabbed the lead, then withstood Coyle's charge to become the third U-M golfer to claim individual medalist honors at the NCAA tournament.

Photo: Michiganensian

Dave Barclay

CHAMPION OF THE WEST

BOB CHAPPUIS

Bob Chappuis erupted onto the Michigan gridiron in 1942 and performed masterfully for the 7-3 Wolverines. The 19-year-old sophomore from Toledo, Ohio, started just one game, yet led Michigan in both passing and total offense. High hopes for the 1943 season were dashed when Chappuis was called to the Air Force because of the war. The young man picked up right where he left off, leading Michigan in passing, rushing and total offense in 1946. His totals were good enough to be the best in the Big Ten in both rushing and total offense, performances that earned him team MVP honors. If Chappuis' efforts for the 6-2-1 Wolverines in 1946 were great, his 1947 statistics were superhuman. Chappuis rewrote the Michigan record book, setting single season records for touchdown percentage, yards per completion and pass efficiency, the latter two which he still holds today. He led both Michigan and the Big Ten in passing and total offense, becoming the only man in Conference history to be a season leader in both passing and rushing. Following his second-place finish in the Heisman Trophy voting, Chappuis ran for 91 yards and passed for 188 more in Michigan's Rose Bowl victory. Selected in the first round of the 1947 AAFC draft, Chappuis went on to play two years in the AAFC with the Brooklyn Dodgers and Chicago Rockets. A three-year letterman in football and baseball, Chappuis was selected to the presitigious National Football Foundation Hall of Fame.

another CHAMPION OF THE WEST

MACK SUPRUNOWICZ

Due to relaxed eligibility rules because of the recently ended World War, Schenectady, New York native Mack Suprunowicz was able to play varsity basketball as a freshman. Though young, Suprunowicz left little doubt remaining about his ability by leading the team in scoring his first season. The six-foot, 180-pound player played in all 20 of the team's games his first year, averaging 11.4 points per game and leading the team to its best Big Ten finish in ten years. Despite being hampered by injury his sophomore year, Mack again led the Wolverines in scoring average and finished seventh in the Conference race in scoring. With his help, Michigan earned its first Conference championship in 19 years and its first ever bid to the NCAA tournament. During his junior season, Suprunowicz finished third in the Conference in scoring as he poured in 247 points. Included in this total was a then single-game record of 28 points Mack scored against Purdue. Mack led the team in scoring average for an unprecedented fourth time in 1949-50, averaging 12.6 points per game over Michigan's 22-game campaign. Having already influenced Michigan basketball history for years to come, the forward etched his name in the record books by becoming Michigan's first-ever 1,000 point scorer. In the season's final contest, Mack posted 19 points against Purdue to deliver a 70-60 win and finish his career with 1,006 career points.

Maize & Blue Item

Nearly 80,000 fans filed into Ohio Stadium expecting to see another hard-fought battle between the two rivals. What they saw was a dismantling of the Ohio State team by a Michigan squad that won its fourth of 25 consecutive games. U-M took a 7-0 lead after one quarter of play, but picked up 20 more points before halftime. Quarterback Bob Chappuis, accounted for 270 of Michigan's yards on 13 completed passes and nine rushes.

M List

Men's Basketball Scoring Leaders

Glen Rice	2,442
Mike McGee	2,439
Gary Grant	2,222
Cazzie Russell	2,164
Rudy Tomjanovich	1,808
Jalen Rose	1,788
Bill Buntin	1,725
Henry Wilmore	1,652
Roy Tarpley	1,601
Antoine Joubert	1,594

America's Time Capsule

October 14, 1947: Captain Chuck Yeager piloted the world's first supersonic aircraft.

December 5, 1947: Heavyweight boxing champion Joe Louis earned a split decision over "Jersey Joe" Walcott.

March 8, 1948: The Supreme Court ruled that religious education in public schools was a violation of the First Amendment.

May 3, 1948: James Michener's *Tales of the South Pacific* and Tennessee Williams' *A Streetcar Named Desire* earned Pulitzer prizes.

August 16, 1948: Babe Ruth, baseball's greatest player, died of cancer.

University Lore

THE UNIVERSITY OF MICHIGAN · ARTES · SCIENTIA · VERITAS · 1817 ™

Drawing on the ancient myth of the bird reborn from its own ashes, the University established the Phoenix Project for exploration of peaceful uses of atomic energy as a living memorial to its 583 war dead. The project raised $7.5 million by 1953. The Phoenix Memorial Laboratory was completed in 1955 and the Ford Research Reactor in 1956. Phoenix funds supported research in the physical, biological and social sciences which led to fundamental scientific discoveries, most notably Donald Glasers' development of the liquid bubble chamber for which he received the Nobel Prize in 1960.

Michigan Moment

MICHIGAN WINS FIRST NCAA HOCKEY TITLE

The 1947-48 school year had already seen Michigan win the Big Ten title and take home the Roses in football, and win the Big Ten and head to the NCAA's in basketball. Meanwhile, the Wolverine hockey team had gotten off to an 11-1-1 start, then had won its final seven games of the year to finish 18-2-1. In any previous season, the 18th win would have been the last of the year. However, the National Collegiate Athletic Association had instituted a national hockey championship to begin play in 1948. Four teams were selected for the inaugural tournament, which was held at the Broadmoor Hotel Ice Palace in Colorado Springs: Dartmouth, Boston College, Colorado College, and Michigan. The Eagles of Boston College were Michigan's semifinal draw, and the two teams battled to a 4-4 tie at the end of regulation. Defenseman Connie Hill recorded a hat trick and future 'M' coach Allen Renfrew added a goal, but the Eagles equalled each point with one of their own. In a non-sudden death overtime, junior Wally Gacek scored just 18 seconds into the extra session, then scored an empty net goal with half a minute left to give Michigan a 6-4 win. The championship game pitted the Wolverines against the best team in the east, the 20-2-0 Dartmouth Big Green. Despite Gacek's two goals in the first two periods of play, the game was deadlocked at 4-4 with one period left. However, Gacek completed his hat trick and Gacek's linemates, Wally Grant and Ted Greer each tallied a goal to secure the championship. Michigan goalie Jack McDonald did not allow a goal in the final period as Michigan cruised to an 8-4 victory. Gacek led all scorers in the championships with five goals and three assists for a total of eight points.

Photo: U-M Athletic Dept.

The NCAA champions, the 1948 U-M hockey team.

CHAMPIONSHIP *Moment*

MICHIGAN FOOTBALL TEAMS HEADS FOR PASADENA

In 1947, Michigan won all nine of its regular season games en route to claiming the Conference title. Holding the top spot in the nation in total offense and passing yards per game, the Wolverines headed to Pasadena for the first time since 1902 to take on Southern California. Coach-of-the-year Fritz Crisler's squad was picked as 15-point favorites over its Western rivals, then backed up the odds by handing the Trojans the worst loss in their history, 49-0. The final tally matched the score of Michigan's 1902 Rose Bowl win. It took ten minutes for Michigan to get on the board on a one-yard run by Jack Wiesenburger, but the team scored often after that. Weisenburger added another one-yard scoring run in the second quarter before Bob Chappuis tossed an 11-yard touchdown pass to Bump Elliott to give the Maize and Blue a 21-0 lead at halftime. Things only improved for Michigan in the second half, as the team recorded a four-touchdown lead on an 18-yard pass from Chappuis to Howard Yerges. U-M would spend the fourth quarter scoring 21 points, securing nine Rose Bowl records and making the audience of the first televised Rose Bowl aware of the Wolverines' dominance. Weisenburger added his third touchdown of the afternoon in the final stanza, as Michigan compiled 268 rushing yards on the day. The final two touchdowns came through the air, 45 yards from Henry Fonde to Gene Derricotte and a 29-yard bomb from Yerges to Dick Rifenburg, giving U-M 223 passing yards and 491 yards of total offense. Meanwhile, the stifling Wolverine defense held USC to just 133 yards of total offense and forced three turnovers.

CHAMPION OF THE WEST

WALLY GRANT

Wally Grant was a three-time All-American for the U-M after establishing a high school playoff record with 13 points at Eveleth High School in Minnesota, a record that remained in the top five in playoff history for over 40 years. When he joined the Wolverines, Grant earned four varsity letters and became a three-time All-American in 1948-49-50 when he returned from United States Military Service after his freshman year. He was a captain of the 1949-50 Michigan squad. Michigan was 80-15-4 in his four seasons, winning a national title in 1948 and placing third in the nation in 1949 and again in 1950. Grant scored 63 goals and 83 assists for 146 career points, fourth best in Michigan history upon graduation. He was a member of the "G Line" that included Wally Gacek at center and Ted Greer at right wing when each scored a goal in the third period of the 1948 NCAA Championship 8-4 win over Dartmouth in 1948. Wolverine hockey coach Vic Heyliger considered Grant "the best two-way hockey player I have ever seen." He graduated with a BBA from Michigan's Business School in 1950 and worked for General Motors for the next 37 years, retiring in 1987 as comptroller of the Warren Division of Hydra-Matic. He and his wife Mickey still reside in Ann Arbor and are both strong supporters of the Wolverine hockey program through the Dekers Club.

Maize & Blue Item

Led by Big Nine scoring champion Murray Weir, Iowa was supposed to be the team to beat in 1948. But the Wolverines, led by standout forward Mack Suprunowicz, were doing their best to break a Conference title drought that had begun in 1929. The Hawkeyes led 29-22 at the half, but the Wolverines seized control, coasting to a 51-35 win and the school's first ever NCAA tournament bid.

M List: Rose Bowl-ing with Michigan

Date	Opponent	Result
January 1, 1902	Stanford	W, 49-0
January 1, 1948	USC	W, 49-0
January 1, 1951	California	W, 14-6
January 1, 1965	Oregon State	W, 34-7
January 1, 1970	USC	L, 3-10
January 1, 1972	Stanford	L, 12-13
January 1, 1977	USC	L, 6-14
January 1, 1978	Washington	L, 20-27
January 1, 1979	USC	L, 10-17
January 1, 1981	Washington	W, 23-6
January 1, 1983	UCLA	L, 14-24
January 1, 1987	Arizona State	L, 15-22
January 2, 1989	USC	W, 22-14
January 1, 1990	USC	L, 10-17
January 1, 1992	Washington	L, 14-34
January 1, 1993	Washington	W, 38-31

America's Time Capsule

November 2, 1948: In a major political upset, Harry Truman defeated Thomas Dewey for the U.S. presidency.

December 15, 1948: Former State Department official Alger Hiss was indicted by a federal grand jury on two counts of perjury.

April 4, 1949: NATO was formed when the North Atlantic Treaty was signed in Washington, D.C.

April 20, 1949: The discovery of cortisone, the hormone promised to bring relief to sufferers of rheumatoid arthritis, was announced.

June 22, 1949: Ezzard Charles defeated "Jersey Joe" Walcott to become the new heavyweight boxing champion.

University Lore

The first fruits of a post-war building boom came on-line in 1948-49. The $2.45 million Administration Building consolidated central administrative and student services offices and also provided a home for the University's new radio station, WUOM. A $2.7 million Business Administration Building and a $2.6 million expansion of the Chemistry and Pharmacy Building provided classroom space. In the Randall Laboratory the 300-million electron volt synchrotron began smashing atoms for Professors David Dennison and H.R. Crane.

Michigan Moment

MICHIGAN GRIDDERS AIM FOR NO. 1

After capturing an undefeated season, a Big Ten title and winning the Rose Bowl in the 1947 season, there was little more that the Wolverines could do in following up that performance. Due to Big Ten rules that permitted a team to go to Pasadena once every three seasons, the Michigan players could make Christmas plans. However, there was still the challenge of a second straight national championship. With just three offensive starters returning, Michigan needed a fourth-quarter touchdown to beat Michigan State, 13-7, in the season opener. In week four, Michigan shut out third-ranked Northwestern, 28-0, to claim the number-one ranking. Two weeks later, the Wolverines dropped to number two in the polls when they were outgained, 296-235, in a 28-20 win over Illinois. Navy became the victim of the Wolverines frustration as the Midshipmen were held to 119 total yards in a 35-0 Maize and Blue win. Back in control of the top spot, Michigan caused Indiana to turn the ball over eight times as the Wolverines won their eighth straight, 54-0. Michigan closed out its season in Columbus, looking for its fourth straight win over the Buckeyes. The Wolverines spotted Ohio State a 3-0 lead, but scored all the rest of the points in a 13-3 win. The season-ending win improved the Wolverines record to 9-0 and cemented their spot at the top of the final Associated Press poll. End Dick Rifenburg, quarterback Pete Elliott and tackle Alvin Wistert all captured All-American honors for the 1948 season, while these three plus captain guard Dominic Tomasi captured All-Big Ten honors.

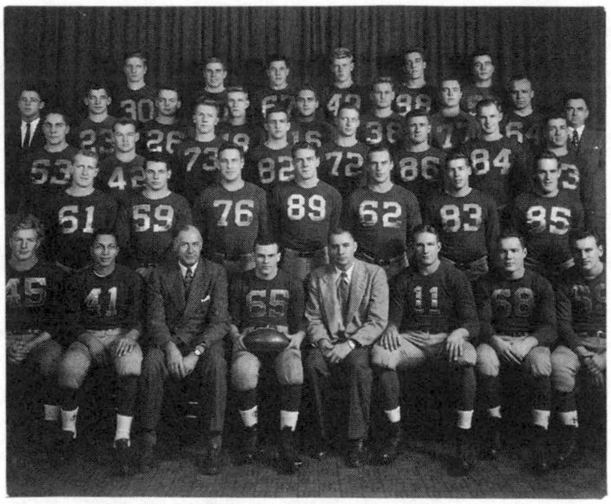

The 1948 Michigan football team.

CHAMPION OF THE WEST

AL RENFREW

While many Michigan legends have made their marks playing and coaching at the University of Michigan, hockey star Al Renfrew accomplished the rare feat of winning a national championship from both sides of the bench. The Toronto native came to Ann Arbor in 1945 and played four years of hockey, rising up to captain's status in his senior year. The wing scored 91 goals and 172 points under coach, and later brother-in-law, Vic Heyliger, as the Wolverines went 70-18-6 while Renfrew was playing. The 1948 squad won the first-ever national championship as Renfrew finished his career second in Michigan history in points. Almost 50 years later, his career totals still rank among the top 20 in the Michigan record books. After his 1949 graduation from the school of education, Renfrew began coaching at Michigan Tech in 1951. He remained in Houghton for five seasons before going to North Dakota for one year. In 1957, he returned to U-M to take over the position vacated by Heyliger. Though his early teams could not meet the lofty record established by their predecessors, Renfrew rebuilt the program, winning five Big Ten titles and the coveted NCAA trophy in 1964. He ended his coaching career after 16 seasons in 1973 with a 222-207-11 record at Michigan before taking over the role of manager of the U-M ticket office.

another CHAMPION OF THE WEST

PETE ELLIOTT

On February 21, 1943, due to the war, the Big Ten Conference allowed freshmen to play intercollegiate athletics. A young blond boy from Bloomington, Indiana, took advantage of this rule, lettering in three different sports in his first year. Before he would graduate with a B.A. in 1949, Pete Elliott would letter each of his four years in football, basketball and golf. Elliott wound up in Ann Arbor purely by chance, as the Navy college training unit was divided into three parts, sending trainees to Michigan, Notre Dame and Northwestern. Pete took to his new hometown, playing backup on the football team, before switching his sights to basketball where the guard cracked the starting lineup as a freshman. When the basketball season ended, Elliott could be found on the golf course, aiding the Maize and Blue as it won three Big Ten titles in his four seasons. Pete Elliott rose up the depth chart to become Michigan's starting quarterback for the 1948 Big Ten and National Championship teams, also seeing playing time on the 1947 squad which captured the Rose Bowl crown. As a junior he was part of the basketball team that won U-M's first hoops title since 1929. Following graduation, Elliott left Michigan, but not the sport of football. He served as head coach at Nebraska, California, Illinois, and Miami (Florida), taking the Illini to the Rose Bowl in 1963. Elliott and his wife Joanne had two sons, Bruce and Dave, both of whom played football under Bo Schembechler in the 1970s.

Maize & Blue Item

Following a 1947 campaign that saw his team go 10-0, Michigan football coach Fritz Crisler was selected as the American Football Coaches Association coach of the year. Then Crisler handed the reigns over to Bennie Oosterbaan, who took the team to a 9-0 finish. The first and only coach to win a national championship in his first season, Oosterbaan was chosen AFCA coach of the year in 1948.

M List: Michigan's All-time, All-Sports Records vs. Big Ten Competition

	W	L	T	Pct.
Chicago	140	49	3	.737
Illinois	452	315	9	.588
Indiana	434	313	5	.580
Iowa	356	247	5	.590
Michigan State	859	504	29	.628
Minnesota	512	396	12	.563
Northwestern	471	231	6	.669
Ohio State	658	406	26	.616
Penn State	88	79	0	.527
Purdue	430	213	6	.667
Wisconsin	482	248	11	.658
Total	4882	3001	112	.618

1949-50

America's Time Capsule

October 9, 1949: The New York Yankees beat the Brooklyn Dodgers to win baseball's World Series.

October 24, 1949: The United Nations headquarters were dedicated in New York.

January 31, 1949: President Truman authorized development of the hydrogen bomb.

April 23, 1950: The Minneapolis Lakers beat the Syracuse Nationals to win the first National Basketball Association championship.

June 27, 1950: President Truman ordered U.S. armed forces to Korea to help South Korea repel the North Korean invasion.

University Lore

Haven Hall, situated at the northwest corner of campus, was destroyed by fire on June 6, 1950. Built in 1863 to house the Law Department, in 1950 it was home to the History, Journalism and Sociology Departments and the Bureau of Government. The fire raged out of control for three hours as a crowd of 15,000 watched. Damages were estimated at $3 million, including many irreplaceable items in the Bureau of Government Library. The new wing of Angell Hall, completed in 1952, reused the name Haven Hall.

Michigan Moment

"M" FOOTBALL TEAM PUTS STREAK ON LINE

As the 1949 football season dawned, the Wolverines were faced with high expectations from the community. Victors in 23 straight games, fans expected nothing less than a third straight Big Ten title, a feat not accomplished since Minnesota's consecutive titles from 1935-37. Due to the "one Rose Bowl every three years" rule in place at the time, Michigan could not return to Pasadena until January 1, 1951. Only a Conference title would satiate the U-M fans. The Wolverines ran their winning streak to 25 games by edging Michigan State, 7-3, and crushing Stanford, 27-7. However, if the streak was to continue, Michigan would have to beat the seventh ranked Army squad. In front of a capacity crowd at Michigan Stadium, the Cadets jumped out to a 14-0 lead in handing Michigan its first defeat since October 1946, 21-7. A week later in Evanston, the Maize and Blue suffered their second straight setback, a 21-20 decision to the Wildcats of Northwestern. With the team 2-2, the hopes for a third straight Conference title were nearly extinguished. Michigan's next scheduled opponent was the 4-0 Minnesota Golden Gophers, a two-touchdown favorite. However, U-M's Chuck Ortmann and Charlie Lentz would rule the day. Ortmann, who accounted for over 90 percent of Michigan's total offense, led Michigan to a 14-0 advantage, while Lentz had three interceptions to keep the Golden Gophers in check. Following the upset, Michigan shut out Illinois 13-0, then forced Purdue to commit seven turnovers in a 20-12 "M" victory. A 20-7 win over Indiana, set up the once unthinkable. To win the Conference, Michigan would simply need to beat Ohio State, a team which was also 4-1 in the Big Ten. The Buckeyes, who had suffered their lone Conference loss in a 27-0 shut out at the hands off Minnesota, were looking for their first trip to Pasadena since 1921. In front of Michigan's fifth 95,000 plus crowd of the year, the U-M jumped out to a 7-0 lead, an edge that held through the first three quarters. Ohio State, needing just a tie to hold off Minnesota in the standings and a Rose Bowl bid, scored with 5:20 left in the contest to even the score at 7-7. The game ended with the same score, leaving Michigan and Ohio State as co-champions.

Photo: U-M Athletic Dept.

Chuck Ortmann

CHAMPION OF THE WEST

THE WISTERTS

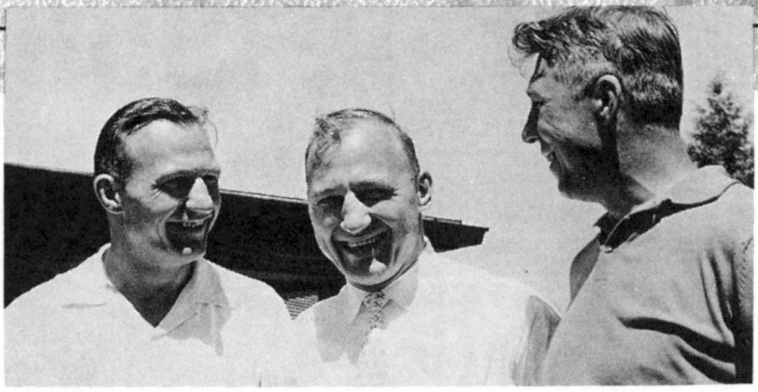

Francis, Albert and Alvin were all tackles, all wore the number 11 jersey and all were voted first-team All-American, an accomplishment that has never been duplicated by three brothers on any level of collegiate competition. The first brother to attain national honors was Francis 'Whitey' Wistert, a member of the 1933 Big Ten and National Championship team. After a brief stint in professional baseball and as an assistant football coach at Michigan, he practiced law then became a vice president for Eltra Corporation of Toledo, Ohio. He died in 1985. Albert "Ox" Wistert played for Fritz Crisler and was chosen to the 1942 All-American team. He went on to play professionally with Philadelphia in the NFL before selling life insurance, and now resides in Thousand Oaks, California. Alvin "Moose" Wistert was the last of the siblings to play at Michigan. He was the oldest man ever to play football at Michigan at the age of 32 following Marine Corps service in World War II. A transfer from Boston University to Michigan, he eventually became a two-time All-American. Upon graduation, Alvin worked in insurance before becoming a manufacturers' rep. He still resides in Northville, Michigan. The Wisterts all have been enshrined in the National Football Foundation Hall of Fame, inducted into the Michigan Hall of Honor and, of course, the number 11 has been retired.

another CHAMPION OF THE WEST

CHARLES FONVILLE

Charles Fonville became the eighth Michigan track and field athlete to win the shot put at the Big Ten championship during the 1947 indoor meet at Champaign, Illinois. But Fonville was no ordinary shot put champion. The Detroit native, who blew the field away at the 1947 Big Ten and NCAA championships, would go on to post a world record mark of 58 feet, 1/4 inch in the spring of 1948. Once again, Fonville sewed up all three titles, the Big Ten Indoor and Outdoor and the NCAA crowns. A sure bet to make the Olympic squad for the games in London, Fonville's career was seemingly finished when he suffered a slipped disc in his back in the early summer of 1948. While American Wilbur Thompson was winning the Olympic shot put with a distance of just 56 feet, 2 inches, Fonville was undergoing surgery to repair his back. He did not compete during 1948-49 and few expected to see him at a collegiate meet again. But at the Michigan AAU relays held in Yost Field House, there was Fonville, returning to the circle he had dominated just 18 months earlier. On his second throw back, he hurled the 16-lb. ball 55 feet, 1 inch, a mark that would have earned him the silver medal at the Olympics. Though he wasn't nearly as dominant as before, Fonville still had enough left in his system to gather the 1950 Big Ten indoor title in the shot put, following William Watson as Michigan three-time winners in that event.

Maize & Blue Item

In 1950, Ray Fisher's baseball squad won its first five Conference games behind the pitching of Ed Grenkoski. The path to the Wolverines' seventh crown in nine years seemed easy until U-M dropped a pair of decisions to Wisconsin. Needing a pair of wins to assure the title, Michigan swept the series in Columbus to assure the title.

M List — NCAA Football All-time Victories

Michigan's football team has claimed 37 conference championships, a Big Ten best. The Wolverines have won 10 national titles and are at the top of the all-time list for victories:

School	Wins
1. Michigan	764
2. Notre Dame	746
3. Alabama	713
4. Texas	713
5. Nebraska	709
6. Penn State	706
7. Ohio State	690
8. Oklahoma	673
9. Tennessee	665
10. Southern California	653

1950-51

America's Time Capsule

September 26, 1950: U.S. troops recaptured Seoul, the capital of South Korea.

October 7, 1950: The New York Yankees defeated the Philadelphia Phillies to win the World Series, four games to none.

February 26, 1951: Congress adopted the 22nd Amendment to the U.S. Constitution, stipulating that no person may be elected to the presidency for more than two terms.

April 11, 1951: President Truman relieved Gen. Douglas MacArthur of his post as supreme commander.

June 25, 1951: The Columbia Broadcasting System (CBS) presented television's first commercial color broadcast.

University Lore

Two new schools appeared in 1950-51. The School of Forestry, established in 1903, was transformed into the School of Natural Resources, offering a much broader curriculum with courses in areas such as regional planning and general conservation. Under Samuel T. Dana and Stanley Fontana, the school became a model for programs at other universities. The School of Social Work was established in March 1951 with Fedele Fauri as dean. Social work courses were first taught in 1921 through the Sociology Department and later through the Institute of Public Administration based in Detroit.

Michigan Moment

SNOW BOWL

Following three straight Big Ten titles and a 25-2-1 record over those seasons, Michiganders looked forward to the 1950 campaign. However, two seven-point losses and a defeat at the hands of number-one ranked Army left the Wolverines with a 2-3-1 record and dim hopes of returning to Pasadena. Two successive wins put the Wolverines in the upper echelon of the Big Nine, but Michigan would need a win over Ohio State in Columbus and a Northwestern victory over Illinois to return to the Roses. When the game began, snow blanketed the field and blew through the air on 28-mile-per-hour winds. The temperature stood at a frigid 10° and just over 50,000 of the 85,200 ticket-holding fans decided to brave the conditions. Ohio State struck first, blocking a punt off the foot of Chuck Ortmann and recovering the ball on the Michigan 8-yard line. Three plays later, a field goal gave OSU a 3-0 lead. The teams exchanged kicks several times, and Michigan would catch the next break. Deep in Buckeye territory, Janowicz attempted a punt, but tackle Al Wahl blocked it and the ball, which caromed out of the end zone for a safety. With 47 seconds left in the half, Ohio State found itself on its own goal line. Following a time out, Janowicz attempted to kick the ball on third down. Center Tony Momsen blocked the kick, and secured the ball in the end zone to record the points for the Michigan special teams unit. Harry Allis converted the extra point, and the Wolverines led at the break, 9-3. Neither team would score in the second half. Ralph Straffon gained 14 yards on 12 carries to lead Michigan in both rushing and total offense. The hero of the game was undoubtedly Michigan kicker who kicked a Big Ten record 24 punts for 723 yards. When the infamous "Snow Bowl" was over, Michigan had zero first downs, zero completed passes, 24 punts, 27 total yards, and yet a victory and a ticket to California.

Harry Allis converts an extra point on the winning touchdown in the "Snow Bowl."

CHAMPION OF THE WEST

VIC HEYLIGER

Ann Arbor News hockey writer Neil Koepke once noted "If the University of Illinois had not scrapped its hockey program in 1943, the history of Michigan hockey might read a lot differently." Fritz Crisler replaced Eddie Lowrey with Heyliger and fought off the sentiments to drop hockey due to the limited opponents during the war years. Heyliger returned to Michigan in 1944 where ten years earlier he skated for U-M. After a 3-6-0 record the first year, he developed Michigan into a national power. Heyliger coached the Wolverines to one third-place NCAA finish, three NCAA runner-up spots, and six national championships. His overall record was 228-61-13. Heyliger also was one of the individuals who drummed up support for an NCAA Championship. Asthma forced Heyliger to leave Michigan and go to Colorado. He coached the U.S. National Team and in 1962, he started the Air Force Academy hockey program. As an athlete, not only did Heyliger play hockey, as a sophomore baseball player, he led the Big Ten in RBIs and was second in batting in the Conference while playing the outfield. In hockey, Heyliger was an all-league center in the Western Hockey League. After graduation, he joined the Chicago Black Hawks and found himself on a Stanley Cup team as a rookie.

another CHAMPION OF THE WEST

EDSEL BUCHANAN

Edsel Buchanan was one of the greatest trampoline artists who ever bounced on a canvas. In 1949 and 1950, Buchanan was a national champion. As a captain in 1951, Buchanan was put to the test. During the Big Ten Championship in that year, Buchanan made a major mistake. He bounced off the net and was disqualified. After Buchanan's disqualification, it was Illinois that breezed to the title. One week later, Buchanan had to try to redeem himself as the NCAA Championships came to the Michigan Intramural Building. Buchanan had extremely tough competition from ex Conference champion Bill Harris of Iowa and the 1951 Big Ten champion from Illinois, Bruce Sidlinger. On March 31, Buchanan used his artistic touch to show the home crowd a truly great performance. Unlike many performers of the time, Buchanan did not try to develop stunts of great difficulty. Since officials judged performance and difficulty on 50-50 basis, Buchanan figured a smooth, graceful approach was the way to win. He used a method called "swing time" to provide continuity to his performance. According to the experts, he was the only known trampoline athlete who could run through his one-minute routine without allowing himself a free bounce to regain stability or attain a greater height. Buchanan's ease and incomparable smoothness that afternoon gave the greatest Michigan trampoline artist his third consecutive NCAA individual crown.

Maize & Blue Item

In the Rose Bowl, the Wolverines played the 9-0-1 California Golden Bears, a team that was hungry after dropping Rose Bowl decisions in both 1949 and 1950. California showed its frustration by dominating the first half. Though California outgained Michigan 192-65 in total yards, the Wolverines were in high spirits knowing that the score was only 6-0. Although Michigan trailed entering the final stanza, the Wolverines scored twice to win 14-6. Don Dufek, who ran for 113 yards on 23 carries, scored both U-M touchdowns.

M List — Statistics About "The Game"

Michigan and Ohio State have matched up for some classic contests in the last 63 years. The following is a breakdown of some of the more important games in the series:

- Games that determined the Big Ten Champion between the two schools: 1942, '44, '49, '50, '54, '55, '64, '68, '69, '70, '72, '73, '74, '75, '76, '77, '80, '86
- Games that helped determine the Big Ten Champion: 1935, '38, '43, '52, '56, '61, '78, '79, '81, '84, '88, '89, '90, '91, '93, '95, '96
- Michigan undefeated seasons ended: 1970, '72, '74
- Ohio State undefeated seasons ended: 1969, '93, '95, '96
- Longest Big Ten winning streak snapped: Ohio State, 17, 1976
- Longest overall winning streak snapped: Ohio State, 20, 1969

1951-52

America's Time Capsule

November 10, 1951: The first transcontinental direct dial telephone service took place when a call was placed from New Jersey to California.

December 20, 1951: A station in Idaho began producing electricity from the first atomic-powered generator.

April 8, 1952: A presidential order prevented a shutdown of the nation's steel mills by strikers.

July 11, 1952: Gen. Dwight Eisenhower and Sen. Richard Nixon were nominated as the presidential ticket for the Republicans.

July 26, 1952: Illinois governor Adlai Stevenson was nominated at the Democratic National Convention as that party's presidential candidate.

University Lore

Harlan Hatcher, a former dean and English professor at Ohio State University, was inaugurated as the University's 10th president, succeeding Alexander Ruthven. Hatcher's 17-year tenure saw dramatic expansion in enrollment and the physical campus. Student population grew from 23,000 to 41,000. Acquisition and development of the north campus began, and the Flint and Dearborn campuses were opened. Controversies over the firing of two faculty members during the McCarthy era and the rise of student activism also marked Hatcher's years.

Michigan Moment

MICHIGAN ICERS REPEAT AS NATIONAL CHAMPS

Except for lacking a tie, Michigan's record at the end of the 1951-52 hockey season was the same as the regular season record of U-M's 1950-51 NCAA championship team. Behind captain Earl Keyes and leading point scorer Bob Heathcott, the Wolverine icers averaged over six goals per game and entered its fifth straight NCAA tournament with a seven-game winning streak Michigan blasted away at St. Lawrence in the semi-final game. Using a five-goal first period, the Wolverines flew to the final on a 9-3 win. John McKennell and Pat Cooney had two goals apiece. In the championship, Michigan squared off against Colorado College, a team with whom U-M had split a pair of games in Colorado Springs earlier in the year. Goals by George Chin, George Philpott and Keyes gave Michigan a 3-0 advantage at the first intermission. Colorado College, who had trailed Yale 3-0 in its semifinal game, attempted to mount a comeback with a goal at the five-minute mark of the second period. However, Graham Cragg scored on a McKennell rebound midway through the period for the final goal of the game. The power-play goal was the final one of the 1952 college hockey season as Michigan coasted to a 4-1 win and a second straight championship.

Photo: U-M Athletic Dept.

The 1952 NCAA-champion U-M hockey team.

CHAMPION OF THE WEST

LOWELL PERRY

A speedy pass receiver with an excellent set of hands, Lowell Perry was one of the best ends ever to play football for Michigan. He made an immediate impact for the Wolverines in his first season, grabbing 21 passes as the team won the 1950 Big Ten Championship and the 1951 Rose Bowl. Perry was named All-Big Ten and All-America in 1951. In addition to playing end, Perry also returned punts and played safety on defense. In three seasons at U-M, Perry had 71 pass receptions for 1,261 yards, 10 touchdowns and 41 punt returns. He also lettered in track. His best single game of his Michigan career was the 1951 Little Brown Jug Homecoming game against Minnesota. Perry caught two touchdown passes from Ted Topor, gained over 100 years passing and returned a punt 75 yards for a touchdown in Michigan's 54-27 victory. After concluding his career at Michigan in 1952, Perry was drafted by the Pittsburgh Steelers after serving in the United States Air Force. In Pittsburgh, he suffered a knee injury in his first season, and then became a coach and scout. He left the Steelers after obtaining his law degree in 1960, and worked for the Chrysler Corporation and Michigan Bell. Lowell and his wife, Maxine, have two sons, Lowell, Jr. and Scott, and one daughter, Merideth. Scott was an assistant basketball coach at U-M and is now the head coach at Eastern Kentucky.

another CHAMPION OF THE WEST

JOHN DAVIES

After finishing fourth in the 200-meter breaststroke at the 1948 Olympics, Australian John Davies decided to tour the United States. Given the name of U-M swimming coach Matt Mann, Davies included Ann Arbor on his list of places to stop while in America. This layover would lead to a legendary U.S. swimming career for the man who at one time held every Australian breaststroke record from 110 to 550 yards. The 1951 Big Ten champion in the 200-yard breaststroke, Davis defended his Conference crown in 1952, while adding a victory in the 100-yard version of the event to his honors. The co-captain, who was never on a scholarship while at Michigan, continued his successful senior season with victories in the 100- and 200-yard butterfly at the NCAA meet. In wrestling away both championships from two-time victor Bill Brawner of Princeton, Davies set national championship bests in each event. As a member of the Australian swim team at the 1952 Helsinki Olympics, Davies took top honors in 200-meter breaststroke, one of two gold medals not won by the Matt Mann-coached United States team. Davies graduated from Michigan in 1953, and returned to Australia for postgraduate work at the University of Sydney. He practiced law in California for over 25 years and has been a United States District Judge in Los Angeles since 1986.

Maize & Blue Item

Sophomore Russ Johnson brought Michigan the 1952 Big Ten golf title, tying a course record with a first-round 70, placing him well ahead of the field. Johnson's four-day total of 307 led U-M to a 16-stroke win over second-place Purdue. Team captain Dean Lind finished fourth overall and teammate Lowell LeClair was fifth as U-M claimed its 12th Conference golf crown.

M List: LONE STAR STATES

Don ZanFagna, who lettered on Michigan's football team in 1951, is the only letter winner in "M" football history from the state of Rhode Island. Here is a list of other states with just one letterwinner and the last year the player lettered:

State	Player, year
Idaho	Rex Wells, 1943
Maine	Charles Carter, 1904
New Hampshire	Eric Phelps, 1975
New Mexico	Roy Johnson, 1919
South Carolina	Harold Goodwin, 1995
Wyoming	Don Bracken, 1983

1952-53

America's Time Capsule

September 23, 1952: Rocky Marciano won his 43rd consecutive bout without a loss, defeating "Jersey Joe" Walcott for the world heavyweight boxing title.

November 4, 1952: Dwight Eisenhower defeated Illinois governor Adlai Stevenson for the presidency of the United States.

December 28, 1952: Led by Bobby Layne, the Detroit Lions won the first of back-to-back NFL championships with a 17-7 win over the Browns in Cleveland.

January 2, 1953: Wisconsin senator Joseph McCarthy, known for his charges of communist infiltration in various organizations, was accused by a senate subcommittee of "motivation by self-interest."

March 18, 1953: Baseball's Boston Braves moved to Milwaukee, Wisconsin.

University Lore

MIDAC, the Michigan Digital Automatic Computer, was unveiled in the summer of 1953. Created by U-M scientists under contract from the Air Force, the University's first computer consisted of 1,200 tubes and 500,000 connections and occupied two rooms at Willow Run Research Center. Though used primarily for classified research, some faculty and students did receive training on the MIDAC. Professor John Carr and others developed several major programs.

Michigan Moment

"M" BASEBALL REIGNS AS NCAA CHAMPS

The 1953 baseball season had started a disappointing 9-8 for the Wolverines, who then rose up and won their last six games to earn the Big Ten crown. The squad's 10-3 conference mark tied it with Illinois, but Michigan grabbed a berth in the District IV NCAA playoffs by virtue of its season sweep of the Illini. U-M swept the Bobcats first with the bats in a 6-5 win, then with pitching in a 7-0 victory. U-M defeated Stanford, Boston College and Texas in the opening games, but the Longhorns bounced back to take a 6-4 decision the following night, then defeated Lafayette to set up a championship game between the two now familiar foes. In the title game, Michigan grabbed the lead in the bottom of the fourth when Bill Mogk and Frank Howell walked, and Mogk scored on Don Eaddy's single. Dan Cline then singled to score Howell, with Eaddy coming home on a throwing error. The 5-2 lead was cut to 5-4 in the seventh, then extended to 7-4 in the eighth. In the last stanza, pitcher Marv Wisniewski was replaced after yielding a run on a double and a triple. His replacement, John Corbett, picked up one out, but walked two batters, loading the bases. Jack Ritter was called upon to quench the fire, and responded with two quick outs to claim the championship.

Photo: Rentschler

U-M's 1953 NCAA champion baseball team.

CHAMPIONSHIP *Moment*

MICHIGAN MATMEN WIN BIG TEN CHAMPIONSHIP

Cliff Keen's matmen had been close in recent years, but had yet to claim their first Big Ten title since 1944. While the Wolverines had not placed lower than third since 1945, they had continued to come up short, including a narrow loss to Illinois at the championship in Ann Arbor in 1952. This group of wrestlers was not to be denied. Six Wolverines would place in the top four in their respective weight classes, including Norvard Nalen and Dick O'Shaugnessy, who took individual titles. Nalen, named the outstanding wrestler of the meet, won the 130-pound class, the weight at which he would take a national title less than a month later. Nalen's title was the second of three consecutive years he would win at the conference meet. O'Shaughnessy, better known as the All-Big Ten center on Michigan's football team took down Iowa's George Myers, a 1952 Olympic Medalist, to win top honors at 177 pounds. Like Nalen, O'Shaughnessy was successful in defending his 1952 title. Additionally, Andy Kaul and Joe Scandura clawed their way into the finals before being defeated, while Miles Lee and Tony D'Amico each won their consolation matches. Michigan ended the meet with 27 points, five better than second-place Michigan State. The Wolverines would return to the victory stand three times in the next seven years as Keen's dynasty rolled along.

CHAMPION OF THE WEST

BURWELL JONES

An outstanding swimmer at Detroit's Redford High School, Burwell "Bumpy" Jones was able to contribute immediately after enrolling at U-M in the fall if 1951. For the first time since World War II, freshmen were allowed to compete in intercollegiate athletics. Jones took full advantage of this opportunity, winning the 150-yard individual medley at both the Big Ten and NCAA levels. The freshman also served as part of Michigan's national champion and record setting freestyle relay. Jones repeated all three of these championships in 1953 and 1954, adding the 200-yard freestyle title at Big Tens in 1953 and the 200-yard breaststroke crown at Big Tens in 1954. His title-winning time of 1:29.7 in the 150-yard IM at the 1954 NCAA meet set an American record and made Jones just the 10th swimmer in NCAA history to be a three-time champion in a single event. The six-time national champion just missed a seventh NCAA title by finishing runner-up by two-tenths of a second in the 200-yard breaststroke in 1954. Jones won two more Big Ten crowns in 1955, defending his 200 breaststroke honor and winning the Conference's first-ever 200-yard butterfly race. During the 10-time All-American's career at Michigan, the Wolverines never finished lower than third at the NCAA championship.

Maize & Blue Item

Michigan, two-time defending NCAA hockey champions, returned to the finals in March 1953. The Wolverines mangled Boston University, 14-2 in the semi-finals behind Junior George Chin's two goals and four assists. Between U-M and a third title, however, stood Minnesota who had already taken three games from U-M. The Wolverines' John Matchefts and Jim Haas each scored a pair of goals in U-M's 7-3 championship win.

M List

All-time Big Ten Baseball Standings (as of July 1997)

	Years	Games	Titles
Michigan	91	824	31
Minnesota	85	719	17
Illinois	102	827	26
Ohio State	85	655	12
Michigan State	47	408	3
Iowa	90	578	7
Wisconsin	93	1173	5
Penn State	6	72	1
Indiana	91	1182	4
Chicago	49	543	5
Purdue	92	481	1
Northwestern	95	463	2

MICHIGAN MOMENT

America's Time Capsule

October 5, 1953: The New York Yankees won baseball's World Series for the fifth consecutive time, defeating the Brooklyn Dodgers.

February 23, 1954: Inoculation of school children against polio began for the first time.

March 1, 1954: An explosion of a hydrogen bomb in the Marshall Islands exceeded all estimates of its power.

March 20, 1954: Bradley was defeated by La Salle in the NCAA basketball championship game.

May 17, 1954: The Supreme Court declared racial segregation in public schools unconstitutional.

UNIVERSITY LORE

The University Television Center acquired new quarters in a former funeral home on Maynard Street. Established in 1950, the TV Center's programs were originally broadcast live from the WWJ studios in Detroit. The new studio and kinescope film equipment enabled the TVC to become a pioneer in educational programming even though it never had an on-air station. The "telecourses" and other programs featuring University faculty and distinguished campus visitors were recorded on film and distributed by mail to commercial stations around the country for local broadcast.

MATT MANN STEPS DOWN

The 1954 Big Ten swimming meet would be Matt Mann's last as the coach of the Wolverine team. At the age of 69, the Englishman was forced to retire by University rules. Though laden with youth, his team hoped it could deliver an unprecedented 17th Big Ten Conference title. In front of a packed house in Ann Arbor, Mann's team finished runner-up for the second straight season, but gave the legendary coach a memorable farewell. Wolverines finished first in four separate events, while eight Michigan entries came in second as Michgan racked up the highest runner-up score ever. Burwell "Bumpy" Jones was Michigan's individual standout, winning the 150-yard individual medley, the 200-yard breaststroke and serving as part of U-M's champion 400 freestyle relay team. Jones' time of 1:29.5 in the 150-yard IM set an American record and was nearly two seconds faster than the second-place finisher. Don Hill was the Wolverines other single event winner, earning top honors in the 50-yard freestyle with a Big Ten record time of 22.1 seconds. Jack Wardrop finished second in three events and Jim Walters took runner-up placings in both diving contests as Michigan took second place overall behind Ohio State. Before the final day of competition, Mann was honored in front of the home crowd. Acknowledging the crowd, Mann said, "You may take Matt Mann out of Michigan, but you'll never get Michigan out of Matt Mann."

Photo: U-M Athletic Dept.

Matt Mann

CHAMPION OF THE WEST

DOUG ROBY

While many Michigan athletes have played major roles in sport, Doug Roby might have been the lone individual to have a worldwide impact on athletics at all levels. In the fall of 1953, Roby became the vice-president of the United States Olympic Committee, a position he held until 1965. Then, the Chicago native out of Wendell Phillips High School became the USOC president, a position he held until 1968. As a young boy, Roby excelled in baseball and football. In 1916, he was granted a scholarship to the Michigan Military Academy in Brighton, Michigan, because of his football talents. Besides helping the MMA remain undefeated, Roby became friends with John Maulbetsch, U-M's All-American football player. When Maulbetsch graduated from Michigan in 1917, he went to Phillips University in Oklahoma and he persuaded Roby to go with him. In 1918 and 1919, with Roby as team captain, Phillips lost only once. In February 1920, Roby entered the University of Michigan. He starred in 1921 and 1922 as a left fielder on the baseball team and a starting fullback on the varsity football team. He graduated with a degree in business administration in 1923. Roby was elected president of the National Amateur Athletic Union of the USA in 1951 while he was an active member of the International Olympic Games. In 1952, he was elected as a member to the International Olympic Committee while he attended games in Finland.

another CHAMPION OF THE WEST

NORVARD "SNIP" NALEN

Only six wrestlers in Michigan history have won three Big Ten titles, while just four have gone on to post two national titles. The first to do so was a 130-pound man from Mason City, Iowa, Norvard Nalen. "Snip," as he was known by many, simply dominated the Big Ten and national scene in wrestling between 1952-54. During his sophomore season, Nalen raised a 5-2 record in dual meets before being awarded the Big Ten title on a referee's decision over Michigan State's Dick Gunner. The victory was sweet revenge for Nalen, who had been taken down by Gunner earlier in the season. In 1953, Nalen rolled through an undefeated dual meet season, then captured his second straight Big Ten title by drilling Iowa's Phil Dugan to the mats. At the NCAA meet in State College, Pennsylvania, Nalen took a 7-4 decision over hometown favorite Dick Lemyre. Named captain for a second time in 1954, Nalen closed out his Big Ten career by decisioning Michigan State's Jim Sinandinos. He ran his career Big Ten mark to 9-0. At the national meet in Norman, Oklahoma, Nalen dropped three competitors to reach the finals, where he decisioned Jim Howard of Ithaca College, 7-2, to become Michigan's first two-time national champion in wrestling. A graduate of the school of education, Nalen still holds the Michigan wrestling record for consecutive wins, collecting his 35th straight victory in his final collegiate meet.

Maize & Blue Item

Presented by Governor G. Mennen Williams in 1953, the six-foot Paul Bunyan Trophy was to be awarded to the winner of the annual Michigan-Michigan State football game. However, as game day got closer, U-M stated that it would not accept the trophy if it won, so as not to tarnish the importance of the Little Brown Jug. MSU, favored by 14 points, grabbed a 14-0 lead, taking 38 plays to drive into the end zone twice and held on to win.

M List: Most Men's NCAA Titles (by Institution)

1. Southern California	68
2. UCLA	60
3. Stanford	45
4. Oklahoma State	42
5. Michigan	28
6. Arkansas	27
7. Yale	25
8. Texas-El Paso	21
9. California, Denver, Indiana, Ohio State	20

America's Time Capsule

October 15, 1954: Hurricane Hazel killed 99 Americans and 249 Canadians.

November 8, 1954: Baseball's Philadelphia Athletics moved to Kansas City.

December 2, 1954: In a vote by U.S. Senators, Sen. Joseph McCarthy was condemned for activities in his anticommunist witch hunt.

May 2, 1955: A Pulitzer prize was awarded to Tennessee Williams for his drama, *Cat on a Hot Tin Roof.*

May 23, 1955: The Presbyterian Church approved the ordination of women ministers.

University Lore

On April 12, 1955, the world's attention was focused on Rackham Auditorium. With the words "safe, effective and potent," Dr. Thomas Francis of the School of Public Health summarized the results of his massive, year-long field trial of Dr. Jonas Salk's polio vaccine. The vaccine was given to 444,000 children the 210,000 received a placebo. Some 1.8 million IBM punch cards containing 144 million bits of data about the children were analyzed at U-M by statisticians and epidemiologists in determing that the vaccine was 60-90 percent effective in preventing poliomyelitis.

Michigan Moment

MICHIGAN TRACK TEAM BACK ON TOP

In the first 27 seasons where Michigan had participated in both the Western Conference indoor and outdoor track championships, the Wolverines had swept the titles 11 times. The Maize and Blue had done so in 1944, before handing over the title of Conference powerhouse to Illinois, who took both championships six times in the next ten seasons, including 1950-53. In those eight meets, Michigan had finished second to the Illini six times. At the 1955 indoor meet in East Lansing, Michigan returned to first place in an easy win over second-place Michigan State. Junior Peter Gray won both the 880-yard and 1000-yard races, while John Moule broke the tape in the one-mile run. Moule's win marked the fourth consecutive meet where a Michigan athlete had finished first in the mile race. Ron Wallingford was the victor in the two-mile race as Michigan swept the distance portion of the meet. Senior James Love took first in the 70-yard hurdles, while Dave Owen began a three-year dynasty as the best in the Big Ten in the shot put. At the outdoor championships in Columbus, Michigan nearly doubled the score of second-place Illinois to win its first outdoor track championship in eleven years. The winners list featured several repeats for the Maize and Blue; Gray in the 880-yard run, Moule in the mile run, and Owen in the shot put. There was additional help as Mark Booth repeated his 1954 win in the high jump, Bob Appleman was victorious in the pole vault and Clarence Stielstra became Michigan's first winner in the outdoor long jump since 1939.

Photo: Rentschler

U-M"s track team in 1955.

CHAMPIONSHIP *Moment*

MICHIGAN HOCKEY ENJOYS ALL-STAR SEASON

The three-year national champion streak of the Michigan hockey team had come to an end with a loss in the semi-finals in 1954. Trying to climb back to the top, the Wolverines closed out the 1954 portion of their 1954-55 season by dropping three of four games on a road trip in Colorado. Two losses in the next six games left the team's record at an un-Michigan-like 8-5-1 with eight games remaining. The Wolverines would roar to victory in each of those contests, winning just one game by less than two goals. Featuring dangerous players as leading scorer Bill McFarland, Mike Buchanan, Dick Dunnigan, Tom Rendall, Bob Schiller and goalie Lorne Howes, the Wolverines invaded the Broadmoor Ice Palace in Colorado Springs in search of national title number five. A 7-3 win over Harvard set up a championship game between Michigan and the Western Intercollegiate Hockey Champion Colorado College Tigers. The Tigers, who had taken two games from U-M in that disastrous Colorado trip in December, were looking for revenge for the 1952 title game won by U-M. The Wolverines took a 4-2 third-period lead on a goal by Jerry Karpinka, but a determined CC team closed the advantage to one with less than three minutes. The Tigers peppered Howes with shots from nearly every angle, but the goalie compiled a game total of 47 saves. The close game came down to the final three seconds when McFarland slammed the puck the length of the ice into an empty Colorado College net for a 5-3 victory.

CHAMPION OF THE WEST

GUS STAGER

In the annals of collegiate swimming history Augustus "Gus" Stager is still one of the great names in the history of the sport. He was named to the coaches' All-American team every year he competed for the Wolverines starting in 1946. Swimming became Stager's life after an outstanding high school career at Newark Academy. After a brilliant collegiate career, Gus took over as the Michigan head coach from the legendary Matt Mann in 1954. He held that position for 25 years, retiring in 1979. During his reign, his teams compiled a 169-39-1 dual meet record. Four times his teams captured NCAA titles and three times they were Big Ten Conference champions. He was called back out of retirement to coach the 1981-82 season. Under his direction were many national champions, including: Carl Robie, Juan Bello, Tony Tashnick, Dick Hanley, Jack Wardrop and Ron Clark to mention a few. In 1960, he was selected as head coach of the United States Swimming Team for the Olympics in Rome. His other honors include the National Collegiate and Scholastic Swimming Trophy, 1979; induction as honoree into the International Swimming Hall of Fame, 1982; induction into the University of Michigan Hall of Honor, 1982 and the Newark Academy Hall of Fame, 1983.

Maize & Blue Item

Mark Jaffe at number two and Al Mann at number five won singles' titles and Michigan swept all three doubles' competitions as the Wolverines won their first Big Ten tennis title since 1945. Barry MacKay and Dick Potter won the number-one title while Mann and Bob Nederlander took number two and Bob Paley and Jaffe took the number-three crown. Coach Bill Murphy's group ended Indiana's three-year domination of the event.

M List

Michigan's Hockey All-Americans

Since 1948, 39 Michigan hockey players have been named All-Americans at least once in their careers. Twelve of those players have been honored two or more times. A list of those honorees appears below:

Wally Gacek	1948-49	Lorne Howes	1955-56
Connie Hill	1948-49	Bill McFarland	1955-56
Wally Grant	1948-49-50	Bob Schiller	1955-56
Ross Smith	1949-50	Bob White	1958-59
John Matchefts	1951-53	Red Berenson	1961-62
George Chin	1952-53	Brendan Morrison	1995-96

1955-56

MICHIGAN MOMENT

America's Time Capsule

September 21, 1955: Rocky Marciano defeated Archie Moore to retain the heavyweight boxing title.

October 4, 1955: The Brooklyn Dodgers beat their cross-town rivals, the Yankees, in Game Seven of the World Series.

February 6, 1956: The University of Alabama's first black student, Autherine Lucy, was suspended, ending three days of campus violence.

April 19, 1956: American actress Grace Kelly was married to Prince Ranier of Monaco.

June 16, 1956: Dr. Cary Middlecoff defeated Ben Hogan and Julius Boros by one stroke to win the U.S. Open golf tournament.

University Lore

In the fall of 1955, plans for development of an upper-level, two-year campus in Flint were approved. The following spring, ground was broken for the John C. and Isabell T. Mott Memorial Building. Instruction began in the fall term of 1956 with 14 full-time instructors and 167 third-year students, most from Flint Junior College. Twenty-eight courses in 13 subjects were offered. A four-year curriculum was instituted in 1965. The campus floundered, however, until 1971, when it became a full college with its own chancellor and increased autonomy and financial support.

"M" HOCKEY TEAM WINS SIXTH NCAA TITLE

Claiming the program's fifth national championship in 1954-55, the Michigan hockey team aimed to repeat its performance in 1955-56. After a 2-1-1 start, Michigan reeled off winning streaks of seven and nine games to enter the tournament with an 18-2-1 record. Michigan allowed only 49 goals during the year, the fewest since 1944, and allowed more than three goals in a game only once. The team was captained by Bill McFarland, who led the team in scoring with 19 goals and 28 assists. In the semifinal matchup at Colorado Springs, Colorado, Michigan faced St. Lawrence, the team the Wolverines had defeated to reach the final in 1952. A goal by Ed Switzer scored just 23 seconds into the opening period. Later in the period, U-M went up 4-2 on Ted Schiller's score at the 13:11 mark. Early in the second period, Michigan Tech scored two goals in less than two and a half minutes early in the second period to take a 5-4 advantage. The lead was short lived as Switzer tied the game at 5-5 with his second goal of the game at 7:58. Neither team scored for over six minutes, before Switzer completed his hat trick with a 20 foot blast at 14:38 and McDonald followed with a goal 11 seconds later. Both goalies made 19 saves in the final stanza as Michigan held on for a 7-5 win and national championship number six. Lorne Howes, who made 76 saves in the two games, was named team MVP and tournament MVP for the 1956 season.

Photo: U-M Athletic Dept.

NCAA champions, the U-M hockey team in 1956.

CHAMPIONSHIP *Moment*

WOLVERINES-HAWKEYES BATTLE ON GRIDIRON

The Iowa Hawkeye football team arrived at Michigan Stadium not having beaten the Wolverines since 1924. A 14-0 lead at the break gave the visitors confidence of their first win in Ann Arbor. However, Michigan came out of the locker room fired up, scoring two touchdowns in two minutes and 37 seconds. A missed conversion after the first score left the Wolverines down 14-13 with 6:11 left in the third quarter. Michigan's chances were dimmed again when Iowa scored just before the end of the third quarter to take a 21-13 lead. The Iowa advantage continued until there was just 8:50 left on the clock, with Michigan faced third-and-20 from its own 34-yard line. Jim Maddock found Ron Kramer with a pass, and Kramer skipped 66 yards into the end zone to complete a 91-yard drive. Now trailing by one, Michigan's offense scored touchdowns by Tom Maentz and Tony Branoff, capping a 20-point spree in nine minutes. U-M's 33-20 victory lifted its season mark to 6-0.

CHAMPION OF THE WEST

RON KRAMER

During his career at Michigan, Ron Kramer was a nine-time letter winner, earning three letters in football, basketball and track. While many fans remember Kramer as one of the all-time great Wolverine football players, it is astonishing to note that Kramer garnered MVP honors for three straight seasons on the hardwood, became the team captain and then set the all-time Michigan scoring mark with 1,124 points. On the football field, Kramer made his name as a hard-nosed, fierce multi-dimensional two-way player. He played offensive and defensive end, running back, quarterback, placekicker and wide receiver—often in the same game. Kramer's phenomenal abilities were recognized by coaches and media around the country, who named him a consensus All-American in 1955 and 1956. The university retired his number 87 after his senior season. In 1957, Kramer joined the Green Bay Packers, playing tight end under coaching great Vince Lombardi. He was a member of the Packers' 1961 and 1962 World Championship teams, earning All-Pro honors both of those years. Kramer finished his pro career with the Detroit Lions from 1964 until 1968. He stayed in the Metro Detroit area working his way to become a Vice President at Paragon Steel. He has also worked as a football color analyst for Michigan football on radio stations WAAM and WWJ. He was inducted into the Michigan Sports Hall of Fame in 1971, the Green Bay Packers Hall of Fame in 1974, the National Football Foundation Hall of Fame in 1978 and received the NCAA's 1981 Silver Anniversary Award. Kramer represents maufacturers in the steel business as the President of Ron Kramer Industries, founded in 1981. He resides in Fenton, Michigan.

Maize & Blue Item

Early in the 1955-56 season, Cliff Keen's wrestlers had dropped three straight dual meets and looked to have little chance to repeat their 1955 Conference title. Eyes opened when the team won six straight meets in February, and the team disproved all doubters by upsetting Iowa in the Big Ten Championship in March. Mike Rodriguez and Jack Marchello each won at their respective weights, while two other Wolverines reached championship finals.

M *List*

M Hockey's Final Four Appearances

Year	Site	Michigan Place	Year	Site	Michigan Place
1948	Colorado Springs, CO	First	1957	Colorado Springs, CO	Second
1949	Colorado Springs, CO	Third	1962	Hamilton, NY	Third
1950	Colorado Springs, CO	Third	1964	Denver, CO	First
1951	Colorado Springs, CO	First	1977	Detroit, MI	Second
1952	Colorado Springs, CO	First	1992	Albany, NY	Tie-Third
1953	Colorado Springs, CO	First	1993	Milwaukee, WI	Tie-Third
1954	Colorado Springs, CO	Third	1995	Providence, RI	Tie-Third
1955	Colorado Springs, CO	First	1996	Cincinnati, OH	First
1956	Colorado Springs, CO	First	1997	Milwaukee, WI	Tie-Third

1956-57

America's Time Capsule

October 8, 1956: Don Larsen of the New York Yankees hurled the first perfect game in World Series history.

November 6, 1956: Dwight Eisenhower defeated Illinois governor Adlai Stevenson in the presidential election.

January 21, 1957: NBC carried the first nationally televised videotaped broadcast, a recording of the presidential inauguration ceremonies.

Spring 1957: Fred Zollner, the owner and founder of the Fort Wayne Zollner Pistons, elected to move his National Basketball Association team to Detroit.

July 12, 1957: Surgeon General Leroy Burney reported that a link between cigarette smoking and lung cancer had been established.

University Lore

On December 17, 1956, the Ford Motor Company donated Henry Ford's Fair Lane estate and 219 acres to the University along with a $6.5 million bequest to establish the Dearborn Center of the University. The combined gifts were the largest ever made by a company to an educational institution. Conceived as a program in cooperative education, combining classroom and shop instruction with practical work in industry, the Dearborn Center opened in the fall of 1959 offering upper level and graduate course work. The Center expanded to a four-year campus in 1971.

Michigan Moment

TENNIS REIGNS AS NCAA KINGS

After compiling its third straight undefeated dual season, Michigan rolled into the 1957 Big Ten tennis championship with a 43-match winning streak and as heavy favorites at Evanston, Illinois. Burdened with heavy expectations, the Wolverines did not disappoint, doubling the score of the second-place Wildcats and capturing their third consecutive Conference title. The Wolverines swept all three doubles matches, behind the duos of Barry MacKay-Dick Potter, Mark Jaffe-John Erickson and Dale Jensen-John Harris. MacKay, Potter, Jaffe, Erickson and Jensen all won singles titles as well in one of the most dominating performances in Conference history. But the Wolverines would not stop at a Conference title in 1957. Under head coach Bill Murphy, the team captured the NCAA crown in Salt Lake City by a single point over second-place Tulane. The second-ranked MacKay captured the singles title with a hard-fought 6-4, 3-6, 6-2, 3-6, 6-3 win over top-ranked Sammy Giammalva of Texas. While MacKay became the first U-M singles player to win an individual championship, his bid for a doubles crown with Potter was stopped in the final round. Erickson and Potter each advanced to the third round in singles competition. Michigan's NCAA tennis crown was the school's second national title of 1957, who also had captured the national swimming crown in March.

Photo: U-M Athletic Dept.

U-M's tennis team in 1957.

CHAMPIONSHIP *Moment*

"M" FOOTBALL STADIUM EXPANDED TO 100,000+

When the 1956 football season opened at Michigan Stadium on September 29, Fielding Yost's original dream had been realized. Stadium capacity was now 101,001, a six-figure number Yost had envisioned when drawing up stadium plans in 1927. The increase from the old capacity of 97,239 had been announced on October 27, 1955, when Athletic Director Fritz Crisler brought the developments into the spotlight. The work included removal of the old press box and creation of a new one. The area where the old press box had stood was replaced with 1,300 seats for spectators. Meanwhile, a new media communication center was put atop and at the edge of the Stadium. The new press box included three television booths, a facility unavailable in the old model. Seating was also added where the 1949 expansion had left off, along the top rows of the stadium. The filling of the gap on the west side made the stadium a perfect bowl. Additionally, one row of box seats was replaced by benches, a move which would eventually claim all the box seats in the 1973 expansion. Michigan first hosted a six-figure crowd when it played Michigan State in front of 101,001 fans on October 6, 1956.

CHAMPIONSHIP *Moment*

MICHIGAN SPOILS IOWA'S PERFECT SEASON

Led by former Michigan quarterback Forest Evashevski, the Iowa Hawkeye team was 5-0 and sailing toward a Rose Bowl bid. The Hawkeyes shrugged off an early Ron Kramer field goal and scored two second-quarter touchdowns to take a 14-3 lead. For the fourth straight year, Evashevski's troops scored two touchdowns before U-M had crossed the goal line. And for the fourth straight season, Michigan would come back to take victory from the jaws of defeat. A 12-play, 69-yard drive brought the Wolverines within four points when Mike Shatusky scored from the 3-yard line. The 26-year-old, who was playing due to an injury to starter Terry Barr, scored the first touchdown of his career. Despite the third-quarter score, Iowa held a 14-10 edge. With 10:17 left in the game, U-M received the ball on its own 20 and began an awe-inspiring drive. After 19 plays and over 10 minutes of ball control, Shatusky scored again, going in from a yard out to break Iowan hearts yet again. The loss would be Iowa's only setback of the season, ultimately advancing to the Rose Bowl.

Mike Shatusky

Maize & Blue Item

At the Big Ten Championship, the swim team finished runner-up for the fifth straight year. However, at the NCAA meet, Dick Kimball reeled in two diving titles and Cy Hopkins placed first in the 200 breaststroke as U-M overcame Yale to win the national title. Fritz Meyers had started U-M out on the right foot when he chopped 42 seconds off his previous best time to win the 1500 meter freestyle event.

M List: Michigan Stadium Expansions

Since being built with a capacity of 72,000 in 1927, Michigan Stadium's capacity has been expanded on six occasions.

Year	Capacity
1927	84,401
1928	85,753
1949	97,239
1956	101,001
1973	101,701
1992	102,501

MICHIGAN MOMENT

WOLVERINE SWIM TEAM DUNKS ITS COMPETITION

Runners-up in the Big Ten swimming standings for five straight seasons, Michigan's 1958 squad focused its sites on breaking the school's 10- year Conference title drought. Following the second day of competition, Tony Tashnick had staked Michigan out to a 20-point lead over second-place Michigan State and Ohio State. The junior had swam the 200 butterfly in 2:06, shaving three seconds off the old Big Ten record. Tashnick followed this performance with an Iowa pool record 2:08.6 in the 200-yard individual medley. Other notable Michigan swimmers on the first day of finals competition included Cyrus Hopkins, the 1957 winner in the 200 butterfly, who finished second in 1958, and Dick Kimball, who placed third in one meter diving. To emerge with the Conference championship, the Wolverines could not let up on the final day. Determined to take the title, the swimmers kept the pressure on. Hopkins repeated his 1957 individual championship in the 200-yard breaststroke to become the sixth Michigan winner in this event in eight years. Tashnick became a three-time individual winner by winning the 100-yard butterfly, and Dick Hanley rounded out the Michigan champions with a first-place finish in the 100-yard freestyle. After finishing in first place by 36 points over Michigan State, the men's swim team would repeat as Conference champions in 1959 and 1960, with second-place finishes every season from 1961 to 1973.

Photo: U-M Athletic Dept.

Tony Tashnick

America's Time Capsule

September 25, 1957: President Eisenhower sent 1,000 Army paratroopers to Little Rock, Arkansas to enforce the desegregation of Central High School.

October 4, 1957: The Soviet Union launched Sputnik I, the first Earth satellite.

October 10, 1957: The Milwaukee Braves beat the New York Yankees in Game Seven of the 54th annual World Series.

January 31, 1958: Explorer I, the first U.S. Earth satellite, was launched from Cape Canaveral, Fla.

March 25, 1958: Sugar Ray Robinson regained the world middleweight boxing title for an unprecedented fifth time, defeating Carmen Basilio.

University Lore

The Undergraduate Library, familiarly known as "the UGLi," opened its doors in 1957. Described in publicity brochures as "one of the most unusual buildings in the world," it was only the second college library designed for use by undergraduates. The $3.1 million building was intended to be a place where students would want to spend many hours. Open stacks, bright colors, comfortable furniture, group study rooms, and audio-visual facilities were among the UGLi's features. It was renamed the Harold and Vivian Shapiro Undergraduate Library in 1995.

CHAMPIONSHIP *Moment*

HOME CROWD ENJOYS "M" SUCCESS

They called it the "Dead Sea." Disgruntled coaches unhappy with the slow times seen at Michigan's Matt Mann Pool assigned it a nickname reserved for non-lively entities. Unlike the implication, the Wolverines were anything but dead in the 1958 NCAA championships, as they won their second straight and eighth overall NCAA title in front of a home crowd. Michigan came into the meet as the favorite of the three teams which had dominated NCAA swimming for the past 20 years, U-M, Yale and Ohio State. The Wolverines hit trouble on the second day when U-M's Tony Tashnick failed to qualify for the 200 indvidual medley by swimming a slow preliminary designed to save his energy for the final. Tashnick responded by setting an American record in the 200 butterfly, but Michigan trailed the Buckeyes, 43-42. A capacity crowd of 3,000 fans was augmented by an extra addition for the final day of competition. Detroit's WJBK-TV brought its cameras for the first-ever televised coverage of a national collegiate swim meet. In front of it all, Michigan scored 29 points as the Buckeyes were shutout. Tashnick gathered his second honor by tying the meet record in the 100 butterfly. Cy Hopkins finished second in both the 200 breaststroke and 200 individual medley while Dick Hanley was the runner up in the 220 freestyle to help Michigan hold off Yale and Michigan State.

CHAMPION OF THE WEST

RAY FISHER

Ray Fisher is a legend in Michigan baseball. He was recommended to take over the coaching reins by Branch Rickey and coached Michigan from 1921 until 1958 going 637-294-8 for a winning percentage of .687. His U-M teams won 14 Big Ten titles and the 1953 NCAA College World Series. Fisher also was a legend in Major League baseball. Born in Middlebury, Vermont on October 4, 1887, Fisher played from 1910 through 1920, compiling a record of 102-98 with a sparkling ERA of 2.38 as a pitcher for both the New York Highlanders (later the Yankees) and Cincinnati Reds. As a Red in 1919, Fisher drew the starting assignment against Dickie Kerr, one of the players untouched by the charges that members of the Chicago White Sox threw the World Series. Kerr bested Fisher in a pitchers' duel, 3-0, in the infamous Black Sox Scandal. When Fisher took the job in Ann Arbor, Cincinnati placed Fisher on the ineligible list. After the 1921 season, Fisher appealed for reinstatement to Commissioner Kenesaw Landis. Landis suspended him for life. While the ban was never lifted, many observers say a close look into Fisher's problems with pro baseball provide an insight into player-owner problems that presently plague major league baseball. He was later reinstated. He died at the age of 95 on November 3, 1982.

Maize & Blue Item

Though in the shadow of Ron Kramer, Jim Pace added to Michigan's football history from 1955-57. As a running back, receiver and punt returner for U-M, Pace's was nearly impossible to stop. He led the Conference in scoring with 10 touchdowns while rushing for 664 yards. The Grand Rapids, Michigan native was also a two-year letter winner for the track team, earning the Big Ten 60-yard dash crown indoors in 1957.

M List

Ray Fisher's All-time "M" Baseball Team

In October 1956, Michigan's Ray Fisher was asked to name his all-time baseball team in his 35 years as head coach. Here were his selections:

First base	Bennie Oosterbaan	1926-28
Second base	Buck Giles	1924-25
	Bud Morse	1927
Third base	Bud Chamberlain	1940-42
Shortstop	Bruce Haynam	1951-53
Outfield	Dick Wakefield	1941
	Ray Neblung	1927-29
	Bill Gregor	1944-45
	Don Lund	1943-45
Catchers	Jack Blott	1922-24
	Ernie Vick	1921-24
Pitchers	Pete Appleton	1924-26
	Bill McAfee	1928-29
	Burger Larson	1935-36
	Johnny Gee	1935-37

America's Time Capsule

September 30, 1958: Arkansas Gov. Orval Faubus defied the Supreme Court's ruling against racial segregation in public schools.

December 28, 1958: The Baltimore Colts won the NFL championship, defeating the New York Giants in overtime.

January 3, 1959: President Dwight Eisenhower proclaimed Alaska as the 49th state,

May 28, 1959: The U.S. Army launched two monkeys into space. They were recovered unhurt from the Caribbean Sea after a 300-mile-high flight.

August 21, 1959: Hawaii was admitted to the union as the 50th state.

University Lore

The State of Michigan's financial crisis had severe repercussions for the University. Beginning in November 1958, the state withheld its monthly disbursements, forcing the University to borrow to meet its operating expenses. By March, $4 million had been borrowed to meet its payroll and banks had informed the University "no further credit can be extended." Talk of "payless paydays" spread throughout campus and deans worried about losing faculty members.

Michigan Moment

"M" TENNIS TEAM RENEWS DOMINANCE

Photo: U-M Athletic Dept.

Jon Erickson

Entering the 1959 Conference championship, Michigan's tennis team looked to be making great strides to take back its title. U-M had disposed of all but one of its dual meet opponents in the regular season, including a spotless mark against Conference schools. The first day of play saw every Michigan athlete sweep his opponent, with the closest Wolverine match involving Gerry Dubie, who fell behind 1-4 in the second set, but rallied for a 6-4 win. Success on the second day followed much the same pattern, with each player subduing his opponent. After Michigan's first four singles players won with ease, Frank Fulton lost the first set to Ohio State's Jake Schlosser, 4-6, and trailed in set two, 4-5. But Fulton rallied to win the last three games, and capped his win with a 6-4 score in the final set. The Wolverine doubles teams easily defeated all comers on day two. Michigan closed the 50th Big Ten tennis tournament by sweeping all of the nine titles en route to becoming only the second team to amass the maximum 87 points. The No. 1 singles title was the most hotly contested, with Michigan's Jon Erickson going up against Iowa's Art Andrews. The grueling 16-game opening set finally ended when Erickson rallied from a 40-15 deficit to take the game and the match, 9-7. Erickson then defeated Art Andrews, 6-4, in the second set as the Wolverines were off and running. Gerry Dubie, Bob Sassone, and Larry Zaitzeff swept past their opponents to earn singles titles. Fulton lost the first set of his match, 1-6, but responded with scores of 6-0 and 6-3 before Wayne Peaock made Michigan six-for-six with a 6-4, 6-4 triumph. In doubles, Erickson and Dubie teamed up to take down Iowa's tandem of Andrews and John Nadig, 6-0, 6-4. Zaitzeff and Peacock blasted a pair from Illinois before Fulton and John Wiley defeated another Illinois duo to close the Michigan sweep.

CHAMPIONSHIP *Moment*

SWIMMING TEAM SHATTERS RECORDS

In the confines of Michigan State's new Intramural Pool, Michigan dedicated the building by scoring a then-record 148 points in the 1959 Big Ten Championships. Four American records, six NCAA records and nine Big Ten marks were shattered as the Wolverines more than doubled the score of second-place Indiana. Junior Tony Tashnick smashed American records in taking both the 200 individual medley and 200 butterfly while also finishing first in the 100 butterfly. Michigan's Ron Clark also set an American record, finishing the 200-yard breaststroke nearly two seconds faster than anyone else had ever achieved. The record-setting Wolverines would continue their prowess in the national forum, racking up a record 137.5 points, in the 1959 NCAA meet at Ithaca, New York, Dave Gillanders, a sophomore, set American records in both the 100 and 200 butterfly events, narrowly beating out Tashnick each time. In a meet where the old marks seemed to fall at will, the Wolverines clinched the team title before the meet hit the halfway mark. Hungarian refugee and Michigan swimmer Jon Urbanchek surprised many with a second-place finish in the meet's opening event, the 1500 freestyle. From there, Michigan would place at least one swimmer in the top three in 15 of 16 events, including Frank Legacki (100 freestyle), Dick Hanley (220 freestyle) and the 400 freestyle relay team, which all copped top honors. Under fifth-year coach Gus Stager, the 1959 Michigan swim team was called, "the greatest collegiate swimming team of all time."

CHAMPION OF THE WEST

DICK KIMBALL

While Dick Kimball's high school and collegiate career took him through three different midwestern states, his coaching tenure has taken the legendary Michigan man across the nation and around the world. Following his high schooling in Rochester, Minnesota, and a year at the University of Oklahoma, Kimball transferred to U-M in 1956. In 1957, Kimball became the first Wolverine in 20 years to win both the NCAA one-meter and three-meter titles as Gus Stager's team claimed the national championship. Kimball would continue as an All-American for the next two seasons while also lettering three years and gaining All-American honors on the trampoline for Newt Loken. In 1960, Kimball was hired on as Harlan's replacement as Michigan diving coach. He has remained with Michigan ever since, rising up to the rank of the Big Ten dean of coaches and adding the women's diving program to his responsibilities. In the 37 seasons in between, Kimball has served as an Olympic coach for five U.S. teams, tutored four Olympic gold medalist divers and seven NCAA champions. He has earned three NCAA diving coach of the year honors and four Big Ten diving coach of the year accolades.

Maize & Blue Item

At the 1959 Big Ten Gymnastics meet, Ed Cole had become Michigan's first-ever three-time champion, taking top honors on the trampoline. Knowing the 1959 NCAA competition in Berkeley, California would be his last, the U-M senior put on a nearly flawless show and captured the national crown. Cole's teammate, Frank Newman finished fourth as Michigan continued its national dominance of the trampoline that would extend through the 1960s.

M List: Collegiate All-Americans Who Are Now Head Coaches at Michigan

Hockey	Red Berenson (Michigan)
Wrestling	Dale Bahr (Iowa)
Cross Country	Mike McGuire (Michigan)
Field Hockey	Marcia Pankratz (Iowa)
Women's Gymnastics	Bev Plocki (Alabama)
Soccer	Debbie Belkin (Massachusetts)
Men's Track	Jack Harvey (Michigan)
Women's Cross Country	Mike McGuire (Michigan)
Men's Swimming and Diving	Jon Urbanchek (Michigan)

1959-60

America's Time Capsule

September 15, 1959: Soviet Premier Nikita Khrushchev arrived in the United States for meetings with President Eisenhower.

October 18, 1959: The Chicago White Sox were beaten by the Los Angeles Dodgers for the World Series title.

January 4, 1960: The United Steel Workers and the nation's steel companies agreed on a wage increase to settle the six-month-long strike.

May 1, 1960: A United States U-2 reconnaissance plane was shot down inside the U.S.S.R., causing Soviet Premier Khrushchev to cancel a planned summit meeting in Paris.

June 20, 1960: Floyd Patterson knocked out Ingemar Johansson to become the first boxer in history to regain the heavyweight championship.

University Lore

The American Voter, a groundbreaking study of the behavior and attitudes of the American electorate, was published by Angus Campbell, Philip Converse, Warren Miller and Donald Stokes, all of U-M's Institute for Social Research. Hailed as "a monumental work by any standard," it used sophisticated demographic survey research and computer analysis techniques to challenge many long-standing beliefs about American politics. Still a standard reference in political science, the study has been updated several times.

Michigan Moment

"M" FOOTBALL MAKES A CHANGE

Though Bennie Oosterbaan's coaching career began smoothly and with success, the dynasty could not last forever. Following Michigan's 1951 Rose Bowl victory, the remainder of the 1950s was not as kind to Michigan football. Though players such as Ron Kramer, Jim Pace, Tom Maentz and Terry Barr met with individual success, the Wolverines as a unit failed to win a single Big Ten title. The 1951 team posted a 4-5 record, Michigan's first losing season since 1936. Michigan posted a winning record in 1952, despite losing its first two games of the season. The middle portion of the season went well, with the Wolverines going 5-1, including an upset of 10th-ranked Purdue. A 4-0 start in 1953 had many fans thinking Rose Bowl early in the season, but Michigan dropped three of its next four games to end those dreams. A 20-0 shutout of Ohio State in the season finale earned Michigan 20th place in the final AP poll. Ron Kramer burst onto the scene in 1954 and helped the Wolverines to a second-place finish. High hopes were held for the Wolverines in 1955 and the preseason polls ranked Michigan third in the nation. The team did not disappoint, starting 6-0, but two losses in the final three games kept the Wolverines away from the Conference title. Another 7-2 finish in 1956 left the Wolverines just short of first place in the Big Ten yet again. Michigan fell to 5-3-1 in 1957, and dropped to 2-6-1 in 1958. Bennie Oosterbaan retired following the season, and former Wolverine star Chalmers "Bump" Elliott was called upon to resurrect the team. While Bump's first team finished only 4-5, better days were ahead.

Photo: U-M Athletic Dept.

U-M football's Stan Noskin in 1959.

CHAMPIONSHIP *Moment*

MICHIGAN WRESTLERS REGAIN BIG TEN TITLE

Cliff Keen's matmen entered the Big Ten championship with a 9-2 dual meet record, aiming to hoist the Conference title in front of its home crowd. The Big Ten wrestling tournament was going to be a dogfight between Michigan, Michigan State, Iowa, and defending champion Minnesota. With undefeated Dennis Fitzgerald (167 pounds) and Karl Fink (177), U-M had the personnel to win. After preliminaries and semifinals, Michigan had placed seven out of its eight wrestlers in either championship or consolation finals and led the pack by 13 points. Four Wolverines advanced to the championship round, Ambi Wilbanks, Fritz Kellerman, Jim Blaker and Fitzgerald. Ironically, the only U-M wrestler eliminated was Fink, who dropped his opening two matches. On the final day of competition, all four Wolverine wrestlers in championship finals copped champion honors. Wilbanks scored the upset of the meet by taking down 1959 champion Norm Young of Michigan State with three seconds remaining. When the dust had settled, Michigan had a Conference record 65 points and won by the biggest margin in 10 years.

CHAMPION OF THE WEST

"BUMP" ELLIOTT

As a Marine trainee during World War II, Chalmers "Bump" Elliott was a three-sport star at Purdue, playing baseball, basketball and football for the Boilermakers. An outstanding player, Elliott was the starting left halfback for the 1943 Purdue football team, which tied for the Big Ten title with Michigan. When the war ended and Elliott was discharged, the Bloomington, Illinois native returned to Michigan, where his brother Pete was the Wolverine quarterback. Elliott played sparingly during the '46 football season and could be found on the baseball diamond in the spring. In 1947, Elliott started all 10 games at right halfback in Michigan's perfect 10-0 season. He was second on the team in rushing and second in punt returns, while his 16 receptions for 318 yards paced the team in both those categories. Elliott was named the Conference MVP by the *Chicago Tribune*. With his playing days over, Elliott chose to return to the gridiron, but on the sidelines as a coach. He took a position as the assistant coach at Oregon State in 1948, then served at Iowa from 1952-56 and U-M from 1957-58. His apprenticeship ended when he was offered Michigan's head coaching job in 1959. Chalmers Elliott finished with a record of 51-42-2 over his 10-year coaching career, including 31-19 over the final five seasons. He eventually served as athletic director at Iowa from 1970 to 1991.

Maize & Blue Item

While Cliff Keen's wrestling squad was winning in Ann Arbor, Don Canham's track team was defending its 1959 Indoor Track title in a snowy Columbus. The Wolverines placed in 13 of 15 events as 13 different runners earned points for U-M. Only one man stood atop the victory stand twice, Michigan's Tom Robinson, who defended his titles in the 60- and 300-yard dash.

M List

Michigan Decade-by-Decade Football Success

The Wolverines have enjoyed six decades where they have won more than three-quarters of the games in that particular 10-year span.

Years	Games	W	L	T	Pct.
1879	2	1	0	1	.750
1880-1889	27	18	9	0	.667
1890-1899	94	72	20	2	.777
1900-1909	93	82	8	3	.898
1910-1919	76	52	18	6	.723
1920-1929	78	58	16	4	.769
1930-1939	83	53	26	4	.663
1940-1949	92	74	15	3	.821
1950-1959	91	52	36	3	.588
1960-1969	97	55	40	2	.577
1970-1979	115	96	16	3	.847
1980-1989	121	90	29	2	.752
1990-1996	85	61	21	3	.735

1960-61

America's Time Capsule

September 26, 1960: Sen. John Kennedy and Vice Pres. Richard Nixon participated in the first of a series of televised presidential campaign debates.

October 13, 1960: Bill Mazeroski of Pittsburgh slammed a game-winning home run against the New York Yankees to give the Pirates the World Series championship.

November 8, 1960: John Kennedy was elected president of the United States in a narrow victory over Richard Nixon.

April 17, 1961: Nearly 2,000 CIA-trained anti-Castro Cuban exiles landed at the Bay of Cochinos in Cuba, in what came to be know as the Bay of Pigs invasion.

May 5, 1961: Alan Shepard made a successful flight in the Project Mercury capsule *Freedom Seven* to become the first American in space.

University Lore

Well after midnight on October 14, 1960, presidential candidate John F. Kennedy arrived at the steps of the Michigan Union. In a short speech he outlined the idea of the Peace Corps, challenging students "to contribute part of your life to this country." By 1966, more than 300 U-M alumni had joined the Peace Corps. U-M grad Jack Hood Vaughn was the Corps' second director. A plaque at the entrance of the Michigan Union commemorates Kennedy's speech.

Michigan Moment

"M" SWIMMERS WIN FOURTH NCAA TITLE IN FIVE YEARS

Entering the 1961 NCAA Men's Swimming Championships in Seattle, Washington, Southern California was the heavy favorite. The Trojans, who had broken Michigan's three-year winning streak in 1960, were led by three-time Olympic champion Murray Rose. Rose would cruise through the championships, breaking records freestyle events, but Michigan would leave Seattle with the designation of national champion. On the second day of competition, Frank Legacki was the first Wolverine champion, tying the NCAA record in the 50-meter freestyle (21.4). After Legacki's victory, Ron Clark led nearly the entire way in the 200 breaststroke. Clark broke his own NCAA and American record of 2:17.6 by an astonishing 4.2 seconds. Dave Gillanders was Michigan's third winner, finishing first in the 200 butterfly with a time of 1:58.6. On the final day of competition, Gillanders set American and NCAA records in the 100 butterfly, finishing first in 52.9 seconds. Don Nelson became the fourth Maize and Blue swimmer to win an individual event with a first-place finish in the 100 breaststroke. Teamwise, Michigan's 85 points was well above second-place USC's 62 or third-place Ohio State's 59, and delivered the Wolverines their fourth NCAA swimming championship in five years.

U-M swimming team in 1961.

CHAMPION OF THE WEST

BILL FREEHAN

An all-state football and baseball player at Bishop Barry H.S. in St. Petersburg, Florida, Royal Oak, Michigan native Bill Freehan decided to stay nearby to play college athletics at the University of Michigan. Though he earned a letter as a sophomore tight end on the football team, Freehan made his loudest noise on the baseball diamond during the 1961 season. In 32 games, the catcher slammed 10 home runs and hit .446 for the 1961 Big Ten Champions. His batting average set a Michigan single-season record, while his .585 Conference mark was a Big Ten record that still stands 35 years later. He also collected Academic All-Big Ten honors in his only collegiate season. Offered a large contract, Freehan signed with the Detroit Tigers during the summer of 1961. He played in four games in the majors in 1961, returning in 1963 and playing through the 1976 campaign, all with the Tigers. Freehan was an 11-time All Star, earning five Gold Glove awards and hitting 200 home runs and driving in 758 runs. He still holds the major league record for career fielding percentage for a catcher (.993). In 1989, Freehan returned to his alma mater and took over the head baseball coaching job, a position he held for six seasons. His coaching highlight came in 1994, when he led the Wolverines to a second-place finish in the Conference playoffs.

another CHAMPION OF THE WEST

JOHN TIDWELL

John W. Tidwell was an explosive scorer with the Wolverine men's basketball team, totaling 1,386 points over his three seasons. A guard, Tidwell burst onto the Michigan basketball scene as a sophomore, averaging 17.6 points and 6.6 rebounds. In both of his last two seasons, Tidwell led the Wolverines in scoring, pouring in 520 points as a junior (21.6 ppg) and 441 as a senior (19.1 ppg). Tidwell was elected captain in 1961 and also earned Michigan's Most Valuable Player Award that season. Tidwell's scoring average of 20.1 places him seventh on the all-time Wolverine record list. Four of the the top 15 Wolverine all-time single-game scoring highs were recorded by Tidwell. He was elected to the Michigan Hall of Honor in 1996. Tidwell is now an OB-GYN for the Mintview Charlotte Women's Specialists in North Carolina.

Maize & Blue Item

At the Big Ten swimming meet in 1961, all eyes were set upon Dave Gillanders, a U-M swimmer who set a world record in the 100-yard butterfly. Gillanders also swam the 200 butterfly in 1:58.4, the second fastest in American history. His heroics would continue at the NCAA meet, as Michigan upset the heavily favored USC Trojans. There he broke his world record in the 100 butterfly (52.9) and earned top honors.

M List: "M" Baseball's Greatest Hitters

In 1961, Bill Freehan st the Michigan standard for highest batting average by hitting .446. Since 1957, 11 Wolverines have hit .400 or higher:

Player	Average	Season
Bill Freehan	.446	1961
Jim Paciorek	.443	1982
Casey Close	.440	1986
Ken Hayward	.432	1985
Hal Morris	.421	1985
Scott Weaver	.418	1995
Mike Watters	.417	1985
Rick Leach	.404	1978
Steve Finken	.404	1988
Tim Flannelly	.402	1990
Ken Tippery	.400	1957

1961-62

America's Time Capsule

October 1, 1961: Roger Maris of the New York Yankees hit his 61st home run, breaking Babe Ruth's single-season record.

February 10, 1962: Jim Beatty became the first American to break the four-minute mile indoors, registering a time of 3:58.9 in Los Angeles.

February 20, 1962: Astronaut John Glenn became the first American to orbit Earth, circling the globe three times aboard *Friendship 7*.

March 2, 1962: Wilt Chamberlain of the Philadelphia Warriors became the first NBA player to score 100 points in a game.

August 5, 1962: Actress Marilyn Monroe, 36, died in her Los Angeles home of an apparent overdose of sleeping pills.

University Lore

The University dedicated its new Botanical Garden in May of 1962. The 200-acre site on Dixboro Road was donated by U-M Regent Frederick C. Matthaei. The herbarium housed specimens of some 700 plants native to the site as well as numerous other North American and exotic species, making it the third-largest University-owned herbarium. Renamed Matthaei Botanical Gardens in 1969, it remains an active research and educational center as well as a popular site for tourists and local plant lovers.

Michigan Moment

MARATHON VICTORY ENABLES U-M TO WIN BASEBALL TITLE

Though the Wolverine baseball squad failed to repeat as Big Ten titlists, Don Lund's 1962 team (24-12) played well enough to garner an at-large regional bid. Senior John Kerr was Michigan's ace in the regionals, pitching 17 innings in one day as the Maize and Blue knocked off Big Ten champ Illinois, 5-1, and Mid-American Conference champion Western Michigan, 3-2 in ten innings. A 7-6 win over the Broncos the next day sent Michigan to the College World Series for the first time since 1953, a year they won the title. U-M beat Texas, Holy Cross and Florida State before meeting the Longhorns in the double-elimination contest. The game was scoreless after six innings, but Texas would romp the rest of the way, holding the Wolverines to just three hits in a 7-0 win. The elimination of Texas the very next day, set up the final game between the Wolverines and Santa Clara. The last game of the college baseball season proved to be a classic. After Santa Clara scored a run in the second inning, Honig homered to even the score. The Broncos brought two runs across in the fifth. Michigan was able to tie the game at 3-3 when starting pitcher Fritz Fisher delivered a key two-out triple. The score remained tied through the 14th inning. Santa Clara reliever Bob Garibaldi retired 14 straight Michigan batters between the 10th and 14th innings, but the Broncos could not muster any offense of their own. Chapman led off the top of the 15th by breaking Garibaldi's string with an infield single. Reliever Jim Bobel, who was batting .143, then drilled a triple to the wall and scored on a wild pitch. The Wolverines led, 5-3, but the Broncos refused to die. The Wolverines let up an infield single, allowing the runner to score on a ground out following a wild pitch, and a throwing error. But Bobel retired the last three men in order, and Michigan claimed its second baseball national championship in the longest title game in history.

Michigan's baseball team in 1962.

CHAMPION OF THE WEST

RED BERENSON

Coming from Regina, Saskatchewan in 1959, Gordon "Red" Berenson had little idea that he would become a part of Michigan's hockey history for the next four decades. Berenson's career would take him from Michigan to the NHL, to an NHL coaching position, and back to Michigan. Berenson's senior year was his best, as he finished with team-leading totals of 43 goals and 70 points. While pacing the WCHA with 41 points en route to league MVP honors, Berenson also picked up his second straight All-American honor. Following his final collegiate game, Berenson headed to Boston to play for the Montreal Canadiens, becoming the first college player to jump immediately to the NHL. Berenson went from the Canadiens to the New York Rangers and then to the St. Louis Blues. On November 7, 1968, Berenson scored four goals in a period and six goals in a game against the Philadelphia Flyers to set a modern-day NHL record. After his playing days ended, Berenson eventually became head coach, winning NHL coach of the year honors in 1980-81. Berenson returned to his alma mater in 1984-85 and recorded 30 season victories six times, five CCHA titles and the 1996 NCAA championship. He has compiled a 334-175-29 record in 12 seasons.

another CHAMPION OF THE WEST

BENNIE McCRAE

As the 20th century entered its latter half, the number of two-sport athletes began to dwindle. While few could keep up with the grueling practices of two sports combined with academic work, even fewer could excel in all three areas. U-M football and track star Bennie McCrae was a notable exception. During the fall season, the Newport News, Virginia native would place the winged helmet upon his head and perform masterfully for the football team. As a sophomore in 1959, the halfback ran for 242 yards and captured All-Conference honorable mention honors. McCrae led the team in rushing as a junior, earning honorable mention accolades once again. An Academic-All Conference selection as a senior, he also climbed his way up to the All-Big Ten first team, averaging over six yards per carry. In the spring, McCrae would shed the pads of football for the less inhibiting apparel of track. McCrae's tackle-evading maneuvers on the gridiron were helpful on the cinders of the track, where the hurdler won three individual Conference championships. In 1961, McCrae set a Conference record of 13.7 seconds in the 120-yard high hurdles, a mark that would stand for over 15 years. As a senior, he would repeat as 120-yard high hurdles champion, in addition to winning the 220-yard low hurdles as U-M claimed a second straight Conference crown. McCrae went on to play 10 years in the NFL with the Chicago Bears and New York Giants.

Maize & Blue Item

Michigan's chances of repeating as Big Ten outdoor track champs seemed remote, as only six of Coach Don Canham's Wolverines qualified for the finals, far shy of Ohio State's and Michigan State's 12 finalists. Bennie McRae won both hurdles events, Rod Denhart set a record in the pole vault, Charles Aquino finished first in the 660 dash, and captain Ergas Leps capped the day by winning the mile and placing second in the 880 dash. When the dust settled, U-M reigned with 48-3/4 points.

M List: Michigan's Singles Champions (Tennis)

Walter Westbrook	1919-20	Joel Ross	1971
Charles Merkel	1923	Victor Amaya	1973-74
Andy Paton	1948	Jeff Etterbeek	1978
Barry MacKay	1956-57	Michaael Leach	1980
Jon Erickson	1959	Dan Goldberg	1986-88
Ray Senkowski	1961	Ed Nagel	1987
Dick Dell	1969	MaliVai Washington	1989
Mark Conti	1970	Peter Pusztai	1996

1962-63

America's Time Capsule

October 1, 1962: James Meredith, escorted by U.S. marshals, became the first black to attend classes at the University of Mississippi. Two men were killed in the ensuing mob violence.

October 22, 1962: President Kennedy addressed the nation on television regarding the Cuban missile crisis. The missile bases were dismantled by the Soviet Union 11 days later.

May 7, 1963: The communications satellite Telstar 2 was launched from Cape Canaveral, Florida and began relaying television signals between the United States and Europe.

June 26, 1963: President Kennedy spoke to a crowd of more than 1,000,000 adjacent to the Berlin Wall in Germany.

August 28, 1963: Dr. Martin Luther King presented his "I have a dream" speech to a crowd of 200,000 from the steps of the Lincoln Memorial in Washington, D.C.

University Lore

The University of Michigan · Artes · Scientia · Veritas · 1817

Groundbreaking for the School of Music marked a new phase in the expansion of the North Campus. The Eero Saarinen-designed building brought together school activities that had been spread over 13 buildings and permitted enrollment to increase for the first time since 1946. Saarinen had created a design plan for the North Campus, but the Music School was the one building he wanted to personally create. He was taken ill and died before completion of the building in 1964, but had watched construction progress from his room in the University Hospital.

Michigan Moment

"M" GYMNASTS CLAIM BIG TEN AND NCAA TITLES

Michigan's two-time defending Big Ten champion men's gymnastics team entered the 1962-63 season attempting to win the program's third Conference title. A 6-0 record in the regular season poised the tumblers for a good showing at the Big Ten meet in East Lansing. There, the Wolverines scored a Big Ten-record 210.5 points in wrapping up a third straight championship. Gil LaRose and Arno Lascari were the stars for Michigan, scoring 119.5 points between them, and thereby outscoring second- place Iowa, which managed just 83.5. Of the nine events, Michigan took first-place honors in six, with Lascari winning the parallel bars, side horse and horizontal bars. LaRose reigned as the Big Ten's best in the presitigious all-around scoring, while tying for first with teammate Mike Henderson in the floor exercise. Fred Sanders rounded out the Michigan champions with first place in the trampoline. LaRose, Ladcari and another Michigan gymnast, Jim Hynds, swept the 1-2-3 spots in the All-Around scoring. At the NCAA meet, the Michigan gymnasts won their first national championship in the program's history by a substantial margin. The Maize and Blue was well represented in the final standings, with Wolverines becoming individual champions in six events, finishing second in two events and coming in third in another. Gil LaRose led the Wolverines with national champion status in the vault, horizontal bar and all-around events. Lascari became the national champion in the parallel bars, and Henderson placed first in the floor exercise. Mike Erwin and Fred Sanders gave Michigan a 1-2 finish nationally on the trampoline.

Michigan's 1962-63 gymnastics team.

CHAMPIONSHIP *Moment*

MICHIGAN-IOWA TIE FOR BIG TEN TRACK TITLE

After finishing second at the Big Ten indoor track championship in 1962, Don Canham's Wolverines looked to return to the top in 1963. Though U-M scored in 12 of 15 events, the only Wolverine to secure first place was Charles Aquino, who ran the 1,000-yard dash in a Conference-record 2:09.9. U-M placed second in the overall standings behind Iowa, by a margin of 43-41. There were high and low moments factoring into Michigan's runner-up finish. Trinidad native Kent Bernard led a near upset of the highly regarded Iowa mile relay team. Bernard's heroics barely overshadowed the disappointment the Wolverines suffered in the 60-yard dash, however. Michigan's entry, Ken Burnley, finished last in a photo finish determined by a judges' decision. Iowa picked up its first title in 34 years as Canham remarked, "If Burnley is fourth, it's a tie meet." Or maybe it was a tie meet. Canham got a hold of a photograph from the *Michigan Daily* which showed Burnley in fourth place. After being reviewed by the Wisconsin athletic department, films of the event were brought to the Big Ten games committee. After reviewing the tapes, Commissioner Bill Reed switched the finishes of Burnley and Illinois sprinter Trent Jackson, giving the former a fourth-place finish. The resulting two-point gain in the standings gave Michigan 43 points to tie Iowa for the title. The co-championship was the first and only in the history of Big Ten Track.

CHAMPION OF THE WEST

GIL LAROSE

While Gil Larose might not have been the biggest competitor on the University of Michigan gymnastics team, he was the one everyone looked up to. The 5-4 Canadian import not only helped the Wolverines capture the Big Ten title in 1961, he became the number one man as a junior and led the Wolverines to another Conference title. His crowning achievement came one year later, when, as the senior captain, Larose won three NCAA titles—high bar, vault and all-around, leading the Wolverines to an NCAA team championship. He also finished second that season in NCAA floor exercise competition to teammate Mike Henderson. Larose arrived in Ann Arbor from Montreal. His sporting background was limited to hockey as a teenager, when he was the right wing on his high school team at Immaculate Conception. Meanwhile, Larose liked to bounce around on the trampoline. At the Immaculate Conception Center, he tried a gymnastic apparatus and his athletic skills made him a dedicated gymnast. As a teenager, Larose began trouping across Canada, engaging in top-flight competition, and in his first major meet in Toronto, Larose won the Novice Division of the Canadian National Gymnastics Championship at the age of 15. Larose and his family reside in Montreal, where he is a high school teacher.

Maize Blue Item

Following second-place Big Ten finishes in 1961 and 1962, the U-M wrestling team went into 1963 with first place on its mind. Cliff Keen's men were so determined at the Big Ten championships that they clinched the top spot before a man even wrestled in the finals. Two Wolverines earned top honors: Rick Bay at 157 pounds and heavyweight Jack Barden.

M List — Gymnastics Champions

The 1962-63 Michigan gymnastics team won the Big Ten meet with individual Conference champions in seven separate events. Six of those Big Ten champions went on to win individual titles at the NCAA meet as well:

Gymnast	1962-63 Big Ten titles	1962-63 NCAA titles
Mike Henderson	Floor exercise (tie)	Floor exercise
Gary Erwin		Trampoline
Arno Lascari	Pommel Horse	Parallel Bars
	Horizontal Bar	
	Parallel Bars	
Fred Sanders	Trampoline	
Gil Larose	Floor Exercise (tie)	Horizontal Bar
	Vault	Vault
	All-Around	All-Around

1963-64

America's Time Capsule

October 2, 1963: Pitcher Sandy Koufax of the Los Angeles Dodgers set a World Series record by striking out 15 New York Yankees in the opening game.

November 22, 1963: President John F. Kennedy was killed by an assassin's bullet in Dallas, Texas.

December 31, 1963: The Chicago Bears won the NFL championship by defeating the New York Giants, 14-0.

February 7, 1964: The Beatles arrived in New York City for an appearance on the *Ed Sullivan Show*.

February 25, 1964: Challenger Cassius Clay defeated Sonny Liston for the world heavyweight boxing title.

University Lore

In "the largest commencement ever," an estimated 80,000 people filled Michigan Stadium to hear President Lyndon Johnson's 1964 commencement address. The President's speech challenged the audience and the country to help build a "Great Society," one that "demands an end to poverty and racial injustice—to which we are totally committed in our time." The speech, regarded by many historians as one of Johnson's most important, laid out a theme and provided a catch-phrase for his domestic policy.

Michigan Moment

KINGS OF THE ICE

Michigan's hockey team had rolled to six titles in the first nine years of NCAA championships. Coach Al Renfrew's 1964 team started the season 6-2, after dropping a 6-5 decision in Minneapolis on January 11. Not only would the team not lose again until February 28, they would spend those next 13 games showing the opposition that they were not to be taken lightly. Following the Minnesota loss, Michigan hosted Loyola of Montreal for two games, winning by double digits. U-M swept the next two weekend series as well, then headed south for its first-ever games with Ohio University and Ohio State. In leaving a trail of destruction, the Wolverines tamed the Bobcats, 14-0, before thrashing the Buckeyes, 21-0. The 21 goals scored represented more points than the combined 1962, 1963 and 1964 U-M football teams had managed against Ohio State. When Michigan Tech finally halted the Michigan juggernaut, the Wolverines had already clinched the Big Ten and WCHA titles. In the Conference playoffs, Michigan beat Michigan Tech, but bowed out to Denver in the second round. Despite the loss, the 22-4-1 Wolverines headed to the NCAA tournament in Denver, Colorado the following week. Versus Providence in the semifinal game, Gary Butler took a pass from Gordon Wilkie and scored with 4:37 left to give Michigan the win. In the championship game against Denver, Wilf Martin scored to give Michigan a 1-0 lead. Most of the work was done by Michigan goalie Bob Gray who stopped 15 Denver shots in the opening 20 minutes. Mel Wakabayashi and Jack Cole tallied goals within a minute of one another as the Wolverines increased the lead to 3-0. Denver later closed the gap to 4-3, but U-M scored twice in the last four minutes to win, 6-3. Wakabayashi and Cole each finished with two goals in the game, but it was Gray, who finished with 31 saves, who was named tournament MVP.

U-M's 1963-64 hockey team.

CHAMPIONSHIP *Moment*

MICHIGAN WINS BIG TEN TITLE FOR FIRST TIME IN 15 YEARS

Since U-M last won a Big Ten title in 1948, the Wolverine cagers had enjoyed just four winning seasons and four finishes in the upper tier of the Big Ten. Led by second-year players Bill Buntin and Larry Tregoning, along with newcomers Cazzie Russell and Oliver Darden, the team jumped out to a 7-0 start, the team's best in 45 years. After the Wolverines finally lost, the quintet reeled off eight more victories. When the season ended, Michigan was perched on top of the Big Ten with Ohio State, holding a 11-3 conference record and a 20-4 mark overall. Behind Russell's 25 points per game and Buntin's 23, Michigan's lowest offensive output during the season was 69 points. Meanwhile, Michigan's scoring defense was the best in the Big Ten. After holding off Loyola, 84-80, and beating Ohio, 69-57 at the Midwest Regional of the NCAA tournament, Michigan was off to the Final Four in Kansas City, Missouri. There the Wolverines met Duke and fell, 91-80. The Blue Devils dominated the boards and grabbed control of the game after the Wolverines had taken an early lead. Russell poured in 31 points and Buntin scored 19. Before the Wolverines squared off against Kansas State for third place, it was learned that Cazzie Russell would not play due to an ankle injury he aggravated against Duke. Despite the absence of their leading scorer, the Wolverines defeated the Wildcats, 100-90. Bill Buntin scored 33 points, while Bob Cantrell filled in admirably for Russell by scoring 20.

CHAMPION OF THE WEST

MOBY BENEDICT

Moby Benedict, born and raised in Detroit, pursued his boyhood dreams by not only playing baseball for the Wolverines, but also becoming the head coach. Benedict began as shortstop for Ray Fisher in 1953. He earned All-Big Ten Conference honors twice and was team captain in his senior season. Upon graduation in 1956, Benedict played minor league ball in the Pioneer League, Eastern League and Sally League for the Detroit Tiger organization. He left pro ball in 1959 and returned to Michigan as the assistant coach under Don Lund. He was with the Wolverines when they won the 1962 NCAA National Championship. In 1963, Lund left coaching and Benedict took over the head coaching duties, compiling a 345-238-5 record from 1963 to 1979. He led the Wolverines to Big Ten titles in 1975, 1976 and 1978, and appearances in NCAA Regional Tournament play four straight years. The 1977 team won 33 games to set a school record (since broken), and the 1978 team placed fifth in the College World Series. A total of 61 players made it to the pro ranks, 21 of those to the majors, including Ted Sizemore, Elliott Maddox, Leon Roberts and Michigan's current head coach Geoff Zahn. In 1979, Benedict retired from coaching baseball at Michigan. He was inducted into the Michigan Hall of Honor in 1994.

Maize Blue Item

At the 1964 NCAA gymnastics meet, Gary Erwin successfully defended his 1963 title on the trampoline. U-M's dominance in the event was shown as the Wolverines spearheaded a 1-2-3 finish, the first time a single team had swept the top three places on the trampoline. Erwin scored a 9.57, nosing out teammate John Hamilton. The Chicago native, also won the Big Ten trampoline title in 1964 and 1965.

M List

On February 7-8, 1964, the Michigan hockey team took a break from a tough WCHA schedule to play at Ohio University and Ohio State. On that trip through the Buckeye State, the Wolverines exploded for 35 goals, allowing 0. Michigan scored the most goals in team history (21), while attempting 143 shots and stopping all of the opponents' 28. Statistics for those games:

February 7

Goals		Shots	
Michigan	7-1-6–14	Michigan	20-18-27–65
Ohio University	0-0-0–0	Ohio University	8-12-2–22

Scoring Leaders: Wakabayashi and Martin-3 goals each

February 8

Goals		Shots	
Michigan	8-8-5–21	Michigan	34-28-16–78
Ohio State	0-0-0–0	Ohio State	3-2-1–6

Scoring Leaders: Martin-4 goals, Wakabayashi-3 goals

1964-65

America's Time Capsule

September 27, 1964: The Warren Commision on the assassination of John Kennedy reported that there was no conspiracy and that Lee Harvey Oswald alone was responsible.

October 15, 1964: Bob Gibson and the St. Louis Cardinals defeated the New York Yankees for the World Series title.

November 3, 1964: Lyndon Johnson defeated Barry Goldwater in the presidential election.

March 8, 1965: The first United States combat forces landed in South Vietnam to guard the U.S. Air Force base at Danang.

June 5, 1965: Astronaut Edward White successfully completed a 20-minute walk in space, the first by an American.

University Lore

On June 3, 1965, James McDivitt Jr. (MSE Aero, '59) piloted the Gemini IV spacecraft in Earth orbit as Edward White (BSE Aero, '59) became the first American to walk in space. White died tragically in the Apollo I launch pad fire in 1967. The plaza at the corner of South and East University was renamed to honor U-M's first astronauts.

Michigan Moment

MICHIGAN BATTLES UCLA IN NCAA BASKETBALL TITLE GAME

Nothing short of a return to the Final Four would suit the Michigan basketball squad in 1965. With four returning starters, there was only one goal for the team. However, the cagers would have to conquer the regular season first. And conquer they did, posting a 21-3 record, including 13-1 in the Big Ten. With Cazzie Russell, Bill Buntin, Larry Tregoning and Oliver Darden all averaging double figures, the Wolverines scored over 100 points four times during the season and was undefeated in Yost Fieldhouse. Russell and Buntin picked up All-Big Ten honors as the team finished the season ranked number one in both national polls, yet all the regular-season glory went out the window when the tournament started. Michigan rolled into Lexington, Kentucky for the East Regional, where it destroyed Dayton, 98-71, before beating Vanderbilt by a close 87-85 margin. The Wolverines then headed to Portland, Oregon for the Final Four. Michigan drew Princeton, led by All-American Bill Bradley, in the semifinal round. Bradley picked up his third foul late in the first half and was forced to the bench, allowing the Wolverines to lead at the half, 40-36. However, Bradley was back for the second half, but when he fouled out with 5:04 left, the Michigan edge ballooned from eight points to 17. Four Wolverines scored in double figures, including Russell with 28 and Buntin with 23, in Michigan's 93-76 win. Defending champion UCLA would be Michigan's opponent in the final game. Though the Wolverines led early, 20-13, they could not contain the Bruins' explosive Gail Goodrich. Despite shooting over 50 percent from the floor, U-M could not make up from the losses of Buntin, Tregoning and Darden, who all fouled out trying to guard Goodrich. UCLA managed to out-rebound the Wolverines, 34-33, and Goodrich scored 42 points in the 91-80 UCLA victory. Goodrich's dominating performance overshadowed an excellent game by Russell, who scored 28 points in Michigan's defeat.

Michigan's Bill Buntin in the 1964-65 season.

CHAMPION
OF THE WEST
BOB TIMBERLAKE

Michigan has had its share of Rose Bowl champions, All-Americans, Big Ten MVP's, All-Big Ten selections and NFL players. However, only one quarterback has achieved all those honors and been named academic All-American, Bob Timberlake. A 6-4, 210-pound signal caller from Middletown, Ohio, Timberlake started the final 19 games of his career, capping it in 1964 when he passed for 884 yards, led the Conference in scoring and was named Conference MVP. In the 1965 Rose Bowl game versus Oregon State, Timberlake passed for 77 yards and ran for 57 more and one touchdown as the Wolverines blitzed the Beavers, 34-7. Following his Michigan career, he played with the New York Giants as a kicker and a back-up quarterback. Later, he enrolled at the Princeton Theological Seminary, completing his Masters of Divinity degree in 1969. After serving as a preacher at a church in Milwaukee, Timberlake went into consulting, then began a career in hospital administration.

another CHAMPION
OF THE WEST
BILL BUNTIN

A 6-7 center from Detroit, Bill Buntin starred for the Michigan basketball team from 1963-65. A s a sophomore, he averaged 22 points and 16 rebounds per game, earning All-Conference honors. The best thing for Buntin was the arrival of Cazzie Russell the following year. While opponents could shut down either Russell or Buntin with double and even triple coverage, there was little chance that both of Michigan's stars could be stopped. With Russell in the backcourt, Buntin scored 627 points, the second highest in Michigan history. Named an All-American, Buntin helped lead Michigan to a third-place finish in the NCAA tournament. Buntin's success spilled over into 1964-65 when he averaged 20.1 points per game. Behind him and Russell, the Wolverines rolled to a 24-4 overall record and second straight Big Ten title. As a senior, Buntin was named an All-American and All-Conference player for the second time. In the Wolverines' second straight Final Four, Buntin was instrumental in getting Michigan to the championship game, keeping the dangerous Bill Bradley in check while scoring 23 points. A first-round territorial pick of the NBA's Detroit Pistons, Buntin played one year in the NBA. In honor of his acheivements, Michigan's best player is annually awarded the Bill Buntin Most Valuable Player Award.

Maize & Blue Item

A shutout by fourth-ranked Michigan over seventh-ranked Ohio State in Columbus sent the Wolverines to the Rose Bowl for the first time in 14 years. In the 1965 New Year's Day classic, Mel Anthony's Rose Bowl record 84-yard touchdown run helped defeat the Oregon State Beavers 34-7. In all, the Wolverine offense ran for 332 yards, while the defense was holding the Beavers to just 64 yards on the ground.

M List: Evolution of Rose Bowl's Record Runs

In the 1965 Rose Bowl, Michigan back Mel Anthony took off on a 84-yard touchdown run, the longest rush in Rose Bowl history. Here are the four most recent record-breaking runs:

Tony Uansa, Pittsburgh	69	vs. USC, 1930
Bob Jeter, Iowa	81	vs. California, 1959
Mel Anthony, Michigan	84	vs. Oregon State, 1965
Tyrone Wheatley, Michigan	88	vs. Washington, 1993

1965-66

America's Time Capsule

October 28, 1965: Workers topped out the Gateway Arch in St. Louis, Missouri.

November 9, 1965: Millions of people in the Northeast were affected by a massive, 13-hour power blackout.

January 31, 1966: President Lyndon Johnson announced that American pilots had resumed their bombing raids on North Vietnam after a 38-day hiatus in hopes of furthering peace negotiations.

April 28, 1966: The Boston Celtics beat the Los Angeles Lakers in Game Seven of the NBA championship series, enabling coach Red Auerbach to retire with his eighth successive title.

June 8, 1966: The National and American football leagues merged, effective in 1970, setting up a Super Bowl game between the league champions.

University Lore

Professor Leslie R. Bassett of the University of Michigan's School of Music was awarded the 1966 Pulitzer Prize in Music for his composition "Variations for Orchestra,"which was premiered by the Philadelphia Orchestra. Bassett, on the UM faculty since 1952, was an internationally recognized composer, having won the Prix de Rome in 1961. Three other UM professors have won music Pulitzers: University Carilloneur Percival Price won the 1934 prize for his "St. Lawrence Symphony"; Ross Lee Finner for a string quartet in 1937; and William Bolcom for "Twelve New Etudes for Piano" in 1988.

Michigan Moment

CAZZIE LEADS "M" CAGERS

After securing back-to-back Big Ten championships for the first time in 1965, the Michigan basketball team looked to raise its third consecutive Conference banner in 1966. If the Wolverines were to claim another league title, they would have do it without the services of Bill Buntin and Larry Tregoning, both of whom had graduated. However, with a team of seniors and juniors, there was no lack of experience. Big Ten MVP Cazzie Russell, captain Oliver Darden and former reserve John Clawson showed that scoring would not be a problem either. Despite opening the season with 100-point games in two of their first three contests, Michigan limped to a 6-4 start. Once the Big Ten schedule began, victories seemed to come at will. The Wolverines rolled to five straight Conference wins before suffering a 99-93 setback to Illinois. After crushing Indiana, Michigan bowled over Wisconsin, 120-102, and slaughtered Purdue, 128-94. The 128 points set a single-game record. Michigan lost to Iowa in its next contest, but then blasted Purdue, the Hawkeyes and Northwestern, scoring more than 100 points in each of those wins. The victory over the Wildcats, a 105-92 beating in Ann Arbor which featured 48 points by Cazzie Russell, clinched Michigan's third straight Conference title. Michigan State closed out Michigan's regular season with an 86-77 win in East Lansing. Russell led the Big Ten in scoring with a 33.2 points-per-game average in Conference play and 30.8 PPG overall, and got lots of scoring support from Clawson (15.8 PPG), Darden (13.8 PPG) and senior forward Jim Myers (13.1 PPG). In their third straight NCAA tournament, the Wolverines faced Western Kentucky in the opening round. Down by one with 11 seconds left, Russell hit two pressure-packed free throws to give Michigan an 80-79 win. U-M's second-round draw was Kentucky, a team that came into the tournament 25-1. Michigan trailed by ten points at halftime, but Russell's game-high 29 points led a second-half comeback that gave the Maize and Blue a 53-52 lead with 12 minutes left. However, a 37.6 field goal percentage dogged the Wolverines and the Wildcats pulled away to win by a score of 84-77.

CHAMPION OF THE WEST

DAVE PORTER

The graduate of Lansing Sexton High School sparkled on both the gridiron and on the wrestling mat for Michigan, winning five "M" letters altogether, but it was in the latter sport where Dave Porter gained his greatest fame. As a grappler for Coach Cliff Keen from 1966-68, the Wolverine heavyweight was a dominant performer. Porter earned NCAA wrestling titles as a sophomore and again as a senior, compiling an amazing 13-1 record in NCAA competition. He also claimed Big Ten individual championships his sophomore and junior seasons and was the Conference runnerup his senior year, racking up an 8-1 career tournament record. The 1968 Michigan Senior Athlete Award winner still holds several Wolverine records, including the dual, Big Ten and NCAA career record for most consecutive falls with seven. A record 14 of Porter's then career-record 32 falls were recorded during his junior season. On three different occasions, the Wolverine giant pinned his opponent in 30 seconds or less. As a football player for Coach Bump Elliott, Porter won two letters as a defensive tackle and was an honorable mention All-Big Ten selection his senior year. He was a starter in the North-South Shrine Game and was drafted by the Cleveland Browns. Porter was among the first 75 individuals inducted into Michigan's Hall of Honor. His 1985 induction class of seven also included Wolverine legends Branch Rickey and Dick Kimball. He currently teaches and coaches at Grand Ledge High School.

another CHAMPION OF THE WEST

CAZZIE RUSSELL

Chicago Carver High School's Cazzie Russell ushered in a new era of basketball at Michigan. In Russell's three All-America seasons—1963-64, '64-65 and '65-66—Michigan equalled the number of Big Ten titles it had won in the previous 46 campaigns. Russell and fellow All-American Bill Buntin led the Wolverines to Conference championships in both '63-64 (23-5) and '64-65 (24-4)and respective finishes of third and second place in the NCAA tournaments. Upon Buntin's graduation, the fate of Michigan's '65-66 season rested largely on Cazzie's shoulders and, predictably, Russell performed masterfully, leading U-M to an 18-8 record and a third consecutive Big Ten title. In the clincher against Northwestern, Russell scored 48 points, a school record that still stands today. The 1966 college basketball player of the year finished his senior campaign with a U-M single-season record of 30.8 points per game and completed his career with school records of 2,164 points and 27.1 points per game. Russell was drafted with the very first pick in the NBA draft by the New York Knicks. He played 12 years as a pro with the Knicks, San Francisco Warriors, Los Angeles Lakers and Chicago Bulls, averaging at least 11 points per game every season but two. On December 11, 1989, Cazzie's #33 was raised to the rafters of Crisler Arena as the only Michigan basketball number ever retired.

Maize & Blue Item

To win its sixth consecutive Big Ten gymnastics championship, Michigan defeated rival Michigan State, 22-21, marking the narrowest margin of victory in 20 years. Though the U-M would record just one event winner in the championships—trampolinist Wayne Miller—it managed to prevail as a team. Three Michigan gymnasts were runners-up, including Rich Blanton on the rings, Ken Williams on the parallel bars and Lloyd Conant on the trampoline.

M List: U-M Big Ten Golf Tourney Individual Champions

M.J. Holdsworth	1924
John Fischer	1932-33-35
Chuck Koscis	1934-36
Ben Smith	1943
John Nenswold	1944
Ed Schalon	1947-49
Bill Newton	1965
Randy Erskine	1970
John Morse	1980
Kyle Dobbs	1997

1966-67

America's Time Capsule

October 13, 1966: U.S. bombers made their heaviest air strike of the war on North Vietnam.

November 11, 1966: The last mission of the Gemini space series was launched as astronauts Jim Lovell and "Buzz" Aldrin successfully rendezvoused with an Agena target vehicle.

January 15, 1967: The Green Bay Packers defeated the Kansas City Chiefs in the first-ever Super Bowl, 35-10.

March 25, 1967: Sophomore center Lew Alcindor led UCLA to the NCAA basketball championship over Dayton, 79-64.

July 23, 1967: Forty-three people were killed in Detroit as the worst race riot in U.S. history erupted.

University Lore

The University marked the 150th anniversary of its founding with a year-long Sesquicentennial Celebration on the theme "Knowledge, Wisdom and the Courage to Serve." The observance brought many distinguished alumni and leading figures from the fields of education, the arts, business and government to campus for a series of symposia, performances and other special events. The University was founded in 1817 as the "Catholepistemiad" of "University of Michigania" with a building in Detroit. It moved to Ann Arbor in 1837.

Michigan Moment

CLANCY PACES 'M' GRID SQUAD

Jack Clancy's first three years at Michigan had given no indication of the player he was. The Detroit native arrived at Michigan as a quarterback, a position he played through the beginning of his sophomore year. Soon after the beginning of fall practice, an accident with a firecracker burned one of his fingers and led to poor ball handling. Clancy became the left halfback for the 1963 season as Michigan compiled a record of 3-4-2, but was forced to redshirt the 1964 season with a disc injury in his back. Entering the 1965 campaign, Clancy found his position filled by Jim Detwiler and was switched to end. The 6-1 senior/junior found his calling at the new spot, setting Michigan records in receptions and receiving yardage. He was tabbed as a "future" draft selection of the Miami Dolphins in 1966, but returned for his senior year at U-M. Clancy opened the 1966 season by reeling in 10 passes for 197 yards as Michigan routed Oregon State. The 197 receiving yards still stands as the high water mark in Michigan history. An eight-catch, 93-yard performance followed against California and Clancy was off and running, collecting All-Big Ten and All-American honors. Clancy's award-winning season included a 10-reception game against Minnesota and an 11-catch contest versus Illinois, where Clancy picked up 179 yards through the air. He finished the season with 76 catches for 1,069 yards, leading the Big Ten and finishing second nationally. Michigan finished with a 6-4 record in 1966 as Clancy set many receiving marks that still lead the Michigan record book.

Jack Clancy

CHAMPIONSHIP *Moment*

ROBIE SMASHES POOL RECORDS

The Wolverines did not win a Big Ten or NCAA swimming title in 1967, but placed a respectable second in the Conference and fifth nationally. However, there was one swimmer who really stood out, Michigan's Carl Robie. The Drexel Hill, Pennsylvania native made a large splash in the Conference competition by setting an NCAA record in the 500 freestyle at the Michigan State pool. Robie's time of 4:43.08 chopped over half a second off the national mark and blasted the old Conference standard by two seconds. But Robie's record-breaking performance on the first day was only a sign of things to come. In a measure of revenge, the senior won the 200 butterfly the following day. Robie's time of 1:53.35 bested that of Indiana's Kevin Berry. At the 1964 Olympics in Tokyo, Berry, then swimming for Australia, bested Robie for the gold medal. Robie would complete the "hat trick" of wins on Saturday night when he set a Big Ten record in the 1650 freestyle. His time of 16:42.76 was not only a pool length in front of his nearest competitor, but sliced eight seconds off the existing Conference record as well. Robie would return to East Lansing three weeks later as the Spartans hosted the NCAA meet. After placing third in the 500 freestyle on the first evening, Robie took top honors in the 200 butterfly the following night. The title was Robie's third national honor, following his top finish in the 400 individual medley in 1965 and 200 butterfly crown in 1966.

CHAMPION OF THE WEST

JACK CLANCY

Jack Clancy's first two years as a Michigan end showed little of the greatness that Clancy would achieve in his last two seasons. As a sophomore, the Detroit native caught just four passes for 78 yards. While the Wolverines won the Big Ten and the Rose Bowl in 1964, Clancy missed the entire year with an injury. Clancy worked his way back in 1965, and not only did the man who missed all of 1964 manage to break into the starting lineup, but he became the first Wolverine to reach the 50-reception plateau. He set Michigan single-season records with 52 receptions for 762 yards and was a bright spot in a dismal 4-6 season. Though it had taken over half a century for any Wolverine to catch more than 50 passes, it would take only a year more for the first Michigan player to top 75. In a year where he would break both Michigan single-season records with 76 catches for 1,079 yards, Clancy was simply unstoppable. He caught more than 10 passes in a game three times in 1966, including 10 receptions for 197 yards against Oregon State. In becoming the first man in Conference history to catch 50 passes in Conference play (50 catches for 698 yards), Clancy led the Wolverine to a third-place finish in the Big Ten. Named an All-American and Michigan MVP in 1966, Clancy finished his college playing days with the most receptions (132) and yards (1919). Though most of Clancy's records have been broken, he still ranks first in single-season catches and owns three of the six best performances for receptions in one game. Drafted in the third round of the 1966 NFL redshirt draft by Miami, Clancy played with the Dolphins from 1967-69 and with the Green Bay Packers in 1970.

Maize & Blue Item

On April 27, 1967, Wolverine hurler Geoff Zahn pitched two complete games of a doubleheader, a feat that had not been accomplished in Big Ten play since 1954. Zahn threw just 93 pitches in a 1-0 win over Northwestern, scattering four hits while striking out seven. Coach Moby Benedict left Zahn in to pitch the second game as well, and Zahn allowed just two runs on three hits. He picked up his second win in Michigan's 8-2 victory.

M List: Michigan Career Receiving Records

No.	Name	Yrs.
161	Anthony Carter	1979-82
143	Amani Toomer	1992-95
134	Desmond Howard	1989-91
132	Jack Clancy	1963-66
125	Derrick Alexander	1989-93
124	Mercury Hayes	1992-95

1967-68

America's Time Capsule

October 2, 1967: Thurgood Marshall was sworn in as the United States' first black Supreme Court justice.

October 12, 1967: The St. Louis Cardinals won Game Seven of the 64th annual World Series, defeating the Boston Red Sox.

January 23, 1968: North Korea seized the Navy intelligence ship U.S.S. Pueblo off its coast. Its crew of 83 was released on December 23.

April 4, 1968: Dr. Martin Luther King Jr. was assassinated by a sniper in Memphis, Tennessee, setting off a week of rioting in several urban black ghettos.

June 5, 1968: Presidential candidate Robert Kennedy was shot in Los Angeles after delivering a speech to acknowledge his victory in the California primary.

University Lore

Robben W. Fleming, Chancellor of the University of Wisconsin and former professor of labor relations, became U-M's eleventh president in January 1968. That background served him well during the tumultuous years from 1968 through 1979. Fleming's patience and genuine sympathy for the concerns of student and faculty, helped Michigan weather the decade.

Michigan Moment

THE HOUSE THAT CAZZIE BUILT

Cazzie Russell's basketball abilities had done more than lift Michigan to the top of the Big Ten standings. They had made the 45-year- old Yost Field House no longer suitable for the cage team and its new throng of followers. After seeing this growth in attendance, the building of a new basketball arena was approved in 1965. On September 18, construction began on the "Varsity Events Center" just northeast of the football stadium. Though the building of the new facility was delayed when a roof beam crashed to the floor, the $7.2 million arena was ready for the first game against Kentucky on December 2, 1967. The building was designed by Dan Dworsky, a star halfback on Michigan's football team from 1945-48.

Containing 13,609 seats arranged telescopically around a maple floor, the brick building was dedicated on February 27, 1968 and renamed in honor of retiring athletic director Fritz Crisler. The home of the basketball, wrestling, gymnastics, and volleyball teams for all or part of the last 30 years, Crisler Arena contains four locker rooms, a wrestling practice room and an assembly lounge. The most interesting part of the construction was the roof, built in "bridge-like" fashion to allow the steel to expand and contract with the changing weather conditions. Under the two 160-ton roof plates, the Michigan men's basketball team has won over 80 percent of its games in "The House that Cazzie built."

CHAMPION OF THE WEST

JOHNNY ORR

A new arena and a new basketball coach were the talk of Ann Arbor in 1968. Crisler Arena was opened and Johnny Orr took over the coaching reins from Dave Strack. One of the most engaging coaches in the profession, Orr starred in basketball on the high school level at Taylorville High School in Illinois. He was second-team All-Big Ten in football and All Conference mention in basketball as a freshman at the University of Illinois. Then, the Armed Services called and when he returned to the collegiate ranks, he entered Beloit College and was an outstanding three-year regular, earning first-team NAIA All-American. He was the number-one draft pick of the St. Louis Bombers of the NBA and also played with the Waterloo Hawks before entering the prep coaching ranks. Orr became the head coach at Massachusetts, then joined Strack as an assistant in 1967-68, and one year later took over the Wolverine top spot. His 12 years as head coach at Michigan included the top-ranked team at the end of the 1977 regular season plus an appearance in the 1976 NCAA Championship game. He won two Big Ten titles, compiling a 209-113 record, the most wins of any Michigan coach. Orr retired as Iowa State's head coach in 1995. He and his wife Rommie still reside in Ames, Iowa.

another CHAMPION OF THE WEST

DAN DWORSKY

In 1950, Dan Dworsky graduated from the University of Michigan and by 1953, he started his own architecture firm. Fifteen years later, his crowning professional jewel, Crisler Arena, was finished and dedicated. While most people remember Dworsky for his professional achievements, he also gained earlier fame as a Michigan athlete. Dworsky was born in Minneapolis, Minnesota and attended public schools in St. Paul, and Sioux Falls, South Dakota, starring in football, basketball, track and gymnastics. He entered the University of Michigan in 1945 as an engineering student, later transferring to Architecture where he became a standout student, winning various awards and earning the Fielding H. Yost Scholarship Award for two years. Along with his scholarly activities, he also earned six varsity letters (four in football and two in wrestling). He played center and linebacker on the great U-M teams of 1947 and 1948. His play in the '48 Rose Bowl at linebacker earned him an outstanding reputation as strong, hard-hitting defender. Upon graduation, he was a first-round draft choice of the Los Angeles Dons of the NFL. Dan and his wife Sylvia reside in Los Angeles.

Maize & Blue Item

U-M had little trouble winning the 1968 Big Ten Championship. The 13-0 squad placed participants in eight of the nine finals matches to post a 47-1/2 victory. All three doubles tandems earned title crowns: Pete Fischbach-Brian Marcus, Dick Dell-Jon Hainline, and Bruce DeBoer-Bob Pritula, while Dell, Hainline and DeBoer also earned singles crowns.

M List: Michigan's Dominating Streaks of Consecutive Big Ten Titles

Sport	Titles	Seasons
Football	5	1988-92
Men's Golf	5	1932-36
Women's Gymnastics	6	1992-97
Men's Gymnastics	6	1961-66
Men's Indoor Track	7	1934-40
Men's Swimming and Diving	10	1986-95
Women's Swimming and Diving	11	1987-97
Men's Tennis	16	1968-83

MICHIGAN MOMENT

America's Time Capsule

October 10, 1968: The Detroit Tigers won the World Series for the first time since 1945, defeating the St. Louis Cardinals in seven games.

November 5, 1968: Republican Richard Nixon won the presidential election, beating Hubert Humphrey by only 500,000 votes.

July 16, 1969: U.S. space capsule Apollo 11 landed on the moon at 4:17 p.m. EDT. Astronaut Neil Armstrong became the first person to set foot on the moon.

July 18, 1969: Senator Edward Kennedy was involved in an auto accident on Chappaquiddick Island, Massachusetts, resulting in the death of his passenger, Mary Jo Kopechne.

August 15, 1969: The Woodstock Music and Art Fair began , drawing a crowd estimated at nearly a half million people.

UNIVERSITY LORE

The new Administration Building, later named the Robben and Sally Fleming Administration Building, was completed in the Fall of 1968. A new campus landmark, "The Cube," also made its appearance. Created by sculptor Bernard Rosenthal (U-M '35), the 2,300-pound revolving steel cube spins on ball bearings around a steel shaft at the slightest push from a passing student. Rosenthal donated his time and talent, and the class of 1965 paid for the materials.

FOOTBALL TRADITION REBOUNDS

After the 1964 Michigan football team had brought home a Rose Bowl victory, the next three Wolverine squads struggled to a combined record of 14 wins and 16 losses. Bump Elliott's 1968 team opened the season with a 21-7 loss to California in Ann Arbor, then reeled off eight coinsecutive wins, behind the impressive running of senior halfback Ron Johnson. Johnson rushed for 205 yards in game two as Michigan bounced back with a 31-10 win over Duke in Durham, North Carolina. He was also a factor in the following week's 32-9 win over Navy, rushing for 121 yards. Johnson's 152 yards on the ground and Jim Mandich's 125 yards receiving enabled the Wolverines to beat Michigan State for the first time in four years, 28-14, to go 3-1 on the season. Michigan improved to 2-0 in the Big Ten under Elliott for the first time ever with a 27-22 win over Indiana. Johnson ran for 163 yards in the game, marking the fourth consecutive game he broke the 100-yard barrier. Michigan cruised out to a 33-0 lead in a win over Minnesota, then notched back-to-back shutouts over Northwestern and Illinois. In posting the first consecutive shutouts since 1954, Michigan improved to 7-1 on the year, 5-0 in the Big Ten. With an NCAA-record 347 yards rushing in a 34-9 against Wisconsin, Johnson helped set up a Michigan-Ohio State contest for the Big Ten title. Though Michigan only trailed 21-14 at the half to the undefeated Buckeyes, the soon-to-be National Champions erupted for 29 second-half points to crush Michigan, 50-14. Tom Stincic recorded 23 tackles for Michigan, but Ohio State racked up 421 rushing yards for its 13th straight win. Despite the beating, optimism reigned in Ann Arbor. The Wolverines were back.

Michigan's Ron Johnson

CHAMPION OF THE WEST

RUDY TOMJANOVICH

In Michigan's 1968-69 season debut, its first game in its new arena, a 6-7 sophomore from Hamtramck, Michigan named Rudy Tomjanovich gave Wolverine fans a preview of what was to come, grabbing a team record-tying 27 rebounds in a loss to Kentucky. It was an auspicious start for a young man who would eventually end his career as the school's all-time leading rebounder (1,039) and No. 2 all-time scorer (1,808 points), second only to Cazzie Russell. For three straight seasons, Rudy T. would pace the team in both categories, averaging 25.1 points and 14.4 rebounds over that span. His single-game highs were 48 points in an overtime win against Indiana and 30 boards versus Loyola, both in 1969. A two-time team MVP and All-Big Ten selection, Tomjanovich earned consensus All-America honors in 1970. He was the number two pick in the 1970 NBA Draft by San Diego, playing 12 seasons with the Rockets, who moved to Houston in 1981. When Rudy retired in 1981, his career totals included a .501 field goal percentage, 6,198 rebounds and 17.4 point per game average. With 13,383 career points, his number 45 was retired by the Rockets. However, Tomjanovich's time in the NBA was far from over. In 1992 he was called upon to be a midseason replacement as head coach for his former team. The following season, Houston claimed a division championship, and in 1994 the Rockets won their first NBA title behind Hakeem Olajuwon. Rudy's Rockets fell to 47-35 in 1995, but came alive in the playoffs to claim their second consecutive NBA crown.

another CHAMPION OF THE WEST

DON CANHAM

When Don Canham became the fifth Michigan athletic director in the history of the school in 1968 , the traditionalists were taken back at his promotional ideas. But Canham's break with marketing tradition was not a break with the great tradition of Michigan. A high jumper on the Wolverine track team from 1939 to 1941, Canham then turned to coaching. While Canham led the Wolverines to several Big Ten titles, he also managed to build a sports supply company on the side, learning the business side of the job in his spare time. And when his career at Michigan ended with his retirement in 1988, Canham didn't break the Wolverines' great tradition, he enhanced its growth with state-of-the-art marketing techniques that made him one of the great athletic directors in the history of college sports. Canham ran college athletics as a business and he was the King of College Marketing. He placed full-page ads in the Detroit newspapers, he took out regional ads in *Sports Illustrated*, and he understood the appeal of mass mailings. Mass mailings increased from 100,000 to 1.6 million pieces and the costs were covered by selling coffee mugs. His first hire was Will Perry, a sportswriter for *The Grand Rapids Press*, as Sports Information Director. He then brought in a football coach from Miami of Ohio by the name of Glenn "Bo" Schembechler. Canham was the AD as Michigan brought in 67 Big Ten championships. Canham still resides in Ann Arbor, helping his son Donald, Jr., run School-Tech, Inc.

Maize & Blue Item

The date November 16, 1968, will be remembered as the day Ron Johnson ran wild. The senior was nearly unstoppable against Wisconsin, carrying the ball 31 times for an NCAA record 347 yards and five touchdowns, a scoring mark no Michigan player had reached since 1917. Johnson had touchdown runs of 67, 60, 50 and 35 yards. His record-setting yardage would be the NCAA standard until 1972, and a Michigan mark that still stands today.

M List: Michigan's Greatest Individual Rushing Performances (Since 1938)

Player	Year	Opponent	Att	Yds	TD
Ron Johnson	1968	Wisconsin	31	347	5
Tim Biakabutuka	1995	Ohio State	37	313	1
Jon Vaughn	1990	UCLA	32	288	3
Ron Johnson	1967	Navy	26	270	2
Butch Woolfolk	1981	Michigan State	39	253	0
Tyrone Wheatley	1993	Washington	15	235	3
Jamie Morris	1988	Alabama	23	234	3
Bill Taylor	1969	Iowa	21	225	2
Tyrone Wheatley	1992	Iowa	19	224	3
Ted Kress	1952	Northwestern	20	218	3

America's Time Capsule

September 22, 1969: Willie Mays of the San Francisco Giants hit his 600th career home run, becoming only the second major leaguer other than Babe Ruth to reach that plateau.

November 16, 1969: More than 450 Vietnam villagers were slain by a U.S. infantry unit in what would be known as the My Lai massacre.

March 18, 1970: The first major postal workers' strike began in the United States.

April 29, 1970: U.S. and South Vietnamese troops invaded Cambodia.

May 4, 1970: Four Kent State University students were killed by National Guard troops during an antiwar demonstration.

University Lore

The Black Action Movement (BAM) called a campus strike in March 1970 to protest the University's record in minority enrollment and services. BAM's demands included increased support service for minority students, establishment of a Center for Afro-American and African Studies, and raising African-American enrollment from the current three to 10 percent. The strike enjoyed wide support in some units and many trade union and service workers honored the picket lines. After eight days, the administration acceded to BAM's essential demands and pledged to increased African-American enrollment to 10 percent by 1973.

Michigan Moment

BO'S WOLVERINES SHOCK THE BUCKEYES

The Wolverines had clinched a Rose Bowl bid the previous week, but the visiting Ohio State Buckeyes weren't at all interested in roses. Prohibited from going to the Rose Bowl because they had gone the previous year, the top-ranked Ohio State Buckeyes were looking for something bigger. Coming into Michigan Stadium as 15-point favorites and averaging 46 points per game, Ohio State was looking for a second straight national championship. Fifteen points was seen as a conservative figure by many, considering that the previous year's matchup between these two teams turned into a 50-14 rout for Ohio State. But in the same year that America saw man walk on the moon, the Jets shock the Colts in the Super Bowl and the Mets walk to a World Series title, there was one more upset to be played out. The game started off in fine fashion for the Buckeyes, as Jim Otis opened the scoring on a one-yard run; OSU missed the conversion. With rookie coach Bo Schembechler on the sidelines, the Wolverines took the ensuing kickoff and marched 55 yards to score on Garvie Craw's three-yard run. When Frank Titas booted the extra point, the Buckeye confidence began to fray. For not only had Michigan become the first team to score on Ohio State in the first period, this marked the first time that the Buckeyes had trailed in a game. Veteran signalcaller Rex Kern then found Jan White open in the end zone and the Buckeye lead was 12-7. A missed two-point conversion kept the score that way, but not for long. The Wolverines threatened to turn the game into a scorefest, taking the Ohio State kickoff, then embarking on a 67-yard drive to go up 14-12 on Craw's second touchdown run of the day. The Buckeyes took the kickoff, but little did they know they would not score again in 1969. Failing to move the ball, Ohio State punted, and Barry Pierson took the ball and returned it 60 yards to the Ohio State three-yard line. It took just two plays for Don Moorhead to take the ball into the end zone, and Michigan led 21-12. Tim Killian would boot a 25-yard field goal to stretch the advantage to the eventual winning margin of 24-12. Though the offensive statistics were nearly equal, Ohio State committed seven turnovers to Michigan's one. At the final gun, the 103,588 who had watched the incredible victory charged the field in celebration of the upset. The victorious Wolverines retreated to the locker room knowing that they were going to the Rose Bowl, not as a second-place replacement, but as Big Ten champions.

Bo Schembechler (left) and Ohio State's Woody Hayes on the sidelines.

Hail! to the victors valiant • Hail! to the conqu'ring heroes • Hail! Hail! to Michigan, the leaders and best • Hail! to the victors valiant • Hail! to the conqu'ring heroes • Hail! Hail! to Michigan, the champions of the West •

In 1991, Desmond Howard joined Tom Harmon as a Heisman Trophy winner from the University of Michigan. *Photo by Duane Black.*

The winningest coach in Michigan football history, Bo Schembechler's teams won or tied an impressive 13 Big Ten championships during his 21-year tenure. *Photo by Per Kjeldsen.*

Tom Dolan (center) and Eric Namesnik (left) won the gold and silver medals respectively, in the 400-meter individual medley at the 1996 Olympics. *Photo by U-M Swimming Coach, Jon Urbanchek.*

Hail! to the victors valiant • Hail! to the conqu'ring heroes • Hail! Hail! to Michigan, the leaders and best •

Hail! to the victors valiant • Hail! to the conqu'ring heroes • Hail! Hail! to Michigan, the champions of the West •

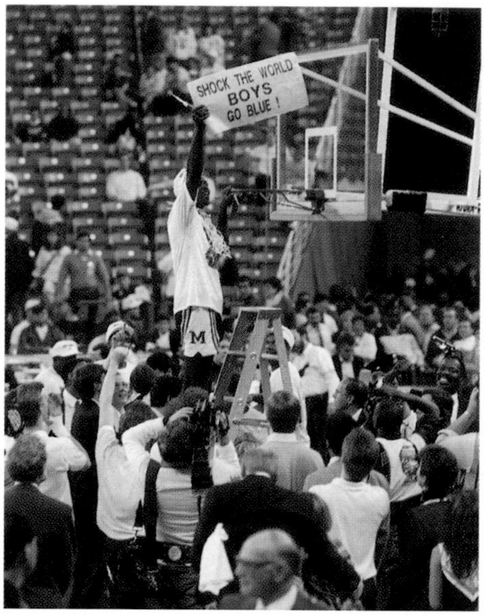

Glen Rice celebrates Michigan's 1989 NCAA basketball championship. *Photo by Duane Black.*

Brendan Morrison's (9) overtime goal against Colorado College in 1996 gave the Wolverines their first NCAA national ice hockey championship in 32 years. *Photo by Joel Hakken.*

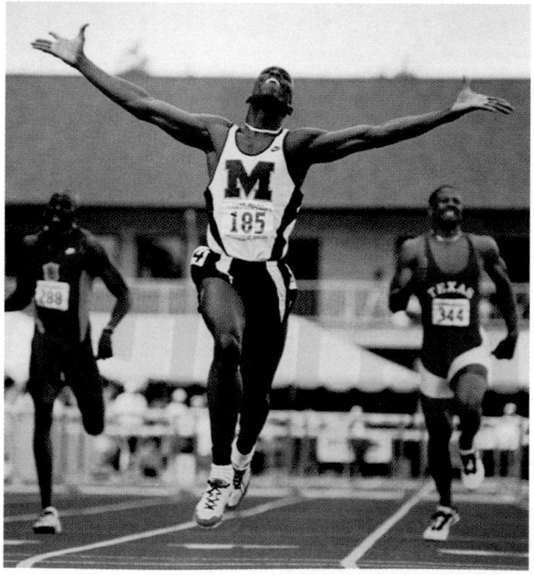

Neil Gardner was the 1996 NCAA champion in the 400-meter hurdles. *Photo by Allsport.*

Hail! to the victors valiant • Hail! to the conqu'ring heroes • Hail! Hail! to Michigan, the leaders and best

• Hail! to the victors valiant • Hail! to the conqu'ring heroes • Hail! Hail! to Michigan, the champions of the West •

Hail! to the victors valiant • Hail! to the conqu'ring heroes • Hail! Hail! to Michigan, the leaders and best • Hail! to the victors valiant • Hail! to the conqu'ring heroes • Hail! Hail! to Michigan, the champions of the West •

MICHIGAN 25 WOMEN 1973-1998

Michigan's 1996-97 women's swimming team captured the school's 11th consecutive Big Ten title in that sport. *Photo by Peter H. Bick.*

The 1996-97 women's basketball team celebrates a home-court victory over Northwestern. *Photo by Bob Kalmbach.*

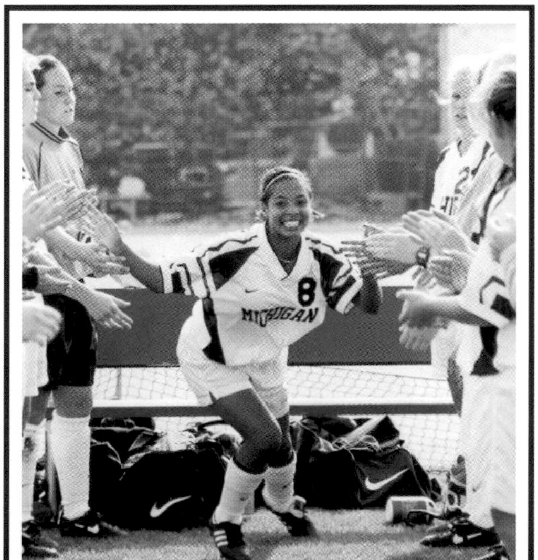

One of the school's newest varsity teams, Michigan's women's soccer squad made its Big Ten debut in 1995. *Photo by Bob Kalmbach.*

Hail! to the victors valiant • Hail! to the conqu'ring heroes • Hail! Hail! to Michigan, the leaders and best • Hail! to the victors valiant • Hail! to the conqu'ring heroes • Hail! Hail! to Michigan, the champions of the West •

THE MICHIGAN ATHLETIC DEPARTMENT
invites you to visit the M DEN
Featuring a unique collection of U of M clothing and giftware
Located at: Briarwood Mall, Michigan Stadium-Gate 2 and Laurel Park Place-Livonia
MICHIGAN STADIUM
To receive your FREE copy of "Hail to the Victors,"
the official U of M Athletic Department/M-DEN Catalog call 1-800-462-5838.
The University of Michigan Athletic Dept. receives a portion of the proceeds from all sales to help fund the many programs of student athletes and the success of Michigan athletics.

CHAMPIONSHIP *Moment*

"M" GYMNASTS CAPTURE NCAA TITLE

Michigan had romped through the regular-season portion of its gymnastics schedule in 1969-70, going 12-0 before wrapping up its ninth Big Ten championship in the past 10 seasons. Led by 1969 NCAA parallel bars champion Ron Rapper, Newt Loken's team qualified for the NCAA team meet along with Temple and Iowa State on April 3. The final competition contained all the excitement that an NCAA championship should contain. Iowa State turned in the top performance on the floor exercise, followed by Michigan. The team reversed positions on the side horse, and then reversed again on the rings. Iowa State took a commanding lead with a first-place finish on the long horse, but Rapper helped Michigan cut that advantage, leading his team to a first-place finish on the parallel bars. The horizontal bar was the final event, as the Wolverines could only watch as Iowa State posted a 27.50 on this piece of apparatus. Michigan needed 27.75 points to win, knowing that it had only scored 27.65 in qualifying the night before. Ted Marti led Michigan's last rotation with a 9.25, followed by Sid Jensen's 8.90 and Rick McCurdy's 9.20. As only the top three scores counted, Michigan needed a 9.35 for the Wolverines to claim a second national team title. Up stepped Ed Howard, a junior from Wilmette, Illinois, whose season average on the horizontal bar was a 9.26. Howard performed his routine, and all nervous eyes turned to the scoreboard. The posted scores of 9.5, 9.5, 9.3, and 9.3 averaged to a 9.40, tying Howard's career best and delivering an NCAA title to Michigan.

CHAMPION OF THE WEST

CLIFF KEEN

Clifford P. Keen was born on June 13, 1901, in a small town called Cheyenne in the then-Oklahoma territory. Keen's beginnings may have started in a small place, but the remainder of his life was spent on a large scale. In his collegiate days, Keen was a three-sport standout at Oklahoma A&M, where he lettered in football, wrestling and track. An All-American on the gridiron, Keen was a national champion wrestler who was selected to the 1924 Olympic team, but forced to withdraw due to injury. From 1925 to 1970, Keen served as the head coach of the Michigan wrestling team, setting a record for longest tenure by any coach in any sport in the history of the NCAA. During that time, he led his squads to a 272-91-10 (.743) record, winning 13 Big Ten titles and finishing lower than third only five times. Under his tutelage, Michigan lay claim to 68 All-Americans and 81 Big Ten Champions. Keen also served as the coach of Michigan's 150-pound football team for 33 seasons, leading his team to the Big Ten title in the only two years the Conference sponsored the sport. A key in developing amateur wrestling around the nation, Keen was selected as head coach of the 1948 U.S. Olympic team. Keen's success was also evident away from the mats. He served three years as a Naval Commander during World War II, received his law degree from U-M, and was a member of the Michigan State Bar. Following his retirement in 1970, he founded Cliff Keen Athletic Products, one of the largest manufacturers of sporting goods in the country. Keen died in Ann Arbor in 1991, soon after having the Varsity Arena renamed in his honor.

Maize & Blue Item

Tom Curtis arrived at Michigan in 1966 as a quarterback, but would never see action at that position as a Wolverine. Switched to safety during his freshman season, Curtis excelled on defense. In 1967, he intercepted seven passes, a mark he surpassed in 1968 when he reeled in a U-M-record 10 interceptions. When Curtis' college days were over, he held the NCAA record in interception yardage with 440 yards on 25 pickoffs. Curtis went on to become a member of two Super Bowl champion teams in the NFL, Baltimore in 1970 and Miami in 1972.

M List: Top NBA Picks

Rudy Tomjanovich was the first-round draft pick (second overall) of the San Diego Rockets following his senior season at U-M. Other Michigan players to be selected in the 15 picks of the NBA draft include the following:

Player	Pick	Team
Cazzie Russell	1	New York Knicks
Chris Webber	1	Orlando Magic
Bill Buntin	*1	Detroit Pistons
Glen Rice	4	Miami Heat
Juwan Howard	5	Washington Bullets
Roy Tarpley	7	Dallas Mavericks
Campy Russell	8	Cleveland Cavaliers
Rumeal Robinson	10	Atlanta Hawks
Tim McCormick	12	Cleveland Cavaliers
Jalen Rose	13	Denver Nuggets
Loy Vaught	13	Los Angeles Clippers
Gary Grant	14	Los Angeles Clippers
Phil Hubbard	15	Detroit Pistons

*-Territorial first pick

America's Time Capsule

November 8, 1970: Tom Dempsey of the New Orleans Saints kicked an NFL-record 63-yard field goal against the Detroit Lions.

December 2, 1970: The Environmental Protection Agency, established in July, was activated.

January 25, 1971: Charles Manson and three of his followers were convicted of the 1969 murders of actress Sharon Tate and six others.

March 29, 1971: William Calley was conviced of the murder of 22 South Vietnamese people at My Lai.

July 30, 1971: Astronauts David Scott and Jim Irwin became the fourth American space team to explore the moon's surface.

University Lore

William D. Revelli retired after 37 years as director of the U-M Marching Band and Symphonic Band. Under his direction, the Marching Band gained international acclaim for its musical abilities, intricate formations and high-stepping style. Revelli's bands were the first to score original music to band shows, to synchronize music and movement, to use an announcer, to do a post-game show, and the first to host a high school Band Day. Revelli died in 1994 at the age of 92.

Michigan Moment

MICHIGAN GYMNASTS CONTINUE DOMINATION OF BIG TEN

The honor of the most dominating Michigan sport of the 1960s had not been with football, basketball or track, but laid in the hands of Newt Loken's gymnastics squad, which had won eight Conference titles in that decade. A Big Ten title in 1970 showed that the gymnasts were not going to give up their power, and so a struggle for the top spot at the 1971 championship in Columbus was expected. Individually, Rick McCurdy was the standout for the Maize and Blue, capturing the All-Around title for the third consecutive year. Just behind him was teammate Ray Gura, while U-M's Ted Marti placed fifth. The final day of competition was almost a mere formality once the Wolverines got started. In the team competition, Michigan won five events and tied the other, scoring at least than 27 points on each piece of equipment. Individual honors were garnered by McCurdy on the horizontal bar and Murray Plotkin on the parallel bars.

Michigan's win marked the 10th Big Ten gymnastics title annexed by Newt Loken and the Wolverines, who had set an NCAA-record score of 165.00 against Michigan State just a week earlier. After a perfect 10-0 regular season, the Wolverines would continue competing at the NCAA gymnastics championship, placing fifth in the national meet held in Ann Arbor.

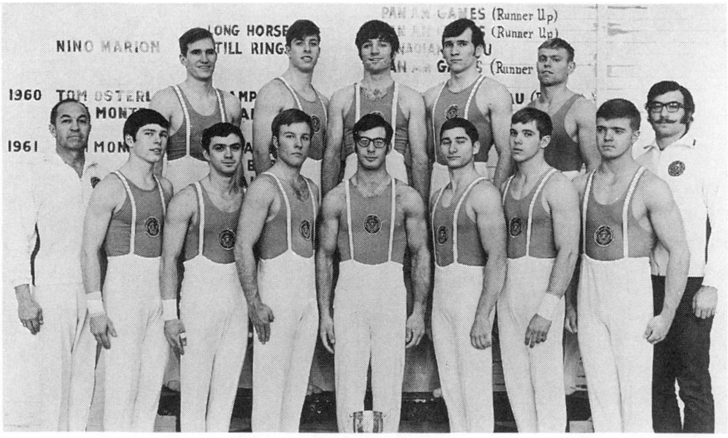

Michigan's Big Ten champions in 1971.

CHAMPION
OF THE WEST
DAN DIERDORF

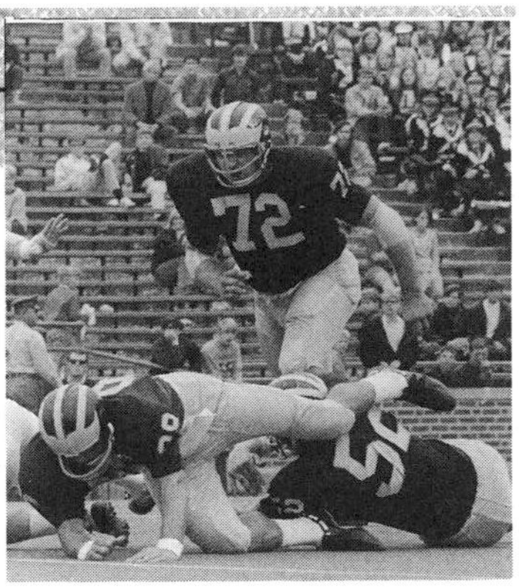

Born and raised in Canton, Ohio, in 1949, Dan Dierdorf would return to his hometown's Pro Football Hall of Fame in 1996 to celebrate a career of accomplishments on the gridiron. Snubbed by Michigan State, Ohio State and Notre Dame, the 6'3", 255-pound tackle arrived in Ann Arbor in 1967 because Bump Elliott was willing to take a chance with the raw talent. Dierdorf took the field as a sophomore as Michigan's record rose from 4-6 to 8-2. He started nine games in his first year, including the Wisconsin affair, where his blocks allowed Ron Johnson to gain 347 rushing yards. In 1969, under new head coach Bo Schembechler, Dierdorf assisted in bringing the Big Ten title back to Ann Arbor. He started eight games, and was honored with an All-Big Ten selection at the end of the season. During 1970, Dierdorf and his linemates continued to pave the way for Michigan's running game. The Wolverines gained over 2,500 yards on the ground in Dierdorf's senior season. Awarded All-American accolades by every major selector, Dierdorf was taken in the second round of the 1971 NFL draft by the St. Louis Cardinals. He played 13 seasons in St. Louis, performing in six Pro Bowl games, being selected to five All-NFL teams and being named NFC offensive lineman of the year three times. He retired from football in 1983, but later rejoined the game as an announcer for ABC's Monday Night Football. In 1996, Dierdorf was enshrined into the Pro Football Hall of Fame and the College Football Hall of Fame.

another CHAMPION
OF THE WEST
WILLIAM REED

William R. Reed was born in Oxford, Michigan, and came to the University of Michigan after graduating from Ann Arbor High School in 1932. Though he only played freshman football for the Wolverines, Reed kept a keen eye on the game as the sports editor of the *Michigan Daily* and working for Michigan's Athletic Public Relations office. After graduating from the Law School in 1937, Reed joined the Big Ten as its Service Bureau Director. He would serve most of the last 32 years of life with the Conference, except for a six-year period where he served in the Navy and in the office of Sen. Homer Ferguson. At the Conference office, Reed was a driving force behind the creation of the Big Ten records book which still exists today. With a talent for being able to explain the most complex of problems in the simplest of terms, Reed was promoted to assistant commissioner in 1951. In 1961, he ascended to become the third commissioner in Conference history, replacing Kenneth Wilson, who had filled the role since 1945. As commissioner, Reed stressed academic success by student athletes, and created the grant-in-aid regulations that affected recruiting rules. The founder of Big Ten all-academic teams, Reed was hampered by rheumatoid arthritis, which curtailed his work in later years. Though he battled to the end, Reed succumbed to the disease in 1971 at the age of 55.

Maize & Blue Item

In high school, Henry Hill played tight end, but the Detroit native was considered too small to play college football. Therefore, the 5-10, 200-pound Hill came to Michigan on an academic scholarship, and attempted to walk on to the football team. He was switched to middle guard and embarked on a legendary career which ended with Hill being named team captain and All-American in 1970. Hill racked up 35 tackles for loss over his three years, a figure that still ranks seventh all-time in Michigan's record books.

M List

Double Success

The following teams have participated in the Rose Bowl and the NCAA Basketball Final Four in the same school year.

Michigan	1964-65
Michigan	1988-89*
Michigan	1991-92%
Michigan	1992-93%
UCLA	1961-62
UCLA	1975-76
Illinois	1951-52
California	1958-59
Southern California	1939-40

*-Won both
%-Hockey team also participated in National Final Four

1971-72

America's Time Capsule

September 13, 1971: A prison riot at Attica State Correctional Facility in New York ended, an uprising that claimed 43 lives.

September 21, 1971: Baseball's Washington Senators announced that the franchise would move to Texas for the beginning of the 1971 season.

February 21, 1972: President Nixon began his historic visit to mainland China.

May 26, 1972: Soviet secretary Leonid Brezhnev and President Nixon signed a treaty on antiballistic missile systems.

June 17, 1972: Police arrested five men involved in a burglary of Democratic Party headquarters, beginning the famed Watergate affair.

University Lore

The Power Center for the Performing Arts was dedicated on October 6 with the premier of a musical version of Truman Capote's play "Grass Harp" starring Celeste Holm. Designed by Kevin Rocke and John Dinkeloo, the 1420-seat theater has a large proscenium stage plus an orchestra pit that can be elevated to form a 28-foot-wide thrust stage. Former university regent Eugene Power and family donated $3 million of the $3.5 million cost of the Center.

Michigan Moment

"M" GRIDDERS WIN BIG TEN, BUT LOSE ROSE BOWL

Photo: U-M Athletic Dept.

Michigan's Billy Taylor

The Michigan's football team's goal at the beginning of the 1971 season was nothing less than the Big Ten title and the Rose Bowl. Northwestern, the team that had tied Michigan for second in the Conference in 1970, was the Wolverines' first opponent, and they were disposed of, 21-6. On the following Saturday, the defense held Virginia to -1 passing yards and the Wolverines romped, 56-0. U-M's defense reigned supreme in shutouts of UCLA and Navy. Though the Wolverines looked mighty in wins over Michigan State, Illinois, Minnesota and Indiana, they could not shake Ohio State in the standings. But as Michigan was scoring 60 points for the second straight game in a 63-7 slaughter of Iowa, MSU handed Ohio State its first loss. Then, as Dana Coin's 25-yard field goal was lifting the Wolverines to a 20-17 victory over Purdue, Northwestern beat the Buckeyes, and Michigan was the Big Ten champion. Even though the game meant little in the standings, for the first time in four seasons, pride would be on the line in the Michigan-Ohio State game. A second-quarter field goal gave Michigan a 3-0 lead at halftime, but the Buckeyes grabbed the lead when Tom Campana ran back a punt 85 yards for a 7-3 Ohio State lead. Billy Taylor gave Michigan hope for its first undefeated season since 1948 when he ran the ball in from 21 yards out with 2:07 remaining. Thom Darden ensured perfection with a late interception as Michigan won the Conference by 2-1/2 games, the largest margin since 1947 and tied for the best ever. The Rose Bowl pitted the Wolverines against 1971 Rose Bowl champion Stanford. Neither team did much offensively early on, and Coin's 30-yard field goal in the second quarter marked the only points scored in the first 30 minutes. Michigan was on the verge of scoring on its first drive of the second half, but the Indians rose up to stop the Wolverines on the one-yard line on fourth down. With the game within reach, quarterback Don Bunce led his troops down the field, ending the drive with a game-tying 42-yard field goal. Early in the last quarter, Michigan mounted a 71-yard drive, with 66 yards coming on rush plays. The Wolverines grabbed a 10-3 lead when Fritz Seyferth burst into the end zone from the one-yard line. On the ensuing drive, Stanford gained 31 yards on a fake punt, later scoring on Jackie Brown's 24-yard run to tie the game at 10-10. Great punt coverage by Ed Shuttlesworth enabled Michigan to get the lead with 3:18 left in the game. Shuttlesworth pulled down returner Jim Ferguson in the end zone for a safety and a 12-10 Michigan advantage. On Stanford's last drive, Bunce led the Indians down the field to the Michigan 14-yard line. With 12 seconds left on the clock, Rod Garcia kicked a field goal through the uprights, giving Stanford a 13-12 victory.

CHAMPION OF THE WEST

HENRY WILMORE

Henry Wilmore grew up in Manhattan, New York then became a high school All-American at Rockwood Academy in Massachusetts. As a sophomore, Wilmore made an immediate impact, scoring 650 points in 26 games for an average of 25.0 points per contest. Standing just 6'3-1/2", Wilmore still managed to grab almost 10 rebounds per game at his forward position. He broke Cazzie Russell's team record for points by a first-year player, and became only the second U-M basketball player to be named All-America in his first season. After a summer stint in the Pan-American games, Wilmore nearly matched his performance in 1972. He averaged 24.0 points per game over his junior season, despite being hampered by a knee injury that sidelined him for four games. He repeated his list of postseason accolades: Team MVP, All-Big Ten pick and All-America honors. Wilmore served as team captain in 1973, and despite being closely guarded by opponents, he averaged 21.8 points per game as the Wolverines ended the season with a 13-11 record. He ended his career with 1,652 points, a figure that still ranks eighth in Michigan's all-time record books. He was a fifth-round pick of the Detroit Pistons in the 1973 NBA Draft.

another CHAMPION OF THE WEST

THOM DARDEN

Thom Darden, a native of Sandusky, Ohio, excelled at defensive back from 1969-71 for Michigan. He was both an out standing pass defender and excellent tackler as Michigan led the Big Ten in scoring defense for his three seasons. As a sophomore in 1969, Darden recorded 82 tackles and two interceptions as Michigan won the Conference title and upset Ohio State. He started nine games in 1970, tying for the team lead in interceptions with five, while leading the team in passes broken up with 10. For his efforts, Darden was named first team All-Big Ten. As a senior, he led the team in interceptions with four, including one he returned for 92 yards against UCLA. He finished his career with 224 interception return yards, a figure that ranked second in the team record books. An All-Big Ten pick and All-American in 1971, Darden was chosen in the first round of the NFL draft by the Cleveland Browns. He played nine years with the Browns and was named to the All-Pro team in both 1978 and 1979. After his retirement, Darden served as the president of a small construction company in Ohio and as an employee of the Cowen and Company brokerage firm. Also active in community affairs, Darden remains a part of Michigan history as part of the record books in interceptions, passes broken up, and punt returns.

Maize & Blue Item

Many Michigan football players have left Ann Arbor to play in the pros, but on August 22, 1971, some of the pros returned to Ann Arbor. Athletic Director Don Canham invited the Detroit Lions to play one of their exhibition games at "The Big House," and the Lions had responded with a game against the defending Super Bowl Champion Baltimore Colts. The "experiment" drew a colossal 91,745 fans. U-M grads Bill Laskey of the Lions and Rick Volk of the Colts made their homecomings on the 90-degree Ann Arbor day.

M List
"M" Basketball All-Americans

In 1972, Henry Wilmore became the eighth Michigan basketball player named as an All-American. Since Wilmore's honor, six other Wolverines have earned such accolades:

Richard Doyle	1926
Bennie Oosterbaan	1927-28
Ernest McCoy	1929
John Townsend	1938
Bill Buntin	1964-65
Cazzie Russell	1964-65-66
Rudy Tomjanovich	1970
Henry Wilmore	1971-72
Campy Russell	1974
Rickey Green	1977
Gary Grant	1988
Glen Rice	1989
Rumeal Robinson	1990
Chris Webber	1993

1972-73

America's Time Capsule

November 7, 1972: The Republican Party enjoyed its greatest landslide victory with the re-election of President Richard Nixon.

December 18, 1972: Paris peace negotiations reached an impasse and full-scale bombing of North Vietnam was resumed by America pilots.

January 22, 1973: An agreement to end the war in Vietnam was signed in Paris by representatives of the United States and North and South Vietnam.

June 9, 1973: Secretariat, called the greatest race horse ever, won the Belmont Stakes and became the ninth Triple Crown winner.

July 16, 1973: The existence of the Watergate tapes was revealed.

University Lore

Groundbreaking ceremonies for the Art and Architecture Building heralded another significant expansion for the North Campus. The 212,065-square foot building was completed in the fall of 1974 at a cost of $8.5 million. Studios and workshops account for 80 percent of the interior space. The building includes a 150-seat lecture hall and an exhibit gallery as well as more than $300,000 in art equipment, including weaving looms, ceramics kilns and potter's wheels, a metal casting furnace, jewelry forges, sandblasting equipment and 30 individual photography dark rooms.

Michigan Moment

MICHIGAN GRAPPLERS GAIN BIG TEN CROWN

In Rick Bay's third year since taking over the reins from the legendary Cliff Keen, Michigan's wrestling squad prevailed at the Big Ten meet in Minneapolis. The win broke a seven-year string of dominance by Michigan State. The Wolverine wrestlers were able to prevail due to their excellent showing in the preliminary rounds. It took only one day of the two-day event to clinch the crown, as seven of the 10 Wolverine wrestlers placed in the finals. Jim Brown, Bill Davids, Jeff Guyton, Jarrett Hubbard, Mitch Mendrygal, Roger Ritzman and Gary Ernst eliminated each of their opponents to render the results of the final competition unimportant. Michigan's contingent did not fare as well in the championship bouts, emerging with just two individual titles. Jeff Guyton outpointed Conrad Calendar of Michigan State, 6-4, to claim the crown at 134 pounds, while Gary Ernst defeated Dave Simonson of Minnesota, 6-2. Defending Conference champions Hubbard and Medrygal were unable to annex another honor, each being decisioned by a single point. Despite the disappointment of the second day's results, the title was a fitting ending to a dual-meet season the Wolverines had finished, 12-0. Michigan would go on to place third at the NCAA championship. In an interesting trivia note, Michigan's Big Ten win was the last Big Ten title by a non-Iowa team, as the Hawkeyes have claimed each championship from 1974-97.

Photo: U-M Athletic Dept.

Michigan's wrestling team.

CHAMPIONSHIP *Moment*

Yost Ice Arena

MICHIGAN ICERS CLOSE OUT COLISEUM

Michigan's ice hockey team rallied for just six wins in 1972-73, but there were bigger problems than simply a poor won-loss record. After 46 years of service, the Coliseum was simply too old to serve the needs of the Wolverines. Standing at the corner of Fifth and Hill, the building had been ahead of its time in 1927, but had lapsed into a state of disrepair as the decades passed. Athletic Director Don Canham was forced to make a decision on the future of the rink following the 1973 season. The choice to renovate the Coliseum was not viable, due to the fact that the structure could not be improved to any great extent. After eliminating the possibility of building a new facility because of the prohibitive cost, Canham moved the team's home further south, to a virtually vacant Yost Fieldhouse. At a cost of $400,000 for an ice surface, a new paint job and some seats, Yost was converted into an 8,000-seat home for the Wolverines in time for the 1973-74 season.

CHAMPION OF THE WEST

JARRETT HUBBARD

Jarrett Hubbard rewrote the Michigan wrestling record books in his four years at U-M. As a freshman, Hubbard, who normally weighed in at 160 pounds, but wrestled at 150, finished with a 23-8 record and a Big Ten championship at his weight. At NCAA's, Hubbard advanced to the semi-finals, finishing fourth in his first appearance at the national level. He continued to improve for his sophomore year, compiling a record of 22-4-1 and claiming his second Big Ten title. He bettered his national finish, coming in second place to Wade Schalles of Clarion State. In 1973, the business major was unable to repeat his Big Ten dominance, finishing second at the Conference championship where Michigan earned top team honors. Hubbard rebounded from this setback by cruising through the national field en route to claiming the NCAA individual title at 150 pounds. The NCAA run began a stretch of 31 consecutive dual meet wins for Hubbard, who did not lose a single dual meet his senior year. He captured the Big Ten and NCAA titles as he recorded a 26-0 mark, becoming the third Michigan wrestler to win two NCAA titles. He finished his career with 78 wins and was named one of the top five student athletes in the country at the NCAA honors luncheon. After finishing up his career at U-M, he returned to his hometown of Joliet, Illinois, where he taught in the local high school.

Maize & Blue Item

A native of Jamaica, Godfrey Murray came to Michigan in 1970 and became the dominant force in Big Ten hurdles. In his three years of competition, Murray won four Big Ten individual titles, two in the indoor 70-yard hurdles and two in the outdoor 120-yard hurdles. In 1971, Murray missed the Conference standard by one-tenth of a second, finishing the 120-yard hurdles in 13.8 seconds. Following his senior year, Murray was named the recipient of the Conference Medal of Honor, recognizing his proficiency in both academics and athletics.

M List

Leaders in NCAA Individual Titles

Most men's NCAA individual titles by institution (by sport): [thru 1995-96]:

1. Southern California	273
2. Michigan	219
3. Ohio State	188
4. Stanford	182
5. UCLA	153
6. Oklahoma State	137
7. Indiana	118
8. Illinois	113
9. Yale	104
10. Iowa	101

1973-74

America's Time Capsule

December 6, 1973: Gerald Ford was sworn in as vice president, filling the void created by Spiro Agnew's resignation on October 10.

February 5, 1974: Patricia Hearst was kidnapped from her California apartment by a group calling itself the Symbionese Liberation Army.

April 8, 1974: Hank Aaron of the Atlanta Braves hit his 715th career home run, breaking Babe Ruth's legendary record.

July 29, 1974: Fred Zollner sells the Pistons to a management group headed by William Davidson for just over eight million dollars.

August 8, 1974: President Richard Nixon announced in a televised address that he would resign, with Gerald Ford sworn in as president the following day.

University Lore

The Bentley Historical Library was formally dedicated on May 4, 1974. The Library houses the Michigan Historical Collections and the University Archives. The library collects and preserves material documenting the history of the state of Michigan and the university. The holdings include 57,000 volumes, over 27,000 linear feet of manuscripts and university records, and 1.5 million photographs. The Library is named for former U-M regent and Congressman Alvin W. Bentley whose widow, Arvella, provided major funding for the building.

Michigan Moment

U-M VOTED OUT, OSU IN

For the second straight year, and fourth season in the last five, Michigan and Ohio State met to determine the Big Ten entrant in the Rose Bowl. Besides the Rose Bowl bid and Big Ten title, the game also carried national championship hopes for number-one ranked Ohio State. Michigan was looking for its first perfect season since 1948 and for retaliation for the Buckeyes' win in 1972. When the game was over, only confusion reigned. The athletic directors' vote at the end of the season had always been a mere formality. Now it was going to be political. Michigan had forced this decision by refusing to wilt in the face of the number-one Buckeyes. Clearly, the Wolverines felt that they belonged in the same class as Ohio State, even if the poll voters ranked Michigan only fourth in the nation. Ohio State threatened to run away early, as Archie Griffin ran for 99 yards in the first half. Though Michigan kept Griffin out of the end zone, the defense could not control Pete Johnson, who went in from five yards away to increase the OSU edge to 10-0. Despite going into halftime losing 10-0, the Wolverines would negate the lead with a 20-yard Mike Lantry field goal and a 10-yard Dennis Franklin run to even the game at ten. The Wolverines were looking for more, and Franklin led the offense into Buckeye territory. However, the junior quarterback was lost for the game when he was tackled after throwing a pass and broke his collarbone. Lantry's 48-yard field-goal attempt was wide left with under two minutes left. An interception by Tom Drake gave the ball back to Michigan, but Lantry's 58-yard attempt with less than thirty seconds left went wide right and the game ended tied. Once the final gun sounded, the debate began. Hadn't Ohio State dominated the first half? But then, hadn't Michigan been in control in the final 30 minutes? Would Franklin be back for the Rose Bowl? Even if he was out, hadn't Larry Cipa stepped in to do an admirable job in the Oregon game earlier in the season, when Franklin was injured? The debate amongst Michigan fans was meaningless at this point, all that mattered was the vote of 10 athletic directors who took the secret ballot that Sunday afternoon. With the Wolverines fairly confident that the bid would go to them, it came as a complete shock when 1973 Rose Bowl participant Ohio State was announced as the Big Ten representative. Michigan would end the 1973 season with a nearly perfect 10-0-1 record and a lot of imperfect feelings toward the Rose Bowl selection process.

Quarterback Dennis Franklin

CHAMPIONSHIP *Moment*

"M" CAGERS WIN BERTH IN NCAA TOURNAMENT

After Cazzie Russell's departure, the Michigan basketball team had suffered some lean years in the late 1960s. Johnny Orr had replaced Dave Strack as coach after the 1967-68 season, and had led the Wolverines to a 12-2 finish in the Big Ten in 1970-71. However, Ohio State finished 13-1 and won the right to go to the NCAA tournament, sending Michigan to the NIT. The Wolverines slumped to third place in 1972 and into the Big Ten's lower tier in 1973. It would be another Russell who would lead Michigan to the top spot in the Conference in 1974. Campy Russell had arrived at Michigan with the reputation of being the best prep player in 1972 and fulfilled those expectations by leading the Maize and Blue in rebounding and placing second in scoring. In 1974, Russell led the Big Ten in scoring with a 24.0 points-per-game average while placing second in rebounding. An All-Big Ten pick and All-America selection, Russell took a team without seniors to a 12-2 Conference record. Assisting Russell was a quartet of starters all averaging double figures in points. Co-captain C.J. Kupec anchored the center spot, with a backcourt of fellow junior Joe Johnson and freshman Steve Grote. Wayman Britt rounded out the starting five for a team that averaged over 80 points per game. Michigan and Indiana ended the season tied atop the Conference with identical 12-2 records. With the season series between the two teams split, a playoff game was arranged in the neutral site of Champaign, Illinois to determine which team would go to the NCAA tournament. Michigan outlasted the Hoosiers, 75-67, earning the playoff berth.

CHAMPION OF THE WEST

VICTOR AMAYA

For three years in the mid-1970s, Victor Amaya kept the Michigan tennis dynasty rolling, claiming two Conference singles titles and two doubles crowns as Michigan ran its Big Ten title streak to eight. The 6'5" lefthander from Holland, Michigan was dominating in nearly every facet of the game, defeating every Big Ten opponent he faced in 1973 and 1974. As a freshman, Amaya capped an excellent season by becoming the tenth Michigan tennis player to capture the Conference singles title. Amaya also teamed up with Jerry Karzen to take the doubles crown. He overpowered his way through the 1974 championship as well, capturing his second Big Ten singles crown with a 6-3, 6-2 defeat of Indiana's Don Sullivan. In doubles competition, Amaya and Eric Friedler narrowly escaped from Phil Kadesch and John Clark of Wisconsin, 7-6, 7-6. In both seasons, Amaya advanced to the quarterfinals of the NCAA championships before bowing out. In 1975, Amaya dropped a match in the Conference finals, falling just short of his third Conference title. After this loss, he decided to test the waters of the pro tour, where he continued his success. The three-time All-Big Ten selection and three-time All-American spent several years ranked amongst the top 15 tennis players in the world.

Maize & Blue Item

On June 23, 1972 Title IX was passed into law, intending to "prevent gender discrimination in any educational program or activity receiving federal financial assistance." This ruling paved the way for women's varsity sports at Michigan, where they had been competing on a club level since the beginning of the century. In its first year of sponsoring women's athletics on the intercollegiate level, U-M provided six sports: field hockey, basketball, swimming, synchonized swimming, volleyball and tennis.

M List

"M" Swimmers Top NCAA List

Most men's NCAA individual titles by institution, one sport: [thru 1995-96]

1. Michigan, swimming	140
2. Ohio State, swimming	117
3. Oklahoma State, wrestling	115
4. Stanford, swimming	107
5. Southern California, outdoor track	102
6. Southern California, swimming	98
7. Indiana, swimming	79
8. Colorado, skiing	60
8. Oklahoma, wrestling	60
9. Yale, swimming	60

1974-75

America's Time Capsule

September 8, 1974: President Gerald Ford pardoned former President Nixon for any crimes he may have committed while in office, calling for an end to the Watergate episode.

October 30, 1974: Muhammad Ali recaptured the heavyweight boxing title with an eighth-round knockout of George Foreman in Zaire.

November 28, 1974: The Denver Broncos defeated Detroit 31-27 in the Lions' last game at Tiger Stadium.

July 5, 1975: Arthur Ashe became the first African-American to win the men's singles title at England's Wimbledon tennis champioships.

July 31, 1975: Former Teamsters leader James Hoffa was reported missing.

University Lore

THE UNIVERSITY OF MICHIGAN · ARTES · SCIENTIA · VERITAS · 1817 ™

The Graduate Employees Organization, certified in the spring of 1974 as the sole bargaining agent for the U-M graduate student teaching and staff assistants, entered its first contract negotiations with the university in the fall of 1974. When talks broke down in February, GEO called a strike that lasted five weeks. The strike settlement granted token concessions to some GEO financial demands but it established the precedent of collective bargaining. GEO is now the oldest continuously functioning and most successful graduate student union in the country.

Michigan Moment

BASEBALL SUCCESS

Over the course of history, Michigan had been proficient in winning Big Ten baseball titles, capturing 21 Conference crowns between 1896 and 1974. However, the current crop of Michigan hitters could would be hard pressed to remember 1961 and the last time Michigan had finished in the top spot in the league. After losing six of its first seven games, it seemed as though Michigan would be hard pressed to break the 14-year drought. But the Wolverines turned it around in Big Ten play, winning their first five contests. A doubleheader sweep at Indiana put the Wolverines a half game ahead of Michigan State heading into the stretch run. Against the Wildcats of Northwestern, Chuck Rogers and Mark Weber pitched back-to-back shutouts to sweep the doubleheader. Rogers struck out 10 NU batters while allowing just four hits in the first game, and Weber struck out seven while pitching a five-hitter in the nightcap. Still, Michigan would need to beat Wisconsin twice to hold off Iowa. In front of a crowd of 1,200 at Ray Fisher Stadium, Michigan took the first game from the Badgers, 4-2, behind Craig Forhan's complete-game performance. In the second game, Wisconsin took a 2-0 lead off Michigan hurler Lary Sorenson. The Wolverines cut the lead to 2-1 in the bottom of the second, then took the lead in the third on a single by Dick Waterhouse and a walk to Randy Hackney, followed by a sacrifice, a fielder's choice and an error. An insurance run in the fifth made the final score 4-2 as Mark Weber pitched the final 3-2/3 innings in relief for the win and a Big Ten title.

Photo: U-M Athletic Dept.

Michigan's 1975 baseball team.

CHAMPION OF THE WEST

THE DUFEK FAMILY

Don Dufek

Bill Dufek

More than 150 family lineages can be traced through the annals of Michigan letter winners. Lately, sister combinations and father-daughter histories have added to the brother pairs and father-son patterns of yesteryear. One of the most notable of these kin connections was the Dufek family, who combined for 14 letters between father Donald and sons Donald Jr. and Bill. The eldest Dufek, a fullback on Michigan's 1948-50 Big Ten title-winning teams, was named the MVP of the 1950 Rose Bowl champion squad. He ran for over 600 yards during that season en route to capturing first-team All Conference honors. He later served as an assistant coach for the Wolverines from 1954-65. Dufek and his wife, Pat, had six children, two of which would continue the great Wolverine tradition. Bill was a four-year letter winner at offensive tackle from 1974-78 and was drafted by the New York Jets, while Don Jr. served as wingback from 1973-75. The pair combined for 50 starts, three All-Big Ten selections and played on four Big Ten champion teams. Don, who also earned four letters in hockey, later and was drafted by the New York Jets.

another CHAMPION OF THE WEST

THE KARZENS

Until 1975, there had been 51 sibling combinations that had participated in intercollegiate athletics at the University of Michigan. In that year, a 52nd tandem was added to that list, and as the first entry on a new list; brother-sister pairs to play at U-M. Jerry and Jan Karzen became the first duo, as Jerry played for the men's tennis team and Jan played for the women's version. As a senior in 1975, Jerry was a part of Michigan's eighth straight Conference title, playing at No. 4 singles. He teamed up with Victor Amaya to claim the 1973 Conference doubles crown, and was named All-Big Ten in both 1973 and 1975. He advanced to the fourth round in singles at the NCAA championship as a sophomore, and went as far as the semifinals in the NCAA doubles tournament in his final season. Jan was just a sophomore in 1975, joining the tennis team as an opportunity to have fun. In her first season, she reached the semi-finals of the Big Ten tournament after winning six of eight regular season matches at No. 2 singles. Karzen went on to play three years for U-M, the last of which she was joined by sister Kathy, the third Karzen to play tennis for Michigan.

Maize & Blue Item

When Michigan began sponsoring cross country in 1971, it took just four years for U-M to rise to the top. Under first-year coach Ron Warhurst, Michigan came in with the low score at the Conference championship meet in Ann Arbor. Greg Meyer led the Michigan charge, coming in second with a time of 29:45.8. Bill Donakowski finished sixth, and Mike McGuire finished eighth for the champion Wolverines.

M List

In trampolining from 1949-70, there was no better team in the nation than the Michigan Wolverines. Michigan gymnasts took home 11 individual national titles in those 22 years, as well as nine runners up and three third-place finishes. On the Big Ten level, Michigan's male gymnasts have been dominant in the trampoline, as well as other events.

Men

Event	"M" Champions	Years	Ind. Champions	Years
Horizontal bar	5	6	3	1971-76
Parallel bars	7	9	4	1956-64
Parallel bars	4	4	3	1968-71
Trampoline	10	12	7	1958-69
Team championships	12	15		1961-75

Women

Event	"M" Champions	Years	Ind. Champions	Years
All-around	7	7	4	1991-97
Uneven parallel bars	6	6	3	1992-97
Balance beam	6	6	6	1992-97
Team championships	6	6		1992-97

America's Time Capsule

September 5, 1975: President Gerald Ford escaped the first of two assassination attempts in a little more than two weeks. Lynette "Squeaky" Fromme was apprehended.

October 1, 1975: Heavyweight boxing champion Muhammad Ali defeated Joe Frazier in the "Thrilla in Manilla".

February 13, 1976: Dorothy Hamill won a gold medal in figure skating at the Winter Olympics in Innsbruck, Austria.

July 4, 1976: The bicentennial of United States independence was celebrated.

July 20, 1976: Viking I, launched 11 months earlier, landed on Mars.

University Lore

In a series of public forums, seminars, and committees, the faculty and U-M community debated the University's policies in regard to recombinant DNA research, the combining of genetic material of one species with that of another. Ethical and safety concerns were weighed against the potential for medical and scientific breakthroughs and the faculty's right to free inquiry. In May, the regents approved a policy permitting "moderate risk" DNA research. Two laboratories were soon remodeled to serve as "moderate risk" containment facilities.

Michigan Moment

MICHIGAN 5 BATTLE HOOSIERS FOR NCAA CROWN

Johnny Orr's basketball squad went through the season with a 25-7 overall record, including a very respectable 14-4 in the Big Ten. However, the performance of the Wolverines was no match for the Indiana Hoosiers, who went through the season undefeated. Thanks to a 1974 ruling by Big Ten officials, a second place finish no longer meant exclusion from the NCAA tournament. For the first-round contest, the Wolverines headed to Denton, Texas, to take on Wichita State. The Shockers held a 60-48 second-half edge. Despite losing Phil Hubbard to fouls with more than seven minutes to go, the Wolverines charged back to within one point with 38 seconds remaining. With six seconds left, Rickey Green nailed a 20-foot jumper for a 74-73 Michigan comeback win. If the Michigan cagers were going to advance to the third round for the first time since 1965, they would have to control Adrian Dantley and the Fighting Irish. U-M fought from behind the entire game, finally taking the lead when Hubbard sank a 15-foot jump shot with 3:43 left. Michigan ultimately prevailed, 80-76, despite Dantley's 31 points. In the third round, it was the opponents' turn to come back. The Wolverines staked out a 50-36 lead over Missouri, but the Tigers roared back to take a 76-71 edge. After evening the score at 77-77, Michigan won 95-88, getting double-doubles from Hubbard (20 points and 18 rebounds) and John Robinson (21 and 16). Now only Rutgers stood in the way of Michigan and the NCAA finals. With a 31-0 record, the Scarlet Knights were a formidable blockade. However, Rutgers' 29.5 field goal percentage in the first half allowed U-M to cruise to an 86-70 victory. All of Michigan's starters scored in double figures. For the first time in NCAA tournament history, two teams from the same Conference were to meet in the final. Michigan's opponent was Indiana, still undefeated and already holding two victories over the Wolverines. Michigan surprised the Hoosiers by taking an early eight-point lead and holding the edge at halftime, 35-29. Behind college basketball Player of the Year Scott May's 26 points and teammate Kent Benson's 25, Indiana managed to pull away in the second half. When Hubbard and Wayman Britt fouled out in the second half, Indiana pulled away to an 86-68 victory.

Michigan's 1975-76 basketball team.

CHAMPIONSHIP *Moment*

MICHIGAN FOOTBALL TEAM GOES TO ORANGE BOWL

On May 12, 1975, the Big Ten assured that no repeat of what happened after the 1973 football season could occur. Except for the stipulation that the second-place team receive a bid before the third-place team, etc., the Conference would now permit a member team to go to a bowl game other than the Rose. The ruling came too late to prevent what happened to the Wolverines in 1972, 1973 and 1974, but was a saving grace in 1975. That season's football team coasted to a record of 8-1-2, but suffered the lone setback to Ohio State, dropping the Wolverines out of sole first place yet again. Despite the loss, there would be a bowl game this year. Michigan became the first Big Ten school to attend a bowl game other than the Rose when it accepted a bid to the Orange Bowl in Miami, Florida. The fifth-ranked Wolverines and third-ranked Sooners matched up in a defensive struggle in the first quarter. Oklahoma finally opened up the scoring in the second period, using a 39-yard reverse by Billy Brooks. A promising Michigan drive in the third quarter ended when freshman quarterback Rick Leach was intercepted in the end zone. Oklahoma was able to extend its lead to 14-0 at the beginning of the fourth quarter on a touchdown run by Steve Davis. The Wolverines cut the deficit to 14-6 after Gordon Bell scored, but that was all U-M could muster. Oklahoma would become the National Champion when Ohio State lost in the Rose Bowl to UCLA.

CHAMPION OF THE WEST

RICKEY GREEN

Raised in Chicago, Rickey Green had already led his prep school team to a state title and become a two-time Junior College All-American at Vincennes Junior College. The guard would continue making his presence felt as he transferred to Michigan for the 1975-76 season. At 6-2, 170 pounds, it was not Green's size that was imposing on the court, it was his unbelievable speed that turned heads. In 1976, Green led the team in points and assists, recording double figures in 31 of 32 games. Green averaged nearly 20 points per game as his presence helped the Wolverines to their first Big Ten title and NCAA finals appearance since the Cazzie Russell years. In 1977, Green was again named an All-Big Ten selection and added All-America honors to his resume by averaging 19.5 points per game. With Green and teammate Phil Hubbard combining for nearly half of the Wolverines' point production, Michigan earned its second straight Conference title and NCAA bid. After completing his career with 1,145 points in two seasons, Green was selected by the Golden State Warriors in the first round of the NBA draft. Green spent 14 years in the NBA, playing for eight teams and setting the Utah Jazz team record for most games played. He also made trivia history by scoring the league's 5,000,000th point. During his time in the pros, Green continued to work on his degree, graduating from U-M in 1981.

Maize & Blue Item

The 1975 homecoming contest versus Indiana is not significant because of the 55-7 final score, but because of the 93,857 fans that braved the 45 degree kickoff temperature. That attendance figure was the last non-six digit attendance figure in the history of Michigan Stadium. Since November 8, 1975, when 102,415 fans were in the stands to see the Wolverines take on Purdue, there have been 135 consecutive games at Michigan Stadium with at least 100,000 people in attendance.

M List: Michigan's Non-Rose Bowl Games

Date	Bowl	Site	Opponent	Result
January 1, 1976	Orange	Miami, FL	Oklahoma	L, 6-14
December 28, 1979	Gator	Jacksonville, FL	North Carolina	L, 15-17
December 31, 1981	Bluebonnet	Houston, TX	UCLA	W, 33-14
January 2, 1984	Sugar	New Orleans, LA	Auburn	L, 7-9
December 21, 1984	Holiday	San Diego, CA	Brigham Young	L, 17-24
January 1, 1986	Fiesta	Tempe, AZ	Nebraska	W, 27-23
January 2, 1988	Hall of Fame	Tampa, FL	Alabama	W, 28-24
January 1, 1991	Gator	Jacksonville, FL	Mississippi	W, 35-3
January 1, 1994	Hall of Fame	Tampa, FL	N.C. State	W, 42-7
December 30, 1994	Holiday	San Diego, CA	Colorado State	W, 24-14
December 28, 1995	Alamo	San Antonio, TX	Texas A&M	L, 20-22
January 1, 1997	Outback	Tampa, FL	Alabama	L, 14-27

1976-77

MICHIGAN MOMENT

America's Time Capsule

September 12, 1976: Jimmy Connors joined Chris Evert as U.S. Open tennis champions.

November 2, 1976: Jimmy Carter defeated incumbent Gerald Ford in the presidential election.

January 17, 1977: A 10-year halt on capital punishment ended in the U.S. when Gary Gilmore was executed by a Utah firing squad.

July 28, 1977: The trans-Alaska pipeline went into full operation.

August 10, 1977: New York City police arrested David Berkowitz as the Son of Sam killer.

University Lore

The Central Campus and North Campus Recreational Buildings opened in the summer of 1976. Together with the Intramural Sports Building and the Sports Coliseum, they gave Michigan the most extensive indoor intramural sports facilities of any university in the country. The completion of the CCRB and NCRB sealed the fate of two campus landmarks. Despite protests from preservationists, the regents ordered Waterman (1894) and Barbour (1896) Gymnasiums torn down to make room for an expansion of the Chemistry Building.

"M" ICERS SKATE TO NCAA FINALS

Dave Debol

After posting three winning seasons in Dan Farrell's first three years as head coach, the Michigan icers hoped to chase a WCHA title in 1977. Not having reached the NCAA tournament or finished higher than fourth in the league since 1964, the goal may have seemed a bit lofty. A 14-7 start gave Michigan good feelings for the remainder of the season, but a seven-game losing streak evened Michigan's record at 14-14 and made a mediocre record seem probable. After an 11-8 loss to Wisconsin, with the season coming apart at the seams, U-M's players came together to post a 12-game winning streak. A pair of losses in the WCHA playoff finals to Wisconsin broke the string, but left the Wolverines with a 26-16 record and an NCAA tournament berth. In the first-round regional playoff in Yost Arena, Michigan bounced Bowling Green, 7-5, behind two goals by both Bill Thayer and Dan Lerg. U-M would not have to travel far to the semifinal, which was being held at Olympia Arena in Detroit. Michigan coasted to a 6-4 win over Boston University and its future Olympian goalie Jim Craig, and the team's ninth trip to the NCAA finals. Michigan's final opponent, Wisconsin, was a very familiar one. U-M and the Badgers had met six times previously in the 1976-77 season, with Michigan winning only the first contest. Wisconsin skated out to a 3-0 lead in the opening 15 minutes of the final game, but Michigan closed to 3-2 on Dave Debol's 42nd goal of the season, just 1:33 into the second period. A minute and a half later, Wisconsin restored the edge to 4-2. There was no further scoring in the second period. Just over a minute into the third period, Wisconsin's Murray Johnson scored his second goal of the game to make the score 5-2. But like it had done earlier in the season, Michigan responded to adversity. Mark Miller scored 26 seconds later, and Debol equalled Red Berenson's single-season record for goals with his 43rd at the 2:14 mark of the third period to make the score 5-4. John Waymann later tied the score at 5-5 with a late goal. The two teams were tied at the end of regulation but it did not take long to determine a winner. Wisconsin's Steve Alley converted a rebound 23 seconds into overtime to give the Badgers the championship. The runner-up trophy claimed by Michigan served notice to the rest of the league never to count out the Wolverines.

CHAMPION
OF THE WEST
ROB LYTLE

Rob Lytle came to Michigan from Fremont, Ohio, and became the newest in a long history of standout running backs at U-M. After seeing limited action in 1973, Lytle exploded onto the scene as a tailback in 1974, collecting 802 rushing yards as Michigan tied for the Big Ten title. After switching to fullback prior to the 1975 season, Lytle bettered his 1974 output, gaining 1,040 yards on 193 carries. The 6-1, 195 pound block of speed scored 10 touchdowns in his junior campaign, including four in a game versus Indiana. During his senior season, Lytle was a dominating force in the Big Ten. He ran for a school record 1,469 yards to increase his career total to a Michigan record 3,317. The running back averaged 6.9 yards per carry, another school record in leading Michigan to its first Rose Bowl since the 1971 season. He led the Conference in rushing yards and was named first-team All-Big Ten, Big Ten MVP, and a consensus All-American. He finished third in the Heisman Trophy balloting following the 1976 regular season. A second-round draft choice of the NFL's Denver Broncos, Lytle played seven years in the NFL, advancing to the Super Bowl with the Broncos in 1977. After retiring in 1983, Lytle returned to Fremont, where he entered private business.

another CHAMPION
OF THE WEST
DAVE DEBOL

When Dave Debol arrived in Ann Arbor in 1974, the hockey team had just posted its first winning season in five years. The St. Clair Shores native walked on and immediately made an impact on the team, scoring 31 points in his freshman season. His 13 goals placed fourth on a team that won 22 games, the most since the 1964 national championship team won 24. Debol played in 33 games without recording a single penalty and earned rookie of the year honors. His success continued into his sophomore season, as Debol placed second on the team with 36 goals and third with 58 points. But Debol would post even higher numbers his junior year, when he exploded for 43 goals and 56 assists for 99 points. His points and assists set school marks while his 43 goals tied the school standard set by Red Berenson. Named an All-American and Michigan's MVP, Debol helped the Wolverines reach the title game of the NCAA championship. The 5'11", 175-pound Debol led the Wolverines in scoring his senior year and ended his career as the Michigan leader in goals, assists and points. After graduating from Michigan, Debol played four years with the Cincinnati Stingers of the WHA and Hartford Whalers of the NHL. He is currently an account representative for Hockey Tech.

Maize & Blue Item

Between 1970 and 1975, Michigan had entered the Ohio State game with a combined record of 57-0-2, including 41-0 in Big Ten play. However, the Wolverines had a record of just 1-4-1 against the Buckeyes in those six seasons, going to Pasadena only once. This time, however, the Ohio Stadium record crowd of 88,250 could do nothing but watch the Buckeyes get shut out for the first time since the Ohio State-Michigan game in 1964. Rob Lytle ran for 165 yards in U-M's 22-0 victory.

M List
Michigan's Football-Basketball Champs

In the 1976-77 school year, Michigan's football and basketball teams both finished on top of the Big Ten Conference. This is a feat that has been accomplished 21 times in Conference history, a half-dozen times by Michigan. Italics denote a team that won both titles outright.

Michigan	1925-26
Michigan	1926-27
Michigan	*1947-48*
Michigan	*1964-65*
Michigan	1973-74
Michigan	1976-77

1977-78

America's Time Capsule

September 13, 1977: The first diesel-engine automobiles were introduced by General Motors.

February 8, 1978: Egyptian President Anwar el-Sadat began a six-day visit to the United States to hasten a Middle East peace settlement.

February 15, 1978: Leon Spinks won a 15-round decision over Muhammad Ali to capture the heavyweight boxing title.

June 10, 1978: Affirmed, ridden by jockey Steve Cauthen, won horse racing's Triple Crown with a victory at the Belmont Stakes.

August 4, 1978: Evacuation of the Love Canal area of Niagara Falls began, a dumping ground for toxic waste in the 1940s and '50s.

University Lore

With his promotion to full professor with tenure in the Department of Microbiology, Albert Wheeler became the first African-American to advance through the ranks to a tenured professorship. A graduate of the School of Public Health (MSPH '38, DrPH '44), Wheeler joined the faculty as an assistant professor in 1952. An activist in civil rights and political causes, Wheeler was instrumental in forming the Michigan Civil Rights Commission and the Ann Arbor Human Rights Commission. He served as mayor of Ann Arbor, 1975-1978.

Michigan Moment

WOLVERINE "9" ADVANCE TO COLLEGE WORLD SERIES

After ending a 14-year drought on Big Ten titles in 1975, the Wolverine baseball team stood atop the Big Ten again in 1976 and 1978. Now came time to end the next dry spell, an appearance in the College World Series. Since winning the national title in 1962, Michigan's attempts at getting back in the tournament had been dashed by regional losses each of the last three seasons. Such was not to be the case in 1978, as the Wolverines blasted Southwest Conference champion Texas A&M in the first game, 8-1, as Steve Howe struck out 10 Aggies. Nearby rival and nemesis Eastern Michigan presented the next hurdle for Michigan to conquer, and the Wolverines obliged with a 6-4 win. After Wolverine pitcher Craig McGinnis walked four of the first five batters he faced, Steve Perry came in to relieve him with just one out in the first. Perry finished the game with 8-2/3 innings of five hit pitching and Michigan erased a 4-1 deficit in the seventh inning to win. U-M needed just one more win to earn a World Series bid, and the Aggies were back for revenge. However, Tom Owens scattered nine hits and Rick Leach's double to open the fourth inning led to two runs in the 3-0 victory. At the World Series, Michigan shut out Baylor, 4-0, as Howe tossed a one-hitter. The season ended the season with losses to Southern California and North Carolina, but marked the beginning of a string where the team would make the College World Series in five of the next seven years.

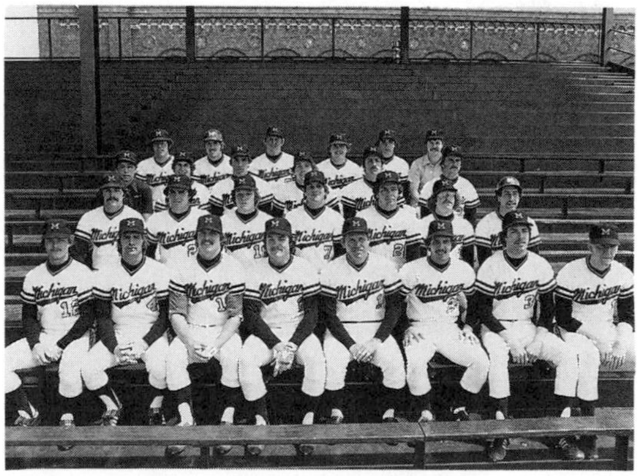

Michigan's 1977-78 baseball team.

CHAMPION OF THE WEST

PHIL HUBBARD

Ohio Basketball Player of theYear, Phil Hubbard averaged 15.1 points and 11.0 rebounds per game during his freshman season at Michigan. The 6-7 Hubbard teamed up with Rickey Green to power U-M's second-place finish at the NCAA Championship. The center recorded international honors during the summer of '76 as he played for the gold medal-winning United States squad at the Summer Olympics in Montreal. Hubbard contributed 10 points in the title game versus Yugoslavia as the Red, White and Blue posted a perfect 7-0 record. Returning to Michigan in 1976-77, Hubbard shot 55.6 percent from the floor and averaged nearly 20 points per game. His achievements on the court led to his selection as both a first-team All-Big Ten pick and first team All-American following his sophomore year. After missing the 1977-78 season due to a knee injury, Hubbard returned to the 1978-79 squad, where he averaged 14.8 points and 8.8 rebounds per game. Despite having a year of eligibility remaining, Hubbard declared himself eligible for the NBA draft, where he was selected with the 15th pick by the Detroit Pistons. In August 1979, Hubbard completed his degree in education and embarked on a 10-year NBA career with the Pistons and the Cleveland Cavaliers. He retired following the 1989 season with a career scoring average of 10.9 points over 665 games.

another CHAMPION OF THE WEST

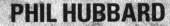

JEFF ETTERBEEK

There were many reasons behind the Michigan tennis team's 16 straight Big Ten titles between 1968 and 1983. In the late-1970s, Jeff Etterbeek was one of the driving forces as the Wolverines continued to batter the rest of the Big Ten. The Holland, Michigan native immediately made an impression, advancing to the second round of NCAA's in both singles and doubles competition. The first-team All-Big Ten pick teamed up with Eric Friedler to earn the Conference doubles title. In 1977, Etterbeek compiled a regular-season record of 17-2 and helped lead a young team to its 10th Consecutive conference crown. He and Judson Shaufler paired up to claim the Big Ten doubles title and advance to the second round of NCAA championships. Etterbeek was nearly unstoppable in 1978, becoming the 11th Michigan netter to win a Big Ten singles crown and pairing up with Matt Horwitch to earn his third straight Conference doubles title. As a senior, Etterbeek made his greatest mark in national competition. In the singles bracket, Jeff reached the national quarterfinals before bowing out to Juan Farrow of Southern Illinois. In doubles, the tandem of Etterbeek and Horwitch approached the round of 16 before losing. During his career, Etterbeek was a four-time All-Big Ten choice.

Maize & Blue Item

Wilmette, Illinois native John Corritore became Newt Loken's 23rd individual champion when the two-time Big Ten champion posted a 19.275 score to win the 1978 parallel bars title. Corritore's 19.275 score enabled him to beat Long Beach State's Yochi Tomata and better his runner-up finish on the parallel bars in 1977. The previous year, Corritore had held the lead heading into the final routine, but missed his dismount and dropped to second place.

M List — Longevity Leaders Among Women's Coaches

Coach	Seasons	Sport
Dick Kimball*	23	Diving
Bitsy Ritt*	13	Tennis
Carol Hutchins*	13	Softball
James Henry*	13	Track
Jim Richardson*	12	Swimming
Sue LeClair	11	Golf
Sandy Vong	11	Volleyball
Bud Van DeWege	8	Basketball
Beverly Plocki*	8	Gymnastics
Gloria Soluk	7	Basketball
Patti Smith	7	Field Hockey

*Still active though 1996-97.

America's Time Capsule

September 15, 1978: Muhammad Ali regained the heavyweight boxing title with a 15-round decision over Leon Spinks.

November 18, 1978: More than 900 people, including 211 children, were found dead in Guyana. Jim Jones, leader of the religious sect, led the group in a mass suicide by poison.

January 16, 1979: The Shah of Iran was overthrown by Ayatollah Khomeni supporters.

March 28, 1979: Three Mile Island, near Harrisburg, Pennsylvania., was the site of a nuclear near-disaster.

May 25, 1979: An American Airlines DC-10 jet crashed shortly after takeoff in Chicago, killing all 272 passengers on board and three other people on the ground.

University Lore

The University lost one of its best known personalities with the death of Dr. Hazel Losh, professor emeritus of astronomy. She received her MA ('22) and PhD ('24) from Michigan and joined the astronomy faculty in 1927. She was best known for her introductory astronomy course for non-majors, teaching nearly 2,000 students per year at her peak. "Doc" Losh was a great supporter of UM athletics and student athletes. She had sideline passes under three football coaches.

Michigan Moment

CHAMPIONS AGAIN

The first ten weeks of the 1978 season saw the Michigan football team roll to a 9-1 record while posting four shutouts. Though the Wolverines suffered their first loss to Michigan State since 1969, Michigan got revenge upon Minnesota for its 1977 win. The Wolverines, Spartans and Buckeyes all entered the final week of the season tied atop the Big Ten at 6-1. Due to NCAA probation, Michigan State was ineligible to go to the Rose Bowl, so the Michigan-Ohio State winner would determine the Conference champion and Rose Bowl entrant. The Buckeyes came in looking for their unprecedented seventh straight Conference title while the Wolverines hoped to continue a more modest two-year streak. Despite a cool, overcast day in Columbus, an Ohio Stadium record crowd of 88,358 was in attendance. Though the Wolverines were held to a regular-season low 14 points, Michigan's defense held the Buckeyes to just a field goal in a 14-3 win. After Ohio State opened the scoring with a 29-yard field goal in the opening quarter, Rick Leach responded with a 30-yard scoring pass to Rodney Feaster to give Michigan a 7-3 lead. The only other score of the game occured in the third quarter, as Leach connected with Roosevelt Smith on an 11-yard scoring pass. Led by Ron Simpkins, who collected 15 tackles, the Wolverine defense held the Buckeyes to just 216 yards of total offense. By winning its second straight game in Ohio Stadium for the first time since 1964-66, Michigan won its 29th Conference title and ninth Rose Bowl bid.

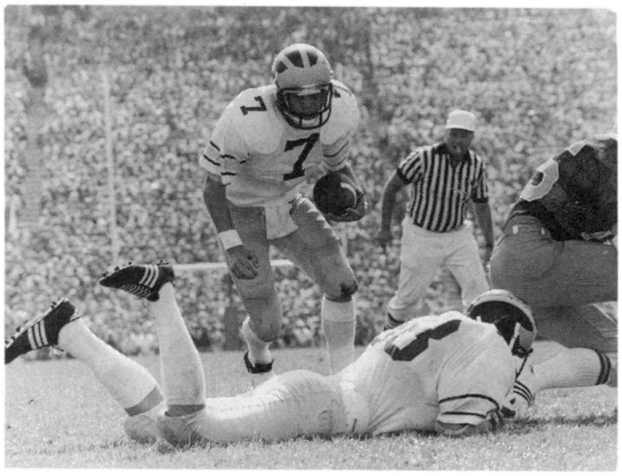

Quarterback Rick Leach

CHAMPION OF THE WEST

MARK CHURELLA

There have been few wrestlers in NCAA history whose record rivals that of Mark Churella.

During his four-year career from 1976-79, the Farmington, Michigan native compiled a record of 127-13, while claiming two Big Ten titles and three national crowns. In his freshman campaign, Churella rolled up a 35-7 mark, finishing second at the Big Ten championship. He capped off his inaugural campaign with a third-place finish at the NCAA's, where his semi-final loss would be the only blemish on an otherwise perfect 22-1 NCAA career record. Almost unbelievably, the 150-pound Churella improved on his freshman year success. His sophomore season included a 30-2 record, a Big Ten title and a NCAA crown, thus becoming U-M's 11th individual wrestling champion. The 1977 All-American repeated all those honors the following season, when he became only the fourth U-M wrestler to win two NCAA championships. For his achievements, he was named the NCAA Outstanding Wrestler for 1978. Moving up to the 167-pound weight class for his senior season, Churella finished 39-2 in his final year. Despite finishing second in the Big Ten, Churella rebounded to capture an NCAA title for the third straight year. Following graduation, Churella served as coach at UNLV for five years before returning to Michigan as an assistant for four seasons.

another CHAMPION OF THE WEST

RICK LEACH

In 1975, for the first time in Michigan football history, a freshman was called upon to be the signal caller. Rick Leach, a Flint native, was ready for the task, steering the Wolverines to an Orange Bowl berth. Following the football season, Leach hung up his helmet temporarily, and took his glove to center field to prepare for the baseball season. He would lead Michigan in batting average as the Wolverines won the Big Ten title. Big Ten championships would become the norm for Leach in football, where he would take Michigan to Rose Bowl berths in his sophomore, junior and senior seasons. He would collect All-Big Ten honors as Michigan finished 10-2 in each of those three seasons. In 1978, Leach set the NCAA record for most touchdowns in a career with 82. After his final game, Leach held 11 Michigan records and three Big Ten bests. Named both Big Ten MVP and an All-American in 1978, Leach finished third in the Heisman Trophy voting and was named co-MVP in the Rose Bowl. A throwback to the days of two-sport stars, Leach continued his success during the spring. He led the team in batting average and his .404 mark in 1978 made him only the third Wolverine to bat .400 in a season in 21 years. He led the Big Ten in batting in 1978 and was a driving force behind Michigan's first College World Series appearance since 1962. An All-Big Ten selection in 1977, 1978 and 1979, Leach was honored with All-American accolades in his senior season. He finished with a career batting average of .348. Drafted by Major League Baseball's Detroit Tigers and the National Football League's Denver Broncos, Leach chose to play baseball. Over a ten-year career, Leach compiled a .268 batting average in 799 games.

Maize & Blue Item

Originally at Michigan on a football scholarship, Jim Paciorek spent four years continuing the baseball juggernaut. The 1982 All-American finished his career ranked first in the Michigan record books in 11 categories, including games played, home runs, and batting average. Though his .443 batting average as a senior was just shy of the U-M record, the Detroit native captured five other Michigan single-season standards.

M List: College Football's All-Time Winningest Teams

School	Years	Games	Wins	Losses	Ties	Percentage
1. Notre Dame	108	1010	746	222	42	.759
2. Michigan	**117**	**1054**	**764**	**254**	**36**	**.742**
3. Alabama	102	1009	713	253	43	.728
4. Oklahoma	102	985	673	259	53	.510
5. Texas	104	1030	713	284	33	.708
6. Ohio State	107	1015	690	272	53	.710
7. USC	107	1030	713	284	33	.708
8. Nebraska	107	1041	709	292	40	.700
9. Penn State	110	1043	706	296	41	.697
10. Tennessee	100	1001	665	283	53	.691

1979-80

America's Time Capsule

September 9, 1979: John McEnroe and 16-year-old Tracy Austin won singles titles at the U.S. Tennis Open.

November 4, 1979: Iranian revolutionaries seized the U.S. embassy in Teheran, taking some 90 hostages, including 65 Americans.

January 20, 1980: President Carter announced that the U.S. Olympic Team would boycott the 1980 Summer Olympics in Moscow, in a protest against the Soviet invasion of Afghanistan.

February 22, 1980: The U.S. hockey team beat the heavily favored Soviet Union, 4-3, advancing to the finals where it defeated Finland for the gold medal.

May 18, 1980: Mt. St. Helens, a volcano that had been dormant since 1857, erupted in Washington, leveling about 120 square miles of forest.

University Lore

Law School professor Allan Smith served one year as interim president before Harold Tafler Shapiro took office as UM's tenth president on January 1, 1980. Canadian by birth and educated at Princeton, Shapiro joined the UM Economics Department in 1964 and co-directed the Research Seminar in Quantitative Economics, famous for its economic forecasting models. "Smaller but better" became the watchword of his tenure as the University experienced a series of budget crises and declining rates of state support. Shapiro resigned in 1987 to become president of Princeton.

Michigan Moment

CARTER STUNS HOOSIER GRIDDERS

In Michigan's 100th season of playing football, the 1979 team added to the vast lore of Wolverine history with a thrilling victory. In front of a capacity homecoming crowd of 104,832, the Wolverines' opponents were the Hoosiers of Indiana, a team that was enjoying a successful season. After not having a winning season since 1968, the 1979 Indiana squad was off to a 5-2 start, 3-1 in the Big Ten. Though Michigan had lost a heartbreaker to Notre Dame in the season's second game, Michigan came into the contest a healthy 6-1 and in the hunt for the Big Ten title once again. Michigan saw a 7-0 first-quarter advantage lapse into a 14-7 halftime deficit. With starting quarterback B.J. Dickey injured, John Wangler was to take his place midway through the game. Lawrence Reid broke a 50-yard touchdown run to tie the game, and Butch Woolfolk ran for two of his 129 yards on the day to give Michigan a 21-14 lead later in the third quarter. The Hoosiers refused to back down, and in search of their first non-loss to Michigan since 1967, tied the game at 21 with 55 seconds left. Eventual Big Ten MVP Tim Clifford found Dave Harangody in the end zone on a two-yard pass to knot the score. If Michigan was going to win, it would have to do so starting from the Wolverine 22-yard line with 51 seconds left. A Wangler pass and two Woolfolk runs left the ball at the "M" 35-yard line with 25 seconds left. A pass to Lawrence Reid and an Indiana penalty put the ball at the Indiana 45-yard line, but with six seconds left, Michigan was forced to go for the touchdown. On the final play, Wangler hit Anthony Carter with a pass over the middle, but Carter stood on the 25-yard line with a number of Indiana players downfield. Utilizing his speed and agility, Carter escaped the first man to grab him, caused another Hoosier to miss and eluded another would-be tackler. Stumbling as he got close to the end zone, Carter managed to find his feet and scamper into the end zone for the unbelievable, improbable victory. The crowd went wild, flooding the field, and no extra point was ever attempted. Nothing more was needed to cap the 27-21 win.

Anthony Carter celebrates game-winning catch in a 1979 game with Indiana.

CHAMPIONSHIP *Moment*

BAND DAY CLASSIC

Michigan Stadium had spent 52 years serving as home to the Michigan football team, but it was Athletic Director Don Canham's idea to allow the mammoth bowl to serve as someone else's home for a single game. Those "someones" were Division III schools Slippery Rock and Shippensburg State as they celebrated the 1979 Band Day with a football game. For several years it had been a Canham tradition to choose a Michigan football game where high school bands could come and play their music. However, with the constant sellouts of Michigan Stadium, it soon became necessary to schedule Band Day when the Michigan team was not at home. Such was the foundation of the Slippery Rock-Shippensburg State game as Canham invited the two schools, the high school bands and anyone looking to see a college football game in Michigan Stadium to come and enjoy the matchup. Nearly 60,000 fans of the teams turned out to catch the inaugural contest, which continued for the next three years. The Ann Arbor-ites' attachment to Slippery Rock had begun years earlier, when public address announcer Steve Filipiak relayed scores of the Rockets' games to the game-day crowd.

CHAMPION OF THE WEST

ANTHONY CARTER

Anthony Carter forever etched his initials into the heart of Michigan fans. Possibly the greatest receiver in U-M history, "A.C." owned 12 major Michigan receiving and return records. In his first game against Northwestern, Carter not only scored his first receiving touchdown, he also returned a punt 78 yards for a touchdown. The Riviera Beach, Florida, native was a two-time Michigan MVP and, as a senior, the *Chicago Tribune* awarded him with the Silver Football emblematic of the Big Ten's MVP. He was a three-time All-American, becoming only the eighth man in Big Ten history to do so, and the first in 36 years. His touchdown catches were a Big Ten record. So good were Carter's numbers that 15 years later, he still owns six records. His pro career spanned 13 years, four teams and two leagues. He started with the Michigan Panthers of the USFL with 1,181 yards in his rookie season. Carter made the NFL Pro Bowl in 1987 and 1988 with the Minnesota Vikings and finished his career with the Detroit Lions, retiring in 1995.

Maize & Blue Item

It is almost inconceivable now, but the first game played in Detroit's Joe Louis Arena was not hockey, not professional and was won by none other than Michigan. On December 12, 1979, 12,319 fans made their way through construction equipment and a very recently swept floor to see Michigan take on the University of Detroit. The teams, which had not been allowed to practice there the day before because the floor was being put down, inaugurated the new building with a tough game, won by Michigan, 85-72. Mike McGee scored 36 points and grabbed 10 rebounds, to lead the Wolverines.

M List

The First 100 Years of Michigan Football (1879-1978)

10 National Championships
10 Bowl Games
14 Coaches
21 Undefeated Seasons
25 NFL First Round Draft Picks
28 Members of the College Football Hall of Fame
29 Big Ten titles
45 Academic All-Big Ten selections (since 1953)
88 All-Americans
107 Opponents
128 All-Big Ten First Team selections (since 1947)
605-200-31 overall record

CHAMPION OF THE WEST

PENNY NEER

Penny Neer came to the University of Michigan on a basketball scholarship, but excelled in all three sports she played during her U-M career. On the basketball court, she played three seasons, scoring 456 points and recording 64 blocks, a figure that still ranks sixth on Michigan's record books. Neer also lettered for one season with the U-M softball team, but Ferry Field is where she made her greatest impression. The discus thrower was a three-time Big Ten champion and two-time AIAW All-American in her four seasons as a track athlete. She became Michigan's first national track champion when she won the AIAW discus throw with a toss of 183 feet in the 1982 Championship. A determined athlete, Neer rebounded from missing the Olympics in 1984 and 1988 to qualify in the discus throw in 1992 at the age of 33. Though she did not place at the games, the Hillsdale, Michigan native was the first U-M female athlete on scholarship to earn a spot on the Olympic track and field squad.

another CHAMPION OF THE WEST

ELAINE CROSBY

Elaine Crosby was a two-sport standout during her career at Michigan, but it was the sport she picked up at 20 years of age that has brought her national attention. First, the Jackson native tried her hand at tennis, lettering during her first two years in Ann Arbor, then she shifted her focus to golf. As a tennis player, Elaine compiled a 13-9 singles record, 5-1 in doubles' action in 1977-78. In 1980-81, she moved over to golf, placing ninth in the Association of Intercollegiate Athletics for Women (AIAW) national tournament in 1980 as the Wolverine team took fourth in the regional. She joined the LPGA Tour in 1984 and has two major tour titles to her credit—the 1989 Mazda Japan Classic and the 1994 Keystone Open. In 1994, Crosby served as the president of the LPGA and she remains active on the tour today.

another CHAMPION OF THE WEST

MICKI KING

When Buck and Rosemary Dawson put together a coed swimming and diving team in Ann Arbor, little did they know that Pontiac native Micki King would eventually bring home the most coveted title in all of amateur sports — an Olympic Gold Medal. While the Dawsons built the team in the 1960s and put together a national championship for women's intercollegiate club teams in 1965 that Michigan won, the women athletes never truly competed for the Wolverines under the Maize and Blue banner. Michigan diving coach Dick Kimball did know talent and he did his best to help the women athletes train under his tutelage. King was one of his great athletes. After graduating from Michigan in 1966, King entered the United States Air Force. She was a lieutenant for the USAF ROTC in Ann Arbor in the late '60s and went on to represent the United States in the 1968 Olympics in Mexico City. Leading the three-meter competition, King broke her left forearm on the board attempting a reverse one- and-a-half layout. She completed her 10th dive but could not hold it together, falling to fourth place in what might have been the most dramatic effort in Mexico City. She returned to the 1972 Olympics in Munich still under the intensive training of Kimball and bounced back to win the Olympic Gold Medal in the three-meter event and place fifth on the platform. King stayed in the Air Force for 26 years, retiring as a full colonel in 1992. The next year she joined the University of Kentucky as an assistant athletic director, a position she holds today.

1980-81

America's Time Capsule

November 4, 1980: Ronald Reagan won the presidential election in a landslide over incumbent Jimmy Carter.

November 21, 1980: More than half of America's television audience tuned in Dallas to see "Who Shot J.R."

January 20, 1981: The Iranian hostage crisis ended when Iran released American captives who were seized at the U.S. Embassy in Teheran 14 months before.

May 24, 1981: The 65th Indianapolis 500 auto race ended in controversy. The next day, Mario Andretti was proclaimed the winner over Bobby Unser because Unser had broken a rule on the race course. Four-and-a-half months later, on October 8, the U.S. Auto Club reversed its decision and gave the victory to Unser.

June 9, 1981: Detroit General Manager Jack McCloskey selected Isiah Thomas with the second selection of the 1981 NBA draft. He would eventually become the greatest Piston ever.

University Lore

A Christmas Eve fire ravaged the historic Economics Building, destroying or damaging many valuable books and manuscripts. Built in 1856 as the Chemical Laboratory, it had been home to the Economics Department since 1909. The department's Leo Scharfman Library was a total loss. Many fire- and water-damaged books and documents were freeze dried in University Food Service trucks and the vacuum chamber at the U-M Aerospace Building. A U-M employee, who had been fired shortly before the blaze, was later charged with arson.

Michigan Moment

MICHIGAN WINS ROSE BOWL

Michigan gridiron men closed out their first season in the 1980s with a 10-2 season, a Big Ten title and a Rose Bowl bid, the fourth trip to Pasadena in five years. The California bowl game had not been kind to the Wolverines since the 1965 contest. Michigan owned a far-less-than-rosy record of 0-5 in Rose Bowls in the last 15 years. This year's New Year's Day opponent was the Huskies of Washington, the team that had sent the Wolverines to a 27-20 defeat in the 1978 Rose Bowl game. Washington drove to a first-and-goal situation on the Michigan eight-yard line in the first quarter. However, Husky back Toussaint Tyler was stopped inside the one-yard line on fourth down. Washington managed to get on the board in the following quarter on a 35-field goal, but Butch Woolfolk scored from the six-yard line to give Michigan a 7-3 edge. Despite another Washington field goal, Michigan went into the intermission with a 7-6 lead. After receiving the second-half kickoff, the Wolverines launched a 83-yard drive which took six minutes off the clock and ended with Ali Haji-Sheikh's 25-yard field goal. Following an unsuccessful Washington drive, Michigan marched to the end zone, taking a 17-6 lead on John Wangler's seven-yard pass to Anthony Carter. With four minutes remaining in the game, Stanley Edwards scored from the one-yard line to increase the edge to 23-6. Though the defense gave up a season-high 374 yards, it managed to deliver Schembechler's first season-ending win in his Michigan coaching career. Woolfolk took Most Valuable Player honors with a 182-yard rushing performance, while Wangler completed 12 of 20 passes for 145 yards and Carter made five catches for 68 yards. Don Bracken kicked a Rose Bowl- record 73-yard punt as Michigan won its ninth game in a row.

The 1981 Rose Bowl champions.

CHAMPIONSHIP *Moment*

FRIEDER TAKES OVER FOR ORR

Saginaw native Bill Frieder came to Michigan in 1960 to get an education, graduating from the Michigan Business School in 1964 and returning to get an MBA in 1965. He served two years as the JV coach at Alpena, later moving to Flint Northern in the same capacity. He was given the head job at Flint Northern in 1970 and compiled a record of 65-9 in three seasons, winning the state championship twice and being named coach of the year in 1972. He returned to U-M as an assistant coach in 1973-74 and was awarded the head job in 1980-81 when Johnny Orr left for Iowa State. In his first season, the Wolverines finished 19-11 and made the NIT before slumping to 8-19 in 1982. Frieder's team rebounded to 16-12 in 1983, then posted a 24-9 mark in 1984 winning the NIT championship with a 83-63 win over Notre Dame. In 1985, Frieder's Wolverines went 26-4, winning the Big Ten title for the first time since 1977. He was named national Coach of the Year by The Associated Press and *Basketball Weekly* as Michigan reached the NCAA tournament after an eight-year absence. Frieder continued successfully recruiting and coaching, earning another Conference title in 1986 and compiling 191 wins and a .687 winning percentage in nine seasons at the helm. Frieder led his team to a 24-7 regular season record in 1988-89, the sixth straight season the Wolverines posted at least 20 wins. As the NCAA tournament was about to begin, Frieder accepted the head coaching job at Arizona State to begin when Michigan's season ended. In response to this, Athletic Director Bo Schembechler handed the reins over to assistant Steve Fisher. Frieder resigned at ASU in September of 1997.

CHAMPION OF THE WEST

MIKE McGEE

Amazingly, Mike McGee did not pick up a basketball until his sophomore year in high school, when football became too rough for him. It did not take long for the Omaha native to develop a love for the game, as he averaged 38.1 points and 15.1 rebounds per game his senior season. Easily adjusting to the college level, the 6'5" McGee averaged 19.7 points per game during his freshman season at U-M, earning All-Big Ten accolades. His scoring average dropped slightly in 1979, but he still led the team with 18.8 points per game. McGee posted a career-best junior year, when he scored an average of 22.2 points in 30 games. He was honored with second-team All-Big Ten honors for his efforts, as he continued to rise on Michigan's all-time scoring list. The forward scored 732 points as a senior to eclipse Michigan's career-scoring record held by Cazzie Russell as well as the Big Ten career scoring mark. McGee also closed his career ranked first in games started and field goals scored. His 2,439 points still ranks as the second-highest point total in Michigan history. In 1981, McGee was the 18th pick in the NBA draft by the Los Angeles Lakers. He played eight seasons in the NBA with the Lakers, Hawks, Kings and Nets before retiring in 1989.

Maize & Blue Item

Jack Harvey was a two-time Big Ten champion in the shot put, capturing All-American honors and Michigan shot put records. Since 1975, Harvey has served as head coach of U-M's track squad, leading 141 U-M trackmen to Conference titles and 76 to All-American status. His teams have captured 10 Conference titles, and Harvey has been named Central Collegiate Coach of the year six times. He was honored as national Coach of the Year in 1980.

M List: Michigan's 1,000-Yard Rushers

Player	# of times over 1,000	High
Jamie Morris	3	1,703
Tyrone Wheatley	3	1,357
Rob Lytle	2	1,469
Butch Woolfolk	2	1,459
Ron Johnson	2	1,391
Gordon Bell	2	1,388
Tshimanga Biakabutuka	1	1,818
Tony Boles	1	1,408
Lawrence Ricks	1	1,388
Jon Vaughn	1	1,364
Billy Taylor	1	1,297
Ricky Powers	1	1,197
Russell Davis	1	1,092
Rick Rogers	1	1,002

CHAMPION OF THE WEST

DEBBIE WILLIAMS

As a freshman in 1979, Debbie Williams became Michigan's first-ever Big Ten champion in track when she threw the javelin 154 feet, 11 inches, bettering the existing record by 20 feet. In 1982, Williams became Michigan's first and only track athlete to win a Conference event every year of her career. The Euclid, Ohio native won the javelin event at the Big Ten Championship each of her four years to etch her name in the U-M record books. Williams, who also threw the discus at Michigan and was a basketball star in high school, later made waves by taking up the sport of golf and playing in several major amateur tournaments. Currently, Williams is attempting to qualify for the LPGA tour.

another CHAMPION OF THE WEST

KENNETH "RED" SIMMONS

The "Founding Father of Michigan Women's Track and Field" is a man whose athletic career still continues into his 80s. A 1933 graduate of Eastern Michigan University, Kenneth "Red" Simmons was a member of the 1932 U.S. Olympic track and field team, qualifying for the 440 hurdle semi-finals at the games. During his college career, Simmons was also a three-time middle-weight boxing and wrestling conference champion and captured two track titles in the low hurdles. After a 25-year stint with the Detroit Police Department, Simmons retired in 1959 and began teaching physical education at U-M. In 1960, he started "The Michigammes," the first Ann Arbor Women's Track Club. His program developed seven national champions, 19 state champions and dozens of other area honorees. When Michigan added women's track as a varsity sport in 1977, Simmons was the team's first coach, a position he served for five years. In 1991, at the age of 81, Simmons competed in the Senior Olympics, winning five gold medals in the long jump, high jump, shot put, discus and javelin. A member of the Michigan women's track and field Hall of Fame, Simmons is a constant fixture at U-M track events. He and his wife, Lois, sponsor three U-M awards to athletes in three different sports.

another CHAMPION OF THE WEST

MELANIE WEAVER

After the Michigan distance running program was developed in the late 1970s, it was Melanie Weaver who helped make the program prestigious in its early years. The Scottsville, Michigan, native was Michigan's leading cross country runner for four years and earned All-America honors running distance events in track. As a freshman, she finished a U-M-best 19th at the Big Ten meet in the opening season of the sport at Michigan. As the seasons changed, she progressed onto the track, where she set five school records. In each of her four cross country seasons, she moved closer to the top of the Conference, ultimately finishing fifth as a senior, when she was named All-Big Ten. She followed this performance with a 33rd-place finish at the national meet, tying teammate Lisa Larsen as U-M's first female NCAA All-Americans. Weaver won her only Big Ten title as a junior, running the 10,000 meters in 35:14.21 to take top honors at the Conference meet. However, she finished second on three other occasions and never lower than fifth in the distance runs. An AIAW All-American in the indoor two-mile race in 1982, Weaver earned All-America track status during her final season, when she finished third nationally in the 10,000 meters.

America's Time Capsule

September 21, 1981: Sandra Day O'Connor became the first female member of the Supreme Court.

January 8, 1982: An eight-year antitrust suit by the Justice Department ended when the American Telephone and Telegraph Company (ATT) agreed to divest itself of its 22 Bell Telephone operating systems.

March 29, 1982: Michael Jordan and North Carolina defeated Patrick Ewing and Georgetown in the NCAA basketball finals.

June 25, 1982: Secretary of State Alexander Haig resigned following disagreements with President Ronald Reagan.

July 3, 1982: Martina Navratilova won her first Wimbledon tennis championship.

University Lore

The subterranean Law School Addition to the 1933 Legal Research Building was designed by Gunnar Birkerts and Associates and dedicated on October 31, 1981. Descending 56 feet into the ground, the new 77,500 square foot library offers dramatic views of the Gothic Revival library above through a 150 x 26 foot V-shaped lightwell. Financed with $9.5 million in private donations, the Addition houses administration and student publication offices, stacks for over 200,000 books, and 300 carrels. Birkerts' design won several architectural awards.

Michigan Moment

LEACH ENDS U-M's 25-YEAR DROUGHT

One of six kids born in the Leach family, Michael enjoyed skiiing, swimming, and music, but it was tennis at which he excelled. In four years with the Wolverine tennis team, Michael Leach compiled a record of 99-18 in singles competition and 80-15 in doubles play. Named an All-Big Ten selection each of his four years, Leach won two number-one doubles and a number-one singles crown from 1979-82 as the Wolverines earned four straight Conference titles. A two-time All-American, Leach's best regular season came in his junior year when he posted a 26-2 singles record and made it to the round of 16 at the NCAA championship before bowing out to the eventual champion, Tim Mayotte. Leach started out his senior year with a 7-5 record in singles play, but won 11 of his final 12 regular-season matches before beginning post-season competition. At number-one singles, he won two matches before suffering a 3-6, 4-6 setback to Ernie Fernandez of Ohio State. In NCAA play, Leach ousted Glenn Layendecker of Yale in the opening round before beating Tom Warneke of Trinity, 7-6, 6-4. The win over Warneke was a bit of revenge for Leach, who had lost to him during the regular season. He bettered his finish from the previous year by blasting Howard Sands of Harvard for the second time in 1982, 6-2, 6-2. Leach then reached the semi-finals by outlasting Glenn Michibata of Pepperdine, 7-5, 6-2. The first Wolverine to reach the semi-finals in singles play since 1975, Leach made the most of his appearance by defeating Christo Steyn, 6-2, 4-6, 7-6. Leach was forced to come back from a 4-5 deficit in the third set to reach the finals. In the final match, Leach swept Brad Gilbert of Pepperdine 7-5, 6-3 to become Michigan's and the Big Ten's first NCAA singles champion since Barry MacKay in 1957.

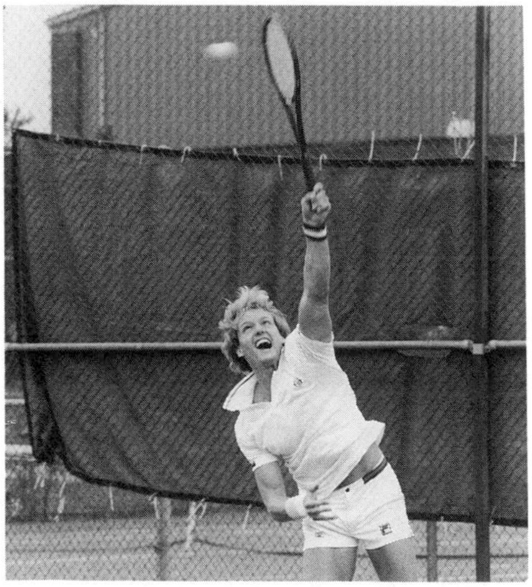

Michigan's Mike Leach

CHAMPION OF THE WEST

BUTCH WOOLFOLK

Highly recruited out of Westfield, New Jersey, Harold "Butch" Woolfolk was a football and track star at Westfield H.S., and owner of the second-fastest 300-yard time in prep history. During his freshman season, Woolfolk patiently waited his turn behind the rest of the Michigan rushing machine. He made his first start against Minnesota and made the most of the opportunity, gaining 131 yards on the ground. After an appearance in the Rose Bowl, he headed to the track finishing second in the outdoor 100-meter and third in the 200-meter races at the Big Ten Championship. He totalled 990 yards and 13 touchdowns his sophomore season before returning to the track, where he won the Conference 200-meter crown. Woolfolk broke the 1,000-yard barrier in 1981, rushing for a team-leading 1,042 yards as Michigan won the Conference title and the Rose Bowl. His 182-yard rushing performance against Washington in Pasadena earned him MVP honors and gave U-M its first Rose Bowl win in 17 years. On the track, he helped the Wolverines to their second straight Conference crown. He closed out his career by running for 1,459 yards and being named an All-American as Michigan won its second straight bowl game. Woolfolk's 3,861 career rushing yards stood as a school record, as did his 718 rushing attempts. After being selected in the first round of the NFL Draft by the New York Giants, Woolfolk ran a leg of Michigan's record-setting 4x100 relay team at the Big Ten Championship. Butch played seven years with the Giants, Houston Oilers and Detroit Lions before settling down with his family in the Houston area.

another CHAMPION OF THE WEST

BRIAN DIEMER

A native of Grand Rapids, Michigan, Brian Diemer proved that Michigan's ability to develop outstanding track and field athletes was not left in the first half of the 20th century. Diemer arrived at Michigan in the fall of 1979 and immediately made an impact on the cross country team, finishing 10th at the Big Ten meet. As a sophomore, Diemer finished runner-up in the Big Ten cross country race, helping lead U-M to a tie for the league title with Indiana. He took top honors in the 3,000-meter steeplechase at the Big Ten track championship in the spring. Diemer's highlight of 1982 came in the NCAA track championships, when he anchored Michigan's distance medley relay team that finished second nationally. He closed out his cross country career by placing third, finishing two seconds behind champion Jim Spivey of Indiana. On the track Diemer, was runner-up in the indoor two-mile, 10,000-meter outdoors and 3,000-meter steeplechase. At the NCAA championship, he became the NCAA steeplechase champion with a U-M-record time of 8:22.13. Michigan's recipient of the 1983 Conference Medal of Honor, Diemer continued to shine with a number-two finish in the 3,000-meter steeplechase at the U.S. Track and Field Olympic Trials, earning him a role on the 1984 Los Angeles Olympic team.. Diemer captured a bronze medal, the first medal won by a Michigan athlete since Eddie Tolan in 1932. A graduate from U-M's school of natural resources, he now works with his father's landscaping firm.

Maize Blue Item

After 20 years in the WCHA, Michigan broke ranks with Minnesota and Wisconsin to become a member of the Central Collegiate Hockey Association. Athletic Director Don Canham said the move was made to acquire a more geographically attractive schedule and reduce costs. Since 1982, the CCHA has boasted the NCAA champion six times, while Michigan has skated to the league title in 1992, 1994, 1995, 1996 and 1997.

M List: Michigan Hockey and the CCHA

School	Years	Titles
Alaska-Fairbanks	since 1995	0
Bowling Green	since 1971	7
Ferris State	since 1979	0
Illinois-Chicago	1982-96	0
Kent State	1992-94	0
Lake Superior State	since 1972	4
Miami	since 1981	1
Michigan	since 1981	5
Michigan State	since 1981	4
Michigan Tech	1981-84	0
Northern Michigan	1977-84	2
Notre Dame	1981-83, since 1992	0
Ohio State	since 1971	1
Western Michigan	since 1975	0

CHAMPION OF THE WEST

DIANE DIETZ

In a four-year basketball career from 1979-82, Orchard Lake, Michigan native Diane Dietz not only put women's athletics on the map at Michigan, she defined a true Wolverine legend for the ages. Though the 5'-9" player originally started as a guard, she took over the forward duties at the beginning of her junior year. A four-year starter, Dietz led the team in scoring each season en route to a record 2,076 career points. She still remains in the top 10 of seven career statistical categories and holds the record for game scoring with a 45-point effort against Illinois. While Dietz was earning first-team All-Michigan AIAW honors three times and state Player of the Year accolades as a senior, she was also excelling in the classroom. She was the recipient of Academic All-America honors during her final three years and was awarded the Conference Medal of Honor in 1982, the first Michigan woman to be so honored. She graduated in 1982 and later earned her law degree. Now a regional director for Comcast Cablevision, Dietz was honored with the prestigious Gerald R. Ford Award in 1995.

another CHAMPION OF THE WEST

SANDY VONG

For its first 11 seasons as a varsity sport, Sandy Vong headed up the Michigan volleyball team, leading the spikers to the top of the first-ever Big Ten tournament in 1981. Born and raised and Shanghai, China, Vong came to the United States to attend college, earning his B.S. in Chemical Engineering from U-M in 1956. Later he returned to Ann Arbor to receive his M.S. in Materials Engineering from Michigan, during which he began a 15-year connection with U-M athletics. He founded the U-M men's volleyball club team in 1968 and expanded his coaching duties to the women's team in 1971. When women's volleyball was made a varsity sport in 1973, Vong became the team's first head coach. He would compile the most wins of any Michigan volleyball coach, ending his career in 1983 with a record of 177-151-7, including a program-record 40-17 mark in 1981. Vong himself played in several national tournaments during the 1970s, later advancing to a coaching role.

CHAMPIONSHIP *Moment*

SUCCESSFUL WOMEN'S TEAMS FROM THE FIRST YEAR—VOLLEYBALL, GYMNASTICS AND SOFTBALL

Though women's sports were first recognized by the Big Ten in 1981-82, Michigan's women's teams wasted little time in jumping to the top of the standings. Two U-M teams claimed Conference titles in that first season, including the volleyball team, which took the first-ever Big Ten crown in any women's sport. Under coach Sandy Vong, the volleyball team compiled a 12-game midseason winning streak to enter the first-ever Big Ten tournament at 23-7. Held in Champaign, Illinois, the tournament was played in a round-robin tournament divided into two pools. Michigan finished 5-1 overall, defeating Ohio State, 15-10, 15-8, 15-12 for the title. Alison Noble and Diane Ratnick were named to the Big Ten's all-tournament team for their performance. The gymnastics team also wasted little time in earning its first Big Ten title. Michigan earned the crown with a score of 140.95, the best in program history. Kathy Beckwith became U-M's first individual event winner, scoring an 8.05 on the vault. She was named All-Big Ten along with teammates Diane Samuelson and Christy Schwartz. Though the softball team would finish second in Big Ten tournament play in 1982, the squad would enjoy success in the final year of the AIAW tournament. Michigan would win the regional and head to the AIAW World Series, where the team would place third. Five Wolverines — Jan Boyd, Laura Reed, Diane Hatch, Sue Birk and Jody Humphries—were selected to the AIAW All-Great Lakes Region team as U-M posted a 31-14 overall record.

America's Time Capsule

September 29, 1982: Seven persons in the Chicago area died from cyanide placed in Tylenol capsules.

October 20, 1982: The St. Louis Cardinals won the seventh and deciding game of the World Series, defeating the Milwaukee Brewers.

December 2, 1982: Barney Clark was the first successful recipient of an artificial heart transplant. He died on March 23, 1983.

March 2, 1983: More than 125 million viewers watched the final television episode of M*A*S*H.

April 12, 1983: Democratic congressman Harold Washington became the first African-American mayor of Chicago.

University Lore

The continuing economic recession and cutbacks in state funding brought across-the-board budget cuts and major cuts in some programs targeted for downsizing. The Geography Department was eliminated. A number of support programs and the schools of Art, Education and Natural Resources underwent review. After a series of public hearings, protests and demonstrations of support, and review committee recommendations, the Art School suffered an 18% cut in general funds, Natural Resources 33% and Education 40%.

Michigan Moment

SIXTEEN IN A ROW!

For 15 years, the sites had changed, the players had changed, the coaches had changed, even the world had changed. But for 15 years, the result of the Big Ten Tennis Championship remained the same, a Michigan win. Since 1968, Michigan had won every Conference tournament, a 15-year string only exceeded by Indiana's dominance in swimming from 1961-80. In 1983, there was new competition from the West. Wisconsin was poised and ready to ascend to the top of the Conference standings, and was helped by the fact that this year's event would be held in Madison. After one day of play, Wisconsin held a 21-1/2 to 21 lead over the Wolverines, as four Michigan singles players and three doubles tandems advanced to the semi-finals. Interestingly, four of these matchups would be head-to-head against the Badgers. Michigan rose to the top of the standings after day two, despite losing singles players Mark Mees and Ross Laser. Jim Sharton and Rodd Schreiber each advanced in singles, while each of Michigan's doubles teams set back its Wisconsin competition. Surprisingly, it was Northwestern that Michigan had to hold off on the final day of competition. The Michigan tandem of Mees and Tom Haney earned the number one doubles title with a 7-6, 6-2 win over their Wildcat counterparts, while Sharton and Laser picked up the crown at number two doubles. Schreiber and Hugh Kwok were unsuccessful in Michigan's bid to sweep the doubles titles, dropping a 5-7, 4-6 decision. In singles play, Sharton was Michigan's only titlist, ousting Jim Nelson of Iowa, 6-4, 4-6, 7-6. Michigan's 45 points overall were five better than Northwestern and Minnesota and placed a 16th trophy next to the others in the tennis trophy case.

Michigan's Mark Mees

CHAMPION OF THE WEST

NEWT LOKEN

Born in Breckenridge, Minnesota in 1919, Newton C. Loken began his association with collegiate gymnastics as an undergraduate in 1940. At the University of Minnesota, Loken was the winner of the high bar event at the 1941 NCAA meet and was the All-Around champion at the 1942 national competition. The two-time Big Ten Champion graduated from Minnesota with a B.S. in 1942. Loken came to Michigan in search of a master's degree in 1944, when the Wolverines did not even have a varsity gymnastics team. After earning his M.A. in 1946, Loken was named the first coach of the resurrected squad in 1947. It would not be until 1984 when any other man would lead Michigan gymnastics. In his 36 years as coach, Michigan won 12 Big Ten and two national championships. Newt compiled a record of 250-72-1, and saw 71 of his gymnasts win Big Ten titles and 21 garner top national accolades. At the time of his retirement, he had won more Big Ten titles than all but two of the other Big Ten schools. When he retired in 1983, Newt was a full professor in Michigan's Department of Physical Education and left an impressive resume behind him. Loken was twice named national coach of the year and spearheaded Michigan's hosting of the 1971 NCAA championship, when a record 25,000 fans came out to watch the three-day event.

CHAMPION OF THE WEST

GREG MEYER

Greg Meyer exemplified Michigan cross country and track during the years from 1973-77. A three-time All-Big Ten selection in cross country, Meyer was the second overall finisher in 1974, and fourth in 1975 as Michigan won back-to-back Big Ten titles. He served as captain and finished third overall when the Wolverines stretched the Conference title string to three in 1976. In track, Meyer was the Michigan recordholder in the 3,000-meter steeplechase from 1976-80. He won the event at the Big Ten Championships as a freshman and as a junior, earning All-American honors in 1976 when he finished fifth at the NCAA meet. Meyer continued building a legacy long after he left Michigan, becoming the first native Michigan runner to run a sub-four minute mile. The holder of the American records in the 15-kilometer and 20-kilometer races, Meyer continued to run marathons across the country. On April 19, 1983, Meyer gained the attention of runners nationwide when he won the Boston Marathon in 2:09.00. His time was the 10th best time ever for a marathon, and beat his previous best by nearly two minutes. Meyer is the last American runner to win the annual Patriots' Day race.

Maize & Blue Item

Powered by Chris Sabo, Barry Larkin and Casey Close, Michigan's baseball team cruised through the 1983 season with a record of 45-7. In the World Series, Michigan posted its best finish since 1962, in third place. U-M used three hits by Sabo to defeat Maine, 6-5, in its opening game. After a loss to Alabama, the Wolverines faced Stanford, scoring seven runs in the ninth inning to blast the Cardinal.

M List: Michigan's Longest Coaching Reigns

Coach	Sport(s)	Years	Seasons	Gms	Wins	Titles
Cliff Keen	Wrestling	1925-42,45-70	42	374	273	12
Ray Fisher	Baseball	1921-58	38	939	637	14
Newt Loken	Gymnastics	1947-83	36	323	250	12
Matt Mann	Swimming	1926-54	28			16
Brian Eisner	Tennis	1970-95	26	557	393	17
Gus Stager	Swimming	1954-79	25			3
Fielding Yost	Football	1901-26*	25	204	165	10
Bert Katzenmeyer	Golf	1947-68	22	na	na	3

CHAMPION OF THE WEST

SUE FOSTER

Sue Foster, an Ann Arbor native, got Michigan's track and cross country programs off "on the right foot" as a two-sport four-time letterwinner from 1980-83. A part of Michigan's first cross country contingent as a freshman, she helped lead the team to an eighth-place finish nationally as a senior, when she was awarded All-Big Ten honors. When the cross country season ended, Foster could be found helping U-M on the track. The six-time Big Ten champion and three-time All-American first tasted success by winning the 800-meter race at the Conference indoor championship in 1981. As a junior, she won at 1,000 yards in Big Ten indoor competition before earning All-American status by placing sixth nationally. Later in 1982, Foster accomplished her best national finish by coming in third in the 1,500 meters outdoors. Foster was named Michigan's female athlete of the year as a senior for a long list of accomplishments, including leading Michigan to a Conference title. She later served as Michigan's women's cross country coach from 1987-91.

another CHAMPION OF THE WEST

ALISON NOBLE

The 1980 Canadian Athlete of the Year, Alison Noble decided to continue her career south of the border, at the University of Michigan. There, the Willowdale, Ontario native wasted little time in bringing U-M to the top of the Big Ten's young women's sports program. In her freshman season, she was named to the Southern Michigan AIAW All-State team for helping lead Michigan to a third-place finish at the tournament. The sophomore was instrumental in leading the Wolverine spikers to the first-ever Big Ten title in 1981, earning All-Big Ten Tournament team honors and All-Midwest AIAW accolades as Michigan finished 40-17 and finished eighth nationally. While she performed admirably on the court, Noble also maintained a near-4.0 average in her major of engineering. She served as team captain during her final two seasons, earning second-team Academic All-America honors and the Big Ten's Conference Medal of Honor as a senior.

CHAMPIONSHIP *Moment*

TRACK SQUAD CAPTURES '83 INDOOR CROWN

Just five years young, the women's track program at the University of Michigan quickly rose into the record books by earning the Big Ten indoor crown in 1983. In doing so, the Wolverines dethroned perennial champion Wisconsin, which had sat atop the standings even before the women's athletics were recognized by the Big Ten.

At Madison, Wisconsin only three Wolverines won individual events, but Michigan garnered enough top eight finishes to deliver the title by 11 points over the Badgers. Senior Lorrie Thornton was one of Michigan's winners, long jumping a Big Ten-best 19 feet, 11-3/4 inches and also finishing fifth in the 60-meter dash. Senior Sue Frederick-Foster set Big Ten and Michigan records in the mile with a time of 4:40.57, while Joanna Bullard successfully defended her high jump title. Joyce Wilson broke a Michigan record in the 600-yard dash as she finished second with a time of 1:20.50. Brenda Kazniec also posted a runner-up placing, doing so in the 300-meter dash. Michigan's women's runners would also enjoy a successful outdoor season, finishing second in the Conference meet.

1983-84

MICHIGAN MOMENT

WOLVERINE CAGERS CAPTURE NIT

Though the Michigan basketball team had posted a winning record in four of its previous five seasons, the squad's best Big Ten finish was sixth place. With Tim McCormick as the only senior on the team, Bill Frieder's 1983-84 squad looked as though it was building a good nucleus, but was far from contention in the tough Big Ten. In non-conference play, the Michigan cagers rolled to an 8-0 start before two one-point setbacks sent then into Conference play 8-2. Inside the Big Ten, Michigan was fast out of the gate, jumping out to a 3-0 start. The joy was short lived as the Wolverines dropped seven of their next ten contests, including a quadruple overtime loss to Illinois. The team regrouped to close out the season 4-1. The loss in that final five- game stretch, a season-ending 54-52 overtime heartbreaker to Northwestern, left Michigan with a 19-9 record and without an NCAA bid. Instead, the second-place team in the Big Ten was headed to the NIT, where the Wolverines had made the third round in both 1980 and 1981. Michigan rolled to easy victories in the first two rounds in Ann Arbor, 94-70 over Wichita State and 83-70 over Marquette. In order to go to New York for the Final Four, the Wolverines had to hold off a determined Xavier team, 63-62. Michigan played a tough game in the semifinals and outlasted Virginia Tech, 78-75. The final game turned out to be a second-half cakewalk for Bill Frieder's team, as Notre Dame was blasted, 83-63, behind 28 points from McCormick. McCormick, who averaged 19.3 PPG over the final four games of the NIT, was named MVP of the tournament.

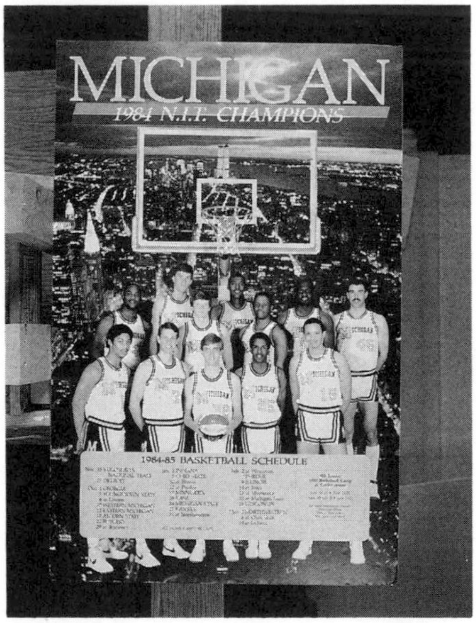

Michigan's 1984-85 basketball poster.

America's Time Capsule

September 1, 1983: A Soviet fighter plane shot down a South Korean airliner, killing all 269 people aboard.

October 23, 1983: An explosive-laden truck blew up outside the U.S. Marine headquarters in Beirut, Lebanon, taking the lives of 241 Marine and Navy personnel.

April 23, 1984: Federal researchers announced the identification of a virus thought to cause acquired immune deficiency syndrome (AIDS).

May 8, 1984: The U.S.S.R. Olympic Committee withdrew from the 1984 Olympics, to be held in Los Angeles, California.

July 28, 1984: The Summer Olympic games began in Los Angeles, highlighted by the performances of Carl Lewis and Mary Lou Retton.

University Lore

Alumnus, screenwriter and film director Lawrence Kasdan (BA '70, MA '72) returned to campus as a writer-in-residence while his movie "The Big Chill" was becoming a box-office hit enroute to a Best Picture academy award nomination. Winner of four Hopwood writing awards at U-M, Kasdan first gained fame as a screenwriter for "Raiders of the Lost Ark" and "Return of the Jedi." He drew heavily on his Ann Arbor experiences for "The Big Chill," a story of eight former college friends coming to terms with life.

CHAMPION OF THE WEST

TIM McCORMICK

An All-American at Clarkston High School, Tim McCormick's 6-10 frame was expected to continue the recent success seen at U-M basketball games. He played all 30 games as a freshman, showing promise for the years to come, but a June operation to remove calcium deposits from both knees sidelined him for his entire sophomore year. He returned as a junior to average 12.3 points and 6.4 rebounds per game, reversing Michigan's sub-.500 record of the previous season. He played in all 28 games, shooting over 55 percent from the field and 80 percent from the line. In his senior year, the center averaged 12.1 points and 5.9 rebounds per game in a season where Michigan improved to 24-9 and a fourth-place finish in the Big Ten. For the first time in three years, U-M was invited to postseason competition, playing in the NIT. Though he only scored two points versus Wichita State in the opening game, the senior averaged 19.3 points over the final four contests, including a 28-point effort which sank Notre Dame and gave U-M the tournament championship. For his efforts, McCormick was named the most valuable player. He was a first-round draft pick of the Cleveland Cavaliers in the 1984 NBA draft and played for six teams over a nine-year NBA career. After recording over 5,000 points for the Sonics, 76ers, Nets, Rockets, Hawks, and Knicks, McCormick went to the broadcast booth, where he is now the color analyst for Creative Sports.

another CHAMPION OF THE WEST

JON URBANCHEK

A native of Hungary, Jon Urbanchek left his homeland in 1956 en route to the United States. Taken in by an Ann Arbor church group, he was enrolled in the University of Michigan in the fall of 1957 and became eligible to swim during the second semester of his sophomore year. He made an immediate impact, placing second in the 1,500-meter freestyle at the 1959 NCAA meet for the national champion Wolverines. Urbanchek would also be a part of Michigan's national championship squad in 1961. After graduating from U-M, Urbanchek went west, where he coached swimming at Anaheim High School and later at Long Beach State University. In 1982 he returned to Ann Arbor to take on a near-impossible job—upholding the oustanding tradition of the Michigan swim team. In the face of that tall order, Urbanchek has excelled, placing the Wolverines among the NCAA's top 10 teams 11 times, including a national championship in 1995. His teams won 10 straight Conference titles from 1986-95 as he has compiled an unbelievable dual meet record of 121-15. A six-time Big Ten coach of the year selection, Urbanchek has sent 25 swimmers to the Olympics and coached 27 NCAA champion event winners. On the international scene, Urbanchek has served on numerous coaching roles, including assistantships at the last four Olympic games.

Maize & Blue Item

The 1984 Michigan baseball team started the season a disappointing 3-7. But the Wolverines rebounded to win 15 of their next 17 games and began Big Ten play with a wild doubleheader split (16-10, 0-16) against Indiana. The Wolverines would win five of their next six games and 11 of 16 overall to take the Conference title. U-M would go on to finish seventh at the College World Series.

M List

Michigan Baseball All-Americans

Since 1953, seven Michigan baseball players were named All-American by the American Baseball Coaches Association. Only one, Barry Larkin, was a two time honoree.

Player	Year(s)
Bruce Haynam	1953
Don Eaddy	1955
Ken Tippery	1957
Bill Freehan	1961
Jim Paciorek	1982
Barry Larkin	1984-85
Casey Close	1986

CHAMPION OF THE WEST

MARY MacTAGGART

Mary MacTaggart was a pioneer for individual honors in U-M's women's tennis from 1981-84. The Port Huron, Michigan native was named to three All-Big Ten teams in singles and two in doubles while participating in two NCAA Championships. The two-time captain began her career by setting a U-M record with 15 consecutive singles wins. She finished her freshman season with first-team All-Conference honors at both singles and doubles. She continued her success during her sophomore season, when she was named the Big Ten's Sportswoman of the Year by Conference athletes and coaches. While completing her nursing degree with a GPA of 3.44, McTaggart also excelled on the courts during her senior year. She posted a 26-8 mark in singles, advancing to the round of 32 at the NCAA Championship and went 20-5 in doubles competition. Named Michigan's outstanding female athlete of the year for 1984, McTaggart finished her career with a 136-68 record on the courts.

another CHAMPION OF THE WEST

SUE CAHILL

As the women's swimming team has won 11 straight Big Ten titles, the early years of the sport at Michigan are often placed aside as pre-dynasty. A closer look at a team that has finished lower than third in the Conference just three times in 25 years would say that the string of success is only continuing. One of the keys of the excellence in the early 1980s was Sue Cahill, an individual medley specialist from Northville, Michigan. Though the multi-talented athlete also swam for U-M in the distance freestyle and 200-yard butterfly events, it would be the IM where she would dominate Big Ten swimming during her four-year career. As a freshman, Cahill finished first in the 400 IM at the Conference meet, a feat which she repeated as a sophomore, setting a Conference record time of 4:20.87. She became a three-time All-American at the AIAW meet, including earning National Championship honors in the 400 IM. After finishing a disappointing fifth in 1983, she bounced back as a senior to break her own record in the 400 IM at the Conference meet. Advancing to the NCAA competition, Cahill became Michigan's second-ever NCAA swimming All-American by placing fifth.

another CHAMPION OF THE WEST

KATHY BECKWITH

Kathy Beckwith, a Richmond Hill, Ontario native was the standout performer for the first 15 years of women's gymnastics at Michigan. Between 1981-84, Beckwith became the first Michigan women's gymnast to win a Big Ten title and the first to advance to nationals, blazing the trail for those who followed her years later. Beckwith became the first Michigan gymnast to qualify for the national AIAW meet in 1981 before having a banner sophomore season. She led the team to a win in the first-ever Big Ten gymnastics meet and helped the squad to a tenth-place finish at the inaugural NCAA competition. On the way, she scored an 8.05 on the vault to become Michigan's first Conference winner and finished first in the All-Around to lead U-M to the NCAA regional crown. Named to the All-Big Ten team three times, Beckwith qualified for NCAA regionals each of her four seasons as a Wolverine. When she graduated from U-M, Beckwith held the school records on the vault, bars, balance beam and the all-around.

1984-85

America's Time Capsule

October 7, 1984: Steve Garvey led the San Diego Padres to the National League pennant over the Chicago Cubs.

October 14, 1984: The Detroit Tigers beat the San Diego Padres, 8-4, at Detroit in Game Five of the World Series to take the title.

November 6, 1984: Ronald Reagan was re-elected president over Walter Mondale in the greatest Republican landslide ever.

March 4, 1985: The Environmental Protection Agency ordered a ban on leaded gasoline.

April 22, 1985: The University of Michigan's Lisa Larsen Weidenback won the women's portion of the Boston Marathon in a time of 2:34:06.

July 13, 1985: President Reagan underwent surgery to remove a cancerous tumor from his colon.

University Lore

The School of Business Administration dedicated two new buildings that also represented significant changes in the school's program initiated by Dean Gilbert Whitaker. The Kresge Library and Computing Resource Center reflected the important role technological change would have in the curriculum of business education. The expanded Executive Education Center was designed to tie the corporate training program closer to the school's other activities. Total cost of the Library and Executive Center was $16.4 million.

Michigan Moment

TARPLEY AND GRANT LEAD MICHIGAN BASKETBALL TEAM

Using the NIT championship as a springboard, the Michigan basketball team jumped out of the gate in 1984-85, at 8-0. With just one senior on the team and a starting nucleus of juniors Richard Rellford, Butch Wade and Roy Tarpley, sophomore Antoine Joubert and freshman Gary Grant, Michigan scored 80 points or more seven times in this span. The young Wolverines then hit a rut, losing three of their next four games, including a 1-2 start in Big Ten play. Following the last of these losses, Michigan would embark on a 16-game winning streak that consumed the rest of the season. Over the first nine games of the stretch, only one was close, a 69-67 triple overtime thriller against Iowa in Crisler Arena. The second half of the streak was marked by close Wolverine wins, with five of the final seven contests being decided by five points or less. When the regular season was done, Michigan was atop the Big Ten for the first time since 1976-77 with a 16-2 record. A number-one ranked seed in the NCAA tournament, Michigan beat Fairleigh Dickinson by a 59-55 score before bowing out to eventual champion Villanova by the same score. After the season, center Roy Tarpley was named Big Ten MVP and an All-American, while coach Bill Frieder was given both Big Ten and National Coach of the Year Honors.

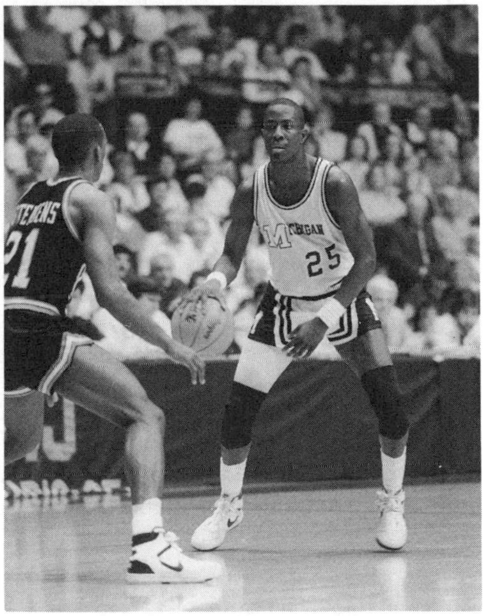

Michigan's Gary Grant

CHAMPIONSHIP *Moment*

BERENSON RETURNS TO HIS ALMA MATER

Since reaching the NCAA final in 1977, Michigan's hockey programs had fallen on lean times, compiling a 115-136-10 record in the last seven seasons. The once-packed Yost Ice Arena was filled with empty seats and the seven NCAA titles Michigan had won were decades behind. Michigan went back two decades to bring in the next coach. Red Berenson, star of Michigan's hockey teams from 1960-62 was offered the job, the third time the former NHL player was lured. The third time was the charm for the Buffalo Sabres assistant coach who gave up a chance to ascend to the top job to take the Michigan position. The move to Berenson was an indication that Michigan was serious about supporting hockey and its high costs in a time of cutbacks. Athletic Director Don Canham had tried to bring Berenson back in 1973 and 1980, but the former Michigan star was not ready to leave his head coaching job with the St. Louis Blues. The 1981 NHL coach of the year returned to U-M in 1984-85 and began the rebuilding phase with a 13-26-1 record his first season. Though it took four years to attain a winning record, Berenson's first fully recruited team posted a 22-19 mark in 1987-88, and the Wolverines have posted at least 22 wins in a season ever since. In the 1990s, seven of Berenson's teams have recorded at least 30 wins, including the 1995-96 squad, which won Michigan's first NCAA hockey championship in 32 years.

CHAMPION OF THE WEST

BARRY LARKIN

Barry Larkin came to Michigan from Cincinnati, Ohio, where he was an all-state infielder and an All-American defensive back in football. He turned down a football scholarship offer from Notre Dame to play baseball at U-M. As a shortstop for the Wolverines, Larkin exploded onto the scene in his freshman season, becoming the MVP of the 1983 Big Ten Tournament. As a sophomore, he hit .363 and was named the Big Ten Conference Player of the Year and an All-American. The top hitter and fielder on the team, Larkin played on the silver medal-winning U.S. Baseball team at the 1984 Los Angeles Olympics. He returned for his junior year to rise even higher, hitting .368 over 65 games. He made just seven errors during the entire season, and his sparkling .975 fielding percentage earned him All-Big Ten honors for the second straight season. Again named an All-American, he also became the first player to be named Conference Player of the Year for two consecutive seasons. Drafted by the Cincinnati Reds in 1982, Larkin jumped to the majors after his senior year. He has played 11 seasons in Cincinnati, winning one World Series title, three Gold Glove Awards, and seven Silver Slugger honors.

Maize & Blue Item

A crowd of 105,403 packed Michigan Stadium to see the Wolverines' season opener and first-ever battle against the top-ranked Hurricanes of Miami. Before the game was over, Wolverines defenders had picked off six Bernie Kosar passes. Michigan's Rodney Lyles, a native of Miami, had three interceptions as U-M's 22-14 victory improved its record to 3-1-1 in its last five games against number-one ranked teams.

M List

Evolution of Michigan's Longest Field Goal

Yards	Player	Opponent
56	Mike Gillette	Ohio State, 1988
53	Mike Gillette	Iowa, 1986
52	Bob Bergeron	Washington, 1984
51	Mike Lantry	Stanford, 1973
50	Mike Lantry	Stanford, 1973
42	Dana Coin	Arizona, 1970
40	Doug Bickle	Iowa, 1961
38	Lou Baldacci	Illinois, 1953
20	Tom Harmon	Illinois, 1940
12	Tom Harmon	Chicago, 1939

CHAMPION OF THE WEST

MELINDA COPP

A four-time Big Ten champion and six-time All-Ameri can, Melinda Copp etched her name on the list of Michigan legends by becoming the first female swimmer to qualify for the Olympic team. The London, Ontario native was a dominant force in both the backstroke and the individual medley from 1981-83. As a freshman, Copp earned top honors in the 200 IM at the Big Ten Championship, a feat which she duplicated in 1982, when she also won the 200 backstroke. Nationally, she finished second in the 200 backstroke in 1982, also picking up All-American honors in the 100 backstroke, 400 IM, 200 IM and as part of the 400-medley relay team. At the 1983 Big Ten Championship, Copp won the 200 backstroke in 2:03.14, a Conference meet record that stood for five years. After redshirting in 1984 to train for the Olympics, Copp qualified for her native Canada by finishing second in the 200 backstroke at the Olympic trials. At the Los Angeles Olympics, she placed fifth in her heat and 19th overall.

another CHAMPION OF THE WEST

ANDREA WILLIAMS

Scarborough, Ontario native Andrea Williams played just two years for the Michigan volleyball team af ter transferring from York University. However, she used those two season to exemplify a U-M athlete, packing a career's worth of honors into just a pair of seasons. The 5-9 setter led the Wolverines in nearly every statistical category in 1984, including kills, kill percentage, digs and assists. She also excelled academically, earning Academic All-Big Ten honors and claiming the Big Ten Conference Medal of Honor in the spring of 1985. With a year of eligibility left, Williams enrolled in graduate school and continued her success in her final season. She led Michigan in seven statistical categories and was named Honorable Mention All-Big Ten, the highest Conference honor received by a Michigan volleyball player at that point. She closed her career in the top three of every Michigan statistical category, including the top spot in kills, assists and solo blocks.

another CHAMPION OF THE WEST

TINA BASLE

Coming from the renowned Nick Bolliteri Tennis Academy in Sarasota, Florida, Tina Basle came to Michigan for an excellent education and a chance to continue her tennis career. After starting her freshman year 7-7, she won eight of her final 10 matches in 1984-85 to finish the season with a 15-9 overall record. Basle was unable to grow from the success of her first year as a hamstring injury sidelined her for the majority of her sophomore season. Expected to be Michigan's competitor at number-one singles during 1986-87, she started with a 5-7 record. Once again, she rebounded to win 15 of her next 17 matches, 13 of them in straight sets. She closed the campaign by winning the Big Ten singles title, collecting All-Conference honors as well as All-Academic accolades. By her senior year, the script was familiar, and Basle cruised through a stretch where she won 22 of 23 matches and her second Big Ten singles title. She garnered All-Conference honors for the second time and was named a co-recipient of the Big Ten's Player of the Year award. With teammate Stacy Berg, Basle also earned first-team All-Big Ten honors in doubles by recording a 24-5 mark. Michigan's 1988 Conference Medal of Honor recipient, Basle graduated from U-M in 1988 with a degree in psychology.

1985-86

America's Time Capsule

September 9, 1985: President Reagan announced trade sanctions against South Africa to protest that country's policy of apartheid.

September 11, 1985: Cincinnati's Pete Rose broke Ty Cobb's major league baseball record for hits when he collected his 4,192nd hit against San Diego.

September 18, 1985: A U.S. hostage in Lebanon, the Rev. Benjamin Weir, was back in the United States after 16 months in captivity.

January 28, 1986: Seven astronauts were killed when the space shuttle Challenger exploded just 74 seconds after liftoff at Cape Canaveral, Florida.

July 11, 1986: Nolan Ryan of the Houston Astros became the first pitcher in major league history to strike out 4,000 batters when he fanned Danny Heep of the New York Mets.

University Lore

After five years of planning and five more of construction, move-in day arrived for the Replacement Hospital Project. On February 14, nearly 500 patients and 3,000 truckloads of equipment were moved into the new hospital. Hospital staff had participated in 800 training sessions to prepare for the move that came off with military-like precision. The $285 million dollar, 615-bed facility was designed by the Albert Kahn Company. Three years later, the 1925 "Old Main" building would be taken down.

Michigan Moment

"M" FOOTBALL SQUAD MAKES RUN AT NATIONAL TITLE

Few thought the 1985 Wolverine football campaign would be one to remember. Based on its disappointing 6-6 season of the year before, Michigan started the season unranked for the first time. Convincing victories over South Carolina and Maryland propelled the Wolverines to the fifth-rated team in the nation. U-M's success continued with lopsided wins over Wisconsin and Michigan State. Now 5-0, the second-ranked Wolverines found themselves against top-rated Iowa. U-M's defense held its opponent without a touchdown, but Rob Houghtlin's 29-yard field goal with two seconds left gave Iowa a 12-10 win. Defeated but undaunted, Michigan bounced back behind Morris' career-high 179 rushing yards and Jim Harbaugh's school-record 283 passing yards to crush Indiana, 42-15. Illinois and Michigan played a 3-3 affair that was preserved when U-M's Dieter Heren tipped Chris White's 37-yard field-goal attempt with no time left. Purdue and Minnesota were defeated and the Wolverines used that momentum to trip up Ohio State, 27-17, in the regular-season finale. The Wolverines headed to Tempe for the 1986 Fiesta Bowl against Nebraska. In a 14-3 hole at halftime, a different U-M team emerged from the tunnel in the second half to deliver the school's first 10-win season since 1980. Running on all cylinders with great play from the offensive, defensive and special teams units, the Wolverines scored 24 points in the third quarter to edge Nebraska by a count of 27-23. U-M's nation's best scoring defense, along with the 1,000-yard rushing performance of Morris and nearly 2,000 yards passing by Harbaugh gave Michigan the number-two ranking in both final polls.

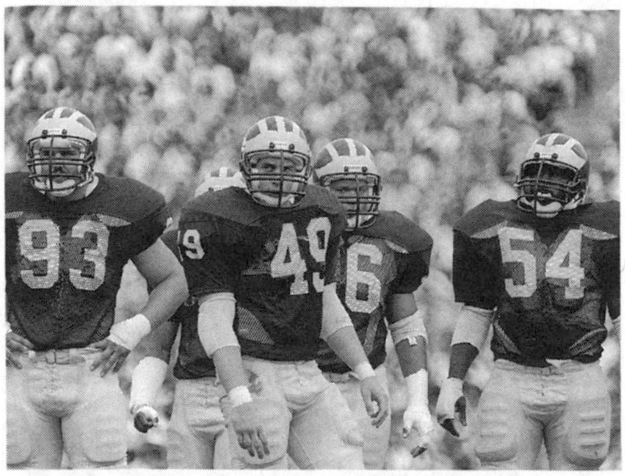

Andy Moeller (#49) led the Wolverines in tackles in 1985 and led a defense that finished second in the nation in total defense.

CHAMPIONSHIP *Moment*

MICHIGAN SWIMMERS BEGIN BIG TEN TITLE STREAK

In the 60 years of Big Ten swimming competiton, Michigan had won 20 swimming titles, but none since 1960 when Gus Stager was coach and Dwight Eisenhower was the U.S. President. Indiana had won 24 of the last 26 Conference championships, and a battle between the defending champions and the up and coming Wolverines was expected at the 1986 competition in Indianapolis. Michigan, which had recorded a 28-1 record over the last four years, ended the first day of competition in third place behind Indiana and Iowa. Two Michigan individuals and the 400 medley relay team finished third to put the Wolverines 47 points behind the Hoosiers. The Wolverines climbed to second on day two, using a 1-2 finish in the 200 freestyle to close the gap with Indiana. Dave Kerska and Joe Parker finished back-to-back in the 200 to complement their 3-4 finish in the 50 freestyle of the previous day. Kerska and Parker also swam on Michigan's second-place 800 freestyle relay team as U-M narrowed to within 43 points of the Hoosiers. Another back-to-back finish by Kerska and Parker, this a 2-3 finish in the 100 freestyle helped the Wolverines on the final day. Jan-Erick Olsen and Bill Kopas earned individual titles in the 200 breaststroke and 1650 freestyle, respectively, while Marc Parrish and Alex Waalingford grabbed a 2-3 finish in the 400 individual medley. The results of the final day left Michigan with a 603-593 edge over Indiana, the closest finish in 25 years. Jon Urbanchek's inaugural Conference title as head coach would be the first of ten straight that the Wolverines would reel off between 1986 and 1995.

CHAMPION OF THE WEST

MIKE HAMMERSTEIN

While Mike Hammerstein's playing career at Michigan started slowly, his statistics blossomed as his playing time increased. After redshirting in 1981, the Wapakoneta, Ohio native saw limited action in his second year at Michigan and saw only slightly more playing time the following season. U-M's defensive tackle began the 1984 campaign with a bang as he intercepted a Bernie Kosar pass to help sink the No. 1-ranked Hurricanes in the season opener. He recorded 55 tackles and 10 tackles for loss. that season, and was named the winner of Michigan's Dick Katcher Award, honoring the top defensive lineman. He opened the 1985 season by sacking Notre Dame quarterback Steve Beurlein four times as Michigan defeated the Fighting Irish, 20-12, and continued as a defensive leader, recording 77 tackles and a team record 23 tackles for loss in a 10-1-1 Michigan campaign. At the end of the '85 season, he was named the team's MVP. Honored with All-Big Ten and All-American status, he added to his accolades in June 1986 when he was awarded the title of Michigan's Athlete of the Year. After starting his final 25 games as a Wolverine, he was a third-round pick of the NFL's Cincinnati Bengals, whom he played with for five years.

Maize & Blue Item

In his first three seasons at Michigan, wrestling's Kirk Trost improved from fourth to second at the Big Ten meet. He had closed out his junior year by finishing second nationally. During his senior campaign, the heavyweight recorded his 100th win, and claimed a Big Ten title before the NCAA competition. There, Trost became 12th U-M individual to win a NCAA title by decisioning John Heropoulos of Iowa State, 6-3.

M List: Michigan's 26 National Runner-up Finishes

Sport	2nd	Years
Men's Basketball	4	1965, 76, 92, 93
Men's Golf	2	1943, 52
Men's Gymnastics	1	1967
Ice Hockey	2	1957, 77
Men's Swimming and Diving	10	1942, 43, 44, 45, 46, 47, 54, 55, 60, 93
Wrestling	4	1928, 29, 67, 74
Women's Swimming and Diving	1	1995
Women's Cross Country	1	1994
Women's Gymnastics	1	1995

CHAMPION OF THE WEST

ELIZABETH "BITSY" RITT

The history of women's tennis at the University of Michigan cannot be touched upon without discussing coach Elizabeth "Bitsy" Ritt, who has headed the Wolverines since 1985. The three-time Big Ten Coach of the Year led the Wolverines to their first Big Ten title, first NCAA regional title and first NCAA Championship appearance in a magical season of 1997. The 1997 squad finished 21-5, the second Ritt-coached squad to win at least 20 matches. The Big Ten champion team also topped Ritt's second-place contingent in a 17-7 1994 season. A native of Milwaukee, Wisconsin, Ritt was a three-year letter winner for the University of Wisconsin. As a Badger, Ritt compiled a 27-8 record in 1982, a mark that still ranks among UW's top ten wins in a season. Her name can also be found under Wisconsin's best doubles tandems. After graduating with a B.S. in education in 1983, Ritt spent two years as an assistant at UW before coming to Michigan, where she has remained the head tennis coach ever since.

another CHAMPION OF THE WEST

JAMES HENRY

As a Michigan track athlete in the late 1970s, James Henry was the Wolverines' premier long jumper, becoming the first U-M track athlete to leap 25 feet. The 1980 Big Ten long jump champion was part of three Conference title squads and qualified for the national meet four times. After graduating with a degree in education in 1980, Henry wasted little time in returning to his alma mater, serving as an assistant track coach to the women's team from 1981-83. In 1984, the New Haven, Michigan native took over the head coaching job for Michigan's women's track team, a role he has continued in to the present day. During that span, he has tutored 33 NCAA All-Americans, including Michigan's 1994 NCAA champion distance relay team. Named the 1994 Big Ten Indoor and Outdoor Coach of the Year for leading Michigan to a sweep of both titles, Henry was also named NCAA District IV Coach of the Year in 1993.

another CHAMPION OF THE WEST

SUE SCHROEDER

In the previous 85 years, several Wolverines had dominated the world of men's track during their stay in Ann Arbor. From 1982-86, Napoleon, Ohio native Sue Schroeder added to the women's portion of the ledger. The track and cross country athlete walked on to the cross country team in the fall of 1982 and finished 22nd at the Conference Championships. She participated in the Big Ten Track Championships during the following winter and spring, competing in several distance races. She continued to fine tune her track abilities while excelling in the classroom, picking up her first of three Academic All-Big Ten honors during her sophomore year. Schroeder finished 14th at the 1984 cross country championships, advancing to the NCAA meet, where she was awarded All-America status. After compiling Michigan records in the 1,500 and 5,000 meter races, Schroeder took second place at the 5,000 meter race at the 1985 NCAA Championship in Austin, Texas. Though she finished just four-tenths of a second behind the champion, Schroeder's finish was a Michigan record and the best place by any Michigan track athlete at the 1984 NCAA's. Michigan's highest finisher at the Conference cross country meet her senior year, Schroeder won the three-mile run at the Conference indoor meet and the 5,000 meters outdoors. She again finished second at the NCAA Championship, earning All-America honors for the fifth time in her career. She graduated from Michigan in 1986 with eight track records and a 3.88 GPA in German.

1986-87

America's Time Capsule

November 3, 1986: The Iran-Contra affair became public when a Lebanese magazine revealed that the United States had been secretly selling arms to Iran in hopes of securing the release of hostages held in Lebanon.

November 22, 1986: Twenty-year-old Mike Tyson became the youngest heavyweight boxing champion in history when he knocked out Trevor Berbick.

March 19, 1987: TV evangelist Jim Bakker admitted that he had an extramarital affair with his church secretary. He was dimissed as minister of the Assemblies of God on May 6.

April 12, 1987: Larry Mize sank a 50-yard wedge shot on the second hole of a three-way playoff against Greg Norman and Seve Ballesteros to win the Masters golf tournament.

August 16, 1987: A Northwest Airlines jet crashed on takeoff from the Detroit Metropolitan Airport, killing 156 of 157 passengers.

University Lore

North Campus gained some desperately needed classroom and office space with the opening of Engineering Building I, later renamed the Electrical Engineering and Computer Science Building. The $30 million building designed by Smith, Hinchman & Grylls was the first fully state-funded construction project in over two decades. Its central atrium soon became a popular student gathering place and site for official receptions. The EECS set the stage for Engineering's move to North Campus.

Michigan Moment

FOOTBALL GLORY DAYS CONTINUE

Following its successful 1985 season, Michigan's football team returned to the more familiar spot as a preseason Big Ten favorite and top 20 team. The Wolverines proved worthy of their ranking with a season-opening win at Notre Dame. Jamie Morris scored three touchdowns and Jim Harbaugh threw for 239 yards to beat the Irish for the second consecutive year. Bo Schembechler became the eighth football coach in NCAA history to reach 200 wins when Michigan defeated Wisconsin in the Big Ten opener. A win over Michigan State set up a battle between undefeated teams Michigan and Iowa. In retribution for the 1985 contest, Michigan's Mike Gillette broke a 17-17 tie with a 34-yard field goal with no time remaining. The victory gave Michigan a 6-0 start, its best since 1977. The Wolverine machine kept rolling, defeating Indiana and Illinois. A 31-7 win over Purdue improved U-M's record to 9-0. Against Minnesota, four Michigan turnovers resulted in 17 Gopher points, leading to a last-minute Minnesota field goal and U-M's first loss to their rival since 1977. The very next Saturday, Michigan beat Ohio State to claim the Rose Bowl bid. U-M then closed the regular season in Hawaii with a 27-10 win against the Rainbow Warriors. On New Year's Day in Pasadena, Michigan faced Arizona State for the first time in school history. Despite leading at one point in the game, 15-3, U-M managed just 53 rushing yards and 225 total yards, ultimately falling, 22-15. Despite the defeat, Michigan's 11 wins marked the most victories in a season for the Maize and Blue since 1971.

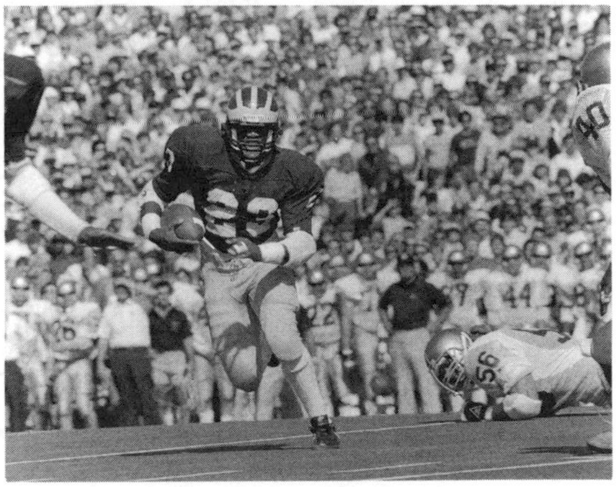

Michigan's Jamie Morris

CHAMPIONSHIP *Moment*

JUST LIKE OLD TIMES

For the first time since 1980, the prize in the season finale between Ohio State and Michigan was a Rose Bowl bid. The Buckeyes grabbed the upperhand early, taking a 14-3 lead after one quarter. A Mike Gillette field goal cut the gap to 14-6, but Michigan could not get any closer before halftime. After receiving the second-half kickoff, the Wolverines marched 83 yards to score the first touchdown the Buckeyes allowed in Ohio Stadium in 1986. Jamie Morris ran the ball in from the four-yard line to close within one point, 14-13. OSU added a field goal, but Michigan rallied for its first lead of the day on the next possession. Morris took the first play from scrimmage 52 yards, then ran in from the eight-yard line two plays later and Michigan led 19-17. The Wolverines added seven more points on their next possession when Thomas Wilcher ran for a seven-yard score. Ohio State was able to close within 26-24, but a late field-goal try went wide left and Michigan emerged with the Conference title and tickets for a trip to Pasadena. Morris was clearly the hero of the day, with 210 yards rushing.

CHAMPION OF THE WEST

JIM HARBAUGH

A three-sport star at Palo Alto High School in California, Jim Harbaugh ended his school career at Ann Arbor's Pioneer High, next door to where his father, Jack, served as defensive coordinator under Bo Schembechler. Harbaugh began showing his power as a sophomore in 1984. He started the season 3-1, including an upset of No. 1-ranked Miami before a broken arm caused him to miss the remainder of the season. Returning to action in 1985, Harbaugh led the nation in passing efficiency as Michigan went 10-1-1 and won the Fiesta Bowl. He continued to excel his senior year, leading Michigan to the Rose Bowl and breaking his own records for yards and completions. Harbaugh was named All-Big Ten, an All-American, Academic All-Big Ten, and was third in the voting for the Heisman Trophy. He ended his Michigan career with 5,449 yards passing, and was a first-round pick of the Chicago Bears in the 1987 NFL Draft. Harbaugh played seven years with the Bears before going to the Indianapolis Colts in 1994, whom he led to the AFC Championship game in 1996. He still maintains connections in Ann Arbor, where he hosts his annual golf tournament.

Maize & Blue Item

After 18 straight wins, Brian Eisner's netters cruised through the tournament to claim the program's 34th Big Ten title. Ed Nagel claimed the singles championship for U-M, which won the league crown for the 18th time in 20 years. In the 21-match streak, Michigan shut out 10 foes, and allowed five others to record just one point.

M List: Michigan's Big Ten Coaches of The Year

Johnny Orr	Men's Basketball	1974,77
Bo Schembechler	Football	1972,76,80,85
Gary Moeller	Football	1991,92
Ron Warhurst	Men's Cross Country	1990,93
Jon Urbanchek	Men's Swimming	1987,90,91,93,94,95
Brian Eisner	Men's Tennis	1987,88,89,95
Mike McGuire	Women's Cross Country	1992,93,94
Bev Plocki	Women's Gymnastics	1992,93,94,95
Carol Hutchins	Softball	1985,92,93,96
Jim Richardson	Women's Swimming	1987,89,92,95
Dick Kimball	Women's Diving	1984,87,88
Bitsy Ritt	Women's Tennis	1988,94, 97
James Henry	Women's Outdoor Track	1993,94
Geoff Zahn	Baseball	1997

CHAMPION OF THE WEST

CAROL HUTCHINS

As a player for Michigan State's 1976 softball team, Carol Hutchins helped the Spartans to the AIAW national title. She played four years for the basketball and softball teams in East Lansing. Hutchins began her coaching career as an assistant softball coach at Indiana in 1981. After leading Ferris State to the NCAA Division II softball tournament in 1982, Hutchins came to Michigan as an assistant under Bob DeCarolis, ultimately succeeding him in 1985. Though her teams posted winning records each season, it wasn't until 1992 that Michigan softball claimed the Big Ten title. Hutchins was named Big Ten Coach of the Year as her team went 22-6 in Conference play. The Wolverines claimed three more Big Ten regular season titles and three Big Ten playoff crowns in the next five seasons. Hutchins received Coach of the Year honors again in 1993 and 1996. In her 13 years as Michigan's head coach, Hutchins has recorded over 500 wins and has led U-M to the College World Series in 1995, 1996 and 1997.

another CHAMPION OF THE WEST

ALICIA SEEGERT

Alicia Seegert, a Manchester, Michigan native played for Ann Arbor's Gabriel Richard H.S. She hit .396 as a U-M freshman, smacking four home runs and driving in 36 runners. The catcher's .418 batting average in Conference play set a Big Ten record, as did her totals for hits, total bases and RBIs. As a sophomore, she hit .338 overall, and finished amongst the five leading hitters in Big Ten play. In 1986, she became the first U-M softball player to be named an All-American as she hit .353 and stroked five home runs. In Seegert's senior season, she hit .351 to be named an All-Big Ten selection for the second straight season. She ended her career holding 10 records in the Michigan softball record books, including career standards for at bats, doubles, home runs, RBI's and batting average. Seegert graduated from U-M in 1988 and was named to the Big Ten Conference's All-Decade team in 1992.

CHAMPIONSHIP Moment

WOMEN'S SWIMMERS END OSU DOMINANCE

Though 14 of the 21 members of the Michigan contingent were freshmen, the young Wolverines were seen by many as the favorite to claim the 1987 Big Ten women's swimming championship. Still, odds were that the road to the championship would be a fight between the Wolverines and five-time defending champion Ohio State. In Indianapolis, Michigan drew first blood, owning the top spot after the first day due to Gwen DeMaat. The freshman, who set a meet record in the 500 free, was also part of U-M's third-place 800 freestyle relay team. On the diving board, Mary Fischbach finished first in one meter diving as Michigan divers placed 1-5-6-7-8. DeMaat set another meet record on the second day, swimming the 200 freestyle in 1:49.35. Though her first-place finish was Michigan's sole championship of the night, U-M continued to hold on to the lead as a team. DeMaat wrapped up swimmer of the meet honors in the competition's final night, touching the wall first in the 1650 freestyle. Christi Vedejs finished first in the 200 breaststroke, avenging her second-place finish in the 100 of the previous day. On the diving board, Fischbach placed third in three-meter diving. Michigan won its first-ever swimming championship and first women's title since 1983 by winning the meet by 115 points. The meet also began a string of luck for the Wolverine swimmers, who have won every one of the seven Big Ten Championships held in Indianapolis.

America's Time Capsule

October 19, 1987: The worst stock crash in the history of the New York Stock Exchange occurred when the Dow Jones industrial average fell 508 points.

November 18, 1987: President Reagan was blamed for failing in his constitutional duty by the Congressional committees' report on the Iran-Contra affair.

February 5, 1988: A federal grand jury in Miami indicted Panamanian General Manuel Noriega in connection with illegal drug dealings.

June 29, 1988: Detroit and Boston set an NBA record as 61, 983 fans attended the game between the two teams at the Pontiac Silverdome.

August 8, 1988: The first night baseball game in the history of Chicago's Wrigley Field took place.

University Lore

The University initiated the Martin Luther King, Jr. Symposium to commemorate the slain civil rights leader and "to reaffirm the striving for social justice that his life embodied." Virginia's Lt. Governor Douglas Wilder delivered the keynote address on January 11 and Eleanor Holmes Norton, Chair of the Equal Employment Opportunities Commission, was the closing speaker. Many University organizations sponsored lectures, workshops, panel discussions, exhibits and concerts as part of the observance. The Symposium has become an annual event.

Michigan Moment

MICHIGAN BASEBALL BOASTS A TEAM OF SUPERSTARS

Michigan's baseball teams comprised a dynasty in the 1980s, finishing first in every method the Big Ten attempted to divide up the teams. From 1981-87, with the baseball programs divided into East and West divisions, Michigan reigned on top of the East each year. In 1980, 1988 and 1989, the Wolverines stood atop the nine other teams combined in one league. While the Wolverines were creating a college dynasty, they were also becoming a major league machine, turning out players who caught on in the pros. With Michigan stars from the 1960s and 1970s such as Rick Leach, Geoff Zahn, Steve Howe, Leon Roberts, Ted Sizemore and Lary Sorenson still in the majors, a new bunch of Maize and Blue batters made it to the big leagues. Barry Larkin and Chris Sabo, teammates on Michigan's 1983 team, played together with the Cincinnati Reds. In 1988, both former Wolverines made it to the All-Star Game as Sabo earned Rookie of the Year honors in the National League. Larkin, whose .296 batting average was sixth best in the league, ended the season with a 21-game hitting streak. In 1990, Hal Morris, a former teammate of Larkin's in 1984 and 1985 joined the Reds, and the trio helped lead Cincinnati to the World Series title in 1990. Two former Wolverines met up on the New York Yankees in the mid-1990s. Pitchers Jim Abbott and Scott Kaminecki helped ressurect a team that had fallen deep in the standings and led it to a wildcard berth in 1995. Other players who made it from Ann Arbor in the 1980s onto a major league team include: Jim Paciorek, Mike Ignasiak, Steve Ontiveros, Ross Powell, and Gary Wayne, each of whom saw at least three years of action in the pros.

Jim Abbott and his 1987 Golden Spikes award.

CHAMPION OF THE WEST

MARK MESSNER

Coming to Michigan from Detroit's Catholic Central in 1984, Mark Messner was redshirted his freshman year. The defensive lineman was part of the starting eleven of Michigan's defense in the 1985 season opener against Notre Dame, and would stay in the starting lineup for the following 48 games. At the end of his career, many Wolverine fans wished the Hartland, Michigan native could remain in the game forever. In his first season of action, Messner set a Michigan record with 11 sacks, while recording 71 tackles and 14 tackles for loss. He was named All-Big Ten as a freshman, a feat he would repeat in each following year. Consistently posting quality numbers, Messner became the first position player in Big Ten history to be named All-Conference for four years. A two-time All-American, Messner set Michigan career records for tackles for loss, tackles for loss yardage and sacks during his four years with the Wolverines. He served as co-captain of the 1988 squad, which went undefeated over its last 10 games and beat USC in the Rose Bowl. He finished his senior season with 26 tackles for loss, another Michigan record. After playing in the Hula and Japan Bowls, Messner was a sixth-round draft pick of the Los Angeles Rams in the 1989 NFL Draft.

another CHAMPION OF THE WEST

JIM ABBOTT

Jim Abbott's arrival at U-M fulfilled a lifelong dream for the Flint native, and the hard-throwing left-hander would continue living that dream while in Ann Arbor. When he left after three seasons, Abbott was among the top 10 in the Michigan record books in innings pitched, wins and strikeouts. But statistics do not tell the whole story behind one of Michigan's greatest pitchers. Born without a right hand, Abbott did not allow this to stop his rapid rise in the game of baseball. A letterman in both football and baseball at Flint Central High School, he continued his success during his freshman year in Ann Arbor. In his first season, he saw action in 14 games, going 6-2 with 44 strikeouts in 50.1 innings. He went 11-3 in his sophomore season, finishing fourth in the Big Ten in ERA and being named to the All-Big Ten second team. Named the winner of the Golden Spikes Award, annually honoring the outstanding amateur baseball player in the United States, Abbott recorded a 9-3 mark with 82 strikeouts in 97.2 innings as a junior. He led the Conference in ERA and was named to both the All-Big Ten and All-American teams. The winner of the Sullivan Award, the Jesse Owens Big Ten Athlete of the Year award and nearly every honor for courage and determination, Abbott jumped to the major leagues following the 1988 campaign. He pitched for the California Angels, New York Yankees and Chicago White Sox in a nine-year major league career, winning more than 100 games.

Maize & Blue Item

Portland, Oregon native Brent Lang burst onto the swimming scene for U-M in 1988 and earned Michigan's first NCAA individual swimming title since 1970. Lang, an Academic All-American and four-time All-Big Ten choice won the 100 freestyle in :42.96. A six-time Big Ten champion, and four-time NCAA titlist, Lang would also lay claim to a gold medal in the 400 freestyle relay at the 1988 Olympics in Seoul.

M List

Football's 40-Start Men

The following is a list of U-M football players who were starters in 40 or more games:

Player	Starts
Mark Messner	49
Greg Skrepenak	48
Vince Bean	48
Rick Leach	47
Jarrett Irons	47
John Vitale	46
John Elliott	45
Erick Anderson	42
Mike Husar	41
Tom Dohring	40
Rod Payne	40

CHAMPION OF THE WEST

JENNY ALLARD

During her four seasons as a member of the Michigan softball team, Irvine, California native Jenny Allard established herself as one of the finest players to wear the Maize and Blue. As a freshman, Allard was named to the Big Ten's first team as she hit .331 with 26 runs batted in. In 1988, she hit .300 and was named to the all-league second team. In 1989, Allard led the Wolverines in nearly every offensive category, including batting average, hits, doubles and RBIs. She also became a force on the mound, recording a 19-9 record in 204 innings with 64 strikeouts and an ERA of 0.75. She led Michigan to the National Softball Tournament Championship and was honored with All-American and Big Ten Player of the Year accolades. As a senior, the utility player hit .300 and cracked 11 doubles while going 10-8 on the mound with an ERA of 1.55. She ended her career in the top four of eight Michigan career statistical categories and was named to the Big Ten Conference's All-Decade team in 1992.

another CHAMPION OF THE WEST

JIM RICHARDSON

A 1971 graduate of Wake Forest University, Jim Richardson's first taste of Big Ten swimming came at the University of Iowa, where he served as an assistant coach for three years. In 1985, he was selected to take over the women's swimming program at the University of Michigan. At a university filled with such legendary swimming names as Matt Mann, Gus Stager and Dick Kimball, Richardson added his name to that list by taking the fledgling women's program to a national power. In 1985-86, Richardson's first team finished fifth in the Big Ten and 31st at the NCAA meet. Since that time, his teams have taken the top Conference spot in every single season and never finished lower than 15th at the NCAA's. Richardson's teams have recorded several milestones, including most consecutive Big Ten titles by a women's team (11) and becoming the first team in the nation other than Stanford, Florida or Texas to finish in the top three places at the NCAA Championship. In 1995, Michigan narrowly missed upsetting Stanford for the National Championship. Boasting a career winning percentage of .791, Richardson's Wolverines won 33 consecutive dual meets between 1987 and 1990. A four-time Big Ten and two-time NCAA Coach of the Year, his teams have been honored by the College Swimming Coaches Association of America four times for All-Academic performance.

another CHAMPION OF THE WEST

MARY FISCHBACH

A four-time state diving champion in Fort Dodge, Iowa, Mary Fischbach was labelled as the country's top diving prospect in 1983. In 1983-84, Fischbach would place second on both the one-meter and three-meter boards at the Big Ten Championship. At the NCAA Championship, the freshman would make an impression by finishing third and fourth on the one- and three-meter boards, respectively. While her success continued in the diving arena, Fischbach was unable to maintain her 3.9 GPA from high school. She did not compete in 1985 or 1986 as she attempted to balance her academic work and diving practice. When she returned to competition in 1987, Fischbach picked up where she left off, earning the Big Ten championship on the one-meter board, then finishing runner-up on both boards at the NCAA Championship. In 1988, Fischbach earned "Big Ten Diver of the Year" honors by winning on the one-meter and three-meter springboards as well as the platform at the Conference championship. After claiming those titles, she advanced to the NCAA meet, where she earned the crown on both springboards and the platform, becoming Michigan's first-ever women's swimmer to win individual champion honors. Fischbach's performance spearheaded Michigan's eighth-place finish nationally, the best ever by a Big Ten team. After the season concluded, she was named Michigan's female athlete of the year and was awarded a place on the Big Ten's All-Decade women's swimming team in 1992.

1988-89

MICHIGAN MOMENT

NCAA CHAMPS!

With a starting five of four juniors and one senior, the 1988-89 Michigan men's basketball team was long on experience. Having lost only Gary Grant from the previous season's sweet sixteen team, the squad was an easy preseason pick as a team to watch. All eyes turned to Bill Frieder's team as it won its first ten games. A loss to unheralded Alaska-Anchorage took the wind out of the Wolverines' sails, but they responded to slam Holy Cross the following night, U-M posted an 11-7 Big Ten record, but a loss to Illinois in the final regular season game of the year left Michigan in third place in the Conference. Frieder was replaced by Steve Fisher and the new coach led U-M to a 92-87 win over Xavier, then to a 91-82 win over South Alabama. Moving to the sweet sixteen, Michigan faced the team that had knocked it out of the tournament the previous two seasons, North Carolina. The Tarheels were set down, 92-87. A 102-65 slamming of Virginia sent Michigan to the Final Four for the first time since 1976. In the semi-final game at Seattle, Michigan faced an all-too-famliar foe. Illinois, who stunned the Wolverines twice during the regular season, had lived up to its number-one tournament seed. Michigan led the thrilling game at halftime 39-38, and the score stood at 81-81 with a few seconds left. Sean Higgins proved valuable in the clutch as he converted his own rebound just before the buzzer sounded for an 83-81 win. On to the finals for the third time in Michigan history, the Wolverines faced another third-seeded team, the Pirates of Seton Hall. The Michigan squad got out to a 37-32 halftime lead, but Seton Hall evened the game at 71-71 at the end of the regulation. Trailing 79-78 with three seconds left to go, Rumeal Robinson stood at the free throw line with two shots to go. The junior nailed both attempts to give Michigan an 80-79 win and their first national championship. Rice led the team in scoring with 31 points, and his 184 points in the tournament netted him most outstanding player honors. Robinson scored 21 in the final game while adding 11 assists.

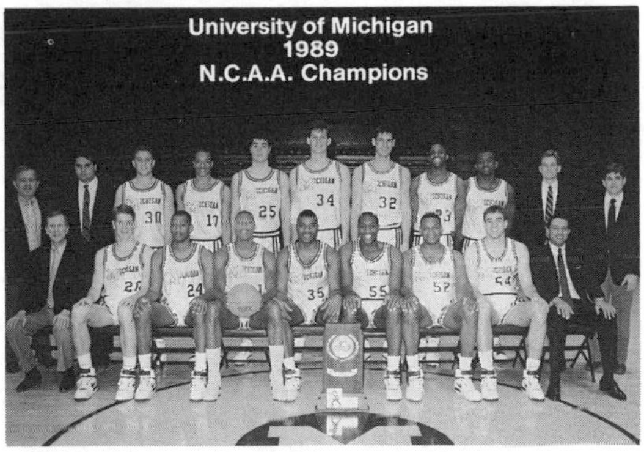

Michigan's 1989 NCAA championship team.

America's Time Capsule

November 8, 1988: Vice President George Bush defeated Governor Michael Dukakis of Massachusetts in the presidential election.

January 22, 1989: The San Francisco 49ers defeated the Cincinnati Bengals, 20-16, in Super Bowl XXIII. Joe Montana passed for a record 357 yards as the 49ers won their third Super Bowl title.

March 24, 1989: The oil tanker Exxon Valdez struck a reef in Prince William Sound, Alaska, leaking more than a million barrels of crude oil into water.

June 13, 1989: Detroit defeated the Los Angeles Lakers 105-97 in Game Four of the 1989 NBA Finals, clinching the first NBA World Championship in franchise history.

August 10, 1989: President Bush nominated Army General Colin Powell to be chairman of the Joint Chiefs of Staff. Powell became the first African-American to hold the nation's highest military post.

University Lore

Interim president James J. Duderstadt was named the University's 11th president. A nuclear engineer by training, Duderstadt had served as dean of the College of Engineering and Vice President for Academic Affairs. Foreseeing a world in which knowledge, globalization, and pluralism would be critical elements, Duderstadt initiated the "Michigan Mandate" to bring more diversity to campus and moved to prepare students for the global economy and information revolution.

CHAMPION
OF THE WEST
MALIVAI WASHINGTON

Born in Glen Cove, New York, just 15 miles northeast of the U.S. Tennis Center, MaliVai Washington moved to Swartz Creek, Michigan, where he attended East Grand Rapids High School. While he got away from the east coast, MaliVai never left the game of tennis, a sport in which he was the boys 12's national claycourt doubles champion. In the spring of 1988, Washington went 23-6, including a 8-1 mark in Big Ten play. He was a member of the tandem that earned the Big Ten doubles title and was named the Big Ten's Freshman of the Year. In 1989, Washington was named an All-American as he compiled a record of 26-5 with an 11-1 slate in the Conference. He was chosen Big Ten Player of the Year, and became the 19th Wolverine to win the Conference singles championship. He left Michigan after his sophomore year to pursue a pro career. His national ranking rose as high as No. 11 in 1992, when he became the first African American to finish in the top 20 since Arthur Ashe. After playing on the U.S. Davis Cup team in 1994, he dropped as low as No. 52 in 1995. The righthander began a comeback in 1996, catching the attention of tennis fans nationwide. In July 1996, Washington reached the finals of Wimbledon and landed a spot on the U.S. Team for the Atlanta Olympic Games.

CHAMPION
OF THE WEST
GLEN RICE

Glen Rice, Michigan's Mr. Basketball in high school, arrived on a Michigan team which had won the Big Ten title the previous year. With the 6'7" freshman forward in the lineup, the Wolverines claimed their second straight Conference title with a 14-4 league mark. Rice saw significantly more playing time in 1986-87, finishing first on the team in rebounding and second in scoring. In 1987-88, Rice averaged 22.1 points per game and led the Big Ten in scoring. Again he was honored with an All-Big Ten selection, as he helped U-M to the third round of the NCAA tournament. As a senior, Rice scored a team-record 949 points. He hit nearly 58 percent of his shots from the floor and more than 50 percent of his shots from beyond the three-point arc to eclipse Mike McGee's Michigan and Big Ten career mark for scoring. An All-Big Ten selection for the third straight year, Rice was a unanimous All-American choice. Rice carried Michigan through the NCAA tournament bracket by scoring a record 184 points (30.7 average) in his six games in the tournament. He scored 31 points in the championship game against Seton Hall as the Wolverines earned their first national title. The fourth pick in the NBA draft by the Miami Heat, Rice has played seven years in the NBA with the Heat and the Charlotte Hornets. An All-Star in 1996 and 1997, he was named the most valuable player of the All-Star affair this past February.

Maize & Blue Item

Before U-M could play its first tournament game, the team was rocked by a surprise announcement, that Bill Frieder would leave for Arizona State following the season. Athletic Director Bo Schembechler immediately relieved Frieder of his duties, handing the job to Steve Fisher, Frieder's assistant since 1982. He became the first interim coach to ever win an NCAA title.

M List

Men's and Women's Career Rebounding Leaders

Athlete	Yrs	Reb	Athlete	Yrs	Reb
Rudy Tomjanovich	68-70	1039	Trish Andrew	90-93	928
Bill Buntin	63-65	1037	Tanya Powell	87-90	820
Loy Vaught	87-90	993	Abby Currier	78-81	747
Phil Hubbard	76-79	979	Jennifer Brzezinski	92-96	
Roy Tarpley	83-86	953	Lorea Feldman	85-87	610

CHAMPION OF THE WEST

AMY BANNISTER

When Northwestern dropped all running sports in 1988, freshman Amy Bannister was a casualty of the cost-cutting measure. But the Bothell, Washington native was able to continue her career at Michigan, a career filled with success and championships. A four-time Academic All-Big Ten selection, Bannister earned All-Big Ten track honors for her performance at the 1991 Big Ten Indoor Track Championship, where she won both the 800 meter race and served as part of U-M's Big Ten champion 3200 meter relay team. Bannister became Michigan's highest national finisher at 800 meters when she finished ninth at the 1991 NCAA meet. Bannister repeated her Conference title at 800 meters at the 1992 Big Ten meet.

another CHAMPION OF THE WEST

ANN COLLOTON

She grew up in Iowa City as a devout fan of the Hawkeyes, but it was at Michigan where she made her mark. Ann Colloton, a seven-time Iowa state champion in swimming, came to U-M in the September 1986 and rewrote the Wolverines' record book in her four years. Between 1987 and 1990, Michigan's women's swimming team won 35 of 36 dual meets and claimed its first four Big Ten titles. The Wolverines finished amongst the top 10 in NCAA's each season and never lost a Big Ten dual meet. Colloton became a five-time Big Ten champion and eight-time All-American. In 1989, Colloton capped a season where she claimed three Big Ten championships by becoming U-M's second women's swimmer to become an NCAA champion. The three-time All-Big Ten selection was Michigan's female athlete of the year in 1989 and 1990. Colloton served as a Graduate Assistant Coach to the swim team in 1991 after graduating with a sociology degree from U-M. On January 28, 1992, she was named Michigan's Female Athlete of the Decade in conjunction with the Big Ten's celebration of 10 years of women's athletics.

another CHAMPION OF THE WEST

MINDY ROWAND

A six-time All-South Jersey selection in track and cross country in high school, Mindy Rowand chose Michigan for its academic reputation and aesthetic beauty. In her four years in Ann Arbor, she would add to U-M's track legendary history — on the women's side. After finishing eighth at the 1987 Conference cross country meet, Rowand finished second in the 5,000 meters at the Big Ten indoor track championship in 1988. The Laurel Springs, New Jersey native missed first place by just .04 seconds. She returned in 1988-89 to place fourth at the Big Ten cross country meet, earning All-Big Ten honors for her performance. She would add All-Big Ten honors in track as the year progressed, winning the 5,000 and 10,000-meter races at the Conference outdoor meet. To her ever-growing list of accomplishments, Rowand added two All-American citations in 1989, one for her fourth-place finish in the NCAA 5,000-meter indoor race and one for a fifth-place finish outdoors. In 1989, Rowand finished third at the Conference cross country race and second in the District IV competition before coming in eighth nationally. After garnering All-Big Ten and All-American honors in cross country, Rowand finished second in both the 3,000 and 5,000 meter runs at the Big Ten Indoor Championship. She came in third at the NCAA meet in the 5,000 meters before closing her career by winning the 5,000 and 10,000 meter races at the Big Ten outdoor meet. Rowand graduated with a degree in physical education in 1990.

MICHIGAN MOMENT

BO STEPS DOWN

After the 1989 season, Bo Schembechler announced that this football campaign had been his last. With 13 Big Ten titles to his credit, Schembechler had the most in Michigan history and tied the Conference record held by Woody Hayes. Only one other football coach in Big Ten history, Fielding Yost, had won a Conference championship in both his first and last seasons at the helm. The 1989 Michigan football team made Schembechler the second coach to do so. After dropping the season-opening contest to Notre Dame, the team headed to Pasadena to face UCLA. In the Wolverines' second 1989 appearance in the Rose Bowl, J.D. Carlson kicked a 24-yard field goal with one second remaining to give Michigan a 24-23 victory over the Bruins. A 41-21 win over Maryland ended Michigan's non-conference season, as they prepared for the Conference season. A 24-0 shutout of Wisconsin started the Wolverines' Big Ten season, followed by a narrow 10-7 win over Michigan State. The next five Big Ten foes went down by at least a two touchdown margin. The last win, a 49-15 win over Minnesota, in which Michigan averaged a record 9.0 yards per play, enabled the Wolverines to secure at least a tie for the Conference title. However, Michigan would need to beat Ohio State to return to the Rose Bowl and become the first team in 23 seasons to win back-to-back Conference titles in football. A 14-0 lead in the second quarter had Michigan thinking Rose Bowl, but the Buckeyes struck back to cut the lead to 14-12 at the end of three quarters. Schembechler, who had won eight of his last 13 games with Ohio State, would not give away his final contest. Jarrod Bunch ensured the U-M win with two fourth- quarter touchdowns, the latter coming with two minutes left in the game. With the 28-18 win, Bo's record in Big Ten games stood at 143-24-3. In its second straight Rose Bowl, Michigan fell behind to USC 10-3 at halftime before tying the game on Allen Jefferson's two-yard touchdown run in the third quarter. The Wolverines bid for a second straight victory was thwarted when the Trojans scored a touchdown with 1:08 left. Despite the 17-10 loss, Schembechler finished his Michigan career with a school-record 194 wins.

Bo Schembechler

America's Time Capsule

September 21, 1989: Hurricane Hugo ravished Charleston, S.C., causing more than a billion dollars in damages.

October 17, 1989: An earthquake measuring 6.9 on the Richter sale hit the San Francisco Bay area and more than 60 people were killed.

January 18, 1990: Washington, D.C. police arrested Mayor Marion Barry on a charge of smoking crack cocaine.

February 28, 1990: Black nationalist Nelson Mandela met with President Bush, just two weeks after having spent 27 years in prison in South Africa.

August 7, 1990: American troops, responding to the crisis in the Middle East, left for Saudi Arabia as Operation "Desert Storm" began.

University Lore

The new Willard Henry Dow Laboratory and renovated Chemistry Building provided the Chemistry Department with state-of-the-art facilities. The 270,000 square-foot, $45 million Dow building contains 14 teaching and 69 research laboratories, a science teaching center and two lecture halls as well as a glass-covered, five-story atrium that joins the building to the Diag. The building is named for Willard Henry Dow (BS Chem 1919), who was president and then chairman of the company, 1920-1949.

CHAMPION OF THE WEST

RUMEAL ROBINSON

Rumeal Robinson grew up in Cambridge, Massachusetts, where he was named an All-American in high school. He saw no action during his first year in Ann Arbor, but made significant contributions in 1987-88, when he started 32 games and averaged almost 10 points per contest. The 6'-2" guard converted 55 percent of his shots from the field while dishing out 158 assists. He continued to display his abilities during 1988-89, averaging nearly 15 points and over six assists per game. In the regional semifinal, Robinson had 17 points and a career-high 13 assists as U-M beat North Carolina then added 14 points while dishing out 12 assists versus Illinois. He scored 21 points against Seton Hall in the championship game, but the final two are the ones that everyone will remember. Michigan was trailing Seton Hall, 79-78, with three seconds left as Robinson was attempting to pass to Mark Hughes for the game-winning basket. Robinson, who had missed two free throws in a similar situation against Wisconsin earlier in the season calmly sank the two shots to give U-M the 80-79 victory and the national championship. Robinson returned to Michigan for his senior year where he completed his degree and averaged 19.2 points per game. Drafted by the Atlanta Hawks in the first round of the 1990 NBA Draft, the 1990 All-American played with five teams in a seven-year NBA career.

another CHAMPION OF THE WEST

BO SCHEMBECHLER

In the spirit of Fielding Yost, Glenn E. "Bo" Schembechler faithfully served the University of Michigan for 22 years between 1969 and 1990. During his 21 years of coaching, Michigan compiled a record of 194-48-5, winning 13 Big Ten Titles and playing in 16 bowl games. He would serve as Athletic Director for 18 months while and after he served as football coach. Schembechler lettered in football and baseball at Miami of Ohio. After a brief stint in the Army, Schembechler was an assistant coach at four schools before taking the head job at Miami in 1963. In six years he went 40-17-3 with two MAC championships. He stepped in to replace Bump Elliott at Michigan after the 1968 season and capped his first regular season in 1969 with a stunning upset of Ohio State. When he retired, Bo was the winningest active coach in Division I-A. With Bo as the athletic director, Michigan won two Big Ten football titles and a NCAA basketball crown. From 1990 to 1992, Schembechler served as the president of the Detroit Tigers baseball franchise, while working as a college football broadcaster for ABC sports. A member of the Miami and Michigan Halls of Fame, Bo is also enshrined in the Rose Bowl Hall of Fame and the National Football Foundation Hall of Fame.

Maize & Blue Item

Matt Mann Pool had been home to Michigan swimming teams for over 30 years. However, completion of Canham Natatorium left the building open for renovation after the 1988 season. Over the next two years, $750,000 was spent to convert the facility into a home for the volleyball, wrestling and gymnastics team. On September 8, 1989, the building was renamed in honor of Cliff Keen before the 1990-91 season.

M List — Bo's Michigan Champs

Year	School	W	L	T	Conf. Pl.	Bowl	AP Finish
1969	Michigan	8	3	0	1st-t	Rose	9
1971	Michigan	11	1	0	1st	Rose	6
1972	Michigan	10	1	0	1st-t		6
1973	Michigan	10	0	1	1st-t		6
1974	Michigan	10	1	0	1st-t		3
1976	Michigan	10	2	0	1st-t	Rose	3
1977	Michigan	10	2	0	1st-t	Rose	9
1978	Michigan	10	2	0	1st-t	Rose	5
1980	Michigan	10	2	0	1st	Rose	4
1982	Michigan	8	4	0	1st	Rose	-
1986	Michigan	11	2	0	1st-t	Rose	8
1988	Michigan	9	2	1	1st	Rose	4
1989	Michigan	10	2	0	1st	Rose	7

CHAMPION OF THE WEST

MARIE HARTWIG

Marie Hartwig was associated with the University of Michigan for more than 50 years, and her contributions in time and effort still have an impact today in the world of women's athletics. Hartwig went to high school in Detroit before attending the University of Michigan, where she received her B.A. in 1929, B.S. in 1931 and her master's in 1938. The following year Hartwig accepted a position in the Department of Physical Education for Women, a post which she held until 1971. During the time she was teaching courses in organization, administration, and outdoor-related topics. In 1974, Hartwig was designated as Michigan's first Director for Women's Collegiate Athletics. She was instrumental in the founding of Michigan's first six varsity sports for women. She retired from her athletic department position in 1976 and from the University in 1977. In her honor, the Marie Hartwig Award is given to the junior class female athlete of the year at U-M. On December 11, 1990, the building that was once Ferry Fieldhouse and later the women's athletics building was renamed the Marie Hartwig Building in her honor.

another CHAMPION OF THE WEST

BEVERLY FRY-PLOCKI

In the fall of 1989, Beverly Fry and the Michigan women's gymnastics program were brought together as the Butler, Pennsylvania native was named the coach of the Wolverines. It was a synergy that has reaped rewards ever since. Fry took the Wolverines out of the basement in her first season and put U-M on top of the Big Ten in 1992, a spot Michigan has yet to relinquish in the five seasons since. Fry, who married Wolverine weight and conditioning coach Jim Plocki in July 1993, has taken the Wolverines to five consecutive NCAA Championships, reaching the "Super Six" each of the last four seasons. Plocki has earned four Conference Coach of the Year citations, two Central Regional Coach of the Year honors and was named the National Coach of the Year in 1994.

CHAMPIONSHIP *Moment*

VAN DE WEGE LEADS WOMEN'S CAGERS

Before 1989-90, the women's basketball team had not posted a winning record since 1981-82. Despite the subpar history, the team grouped together to win 20 games and make Michigan's first appearance in the NCAA tournament. Led by seniors and augmented by freshmen, the Wolverines won their first six games and entered the Big Ten season 8-2. After a Conference win over Minnesota, coach Bud VanDeWege's troops would lose the next four games. However, the Wolverines refused to wilt under the pressure and won nine of their next ten games, eventually finishing fourth in the Conference. For the turnaround, VanDeWege was named Big Ten Coach of the Year. Earning a berth to the NCAA tournament, Michigan travelled to Oklahoma State to take on the higher-seeded Cowgirls. There, the Wolverines stunned the home team, taking a 77-68 decision behind Carol Szczechowski's 21 points and Tanya Powell's 19 points and 14 rebounds. Though Michigan would fall to North Carolina in the next round, the accomplishments made during the season would not be forgotten. Statistically, Powell led the team in points, rebounds and assists, while Szczechowski paced the squad in steals. Freshman Trish Andrew began a legendary career by leading Michigan and the Big Ten in blocked shots.

1990-91

America's Time Capsule

November 8, 1990: President Bush doubled U.S. forces in the Persian Gulf region to nearly a half million troops.

January 16, 1991: U.S. and allied planes attacked Iraq's communications systems and chemical weapons plants.

February 27, 1991: The United States and allied forces claimed an overwhelming victory, pushing back the Iraqi army.

March 3, 1991: Los Angeles policemen stopped and beat African-American motorist Rodney King, and an observer recorded the event on videotape.

June 12, 1991: Michael Jordan led the Chicago Bulls to its first-ever NBA championship, beating the Los Angeles Lakers, four games to one.

University Lore

Sunrunner, the U-M student-designed and constructed solar car, finished first among the 32 university teams in the first SunRayce, a three-day race from Florida to Michigan sponsored by General Motors. The U-M team qualified for the World Solar Challenge held in Australia in November 1990. Competing against a field of 36 cars, including entries from Japanese auto companies, Sunrunner finished the 1,900-mile course in third place. The team included more than 100 students from engineering, business and the sciences.

Michigan Moment

HOCKEY GLORY RETURNS

Red Berenson's ability to choose and develop talent was evidenced by his 1988-90 teams each posting winning records. In 1991, the team took the next step, returning to the NCAA tournament for the first time since 1977. With Denny Felsner, David Roberts and Brian Wiseman anchoring the offense, Michigan's shots found the back of the net more often than at any time in 14 years. Freshman Steve Shields defended his goal to the extent of Michigan's lowest goals against average in two decades. Michigan opened the season with an 11-1, 9-3 sweep of Miami, and stood at 12-5-3 midway through the campaign. After tying Lake Superior, 4-4, the puckmen headed to Joe Louis Arena in search of their third-straight GLI title. The 2-1 defeat of Michigan Tech and 3-1 win over Maine not only gave Michigan the trophy, but began a 15-game winning streak that would lift the Wolverines to near the top of the CCHA standings. Although the Wolverines would fall one point short of Lake Superior, their second-place finish in the CCHA was the school's best. In the CCHA playoffs, U-M reached the title game before losing a 6-5 overtime heartbreaker to Lake Superior. Despite the loss, the Wolverines made the playoffs, facing Cornell in the best-of-three series at Yost Arena. After losing the first game, 5-4, Michigan defeated the Big Red, 6-4, 9-3 to advance to the next round. Michigan was overmatched by Boston University in a pair of losses in Boston, but the experience gained would help the Wolverines in coming years. Felsner led U-M with 40 goals and 75 points, while Roberts paced the team with 45 assists.

Michigan's 1990-91 hockey team.

CHAMPION OF THE WEST

MIKE BARROWMAN

From the time Mike Barrowman was introduced to the water at the age of six months, his love of swimming became an integral part of his life. About 16 years later, Barrowman gained notoriety as an All-American at Potomac, Maryland's Winston Churchill High School. By the time he arrived at the University of Michigan in 1987, Barrowman's talent as a breaststroker was beginning to peak. A Big Ten champion as a freshman, he soon after entered the U.S. Olympic trials, where he set an American record to claim a spot on the team. Barrowman managed a fourth-place finish at the Seoul Summer Olympics, vowing to better that mark in 1992 at the Games in Spain. Meanwhile, at Michigan, he continued to perfect his stroke, capturing the 200-yard breaststroke at both the Big Ten and NCAA meets each of the next three years. The 1990 NCAA Swimmer of the Year and 1991 Big Ten Conference Male Athlete of the Year also was a whiz in the classroom, receiving a 1991 NCAA post-graduate scholarship. Even with all those accolades, Barrowman still had his sights set on a gold medal in Barcelona. That's exactly what he would accomplish, swimming the 200 breaststroke in 2:10.16, his sixth world record-breaking time. Barrowman was inducted into the Swimming Hall of Fame in 1997, the first year in which he was eligible.

CHAMPION OF THE WEST

JACK WEIDENBACH

Jack Weidenbach stepped in as Michigan's seventh Athletic Director when Bo Schembechler retired in January 1990. After attending Western Reserve University in Ohio, the former Air Force captain had spent 20 years in aviation management. Weidenbach arrived at U-M in 1966 and served in various administrative positions, including director of business operations and manager of the entire physical plant. In 1988, Weidenbach was named the senior associate director of athletics as Bo Schembechler ascended to the Athletic Director position. When Schembechler left to become president of the Detroit Tigers, Weidenbach moved into the AD position at the age of 65. He was able to turn around a department that had posted a $1.3 million shortfall in 1989-90 into a $500,000 profit the following year. During his four-year tenure, Michigan's sports continued to excel, with the football team winning three Big Ten titles, the basketball team going to two Final Fours and the hockey team earning its first CCHA title. He oversaw major renovations of the U-M golf course, Yost Ice Arena and the Athletic Administration Building, the last of which was renamed in his honor. Weidenbach retired in February of 1994, giving up his position to Joe Roberson.

Maize & Blue Item

Fielding Yost, Bennie Oosterbaan and Bo Schembechler had all done it, and in 1990, Gary Moeller would match the feat of that legendary list: winning a Big Ten title in his first season. Moeller got off to a shaky 3-3 start. However, the Wolverines won their final five regular season contests, including a 16-13 thriller over Ohio State to place U-M in a four-way tie for the championship.

M List — Winter Sports Team Records

Michigan's hockey team posted a team record for wins during the 1990-91 season (since broken). Here are other Michigan winter sports teams' records for wins in a season:

Sport	Wins	Season
Men's Basketball	31	1992-93
Women's Basketball	20	1989-90
Men's Swimming	13	1978-79
Women's Swimming	13	1986-87
Wrestling	20	1988-89
Men's Gymnastics	12	1969,1970,1989,1994
Women's Gymnastics	27	1993-94
Hockey	35	1996-97

CHAMPION OF THE WEST

TRISH ANDREW

A native of Winnetka, Illinois where she was a high school All-American, Trish Andrew brought her abilities to the U-M in 1989-90. As a freshman, the 6'2" forward/center had 64 blocks to place her fourth in the Michigan record books after just one season. Andrew averaged 7.9 points in Michigan's first-ever run in the NCAA tournament. Midway through her sophomore season, Andrew broke the Michigan record for career blocks and began a crusade to set the Conference standard. By her junior year, the Big Ten record for blocks was in Andrew's possession, when she rejected her 255th shot against Wisconsin. She closed out her career by averaging 19.0 points and 11.5 rebounds per game for her senior season, as she blocked 79 more shots to bring her career total to 367. An All-Big Ten second-team choice, Andrew was also an Academic All-Big Ten selection in 1992-93. Second on Michigan's career rebounding and career scoring charts, Andrew graduated from U-M in 1993 with a degree in English before playing basketball overseas.

another CHAMPION OF THE WEST

PATTI BENEDICT

A native of Allendale, Michigan, Patti Benedict never gave college softball a serious thought until her freshman year in high school. After claiming first-team All-State honors each of her four high school seasons, softball would never be an afterthought in Benedict's life again. Such a transformation was Michigan's luck, as the outfielder would spend her four years in Ann Arbor helping U-M to its first Big Ten title. She collected 1990 Big Ten Freshman of the Year accolades as she placed second on the team with 18 RBIs, but that was only the tip of the iceberg. Benedict was named All-Big Ten in 1991 as she hit .345 and shared the Conference batting crown by hitting .403. Her statistics got better in the latter half of her career, leading up to a senior campaign where she hit .421 and batted in 47 runs. The 1992 and 1993 Big Ten Player of the Year, Benedict was a third-team All-American as a junior and first-team All-American in her final season. She remains in the top 10 of eight Michigan career statistical categories, but has continued to excel in the national forum since leaving U-M.

another CHAMPION OF THE WEST

KALLI & LELLI HOSE

Kalli Hose

Lelli Hose

A duo from Del Mar, California, Kalli and Lelli Hose "twinned" up for a successful four years for the Michigan field hockey program. During their tenure, the team finished 44-31-2, a period of excellence matched only once in U-M field hockey history. The pair played in every U-M field hockey game between 1990 and 1993, combining for 20 goals, 30 assists and six Academic All-Big Ten selections. Kalli, a foward, tallied only one goal during her freshman and sophomore years, but exploded for seven markers during 1992, when she finished second on the team in scoring. She scored seven goals again during her senior season, leading the Wolverines in that department and in points. Lelli, a defender, scored only four goals in her career, but kept opponents away from the Wolverine nets while adding 13 assists. She was named to the All-Big Ten second team as a junior and again as a senior when she made the list along with Kalli. Both engineering majors were also named to the All-Midwest Region second team as seniors in 1993.

America's Time Capsule

September 9, 1991: Boxing champ Mike Tyson was indicted on rape charges by a Marion County (Indiana) grand jury.

November 7, 1991: Basketball's Magic Johnson retired after announcing that he had tested positive for the HIV virus.

December 25, 1991: Mikhail Gorbachev resigned his position as leader of the Soviet Union.

January 5, 1992: The Detroit Lions hosted the first playoff game in the Pontiac Silverdome and first home playoff since 1957. Detroit defeated the Dallas Cowboys, 38-6, for its first playoff win since 1957.

May 1, 1992: President Bush ordered federal troops to enter riot-torn Los Angeles. The unrest was triggered when a jury acquitted four policemen charged with beating Rodney King.

University Lore

A U-M delegation to South Africa finally was able to present Nelson Mandela the honorary degree he had been awarded in 1987. The leader of the African National Congress had been unable to accept the honorary doctor of law degree because he was in prison for activities against the apartheid system of South Africa. Mandela was released from prison in 1990 and would go on to become president of South Africa. The U-M delegation also laid the groundwork for later cooperative ventures and exchanges with South African universities.

Michigan Moment

FAB FIVE FROSH MAKE THEIR MARK

The 1991-92 Michigan basketball squad looked to build on experience, utilizing the seven seniors listed on its roster. While it was the seniors who provided leadership and guidance, it was a quintet of freshmen, Chris Webber, Juwan Howard, Jalen Rose, Ray Jackson and Jimmy King, who would lead U-M's quick turnaround to the upper division. In Michigan's opening game of the 1991-92 season, the Wolverines shot over 60 percent from the floor in a 100-74 win over Detroit Mercy, but committed 34 turnovers. The turnovers dwindled, but the hoopla surrounding this group of freshmen only intensified. On February 9, 1992, the Wolverines entered the Joyce Fieldhouse to take on Notre Dame and history was made as the quintet assumed the five starting roles. The youngsters accounted for all of Michigan's points in a 74-65 win over the Irish, and the lineup would stay virtually the same for the rest of the season. With a 20-8 record, Michigan reached the NCAA tournament, and the "Fab Five" wore down Temple and East Tennessee State to advance to the "Sweet 16." Moving on to Lexington, the Wolverines subdued Oklahoma State before defeating Ohio State for the first time all season, 75-71 in overtime. In the Final Four game versus Cincinnati, senior leadership became important. Senior James Voskuil broke a 58-58 tie with five minutes left as U-M held off the Bearcats, 76-72. The Wolverines fell to a more experienced Duke team in the final game, 71-51, the only time five freshman started for one team in NCAA Final Four history.

Michigan's Chris Webber (#4)

CHAMPION OF THE WEST

DESMOND HOWARD

A two-way player at St. Joseph High School in Cleveland, Ohio, Desmond Howard redshirted his freshman year, then saw limited kickoff return and receiving action during his second season. Howard's numbers and playing time increased significantly in 1990. He neared team records with 63 receptions for 1,161 yards and 11 touchdowns, while finishing atop the Conference in kickoff return average. Howard met high expectations as a junior by catching 62 passes, including unbelievable receptions against Notre Dame and Indiana, for 985 yards and 19 touchdowns. He blasted Tom Harmon's 51-year-old U-M record for points in a season and became the first receiver to lead the Conference in scoring. As a receiver and return man, Howard set or tied five NCAA records and 12 Michigan standards. A consensus All-Big Ten selection and All-America pick, he won the Heisman Trophy by capturing the highest percentage of first-place votes in the history of the award. He also was the recipient of the Walter Camp Trophy, the Maxwell Trophy, Dunlop Amateur Athlete of the year and Player of the Year accolades from the Big Ten, AP and UPI. After five quiet years in the NFL, Howard was rediscovered as a dangerous return man for the Green Bay Packers. His abilities were shown nationwide as he returned a kickoff 92 yards for a touchdown in Super Bowl XXXI, earning him MVP honors.

another CHAMPION OF THE WEST

BRIAN WINKLER

Brian Winkler already had an impressive resume when he came from Sarasota, Florida to Ann Arbor in the fall of 1991. At Riverview H.S., Winkler was a four-time Florida state champion. Winkler began expanding his success into the national forum immediately upon stepping onto the mats at Cliff Keen Arena. The engineering major posted Michigan's high scores in the floor exercise, vault and all-around during his freshman campaign. At the Big Ten Championship in Champaign, Illinois, Winkler became U-M's first individual Conference champion in five years as he scored a 9.825 on the floor to take top honors. At the NCAA Championship, he finished fourth in the vault and later, he scored a 9.95 on the floor exercise to win the NCAA individual championship in this event, the first Michigan NCAA individual champion since 1978. Hampered by a back injury his sophomore season, Winkler worked hard to return to his previous form. He finished second on the vault and seventh in the floor exercise at the Big Ten Championship his junior year, then closed out his career at U-M with a runner-up finish in the floor exercise and fourth on the parallel bars. He came in first in the floor exercise at the NCAA Regional in 1995.

Maize & Blue Item

Desmond Howard's Heisman Trophy was not the only piece of hardware brought back to Ann Arbor in 1991. Defensive linebacker Erick Anderson was given the Butkus Award, honoring the best linebacker in the nation. The Glenview, Illinois native recorded a team-leading 130 tackles, 13 tackles for loss and eight pass breakups. The Glenview, Illinois native was a key factor in U-M's defense, which led the Conference in rushing and scoring defense.

M List: Most Individual Big Ten Women's Swimming Titles

Alecia Humphrey	8
Debby Brevitz	8
Mindy Gehrs	6
Gwen DeMaat	6
Katy McCully	5
Sue Collins	4
Ann Colloton	4
Lara Hooiveld	4
Christi Vedejs	4
Maggie Stevens	4
Talor Bendel	4
Anne Kampfe	4

CHAMPION OF THE WEST

MELINDA "MINDY" GEHRS

Between 1990 and 1993, four-time Tennessee state champion Melinda "Mindy" Gehrs continued the tradition built up with the Michigan swimming program while adding her personal mark on the pool. The Oak Ridge native helped U-M to its fourth consecutive Big Ten championship as a freshman, serving as part of three first-place relay teams. Those same relay teams earned All-American status at the NCAA meet, taking Michigan to its second-highest finish ever. Two years later, Gehrs became Michigan's third-ever Big Ten Swimmer of the Year by finishing first in three individual events and two relays at the Conference Championship. She followed this with her best performance at the NCAA's, earning All-American status in five events. As a senior, Gehrs won three events at the Big Ten Championship, but saved her shining moment for the NCAA's, when she was first to the wall in the 400 individual medley. Along with the national champion honor, she took three more All-American citations from her final meet, where Michigan finished a program-best fifth place. A three-time Academic-All Big Ten selection, Gehrs was honored with a NCAA postgraduate scholarship and the Big Ten Conference Medal of Honor for her excellence both in the pool and in the classroom. She was also chosen by the NCAA as the State of Michigan's "Woman of the Year" for 1993.

another CHAMPION OF THE WEST

LARA HOOIVELD

The 15th-place competitor in the 100 breaststroke at the 1988 Olympics, Lara Hooiveld had already competed nationally in her native Australia. Arriving at Michigan in the fall of 1991, she met with similar success in the pools of the United States. In her first season, she won four Big Ten titles and earned All-American status in five events at the NCAA meet. Specializing in the breaststroke, Hooiveld began the postseason of 1993 by becoming a four-time Big Ten champion at the Conference meet. She advanced to the NCAA meet, where she became a national champion in both the 100 and 200 breaststrokes. Her time of 1:00.47 in the 100 broke the pool, Big Ten and NCAA marks for the event. She earned All-America status in two other events en route to being named the NCAA Swimmer of the Year, the first Michigan woman to be so honored. Hooiveld ended her collegiate swimming career in 1994 with seven All-America designations, eight Big Ten champion accolades, and two Academic All-Big Ten certificates.

CHAMPIONSHIP *Moment*

Patti Benedict

SOFTBALL TEAM WINS FINAL EIGHT TO SNARE BIG TEN CROWN

Though the Michigan softball team had never finished below .500, it had never finished atop the standings either, settling into second place four times between 1985-91. The 1992 season would continue the history of a winning team, and add a Big Ten championship as well. Despite a roster that was loaded with experience, the team struggled in the early part of the season. The Wolverines did not meet with any more success on their first homestand, splitting a four-game series with Northwestern. After splitting a pair of games with Bowling Green, Michigan finally found its touch, winning 12 of 13 games, including 10 straight Conference contests. Despite losing three games of a four-game set with Iowa, Michigan rebounded to win its final eight Big Ten games, earning its first league crown by a scant one-game margin over the Hawkeyes. Coach Carol Hutchins was named Big Ten Coach of the Year as the Wolverines also laid claim to the Conference Player of the Year (Patti Benedict), Pitcher of the Year (Kelly Kovach) and Freshman of the Year (Kovach). Benedict was named a third-team All-American as she led U-M in hits, doubles, home runs, runs batted in, stolen bases and batting average. From the mound, Kovach won 19 games and struck out 119 batters while compiling a 1.31 ERA. Despite a quick exit from the NCAA regional tournament, the first step to a nationally prominent program had been made.

1992-93

MICHIGAN MOMENT

America's Time Capsule

November 3, 1992: Bill Clinton won the presidential election, defeating incumbent George Bush and independent candidate Ross Perot.

December 8, 1992: The first United Nations-authorized troops landed in Somalia to assist the starving populace.

February 26, 1993: New York City's World Trade Center was bombed by terrorists.

April 19, 1993: Nearly 100 people perished in a fire ending the 51-day standoff of David Koresh's Branch Davidians against federal agents.

June 20, 1993: The Chicago Bullls defeated the Phoenix Suns, 99-98, to win their third consecutive NBA championship.

University Lore

CBS and "60 Minutes" reporter Mike Wallace and nearly 1,000 members of "Team Michigan" gathered at the Power Center on September 20 to launch the Campaign for Michigan, a five-year, one billion dollar fund-raising effort. Wallace, a 1939 journalism grad, was co-chair of the campaign. He announced that nearly $300 million dollars already had been pledged by 40 donors. The one billion dollar mark was reached in the fall of 1996.

"FAB FIVE" BIDS FOR NCAA BASKETBALL TITLE

After their tournament run of a year earlier, great things were expected of the "Fab Five" and Michigan basketball team, which was pegged as the preseason No. 1 choice. Chris Webber, Juwan Howard, Jalen Rose, Ray Jackson and Jimmy King did not disappoint the 13,000 plus fans who filled Crisler Arena each game as the team started the season 12-1. The Wolverines rolled to a 26-4 overall record, including 15-3 in the Conference. A pair of one-point losses to Indiana denied U-M a shot at the Big Ten title, but the Wolverines qualified as NCAA's No. 1 seed in the west bracket. Michigan crushed Coastal Carolina, 84-53, before taking on an old nemesis, UCLA. The Bruins took a 52-39 halftime lead, but the Wolverines refused to die, using a 23-4 second half run to send the game into overtime. With two seconds remaining in the extra session, King converted a three-foot jumper and U-M was back in the "Sweet 16." There, Michigan ended George Washington's season, then upended Temple. In both games, each of the "Fab Five" scored in double figures. Entering the Final Four for the second straight season, Michigan now faced Kentucky. The Wolverines used Webber's 27 points to defeat U-K in overtime, 81-78. In the final game, U-M dropped a close contest to North Carolina, 77-71. However, the back-to-back finals appearances permanently placed the "Fab Five" amongst the greatest NCAA tournament quintets of all time.

Photo by Per Kjeldsen

The Fab Five: (front to back) Chris Webber, Juwan Howard, Jalen Rose, Ray Jackson and Jimmy King.

CHAMPIONSHIP Moment

Tyrone Wheatley

ROSE BOWL VICTORY CAPS UNDEFEATED SEASON

Michigan's football team managed to do something in 1992 that it had not done since 1973 ... finish the season undefeated. Perfection, however, did not come easy, as five contests were decided by seven points or less, including three ties. Following a 17-17 tie with Notre Dame in the season opener, quarterback Todd Collins helped U-M to two non-conference victories. As the Wolverines opened up the Big Ten season 4-0, a new star emerged. In these four contests, a sophomore tailback named Tyrone Wheatley filled the hero role vacated by Desmond Howard by rushing for 678 yards and eight touchdowns. Victories over Purdue and Northwestern set up a Rose Bowl-clinching tie against Illinois. The annual season finale versus Ohio State, played on a muddy field in Columbus, ended in a 13-13 tie. Wheatley starred in Michigan's Rose Bowl rematch against defending national champion Washington, as the game MVP ran for 235 yards and three touchdowns on just 15 carries, including a record 88-yard scamper. A goal-line stand forced Washington to attempt a field goal, which was missed, and Michigan took over on its own 20-yard line. In five minutes, the Wolverines drove 80 yards and took the lead when Grbac found Tony McGee for a 15-yard scoring pass. The defense prevailed from there, and the 38-31 Michigan victory clinched a 9-0-3 season.

CHAMPION OF THE WEST

FAB FIVE

In September of 1991, they were simply recruits, two from Michigan, two from Texas and one from Illinois. Two guards, two forwards and a center, all of whom had averaged over 19 points and seven rebounds per game in high school. Ranging in height from 6'5" to 6'9" and in weight from 200 to 245 pounds, they came in as individuals, but they would leave as parts of a clan forever etched into the annals of college basketball, the "Fab Five." Chris Webber from Detroit's Country Day H.S., was the center of the bunch. He led the Wolverines in points, rebounding and blocks in 1992-93. He left U-M after his sophomore year and was the first pick in the NBA draft by the Orlando Magic. Jalen Rose, a high school All-American at Detroit's Southwestern H.S., led the Wolverines in scoring in 1991-92 and 1993-94, and in assists for all three of his seasons. He opted for the NBA after his junior year, being picked by the Denver Nuggets in the first round of the NBA draft. Forward Juwan Howard averaged double figures in scoring in each of his three seasons and was chosen with the fifth pick in the 1994 NBA draft by the Washington Bullets. Jimmy King and Ray Jackson both played four years for Michigan, with Jackson leading the team in scoring in 1995.

Maize & Blue Item

Ranked first in the country entering the season, Michigan used a nucleus of experienced players and goalie Steve Shields to post a 30-7-3 record in 1992-93. Though the Wolverines missed out on capturing their second straight CCHA title by a single point, they were able to advance to the NCAA playoffs for the third consecutive year and into the Final Four after an overtime win against Wisconsin.

M List

Michigan's Big Ten Title Leaders

Sport	Conference Titles	Most Consecutive
Football	37	5, 1988-92
Men's Tennis	36	16, 1968-83
Baseball	31	3, 1948-50
Men's Outdoor Track	30	4, three times
Men's Swimming	30	10, 1986-95
Men's Indoor Track	26	7, 1934-40
Women's Swimming	14	11, 1987-97
Men's Gymnastics	12	6, 1961-66
Men's Golf	12	5, 1932-36
Men's Basketball	12	3, 1964-66

CHAMPION OF THE WEST

COURTNEY BABCOCK

A native of Chatham, Ontario, Courtney Babcock followed in her father's footsteps by coming south to the University of Michigan. As a freshman, Babcock added one of the final pieces to a cross country team that took its first-ever Big Ten championship. After the fall season, she took her attention to the track where she was an All-American in the 3,000 meters, both indoors and outdoors. In 1993-94, Babcock helped keep the Big Ten cross country title in Ann Arbor and earned All-American honors by placing 13th in the national meet. In track, she compiled one of the best seasons in Michigan women's track history by winning two Conference events, the mile indoors and 3,000 meters outdoors. Nationally, she was part of Michigan's first- ever NCAA champion track contingent, part of a foursome that won the distance medley relay. Additionally, she took All-American honors at 5,000 meters indoors and 3,000 meters outdoors. The three-time All-Big Ten selection would also collect two All-America citations in 1996, and finished her career with six Academic All-Conference awards.

another CHAMPION OF THE WEST

ALECIA HUMPHREY

Three NCAA championships, 12 All-American citations, two Swimmer of the Year designations. Michigan swimmer Alecia Humphrey garnered all these honors individually during her four-year span of glory from 1992-95. The Poughkeepsie native made a big splash as a freshman, winning four Big Ten titles and setting Conference records in the 100 and 200 back. As a sophomore, Humphrey won four Conference crowns and earned five All-America certificates and the 1993 Conference Swimmer of the Year. She was the Big Ten's Swimmer of the Year again in 1994, bringing her career total to 16 Conference titles with four more crowns at the Big Ten meet. In the NCAA competition, the U-M senior won the 100 and 200 backstroke individually and served as part of U-M's champion 400 medley relay contingent. Her performance sparked Michigan to a program best second-place finish at the NCAA's.

CHAMPIONSHIP *Moment*

FROM WORST TO FIRST

From a last-place finish in 1988 and 1989, the woman's gymnastics team climbed up to first place by the 1992 season. In 1993, the Wolverines made it clear that they had no intention of yielding their lofty status, blasting the competition and claiming a second-straight Big Ten title. During the season, U-M posted a 25-3 mark, losing only in invitational meets to Michigan State, Alabama and Florida. The team set records in three events and set an all-time record high team score of 193.45 against Central Michigan. At the Big Ten Championship, it was Beth Wymer who led the Wolverines, setting Big Ten records in the all-around, balance beam and uneven bars. She was named to the All-Big Ten team along with Wendy Marshall, who finished sixth in the all-around. LiLi Leung also placed among the top nine finishers on three pieces of apparatus. While coach Bev Plocki earned her second Coach of the Year designation, her team did not stop at the Big Ten meet. By virtue of one of the nation's top 12 scores at the NCAA Central Regional, Michigan advanced to the NCAA championship for the first time since 1982. The Wolverines finished ninth in the nation, the program's second-ever top-10 finish.

1993-94

America's Time Capsule

October 6, 1993: Michael Jordan shocked professional basketball by announcing his retirement from the Chicago Bulls.

October 23, 1993: Joe Carter hit a three-run home run in the bottom of the ninth inning off Philadelphia's Mitch Williams to give the Toronto Blue Jays their second consecutive World Series title.

January 17, 1994: An earthquake in southern California killed 57 people.

June 17, 1994: Former football star O.J. Simpson, charged with two counts of murder, led a convoy of police cars on a 60-mile chase before returning to his home.

August 12, 1994: Major league baseball players went on strike. The balance of the season, including the World Series, was canceled on September 14.

University Lore

The Dalai Lama, the exiled spiritual and secular leader of Tibet, delivered the 4th annual Raoul Wallenberg Lecture and received the Wallenberg Medal. The lecture and medal commemorated Wallenberg's efforts to save thousands of Hungarian Jews from Nazi extermination in 1944. The Swedish diplomat was arrested by Soviet troops liberating Hungary in 1945 and disappeared into the Soviet prison system. Wallenberg received a bachelor's degree in architecture from the U-M in 1935.

Michigan Moment

WOLVERINE HARRIERS BREAK BADGERS' STREAK

Though Ron Warhurst's cross country team had finished second six times since tying Indiana for the Big Ten cross country title in 1980, the first-place spot had been elusive to U-M's harriers. Entering the 1993 season, the Wolverines had finished runner-up to Wisconsin for three consecutive years, including a narrow defeat in 1990. Despite losing top runner Matt Smith to graduation, the experienced team had just one freshman addition to a squad which finished fifth nationally in 1992. It was that one new face, Kevin Sullivan, who helped the Wolverines sing "The Victors" on the winner's stand. At the Conference championship in East Lansing, it was Sullivan who crossed the line ahead of the field, earning Athlete and Freshman of the Year honors with a time of 24:15.89. Less than 30 seconds later, teammate Scott MacDonald finished fourth, also laying claim to All-Big Ten honors. Maize and Blue runners Matt Schroeder and Theo Molla came in back-to-back at 12 and 13 to comprise four of the five runners that would determine Michigan's score. The Wolverines did not have to wait much longer, as Jim Finlayson finished 20th in a time of 25:27.33. U-M's Shawn McKay was just two seconds behind Finlayson, adding to Michigan's dominance despite not affecting the score. Warhurst was named the Big Ten Coach of the Year as the Wolverines broke Wisconsin's eight-year stranglehold on the top spot.

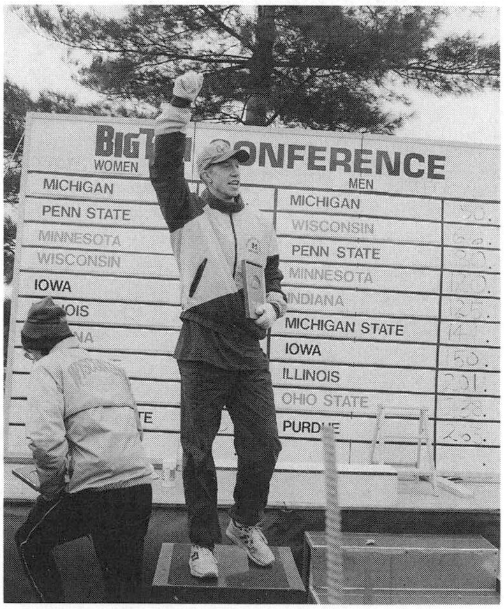

Big Ten Champion Kevin Sullivan

CHAMPIONSHIP *Moment*

Steve Shields (31) and David Oliver (26)

"M" ICERS SHINE AGAIN

With the addition of Brian Wiseman, Steve Shields and David Roberts, the Wolverines took the step to become the most successful hockey program of the 1990s. While Shields was anchoring the defense, Wiseman played in all of Michigan's 47 games, scoring 58 points from his center spot. The league freshman of the year center was complemented by right winger David Oliver, who joined Wiseman on the CCHA All-Rookie team. The trio, who delivered U-M to its first NCAA appearance in 13 years in 1990-91, continued to develop as sophomores. Wiseman recorded 71 points, while Oliver scored 31 goals for the 32-9-3 Wolverines. Michigan was helped to its first-ever CCHA title by Shields, who allowed just 2.84 goals per game. After the season of milestones, U-M advanced to the hockey final four for the first time since 1977. Shields' GAA dropped to 2.22 his junior season, while Wiseman and Oliver each contributed 50 points. The Wolverines won 30 games for the third straight year and returned to the NCAA Final Four. In 1993-94, the trio helped Michigan to a 33-7-1 record and a second CCHA title. Wiseman and Oliver finished one-two on the team in scoring with 69 and 68 points, respectively, while Shields saved over 89 percent of the shots he faced. All three were honored with first-team All-CCHA selections and Oliver was named CCHA Player of the Year. After leading U-M to its first CCHA playoff title, all three players were named semifinalists for the Hobey Baker Award, honoring the best player in college hockey.

CHAMPION OF THE WEST

GUSTAVO BORGES

Standing a towering 6'-7", Gustavo Borges could have been mistaken for a basketball player when seen around Ann Arbor. But once the Brazilian hit the pool, there was no mistaking at which sport he excelled. In his four years at Michigan, Borges helped the Wolverines win four Big Ten titles and their first NCAA title in 34 years in 1995. A four-time All-Big Ten selection, Borges specialized in the freestyle, where he won nine individual Conference titles. He set Big Ten records in the 100-yard and 200-yard freestyle, in which he earned the crown every year from 1992-95. Borges was also a force nationally, winning eight NCAA individual titles in freestyle events. A champion each of his years in the 100-yard freestyle, Borges also won three 200-yard freestyle titles and served on two champion 800-yard freestyle relay teams. A two-time Olympian for his native Brazil, Borges competed in seven separate events in the Barcelona and Atlanta Summer Olympics. In 1992, he claimed the silver medal in the 100 freestyle, while also swimming on Brazil's 400 and 800 free relay teams. Four years later, he added to his medal collection with a silver in the 200 free and bronze in the 100 free. A three-time Big Ten swimmer of the month and the 1995 Big Ten swimmer of the championship meet, Borges finished his career with 20 Big Ten championships and 22 All-American accolades. He was Michigan's Male Athlete of the Year in 1994.

Maize & Blue Item

Carrying a respectable yet disappointing 7-4 record into the season finale against Ohio State, Michigan's football team had a tremendous amount of pride on the line. The fifth-ranked Buckeyes, 9-0-1 and looking for their first Rose Bowl bid since 1984, were heavily favored. However, a total team effort by the Maize and Blue treated the NCAA-record crowd of 106,867 to a 28-0 victory, one of its most satisfying in years.

M List — Michigan's Retired Numbers

On December 13, 1993, Cazzie Russell's number 33 was raised to the rafters and retired forever from the annals of Michigan basketball. Only nine other Wolverines in any sport have had their jersey number retired:

Retired Number	In Honor of:
1	Moby Benedict, baseball
11	Bill Freehan, baseball
11	Alvin, Albert and Francis Wistert, football
33	Cazzie Russell, basketball
47	Bennie Oosterbaan, football
48	Gerald Ford, football
87	Ron Kramer, football
98	Tom Harmon, football

CHAMPION OF THE WEST

MOLLY McCLIMON

One of the athletes who has made her mark on U-M women's athletics forever is Madison, Wisconsin native Molly McClimon. A member of four Michigan championship cross country and track teams, McClimon earned All-America honors eight times and All-Big Ten honors on six occasions during her stay in Ann Arbor. As a junior, knee surgery curtailed her 1991 season, but she bounced back in 1992 to play a part in Michigan's first-ever Big Ten cross country title. In track, McClimon was a champion in the 5,000 meters outdoors and the 3,000 meters indoors. Few honors escaped McClimon during her stellar senior season in 1993-94. On the cross country circuit, she finished first overall at both the Big Ten meet and the NCAA District IV race and, placed fourth at the NCAA meet. Behind her performance, the Wolverines won a second straight Conference title and posted their best ever finish nationally. Following her final season, McClimon was named Michigan's Female Athlete of the Year and the Big Ten's Conference Medal of Honor recipient.

another CHAMPION OF THE WEST

BETH WYMER

During Beth Wymer's career with Michigan's women's gymnastics team, the Wolverines won four Big Ten championships and placed fourth at the NCAA meet. The 14-time Big Ten champion was a multiple winner in the all-around, uneven bars and floor exercise events. In 1993, Wymer won the same three events at the Big Ten Championship meet as Michigan claimed its second straight crown. At the 1993 NCAA Central Regional, Wymer became the first Michigan gymnast in U-M history to record a "10," garnering the perfect score on the uneven bars. At the national meet, she became the first Michigan gymnast to win an individual event, taking top honors on the uneven bars. Wymer was simply perfect as a junior, recording eight "10's", including the first-ever perfect scores for U-M on the floor exercise and vault. Following her third Big Ten Gymnast of the Year designation in 1995, she won the NCAA uneven bars title for an unprecedented third time to drive Michigan's best ever second-place finish. Michigan's 1995 Athlete of the Year, Wymer ended her career holding at least a share of every Michigan and Big Ten gymnastics record. The prolific gymnast also excelled in the classroom, earning three Academic All-Big Ten citations, Academic All-American status and Michigan's 1995 Conference Medal of Honor.

CHAMPIONSHIP Moment

TRACK WINS TRIPLE CROWN

Entering the 1993-94 school year, only one Big Ten school, Wisconsin, had ever won the women's track triple crown. In the successful seasons that ensued, Michigan's cross country, indoor track and outdoor track teams would combine for three Big Ten titles and a special place in history. The cross country team was U-M's success of the fall, claiming its second consecutive title. Molly McClimon and Courtney Babcock finished 1-2 in the Conference race, both earning All-Big Ten honors, while McClimon took Athlete of the Championship laurels. U-M's Karen Harvey came in eighth as the Wolverines won by a substantial margin. After winning the District meet, U-M would go on to place sixth nationally. In the winter, the indoor track team beat out Illinois in a two-team race atop the standings. Four Wolverines earned individual championships. Molly McClimon was Michigan's only two-time champion, earning top honors in the 3,000-meter and 5,000-meter runs en route to claiming Athlete of the Championship honors. Though the climate may have changed for springtime, Michigan's finish in the track standings did not. The Wolverines dominated the outdoor field, as six U-M athletes won individual events. Leading the way was Athlete of the Championship Richelle Webb, who finished first in both the 100- and 200-meter runs. Cross country coach Mike McGuire and track coach James Henry collected Big Ten Coach of the Year honors for their champion tutoring during their sports' seasons.

MICHIGAN MOMENT

America's Time Capsule

September 8, 1994: USAir flight 427 crashed near Pittsburgh, killing all 132 passengers on board.

November 5, 1994: Forty-five-year-old George Foreman became boxing's oldest heavyweight champion.

November 8, 1994: The Republicans won control of both houses of Congress for the first time in 40 years, rebuking Democratic President Bill Clinton.

January 29, 1995: The San Francisco 49ers won an unprecedented fifth Super Bowl title, beating the San Diego Chargers, 49-26.

April 19, 1995: One-hundred sixty-eight persons, including several children, were killed when the Federal Building in Oklahoma City was bombed by terrorists. It was the deadliest terrorist attack ever on U.S. soil.

University Lore

The University began "pulling the plug" on its main-frame computer in 1994-95. Thousands of U-M students had cut their computing teeth on MTS (Michigan Terminal System), a pioneering operating system developed by the U-M Computing Center. With the development of powerful personal computers, U-M began moving to a distributed computing environment. Campus was rewired with a fiber optic "backbone" that would connect more than 30,000 personal computers to the campus network, including more than 1,300 in Public Computing Sites.

DOLAN'S FOUR TITLES LEAD "M" SWIMMERS TO NCAA TITLE

Despite the fact that Michigan owned the second-most NCAA swimming championships with 10, it had been 34 years since the Wolverines last raised the banner. In 1982, Jon Urbanchek had been lured back to Michigan with the hopes of putting U-M on top for the first time since the early days of the Kennedy administration. While the former Michigan swimmer had brought Michigan as high as second, the first-place spot still eluded the Wolverines. The years of waiting came to a halt in 1995 as U-M led the competition from start to finish, taking a 25-point lead from day one and extending it to an 86-point margin over defending champion Stanford. The first event of the three-day competition gave a hint of things to come as Maize and Blue swimmers finished 1-3-4-5 in the 500 free. Michigan's dominance was evident throughout the rest of the meet, with a 1-4-5 finish in the 1,650 free and 1-3-4-5 placing in the 400 individual medley. Tom Dolan led the pack with four national titles, including three NCAA and American records. Senior Gustavo Borges went out in style by touching the wall first in the 50, 100 and 200 freestyle events. Michigan's 800 freestyle relay team of Dolan, John Piersma, Owen von Richter and Chris Rumley set an NCAA record and marked the third consecutive year U-M won this event. Jason Lancaster earned six All-American citations to lead the Wolverines.

Michigan's Tom Dolan

CHAMPION
OF THE WEST

KEVIN SULLIVAN

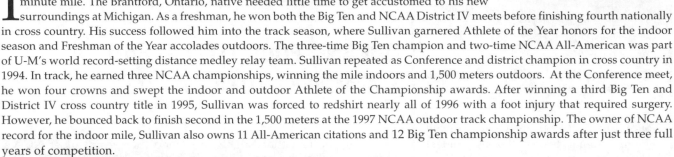

In high school, Kevin Sullivan became just the second high school Canadian to run a four-minute mile. The Brantford, Ontario, native needed little time to get accustomed to his new surroundings at Michigan. As a freshman, he won both the Big Ten and NCAA District IV meets before finishing fourth nationally in cross country. His success followed him into the track season, where Sullivan garnered Athlete of the Year honors for the indoor season and Freshman of the Year accolades outdoors. The three-time Big Ten champion and two-time NCAA All-American was part of U-M's world record-setting distance medley relay team. Sullivan repeated as Conference and district champion in cross country in 1994. In track, he earned three NCAA championships, winning the mile indoors and 1,500 meters outdoors. At the Conference meet, he won four crowns and swept the indoor and outdoor Athlete of the Championship awards. After winning a third Big Ten and District IV cross country title in 1995, Sullivan was forced to redshirt nearly all of 1996 with a foot injury that required surgery. However, he bounced back to finish second in the 1,500 meters at the 1997 NCAA outdoor track championship. The owner of NCAA record for the indoor mile, Sullivan also owns 11 All-American citations and 12 Big Ten championship awards after just three full years of competition.

CHAMPION
OF THE WEST

TOM DOLAN

Despite competing in a non-revenue sport, Tom Dolan turned many eyes to Michigan's swimming program during his three-year stay in Ann Arbor. The 6'6" Arlington, Virginia native showed his skills as a freshman, winning four titles at the Big Ten championships to give U-M its ninth consecutive Conference crown. He was awarded Big Ten Freshman and Swimmer of the Year honors for his performance there before becoming a four-time All-American at the NCAA championship. Dolan was honored as the United States Swimmer of the Year after posting a world record time in the 400 individual medley at the World Championships. As a sophomore in 1995, Dolan was a major force in bringing the NCAA championship banner back to Ann Arbor for the first time in 34 years. He won four events at the national meet — the 500 freestyle, 1,650 freestyle, 400 IM and as part of the 800 free relay — en route to being named as the NCAA Swimmer of the Year. This performance came on the heels of three crowns at the Big Ten meet and led to Dolan receiving the U.S. Swimmer of the Year award for a second time, only the third individual ever to do so. His accomplishments led to his naming as the Big Ten Male Athlete of the Year. Dolan also won the same four events at the 1996 NCAA championship, while earning All-America honors in two other events to bring his career totals to nine championships and 14 All-American plaques. However, he would rise to even greater fame as an Olympian, claiming the gold medal in the 400 IM at the 1996 Summer Olympics in Atlanta.

Maize & Blue Item

After a successful season, Michigan's hockey team had climbed into the NCAA semi-final game. At the end of regulation against Maine, the score was 3-3. It stayed that way until the third overtime when Maine's Dan Shermerhorn slipped a shot past Michigan goalie Marty Turco. In 100 minutes and 28 seconds of action, Turco had turned aside 52 shots and Maine's Blair Allison 47, but ultimately it was Michigan's hopes that would be turned aside once again.

M List

Michigan Home Run Leaders

The following is a list of Michigan baseball's most prolific sluggers:

Casey Close	46	1983-86
Phil Price	33	1987-90
Ken Hayward	33	1982-85
Jim Paciorek	32	1979-82
Chris Sabo	30	1981-83
Barry Larkin	26	1983-85
Steve Finken	22	1986-88
Jeff Jacobson	21	1980-83
Brian Simmons	20	1993-95
Nate Holdren	20	1991-93
Dan Ruff	20	1988-91
Hal Morris	20	1984-86

CHAMPION OF THE WEST

KELLY KOVACH

Before 1991, Michigan's softball program had never won a Big Ten title, or reached the Women's College World Series. With the addition of Kelly Kovach, the Wolverine program would accomplish all those feats. During her first two seasons as a U-M pitcher, Kovach compiled a record of 39-18, winning Big Ten team titles both years. While enjoying success on the mound as a junior, Kovach also made her presence felt at the plate, hitting .306. In her final season in 1995, Kovach claimed Big Ten pitcher of the year honors by going 18-4 with a 1.58 ERA. At the plate, she hit .340 with five home runs and 61 runs batted in. Named All-Big Ten and All-American, Kovach also claimed her third Academic All-Big Ten award. She finished her career in the top three of seven Michigan career statistical categories, including wins, innings pitched, strikeouts, home runs and runs batted in. Following graduation, Kovach returned to Michigan as an assistant softball coach.

another CHAMPION OF THE WEST

MICHELLE SMULDERS

The product of a family of field hockey players, Michelle Smulders participated in track, soccer and field hockey during her high school career. Once it came to the college game, however, there was no doubt as to which sport the Houston, Texas native would play. She played in 19 of the Wolverines' 20 games in 1993, but failed to record a point for U-M. Smulders led the team in goals with eight in 1994. During her junior year, Smulders started all 21 games for the Wolverines, finishing the season with eight goals. She was named a second-team All-Big Ten selection as Michigan started the season 7-2 en route to a 12-9 overall record. With three seasons of experience behind her, she was nearly unstoppable her senior season. Smulders exploded for 17 goals in 1996, tying the third-best mark ever in program history. This mark included a 14 goals-in-eight-games stretch in October, as she worked her way to All-Big Ten, Midwest Regional All-American and national second-team All-American accolades.

CHAMPIONSHIP Moment

WOLVERINE WOMEN ENJOY THEIR FINEST SEASON

The year 1994-95 would turn out to be a magical year in the history of U-M women's sports. Though the Wolverines could not capture their first national championship, they did finish runner up in three sports, a feat that has only been matched by eight schools in NCAA history. The successful season began with the cross country team, which finished second to perennial power Villanova at the NCAA meet in Arkansas. Three Wolverines earned All-America status, Deanna Arnill, Pauline Arnill and Jessica Kluge. Before advancing to the national forum, Mike McGuire's harriers won their second straight NCAA District IV title and third straight Conference crown. After capturing its ninth consecutive Big Ten title, the women's swimming and diving squad nearly toppled Stanford from its perch on top of the standings. However, the Wolverines posted a program-best finish, coming in just 19 points behind the Cardinal. Backstroker Alecia Humphrey earned three individual national titles, the last coming as part of U-M's 400-medley relay team. In a season of bests, 14 Wolverines earned All-America honors, including seven-time honoree Taylor Bendel. The gymnastics team was the third to finish second, tying Alabama for the runner-up spot behind Utah. At the NCAA meet, the Wolverines placed three members in the top 10 of the all-around, Wendy Marshall, Heather Kabnick and Beth Wymer. Wymer claimed the national title on the uneven bars for the third straight year. Prior to the NCAA meet, the gymnasts laid claim to their fourth consecutive Big Ten Conference title.

1995-96

America's Time Capsule

October 3, 1995: The "Trial of the Century" came to end in Los Angeles when the jury, sequestered for 266 days, deliberated less than four hours and found O.J. Simpson not guilty of double murder.

April 3, 1996: Federal agents seized the home of Theodore Kaczynski, thought to be the notorious Unabomber, sought for over 17 years in connection with a series of mail bombs that killed three and injured more than 20.

July 17, 1996: TWA Flight 800, traveling from New York City to Paris, exploded and crashed into the Atlantic Ocean off the coast of Long Island, killing all 230 people aboard.

August 4, 1996: The Summer Olympic Games, held in Atlanta, come to a close. Highlights included Carl Lewis' fourth consecutive gold medal in the long jump and Michael Johnson's victories in the 400- and 200-meter races.

University Lore

On September 28, 1995, U-M President James Duderstadt unexpectedly announced his resignation as president effective June 30, 1996. A sense of having accomplished most of the goals he set for his administration and a desire to return to teaching and research prompted the resignation. In January, Homer Neal was named interim president. Neal received his Ph.D. in physics from U-M in 1966, joined the faculty in 1987 and was appointed vice president for research since 1993.

Michigan Moment

"M" HOCKEY TEAM CLAIMS NCAA CHAMPIONSHIP NO. 8

For Michigan, the hockey team with the best winning percentage in the 1990s, winning had never been a problem. The Wolverines were red hot at the beginning of the 1995-96 campaign, jumping off to a 10-1 start. Jason Botterill, Warren Luhning, John Madden and Bill Muckalt were Michigan's scoring stars, while captain Steven Halko anchored the defense and Marty Turco sparkled in goal. Michigan rolled through the CCHA playoffs to face Lake Superior State in the championship game. With the contest tied 3-3 late in the third period, freshman walk-on Bobby Hayes scored to bring U-M the league playoff trophy. Off to East Lansing for an NCAA tournament game with Minnesota, the Wolverines trailed the Gophers, 2-1, before Mike Legg electrified the crowd with a lacrosse-style goal. With the game tied and just two minutes left in the third period, Muckalt took a pass from Morrison to score the game winner. Against tough Boston University in the NCAA semifinal, U-M posted a 4-0 record to advance to the championship game against Colorado College. Colorado College scored twice in a two-minute span in the second period to take a 2-1 lead, but Michigan evened the score on Mike Legg's power-play goal 6:54 into the third period. Both teams had opportunities as time dwindled, but neither the Tigers nor U-M could convert, and the game headed to overtime. Just 3:30 into the extra session, Muckalt took a pass from Crozier and fired a shot from the left faceoff circle. Tiger goalie Ryan Bach stopped the shot, but it rebounded out in front of the right post where Morrison slammed the puck home. Thirty-two years of frustration had finally ended and the Wolverines had their eighth NCAA hockey championship.

Defenseman Mark Sakala hoists the national championship trophy.

CHAMPIONSHIP *Moment*

MICHIGAN TENNIS TEAM REGAINS ITS CHAMPIONSHIP TOUCH

Though Michigan led the Big Ten with 35 men's tennis championships, the Wolverines had been title-less since 1988. In both 1994 and 1995, the Wolverines had ascended to the finals where they had dropped the final match to Minnesota. Entering the 1996 season, Michigan had not beaten the Golden Gophers since 1989. After getting off to a 6-6 start under coach Brian Eisner, Michigan took on the four-time defending champions at the Liberty Sports Complex. Led by a win at No. 1 singles by Peter Pusztai, the Wolverines gave Eisner his 400th Michigan win, 5-2. U-M would win eight of its nine final regular season matches to enter the Big Ten championship in West Lafayette as the top seed. The Wolverines easily defeated Ohio State, 4-0, in their first-round match. Despite splitting the singles matches, U-M used its doubles strength to oust Northwestern, 4-3. The tandems of Geoff Prentice/Arvid Swan and William Farah/Jake Raiton claimed victories over their Wildcat opponents, while Swan, Prentice and John Costanzo helped Michigan in singles competition. Suprisingly, Michigan's final opponent would not be Minnesota, but rather Illinois, who had upset the second-seeded Golden Gophers in the semi-finals. The Wolverines won five of the six singles matches, as Pusztai, Costanzo, Swan, Farah and David Paradzik each won to deliver a 5-2 win. Pusztai, who would win the overall singles competition, would be named the Conference Player of the Year, while Swan and Costanzo were chosen as All-Big Ten selections.

CHAMPION OF THE WEST

BRENDAN MORRISON

Brendan Morrison joined a Michigan team already loaded with talent in 1993-94. Not only would Morrison rise to the top of the Michigan pack, he would gain nationwide attention in becoming the Wolverines' first winner of the prestigious Hobey Baker Award following his senior year. In 1993-94, Morrison scored 20 goals en route to claiming CCHA Rookie of the Year honors. As a sophomore in 1994-95, the nation's and the CCHA's leading scorer was named an All-American and a Hobey Baker finalist. Despite being hampered by a wrist injury his junior year, Morrison was named the U.S. College Hockey Player of the Year by the *Hockey News*. Perhaps his biggest highlight came in the 1996 NCAA title game when Morrison scored the game-winning goal that delivered Michigan's first hockey crown in 32 years. A 1993 second-round selection of the New Jersey Devils, Morrison set personal bests with 31 goals and 57 assists, leading to his second CCHA Player of the Year trophy. An All-American for the third straight season, he capped off four successful years by winning the Hobey Baker Award in March of 1997.

Maize & Blue Item

The second-ranked Ohio State Buckeyes, starring eventual Heisman Trophy winner Eddie George, needed a win to secure the Big Ten title and a Rose Bowl berth. However, the road to the crown went through Michigan. A career-best rushing performance by Tshimanga Biakabutuka (313 yards) shelved OSU, 31-23, handing Northwestern its first outright Big Ten title in 48 years.

M List

Michigan Swimming Domination

Michigan's men and women both lead the Big Ten in team swimming championships won as well as individual championships won. Following is a list of those events the Wolverine women have dominated, the number of champions Michigan has had in the given number of years, and the number of Michigan individual champions in that event during that span.

Women'sEvent	'M' Champions	Years	Ind. Champions	Years
100 backstroke	5	6	2	1990-95
200 backstroke	6	7	2	1989-95
100 breaststroke	6	7	5	1989-95
200 breaststroke	10	11	5	1985-95
200 individual medley	6	7	3	1989-95
200 medley relay	5	6		1990-95
400 medley relay	7	7		1989-95
Team championships	9	9		1987-95

CHAMPION OF THE WEST

WENDY MARSHALL

With four consecutive Big Ten Championships to defend, a lot of pressure was placed on the 1996 Michigan women's gymnastics team to continue the school's reign atop the Big Ten. In the face of great expectations, senior Wendy Marshall answered the call and led the Wolverines to the winner's stand. Marshall earned Big Ten Gymnast of the Year honors for her performance, finishing first on the vault and 11th in the all-around. She continued her farewell performance by leading Michigan to the "Super Six" with three All-American finishes, coming in fifth in the all-around, eighth in the floor exercise and ninth on the balance beam. Sometimes in the shadow of teammate Beth Wymer, Marshall had been proving her abilities all along, earning All-Big Ten recognition during each year of her career. At the 1995 NCAA meet where Michigan came in second, the Hicksville, New York native had garnered three All-American citations.

another CHAMPION OF THE WEST

MIKE McGUIRE

In just six years as the Wolverines women's cross country coach, Mike McGuire has established a record of success that has extended the Michigan legacy even further. Since taking over the head coaching position in 1992, McGuire's teams have finished no lower than third at the Big Ten meet, including first-place finishes in his first three seasons. The three-time Big Ten and NCAA District IV Coach of the Year has tutored nine All-Americans and led the team to three first-place district finishes. From 1992-96, McGuire's team finished no lower than eighth nationally, including a NCAA runner-up finish in 1994. McGuire, who also coaches the distance runners of the track team, is no stranger to Michigan athletics. The New Jersey native was a member of U-M's track and cross country teams from 1974-78, winning two Big Ten individual titles and earning All-American status as a harrier in 1974. The winner of the 1981 *Detroit Free Press* Marathon, McGuire served as an assistant track coach at both Kansas and Eastern Michigan before returning to the Wolverines as an assistant in 1990.

another CHAMPION OF THE WEST

PHYLLIS OCKER

Phyllis Ocker, who made her presence felt from coast to coast, helped place women's athletics on the map at Michigan, where she worked for 30 years. Born in Spokane, Washington, Ocker received a bachelor's degree in physical education from the University of Washington. A few years later, she headed to Smith College in Massachusetts, where she coached softball and played field hockey while attaining her master's degree. Later she taught at the University of Texas and at Oregon State before accepting a position as a physical education teacher at U-M in 1961. Ocker, who continued to teach until 1989, took on more duties during her career in Ann Arbor. From 1974-78 she was the head coach of Michigan's field hockey team, which compiled a 33-33-3 record under her direction. She gave up her coaching duties soon after being named Michigan's third Director of Women's Athletics in July 1977. During Ocker's tenure, spending on women's sports at U-M increased from $100,000 to almost $2.5 million. She helped oversee the building of Canham Natatorium and the renovation of Cliff Keen Arena. Scholarship money for women increased 50 times between Ocker's naming as an administrator for women's sports and her retirement in January of 1991. On October 8, 1995, the brand new Michigan field hockey field was renamed Ocker Field in honor of her service to women's athletics.

1996-97

America's Time Capsule

November 5, 1996: Bill Clinton was reelected to a second term as U.S. President, easily defeating former Kansas senator Bob Dole. Clinton won 31 states.

April 13, 1997: Tiger Woods, at the age of 21, became the youngest person in history to win the Masters' Golf Tournament. His 12-stroke victory was the largest in the history of the event.

June 2, 1997: Timothy McVeigh was found guilty of the worst act of domestic terrorism in American history, the bombing of the Alfred P. Murrah Federal Building in Oklahoma City that killed 168 people in 1995.

June 7, 1997: The Detroit Red Wings defeated the Philadelphia Flyers 3-2 to win their first Stanley Cup in 42 years.

University Lore

The University of Michigan · Artes · Scientia · Veritas · 1817 ™

Former Law School Dean, Lee C. Bollinger became the 12th president of the University in February 1996. Bollinger began his academic career in 1972 as an assistant professor in the Law School. He became a recognized authority on the first amendment and authored several books on free speech issues. He served as dean of the Law School from 1987-1994 before leaving to become provost of Dartmouth University.

Michigan Moment

UNDERDOG WOLVERINES UPSET OSU AGAIN

The Buckeyes were 10-0, second ranked in the nation, Rose Bowl bound, and playing at home in front of a capacity crowd. The Wolverines were losers of two straight, 4-3 in the Conference and 17-point underdogs. There were no surprises after one half of play. The Buckeyes led, 9-0, and it would have been more had the Wolverine defense not dug in and held Ohio State to three field goals. Averaging nearly 43 points per game, Ohio State seemed poised to make a run for the national title. Then Michigan erupted for 13 second-half points, dashing OSU's dreams for the second straight season. A total team effort blanked the Buckeye offense in the latter half, and the Wolverines exited Ohio Stadium with a 13-9 victory. A second-half opening 69-yard touchdown reception from Brian Griese to Tai Streets was the only crossing of the goal line all afternoon and closed the gap to 9-7. Remy Hamilton added two field goals for the go-ahead and insurance scores for the victors. If the Buckeyes dominated the first half statistically, they were manhandled in the second part of the game. Head coach Lloyd Carr's team outgained OSU, 237-84, including a 123-5 difference on the ground. Chris Howard became the first player to run for over 100 yards against Ohio State in 1996 and the first since Tshimanga Biakabutuka ran for 313 yards vs. the Buckeyes in 1995.

Tai Streets (86) and Charles Woodson (2) enter Ohio Stadium.

CHAMPION
OF THE WEST

NEIL GARDNER

Though Michigan's track history has been illustrious to say the least, it had lacked great hurdlers until the 1994 arrival of Neil Gardner. The Kingston, Jamaica native not only set marks as Michigan's greatest hurdler of the day, but twice placed his name among the nation's best. Gardner won the 110-meter hurdles at the Big Ten outdoor meet in 1995 while coming in second in the 400-meter version of the event. In 1996, Gardner reversed his fortunes at the outdoor Conference championship, winning the 400-meter hurdles and finishing runner-up in the 110-meter version. He thus became the first-ever Wolverine athlete to win the 400-meter event. Three weeks later, Gardner became the first Michigan athlete in 60 years to become a national champion in the hurdles, winning the 400-meter intermediate event with a time of 49.27 seconds. Following a summer with the Jamaican Olympic team, Gardner continued his dominance of hurdles as a senior. In 1997, he repeated as Big Ten 400 I.M. hurdles champion at the outdoor meet. At the NCAA's, he closed a storied Michigan career by winning the 55-meter hurdles, becoming the first person in NCAA history to win both the 55-meter and 400-meter hurdles in a career.

CHAMPION
OF THE WEST

GEOFF ZAHN

Though separated by 30 years, Geoff Zahn's legendary Michigan career sandwiched a 13-year major league stint with four teams. As a part of Michigan's baseball team in 1966 and 1967, the Toledo, Ohio native set one Wolverine single-season record and tied another during his two-year pitching career. Following a 3-1 mark in 1966, Zahn was nearly unbeatable in 1967, compiling a 9-1 record with a 1.19 ERA. He tied for the league lead in wins and complete games for the third-place Michigan squad. Drafted by the Los Angeles Dodgers in January of 1968, Zahn closed his Wolverine career with a then-record .857 winning percentage. In the majors, Zahn compiled a 111-109 record in 304 games with the Dodgers, Cubs, Twins and Angels. He enjoyed his best success in 1982 when he finished 18-8 record and placed sixth in the Cy Young voting. After serving as an assistant at Pepperdine in 1995, Zahn was asked to return to his alma mater as head baseball coach for the 1996 season. In his inaugural campaign, Zahn took the last-place team and led them to a playoff berth and a fourth-place finish the Big Ten. He continued to show his coaching excellence in 1997, when he took the Wolverines to their first Big Ten title of the decade with a 17-9 Conference mark. The two-year last-to-first turnaround has been matched only once in Big Ten history.

Maize Blue Item

Nineteen-ninety-seven was a magical year for former Wolverines as U-M became the answer to the question, "Name the only school to have a Super Bowl MVP and NBA All-Star game MVP in the same year". Desmond Howard's 99-yard kickoff return helped Green Bay win the Super Bowl, while Glen Rice's 26-point performance in the NBA All-Star Game led the East to a come-back victory.

M List: Coaches Who Have Won Both the NCAA and the NIT

Coach	School
Steve Fisher	Michigan
Al McGuire	Marquette
Dean Smith	North Carolina
Adolph Rupp	Kentucky
Joe Hall	Kentucky
Bob Knight	Indiana

CHAMPION OF THE WEST

KELLY HOLMES

Entering the 1997 season, Kelly Holmes was a dependable number-two pitcher behind 1996 Big Ten Pitcher of the Year Sara Griffin for the powerhouse Wolverine softball team. During the early portion of the season, Holmes performed well, but her job was redefined when Griffin broke her wrist in Michigan's Big Ten opening series at Iowa. With much of the team's fate on her arm, the senior did not wilt in the face of pressure. Instead, she won 24 of her final 27 starts, including 22 in a row from April 8 to May 18. Holmes won her last 15 Big Ten games and finished with a Conference low 1.07 ERA en route to claiming Big Ten Pitcher of the Year honors. Following this honor, Holmes led Michigan to its third straight Women's College World Series, where the Wolverines finished a program-best tied for fifth place.

another CHAMPION OF THE WEST

ANNE KAMPFE

Michigan is famous for its athletic talent, its academic excellence and the spirit intertwined with the Maize and Blue. Few Wolverines have accomplished all three qualities better than U-M swimmer Anne Kampfe. Kampfe was a member of four Big Ten championship teams, scoring 57 points at the Big Ten Championship as a senior when she served as co-captain. A seven-time All-American in the 400-meter individual medley, the 200 backstroke and as part of the 800-medley relay, Kampfe won five Conference titles during her four-year stay in Ann Arbor. She finished second in the 400 IM at the NCAA's her freshman year and was Michigan's highest finisher at the 1996 Olympic Trials. By virtue of her third- place finish at 1997 nationals, Kampfe became the first Michigan swimmer to be All-America in one event all four years of her career. Known for her ability to energize the team, Kampfe was also an excellent performer in the classroom, earning Academic All-Big Ten honors three times and being named Academic All-District as a senior.

another CHAMPION OF THE WEST

SARAH CYGANIAK

A native of Mequon, Wisconsin, Sarah Cyganiak followed her sister to the University of Michigan women's tennis team. With Sarah joining her junior sister, Elizabeth, on U-M's 1993-94 team, the Wolverines posted a best-ever second-place finish. Sarah was named the Conference's Freshman of the Year as she posted a singles record of 16-11 and a 18-6 mark in doubles. Despite playing for the same school, the two sisters did have to face off against each other, when Sarah defeated Elizabeth at the U.S. National Amateur Tennis Championship Finals in June 1994. As a sophomore, Cyganiak was named the Big Ten's Player of the Year as she went 34-14 in singles play. She gathered All-Conference honors as a junior for the third consecutive year by going 22-9 in singles play and 19-5 in doubles action. But she surely made her mark on the Michigan women's tennis program as a senior, earning Big Ten Player of the Year honors and All-Big Ten accolades again. As co-captain and No. 1 singles player, Cyganiak led U-M to its first Big Ten championship, first NCAA regional championship and first NCAA appearance. She closed her career with a 99 singles wins, a Michigan record.

1997-98

MICHIGAN MOMENT

THE TRANSITION BEGINS

On September 8, 1997, Tom A. Goss was named the University of Michigan's ninth Director of Intercollegiate Athletics by U-M President Lee Bollinger. Goss replaced M. Joe Roberson after a four-year stay in athletics at Michigan.

TOM A. GOSS

While a student at Michigan, Tom Goss was a varsity football player who earned All-Big Ten honors at left tackle under head coach Bump Elliott in 1968. He started all 10 games as a senior and earned his third varsity letter. Goss ranked third on the team in tackles with 54 solo hits and 31 assists. He was an all-state high school player and two-time team captain under coach George Lennon at Austin High in Knoxville. Since graduating from the University, Goss has remained an active alumnus, serving as the University's alumni representative to the Big Ten Conference, being a member of the President's Advisory Committee and sitting on the board of directors of the Alumni Association. A resident of Oakland, California and a native of Knoxville, Tennessee, the 51-year-old Goss was a managing partner of The Goss Group, Inc. and previously was president and chief operating officer of PIA Merchandising Co., the nation's largest supplier of regular scheduled merchandised services. Tom and his wife, Carol, have three daughters: Anika, Fatima and Maloni.

DR. M. JOE ROBERSON

On September 3, 1993, University of Michigan President Dr. James J. Duderstadt named M. Joe Roberson as Michigan's eighth athletic director. Roberson assumed his duties officially on Feb. 1, 1994. During his tenure the U-M was one of the first schools to be officially certified by the NCAA. Roberson also helped the athletic program achieve gender equity, established a student-athlete alcohol policy, and watched as both the U-M men's swimming team and ice hockey team brought home NCAA championships. Before becoming U-M's Director of Athletics, he was executive director of the Campaign for Michigan, a fund-raising effort that has raised more than $1 billion from private donations. From 1976 to 1984, Roberson served the University on the Flint campus, ending his tenure as acting chancellor. He started his career in 1966, serving U-M for more than 31 years. After attending Flint Northern High School, Roberson entered professional baseball in 1953 as a left-handed pitcher with the Brooklyn Dodgers. In his five-plus years of professional minor league baseball, he played and trained with many future professionals, including Tommy Lasorda. An arm injury sent Roberson back to U-M, where he earned his undergraduate degree at Flint and his masters and Ph.D in Ann Arbor. Married to the former Carolyn Black in 1994, Roberson plans to winter in Florida and spend the summer in Michigan. He has a son, Marvin, and a daughter, Kimberly, from his marriage to the late Barbara Roberson, who died in 1989.

Year-by-Year Summaries

The following is a year-by-year summary of University of Michigan athletic teams through the 1996-97 season.

Baseball

Year	Overall Record	Big Ten Record	Big Ten Finish
1866	3-0		
1867	4-1		
1868	2-0		
1869-71	No record of scores		
1872	1-0		
1873-74	No record of scores		
1875	2-2		
1876	No record of scores		
1877	1-1		
1878	1-0		
1879	No record of scores		
1880	2-4		
1881	3-3		
1882	10-3-0		
1883	3-3		
1884	8-1-1		
1885	2-1		
1886	5-2		
1887	3-4		
1888	6-3-1		
1889	4-3		
1890	8-3		
1891	10-3		
1892	12-6-1		
1893	14-4		
1894	11-8		
1895	19-3-1		
1896	17-4-1	6-3	2nd
1897	4-8	2-6	4th
1898	15-6	7-3	2nd
1899	14-5	5-2	1st
1900	12-9-1	6-5-1	3rd
1901	13-8	8-2	1st
1902	8-10	1-7	5th
1903	12-5	7-3	2nd
1904	10-5	4-5	4th
1905	16-3	9-3	1st
1906	12-7	5-3	2nd
1907	11-4-1		
1908	12-4		
1909	18-3-1		
1910	17-8		
1911	16-10-1		
1912	14-10-2		
1913	21-4-1		
1914	22-6		
1915	16-7-3		
1916	9-12-2		
1917	No season–World War I		
1918	16-1	9-1	1st
1919	13-1	9-0	1st
1920	17-6-1	9-1	1st
1921	21-4	10-2	2nd
1922	21-6	9-3	2nd
1923	22-4	10-0	1st
1924	13-3	8-2	1st
1925	17-8	7-4	4th
1926	16-7	9-2	1st
1927	16-8	8-4	3rd
1928	22-5	11-1	1st
1929	15-6	7-2	1st
1930	9-15-1	3-6	7th
1931	11-7	5-4	5th
1932	19-15-1	4-5	7th
1933	12-4	8-2	2nd
1934	15-9	6-6	3rd
1935	11-11	6-5	5th
1936	20-5	9-1	1st
1937	16-8	5-6	6th
1938	14-12	4-6	8th
1939	18-9-2	8-4	3rd
1949	10-12	7-5	5th
1941	24-8	10-2	1st
1942	17-9	10-2	1st-T
1943	8-4	3-2	6th
1944	15-4-1	8-0	1st
1945	20-1	8-0	1st
1946	18-3	6-2	2nd
1947	18-10	7-4	3rd
1948	21-6	10-2	1st-T
1949	18-9-2	8-4	1st-T
1950	18-9	9-3	1st-T
1951	13-10	4-8	8th-T

Baseball Cont.

Year	Overall Record	Big Ten Record	Big Ten Finish
1952	16-7	8-4	1st-T
1953	21-9	10-3	1st-T+
1954	22-9	10-5	3rd-T
1955	17-11-1	8-7	5th
1956	17-9	6-5	4th
1957	17-7	7-4	3rd
1958	18-12	7-8	6th-T
1959	10-17-2	5-7	7th
1960	19-12-1	7-7	5th
1961	20-11	10-2	1st
1962	34-15	12-3	2nd+
1963	21-11	7-7	6th
1964	19-16	10-4	2nd
1965	18-14	10-5	2nd
1966	22-10	10-3	3rd
1967	24-12	10-4	2nd
1968	17-16	9-5	4th
1969	14-21-1	8-8	5th-T
1970	16-18	7-7	5th
1971	23-13-1	10-5-1	2nd
1972	18-13-1	9-5	3rd
1973	22-16	12-6	2nd
1974	18-14-1	7-5	3rd
1975	28-12	13-3	1st
1976	22-19-1	9-4	1st
1977	33-15	14-4	2nd
1978	30-17	13-3	1st
1979	22-14	10-4	3rd
1980	36-18-1	14-2	1st
1981	41-20	10-4	East-1st
1982	44-10	13-3	East-1st-T
1983	50-9	13-2	East-1st
1984	43-20	11-5	East-1st
1985	55-10	14-2	East-1st
1986	47-12	13-3	East-1st
1987	52-12	13-3	East-1st
1988	48-19	20-8	1st
1989	49-16	21-6	1st
1990	33-24	14-14	5th-T
1991	34-23-1	15-13	5th
1992	21-32	11-17	8th-T
1993	25-30	13-14	7th
1994	29-29	13-15	3rd-T
1995	24-29	10-16	10th
1996	24-30	17-11	4th
1997	36-22	17-9	1st

+ College World Series champions

Men's Basketball

Year	Overall Record	Big Ten Record	Big Ten Finish
1909	1-4		
1918	6-12	0-10	10th
1919	18-6	5-5	4th
1920	10-13	3-9	7th-T
1921	18-4	8-4	1st-T
1922	15-4	8-4	2nd-T
1923	11-4	8-4	3rd
1924	10-7	6-6	7th
1925	8-6	6-5	5th
1926	12-5	8-4	1st-T
1927	14-3	10-2	1st
1928	10-7	7-5	5th
1929	13-3	10-2	1st-T
1930	9-5	6-4	3rd
1931	13-4	8-4	2nd-T
1932	11-6	8-4	4th
1933	10-8	8-4	3rd-T
1934	6-14	4-8	8th-T
1935	8-12	2-10	9th
1936	15-5	7-5	3rd-T
1937	16-4	9-3	3rd
1938	12-8	6-6	5th-T
1939	11-9	4-8	7th-T
1940	13-7	6-6	6th
1941	9-10	5-7	7th
1942	6-14	5-10	7th-T
1943	10-8	4-8	8th
1944	8-10	5-7	6th-T
1945	12-7	5-7	5th
1946	12-7	6-6	7th
1947	12-8	6-6	5th
1948	16-6	10-2	1st
1949	15-6	7-5	3rd
1950	11-11	4-8	6th-T
1951	7-15	3-11	9th-T
1952	7-15	4-10	8th-T
1953	6-16	3-15	9th-T
1954	9-13	3-11	9th-T
1955	11-11	5-9	6th-T
1956	9-13	4-10	8th-T
1957	13-9	8-6	5th-T
1958	11-11	6-8	7th
1959	15-7	8-6	2nd-T
1960	4-20	1-13	10th
1961	6-18	2-12	10th
1962	7-17	5-9	8th
1963	16-8	8-6	4th-T

Men's Basketball Cont.

Year	Overall Record	Big Ten Record	Big Ten Finish
1964	23-5 •	11-3	1st-T
1965	24-4 •	13-1	1st
1966	18-8	11-3	1st
1967	8-16	2-12	10th
1968	11-13	6-8	6th-T
1969	13-11	7-7	4th
1970	10-14	5-9	6th-T
1971	19-7	12-2	2nd
1972	14-10	9-5	3rd-T
1973	13-11	6-8	6th-T
1974	22-5	12-2	1st-T
1975	19-8	12-6	2nd
1976	25-7 •	14-4	2nd
1977	26-4	16-2	1st
1978	16-11	11-7	4th-T
1979	15-12	8-10	6th
1980	17-13	8-10	6th-T
1981	19-11	8-10	7th

Year	Overall Record	Big Ten Record	Big Ten Finish
1982	8-19	7-11	7th-T
1983	16-12	7-11	9th
1984	24-9#	11-9	4th
1985	26-4	16-2	1st
1986	28-5	14-4	1st
1987	20-12	10-8	5th
1988	26-8	13-5	2nd
1989	30-7%	12-6	3rd
1990	23-8	12-6	3rd
1991	14-15	7-11	8th
1992	25-9 •	11-7	3rd-T
1993	31-5 •	15-3	2nd
1994	24-8	13-5	2nd
1995	17-14	11-7	3rd
1996	20-12	10-8	5th-T
1997	24-11	9-9	6th

• NCAA Final Four
% Won NCAA title
# Won NIT title

Women's Basketball

Year	Overall Record	Big Ten Record	Big Ten Finish
1974	3-8	0-1	
1975	3-7	0-2	
1976	12-6	3-2	
1977	8-15	1-4	8th-T*
1978	8-16	1-7	7th-T*
1979	13-14	3-6	7th-T*
1980	8-20	0-7	
1981	12-15	4-5	5th-T*
1982	17-9	3-3	
1983	4-24	2-16	9th-T
1984	4-22	2-16	9th
1985	7-21	1-17	10th
1986	14-14	8-10	7th

Year	Overall Record	Big Ten Record	Big Ten Finish
1987	9-18	2-16	10th
1988	14-14	7-11	6th-T
1989	11-17	5-13	8th-T
1990	20-10 •	11-7	4th-T
1991	11-17	4-14	9th
1992	7-21	3-15	9th-T
1993	2-25	1-17	11th
1994	3-24	0-18	11th
1995	8-19	3-13	10th-T
1996	7-20	1-15	10th
1997	15-11	7-9	8th-T

* Indicates non-Big Ten sanctioned championship play
• NCAA appearance

Men's Cross Country

Year	Dual Meet Record	Big Ten Finish	NCAA Finish
1919		6th	
1920	2-1	7th	
1921	1-2	5th	
1922	2-0	1st	
1923	2-0	5th	
1924	1-1	3rd	
1925	1-1	5th	
1926	2-0	5th	
1927	1-1	7th	
1928	0-2	3rd	
1929	0-3	3rd	
1930	1-2	5th	
1931	1-3	3rd	
1932	1-1	6th	
1933-49	No Big Ten Championships held		
1950		4th	
1951		3rd	
1952	Team did not compete in Big Ten Championship		
1953		4th	
1954		1st	
1955-56	Team did not compete in Big Ten Championship		
1957		6th	
1958	Team did not compete in Big Ten Championship		
1959		5th	
1960	Team did not compete in Big Ten Championship		
1961		8th-T	
1962-65	Team did not compete in Big Ten Championship		
1966		5th	
1967		6th	
1968		7th	
1969-70	Team did not compete in Big Ten Championship		
1971	1-1	3rd	
1972	0-0	2nd	
1973	0-0	3rd	
1974	2-0	1st	12th
1975	1-0	1st	22nd
1976	2-0	1st	18th
1977	1-0	4th	
1978	1-0	2nd	21st
1979	2-0	3rd	13th
1980	1-0	1st-T	7th
1981	1-0	4th	
1982	1-0	2nd	6th
1983	1-0	2nd	17th
1984	1-0	2nd	8th
1985	0-0	6th	
1986	0-0	5th	
1987	0-0	6th	
1988	0-0	3rd	
1989	0-0	8th	
1990	0-0	2nd	13th
1991	1-0	2nd	6th
1992	0-0	2nd	5th
1993	0-0	1st	10th
1994	0-0	2nd	7th
1995	0-0	2nd	11th
1996	0-0	2nd	14th

Women's Cross Country

Year	Dual Meet Record	Big Ten Finish	NCAA Finish
1979	0-0	7th*	
1980	1-0	6th*	
1981	2-0	5th	
1982	0-1	3rd	8th-T
1983	0-0	9th	
1984	0-0	3rd	
1985	0-0	3rd-T	
1986	0-0	4th	
1987	0-0	5th	
1988	0-0	3rd	7th
1989	0-0	3rd	15th
1990	0-0	3rd	17th
1991	2-0	3rd	14th
1992	0-0	1st	8th
1993	0-0	1st	6th
1994	0-0	1st	2nd
1995	1-0	2nd	7th
1996	1-0	2nd	

* Indicates non-Big Ten sanctioned championship play

Fencing

Year	Overall Record
1928	1-3-1
1929	No meets
1930	5-0
1931	6-2
1932	3-2
1933	6-0

Field Hockey

Year	Overall Record	Big Ten Record	Big Ten Finish
1974	2-8		
1975	5-6		
1976	8-3		
1977	7-8-3		
1978	11-8		5th*
1979	12-8-1		2nd*
1980	11-8		7th*
1981	11-8-1		6th*
1982	13-3	3-2	3rd
1983	9-7	3-7	4th
1984	1-13-5	0-7-3	5th
1985	1-14-2	1-8-1	6th
1986	8-11-1	1-8-1	5th
1987	11-6-3	2-6-2	5th
1988	6-10-4	1-6-1	4th
1989	9-9-2	3-7	4th
1990	12-7-2	3-6-1	5th
1991	9-9	4-6	4th
1992	10-8	3-7	4th
1993	13-7	4-6	4th
1994	9-11	4-6	5th
1995	12-9	4-6	4th
1996	7-11	2-8	6th

* Indicates non-Big Ten sanctioned championship play

Football

Year	Overall Record	Big Ten Record	Big Ten Finish	Bowl
1879	1-0-1			
1880	1-0-0			
1881	0-3-0			
1882	No games			
1883	2-3-0			
1884	2-0-0			
1885	3-0-0			
1886	2-0-0			
1887	3-0-0			
1888	4-1-0			
1889	1-2-0			
1890	4-1-0			
1891	4-5-0			
1892	7-5-0			
1893	7-3-0			
1894	9-1-1			
1895	8-1-0			
1896	9-1-0	2-1-0	2nd-T	
1897	6-1-1	2-1-0	3rd	
1898	10-0-0	3-0-0	1st-T	
1899	8-2-0	1-1-0	3rd-T	
1900	7-2-1	3-2-0	5th	
1901	11-0-0#	4-0-0	1st-T	Rose
1902	11-0-0#	5-0-0	1st-T	
1903	11-0-1#	3-0-1	1st-T	
1904	10-0-0#	2-0-0	1st-T	
1905	12-1-0	2-1-0	2nd-T	
1906	4-1-0	1-0-0	1st-T	
1907	5-1-0			
1908	5-2-1			
1909	6-1-0			
1910	3-0-3			
1911	5-1-2			
1912	5-2-0			
1913	6-1-0			
1914	6-3-0			
1915	4-3-1			
1916	7-2-0			
1917	8-2-0	0-1-0	8th-T	
1918	5-0-0	2-0-0	1st-T	
1919	3-4-0	1-4-0	7th-T	
1920	5-2-0	2-2-0	6th	
1921	5-1-1	2-1-1	5th	
1922	6-0-1	4-0-0	1st-T	
1923	8-0-0#	4-0-0	1st-T	
1924	6-2-0	4-2-0	4th	
1925	7-1-0	5-1-0	1st	
1926	7-1-0	5-0-0	1st-T	

Football Cont.

Year	Overall Record	Big Ten Record	Big Ten Finish	Bowl
1927	6-2-0	3-2-0	3rd	
1928	3-4-1	2-3-0	7th-T	
1929	5-3-1	1-3-1	7th-T	
1930	8-0-1	5-0-0	1st-T	
1931	8-1-1	5-1-0	1st-T	
1932#	8-0-0	6-0-0	1st-T	
1933	7-0-1	5-0-1	1st-T	
1934	1-7-0	0-6-0	10th	
1935	4-4-0	2-3-0	5th-T	
1936	1-7-0	0-5-0	8th-T	
1937	4-4-0	3-3-0	4th-T	
1938	5-1-1	3-1-1	2nd-T	
1939	6-2-0	3-2-0	4th-T	
1940	7-1-0	3-1-0	2nd	
1941	6-1-1	3-1-1	2nd	
1942	7-3-0	3-2-0	3rd-T	
1943	8-1-0	6-0-0	1st-T	
1944	8-2-0	5-2-0	2nd	
1945	7-3-0	5-1-0	2nd	
1946	6-2-1	5-1-1	2nd	
1947	10-0-0#	6-0-0	1st	Rose
1948	9-0-0#	6-00	1st	
1949	6-2-1	4-1-1	1st-T	
1950	6-3-1	4-1-1	1st	Rose
1951	4-5-0	4-2-0	4th	
1952	5-4-0	4-2-0	4th-T	
1953	6-3-0	3-3-0	5th-T	
1954	6-3-0	5-2-0	2nd-T	
1955	7-2-0	5-2-0	3rd	
1956	7-2-0	5-2-0	2nd	
1957	5-3-1	3-3-1	6th	
1958	2-6-1	1-5-1	8th	
1959	4-5-0	3-4-0	5th-T	
1960	5-4-0	2-4-0	5th-T	
1961	6-3-0	3-3-0	6th	
1962	2-7-0	1-6-0	10th	

Year	Overall Record	Big Ten Record	Big Ten Finish	Bowl
1963	3-4-2	2-3-2	5th-T	
1964	9-1-0	6-1-0	1st	Rose
1965	4-6-0	2-5-0	7th-T	
1966	6-4-0	4-3-0	3rd-T	
1967	4-6-0	3-4-0	5th-T	
1968	8-2-0	6-1-0	2nd	
1969	8-3-0	6-1-0	1st-T	Rose
1970	9-1-0	6-1-0	2nd-T	
1971	11-1-0	8-0-0	1st	Rose
1972	10-1-0	7-1-0	1st-T	
1973	10-0-1	7-0-1	1st-T	
1974	10-1-0	7-1-0	1st-T	
1975	8-2-2	7-1-0	2nd	Orange
1976	10-2-0	7-1-0	1st-T	Rose
1977	10-2-0	7-1-0	1st-T	Rose
1978	10-2-0	7-1-0	1st-T	Rose
1979	8-4-0	6-2-0	3rd	Gator
1980	10-2-0	8-0-0	1st	Rose
1981	9-3-0	6-3-0	3rd-T	Bluebonnet
1982	8-4-0	8-1-0	1st	Rose
1983	9-3-0	8-1-0	2nd	Sugar
1984	6-6-0	5-4-0	6th-T	Holiday
1985	10-1-1	6-1-1	2nd	Fiesta
1986	11-2-0	7-1-0	1st-T	Rose
1987	8-4-0	5-3-0	4th	Hall of Fame
1988	9-2-1	7-0-1	1st	Rose
1989	10-2-0	8-0-0	1st	Rose
1990	9-3-0	6-2-0	1st-T	Gator
1991	10-2-0	8-0-0	1st	Rose
1992	9-0-3	6-0-2	1st	Rose
1993	8-4-0	5-3-0	4th	Hall of Fame
1994	8-4-0	5-3-0	3rd	Holiday
1995	9-4-0	5-3-0	3rd-T	Alamo
1996	8-4-0	5-3-0	5th-T	Outback

National Champions

Men's Golf

Year	Overall Record	Big Ten Place	NCAA Place
1920	0-0	5th	
1921	0-0		
1922	3-0	2nd	
1923	2-0	5th	
1924	4-1	2nd	
1925	6-0	2nd	
1926	4-2	4th	

Year	Overall Record	Big Ten Place	NCAA Place
1927	5-1	2nd-t	
1928	5-0	2nd	
1929	6-0	2nd	
1930	5-3	2nd	
1931	5-0-2	2nd	4th
1932	6-1	1st	2nd
1933	7-0	1st	

Men's Golf Cont.

Year	Overall Record	Big Ten Place	NCAA Place
1934	8-0	1st	1st
1935	5-1	1st	1st
1936	6-1	1st	
1937	6-1	2nd	
1938	14-1	3rd	
1939	10-4	2nd	8th
1940	11-0-1	2nd	13th
1941	8-4	2nd-T	
1942	5-3-1	1st	9th
1943	4-2	1st	2nd
1944	6-2	1st	3rd
1945	6-1	3rd	3rd
1946	8-3	1st	2nd
1947	13-4	1st	5th-T
1948	10-3	4th	6th
1949	6-5-1	1st	4th
1950	8-6	3rd	
1951	9-4-1	4th	
1952	9-5	1st	2nd
1953	10-3-1	2nd	
1954	7-9	9th	
1955	5-6-2	4th	
1956	8-6	2nd	16th
1957	6-8	3rd	
1958	3-8	9th	
1959	10-6	2nd	
1960	2-5	8th	
1961	2-1	7th	
1962	5-4	3rd	
1963	3-0	4th	
1964	2-4-1	3rd	11th-T
1965	1-0	2nd	22nd
1966	3-1	2nd	16th
1967	1-1	2nd	
1968	0-2	3rd	14th-T
1969	0-0	6th	
1970	0-0	8th	
1971	0-0	7th	
1972	0-0	4th	
1973	0-0	6th-T	
1974	0-0	4th	
1975	0-0	4th	
1976	0-0	4th	
1977	0-1	5th	
1978	0-0	3rd	
1979	0-0	6th	
1980	0-0	2nd	
1981	0-0	7th	
1982	0-0	9th	
1983	0-0	6th	
1984	0-0	8th	
1985	0-0	3rd	
1986	0-0	9th-T	
1987	0-0	6th	
1988	0-0	3rd	
1989	0-0	8th	
1990	0-0	7th-T	
1991	0-0	7th	
1992	0-0	7th-T	
1993	0-0	7th	
1994	0-0	9th	
1995	0-0	3rd	
1996	0-0	4th-T	
1997	0-0	3rd	25th

Women's Golf

Year	Big Ten Place
1977-82	No Big Ten competition
1983	9th
1984	9th
1985	9th
1986	8th
1987	9th
1988	9th
1989	9th
1990	7th
1991	8th
1992	9th
1993	10th
1994	10th
1995	7th
1996	5th
1997	4th

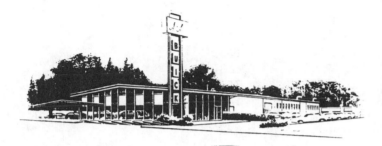

Men's Gymnastics

Year	Overall Record	Big Ten Finish	NCAA Finish
1931	0-5	5th	
1932	1-4	4th	
1933	0-1	4th	
1948	5-2	3rd	6th
1949	6-1	3rd	9th
1950	7-0	2nd	4th
1951	2-4	7th	9th
1952	4-2	4th	10th
1953	4-3	6th	
1954	7-2	3rd	14th
1955	5-2	5th	
1956	7-0	2nd	5th
1957	7-2	2nd	6th
1958	6-2	4th	5th
1959	9-1	2nd	5th
1960	7-4	5th	12th
1961	7-0	1st	4th
1962	7-1	1st	3rd
1963	6-0	1st	1st
1964	3-2-1	1st	3rd
1965	6-0	1st	
1966	8-1	1st	5th
1967	8-1	2nd	2nd
1968	8-1	1st	
1969	12-0	1st	
1970	12-0	1st	1st
1971	10-0	1st	5th
1972	10-1	2nd	
1973	7-2	1st	
1974	7-0	2nd	
1975	6-2	1st	5th
1976	9-1	2nd	
1977	6-2	3rd	
1978	4-5	3rd	

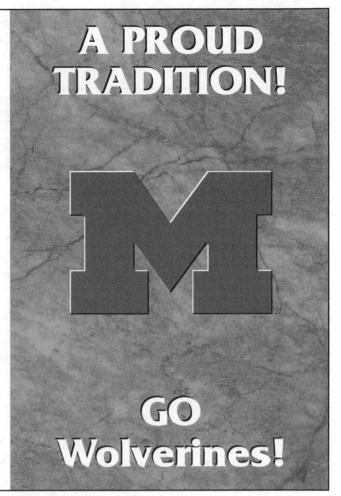

Men's Gymnastics Cont.

Year	Overall Record	Big Ten Finish	NCAA Finish
1979	5-3	3rd	
1980	10-6	3rd	
1981	4-9	5th	
1982	7-3	5th	
1983	2-6	5th	
1984	2-7	5th	
1985	2-7	7th	
1986	9-4	6th	
1987	8-10	6th	
1988	1-11	7th	
1989	12-15	6th	
1990	5-7-1	7th	
1991	8-7	7th	
1992	5-7	6th	
1993	9-14	5th	
1994	12-5	5th	
1995	3-6	6th	
1996	0-11	7th	
1997	0-6	7th	

Women's Gymnastics

Year	Overall Record	Big Ten Finish
1976	1-1	7th
1977	2-3	5th
1978	4-3	4th
1979	20-3	3rd
1980	11-3	4th
1981	6-5	3rd
1982	13-4	1st
1983	9-18	5th
1984	14-7-1	4th
1985	15-16	4th
1986	5-15	6th
1987	12-10	5th
1988	8-16	7th
1989	2-19	7th
1990	7-15	6th
1991	13-12	3rd
1992	20-3	1st
1993	25-3	1st
1994	27-1	1st
1995	24-2	1st
1996	21-6	1st
1997	20-5	1st

Ice Hockey

Year	Overall Record	League Finish
1923	4-7-0	
1924	6-4-1	
1925	4-1-1	
1926	3-5-2	
1927	9-4-0	
1928	2-10-0	
1929	5-11-1	
1930	12-7-2	
1931	10-5-2	
1932	9-6-2	
1933	10-4-2	
1934	10-6-0	
1935	12-3-2	
1936	7-9-0	
1937	11-6-1	
1938	13-6-0	
1939	8-8-2	
1940	5-14-1	
1941	2-14-1	
1942	2-14-2	
1943	1-10-2	
1944	5-3-0	
1945	3-6-0	
1946	17-7-1	
1947	13-7-1	
1948	20-2-3%	
1949	20-2-3 •	
1950	23-4-0 •	
1951	22-4-1%	
1952	22-4-0%	
1953	17-7-0%	MIHL-2nd
1954	15-6-2 •	WIHL-2nd
1955	18-5-1%	WIHL-2nd
1956	20-2-1%	WIHL-1st
1957	18-5-2 •	WIHL-2nd
1958	8-13-0	WIHL-6th
1959	8-13-1	
1960	12-12-0	WCHA-5th
1961	16-10-2	WCHA-3rd
1962	22-5-0 •	WCHA-3rd
1963	7-14-3	WCHA-7th
1964	24-4-1%	WCHA-1st
1965	13-12-1	WCHA-5th
1966	14-14-0	WCHA-5th
1967	19-7-2	WCHA-4th
1968	18-9-0	WCHA-4th
1969	16-12-0	WCHA-4th
1970	14-16-0	WCHA-6th
1971	9-21-0	WCHA-9th

Ice Hockey Cont.

Year	Overall Record	League Finish
1972	16-18-0	WCHA-6th
1973	6-27-1	WCHA-10th
1974	18-17-1	WCHA-7th
1975	22-17-1	WCHA-6th
1976	22-20-0	WCHA-4th
1977	28-17-0 •	WCHA-3rd
1978	15-20-1	WCHA-9th
1979	8-27-1	WCHA-10th
1980	23-13-2	WCHA-4th
1981	23-17-0	WCHA-5th
1982	18-15-5	CCHA-4th
1983	14-22-0	CCHA-9th
1984	14-22-1	CCHA-9th
1985	13-26-1	CCHA-9th
1986	12-26-0	CCHA-8th
1987	14-25-1	CCHA-7th
1988	22-19-0	CCHA-5th
1989	22-15-4	CCHA-4th
1990	24-12-6	CCHA-4th
1991	34-10-3	CCHA-2nd
1992	32-9-3 •	CCHA-1st
1993	30-7-3 •	CCHA-2nd
1994	33-7-1	CCHA-1st
1995	30-8-1 •	CCHA-1st
1996	34-7-2%	CCHA-1st-T
1997	35-4-4 •	CCHA-1st

• NCAA Final Four
% Won NCAA title

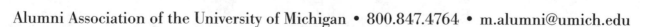

Women's Soccer

Year	Overall Record	Big Ten Record	Big Ten Place
1994	11-7-1	1-6	7th
1995	7-11-2	1-5-1	8th
1996	10-7-3	3-3-1	4th

Men's Swimming and Diving

Year	Overall Record	Big Ten Finish	National Finish
1922	0-1		
1923	1-2	6th	
1924	1-2-1	2nd	
1925	5-0	3rd	
1926	6-1	2nd	
1927	5-0	1st	1st
1928	11-3	1st	1st
1929	6-1	1st	
1930	9-0	2nd	
1931	9-0	1st	1st
1932	10-1	1st	1st
1933	4-1	1st	
1934	9-2	1st	1st
1935	9-0-1	1st	1st
1936	6-1	2nd	1st
1937	8-0	1st	1st
1938	6-2	2nd	1st
1939	7-0-2	1st	1st
1940	9-0	1st	1st
1941	10-0	1st	1st
1942	10-1	1st	2nd
1943	4-0	2nd	2nd
1944	4-2	1st	2nd
1945	4-1	1st	2nd
1946	7-2	2nd	2nd
1947	6-1	2nd	2nd
1948	8-0	1st	1st
1949	6-1	3rd	3rd
1950	4-2	2nd	4th
1951	4-2	3rd	8th
1952	8-1	3rd	3rd
1953	8-0	2nd	3rd
1954	5-1	2nd	2nd
1955	9-0	2nd	2nd
1956	1-4-1	2nd	2nd
1957	7-0	2nd	1st
1958	8-0	1st	1st
1959	10-0	1st	1st

Year	Overall Record	Big Ten Finish	NCAA Finish
1960	7-1	1st	2nd
1961	5-2	2nd	1st
1962	5-2	3rd	4th
1963	5-2	2nd	3rd
1964	7-3	2nd	4th
1965	7-0	2nd	3rd
1966	8-1	2nd	3rd
1967	4-3	2nd	5th
1968	5-2	2nd	6th
1969	7-3	2nd	4th
1970	10-1	2nd	5th
1971	10-1	2nd	10th
1972	8-2	2nd	10th
1973	8-1	2nd	7th
1974	8-3	3rd	15th
1975	8-2	3rd	11th
1976	11-2	3rd	13th
1977	7-1	4th	14th
1978	5-2	4th	15th
1979	13-1	2nd	10th
1980	7-1	2nd	15th
1981	7-3	4th	17th
1982	5-1	3rd	15th
1983	6-0	3rd	16th
1984	5-1	3rd	11th
1985	8-0	2nd	15th
1986	9-0	1st	25th
1987	9-0	1st	6th
1988	8-0	1st	5th
1989	10-1	1st	3rd
1990	10-2	1st	4th
1991	7-1	1st	6th
1992	9-1	1st	10th
1993	7-1	1st	2nd
1994	9-3	1st	3rd
1995	9-1	1st	1st
1996	8-1	2nd	3rd
1997	6-2	1st	7th

Synchronized Swimming

Year	Dual Meet Record	Regional Finish	National Finish
1975	0-0	3rd	
1976	2-0	2nd	
1977	2-0	2nd	2nd
1978	0-0	2nd	2nd
1979	0-0	2nd	3rd
1980	0-0	2nd	3rd
1981	0-0	2nd	3rd
1982	0-0		

Men's Tennis

Year	Overall Record	Big Ten Finish	NCAA Finish
1893	0-0	1st	
1894	No team		
1895	No team		
1896	No team		
1897	0-0	1st	
1898	0-0	2nd	
1899	1-0		
1900	0-1		
1901	0-0	1st	
1902	1-0		
1903	1-0	1st	
1904	3-0	1st	
1905	1-0		
1906	No team		
1907	1-0		
1908	5-1-1		
1909	3-1		
1910	2-0-1		
1911	1-3-1		
1912	5-1		
1913	3-2		
1914	2-5-1		
1915	5-2		
1916	3-3-1		
1917	No season		
1918	1-2		
1919	4-0	1st	
1920	0-0	1st	
1921	8-3		
1922	9-3-1		
1923	9-1-2	1st	
1924	9-2-1	2nd	
1925	7-3-1		
1926	8-2		
1927	8-0		
1928	4-1		
1929	4-0		
1930	9-1		
1931	6-2		
1932	4-2-2		
1933	5-7-1		
1934	5-4-1	2nd	
1935	10-2-1	7th	
1936	3-9-1	3rd	
1937	7-6	4th	
1938	10-8	8th	
1939	17-3	3rd	
1940	11-5	4th	
1941	17-3	1st	
1942	10-1	2nd	
1943	4-5	5th	
1944	8-1	1st	
1945	8-0	1st	
1946	9-4	5th	
1947	11-5	3rd	
1948	9-4	2nd	
1949	8-0	2nd	
1950	9-0	3rd	
1951	6-2	2nd	
1952	6-4	5th	
1953	8-3	3rd	
1954	11-3-1	2nd	
1955	13-0	1st	6th-T
1956	12-0	1st	6th-T
1957	12-0	1st	1st
1958	8-2	3rd	8th-T
1959	9-1	1st	8th-T
1960	7-4	1st	
1961	9-3	1st	6th-T
1962	8-2	1st	5th
1963	7-6	2nd	6th-T
1964	9-4	2nd	9th-T
1965	10-4	1st	15th
1966	10-0	1st	12th-T
1967	9-3	2nd	
1968	13-0	1st	13th-T
1969	15-2	1st	16th-T
1970	13-4	1st	16th-T
1971	17-4	1st	25th-T
1972	15-3	1st	18th-T
1973	18-3	1st	9th-T
1974	14-1	1st	3rd

Men's Tennis Cont.

Year	Overall Record	Big Ten Finish	NCAA Finish
1975	16-1	1st	4th
1976	14-4	1st	26th-T
1977	16-4	1st	9th-T
1978	14-5	1st	
1979	19-2	1st	9th-T
1980	18-1	1st	10th
1981	17-4	1st	19th
1982	16-9	1st	9th-T
1983	13-12	1st	9th-T
1984	9-7	5th	
1985	13-4	1st	9th-T
1986	13-8	2nd	

Year	Overall Record	Big Ten Finish	NCAA Finish
1987	28-3	1st	5th-T
1988	26-5	1st	3rd
1989	15-10	2nd	
1990	11-15	6th	
1991	12-8	8th	
1992	6-16	8th	
1993	8-14	8th	
1994	15-8	2nd	
1995	17-9	2nd	
1996	18-8	1st	
1997	9-14	6th	

Women's Tennis

Year	Overall Record	Big Ten Record	Big Ten Finish
1974	5-0	0-0	6th*
1975	4-1	0-1	6th-T*
1976	11-0	2-0	5th*
1977	10-2	4-2	2nd*
1978	11-2	5-1	5th*
1979	18-5	8-2	3rd*
1980	4-12	5-6	4th*
1981	19-9	8-6	4th*
1982	11-8	7-3	3rd
1983	11-9	6-5	5th
1984	15-8	8-3	3rd
1985	9-13	4-11	8th
1986	10-18	2-13	10th
1987	11-16	3-11	10th
1988	18-9	7-7	5th
1989	9-14	5-7	10th
1990	20-9	7-6	5th
1991	15-8	7-5	4th
1992	14-9	9-4	5th
1993	12-11	7-6	6th
1994	17-7	11-2	2nd
1995	16-7	10-3	5th
1996	8-12	6-5	5th
1997	21-5	10-0	1st

* Indicates non-Big Ten sanctioned championship play

Men's Indoor Track

Year	Big Ten Finish	NCAA Finish
1918	1st	
1919	1st	
1920	2nd	
1921	2nd	
1922	5th	
1923	1st	
1924	2nd	
1925	1st	
1926	2nd	
1927	4th	
1928	5th	
1929	5th	
1930	4th	
1931	1st	
1932	2nd	
1933	2nd	
1934	1st	
1935	1st	
1936	1st	
1937	1st	
1938	1st	
1939	1st	
1940	1st	
1941	2nd	
1942	4th	
1943	1st	
1944	1st	
1945	1st	
1946	2nd	

Men's Indoor Track Cont.

Year	Big Ten Finish	NCAA Finish
1947	3rd	
1948	4th	
1949	7th	
1950	2nd	
1951	2nd	
1952	2nd	
1953	2nd	
1954	3rd	
1955	1st	
1956	1st	
1957	4th	
1958	8th	
1959	1st	
1960	1st	
1961	1st	
1962	2nd	
1963	1st-T	
1964	1st	
1965	3rd	25th-T
1966	4th	28th-T
1967	5th	8th-T
1968	2nd	11th-T
1969	3rd	11th
1970	5th	28th-T
1971	8th	31st-T
1972	5th	34th-T
1973	2nd	8th-T
1974	5th	44th-T
1975	4th-t	44th-T
1976	1st	10th-T
1977	2nd	
1978	1st	6th-T
1979	3rd	31st-T
1980	2nd	9th
1981	2nd	15th-T
1982	1st	26th-T
1983	2nd	15th-T
1984	2nd	39th-T
1985	4th	50th-T
1986	3rd-t	13th-T
1987	4th	
1988	6th	44th-T
1989	4th	10th-T
1990	8th	
1991	4th	11th
1992	7th	
1993	7th	
1994	1st	17th
1995	3rd	4th
1996	6th-t	30th-T
1997	5th	13th

Men's Outdoor Track

Year	Overall Record	Big Ten Finish	NCAA Finish
1896	1-0		
1897	1-0		
1898	1-0-1		
1899	1-0		
1900	1-0		
1901	3-0	1st	
1902	2-1	1st	
1903	3-0	1st	
1904	2-0	1st	
1905	2-1	2nd	
1906	2-0	1st	
1907	1-0		
1908	1-0		
1909	1-0		
1910	3-0		
1911	1-2		
1912	1-2		
1913	3-1		
1914	2-2		
1915	4-0		
1916	2-1		
1917	1-1-1		
1918	4-0	1st	
1919	4-0	1st	
1920	2-2	2nd	
1921	4-2	2nd	11th
1922	3-2	7th	6th
1923	3-1	1st	1st
1924	2-1	3rd	
1925	4-0	1st	

Men's Outdoor Track Cont.

Year	Overall Record	Big Ten Finish	NCAA Finish
1926	3-0	1st	
1927	4-0	2nd	
1928	2-2	4th	8th
1929	3-1	3rd	7th
1930	2-2	1st	7th
1931	4-0	3rd	6th
1932	2-1	1st	5th
1933	4-0	1st	5th
1934	3-0	3rd	
1935	5-1	1st	7th-T
1936	4-2	2nd	5th
1937	6-0	1st	8th
1938	0-0	1st	3rd
1939	5-0	1st	3rd
1940	4-1	1st	8th
1941	4-0	2nd	13th
1942	3-1	6th	26th-T
1943	2-1	1st	9th
1944	3-0	1st	3rd
1945	1-1	2nd	2nd
1946	2-3	3rd	
1947	2-5	3rd	10th-T
1948	1-2-1	2nd	6th-T
1949	3-2	6th	16th-T
1950	3-1	6th	15th-T
1951	5-0	4th	12th-T
1952	3-1	2nd	8th
1953	2-1	2nd	6th-T
1954	2-1	2nd	6th-T
1955	7-0	1st	11th-T
1956	2-0	1st	8th
1957	3-2-1	3rd	14th-T
1958	1-1	8th	42nd-T
1959	3-1	2nd	19th
1960	3-0	2nd	21st-T
1961	2-0	1st	6th-T

Year	Overall Record	Big Ten Finish	NCAA Finish
1962	1-0	1st	
1963	2-0	3rd	
1964	3-0	2nd	16th
1965	5-0	2nd	
1966	2-0	3rd	
1967	2-0	3rd	
1968	3-0	2nd	
1969	4-0	3rd	
1970	3-1	5th	39th-T
1971	0-5	5th	51st-T
1972	3-2	4th	
1973	3-2	2nd	
1974	0-3	2nd	
1975	2-1	6th-t	
1976	1-0	1st	43rd-T
1977	3-1	5th	
1978	1-1	1st	31st-T
1979	2-0	2nd	46th-T
1980	1-1	1st	41st
1981	0-1	1st	52nd-T
1982	1-1	1st	
1983	2-0	1st	20th
1984	0-0	3rd	
1985	0-0	4th	34th-T
1986	0-0	5th	51st-T
1987	1-0	4th	36th-T
1988	2-0	5th	25th-T
1989	0-0	6th	30th
1990	1-0	6th	
1991	1-0	4th	
1992	0-0	7th	59th-T
1993	0-0	7th	
1994	0-0	4th	42nd-T
1995	1-0	2nd	19th-T
1996	1-0	7th	18th
1997	0-0	3rd	13th-T

Women's Indoor Track

Year	Dual Meet Record	Big Ten Finish	National Finish
1978	0-1	7th*	
1979	1-3	8th*	
1980	2-1	5th-T*	
1981	2-0	7th*	
1982	0-0	4th	21st
1983	0-0	1st	33rd
1984	0-0	6th	34th
1985	0-0	6th	29th-T
1986	0-0	6th	19th-T
1987	0-0	8th	15th-T
1988	0-0	6th	
1989	0-0	7th	
1990	0-0	5th	
1991	0-0	7th	
1992	0-0	6th	
1993	0-0	3rd	33rd-T
1994	0-0	1st	7th
1995	1-0	3rd	37th-T
1996	0-0	3rd	33rd-T
1997	0-0	2nd	

* Indicates non-Big Ten sanctioned championship play

Women's Outdoor Track

Year	Dual Meet Record	Big Ten Finish	National Finish
1978	0-1	8th*	
1979	0-0	7th*	
1980	0-0	7th*	
1981	1-0	4th*	
1982	0-1	2nd	5th
1983	0-0	2nd	16th
1984	0-0	6th	
1985	0-0	8th	27th-T
1986	0-0	4th	23rd-T
1987	0-0	7th	
1988	0-0	8th	30th-T
1989	0-0	4th	
1990	0-0	5th	
1991	0-0	9th	
1992	0-0	8th	
1993	0-0	1st	19th
1994	1-0	1st	23rd-T
1995	0-0	5th	
1996	0-0	3rd	25th-T
1997	0-0	2nd	36th-T

* Indicates non-Big Ten sanctioned championship play

Volleyball

Year	Overall Record	Big Ten Record	Big Ten Finish
1973	7-9		
1974	6-10		
1975	5-6		
1976	14-15		
1977	12-17		
1978	15-15-2		
1979	23-14-5		
1980	26-17		
1981	40-17		1st
1982	11-18	3-10	4th-East
1983	18-13	4-9	4th-East
1984	11-16	1-12	5th-East

Year	Overall Record	Big Ten Record	Big Ten Finish
1985	18-18	6-12	8th
1986	13-20	3-15	10th
1987	20-20	3-15	9th
1988	11-23	1-17	10th
1989	6-20	1-17	10th
1990	6-25	2-16	10th
1991	19-12	10-10	6th-T
1992	19-13	11-9	5th
1993	11-18	7-13	7th-T
1994	8-23	4-16	9th-T
1995	19-15	11-9	6th
1996	14-17	9-11	6th

Wrestling

Year	Overall Record	Big Ten Finish	NCAA Finish
1922	4-1		
1924	1-6		
1925	0-7		
1926	3-3	2nd	
1927	6-2	2nd	
1928	7-1	2nd	2nd
1929	5-1-1	1st	2nd
1930	7-1	2nd	5th
1931	4-1	2nd	8th
1932	3-3	3rd	6th
1933	4-3	2nd	
1934	4-2	4th	7th
1935	3-5	6th	
1936	5-4	5th	12th
1937	8-1	2nd	9th
1938	7-1	1st	
1939	7-0	3rd	3rd
1940	5-2-1	2nd	3rd
1941	5-3	4th	
1942	5-1-1	3rd	4th
1943	5-2	2nd	
1944	4-0	1st	
1945	3-1-2	7th	
1946	4-3	3rd	5th
1947	5-3	4th	10th
1948	4-3-1	4th	
1949	2-5	3rd	
1950	8-2	3rd	
1951	9-0-1	2nd	
1952	6-2-1	2nd	16th
1953	8-1	1st	7th
1954	9-1	2nd	7th
1955	6-2	1st	7th
1956	6-3	1st	12th
1957	3-6	2nd	6th
1958	3-6-1	6th	13th
1959	6-4-1	4th	

Year	Overall Record	Big Ten Finish	NCAA Finish
1960	9-2	1st	18th
1961	9-1	2nd	10th
1962	7-2-1	2nd	
1963	9-1	1st	3rd
1964	12-0	1st	5th
1965	10-0	1st	6th
1966	9-1	2nd	5th
1967	10-0	2nd	2nd
1968	10-2	3rd	9th
1969	13-2	3rd	9th
1970	7-5-1	3rd	10th
1971	8-2-2	3rd	14th
1972	9-3-1	3rd	15th
1973	12-0	1st	3rd
1974	14-0	2nd	2nd
1975	14-4	4th	12th
1976	16-6	4th	8th
1977	8-3	4th	9th
1978	5-9	5th	10th
1979	10-6	5th	10th
1980	11-6-1	6th	28th
1981	7-9	4th	25th
1982	9-7	5th	24th
1983	8-8	4th	38th
1984	7-9	5th	18th
1985	17-2	3rd	5th
1986	8-7	3rd	10th
1987	9-6-1	7th	19th
1988	14-3	2nd	6th
1989	20-2	3rd	5th
1990	11-4	6th	30th
1991	11-6	2nd	12th
1992	13-4-1	6th	25th
1993	13-5	5th	11th
1994	6-9	4th	5th
1995	7-3-2	5th	22th
1996	12-5-1	7th	9th
1997	10-5	5th	22th

Personnel History of the Department of Intercollegiate Athletics--University of Michigan

Faculty Representatives

1896	Dr. Joseph Nancrede
1896-97	J.C. Knowlton
1898-05	A.H. Pattengill
1906-07	V.H. Lane
1907	G.M. Bates
1908	G. W. Patterson
1917-55	Ralph Aigler
1955-79	Marcus Plant
1979-82	Tom Anton
1981-90	Gwen Cruzat
1983-89	Paul Gikas
1989-91	Douglas Kahn
1990-	Percy Bates

Directors of Athletics

1898-08	Charles Baird
1909-20	Philip Bartelme
1921-41	Fielding Yost
1941-68	Herbert (Fritz) Crisler
1968-88	Don Canham
1988-90	Glenn (Bo) Schembechler
1990-94	Jack Weidenbach
1994-97	Joe Roberson
1997-	Tom Goss

Women's Athletic Directors

1973-76	Marie Hartwig
1976-77	Virginia Hunt
1977-91	Phyllis Ocker
1991-	Peggy Bradley-Doppes

Dick Kimball, the dean of all Michigan coaches, has tutored four Olympic gold medalist divers.

Athletic Media Relations Directors

1925-38	Phil Pack
1938-39	William Reed
1940-44	Fred DeLano
1944-68	Les Etter
1968-80	Will Perry
1980-82	John Humenik
1982-	Bruce Madej

Baseball Coaches

1891-92	Peter Conway
1893	H.G. Cleveland
1894	George Caldwell
1895	E.C. Weeks
1896	Frank Sexton
1897-01	Charles Watkins
1902	Frank Sexton
1903	S. Roach
1904	Jerome Utley
1905-06	L.W. McAllister
1907	R.L. Rowe
1908-09	L.W. McAllister
1910-13	Branch Rickey
1914-20	Carl Lundgren
1921-58	Ray Fisher
1959-62	Don Lund
1963-79	Moby Benedict
1980-89	Bud Middaugh
1990-95	Bill Freehan
1996-	Geoff Zahn

Basketball Coaches - Men's

1909	G.D. Corneal
1917-18	Elmer Mitchell
1919-28	E.J. Mather
1929-30	George Veekner
1931-37	Franklin Cappon
1938-46	Bennie Oosterbaan
1947-48	Ozzie Cowles
1949-52	Ernie McCoy
1953-60	Bill Perigo
1961-68	Dave Strack
1969-80	Johnny Orr
1981-89	Bill Freider
1989-	Steve Fisher

Basketball Coaches - Women's

1973-74	Vic Katch
1975-77	Carmel Borders
1978-84	Gloria Soluk
1985-92	Bud Van DeWege
1993-96	Trish Roberts
1997-	Sue Guevara

Crew Coaches

1997-	Mark Rothstein

Cross Country Coaches - Men's

1919-29	Stephen Farrell
1930-32	Charles Hoyt
1971-73	Dixon Farmer
1974-	Ron Warhurst

Cross Country Coaches - Women's

1979-81	Red Simmons
1982-83	Francie Goodridge
1984-86	Sue Parks
1987-91	Sue Foster
1992-	Mike McGuire

Diving Coaches - Men's

1951-59	Bruce Harlan
1960-	Dick Kimball

Diving Coaches - Women's

1974-	Dick Kimball

Fencing Coaches

1927-33	John Johnstone

Field Hockey Coaches - Women's

1973	Phyllis Weikart
1974-78	Phyllis Ocker
1979-83	Candy Zientek
1984-88	Karen Collins
1989-95	Patti Smith
1996-	Marcia Pankratz

Football Coaches

1891	Mike Murphy and Frank Crawford
1892-93	Frank Barbour
1894-95	William McCauley
1896	William Ward
1897-99	Gustave Ferbert
1900	Langdon (Biff) Lea
1901-23	Fielding Yost
1924	George Little
1925-26	Fielding Yost
1927-28	Elton (Tad) Wieman

Brian Eisner, U-M's tennis coach since 1970, has led the Wolverines to 18 Big Ten team titles.

1929-37	Harry Kipke
1938-47	Herbert (Fritz) Crisler
1948-58	Bennie Oosterbaan
1959-68	Chalmers (Bump) Elliott
1969-89	Glenn (Bo) Schembechler
1990-94	Gary Moeller
1995-	Lloyd Carr

Golf Coaches - Men's

1921-35	Thomas Trueblood
1936-44	Ray Courtright
1945-46	William Barclay
1947-68	Bert Katzenmeyer
1969-78	William Newcomb
1979-82	Tom Simon
1983-	Jim Carras

Golf Coaches - Women's

1977-82	Tom Simon
1983-93	Sue LeClair
1994-	Kathy Teichert

Gymnastics Coaches - Men's

1930-32	Wilbur West
1947-83	Newt Loken
1984-96	Bob Darden
1997-	Kurt Golder

Gymnastics Coaches - Women's

1975	Newt Loken
1976-78	Anne Cornell
1979	Scott Ponto
1980-84	Sheri Hyatt
1985-89	Dana Kempthorn
1990-	Beverly Plocki

Ice Hockey Coaches

1923-27	Joseph Barss
1928-44	Edward Lowrey
1945-57	Vic Heyliger
1958-73	Al Renfrew
1974-80	Dan Farrell
1980	Wilf Martin
1981-84	John Giordano
1985-	Red Berenson

Soccer Coaches - Women's

1994-	Debbie Belkin

Softball Coaches

1978-80	Gloria Soluk
1981-84	Bob DeCarolis
1985-	Carol Hutchins

Swimming Coaches - Men's

1922	John Jerome
1923-24	William Sterry Brown
1925	Gerald Barnes
1926-54	Matt Mann
1955-79	Gus Stager
1981	Bill Farley
1982	Gus Stager
1983-	Jon Urbanchek

Swimming Coaches - Women's

1974-75	Johnanna High
1974-83	Stu Isaac
1984-85	Peter Lindsay
1986-	Jim Richardson

Synchronized Swimming Coaches

1973-83	Joyce Lindeman

Tennis Coaches - Men's

1913-15	A.O. Lee
1918	Chris Mack
1921	Walter Westbrook
1922	Thomas Trueblood
1923	Paul Leidy
1924	Robert Angell
1925	Henry Hutchins
1929-36	John Johnstone
1937-47	LeRoy Weir
1948	Robert Dixon
1949-69	William Murphy
1970-	Brian Eisner

Tennis Coaches - Women's

1973	Janet Hopper
1974-75	Carmen Brummet
1976-77	John Atwood
1978	Theo Shepard
1979-84	Oliver Owens
1985-	Elizabeth Ritt

Track and Field Coaches - Men's

1898-10	Keene Fitzpatrick
1911-12	Alvin Kraenzlein
1913-29	Stephen Farrell
1930-39	Charles Hoyt
1940-48	Kenneth Doherty
1949-67	Don Canham
1968-71	David Martin
1972-74	Dixon Farmer
1975-	Jack Harvey

Track and Field Coaches - Women's

1979-81	Red Simmons
1982-83	Francie Goodridge
1984-	James Henry

Volleyball Coaches - Women's

1973-83	Sandy Vong
1984-85	Barb Canning
1986-89	Joyce Davis
1990-91	Peggy Bradley-Doppes
1992-	Greg Giovanazzi

Wrestling Coaches

1922	Hevery Thorne
1923-24	Richard Barker
1925-43	Cliff Keen
1943-44	Ray Courtright
1945	Wally Weber
1946-70	Cliff Keen
1971-74	Rick Bay
1975-78	Bill Johannesen
1979-	Dale Bahr

Michigan's Jack Harvey enters his 25th season as men's track coach in 1997-98.

Michigan's Hall of Honor

The University of Michigan Hall of Honor was established in 1978 to recognize those persons who have made significant contributions as athletes, coaches and administrators to the tradition of Wolverine athletics and, in doing so, have enhanced the image and reputation of the University of Michigan.

Those inducted into the Hall of Honor have earned All-America recognition in a team or individual sport or, as individuals, have established an NCAA, American or World record; won an NCAA title, or made significant contributions to the Michigan Athletic Department as a coach or administrator.

1978 Inductees

Gerald R. Ford	Football
Bill Freehan	Baseball
Tom Harmon	Football
Bennie Oosterbaan	Football
	Basketball
	Baseball
	Football Coach
	Basketball Coach
Cazzie Russell	Basketball
Bob Ufer	Track

1979 Inductees

Fritz Crisler	Football Coach
	Athletic Director
Ray Fisher	Baseball Coach
Charlie Fonville	Track
* Willie Heston	Football
* DeHart Hubbard	Track
Chuck Kocsis	Golf
Ron Kramer	Football
	Basketball
	Track
Adolph (Germany) Schulz	Football
* George Sisler	Baseball
Rudy Tomjanovich	Basketball
* Fielding H. Yost	Football Coach
	Athletic Director

1980 Inductees

Bill Buntin	Basketball
Dick Degener	Diving
John Fischer	Golf
Benny Friedman	Football
Buck Giles	Baseball
Vic Heyliger	Hockey
Cliff Keen	Wrestling Coach
Barry MacKay	Tennis
* Matt Mann	Swimming Coach
* Eddie Tolan	Track
John Townsend	Basketball
	Track

1981 Inductees

Ed Don George	Wrestling
Paul Goebel	Football
Harry Holiday	Swimming
* Harry Kipke	Football Coach
	Football
	Basketball
	Baseball
Newt Loken	Gymnastics Coach
John Sherf	Hockey
* Thomas Trueblood	Golf Coach
Willis Ward	Track
Wally Weber	Football
Albert Wistert	Football
Alvin Wistert	Football
Francis Wistert	Football
	Baseball

1982 Inductees

* Ralph W. Aigler	Faculty Rep
Robert J. Brown	Football
B.F. (Bud) Chamberlain	Baseball
Dr. Julius Franks Jr.	Football
Marcus Plant	Faculty Rep
Edward I. Schalon	Golf
Augustus (Gus) P. Stager	Swimming
Jack Tompkins	Hockey
	Baseball
* Henry (Ernie) Vick	Football
* William Watson	Track
* Robert Westfall	Football

1983 Inductees

Gordon (Red) Berenson	Hockey
* Elmer Gedeon	Track
	Baseball
George Lee	Basketball
Maynard Morrison	Football
Bill Murphy	Tennis Coach
Harry Newman	Football
Harold Nichols	Wrestling
Bob Osgood	Track
Dick Wakefield	Baseball

1984 Inductees

Bob Chappuis	Football
	Baseball
* Archie Hahn	Track
Elroy Hirsch	Football
	Basketball
	Baseball
	Track
Don Lund	Baseball
	Football
	Basketball
Bill Orwig	Football
	Basketball
Doug Roby	Football
	Baseball
Dave Strack	Basketball Coach

1985 Inductees

Connie Hill	Hockey
Dick Kimball	Diving Coach
Dave Porter	Football
	Wrestling
* Branch Rickey	Baseball Coach
Tom Robinson	Track
Ben Smith	Golf
Roger Zatkoff	Football

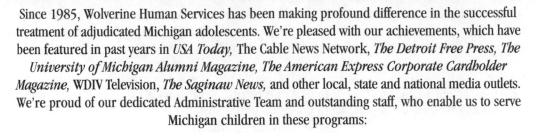

1986 Inductees

* Bill Combs	Wrestling
Chalmers (Bump) Elliott	Football
	Basketball
	Baseball
Pete Elliott	Football
	Basketball
	Golf
Micki King	Diving
* Ernie McCoy	Basketball Coach
Dave Nelson	Football
	Baseball
Al Renfrew	Hockey Coach

1987 Inductees

Don Canham	Track
	Athletic Director
Wally Grant	Hockey
Gene Derricotte	Football
Ralph Heikkinen	Football
Dave Barclay	Golf
* Jack Blott	Football
	Baseball

1988 Inductees

Don McEwen	Track
Ed Frutig	Football
Merv Pregulman	Football
Francis Heydt	Swimming
Harold Donahue	Wrestling
Bruce Haynan	Baseball
M.C. Burton	Basketball

1989 Inductees

Randy Erskine	Golf
John Greene	Wrestling
	Football
Bob Harrison	Basketball
Marie Hartwig	Administration
Ron Johnson	Football
Frank Nunley	Football
	Basketball
Lowell Perry	Football
Richard Volk	Football
Robert Webster	Swimming
Gordon Wilkey	Hockey

1990 Inductees

Forest Evashevski	Football
	Baseball
H. Ross Hume	Track
Robert H. Hume	Track
Willard Ikola	Hockey
Jim Skinner	Swimming
Mack Suprunowicz	Basketball

1992 Inductees

Jack Clancy	Football
Ed Gagnier	Gymnastics
* Henry Hatch	Equipment Manager
* Bruce Hilkene	Football
Phil Hubbard	Basketball
Dick Kempthorn	Football
Gordon McMillan	Hockey
Glenn (Bo) Schembechler	Football Coach
John Schroeder	Golf
Jack Weisenburger	Football

1994 Inductees

Terry Barr	Football
Milbry (Moby) Benedict	Baseball
Francie Goodridge	Track
Rickey Green	Basketball
Frank Legacki	Swimming
John MacInnes	Ice Hockey
Tom Maentz	Football
Jim Mandich	Football
Dominic Tomasi	Football
	Baseball

1996 Inductees

Steve Boros	Baseball
Mark Churella	Wrestling
Dave Debol	Hockey
Dan Dierdorf	Football
Diane Dietz	Basketball
Elaine Crosby	Tennis
Len Ford	Football
Ray Senkowski	Tennis
John Tidwell	Basketball

There were no inductions made in 1991, 1993, 1995 and 1997.
* Elected posthumously

All-Time Wolverine Letter Winner List

As with any list of this magnitude, there could be inadvertent errors or omissions. Please contact the U-M athletic media relations office should you discover a mistake.

KEY TO ABBREVIATIONS

BB - baseball
FB - football
FH - field hockey
IHO - ice hockey
MBK - men's basketball
MCC - men's cross country
MD - men's diving
MGO - men's golf
MGY - men's gymnastics
MSW - men's swimming
MTN - men's tennis
MTR - men's track and field
SB - softball
SS - synchronized swimming
VB - volleyball
WBK - women's basketball
WCC - women's cross country
WCR - women's crew
WGO - women's golf
WGY - women's gymnastics
WR - wrestling
WSOC - women's soccer
WSW - women's swimming
WTN - women's tennis
WTR - women's track

A		
Abbett, John	IHO	1928,29
Abbey, Vincent H.D.	IHO	1944
Abbot Jr., Waldo M.	MTR	1938
Abbot, Howard	FB	1889,90,91
Abbott, Howard T.	BB	1891
Abbott, James A.	BB	1986,87,88
Abdul-Raheem, A. Rasool	FB	1975
Abell, Jennifer	WSW	1992
Abraham, Joseph F.	MTR	1970,71,72,73
Abrahams, Morris M.	FB	1969
Abrams Jr., Bobby E.	FB	1986,87,88,89
Abruzzi, Daniel	MSW	1992,93,94,95
Ackerman, James H.	MTR	1949,50
Ackerman, Wilbert E.	MTR	1940,41,42
Adam, Frederika	WTN	1989,90,91,92
Adami, Zachary	FB	1994,95,96
Adams Jr., Thomas B.	MTR	1940
Adams, Thomas R.	BB	1918
Adams, Amy	SS	1978,79
Adams, Arthur S.	BB	1973,74
Adams, Charles M.	MBK	1962,65
	BB	1962,63
Adams, Cuthbert	MTR	1898,99
Adams, Franklin H.	MGY	1952,53,54,55
Adams, Lisa D.	WTR	1990,91,93
Adams, Mary	SB	1994,95,96,97
Adams, Neville	MSW	1946
Adams, Peter N.	BB	1962,63,64
Adams, Stephen Q.	MTR	1971,72,73,74
Adams, Theo	FB	1918
Adamski, Donald F.	MSW	1955,56,57
Adamson, Laura S.	WSW	1976,77
Adler, Andrew F.	MTN	1988,89
Affoon, Ronald R.	MTR	1979,80
Agemy, James M.	BB	1984,85,87
Aghakhan, Ninef	FB	1991,92,93
Agnew, Douglas J.	FB	1979,81
Agnew, James K.	WR	1959
Agnew, Peter K.	MD	1973,74
Agosta, Anthony	BB	1992
Ahern, Thomas R.	MGO	1959,61,62
Ahlholm, Cynthia L.	WD	1987,88
Aigler, William F.	MTR	1938
Aikens, Frank W.	MTR	1935,36
Akehi, Meg	VB	1995,96
Akers, Jeffery L.	FB	1983,84,85
Aland, Lindsay	WTN	1990
Albertson, John W.	FB	1991
Alcaraz, Jason R.	BB	1996
Aldinger, Edward T.	WR	1930
Aldinger, Harry E.	BB	1904
Aldrich, William	FB	1893
Alexander, Martin M.	MTR	1933,35
Alexander, Derrick S.	FB	1989,90,92,93
Alexander, Morris	FB	1970,71
Alexander, Thomas L.	MGY	1984
Algyer, Durwin D.	MTN	1927,28
Aliber, James A.	FB	1943,44
Alix, Dennis R.	FB	1963
Alix, Neree D.	MTR	1934,35,37
Alkon, Leonard W.	MTR	1943
Allard, Jennifer	SB	1987,88,89,90
Allen III, Cyril R.	FB	1976
Allen, Boyd E.	MTR	1933,36
Allen, Bruce A.	MSW	1941,42
Allen, Bruce B.	MBK	1952,53,54
Allen, Carl L.	MCC	1982
	MTR	1982
Allen, Charles M.	MTR	1933
Allen, Earl F.	FB	1984
	MTR	1982
Allen, Edwin	IHO	1938
Allen, Eugene	BB	1950
Allen, Frederick J.	MBK	1933,34
Allen, Frank	FB	1878,79,80,81
Allen, G. Wesley	MTR	1938,39,41
Allen, Jay	FB	1979
Allen, Linda A.	SB	1984,85
Allen, Michael G.	MSW	1968,69
Allen, Robert A.	WR	1942,44
Allerdice, Dave	FB	1907,08,09
	MTR	1908
Allis, Harry D.	FB	1948,49,50
	MTR	1948,49
Allis, Carol	SB	1983
Allison, Anne	WSW	1975
Allison, Katie	FH	1990,91,92
Allman, Albert F.	IHO	1945
Allmendinger, Charles G.	BB	1882
Allmendinger, Ernest	FB	1911,12,13
Allor, Deborah	WBK	1978,80
	SB	1978
Allore, Joseph	FB	1993,93,95,95
Allred Jr., John P.	FB	1947
	MGY	1948
	WR	1946,47
Almeida, Jennifer	WSW	1992,93,94,95
Almeida, Thomas	MSW	1994,95,96
Almonte, Ramon M.	MTN	1968,69,70,71
Almquist, Shellee	FH	1973,75
	WBK	1974
Altenhof, Raymond F.	MBK	1931,32,33
Alvizuri, Alejandro L.	MSW	1986,87,88,89
Amaya, Victor C.	MTN	1973,74,75
Ambroe, Mark	MGY	1989,90
Ames, Amy	SB	1979,80,81
Amine, Michael N.	WR	1986,87,88,89
Amine, Sam	WR	1988,89,90
Ammerman, Albert J.	MTR	1961,62,63,64
Amrine, Robert Y.	FB	1934
Amstutz, Ralph H.	FB	1942,43
Anair, Ryan S.	MGO	1986
Andersen, Ashley	WCR	1997
Anderson Jr., Gordon R.	IHO	1943,44
Anderson, Robert E.	FB	1969,71
Anderson, Adam	MGO	1995,96,97
Anderson, Charles R.	WR	1953,54,56
Anderson, Deollo	FB	1993,94,95
Anderson, Erick S.	FB	1988,89,90,91
Anderson, Francis F.	MSW	1945
Anderson, John L.	MBK	1976,77,78,79
Anderson, Kyle	FB	1986,87
Anderson, Lisa	WSW	1989,90,91,92
Anderson, Mark J.	MSW	1972,73,74,75
Anderson, Mauritz G.	WR	1942
Anderson, R. John	FB	1974,75,76,77
Anderson, Robert	IHO	1923
Anderson, Robert O.	IHO	1935
Anderson, Scott E.	BB	1977,78
Anderson, Steven M.	FB	1976
Anderson, Suzanne E.	WSW	1980,81
Anderson, Thomas J.	FB	1976,77,78,79
Anderson, Timothy J.	FB	1982,83,84
Anderson, Tomas K.	MTN	1985
Andres, John M.	MSW	1984,85,86
Andrew, Patricia	WBK	1990,91,92,93
Andrews, Allen Jr.	MTN	1912,13,14
Andrews, Elmore L.	MTN	1913
Andrews, Harold P.	MGO	1953,54,55
Andrews, Mark J.	FB	1977,78
Andrews, Phil	FB	1976
Andrews, Susan	WSW	1977
Andronik, Edmund L.	BB	1938
Andrus, Linda	VB	1974,75
Anes, John	FB	1996
Angell, Allen D.	MTR	1978,79
Angell, James R.	MTN	1886,87,89
Angelotti, Anthony G.	MGY	1987,88,89,90
Angood, David S.	FB	1976,79
Anstaett, Jay K.	MCC	1974,75,77
	MTR	1976
Ansted, John C.	BB	1987
Anthony, Melvin	FB	1962,63,64
Antle, Robert C.	MBK	1942
Antle, Thomas P.	BB	1881,82
Antonick, Gary M.	MSW	1983,84,85,86
Antonides, Jon C.	MBK	1981,83,84
Antrum, Curtis M.	FB	1979,82
Aparo, Brian	WR	1995
Appelhans, Amy	WSW	1987,88
Appelt, Joseph E.	MTN	1933,34
Appleman, Robert M.	MTR	1953,54,55,56
Appleton, Peter W.	BB	1924,25,26
Aquino, Charles F.	MTR	1960,61,62,63
Aranha, Jose R. D.	MSW	1972,73,74
Arbeznik, John C.	FB	1977,78,79
Arbour, Dale F.	MCC	1971
	MTR	1969,70,71
Arbuckle, John H.	MSW	1948,49,50,51
Arcure, Joseph H.	WR	1962,63,64
Aretakis, Sylvia	FH	1973,74,75,76
Ahrendt, Suzanne	WSW	1978
Armelagos, Nick	WR	1960,61,62,63
Armelogos, James	FB	1948
Armento, Diane J.	WGY	1989,90,91,92
Armer, Harry M. (Chip)	MBK	1991,92
Armour, James	FB	1973,74
Armstrong, Aikman L.	MTR	1900,01,02
Armstrong, Gregory L.	FB	1982,83,84
Armstrong, Jennifer	WCC	1990
Armstrong, L. Paul	MTR	1967,69,70
Armstrong, Robert L.	MGY	1955,56,57
Armstrong, Robert N.	BB	1976
Arndt, Kirk S.	WR	1978
Arndt, Raymond A.	MTR	1922,23
Arnold, Catherine	VB	1984
Arnold, David P.	FB	1985,86,87,88
Arnold, John D.	IHO	1993,94,95,96
Arnold, Mark F.	MTR	1988
Artley, James M.	MTR	1945
Artz, Avon S.	BB	1932,33,34
	IHO	1933,34
Artz, Gregory	MTN	1992,93
Arusoo, Toomas	MSW	1966,67,68,69
Arvai III, John J.	BB	1966,67,68,69
Arvai IV, John J.	BB	1993,94,95,96
Arvai, Charles L.	BB	1980
Arvia, Lesa	SB	1992,93,94,95
Asbeck, Frederick	BB	1927,28,29
Asbury, Elizabeth G.	SS	1979
Ash, Rudolph T.	BB	1923
Ashare, Erin	WTN	1985,86
Ashare, Kristen	WTN	1988
Ashcraft, Dianne	SB	1980,81
Ashford, Georgianne	WGY	1984
Ashworth, Roy A.	IHO	1970,72,73
Aster, George H.	MTR	1955
Atamian, Elliott L.	MGO	1942
Atchison, James L.	FB	1948,49
Atchison, Walter D.	MTR	1949,50,51,52
Athens, John W.	IHO	1943,44
Atkins, Joseph J.	WR	1952,53
Attar, Paul A.	MD	1961,62,63
Aubuchan, Jon	MTR	1996
Auer, Howard	FB	1929,30,31
	WR	1930
Aug, Vincent J.	FB	1934,35
Augimeri, Vincent E.	IHO	1981
Ault, Garnet W.	MSW	1928,29,30
Austin, Joseph P.	MTR	1929,30,31
Austin, Robert O.	MTR	1893,94
Austin, Thomas D.	FB	1932,33,34
Austin III, William F.	MSW	1948,49,50
Avery, Waldo A.	MTR	1899,1900
Axley, Betsy	WSOC	1994,95
Axon, Margaret	WGY	1977,78,79
Ayers, Frank C.	MTN	1908,09,10
Ayers, J.C.	BB	1875
Ayers, Norwood	FB	1896,97
Ayler, William G.	MBK	1972,73,74
Ayres, John	FB	1881
Azcona, Eduardo	FB	1990,91,92
B		
Babcock, Dick	FB	1923,24,25
Babcock, Courtney	WCC	1992,93,95
	WTR	1992,93,94,96
Babcock, Larry R.	IHO	1960,61,62,63
Babcock, R.S.	FB	1887
Babcock, Samuel	FB	1925
Babcock, Traci	WCC	1985,86,87,88,
	WTR	1986,87,88,89
Bach, Natasha	FH	1990
Bachman, Julie	WD	1978,79,80,81
Bachmann, Edward B.	BB	1924,25
Bacon, Howard W.	MTN	1941
Bacon, Marvin A.	MTN	1929
Bade, William G.	BB	1919
Badger, Carl M.	MGY	1975,77,78
Badran-Grycan, Erica L.	VB	1990,91,92,93
Baer Jr., Frederick N.	FB	1952,53,54
Baer, Ray	FB	1925,26,27
Baer, Russell	BB	1913,14
Baessler, Arthur A.	MGY	1964,65,66,67

Terry Barr lettered at U-M from 1954-56, then starred for the Detroit Lions.

Bagley, April	SB	1985,86,87,88
Bagnell, D. Karl	IHO	1969,70,71,72
Bahlow Jr., Edward H.	FB	1946
Bahna, Ralph M.	WR	1961,62,63,64
Bahr, David	WR	1990
Bahrych, Maximillian M.	IHO	1941,42
Bailey, Debi	VB	1986
Bailey, Donald A.	FB	1964,65,66
Bailey, Eric R.	MSW	1989,90,91,92
Bailey, Harold W.	MSW	1929
Bailey, J. Brent	MGO	1972,73
Bailey, Reeve M.	MSW	1933
Bair, Richard C.	BB	1981,82,83,84
Baird, Geoffrey J.	MTN	1991
Baird, James	FB	1893,94,95
	BB	1894
Baird, Robert J.	IHO	1965,66,67
Baker, Fred	FB	1895,96
Baker, G. Robert	MBK	1946
	MTR	1946
Baker, John F.	MSW	1962
Baker, Joseph L.	MTR	1918,19,20
Baker, Kraig	FB	1994
Baker, Merle C.	BB	1925
Baker, Roy J.	BB	1913,14
Baker, Russell C.	WR	1925,26,27
Baker, W. Sean	IHO	1985,86,87,88
Baker, Willard K.	BB	1948,49
Baker, William	FB	1897,98
	MTR	1898
Balaze, Brian L.	BB	1970,72,73
Balaze, Patrick D.	BB	1979,80
Balcom, Jason R.	WR	1995
Baldacci, Louis G.	FB	1953,54,55
Baldwin, Edward P.	FB	1967,70
Baldwin, Henry	MTR	1898,99,00
Baldwin, Ralph B.	MTN	1933
Baldwin, W.E.	MTR	1898,99
Balestri, George	IHO	1947
Ball, Louis	MGY	1989
Ball, Reginald A.	BB	1970,71,72,73
Ball, William	FB	1888,89
Ballantine, James J.	IHO	1988,89,90,91
Balliet, Gary A.	MGO	1969,70,71,72
Ballou, Robert M.	FB	1946
Balog, James T.	FB	1951,52,53
Balourdos, Arthur	FB	1981,82,83,84
Balourdos, John S.	FB	1986
Balsamo, Joseph J.	MBK	1929
Balyeat, Phil E.	MTR	1939,40
Balza, David W.	MBK	1989,90,91
Balzhiser, Richard E.	FB	1952,53
Banar, James F.	FB	1968,69
Bankey, Dennis J.	MBK	1964,65,66,67
	BB	1964
Banks, Charles	FB	1885,86
Banks, Harry	FB	1971,72,74
Banks, Larry L.	FB	1974
Banks, Theodore	FB	1920,21
Bannister, Amy	WCC	1989,90,91
	WTR	1989,90,91,92
Bara, Allan A.	BB	1963,64,65,66
Barabe, Clifford	FB	1897,98
Baranyi, Jeff	MSW	1994,94
Barber, Jennifer	WCC	1993,94,95,96
	WTR	1994,95,96
Barbero, James W.	MGY	1952,53,54
Barborek, Susan	WGY	1982
Barclay, David D.	MGO	1946,47,48
Barclay, Robert L.	MGO	1964,65,66,67
Barclay, William C.	MBK	1937,38
	FB	1935,36,37
	MGO	1936,37,38

Bardakian, Carl	MBK	1991,92,93
Barden, John H.	WR	1960,61,62,63
Baribeau, Roy H.	BB	1912,13,14
Barker, Charles L.	MSW	1939,40,41
Barker, V. Robert	MTN	1962,63,64,65
Barkhordari, Roozbeh	IHO	1992,92
Barley, Elbert R.	MBK	1929
Barlow, Alfred	FB	1905
Barmore, Edmund	FB	1879,80
Barnard, Frank E.	MSW	1935,36,37
Barnard, Richard P.	MTR	1944,45
Barnard, Robert A.	MTR	1940,41
Barnes, Charles O.	MSW	1946
Barnes, Karen S.	WSW	1991,92,93,94
Barnett, David	MCC	1993,94,95,96
	MTR	1994,95,96
Barnett, Herbert P.	WR	1941,42
Barnett, Jeffery S.	MCC	1986,87,90
	MTR	1988,89,90,91
Barnhart, Clyde R.	BB	1962,63,64,65
Barquist, Bradley N.	MCC	1986,87,88,90
	MTR	1987,88,89,91
Barr, David	BB	1908,09
Barr, John B.	MGO	1941
Barr, Terry A.	FB	1954,55,56
Barrack, Eugene J.	MTN	1950,51,52
Barrett, Arthur	MTR	1899,01,02
Barritt, Edward P.	MTR	1939,40
Barron, James W.	MBK	1953,54,55,56
Barron, Kathleen	FH	1983
Barron, Sandra	WGO	1982,83,84
Barrow, D.W.	MGO	1907
Barrowman, Michael R.	MSW	1988,89,90,91
Barry, John G.	BB	1938,39,40
Barry, Paul J.	FB	1995
Barstow, Pamela	WCC	1987,89
Bartells, A.D.	FB	1893
Barten, Herbert O.	MTR	1946,47,48,49
Barthell, John P.	MGY	1948,49,50
Bartholomew, Bruce A.	FB	1951
Bartlett, William H.	FB	1948,49
Bartlett, James M.	BB	1981
Bartnick, Gregory D.	FB	1976,77,78
Barto, Judith	WSW	1991,92,94
Barton, Charles	FB	1912
Barton, Horace J.	MTN	1927,28,29
Barton, William J.	MTR	1951,52,53,54
Bartsch, Edward C.	MSW	1962,63,64,65
Bartz, Nicholas B.	MTN	1919
Baseotto, Bruno A.	IHO	1980
Basford, Sarah	WBK	1985,86,87,88
Basle, Tina	WTN	1985,86,87,88
Basmajian, Steve	WR	1997
Bass, Michael T.	FB	1964,65,66
	MTR	1964
Bassey, Albert	IHO	1949,51
Bassler, Leigh	WSW	1994,95
Bastein, Clyde E.	MTR	1916
Bastian, Clyde	FB	1914,15
Baston, Maceo	MBK	1995,96,97
Bates, Bradley J.	FB	1980
Bates, Charles C.	MGY	1956
	MD	1952,54,55,56
Bates, James V.	MBK	1952
	FB	1952,54,55
Bates, William C.	FB	1936
Batsakes, John J.	FB	1958
Batter, Clarence	MSW	1926,27,28
Bauer Jr., Carl J.	FB	1928,29
Bauer, Dennis D.	WR	1977,78
Bauer, Joseph G.	MSW	1974,75,76,77
Bauer, Marie	WSW	1978
Bauer, Melissa	WGO	1983,84,85,86
Bauer, Patrick J.	MSW	1972,73,74,75
Bauerle, William S.	MBK	1948
Bauman, Clem	FB	1943,44
Bauman, Robert T.	MSW	1974,75,76
Baumgart, Cynthia	WBK	1981,82
	SB	1981
Baumgartner, James E.	MCC	1978
	MTR	1976,77,78,79
Baumgartner, Robert	FB	1967,68,69
Bauss, Dennis C.	WR	1933
Baur, Adelbert	BB	1891
Bautista, Mark F.	MGY	1977,78
Bavinger Jr., William F.	MGO	1940
Bawol, Shelley	SB	1989,90,91,92
Baxter, David	MBK	1975,76,77,78
Bay, Richard M.	WR	1962,63,64,65
Baydarian, Varskin	FB	1946
	MTR	1948,49
Bayerl, Michael G.	MD	1987,88,89,90
Bayless, Tom A.	IHO	1949
Bazelon, Stephen B.	MBK	1970,72

Beach, David	IHO	1938
Beach, Elmer	FB	1882,83
Beach, Jonathan W.	MD	1981,82
Beach, Raymond	FB	1882,83,84,85
Beach, Thomas E.	MTN	1959,60,61,62
Beahrs, Michele	WCR	1997
Beal, Robert H.	MTN	1929,30
Beals, Albert T.	MTR	1927
Beaman, Fred T.	MTR	1928
Beamon, Kalei	WTN	1990,91,92,93
Bean, Azel E.	MTR	1925,26
Bean, Leslie C.	SB	1983,84
Bean, Vincent L.	FB	1981,82,83,84
	MTR	1981,82,83,84
Beard, Chester	FB	1933,34
Beard, Lisa	SB	1997
Beard, Willard F.	MGY	1955
Beardsley, Raymond R.	MTR	1917,18,20
Bearss, Glen D.	FB	1954
Beath, Douglas B.	MGO	1948
Beauchamp Jr., George A.	BB	1954
Beaudry, Nicole	WBK	1990,91,92,93
Beaumont, J.A.	FB	1877
Becerra, Carlos R.	MSW	1982
Bechard, Warren D.	MTR	1967,68,69,70
Bechtel, Thomas B.	MSW	1959,60
Beck, Daniel L.	MCC	1979,80,81
	MTR	1979,80,81,82
Becker, (first name n/a)	MGO	1905
Becker, James C.	MGO	1981
Becker, Kurt F.	FB	1978,79,80,81
Becker, Marvin H.	WR	1942
Becker, Otto R.	BB	1940
Beckman, Theresa	SS	1981
Beckman, Thomas C.	FB	1969,70,71
Beckstein, Leslie	WSW	1982,83
Beckwith, Katherine	WGY	1981,82,83,84
Bednarek, Jeffrey T.	FB	1976,79
Beebe, Leo C.	MBK	1937,38,39
	BB	1937,38,39
	FB	1935
Beebe, William F.	MSW	1939,40,41
Beer, Laura	FH	1988
Beermann, Kirk	BB	1994,95,96
Begle, Ned	FB	1900
Behm, Andrew	WR	1995
Beier, Michael R.	FB	1965,66,68
Beilstein, Kristin	WGO	1989,90,91,92
Beison, Richard A.	FB	1951,52,53
Beistle, Clayton W.	BB	1900
Beljan Jr., John R.	WR	1979,80,82
Belknap, John T.	WR	1969,70
Bell, F. Cortez	BB	1919
Bell, Frank E.	FB	1975
Bell, Gene R.	FB	1977,78
Bell, Gordon G.	FB	1973,74,75
Bell, Joseph J.	BB	1911,12,13
Bell, Maryann	FH	1983,84,85,86
Bell, Timothy A.	MCC	1975
Bello, Juan C.	MSW	1968,69,70
Belsky, Jerome	FB	1936,37
Bement, George W.	MSW	1927
Benbrook, Al	FB	1908,09,10
	MTR	1909,10
Benedict, Milbry E.	BB	1953,54,55,56
Benedict, Patricia	SB	1990,91,92,93
Benedict, Theodore W.	MTR	1963,64,65,66
Benham Jr., Hal T.	MSW	1938,39,40
Benintendi, Kelly	WBK	1985,86
Benjamin, Bonnie	WSW	1994
Benjamin, Harry S.	BB	1932
Benner, H. Thomas	MSW	1951,52,53,54
Benner, Kathryn	WTR	1978,80
Bennett, Donald C.	FB	1951,52,53,
	WR	1950
Bennett, Edwin	FB	1898
	BB	1900
	MTR	1896,97,98
Bennett, John	FB	1896,97,98
	MTR	1896,97,98
Bennett, Richard C.	FB	1937
	MTR	1939
Bennett, Robert R.	WR	1931
Bennett, Steven L.	WR	1977,78,79,80
Benninger, Stephen J.	WR	1991
Bensing, Barbara	VB	1982,83
Benson, Clarence	MCC	1928,29
Benson, Jerry S.	BB	1924,25
Benton, Leland	FB	1913,14,15
	BB	1913,14,15
Benton, Lou	FB	1914
	BB	1914,15
Bentz, Warren W.	FB	1944,45
	MTR	1945
Benz, William	WR	1930,31

Berce, Ted	MBK	1945
	BB	1948,49,50
Berenson, Gordon A.	IHO	1960,61,62
Berenzweig, Bubba	IHO	1996
Beresford, James	IHO	1923,24
Berg, Stacy	WTN	1988,89,90,91
Bergelin, John	MGO	1927,28,29
Bergen, Tom E.	MBK	1976,77,78
Berger, Alvin	MGY	1979,80,81,82
Berger, Thomas E.	FB	1956,57
Bergeron, Robert D.	FB	1983,84
Bergesen, Arthur G.	BB	1942
Bergman, Milton E.	FB	1928,29
Bergman, Richard J.	MGY	1953,54
Berke, Kenneth E.	MGO	1948
Berline, James H.	BB	1966
	FB	1967
Berman, Robert L.	MTN	1953
Berman, Deborah	WGY	1992,93,94,95
Berman, Hyman	FB	1948
Berman, Sari L.	VB	1974
Bernard, Charles	FB	1931,32,33
Bernard, Kent B.	MTR	1962,63,64,65
Berne, Laura	SS	1982
Bernoudy, Monique	WBK	1979
Berra, James A.	MBK	1975
	BB	1975,76,77,78
Berrigan, Kathleen	SB	1993,94
Berry, Frank	MSW	1962,63
Berry, Gordon	MGO	1902,03
Berry, Paul	FB	1994,95
Berryman, Brian	BB	1996
Berryman, Richard	IHO	1935
Bert, Kelli G.	WCC	1983,84,85,86
	WTR	1986,87
Bertoncin, Teresa	WGY	1979,80,81
Berutti, William J.	FB	1969,70
Besancon, John	MGY	1992
Besco, Bryan	BB	1995,96
Besco, Derek	BB	1995,96
Beshke, C.J.	BB	1983,84,85
Best, Edgar	BB	1983,84
Bettis, Roger A.	FB	1977
Betts, Norman J.	FB	1979,80,81
Betts, N. James	FB	1968,69,70
Betz, Michael P.	BB	1984
Betzig, Robert E.	WR	1947,48,49
Beuche, Jeffrey	MTR	1994,95,96
	MCC	1994
Beyer, Brenda	WBK	1980
	SB	1980
Biagi, Gia	FH	1992,93,94,95
Biakabatuka, Tshimanga	FB	1993,94,95
Bickle, Douglas G.	FB	1961
Bickner, Brian	FB	1992,92
Bickner, Kevin	FB	1993,93
Bieber, William F.	IHO	1961,62,63,64
Bierley, Brian	MBK	1991,92,93
Bigelow, Steven	MSW	1990,91,92
Biggert, Chad	WR	1993,94,95
Biggs, Evelyn	VB	1973
Bigler, Wendy	WGO	1990,91,92,93
Bigras, Richard J.	MGY	1973,74,75,76
Bikoff, Morris I.	MBK	1942
Billings, William	FB	1951
	BB	1951,52,53
Binnie, Randall R.	IHO	1966,67,68,69
Bird, James	FB	1892
Bird, Lester B.	MTR	1958,59,60,61
Bird, Mary Beth	FH	1990,91,92
Bird, Thomas	BB	1903
Birdsall, Charles K.	MTR	1944,45,46,47
Birks, Howard M.	MBK	1922,23,24
Birleson, Stanley R.	MTR	1935,36,37
Bisbee III, Leland S.	MSW	1966,67,68,69
Bischoff, Paul	MGY	1995
Bishop, Allen B.	FB	1984,86,87
Bishop, Arthur G.	BB	1870
Bishop, Harry	FB	1906
	MTR	1906
Bishop, Michele	WTR	1990,91
Bishop, Steven M.	MTR	1966,67,68
Bissell, Frank S.	FB	1934,35
	WR	1933,35,36,37
Bissell, Geoffrey J.	FB	1987
Bither, Richard L.	MGO	1955,58
Bitkowski, Mary	SB	1982,83,84,85
Bitner, Harry	FB	1881,82
Bjorkman, John M.	IHO	1984,85,87
Black Jr., William F.	MGO	1938,39,40
Black, James S.	MD	1977
Black, Monika	WTR	1993,94,95,96
Black, Ward E.	MGY	1970,71,72,73
Blackett, Charles T.	MGO	1954,58,59
Blackmore, Edmund T.	BB	1912

Blackwell, Brent	FB	1994,95
Blaine, Phillip	MTR	1961
Blair, Jack M.	FB	1969,72
Blair, Tina	WGY	1990
Blake, Amy	VB	1980
Blake, Richmond S.	MSW	1934,35,36
Blake, Thomas	MSW	1992,93,94,95
Blakenship, Joel A. (Tony)	FB	1991,92,93
Blaker, James R.	WR	1958,59,60,61
Blakley, Pamela	SB	1981,81
Blanchard, Donald R.	FB	1962
Blanchard, R. Bruce	BB	1943,44
	MTR	1944
Blanco, Orlando L.	BB	1976
Blanding, Fred J.	BB	1909,10
Blanks, James D.	WR	1970,73
Blanton, Richard E.	MGY	1963,65,66
Blanzy, Russell P.	IHO	1974,75,76,77
Blencoe, Guy	BB	1901
Blessing, Leigh Ann	WSW	1989
Bliss, Frank E.	BB	1872
Block, Brian M.	MTR	1970,71
Block, Earl F.	BB	1946
Blom, Joel F.	MBK	1972,73,74
Bloodworth, Richard L.	MBK	1967,69,70
Bloomfield, L.G.	MGO	1902,03,05
Bloomingston, John	FB	1895
	BB	1895,96
Blott, Jack	FB	1922,23
	BB	1922,23,24
Blue, James C.	FB	1975
Blum, John J.	IHO	1978,79,80,81
Blumenfled, Albert M.	MTR	1933
Blumenstein, Walter	WR	1945
Blunt, Alana Davis	WTR	1987,88,89,90
Bobel, James M.	BB	1961,62,63,64
Bochen, Steve J.	IHO	1957,58,59,60
Bochnowski, Alexander H.	FB	1956,57
Bockstahler, Karen	WSW	1977,78
Bock, Ernest F.	FB	1987
Boden, Marshall H.	FB	1928
Bodnar, Mark J.	MBK	1978,79,80,81
Bodnar, Martin J.	MBK	1978,79,80,81
Bodolay, Geza	MSW	1962,63,64

Body, Marion	FB	1979,80,81,82
Bodycombe, Richard	BB	1947,48
	FB	1947,48
Boehmer, Michael G.	MTR	1977,78,79,80
Bogaerts II, Alexander	MSW	1993,94,95,96
Bogard, Richard H.	BB	1950
Bogle, Darlynda Key	WTR	1978,79,80
Bogle, Thomas	FB	1910,11
Bohlke, Mark W.	MTR	1976
Bohn, Christopher R.	FB	1988,89,90
Bohnert, Amy	WSW	1991,92,93
Bohnsack, Arthur W.	MTR	1908,09,10
Bohrer, Jan	WSW	1983,83
Boice, William K.	MSW	1934
Boila, Remus	MGY	1950,51,52,56
Boim, Irving Pro	BB	1942,43,46
Bolach, Mark	FB	1993,94,95,96
Bolas, George A.	BS	1933
	FB	1934
Bolden, James M.	FB	1974,75,76
Boldt, Clarence J. Jr.	MSW	1930
Boles, Anthony L.	FB	1988,89
Bolhouse, Rick A.	MSW	1970,71
Bolles, Roy E.	IHO	1973
Bolster, Michelle	SB	1985,86,87,88
Bolster, William P.	MCC	1971,72,73
	MTR	1971,72,73,74
Bolton, Phillip L.	MGY	1961,62,63,64
Bond, James E.	MTR	1913,14
Bond, Lonjyno	MBK	1975
Bond, Lyle W.	BB	1939,40
Bond, Neal W.	MSW	1982
Bond, Richard E.	WR	1968,69,70,71
Bondy, Scott	IHO	1975
Bonelli, John B.	MD	1966
Boniforti, Christian	MGY	1992,93
Bonisteel, Roscoe O. Jr.	MGO	1943
Bonnell, William	FB	1982
Bonner, Lukas A.	BB	1996
Booker, Ethan	MSW	1994,95,96
Boor, Don	FB	1941,42
	BB	1942
Booth, Frederick C.	WR	1945
Booth, Mark F.	MTR	1953,54,55,56

Booth, Walter	BB	1886,87,88,89,
		90,91
Boothman, Edward H.	MSW	1962,63,64,65
Borcherts, Monica	WTN	1983,84,85,86
Borden, Hugh	FB	1882,83
Boren, Michael L.	FB	1980,81,82,83
Borges, Gustavo	MSW	1992,93,94,95
Borgmann, William F.	MBK	1933
	FB	1933,34
Boring, Jennifer	WGO	1989,92
Borinstein, Wilfred R.	MTN	1919,20
Borleske, Stanley	FB	1910,11
	BB	1911
Bormet, Sean	WR	1991,92,93,94
Boros, Jr. Stephen	BB	1955,56,57
Borowski, Andrew E.	FB	1985,86,87
Borst, Mary E.	FH	1973
	WBK	1974
Boschan, M.G.	WR	1922
Boshoven, Robert J.	FB	1957
Bossard, Jason G.	MBK	1991,92,93,94
Bostic, W. Keith	FB	1979,80,81,82
	MTR	1983
Bostic, Carlitos R.	FB	1987
Botterill, Jason	IHO	1994,95,96,97
Bottoms, Kenneth P.	FB	1953
	MTR	1954,55,56
Bouchard, Jean-Paul	MGY	1971,72,73,74
Boucher, Roy D.	MTN	1943,44,45
Boulding, Wiley C.	MTR	1986,87,88,89
Bourke, Peter	IHO	1994,95,96,97
Bourke, William T.	MTR	1938
Bouma, Edward	MTR	1917,18,19
Bourne, Roger A.	IHO	1979,80,81
Bourquin, James F.	MTN	1942
Boutell, Benjamin R.	MTN	1929
Boutwell, Ben	FB	1889
Bovard, Alan	FB	1927,28,29
Boville, Edwin	FB	1918
Bowen, John A.	MCC	1921,22,23
Bowen, Michael G.	BB	1968,69,70,71
Bowens, David	FB	1995,96
Bower, Robert K.	BB	1969,72

Bower, Timothy	MSW	1991,92
Bowerman, Edward B.	BB	1919
Bowerman, Frank	BB	1892
Bowers, David C.	FB	1956,57
Bowers, Douglas E.	BB	1976
Bowles, William H.	MTN	1934
Bowman Jr., Bliss	BB	1944,45,46
Bowman, Charles	BB	1912
Bowman, James N.	FB	1955
Bowman, Kevin	MTR	1996
Bowman, Martin	MTR	1996
Bowman, Victor L.	MBK	1975,76
Boyd, Alan	FB	1916,17
	MBK	1918
Boyd, Ann J.	WTR	1981
	WCC	1981
Boyd, Carol	WCC	1988
	WTR	1990
Boyd, Jan	SB	1982,83
Boyden Jr., Joel M.	FB	1988
Boyden, Jacquelyn	WBK	1976
Boyden, Joel M.	FB	1956,57
	MTR	1958,59
Boyer, Dara	SS	1981,82
Boyer, Stewart	BB	1923
Boyle, Michael	FB	1912
Boyle, Patrick	BB	1904
Boyle, Scott N.	FB	1985,85,87,87
Boynton, Charles M.	MTR	1942
Boynton, Robert C.	MTR	1982,83,84,85
Boys, Terry R.	MGY	1970,71,72,73
Boysen, Robert F.	IHO	1964,65,66,67
Bozo, Brian	MTR	1990,91,92,93
Brace, Fredric F.	MTN	1930,31
Brach, Michele	WSOC	1995,96
Bracken, Donald C.	FB	1980,81,82,83
Bracken, Jeffrey W.	MTR	1969,72
Bradbury, David A.	FB	1947
Braden, Howard	MTR	1931,33
Bradetich, Wendy	WBK	1983,84,85,86
Bradford, Reginald A.	MTR	1969,70,71,72
Bradford, Wes	FB	1950,51
Bradley, Dedra	WTR	1984,85,86,87
Bradley, G. Curtis	FB	1947

Jim Brandstatter, the popular host of Michigan Replay, lettered in football from 1969-71.

Bradley, Robert S.	MBK	1938,38
Bradley, Roy K.	IHO	1942,43
	MTN	1943
Bradshaw, James D.	MBK	1957
	BB	1957,58,59,60
Brady, Carrie	WSOC	1995
Brady, Kenneth R.	MBK	1971,72,73
Brady, William J.	MCC	1981,82,83,84
	MTR	1982,83,84,85
Braendle, Eugene	BB	1931,32,33
Brakus, Dan	MTN	1991,92,93,94
Braman, Mark A.	FB	1977,78,79
Branch Jr., Robert E.	MSW	1944
Brand, Hendrikus H.	IHO	1964,65,66
Brandell, Elmer	BB	1915,16,17
Brandon, David A.	FB	1973
Brandrup, Paul E.	IHO	1979,80,81,82
Brandstatter, James P.	FB	1969,70,71
Brandt, Stephen C.	MCC	1979,80,81
	MTR	1979,82
Branoff, Tony D.	BB	1954,55
	FB	1952,53,54,55
Brauer Jr., William W.	IHO	1983,84,85,86
Breakey, Barry A.	FB	1946,47,48,49
Breaugh, James W.	FB	1979,80
Brecht, Carrie	WCR	1997
Breen, William C.	MSW	1945
Brefeld, Joseph H.	BB	1959,60,61
	FB	1957,58
Breidenbach Jr., Warren	MTR	1939,40,41
Breitmeyer II, Philip	IHO	1944
Brelsford, Clayton E.	MTR	1935,36,37
Brennan, David K.	IHO	1977,78,79,80
Brennan, John	FB	1936,37,38
Brereton, P.M.	MGO	1907
Brevitz, Debra	WTN	1974
	WSW	1974,75,76,77
Brewer, Chauncey	MTR	1902
Brewer, Donald C.	BB	1936,37,38
Brewer, Eugene	MTR	1902,03,04
Brewer, Jodi	WTN	1993,96
Brewer, Robert B.	MTN	1940
Brewster, Christopher J.	MCC	1983,84,85,86
	MTR	1984,85,86,87
Brewster, David	FB	1981,81
Brick, Ernest G.	MTN	1924
Bridges, Catherine	WTR	1984,85
Brielmaier, Gerald E.	FB	1944
Brieske, Jim	FB	1942,46,47
Briggs, Clayton B.	MCC	1924,25,26
Briggs, Karl R.	WR	1975,76,77,78
Briggs, Kevin P.	MTR	1975,76
Brigstock, Thomas S.	FB	1965
Brink, Daniel B.	WR	1974,75
Briskin, Gerald J.	FB	1948
Brisson, Joseph	MGO	1959,60,61
Brisson, Noel	WGO	1987,88
Bristol, George H.	MTR	1906,07
Bristol, Hubert M.	MBK	1937
Britt, Wayman P.	MBK	1973,74,75,76
Broad, Tonya	WTR	1993
Broadnax, Stanley E.	FB	1967,68
Brock, Henry	FB	1884
	MTR	1884
Brock, Russell A.	BB	1989,90,91
Brock, Thomas J.	BB	1988
Brockington, Fred D.	FB	1980,81
Brockway, Bradley J.	MSW	1974,76
Brockway, Christopher	MGO	1994,95,96
Brod, David F.	MGY	1963,64
Broderick, (first name n/a)	MGO	1924
Brodson, John N.	MTN	1961
Brody, Ralph B.	MTN	1928
Brogan, Herbert A.	MBK	1940,41
Bromberg, Stephen A.	MTN	1950
Bromund, Ralph E.	MGY	1961,62
Brook, Allan H.	IHO	1966,67,68,69
Brooker, James K.	MTR	1923,24,25
Brookfield, Arthur D.	MTR	1898,99,00
Brooks, Booker	MTR	1929,30,32
Brooks, Charles E.	FB	1954,55,56
Brooks, Kevin C.	FB	1982,83,84
Brooks, Todd A.	FB	1995,96
Brost, Todd A.	IHO	1986,87,88,89
Brothers, Kenneth J.	IHO	1988,89,90,91
Brow, Shawne L.	WBK	1985
Brown, Bruce P.	MD	1963,64,65,66
Brown, Corwin	FB	1989,90,91,92
Brown, Cory	MTR	1995,96
Brown, Daniel P.	MBK	1963,65,66
Brown, David E.	BB	1958,59,60
	FB	1956,57
Brown, David S.	FB	1972,73,74
Brown, Demetrius J.	FB	1987,88
Brown, Dennis M.	FB	1967,68
Brown, Ellen	SS	1978,79
Brown, Eugene	MTR	1969,70,71,72
Brown, Fred R.	MD	1965,66,67,68
Brown, Gabe	MBK	1991,92,93
Brown, Harry E.	MTR	1913
Brown, Henry	FB	1898,1900
Brown, James R.	MGY	1958,59,60,61
Brown, James R.	WR	1972,73,74,75
Brown, James R.	BB	1946
Brown, Jeffrey F.	FB	1985,86,87,88
Brown, John G.	FB	1979,82
Brown, Keith	MCC	1971,72,73,74
	MTR	1972,74
Brown, Lawrence H.	MTN	1956
Brown, Leo J.	MBK	1980,81,82,83
Brown, Merle E.	MTN	1943
Brown, Philip S.	FB	1974
Brown, Randolph	FB	1880
Brown, Richard T.	BB	1953
	IHO	1956
Brown, Rick W.	FB	1969
Brown, Robert D.	MTR	1953,54,55,56
Brown, Robert F.	MBK	1958,59,60
Brown, Robert I.	FB	1973,74,75,76
	IHO	1975,76
Brown, Robert I.	FB	1923,24,25
Brown, Robert M.	MBK	1959,60,61,62
	FB	1961,62
Brown, Robert T.	IHO	1987,88,89,90
Brown, Roberta	WTR	1978
Brown, Tempie	WBK	1987,88,89,90
Brown, Willie L.	MTR	1966
Brown, Woodward A.	FB	1977
Browne, Brian	MSW	1957,58
Browne, Leslie C.	MBK	1974
Brownlee, Shannon	VB	1993,94,95
Brubaker, Burt C.	MTR	1930
Bruce, Andrew A.	MTR	1979,80,81,82
Brueger, Maura	FH	1983,84
Bruinsma, Ellen	FH	1973
Brumbaugh, Philip J.	FB	1975
Brumm Jr., Leonard W.	IHO	1948,49,50
	MTN	1949,50
Brundage III, Howard A.	MSW	1964,66
Bruner Jr., Van B.	MTR	1950,51,52,53
Brunsting, Carl D.	MBK	1950,51,52
	FB	1949
Bruzzese, James R.	MSW	1984
Bryan, Fred J.	FB	1943
Bryant, Baker L.	MSW	1937,38
Bryant, Clarence	IHO	1928,29,30
Bryant, Jason G.	MTR	1982,83
Bryant, Kevin	FB	1996
Bryant, Michael D.	BB	1977,78,79
Bryson, Edward F.	BB	1969,70
	MTR	1969
Brzezinski, Jennifer	WBK	1993,94,95,96
Brzoznowski, Toby	BB	1990,91,92,3
Buchalter, Fredric D.	FB	1974
Buchanan, H. Edsel	MGY	1948,49,50,51
Buchanan, Michael	IHO	1955,57
Buchanan, Neil E.	IHO	1953,54,55,56
Buchanan, William H.	MTR	1938
Buchholz, Amy	WCC	1989,90,91,92
	WTR	1989,90,92,93
Bucholz, William E.	BB	1949,50
Buckley, H.N.	MGO	1907
Buckley, Kristin	WSOC	1995
Budyk, Aaron	FB	1947
Buell, Bruce	MTR	1919
Buell, J. Lawrence Jr.	BB	1927
Buerkel, Steven M.	BB	1989,90,91,92
Bueter, James T.	FB	1971,72,73
Buff, Ronnie L.	FB	1992,93
Bullard, Anna	SB	1978
Bullock, Louis	MBK	1996,97
Bunch, Jarrod R.	FB	1987,88,89,90
	MTR	1990
Buntin, William	MBK	1963,64,65
Burak, Chris W.	BB	1973,74
Burak, Sandra	WGY	1976,77
Burch, Alfie	FB	1991,92,93
Burchfield, Jack E.	MGY	1954,55,56
Burdick, Janet	SS	1974,75
Burford, Gilbert P.	IHO	1948,49,50,51
Burg, George R.U.	FB	1944,46
Burgei, Gerald R.	FB	1980,81,82
Burgess, Fritz L.	FB	1982,83
Burgett, Michael N.	IHO	1973,74
Burgett, Roger A.	MGY	1973,74
Burinskas, Judith	FH	1986,87,88,89
Burkholder, Marc J.	FB	1990,91,92,93
Burkholder, Paul W.	MTR	1919,20,21
Burk, Sue	SB	1979,80,81,82
Burke, Burt S.	MTR	1922,23
Burks, Roy	FB	1972,73
Burnett, Grady	MTN	1992,93,94,95
Burnett, Robert	MTN	1992,93,94,95
Burnham, Charles C.	MGO	1970,71,72,73
Burnham, David L.	MGO	1974,76
Burnham, Todd	MTR	1993,94,95,96
Burnley, Kenneth S.	MTR	1961,62,63,64
Burns, Jerome M.	MBK	1948
	FB	1948,49,50,51
Burns, Leo A.	MTR	1921
Burns, Richard R.	IHO	1965,68
Burns, Ronald S.	MTN	1966
Burns, Thomas R.	MSW	1963
Burress, William J.	MBK	1974
Burrows, Bradley	FB	1987
Burry, Roy D.	MSW	1962,63
Burt, Eric A.	MTR	1976
Burt, Ryan	MCC	1993,94,95,96
Burton, M.C.	MBK	1981
Burton Jr., M. C.	MBK	1956,57,58,59
Burton, Jim S.	BB	1968,69,70,71
Burton, Tirrel	FB	1969,71
Burton, William D.	MSW	1941,42
Busch, William C.	IHO	1968,69
Bush, Eric A.	BB	1990
	FB	1988,90
Bush, Harvey	BB	1886
Bush, Kenny D.	FB	1974,77
Bushnell, Thomas	FB	1912,13,14
Bushong, Jared L.	MBK	1957
	FB	1957,58,59
	MTR	1958,59,60
Bushong, Reid J.	FB	1958,59,60
Buss, Gregory A.	MBK	1970,72,73
	BB	1970,71,72,74
Butler, John E.	BB	1895,97,98
Buss, John F.	MGY	1960,62
Butler, Lawrence C.	BB	1919,20,21
Butler, Lawrence F.	BB	1930,31,32
Buster, Russell	FB	1947
Butler, Abraham L.	MTR	1973,74,75,76
Butler, David C.	FB	1964
Butler, Gary D.	IHO	1962,63,64
Butler, Matthew W.	MTR	1986,87,88
Butler, Natalie	WTN	1987,88
Butler, Sheila	WBK	1977
Butler, W. Jack	FB	1940
Butterfield, Tyrone A.	FB	1995,96
Buttrey, Stephanie	FH	1975,76
Butts, Michael	FB	1981
Butts, W. David	IHO	1960,61,62,63
Butts, William W.	MBK	1986
Butzlaff, Lisa	WSW	1994,95
Buyukuncu, Derya	MSW	1995,96
Buzynski, John	FB	1966
Byberg, Robert C.	MSW	1948,49,50,51
Byerly, James A.	MTR	1943
Byers, James A.	FB	1956,57,58
Byrnes, Julie Kay	VB	1973

C

Cable, Ben	FB	1874
Cachey, Theodore J.	FB	1952,53,54
Cade, Mike R.	FB	1979
Caffrey, Frederick R.	FB	1951,52
Cahill, Susan	WSW	1981,82,83,84
Cain, William C.	BB	1942,43
Calandrino, Gaspare L.	FB	1978
Caldarazzo, Richard J.	FB	1966,69
Caley, William	FB	1898
Calin, Peter J.	FB	1970,71,72
Calip, Demetrius R.	MBK	1988,89,90,91
Call, Norm	FB	1940
Callahan, Alexander J.	FB	1957,58,59
Callahan, Robert F.	FB	1945,46
Callahan, Roy H.	MCC	1924,25,26
	MTR	1924,25,26
Callam, Alexandra K.	FH	1978,79,80
Callam, Mary	FH	1976,77,78,79
Calloway, Christopher F.	FB	1987,88,89
Calvert, Lawrence A.	IHO	1939,40
Camacho, Jorge	MGY	1991,92,93
Cameron, C. Paul	WR	1936,37,38
Cameron, David G.	MGO	1961,62,63
Cameron, Denise	WBK	1977,78
Cameron, Donald L.	FB	1975
Camp, Craig L.	MTR	1981,82
Campana, Mary Louise	SB	1991,92,93,94
Campbell, Alec J.	MSW	1985,86,87,88
Campbell, Charles	FB	1878,79
Campbell, Charles F.	BB	1902,03,04,05
Campbell, Darrin	BB	1986,87,88
Campbell, David W.	BB	1962,63,64
Campbell, George	MBK	1951
Campbell, Herbert	BB	1902,03,04,05
Campbell, Holly	MTR	1927,30
Campbell, Howard H.	BB	1909,10,11
Campbell, J. Erik	FB	1984,85,86,87
Campbell, Janie	SS	1974
Campbell, John	BB	1910
Campbell, John T.	MTR	1930,31,32
Campbell, Laura	VB	1973
Campbell, Mark J.	FB	1995,96
Campbell, Oscar J.	BB	1865
Campbell, Robert	FB	1935,37
	BB	1937,38
Campbell, S.	WR	1922
Campbell, Scott	MTR	1995,96
Canady, Alan L.	FB	1974
Canales, Fernando J.	MSW	1978,79,80,82
Canales, Harry N.	MSW	1984
	FB	1987
Canamare, George J.	MTR	1964,65,66
Candler, John	MD	1962,63
Canfield, William	IHO	1940
Canham, Donald B.	MTR	1939,40,41
Canja, Alexander	MD	1942,43,46,47
Cannavino, Andrew J.	FB	1978,79,80
Cantor, Sharon	FH	1986,87,88,89
Cantrell, Robert J.	MBK	1961,62,63,64
	BB	1961
Cantrill Jr., Cecil E.	FB	1931,32
Canty, Thomas J.	WR	1977,79
Capoferi, Alfred	BB	1947
Capoferi, James A.	BB	1976,77,78,79
Cappon, Frank	FB	1920,21,22
	MBK	1923
Caputo, David F.	FB	1989
Caputo, Matthew A.	FB	1972,75
Carey, Brian L.	MGY	1976,77,78,80
Carey, Shelby	WSOC	1994
Carfora, Kelly	WGY	1992,93,94,95
Cargile, William	FB	1974
Carian, Robert L.	FB	1975
Carlile, Todd M.	IHO	1983,84,85,86
Carlisle, Russell E.	MSW	1950,51,52
Carlson, Elizabeth	WGY	1977
Carlson, Glen A.	MTR	1928
Carlson, James W.	FB	1970
Carlson Jr., John D.	FB	1989,90,91
Carlson, Philip F.	WR	1947,48,49
Carlson, William S.	MCC	1927
Carna, Anthony R.	MCC	1987,88,90
	MTR	1988,89,91,92
Carpell, Otto	FB	1911,12
Carpenter, Brian M.	FB	1979,80,81
Carpenter, Jack C.	FB	1946
Carpenter, Michael R.	MGY	1967,68
Carpenter, Robert B.	BB	1951,53
Carpenter, William B.	BB	1886,87
Carr, Bert	FB	1895,96,97
Carr, Jason	FB	1993,94,95
Carr, John D.	FB	1980,81,81
Carr, Tracy	SB	1993,94,95,96
Carr, William	FB	1993,94,95,96
Carras, James W.	MGO	1995,96
Carraway, Winfred J.	FB	1979,80,81,82
Carrier, Timothy D.	FB	1978,79,80
Carroll, H.L.	MCC	1915,16,17
Carroll, John F.	MTR	1951,52,53,54
Carroll, Katherine	WSW	1978,80
Carrothers, Edgar M.	BB	1903
Carrow, Mark E.	BB	1968,69,70,71
Carscallen, Charles H.	MSW	1956,57
Carson, Franklin R.	BB	1883,84
Carson, James	MGO	1990,91,92,93
Carson, Michael E.	MTR	1990,91,92,93

Carter, Richard L.	MD	1977
Carter, Anthony	FB	1979,80,81,82
Carter, Charles	FB	1902,04
Carter, Daryl, J.	MBK	1974
Carter, Gary B.	MTR	1978
Carter, Keith L.	IHO	1981
Carter, Richard E.	MBK	1969,70
Carter, Willis R.	MBK	1982
Carthens, Milton B.	FB	1982,83
Cartier, Jean-Yves G.	IHO	1969,70,71,72
Cartmill, William J. Jr.	MBK	1940,41,42
	BB	1941,42
Catrabone, Jeff	WR	1995,96,97
Cartwright, Joseph M.	BB	1897
Cartwright, Oscar	FB	1917
Cartwright, Sherry	WSW	1983,84,85
Carver, Harry C.	MTR	1914,15
Cary, John	FB	1919
Case, Thomas B.	MSW	1953
Casey, Kevin B.	MBK	1971
	FB	1971
Casey, Michael A.	MSW	1968,69
Casey, William	FB	1907,08,09
Cash, Lisa	WSW	1987
Cashion, Nickolas F.	FB	1969,72
Cashion, Timothy	FB	1974
Cashman, John E.	MGY	1963,64,65,66
Casselman, David B.	MGO	1972,75
Cassidy, Susan	SS	1978,79,80
Casto, Dorr C.	MTR	1961,63,64
Caswell, Harrison H.	BB	1915,16
Catallo, Giulio	FB	1967
	MTR	1968,69,70
Catlett, James	FB	1913,14,15
	MTR	1915,16
Ceballos, Ruben J.	MBK	1989
	MGY	1989,90,91,92
Cecchini, Gene	FB	1986
Cecchini, Thomas A.	FB	1963,64,65
Cech, Timothy J.	WR	1969,70
Ceddia, John E.	FB	1976
Cederberg, Jon C.	FB	1973
Ceithaml, George F.	FB	1940,41,42
Celley, Neil R.	IHO	1949,50,51
Cender, Natasha	WBK	1977,78
Centanni, Anthony F.	BB	1929
Cephas, Richard A.	MTR	1958,59,60,61
Cercone, Leonard P.	MTR	1960
Ceresa, Robert M.	MSW	1987,88
Cerezo, Antonio	MSW	1983
Cernak, Robert A.	FB	1987
Cervenak, Michael C.	BB	1996
Chadbourne, Thomas	FB	1890
Chadwell, John T.	MSW	1955
Chadwick, Alfred	IHO	1938,39
Chaffee, Donald	IHO	1932
Chalfant, Donald C.	MTR	1958,59,60,61
Chamberlain, B. Francis	BB	1940,41,42
Chambers, Edward W.	MBK	1925,26,27
Chambers, John H.	MCC	1983,84,85
	MTR	1985,86
Chandler, Darcy S.	WGO	1988,89,90,91
Chandler, M. Robert	FB	1961,62,63
Chang, George J.	MBK	1978
Chapel, H. Daniel	BB	1976
Chapman, Chad	BB	1992,93,94,95
Chapman, David P.	BB	1975,76,77,78
Chapman, Eric T.	MTR	1970,71,72,73
Chapman, George A.	MTR	1893
Chapman, Gil	FB	1972,73,74
Chapman Jr., Harvey E.	BB	1962,63
	FB	1960,61,62,63
Chapman, Harvey Sr.	FB	1932,33
	BB	1934
	IHO	1932,33,34
Chapman, Richard M.	MTR	1928,30
Chapman, Robert C.	MBK	1928,29,30
Chappuis, Robert R.	BB	1946,48
	FB	1942,46,47
Chard, Kelly	WCC	1991,92,94,95
	WTR	1992,93,95,96
Chardavoyne, David G.	FB	1969,70,70
Charles, Jean Agnus	FB	1992,93,94,95
Chase Jr., Edward C.	IHO	1933,37,38
Chase, J.G.	MGO	1907
Chase, John	FB	1878,79,80
Chase Jr., John M.	MD	1951,52,53,54
Chase, Karen	VB	1995,96
Chase, William K.	IHO	1933,35,37,38
Checkley, G. Robert	MGY	1949,50,51
Cheever, Walter H.	BB	1874
Chelich, C. Matthew	MD	1976,77,78,79
Cherney, Luanne	WGO	1982,83,84
Cherry, John A.	FB	1973
Cherry, Royal F.	MBK	1924,25
	BB	1925
Chester, David D.	FB	1985,86,87,88
Chevillet, Donald L.	MTR	1982
Chiames, George J.	FB	1945
	WR	1946
Chiamp, Mark A.	IHO	1982,83,84,85
Chiesa, Robert G.	FB	1978,79
Child, Luis M.	MSW	1950,51
Childs, Chris P.	MCC	1989,90,91,92
	MTR	1990,91,92,93
Childs, Jack W.	MTR	1934
Childs, K. Ross	IHO	1956,57,58,59
Chilvers, Clifford R.	MGY	1964,65,66
Chin, George E.	IHO	1951,52,53,54
Chipman, Gordon N.	BB	1965
Chipokas, Scott J.	MGO	1984,85,86,87
Chisholm, Arnett B.	MTR	1976,77,78,79
Christenson, Mark W.	MGO	1967,68,69
Christenson, R. Wayne	BB	1941,42
Christian, Charles I.	FB	1979,80
Christiansen, Roy H.	MTR	1951,52,53,54
Christie, Eugene F.	MTR	1957,58
Christman, Gerald L.	MBK	1967
	BB	1967,68,69
Chubb, Ralph L.	FB	1944,46
	MSW	1945
Church, Harrison A.	MTR	1937
Church, Merton W. Jr.	MSW	1943,44,45
Churella, Mark B.	WR	1976,77,78,79
Chute, George M.	MCC	1922
Cipa, Lawrence A.	FB	1971,72,73
Clancy, John D.	FB	1963,65,66
Clancy, Sean	MTR	1993,94,95
Clark, Ronald L.	MSW	1958,59,60,61
Clark, Andrea	FH	1979,80
Clark, David W.	MSW	1970
Clark, Fay	FB	1909
Clark Jr., Goodwin	MGO	1940
Clark, James E.	BB	1954,55,56,57
Clark, Julie	SB	1984,85,86,87
Clark, Justin	IHO	1996
Clark, Kenneth M.	MGO	1983,84,85
Clark, Kim	SB	1992,93,94
Clark, Ned R.	MTR	1906
Clark, Oswald	FB	1948,49,50
Clark, Richard K.	MBK	1959,60
	BB	1959
Clark, Rollin W. Jr.	MTN	1930,32
Clark, Ronald L.	MTR	1969
Clark, Sara	FH	1985,86,87,88
Clark, Thomas B.	MGO	1961,63,64
Clark, William	FB	1904,05
Clark, William A.	FB	1947
Clarke, Harvey W.	MTR	1937,38,39
Clarke, John H.	MCC	1932
Clarke, Peter D.	MGO	1969,70,72
Clarke, Robert W.	MTN	1930,31
Clarkson, Charles B.	MGY	1956,57,58,59
Clarkson, Julie	SB	1991,92
Clawson, John R.	MBK	1963,64,65,66
Clay, Tanya	WTR	1992,93,94,95
Clayton, Ralph D.	FB	1977,78,79
Cleary, Sue Anne	WBK	1989
Clegg, Edward M.	BB	1974,76
Clem, John D.	BB	1982
Clement, Benoit R.	MSW	1983,84
Clement, Carl	FB	1906
Clifford, Julie	WTR	1978,79,80,82
	WCC	1979
Cline, J. Daniel	BB	1952,53,54,55
	FB	1952,53,54
Clinton, Mark J.	BB	1978,79,80,81
Clinton, R. Kevin	BB	1977
Close, Bart	BB	1993
Close, Casey R.	BB	1983,84,85,86
Clover, Kimberly	VB	1986,87,88,89
Cluff, Jason	WR	1992,93
Clymer, Carolyn	WSW	1980,81,82
Cmejrek, Carl G.	BB	1965
	FB	1963
Coakley, Gary R.	FB	1971,72

Coates, Ross A.	MTR	1952,53
Coates, Thomas	MSW	1947,48,49
Cochran, Bradley M.	FB	1983,84,85
Cochran, Harold C.	MTR	1924
Cochran, William	FB	1913,14,15
Cocozzo, Joseph T.	FB	1989,90,91,92
Cocuzza, Carol	VB	1977
Codd, George P.	BB	1890
Codere, John C.	MGO	1985,86,87
Codwell Jr., John E.	MBK	1951,52,53,54
	BB	1951
Cody, Frederick K.	MSW	1935,37
Coe, Harry L.	MTR	1905,06,07,08
Coe, William W.	MTR	1906
Coffin, Kenneth R.	MTR	1965,66,67,68
Coffman, Michael P.	IHO	1976,77,78,79
Cohen, David C.	MGY	1960
Cohen, Heidi	WGY	1984,85,86,87
Cohen, Jeffrey A.	FB	1980,82,83
Cohen, Patricia	FH	1975,76,77
Cohen, Richard S.	MTN	1954,55,56,57
Cohen, Samuel L.	MTN	1915
Cohen, Todd S.	MTN	1984
Cohn, Abe J.	FB	1917,18,20
Coin, Dana S.	FB	1969,70,71
Coke, Elizabeth	FH	1978,79,80,81
Colbert, Karyn	WGO	1980,81,82
Colby, Branch	FB	1876
Coldren, Charles H.	BB	1870
Coldren, Rebecca	WGY	1977
Cole, Edward W.	MGY	1957,58,59
	MD	1957,58
Cole, G. Thomas	MBK	1960,61,62,63
	BB	1960
Cole, Harry	FB	1912
Cole, John D.	IHO	1962,63,64
Cole, Phillip	MTR	1984
Cole, Ralph M.	MGO	1926,27,28
Cole, Walter	FB	1913
Cole, Wheaton	FB	1910
Cole, William C.	BB	1903
Coleman Jr., Horace	MTR	1949,50,51,52
Coleman Sr., Horace	MTR	1946
Coleman, Donald A.	FB	1972,73
Coleman, James E.	FB	1948
Coleman, Leo W.	BB	1925
Coleman, Robert L.	IHO	1964
Coleman, Wallace	FB	1989
Coles, Cedric C.	FB	1979,80,81
Collette, William	FB	1912
Collia, Philip	MTR	1944
Collias, Joanna	VB	1990,91,92,93
Collins, Alexis	WTR	1992,93
Collins, Jerrold M.	FB	1975
Collins, Robert	IHO	1940,41,42
Collins, S. Autumn	VB	1988,89,90,91
Collins, Shawn	FB	1992
Collins, Todd	FB	1991,92,93,94
Collins, Sue	WSW	1978,79,81,82
Colloton, Ann	WSW	1987,88,89,90
Colombo Jr., Louis J.	FB	1932
Colombo, James F.	FB	1937
Colombo, Paula	WSW	1987,88,89,90
Colombo, Sharon	WSW	1989,90
Colton, William O.	MTR	1966,67
Colvin, Jason	MTR	1990,91
Colvin, Jason	MCC	1990
Colwell, Chris B.	MTN	1985,88
Colwell, W. Paul	MCC	1927,28
Comb, Raymond L.	IHO	1927
Combs, William B.	WR	1939,40

Ann Colloton was named Michigan's Female Athlete of the Decade for the 1980s.

Comby, Denise	FH	1980,81,82,83
Comeau, Wendy A.	WGY	1987,88,89,90
Comin, Melvin	MBK	1941,42,43
Compton, William V.	BB	1930,31
Comstock, Howard M.	MBK	1974,75
Conant, James R.	MTR	1943
Conant Jr., Lloyd V.	MGY	1965,66,67
Concaugh, Jacqueline	WCC	1993,95
Condon, Carl	MGO	1991,92,93,94
Condon, Frank C.	BB	1897,98,99,01
Condon, John C.	BB	1895,96
Condon, William D.	BB	1883,84,85,86
Confer, Wendy S.	VB	1984
Conger, Seymour B.	MTR	1899,1903,04
Conkin, Fredric	FB	1909,10,11
Conlan, Travis	MBK	1995,96,97
Conley, James P.	FB	1962,63,64
Conlin, John W.	FB	1951,52
Conlin, Theresa A.	WBK	1975,76,77,78
	SB	1978
Connally, William T.	FB	1948
Connell, Dennis P.	FB	1968,69,70,71
Connelly, Gary N.	IHO	1971
Conney, Lisa	WGO	1980
Connor, Addison D.	MGO	1926,27,28
Conrad, Traci	SB	1996,97
Conti, Mark S.	MTN	1968,69,70
Conway, Michael W.	MTR	1988
Conway, William L.	BB	1891
Coode, Jim	FB	1971,72,73
Cook, Harold A.	MTN	1946,47
Cook, John D.	MTR	1989,90
Cook, Robert	MTR	1918,19,20
Cooke, George	IHO	1937,38,39
Cooley, Edgar L.	BB	1897,98
Cooley, Eugene F.	BB	1867,70
Cooley, Keith W.	MGY	1966
Cooley Jr., Willard	MSW	1944
Cooney, Patrick M.	IHO	1951,52,53,54
Cooper, David L.	MTR	1964,65,66
Cooper, Donald M.	MTR	1927,28
Cooper, Evan	FB	1980,81,82,83
Cooper, Howard J.	FB	1949
Cooper, Julie	SB	1988,89,90,91
Cooper, Keith B.	FB	1987
Cooper, Maggie	VB	1996
Cooper, Pierre	FB	1993,94
Cooper, Robert E.	FB	1936
	MTR	1935
Cooper, Roland	BB	1918,19
Cooperrider, Daniel J.	MBK	1976
	BB	1976,77,78,79
Copeland, Ernie	1876	
Copeland, Glenn K.	IHO	1927,28
Copeland, J. Todd	IHO	1988,89,90
Copenhaver, Clint C.	FB	1995,96
Copley, Almon L.	WR	1941
Copley, Everett C.	MGO	1935
Copley, Julie	WTR	1993
Coplin, Haskell R.	MTR	1947
Copp, Matthew	BB	1990,91,92,93
Copp, Melinda	WSW	1981,82,83,85
Corbett Jr., John A.	BB	1951,52,53,54
Corbin, Cecil B.	MTR	1915
	BB	1912
Corbin, J. Scott	FB	1974,75
Corey, George R.	FB	1954,55
Coristine, Ronald C.	IHO	1961,62,63,64
Cormier, Daniel	IHO	1976
Cornell, Peter M.	FB	1965,66
	WR	1966,67,68,69
Cornwell, Alan I.	MTR	1971,72,73
Cornwell, Arthur	FB	1910
Cornwell, Francis	FB	1928,29,30
Cornwell, Norman S.	MTR	1969,70
Corona, Clement L.	FB	1955,56
Corp, Michael B.	BB	1970,72,73
Corriden, Donald J.	BB	1926,28,29
Corriere, Donald B.	WR	1958,59,61,62
Corritore, John J.	MGY	1976,77,78
Corson, John R.	IHO	1940,42
Corwin, Henry R.	MTN	1938
Cory Jr., John W.	BB	1913
Cory, Ace R.	MSW	1943,44
Cosby, Baden L.	IHO	1955,56
	MTR	1954
Cossalter, Clement	IHO	1946,48
Costa, James P.	FB	1947
Costanzo, John	MTN	1993,94,95,96
Costello, Jeffery M.	MCC	1983
	MTR	1984,85
Coston, Sean	BB	1993,94,95
Courtis, Thomas M.	IHO	1929,30,31
Courtis, Walter F.	IHO	1933,35

Courtright, William E.	MGO	1942,46,47
	WR	1941,42,46,47
Coventry, Markham	IHO	1933
Cowan, Keith E.	FB	1959,60
Cowan, Keith F.	FB	1984,85
Cowan, Van S.	MTR	1990,91,92,93
Cox III, Stanley C.	MD	1960,61,62,63
Cox, Ramona	VB	1995
Cox, Roderick H.	FB	1930,32
	MTR	1931,32,33
Coyle, James A.	IHO	1958,59,60,61
Coyle, Thomas J.	FB	1970,71,72
Coyne, Michael T.	FB	1972,74
Cragg, Graham S.	IHO	1949,50,51,52
Cragin, Raymond	FB	1928
Cramer, Suzanne	VB	1977
Craig, Jim	FB	1911,12,13
	MTR	1912,13
Craig, Ralph C.	MTR	1909,10,11
Craine, Donald W.	MD	1974,75,76
Crandell, John S.	FB	1943
Crane, Fenwick J.	FB	1943,46
Crane, Mark G.	BB	1971,72,73
Crane, Richard	MTN	1924,25,26
Craw, Garvie T.	FB	1967,68,69
Crawfis, Karen	SB	1982,83
Crawford, Charles	MTN	1915,16
Crawford, Bobby	MBK	1994,95
Crawford, Frank	BB	1892,93
Crawford, Joseph L.	MD	1970,71,72,73
Crawford, Scott A.	MTR	1984,85,86,87
Creaser, Michael J.	MSW	1985,86,87,88
Creede, James R.	MD	1969,71
Creek, Robert J.	MGY	1975,77,78,79
Creighton Jr., John W.	MSW	1938
Creighton, Katherine R.	WSW	1989,90,92
Cress, Elmer	FB	1919
Cribari, Lisa	WD	1990,91,92
Crispin, David	FB	1996
Crispin, William H.	MSW	1947,48
Cristy, James C. Jr.	MSW	1932,33,34
Crittenden, Willard C.	MSW	1935
Crociata, Kevin	BB	1991,92,93,94
Crocker, Kimberly	WGY	1989,90,91,92
Crocker, Tami	WGY	1991
Crockett, Laurence R.	FB	1976
Crooks Jr., William A.	MBK	1960
Crosby, Elaine	WGO	1979,80
	WTN	1977,78
Crosby, M.S.	MGO	1923,24
Cross, Arthur G.	MTR	1918,19,20
Cross, Cecli F.	MTR	1915,16,17
Cross, Jonathan P.	MCC	1972,73,74,76
	MTR	1972,73,74,75
Crossland, Hugh J.	FB	1956,57,58
	IHO	1962
Crossman, Keith K.	IHO	1931,32,33
Crouther, Charles L.	MTR	1976,77,78
Crowder III, R. Scott	MSW	1979,80,81,82
Crowe, Charles W.	BB	1939
Crowe, La Shawnda	VB	1991
Crownley, Erwin W.	FB	1956,57
	MTR	1957,58,59
Crozier, Greg	IHO	1996
Cruikshank, Charles L.	MTR	1920,21
Crumpacker, Maurice	FB	1908
Cruse, William	FB	1917,18
Culbertson II, Carey	MGY	1973,74,75,76
Culbertson, Carla	WGY	1983
Cullen, Gordon F.	IHO	1973,74
Cullen, Terry C.	IHO	1979
Culligan Jr., William L.	FB	1944,46
Culver, Carl A.	MTR	1939,40
Culver, Fred C.	MTR	1939
Cummins, Scott M.	WR	1977
Cunningham, Leo P.	FB	1941
Cunningham, Linda	VB	1978,79,80,81
Cunningham, Robert K.	WR	1948,49
Cunningham, William	FB	1896,97,98,99
Cuppett, Scott	MTN	1991
Curby, David G.	WR	1972,73,74,75
Curby, Jerome H.	WR	1987,88
Curhan, Robert P.	MTN	1950,51,52,53
Curran, Louis	FB	1921,22,23
Currier, Abby A.	WBK	1978,79,80,81
	WTR	1978
Curry, Mathew D.	MSW	1987
Curtis III, George H.	WR	1944,47,48
Curtis, Guy P.	FB	1959,60,61
	WR	1958,60,62
Curtis, John S.	MTR	1905,06
Curtis, Thomas	IHO	1929,30,31
Curtis, Thomas N.	FB	1967,68,69
Cusak, Michael	IHO	1986
Cushing, Carl F.	MTR	1923

Cushing, David G.	MTR	1930,31
Cushing, Ellwood L.	MBK	1929
Cushing, Patrick E.	IHO	1958,59,61
Cutler, Barry	IHO	1960
Cutro, Joseph E.	MBK	1964
Cutting, Robert M.	BB	1900,03
Cyganiak, Elizabeth M.	WTN	1992,93,94,95
Cymbalski, Brent	BB	1991
Czachorski, Robert	MTR	1991,92
Czak, Edward W.	FB	1939,40
Czarnecki, Diane	WTN	1974,75
Czarnota, Michael A.	FB	1981
Czirr, James C.	FB	1973,74,75
Czupek, Joseph D.	MBK	1986,87,88

D

D'Agostino Jr., Alfred A.	MTR	1970,73
D'Agostino, Michael	MCC	1974,75
	MTR	1973,74,75,76
D'Amura, Randy	MGY	1996
D'Anna Jr., Edward O.	MCC	1929
D'Atri, Geoffrey A.	MSW	1964
D'Eramo, Paul J.	FB	1965,66
	MTR	1965
D'Esposito, Christopher J	FB	1986
Daane, Martin H.	MTR	1904,05,06
Dadabbo, Mark J.	BB	1982,83,84
Daggs, LeRoy W.	MTR	1946
Dahlem, Alvin G.	FB	1928,29
	MTR	1930
Dahlinger, Dawnanne	WSW	1981,82
Dale, Jonathan O.	MGO	1971,73,74
Dale, Sandra	SS	1980,81,82
Dale, William B.	MTR	1943,44
Daley, William E.	FB	1943
Dalrymple, OgdenR.	MSW	1934,35
Dalton, Becky	WSOC	1994
Dalton, John M	BB	1954,55
Daly, John	MSW	1975,76,77
Dameron, David F.	WR	1987,88
Dames, Michael K.	FB	1985,86,87,88
Damiani, Daniel A.	BB	1973,74,75,76
Damken, Michael L.	MBK	1978
Damm, Frederick R.	MSW	1964
Damm, Russell	FB	1932
Damon, Donald A.	BB	1945
Damron, Carroll G.	FB	1969,72
Dana, Robert F.	FB	1980,83
Dance, William H.	IHO	1942,43
Danforth, Henry T.	MTN	1901,02,03
Danforth, Robert S.	MTN	1896,97,98,99
Danhof, Jerome A.	FB	1966
Daniels, John D.	FB	1970,72
Daniels, Marcus L.	MSW	1931,32,33
Daniels, Norman J.	MBK	1930,31,32
	BB	1930,31,32
	FB	1929,30,31
Dankow, Mark	WR	1993,94
Danks, Chris	WCC	1988
	WTR	1988
Dannenfelser, Frederick	MGO	1940,41
Danner, Harland F.	WR	1937,38,40
Danner, Harley J.	MGY	1975,76
Danuff, Laura	WTN	1979
Darden, Oliver M.	MBK	1963,64,65,66
Darden, Robert K.	MGY	1973,74,75,76
Darden, Thomas V.	FB	1969,70,71
Dardick, Harold A.	MGY	1978
Darien, Andrew	MTR	1990,91,92
Darin, Lynn	FH	1977,78
Darland, Michael W.	MD	1977
Darnall, Carl R.	MSW	1926,27,28
Darnton, William T.	MSW	1960,61,62
Darr, Bradford W.	MTR	1989,90,91,92
Darrow, George F.	WR	1945
Daugherty, R. Douglas	FB	1989
Dauw, Michael W.	MSW	1980,81
Davenport, Juston B.	MGY	1956
Davey, Frank P.	MTR	1906,07
David Jr., George	MGO	1933
	IHO	1932,33,34
David, Lawrence J.	MGO	1934,35,36
	IHO	1933,34,35,36
Davids, Thomas A.	WR	1980
Davids, William F.	WR	1971,73,74
Davidson Jr., Howard R.	MTR	1935,36,37
Davidson Jr., Richard S.	MGY	1950,51
Davidson, Fiona	VB	1990,91,92,93
Davidson, Harold E.	MTR	1937,38,39
Davidson, Marie-Ann	VB	1985,86,87,88
Davidson, Omar B.	MTR	1985,86,87,88
Davie, Cathy	SB	1996,97
Daviera, Mary Ann	SB	1986,87,88,89
Davies, James H.	FB	1955,56,57
Davies, John G.	MSW	1950,51,52

Davis, Harry L.	MCC	1922,23
Davis III, Russell	FB	1975,76,77,78
Davis III, William J.	MTR	1984,85,86
Davis, Douglas J.	MGO	1975,76,77,78
Davis, Edward	FB	1992,93,94,95
Davis, J. Nathaniel	FB	1982
Davis, Martin J.	FB	1989,90,91,92
Davis, Michael	FB	1976,79
Davis, Rickey D.	FB	1982
Davis, Timothy F.	FB	1973,74,75
Davison, Samuel	FB	1908
Dawson, Scott A.	BB	1980
Day, Floyd A.	FB	1965
Day, Lawrence J.	MSW	1970,71,72,73
Day, Michael J.	FB	1973
Day, Richard B.	IHO	1963,64
Dayton, Edwin	MGO	1932,33,34
Dayton, Joseph D.	FB	1965,66,67
Dayton, Michael S.	MTN	1947
De Kay, W. Todd	MTR	1989
DeBaker, Charles E.	FB	1930,31,32
	MTR	1931,32,33
DeBoer, Bruce A.	MTN	1968,69,70
DeBoer, Michael S.	FB	1986,87
DeBoo, James C.	MGY	1967,68,69
DeBryn, Ihor A.	MTN	1978,79,80 81,82
DeCou, Michael R.	BB	1971,72,73,74
DeFelice, Vincent A.	FB	1980,82,83,84
DeGain, Joseph	WR	1997
DeGlopper, Charles K.	MBK	1985,87
DeHaven, George	FB	1887,88,89
DeJesus, Federico R.	MTN	1973,74,75,76
DeKuiper, Ryan	MBK	1995,96,97
DeLamielleure, Richard J.	BB	1959,60,61
DeLeon, Gregory	WR	1995,96
DeMaat, Gwen	WSW	1987,88,89,90
DeMartino, John T.	IHO	1983,84
DeMassa, Thomas A.	FB	1959
DePont, Edward	FB	1891,92
	MTR	1891,92
DePuy, Richard	FB	1878,79,80, 81,82
DePuy, William	FB	1881
DeSantis, Mark E.	FB	1976,77,78
DeStefano, Guy J.	FB	1960
DeVasher, Damon	MTR	1994,95,96
DeVine, Edmond F.	MTR	1934,37
DeVries, Lisa	WTR	1987,88,89,90
DeVries, Richard J.	FB	1962
DeWitt, Mark J.	MGO	1980,83
DeYoung, Derk D.	FB	1974
DeYoung, Matthew	FB	1996
Deacon, Andrew	FB	1876,77,78
Dean, D. Jarvis	MTN	1935,36,37
Dean, Walter	FB	1921
Deane, Raymond E.	WR	1941,42
Deardorff Jr., Earl W.	MTR	1957,58,59,60
Dearing, Carla E.	VB	1982,83
Deasley, Bryan T.	IHO	1987,88
Deaver, Angela	WGY	1980,81,82,83
Deaver, Caren	WGY	1982,83,84,86
Deaver, Dorian L.	MGY	1976,79,80
Debol, David C.	IHO	1975,76,77,78
Debryn, Ihor A.	MTN	1978,79,81,82
Dechaine, Pierre A.	IHO	1963,64,65
Decker, Alfred R.	MGY	1931
Decker, Charles W.	MTR	1938,39,40,41
Decker, Daniel	FB	1983
Deeks, Donald H.	IHO	1967,68,69,70
Defoe, George L.	WR	1922
Degener, Richard K.	MSW	1932,33,34
Dehlin Jr., C. Barry	FB	1963,64,66
Deibler, Kathryn	WSW	1990,91,93,94
Deitrick Jr., F. Lee	WR	1962,63,64
Delaney, J. Michael	MSW	1954,55,56
Dell, Richard P.	MTN	1966,67,68,69
Delzer, Marc F.	MBK	1964,67
DenBoer, Gregory L.	FB	1972,73,74
DenHerder, Christine	WSW	1976,77
DenHouter, Willard D	BB	1950,51
Denby, Edwin	FB	1895
Dendrinos, Peter C.	FB	1947
	MTR	1948,49,50
Deng, Roy F.	MBK	1924
Denhart, Rodney E.	MTR	1961,62
Denk, Gene F.	MGO	1967,68,69
Dennis, James L.	MTR	1965,66,67
Dennis, Kathleen A.	FH	1974,75,76,77
Densham, Robert L.	MTR	1963,64,65,66
Denson, Damon	FB	1993,94,95,96
Denton, John	IHO	1927
Denzin, J. David	FB	1968
Deppe, Daniel F.	WR	1954,55,56,57
DerGarabedian Jr., Michael	WR	1983,84,85

Derks, James F.	MSW	1979
Derleth, Douglas P.	MBK	1974,75
Derleth, Robert J.	FB	1942,43,45,46
	IHO	1943,44
Derr, Bree	FH	1993,94,95,96
Derricks, Leon	MBK	1993,94
Derricotte, Gene A	FB	1944,46,47,48
Dersch, John W.	MSW	1934
Deskins Jr., Donald R.	FB	1958,59
	MTR	1957,58,59
Desmarais, Rene F.	MGO	1972,73,74
	IHO	1971
Detwiler, James R.	FB	1964,65,66
Detwiler, Melvin L.	MTR	1944
Dever, David S.	FB	1987
Devich, David L.	FB	1974,75
Devine, Deborah	FH	1984,85,86,87
Dewey, Richard S. (Syd)	FB	1924,25,26
Dewhirst, Daniel J.	MSW	1986,87,88,89
Di Pasquale, Richard M.	MBK	1978
Di Pietro, Marcus M.	MD	1985
DiGiacinto, Catherine	WBK	1994,95,96,97
DiMascio, Jennifer	FH	1990,91,92,93
DiMatteo, Lisa	WGO	1983,84,85,86
DiNunzio, Daniel J.	BB	1962,64,65
DiPaolo, Donald G.	FB	1975,76,77
Diaz-Perez, Leticia	WTN	1978
Dibble, William B.	MTR	1933
Dickerson, Marianne M.	WTR	1979
Dickerson, Marshall L.	MTR	1958,59,60,61
Dickey, Brian J.	FB	1977,78,79,81
Dickey, James A.	BB	1957,58,59
	FB	1956,57,58
Diebolt, David P.	FB	1988,89,90,91
Diefendorf, Daniel L.	MSW	1935,36
Diemer, Brian L.	MCC	1979,80,82,83
	MTR	1980,81,82,83
Dierdorf, Daniel L.	FB	1968,69,70
	MTR	1968
Dietrich, William F.	MBK	1946
Dietz, Anthony E.	MGO	1990,91,92,93
Dietz, Diane M.	WBK	1979,80,81,82
Dietz, Suzanne	WBK	1982
Diffley, Michael J.	BB	1931,32,33
Diggins, John H.	BB	1979
Diggs, Gerald C.	FB	1978,79,80
Dill, Craig H.	MBK	1964,65,66,67
Dill, Scott	MSW	1994,95
Dill, Susan	WSW	1987,88
Dillard, Roosevelt	FB	1981
Dillay, Jeannette	SB	1979
Diller, Andrew P.	MTR	1988,89,90,91
Dimcheff, David	MCC	1989
Dingman, Dean R.	FB	1987,88,89,90
Dingman, Robert W.	FB	1951,52
Diorio, Gerald J.	FB	1980,81,82,83
Disher, Dan C.	BB	1983,84,85,86
Ditchendorf, Heidi	FH	1980,81,83
Dixon, Thomas M.	FB	1980,81,82,83
Dixon, William R.	MTN	1963,64,66
Doane, Thomas E.	FB	1968
Dobbins, Sean B.	MBK	1990,91,93
Dobbs, Kyle	MGO	1994,95,96,97
Dober, Bernard	MTN	1940
Dobosy, Lynn B.	MTR	1975,76,77,78
Dobreff, David	FB	1990,92
Dobson, John S.	MTR	1939,40,41
Dobson, Russell T.	MBK	1939
	BB	1939,40
Dobson, W. Teddy	MTR	1977,78,79,80
Dobson, Warren T.	MTR	1977,78,79,80
Dobson, William T.	MTR	1940,41
Dodd, William A.	MBK	1961
	FB	1962,63
Dodge III, Charles H.	BB	1984,85,87,88
Dodge, Henry R.	MTN	1892
Doherty, Robert C.	FB	1989,90,91,92
Dohring, Thomas E.	FB	1987,88,89,90
Dolan, James L.	MTR	1965,66,67,68
Dolan, Thomas I.	MTR	1948,49
Dolan, Tom	MSW	1994,95,96
Dole III, Arthur	BB	1947,48
Dollenberg, Eric P.	MGO	1962,65
Dollwet, Helmar H.A.	MTR	1955,56,57
Domhoff, Vic	FB	1924,26,27
Domm, Paul D.	IHO	1966,67,68,69
Domzal, David A.	MTN	1969,71
Don Carlos, Barbara	WSW	1979,80
Donahoe, Theron	WR	1926,27,28
Donahue, Mark J.	FB	1975,76,77
Donakowski, Gerard A.	MCC	1978,81,82
	MTR	1981,82,83
Donakowski, William J.	MCC	1974,75,76,77
	MTR	1975,76,77,78
Donaldson, Kirk	MD	1975

Donati, Autumn	WGY	1994,95,96,97
Donley, Richard C.	MBK	1958,59,60,61
Donnelly, Robert J.	MTR	1963,65,66
Donovan, Mary	WBK	1978
Donovan, Patrice	WBK	1981,82
Donovan, Percy J.	MTN	1910
Dooley, Geoffrey H.	MTR	1952,53,54,55
Dopp, Richard	MGY	1992,93,94,95
Dorgan, Jill	WSW	1987,88
Dorn, Edward	FB	1884
Dorney, Richard W.	MSW	1970,72,73
Dorney, William A.	MSW	1968
Dott, Richard	FB	1880
Dottin, Lance D.	FB	1988,89,90,91
Doty Jr., Alfred L.	FB	1967
Doty, Jane	VB	1976,77,78,79
Dotzauer, Barry S.	FB	1971,72,73
Dougall, William R.	MTR	1931
Dougall Jr., William R.	FB	1961
Doughty, Glenn M.	FB	1969,70,71
Douglas, Donald C.	MTR	1921,22
Douglas, Jerry L.	MSW	1989
	MTR	1990,91
Douglass, Leslie	FB	1930,31
Douglass, Prentiss	FB	1908
Dougovito, Carl	WR	1929,30,31
Doutt, Connie	WBK	1982,83,84,85
Dow, Peter A.	MSW	1953,54,55
Downes, Harold	IHO	1950,51
Downey, Ryan	MSW	1991
Downie, Gordon H.	MSW	1974,75,76,77
Downing Jr., Franklin G.	IHO	1983,84,85,86
Downing, Joe K.	MBK	1931
Downing, Matthew M.	IHO	1987,88,89
Downing, Stuart F.	MGY	1981,83,84,85
Downing, Walter T.	FB	1975,76,77
Doyle, Leo H.	MBK	1941,42,43
Doyle, Richard F.	MBK	1924,25,26
	MTR	1925,26
Doyle, William A.	MBK	1949,50
Dozauer, Wolfgang	MGY	1957,58,59,60
Dozeman, David L.	WR	1962,63,65,66
Dozzi, Delky	IHO	1958
Drake, Donald D.	MSW	1945
Drake, Thomas E.	FB	1971,73,74
Draveling, Leo	FB	1928,29,30
Drehmann, Peter C.	FB	1967,68
	WR	1967,68
Dreifus, John	WR	1947
Dreisbach, Scott T.	FB	1995,96
Dresbach, Martha	WSW	1984,85,86
Drew, Charles	MSW	1935,36
Drew, George J.	MTR	1970,71
Drew, Susan	SS	1978,79
Drews, Michael W.	FB	1983,84
Dreyer, Walter O.	FB	1943
Dries, Raymond M.	IHO	1983,84,85
Drillock, Linda R.	WGO	1979,80,81
Driskell, Lance C.	WR	1976
Driver, John J.	BB	1931
Droste, John L.	IM-L	1940
Drouillard, Paul J.	WR	1975
Droulard, Nelson R.	MTR	1935,36
Drucker, Michael	MBK	1988,89,90
Drysdale, Taylor	MSW	1932,34,35
Dubie, Gerald	MTN	1958,59,60,62
Dubreuil, Sophia	WTR	1988,89,90
Duckworth, Julie	WGY	1987,88,89
Dudeck, Diane	WSW	1982,83,84
Dudlar, Gannon	FB	1991,92,93
Dudley Jr., E. Gerry	FB	1952
Dudley Jr., E. Samuel	MGY	1950
Dudley Jr., Thomas D.	MSW	1979,80,81,82
Dudley Sr., Thomas D.	MSW	1962,63,64
Duerr, John M.	FB	1987
Dufek, Donald E.	FB	1948,49,50
Dufek, Donald P.	FB	1973,74,75
	IHO	1973,74,75,76
Dufek, William F.	FB	1974,75,76,78
Duff, Gayle A.	MTR	1906,07,08,09
Duff, William	FB	1884
Duffy, Gregg A.	MTR	1988,89,90,92
Duffy, Ignatius	FB	1896
Duffy, James	FB	1885
Duffy, John	FB	1885,86,87,88
Duffy, Mark F.	FB	1971
Dugger, Don	FB	1951,52,53
Duke, Ned E.	MGY	1963,64,65,66
Dumont, John H.	MSW	1960,61,62,63
Dunagan, A. Scott	BB	1912,13
Dunakin, Fred D.	MSW	1925,26
Dunaway, Craig C.	FB	1980,81,82
Dunayczan, Walter S.	WR	1987
Dunbar, Peter G.	IHO	1972,73,74
Duncan, Debbie	WTR	1985,86

Don Dufek, Sr. is the patriarch of one of Michigan's most famous athletic families.

Dunlap, David L.	MTR	1903,04,05,06
Dunleavy, George	FB	1922
Dunn, Douglas B.	IHO	1952,53,54
Dunn, John	FB	1920
Dunn, Roland	FB	1916,19
Dunne, Arthur L.	FB	1949,50,51,52
Dunne, Maurice	FB	1914,15,16
Dunne, Robert	FB	1918,19,20,21
	MBK	1920,21
	MTR	1920,21,22
Dunnigan, G. Richard	IHO	1954,55,56,57
Dunston, Robert L.	BB	1961,62,64
Dunton, Krista M.	WGO	1987,88
Dunton, Thomas H.	MBK	1977
Durand Jr., Harvey S.	MTN	1934
Durand, Charlotte	WBK	1989,90,91,92
Durham, James T.	BB	1986,87,88,89
Durr, John F.	MGO	1941
Durst, Michael S.	MTN	1971
Durst, Samuel J.	MTN	1939,40
Dutcher, Gerald E.	FB	1970
Duttenhofer, Stephen M.	MSW	1990,91,92,93
Dutter, George S.	MBK	1951
	FB	1952,53
Dvorak, Charles M.	MTR	1900,01,02
Dworsky, Daniel L.	FB	1945,46,47,48
	WR	1946,47
Dworsky, Leonard B.	MTR	1936
Dwyer, Glen R.	FB	1980
Dye, James L.	WR	1987,88,89,90
Dyer, Horace	FB	1893,94
Dygert, George	FB	1891,92,93,94
Dyhaldo, Chris	VB	1973,74
Dykema, Charles M.	MTR	1945
Dyksterhouse, Sara	SB	1987,88,89,90
Dyson Jr., Matthew	FB	1991,92,93,94
Dzenowagis, Anastasia	SS	1981
Dzenowagis, Joan	SS	1974,75,76,77

E

Eaddy, Donald J.	MBK	1952,53,54,55
	BB	1952,53,54,55
	FB	1951
Eagan, Elizabeth M.	FH	1973
Earle, George N.	MTR	1919,20
Eason, William H.	MTN	1936
Eastman Jr., Harry	BB	1929,31
	FB	1930
Eaton, D.	MGO	1903
Eaton, Donald R.	FB	1970,71,73
Eaton, Stanley H.	MTN	1915
Eaves, Murray J.	IHO	1979,80
Ebert, Linsey	VB	1995,96
Eccleston, Michael G.	MTR	1990,91,92,93
Eck, Jennifer	WSW	1987,88,89,90
Eckle, John J.	MGY	1953,57,58
Eckner, Charles	MTR	1931
Eddy, Darryl K.	MCC	1987,88,89
	MTR	1988
Eddy, David G.	MCC	1971,73
	MTR	1971
Eddy, William D.	MD	1977
Eder, Joyce Wilson	WTR	1983,84,85,86
Edgar, Vernon G.	BB	1925,26
Edmunds, William	FB	1909,10
Edwards, Kimbery	VB	1982,83,84
Edwards, Mike	MTR	1996
Edwards, R.T.	BB	1877
Edwards, Stanley J.	FB	1977,79,80,81
Edwards, Thomas	FB	1924,25
Edwards, Tom	FB	1877,78,79
Edwards, Willie L.	MBK	1966,67,68,69

Efstatos, John N.	MTN	1982,83
Egan, John	FB	1895
Egert, Howard E.	MTR	1940
Eggle, Christopher	MTR	1993,94
	MCC	1993,94,95
Egleston, Hawley	MTR	1931,32,33
Ehle, Craig B.	MGY	1985,86,87,88
Ehresman, Charles J. Jr.	BB	1934
Einbinder, Irving M.	MSW	1943,47,48
Eisley, John	MTR	1944
Elam, Vincent S.	BB	1980,81
Elbin, William J.	WR	1983,84,85
Elconin, Elise	WGO	1981
Eldred, Dale L.	FB	1955
Eldridge, Clarence	BB	1910
Eldridge, Morton	WR	1950
Elezovic, Peter	FB	1992,93
Elias, Harry M.	MTR	1969,72
Ellerby Jr., H. Thomas	MTR	1932,33,34
Ellerby, Richard G.	MTR	1934
Elliot, Harold W.	BB	1922
Elliot, Irwin E.	IHO	1936
Elliot, Sue	WSW	1980
Elliott, Bruce N.	FB	1969,70,71
Elliott, Chalmers W.	BB	1947,48
	FB	1946,47
Elliott, Daniel R.	MTR	1982,83,84
Elliott, David L.	FB	1971,73,74
Elliott, E. Matthew	FB	1988,89,90,91
Elliott, Edwin M.	WR	1928,29
Elliott, John	FB	1984,85,86,87
Elliott, Jonathon M.	IHO	1982,83,84,85
Elliott, Marc	FB	1991,92
Elliott, Peter R.	MBK	1945,46,47,48
	FB	1945,46,47,48
	MGO	1946,47,48,49
Elliott, Richard G.	MTN	1925
Elliott, Stephen J.	MCC	1975,76,78
	MTR	1976,77,78,79
Elliott, Stewart C.	MSW	1950,51,52
Ellis, David J.	MSW	1977,78,79
Ellis, Gregory A.	FB	1970,71,72
Ellis, Joseph	FB	1934
Ellison, John	BB	1991
	FB	1991
Ellison, Vickie	WGY	1978
Ellman, Seymour S.	MTN	1940
Ellsworth, Carl R.	MGY	1931,32
Ellsworth, Michael K.	WR	1993,94,95
Elmblad, Thomas R.	MTR	1948,50,51
Elston, Michael	FB	1994,95,96
Elwood, Michael H.P.	BB	1970,71,72
Ely, Gilbert C.	MBK	1922,23
Ely, William H.	MGO	1975,76
Elzinga, Mark G.	FB	1974,75
Embs, William	FB	1907,08
Emerling, Stanley J.	FB	1948
Emerman, Maxwell V.	BB	1906,07
Emery, John H.	MBK	1918,19
Emery, John R.	MGO	1937,39,40
Emmett, Robert A.	MSW	1937
Emmons, Harold H. Sr.	BB	1899
Emmons, Walter T.	BB	1914,15
Engebous, Doris	VB	1973
Engel, I. Jeffrey	MTR	1959,60,61
Engelbrecht, Kirsten	WTR	1987,88,89,90
Englander, Meryl E.	FB	1947
Englehart, Harry A.	MGO	1966,67
English, Anne	VB	1985
English, Joseph C.	FB	1982
Enzenroth, Clarence H.	BB	1908,09,10
Epler, Katherine	FH	1990
Epstein, Robert A.	MTN	1971
Erben, Robert F.	MBK	1948
	FB	1948,49
Erdmann, Frederick W.	BB	1980,81,82,83
Erenberg, Mark E.	MGY	1961
Erhardt, Mark D.	FB	1987
Erickson, Arnie	MTR	1929
Erickson, Jon D.	MTN	1956,57,58,59
Eriksson, D. Scott	MTR	1981,82,83,84
Erley, Duncan S.	MGY	1951,52
Ernst, Gary C.	WR	1971,72,73,74
Ernst, Robert E.	MGO	1945
Ernsting, Thomas D.	MSW	1979,80,81,82
Erpenbeck, Anthony W.	BB	1980
Erskine, A. Randy	MGO	1967,68,69,70
Erwin, Gary L.	MGY	1962,63,64,65
Eskie, Milton J.	MTN	1935
Espie, Solomon	MTR	1967,68,69
Esselstyn, Caldwell B.	MSW	1987,88,89
Esselstyn, Jane	WSW	1984,85
Estes, L.E.	MGO	1907
Etchells, E. Widmer	IHO	1933
	MTR	1934,35,36
Etterbeek, Jeffrey J.	MTN	1976,77,78,79
Ettl, Conrad J.	MGY	1949,50,51,52
Evans, Allison B.	MTN	1932
Evans, Anthony J.	BB	1980,81,82
Evans, Arthur L.	MBK	1934,35,36
Evans, Douglas B.	IHO	1989,90,91,92
Evans, Gilbert	MD	1943,46,47,48
Evans, James R.	MTN	1946
Evans, Laura	WSW	1987,88
Evans, Lynn R.	FB	1957,57
Evans, Michael J.	FB	1988,89,90,91
Evans, Richard E.	MGO	1949,50,51,52
Evans, Robert L.	MTR	1950,51,52,53
Evans, Stephen	FB	1994
Evans, Steven L.	BB	1967,68
Evashevski Jr., Forest	FB	1962,63,64
	MGO	1963,64,65
Evashevski Sr., Forest J.	BB	1938,39,40
	FB	1938,39,40
Evashevski, James A.	FB	1962
	MGO	1965,66
	WR	1963,64
Evashevski, Tom H.	WR	1973,74,75
Evashevski, William L.	WR	1977,78
Eveland, DeForest H.	MBK	1931,32,33
Eveland, Thomas S.	MBK	1960,61
Everhardus, Chris	FB	1934,35
Everhardus, Herman	FB	1931,32,33
Everhardus, John A.	MGO	1958,60
Everitt, Steven M.	FB	1989,90,91,92
Everly, David F.	BB	1988,89,90,91
Everson, Gregory C.	BB	1985,86,87
Ewend, Kurt	MBK	1957
Ewing, Donald J.	MD	1965
Eyke, Walter	FB	1906
Eyster, George W.	MD	1949,50

F

Fabello, John T.	IHO	1936,37,38
Fabian, Richard R.	MSW	1986,87
Fabergas, Troy P.	MGY	1989
Fabyan, August E.	FB	1936
	MTR	1939
Faculak, Scott	MTR	1994,95
Fagan, Timothy W.	WR	1980,81,82,83
Fagge Jr., Ralph D.	BB	1952,53,54,55
Fairclough, Neil A.	MTR	1979,80
Fairman, Andrew R.	BB	1989,90,91
Fairman, Paul C.	MSW	1974
Fairservis, Walter	MTR	1945
Falb, R. Montgomery	MGY	1971,72,73,74
Falconer, Robert P.	IHO	1971,72,73,74
Falk, Merle W.	IHO	1968,69,70,71
Fallek, Stacey	WTN	1981
Faller, Courtney	MSW	1993,94,95
Fancett, Robert V.	BB	1950
	MTR	1947,50
Fancher, Paul S.	BB	1950,51,52,53
Farabee, Ben G.	FB	1962,63,64
Farabee, David A.	FB	1965,66,67,68
Farah, William	MTN	1996
Fardig Jr., David J.	MGO	1979,80,81
	IHO	1981
Fardig, Don R.	MGO	1973,74,75
	IHO	1973,74,75,76
Farley, Patricia	FH	1988,89
Farley, William W.	MSW	1963,64,65,66
Farnick, Myron M.	BB	1943,44
Farmer, Douglas	FB	1937
Farnham, Thad	FB	1895,96
Farnsworth, William H.	MSW	1937,38
Farquhar, Leslie	WSW	1981
Farrand, Royal	FB	1887
	MTR	1887,88
Farrell, Sanford W.	MTR	1938
Farrer, Richard D.	FB	1948,49,50
Farris, Lovell L.	MBK	1957,58,59,60
Fashbaugh, Richard H.	MGY	1948,49
Faul, Lawrence J.	FB	1955,56,57
Faulkner, Ross H.	MTR	1937,38,39
Fauquier, Henry E.	MTN	1961,62,63,64
Fay, Stanley	FB	1931,32,33
Fead Jr., George S.	BB	1957,58,59,60
Feaster, Rodney L.	FB	1978,79
	MTR	1980
Feaster, Curtis D.	FB	1989
Feazell, Juaquin L.	FB	1995,96
Federico, Eric C.	FB	1968,69
Federov, Anton	IHO	1994
Fediuk, Arthur W.	FB	1973
Fedrigo, Laura	WSOC	1995
Feely, Fred	MGO	1924,25,26
Feely, Thomas J.	FB	1995,96
Fegan, Thomas J.	MBK	1954,55,56,57
Fehrs, Robert L.	WR	1964,65,66,67
Fehsenfeld, Frank B.	MD	1935,36
Feinberg, Barry N.	MGY	1957,58,59,60
Feinberg, Martin	MBK	1946
Feinsinger, Nathan P.	MTR	1925,26
Feiock, W. Anthony	WR	1962,63,64,65
Feiock, Jennifer	WGY	1985
Feldman, Brian	BB	1991
Feldman, Evan	MGY	1993,94
Feldman, Lorea	WBK	1985,86,87
Feldman, Zachary	WR	1995
Felker, Crawford L.	MTR	1928,29
Felker, H.	MGO	1902,03
Fellin, Phillip C.	FB	1985
Felsner, Dennis W.	IHO	1989,90,91,92
Felten, Jeffrey L.	FB	1979,80
Felver, Howard	FB	1896,97
Fenner, Lewis T.	MGY	1961,62
Fenske, Frederic C.	MSW	1931,32,33
Fenson, Rebecca R.	WSW	1986,87,88,89
Fenton, James M.	MCC	1978
Ferar, Robert D.	MGY	1933
Ferbert, Gustave	FB	1893,94,95,96
Ferchau, Thomas D.	FB	1969,72
Ferens, John A.	FB	1983
Ferguson, Charles W.	BB	1914,15
Ferguson, Donald L.	MSW	1954
Ferguson, Howard S.	BB	1932
Ferguson, Kent M.	MD	1982,83,84,85
Ferguson, Philip L.	MTR	1986,87,88,90
Ferguson, Robert B.	IHO	1963,64,65,66
Ferner, Carl F.	BB	1936
Fernstenfeld, Adolf	MSW	1938,39
Ferrelli, Marcus A.	BB	1953,54,55,56
Ferris, John H.	MTR	1914
Fertig, Melinda	WBK	1976,77
	WTN	1976,77
Ferullo, Matthew	BB	1993,94,95
Fester, Thomas W.	FB	1977,78
Feustel, Robert K.	MTR	1931
Fichtner, Rustin W.	FB	1988,89
Field, Jayson	MSW	1991
Fielder, Kris L.	MBK	1978
Fielding, Jaimie L.	WTN	1992,93,94,95
Fields, Chris	MBK	1994
Fiero, Carl D.	WR	1934
Fife, Danny W.	MBK	1968,69,70
	BB	1968,69,70,71
Fife, Dugan	MBK	1992,93,95,96
Fife, Robert	IHO	1941
	MGO	1941,42,43
Filer, Edward L.	MTN	1985,86,87
Filip, Donald J.	MGY	1964
Fillichio, Michael E.	FB	1957,58,59
Fillion, Thomas J.	WR	1974,75
Finch, Macklyn W.	BB	1952,53,54
Fine, Jerome L.	FB	1971,72,72
Fink, Karl V.	WR	1958,59,60,61
Finkbeiner, Dean E.	BB	1954,56,57,58
Finken, Steven M.	BB	1986,87,88
Finlayson, James	MCC	1991,92,93
	MTR	1992,93,94
Finn, Michael J.	MTR	1980,81,82
Fischbach, Mary	WD	1984,87,88
Fischbach, Peter	MTN	1966,67,68,69
Fischburg, Paul R.	MGY	1978
Fischer, Bradley C.	FB	1981
Fischer, Bruce N.	MTR	1957,58,59
Fischer, John Jr.	MGO	1932,33,35
Fischer, Richard O.	MTR	1921
Fischer, Robert H.	FB	1943
Fischley, Barbara S.	WTN	1979
Fish, David J.	FB	1971,72,72
Fishbach, Peter	MTN	1966,67,68,69
Fishburn, Dan G.	MSW	1971,72,73,74
Fisher II, Andrew E.	BB	1965,66,67,68
Fisher II, Frederick B.	BB	1960,61,62,63
Fisher, David R.	FB	1964,65,66
Fisher, James	IHO	1926,27,29
Fisher, John G.	WR	1985,87,88,89
Fishleigh, Walter T.	MTR	1901,02
Fishman, Benjamin	MSW	1930
Fishman, Emanuel	MBK	1933,34
Fishman, Herman	BB	1936,37,38
Fishman, Milton	BB	1942,43
Fishman, Steven F.	MBK	1967,70
Fitch, Alan D.	FB	1949
Fitzgerald, J. Dennis	FB	1959,60
	WR	1958,59,60,61
Fitzgerald, J. Patrick	FB	1987
Fitzgerald, Wayne R.	MBK	1940
Fitzgibbons, David W.	MCC	1930
	MTR	1930
Fitzhugh, E. Lee	MSW	1956,57,58
Fitzpatrick, Bridget	SB	1989,90

Randy Erskine (1968-70) was a two-time All-American selection in golf for Michigan.

Fitzpatrick, Christopher	MTR	1981,82,84,85
Fitzsimmons, Thomas R.	MTR	1988
Flagg, Thomas L.	MTR	1968,69,71
Flaherty, Debbie	WSOC	1994,95
Flaherty, Sharon	WSW	1978,79,80,81
Flanagan, Dennis	FB	1965
Flannelly, Timothy M.	BB	1989,90,91
Fleischman, M. Richard	FB	1948
Fleisig, Jonathan D.	BB	1986
Fleming, Al	MSW	1996
Fleming, Kim	WSW	1977,78,79,80
Fleming, Peter B.	MTN	1974
Fleming, Richard H.	MGY	1934
Fleming, Robert S.	IHO	1948,49
Fleming, William W.	MBK	1983,84
Flermoen, Jeff	MSW	1996
Flesher, Marion B.	BB	1899,1900,01
Fleszar, Thomas J.	BB	1968,69,70,71
Fletcher, Harold K.	MTR	1944,45
Fletcher, Owen R.	IHO	1974
Fleury, Matthew J.	BB	1994,95,96
Flick, Jesse E.	MTN	1936,37
Floden, Dennis E.	MSW	1959,60,61,62
Flodin, Richard H.	MTR	1954,55,56,57
Floersch, Harold J.	BB	1937
	FB	1936
Flom, Sara A.	WGY	1977,78,79,80
Flood, Brian M.	MTN	1962,63,64,65
Flora, Robert L.	FB	1939,40,41
Flora, William	FB	1924,25,26
Florence, William C.	WR	1961,62
Floreno, Annemarie	WTN	1987
Flourney, Thomas	MTR	1897,98,99,00
Flowers II, Carl V.	BB	1967
	MTR	1968
Floyd, Christopher M.	FB	1994,95,96
Fogarty, Richard B.	FB	1929
Foley, Jennifer	FH	1992
Folkertsma, David L.	FB	1985,86,87
Folse, Bectel	WGY	1978
Foltz, James	FB	1945
Fonde, Henry	FB	1945,46,47
Fontanna, Stanley G.	MTR	1916,17
Fonville, Charles	MTR	1946,47,48,50
Forbes, David A.	MTR	1918,21
Forbis, Kelly	SB	1990,91,92,93
Ford, George B.	MBK	1934
	BB	1935
Ford, Gerald R.	FB	1932,33,34
Ford, Gregory M.	MBK	1975
Ford, James A.	MSW	1952,53
Ford, Jody	WSW	1978,79
Ford, Len	FB	1945,46,47
Ford, Rodney A.	MBK	1968,69,70,71
Ford, William Clay	MTN	1944
Forhan, Craig G.	BB	1972,73,74,75
Forhan, Gary D.	BB	1976
Forrest, George H.	IHO	1961,63,64
Forrestal, Mary	FH	1973,74
Forrestel, Colleen	WGY	1978,79
Forrestel, Julia	FH	1980,81
Forrestel, Richard E.	MTR	1944,45,47
Forrestel, Sara	FH	1980,81,82
Forsyth, Ian	MCC	1991,92,93,94
	MTR	1992,93,94,95
Forsythe, Steven A.	BB	1966,67,68,69
Fortman, Darlene	WTR	1983,84
Fortune, William	FB	1917,18,19
Fortus, Robert S.	MTR	1971
Fosdick, Ann	SS	1974
Foss, Randall E.	MTR	1975,76,77,78
Foster, Brian	FB	1992

Foster, Che	FB	1992,93,94
Foster, Christine	WTR	1993
Foster, Julie A.	SB	1989,90,91
Foster, Mari	SB	1984,85,86,87
Foster, Mark C.	MCC	1974,75,76,77
	MTR	1975,76,77,78
Foster, Paul A.	MSW	1973,74,76
Foster, Suzanne C.	WCC	1979,80,81,82
	WTR	1980,81,82,83
Foster, Walter S.	MTR	1901,02
Fountain, John R.	BB	1909
Foussianes, George B.	BB	1977,78,79,80
Fox, Bruce A.	BB	1955,56,57
Fox, Chris	IHO	1995,96
Fox, George B.	MTR	1915,16
Fox, Gregory B.	IHO	1973,74,75,76
Fox, James W.	FB	1953,54,55
Fox, John P.	FB	1975,76
Fox, William W.	MTR	1966
Fracassi, Todd	BB	1992
Fraleigh, Timothy L.	MCC	1987
France, Richard	FB	1898,99
Francis III, Thomas	MGY	1958,60
	MDV	1958
Francis, Alan J.	FB	1968,69
Francis, Ann Louise	WSW	1991,92,94
Franden, Meredith	FH	1993,94,95,96
Frangione, Rob	MTR	1996
Frank, Karen E.	SB	1979
Franklin, Dennis E.	FB	1972,73,74
Franklin, Glenn A.	FB	1971,74
Franklin, Wilbert A.	BB	1959,60
	FB	1958
Franks Jr., Julius	FB	1941,42
Franks, Dennis J.	FB	1972,73,74
Fraser, John	MGO	1950,51,52
Fraser, John H.	MTN	1963,64,65
Fraser, Steven H.	WR	1977,78,79,80
Fraumann, Harlin E.	FB	1940,41
Fraumann, Willard G.	MBK	1967,68,69,70
Frazer, Richard D.	FB	1984
Frazier, Raymond V.	MTR	1936
Frecska, Sandor A.	MGY	1963,64,65
Fredal, Thomas M.	BB	1980
Frederick, Michael J.	MTR	1986
Freeborn, Guy C.	MTR	1925
Freed, Eugene	FB	1947
Freedman, Mark I.	MTN	1977
Freedman, Seymour	WR	1933,34
Freedman, Zack	FB	1993
Freedson, Patty	WTN	1974
Freehan, Tim	BB	1995,95
Freehan, William A.	BB	1960,61
	FB	1960
Freeman, Barbara	WTN	1979
Freeman, Brian K.	WR	1994
Freeman, Dwayne	FB	1986
Freeman, Elaine	WSW	1982
Freeman, Ernest	IHO	1933
Freeman, J. Paul	FB	1918
Freeman, Richard H.	WR	1945
Freeney, Charles	FB	1909
Freese, Ernest J.	MTR	1929
Freihofer, Cecil	FB	1944,45
Freihofer, Walter B.	FB	1942
French, Edward B.	MTR	1905,06,07
French, Maurice P.	BB	1879,80
Frescoln, Christopher	IHO	1994,95,96,97
Freund, Raynor	FB	1892,93,94,95
Freyberg, Richard H.	MTR	1924,25,26
Fricker, Paul D.	IHO	1980,81
Friedberg, Linda	WSW	1987
Friedler, Eric M.	MTN	1973,74,75,76
Friedman, Benny	FB	1924,25,26
	BB	1925
Fries, Charles C.	MSW	1943,44,45,46
Fries, Peter H.	MSW	1957,58,59
Fritz, Ralph C.	FB	1938,39,40
Froeming, Charles S.	MGY	1967,68,69
Froemke, Gerald	FB	1917,18
	BB	1919,20
Froemke, Harlan	BB	1925
Frohock, Stephani S.	WTR	1990,91
Frolik, James R.	MTN	1944
Fromm, Charles B.	FB	1980,81,82
Fronczak, Richard S.	WR	1958,59,60
Froning, Charles C.	BB	1981,82,83,84
Frosheiser, Edwin W.	BB	1948,50
Frowick Jr., Lawrence H.	MGY	1970
Frumkes, Joseph	IHO	1932
Fruth, Stacie J.	WSW	1986,87,88,89
Frutig, Edward A.	MGO	1982
Frutig, Edward C.	FB	1938,39,40
Fry, Jamie	FH	1982,83,84
Fryling, C. Victor	BB	1948,49,50
Frysinger, Terry R.	FB	1968
Fudala, Lynn	WCC	1979,80,81
	WTR	1980,81
Fulkman, Edward A.	MSW	1945
Fuller, Charles R.	MGY	1964,65,66,67
Fuller, Frederic	FB	1925,27
Fuller, J. Philip	MGY	1964,65,66,67
Fulton, Barbara	SS	1975,76
Fulton, John A.	BB	1870
Fulton, Frank A.	MTN	1957,58,59,60
Funk, Kim	SB	1987
Fuog, Russell J.	FB	1932,33,34
Fuqua, Dwayne	MTR	1995,96
Furdak, Edward J.	MSW	1953,54
Furgason, Mary	SB	1980
Furlong, Christine A.	WGY	1988,89,90
Furst, David A.	MTR	1975,76,77

G

Gabel, Norman	FB	1925,26,27
Gabler, Cornelius	IHO	1926,27,33
Gabler III, Wallace F.	FB	1965
Gabler Sr., John H.	FB	1967,68,69
Gacek, Walter F.	IHO	1946,47,48,49
Gafill, David L.	MTR	1931
Gagalis, Peri	FB	1952,53,54
Gage III, Walter H.	MSW	1979,80,81,82
Gagin, Christopher J.	BB	1987,88,89
Gagnet, Alan J.	MD	1970
Gagnier, Edward R.	MGY	1955,56,57,58
Gagnon, Bernard J.	HO	1969,70,71,72
Gagnon, Jean C.	WGY	1972,73,74
Galbraith, Douglas D.	IHO	1966,67,68,69
Galbreath, Andy	BB	1996
Galipeau, Roger C.	IHO	1962,64
Gallagher Jr., John M.	FB	1943
Gallagher, David D.	FB	1971,72,73
Gallagher, James T.	MTN	1975,76
Gallagher, Sean W.	MSW	1988,89
Gallaher, James F.	BB	1879,80,81,82
Galles, James O.	WR	1940,41,42, 44,45
Gallier, Michelle	WTR	1986,87
Gallo, Doris	WGO	1982
Gallon, Jack E.	WR	1950,51,52,53
Galster, Andrew	WR	1926
Galt, Martin	FB	1913
Gamble, Hugh	MTR	1911,12
Gamble, Walter	MTR	1891
Gamon, Thomas H.	MTN	1940,41,42
Gamsby, Paul C.	IHO	1968,69,70,71
Gannon, Cindy	WSW	1984
Gant, Anthony K.	FB	1982,83,84, 85,86
Garbar, Jesse G.	FB	1935,36
Garcia, Ricardo A.	MTN	1977
Gardner Jr., Jack F.	WR	1975
Gardner, Kenneth	MTR	1978,79,80,81
Gardner, Linda F.	WBK	1977
Gardner, Neil	MTR	1994,95,96,97
Gardner, Robert L.	MTR	1943
Gardocki, Theresa	SB	1978,79,80
Garfield, Marshall P.	MGY	1978,80,81
Garfield, Stephen	FB	1922
Gariepy, Fred A.	BB	1920
Garner, James E.	MBK	1932,33
Garner, Thad J.	MBK	1979,80,81,82
Garrels, Allen	FB	1911
Garrels, John	FB	1905,06
	MTR	1904,05,06,07
Garrett, Edward B.	FB	1982,83,84
Garrett, Thomas C.	BB	1918,19
Garris, John B.	MBK	1979,80
Garrity, Thomas J.	FB	1979,81,82
Garvey, Willard W.	MSW	1941
Garza, Mario Jr.	BB	1996
Gascoigne, Louis	BB	1884,85
Gaskins, Tracy	FH	1983,84,85,86
Gasperoni, Sergio	FB	1993
Gast, Warren E.	MBK	1949
	MGO	1953
Gaudette, Roger G.	FB	1976
Gault Jr., Frederick P.	MCC	1972,73
Gauthier, Amanda	WSOC	1994,95
Gavin, Robert F.	MSW	1971
Gawne, Samuel E.	MBK	1927,28
	BB	1928
Gawrych, Garrick A.	BB	1980
Gaxiola, Alejandro	MSW	1959,60,61
Gaxiola, Alvaro	MD	1958
Gaylord, Louis K.	WR	1925
Gaynor, Michael	BB	1988,89
	IHO	1989
Geahan, Robert R.	MBK	1945
Gear, Kenneth A.	FB	1980
Geary, Warren F.	MTR	1893
Geddes, John D.	MGY	1965,66,67
Gedeon, Elmer	FB	1936,37,38
	MTR	1938,39
	BB	1938,39
Gedeon, Walter	FB	1928
Gee, John A.	MBK	1935,36,37
	BB	1935,36,37
Gehrs, Melinda	WSW	1990,91,92,93
Geiger, Deborah A.	WGY	1990,91,92,93
Geiger, Franz A.	MTN	1985,86,88
Geisler, Stephen H.	FB	1980
Geist, Franklin H.	MTR	1958,59,60,61
Geisthardt, Rachael	FH	1992,93,94,95
Gelderloos, Allen B.	MSW	1985
Geller, Andrew L.	MTN	1971,72
Gembis, Joseph	FB	1927,28,29
Gemmell, Bruce M.	MSW	1980,81,82,83
Gemmell, Robert	FB	1882,23
Gendler, Wendy	WSW	1994,95,96,97
Genebach, Lowell	FB	1917
	BB	1918,20,21
Genova, Robert	MSW	1993,94
Gentile, Melissa	SB	1997
Gentles, Lukeland S.	MTR	1990,91,92,93
Genyk, George W.	FB	1957,58,59
George, Edward	WR	1926,29
Gereg, Bud	FB	1987
Gerich, Bryn	WTR	1992,93
Gerich, Jerry W.	MTR	1960,61
Gerlach, Jozsef	MD	1959,60
Gerometta, Robert M.	MTR	1964,65,66,67
Gerring, Joel	FB	1995,95
Gess, Richard S.	MGY	1953
Geyer, H. Ronald	FB	1952,53,54
Geyer, Paul W.	MBK	1950,51
	BB	1950
Ghekas, Paul M.	FB	1983,84
Ghindia, John R.	FB	1984
Ghindia, John V.	FB	1948,49
Ghio, Craig L.	MGO	1971,72,73,74
Ghiron, Karen	WGY	1985,86
Gholston, Darold	MTR	1978,80,81
Giancamilli, Vanessa	WCR	1997
Gibas, Ronald T.	MBK	1983,85,86,87
Gibbs, Douglas R.	MTR	1973,75,76,77
Gibbs, Lisa	WTN	1987
Gibbs, Tracy	FH	1979,80
Gibert, Ralph W.	MBK	1943
Gibson Jr., E. Clark	IHO	1955
Gibson, Edward C.	BB	1923
Gibson, Edzra	MTR	1994,95,96
Gibson, L. Bryan	MTR	1958,59,60,61
Gibson Jr., Mamon	MTR	1957,58,59
Gibson, Robert D.	MTR	1923
Giddings, Allan M.	BB	1907,08
Giesler, Jon W.	FB	1976,77,78
Gilbert, M. Allen	MTN	1942
Gilbert, Jennifer	WTR	1991
Gilbert, Joseph	WR	1991,92
Gilbert, Louis	FB	1925,26,27
Gilbert, Monroe	MTN	1942
Gilbert, Robert K.	MBK	1943,44
Gilchrest, George C.	MTR	1971,72
Giles, Gregory M.	IHO	1969
Giles, William b.	BB	1924,25
Gilfillan, Gray	FH	1973
	WBK	1974
Gilhooley, Robert M.	BB	1963,64,65,66
Gilhooly, Karen	WBK	1977
Gill, David	FB	1899
Gillanders, J. David	MSW	1959,60,61
Gillard, Ellsworth	WR	1922
Gilles, Kevin S.	BB	1985,86
Gillette, V. Michael	BB	1986,87,88
	FB	1985,86,87,88
Gillis, John C.	IHO	1941,42
	MSW	1940
Gillispie, Nannette	WBK	1986,87
Gilmore, Keith L.	FB	1976
Gilmore, Tom	FB	1881,12,83
Ginn, Douglas R.	MBK	1925,26
Gipson, Frederick V.	MBK	1942,43
Girard, Katherine	WSW	1991,92
Girardin, Glenn H.	BB	1954,55,56,57
Girgash, Paul E.	FB	1979,80,81,82
Giroux, Philip H.	MBK	1982,83,84,85
Gittins, Robert B.	WR	1944,45
Glading, Ben	MTR	1931,32
Gladstone, Edwin G.	FB	1918
Glas, Wayne	MTR	1942,43,44
Glass, Kevin	MSW	1991,92
Glasser, Joseph H.	MBK	1940,41
Gleason, Bridget	WTR	1986
Gleason, Kathryn	SB	1993,94,95,96
Glendinning, Wil	IHO	1968,69
Glenn, Burdette	BB	1918,19
Glidden, Dean E.	BB	1938
Glidden, Steve	FB	1889
Glinka, David J.	FB	1960,61,62
Glover, Fred Jr.	MGO	1925,26,27
Gluck, Myron H.	MGY	1968,69,71
Gluppe, George R.	MTR	1954,56,57
Gnatkowski, Lori	WBK	1981,82,83,84
Goble, Rodney	BB	1992,93,94,95
Goch, David P.	MSW	1985,86,87,88
Godfrey, Christopher J.	FB	1978,79
Godfrey, William J.	MTN	1982
Goebel, Jerry	FB	1954,55,57
Goebel, Paul	FB	1920,21,22
Goetz, Angus	FB	1917,18,19,20
Goff, Daniel G.	IHO	1984,85
Goff, Patrick M.	IHO	1983,84,85,86
Gold, Gary W.	MTR	1967,69
Gold, Ian	FB	1996
Goldberg, Daniel E.	MTN	1986,87,88,89
Goldberg, Jan	VB	1973
Golder, Kurt M.	MGY	1975,76,77
Goldfarb, Jennifer	WTN	1990
Goldman, Edward	IHO	1920,21
Goldsmith, DuVal	FB	1931
Goldsmith, Jack	MGY	1931
Goldsmith, Joseph	MTN	1927
Goldsmith, Paul H.	IHO	1940,41,42
Goldsmith, Robert C.	MSW	1929,30
Goldstein, Louis	WR	1925
Goldthwaite, David L.	FB	1975
Goldwater, Leonard J	MTR	1923
Golen, Greg J.	FB	1973
Golombisky, Jeffrey L.	FB	1974
Gonzales, Andrea	WTN	1987
Gonzales-Virgil, Augusto	MSW	1972
Gooch, Gregory	MSW	1990,91,92,93
Good, Patricia	WGO	1990,91,92,93
Goode, Michael M.	MGO	1959,61,63
Goodill, William E.	WR	1981,82,83,84
Gooding, Cecil	FB	1903
Goodlow, Amos L.	WR	1976,77
Goodson, Calvin A.	MTR	1985,86,87
Goodwell, John	FB	1916,17
Goodwin, Harold	FB	1995,96
Goodwin, Irving	MTR	1904,05,06
Gora, Ronald F.	MSW	1952,53,54,55
Gordon Sr., Aaron Z.	MTR	1949,50,51,52
Gordon, Christopher	IHO	1991,92,93,94
Gordon, Eva	WGY	1990,91
Gordon, Jeffrey D.	MSW	1984,85,86,87
Gordon, Robb	IHO	1995
Gorman, Paul J.	MTR	1934,35
Gorte, C. Michael	FB	1964
Goshorn, Gregory K.	MSW	1969,70
Gosier, Harry L.	FB	1980,83
Goss, Thomas A.	FB	1966,67,68
Gotcher, Larry C.	WR	1988,89,90
Gottlieb, Susan	WSW	1974,75,76
Gottschalk, Luther	FB	1885
Gould, H. Mason	BB	1941
Gould, Jay	IHO	1954,55,56
Goulish, Thomas J.	BB	1949,51,52
Gourley, Donald	IHO	1957,58,59
Gow, John L.	MSW	1925,26
Grabiec, Wayne L.	MBK	1969,70,71,72
Grabovez, Leigh Anne	WSW	1983,84,85,86

Dan Goldberg (1986-89) won the Big Ten singles title twice and later served as U-M's assistant tennis coach.

Grabowski, John F.	MTR	1976
Grace, Charles	IHO	1929
Grace Jr., James	MTR	1975,76,77,78
Gracey, Clifford	FB	1916
Grade, Jeffrey D.	IHO	1982
Grady, Ben F.	MSW	1935,36,37
Graff, David A.	MGO	1965,66,67
Graff, Tara	WTN	1993,94,95,96
Graham, Henry C.	MTN	1928
Graham, Nelson A.	MTR	1965,67,68
Graham, Robert C.	IHO	1945
Graham, Walter	FB	1904,05,06,07
Grainger, Robert C.	MTR	1982,83,84,85
Grambau, Fredrick E.	FB	1969,71,72
Grand, Eric	MTN	1991,92
Grant, Corey	WR	1996,97
Grant, Emory L.	BB	1864,65,66
Grant, Gary D.	MBK	1985,86,87,88
Grant, James J.	FB	1986,87,88,89
	MTR	1986
Grant, Todd	FB	1959,60,61
Grant, Wallace D.	IHO	1946,48,49,50
Grathwohl, Casper O.	FB	1955
Graver, Herb	FB	1901,02,03
Graves III, William H.	BB	1946,47
Graves, Eric	FB	1992
Graves, Steven	FB	1976,77
Gray, J. Cameron	MTR	1958
Gray, James P.	FB	1958
Gray, Joseph C.	FB	1982,83,84
Gray, Martha	WTR	1981,82,83,84
Gray, Paul R.	BB	1889,90
Gray, Peter M.	MTR	1953,54,55,56
Gray, Ralph M.	MTR	1956
Gray, Robert G.	IHO	1961,62,63,64
Gray, Sarah	WCC	1986,87
Gray, Yeshimbra	WBK	1992,93,94
Grayson, Howard H.	BB	1940
Grbac, Elvis	FB	1989,90,91,92
Green, Donald	FB	1909,10
Green, James R.	FB	1962,63
Green, Joanne E.	FH	1988,89
Green, John B.	MTR	1939
Green, John C.	MTR	1955,57
Green, Lanny	WR	1990,91,92,93
Green II, Merritt W.	FB	1949,50,51,52
Green, Rickey	MBK	1976,77
Greenblatt, Bethany	WSOC	1995
Greenbury, Donna	WGO	1987,88
Greene, John J.	FB	1943
	WR	1942,43,44
Greening, Charles B.	IHO	1959
Greenleaf, George	FB	1893,94,95,96
Greenstein, Gail	WSW	1974,75
Greenwald, Harold	FB	1926
Greenwold, Douglas J.	MBK	1961,63,64
Greenwood, John	FB	1955,56
Greer Jr., Edward R.	FB	1944
	IHO	1944,45,47,48
Greer, W. Curtis	FB	1976,77,78,79
Gregg, John M.	MTR	1958,59,60,61
Gregor Jr., William C.	MBK	1945
	BB	1944,45
Gregory, Bruce	FB	1924,25
Gregory, George	FB	1901,02,03
Greiner, Jayna	WTR	1994,95,96
Greiner, Waldo K.	MTN	1925
Grenkoski, Edwin A.	BB	1949,50
Grenkoski, Mark E.	BB	1974,75,76,77
Gresko, Sandy	WTR	1985,85
Gretsch, Richard F.	MTR	1929
Grettenberger, John O.	BB	1984,85,86,87
Greyer, Julie	WD	1989,90
	WSW	1989,90,91,92
Griese, Brian	FB	1994,95,96
Griest, Walter F.	MTR	1916
Grieves, Christopher P.	FB	1975,76,77
Grieves, Steven	FB	1977,78
Griffin, Charles	FB	1891,92,93
Griffin, George H.	MTR	1924
Griffin, John	IHO	1949
Griffin, Michael G.	MBK	1987,88,89,90
Griffin, Pamela	VB	1985
Griffin, Sara	SB	1995,96,97
Griffith, Paul W.	MSW	1977,78,79,80
Griffiths, William A.	MGO	1937
Grimes, Edwin T.	WR	1948
Grimes, Michael C.	BB	1987,88,89
Grimshaw, Frederick J.	MSW	1929
Grinnell, Henry S.	FB	1926,27
Grinnelli, Mark P.	BB	1976
Grissen, James	MBK	1940
Groce, Alvin V.	FB	1957,58
	MTR	1957
Grodsky, Isadore	MTR	1928,29
Groffsky, Paul	MBK	1952,53,54,55
Groft, William E.	MSW	1964,66,67
Groleau, Kimberly	WSW	1977,78,80
Grosh, Lawrence	FB	1890,90,92,93
Gross, Philip G.	IHO	1966,67,68,69
Grote, Stephen J.	MBK	1974,75,76,77
Grove, Frederick W.	MTR	1965,66
Grover, Tony	MTN	1987
Groves, Frank W.	MGO	1965,66,67,68
Grube, Charles	FB	1923,24,25
Gruber, Michael T.	MD	1983,84
Grundstein, Leon D.	MTR	1967,68,69
Grunow, Robert N.	MCC	1928
Grzymkowski, Aaron J.	MTR	1990,91,92,93
Gubow, David M.	IHO	1968,71
Guidi, Larry	BB	1965,66,67,68
Guillemette, Mara	WCC	1995,96
	WTR	1996
Guinness, William M.	MTR	1957,58,59
Guise Jr., Robert F.	MTR	1950,51,52
Gulick, Merle L.	MTN	1944
Gunn, Brian	MSW	1990,91,92,93
Gupta, Minoo	WSW	1988,89,90
Gura, Raymond P.	MGY	1970,71,72,73
Gusich, Frank J.	FB	1969,70,71
Gust, Christopher L.	BB	1983,84,85,86
Gustafson Jr., Lawrence J.	BB	1974
	FB	1971,72,73
Gustin, Rachel	WSW	1994,95,96
Guthmann, Lisa	WGY	1977
Guthrie, Anne	WSW	1978
Gutowski, Frank W.	MBK	1950,51
Gutzwiller, Mark G.	FB	1988
Guynes, Thomas	FB	1993,94,95,96
Guyton, Jeffrey R.	WR	1973

H

Haas, James J.	IHO	1951,52,53,54
Hackett, James P.	FB	1976
Hackney, Randy J.	BB	1975
Hackstadt, John F.	BB	1944,45
Haddan, Luiey	WR	1997
Hadden, Harry	FB	1894
Haeger, Gregory C.	BB	1988,89,90
Haff, Carroll B.	MTR	1911,12,13
Hafner, Angela	WTR	1983,84,85,86
Hagan, James J.	WR	1969,70,71,72
Hager, harold	WR	1929
Haggarty, George S.	MBK	1923,24,25
Hagle, Anson	FB	1888,89
Hahn, Archibald	MTR	1901,02,03,04
Hahn, Richard P.	FB	1962,63,64
Haidler, William B.	MTR	1946
Haigh, John H.	MSW	1938,39,40
Haigh, R. Allyn	MTR	1917
Haimbaugh, Raymond	MTR	1911,12,13
Haines, Deborah	SB	1979,80,81,82
Hainline, Jon S.	MTN	1967,68,69,70
Hainrihar, Gary C.	FB	1972,73
Haji-Sheikh, Ali S.	FB	1979,80,81,82
Hakken, Jed	MTN	1985,86
Haldane, Mark T.	FB	1976
Halko, Steven	IHO	1993,94,95,96
Hall, Antoinette	VB	1985,86
Hall, B. Lee	FB	1959,60,61
Hall, C.H.	MTR	1911
Hall, David	MGO	1992,93
Hall, David A.	MBK	1982
	FB	1980,82,83
	MTR	1981,83,84,85
Hall, Forrest	FB	1895
Hall, Geoffrey	MTR	1939,40,41
Hall, James	FB	1996
Hall, James D.	FR	1974,75
Hall, Jon K.	MBK	1959,60,61,62
Hall, Michelle	WBK	1991,92
Hall, Morris	MTR	1901,03,04
Hall, Robert	MTN	1912,13,14
Hall, Theresa	WTR	1993,94
Hall, Valerie	WBK	1986,89,90

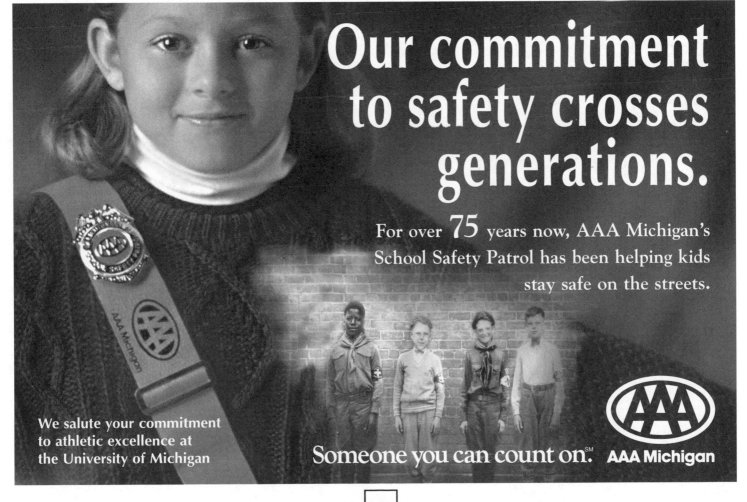

Hall, Werner W.	FB	1968,69,70
Haller, Kenneth F.	MGY	1985,86,87,88
Haller, T.	WR	1922
Hallfrisch, Janet	WTR	1978
Hallock, William W.	MGO	1960,62
Halstead, John C.	BB	1959,61
	FB	1958,59,60
Halsted, J.M.	MSW	1926,27
Halsted, Robert	MSW	1926,27
Haluscsak, Kimberly	WCC	1988,90
	WTR	1989,90
Ham Jr., Douglas K.	FB	1981,82,83
Hamady, Lloyd K.	WR	1954,56,57,58
Hamdan, Jehad	WR	1992,93,94,95
Hamer, Hiram J.	MTN	1918
Hamerski, Stephen M.	MD	1990,91
Hamilton, John A.	MD	1969,71
Hamilton, John C.	MGY	1962,63,64,65
Hamilton, Remy	FB	1994,95,96
Hammels, James V.	FB	1919
Hammer, Edward J.	MTN	1929,30,31
Hammerstein, Mark S.	FB	1983,84,85,86
Hammerstein, Michael S.	FB	1981,82,83, 84,85
Hammett II, A. Lawton	MTN	1941,42
Hammond, Dennis C.	FB	1978,79,80
Hammond, Donald J.	FB	1984,85
Hammond, George L.	MTR	1953
Hammond, Harry	FB	1904,05,06,07
Hammond, Thomas	FB	1903,04,05
Hampson, Gordon E.	IHO	1978,79,80,81
Hams, William	MSW	1990
Han, Richard	MSW	1961
Hanavan, Edmond M.	MTR	1911,12
Hancock, Walter D.	BB	1948
Hand, Eugene A.	MGO	1931,32
Handel, Michael J.	IHO	1987,88,89
Hanel, Scott A.	FB	1990
Haney, Donald J.	WR	1953,54,55,56
Haney, Thomas W.	MTN	1980,81,82,83
Hanish, Joseph	FB	1916,17
Hankins, Woodrow	FB	1993,94,95,96
Hankwitz, G. Michael	FB	1967,68,69
Hanley, Richard D.	MSW	1956,57,58,59
Hanlon, Jerry F.	FB	1969,71
Hanlon, T. Michael	FB	1982
Hanna, Bernard W.	IHO	1954,55,56,57
Hanna, Henry D.	FB	1965
Hanna, Michael R.	MGY	1931
Hanna, Robert L.	WR	1967
Hannah, Donald W.	FB	1959,60
Hannan, Frederic	FB	1897
Hannan, William W.	BB	1876
Hannifin, Gerald	MTR	1992
Hansen Jr., Rupert P.	MGY	1971,72,73,74
Hansen, Amy	WD	1987,88,89,90
Hansen, Christopher A.	MSW	1971,72,73,74
Hansen, Kirk S.	MTR	1968,70
Hansen, Kris	WBK	1979
Hansen, Lars T.	IHO	1966,67,68,69
Hansen, Wayne H.	WR	1965,66,67,68
Hanshue, Cloyce E.	FB	1934,35
Hanson, Kathryn	WGO	1994
Hansz, Andrew	MSW	1992
Hanzek, Morris F.	BB	1948
Hanzlik, Robert L.	FB	1943
Happel, Bryan	MTR	1993,94,95,96
Haratsaris, Nick	MBK	1997,97
Harbaugh, James J.	FB	1983,84,85,86
Hardell, Elmer P.	MTR	1917
Harden, Linwood	FB	1972
Harden, Michael	FB	1977,78,79
Harder Jr., Keith C.	MBK	1945,46
Harding, David M.	FB	1977
Harding, Frank	FB	1892,93
Hardy Sr., William C.	FB	1965,66
Hardy, Alan T.	MBK	1976,77,78,79
Hardy, William	BB	1992
Harless, William	FB	1886,87,90
Harlock, David	IHO	1990,91,92,93
Harmon, Tom	FB	1938,39,40
	MBK	1939
Harmony, Robert W.	MSW	1967,70
Harms, George W.	BB	1940,41,42
Harper, Brian	WR	1991,92,93,94
Harper, Darrell L.	FB	1957,58,59
Harper, Derek D.	MTR	1981,82,83,84
Harpring, Jack J.	FB	1968,69,70
Harrigan, Frank	FB	1927
	MBK	1926,27,28
Harrington, Gerald C.	BB	1916
Harris, Barry C.	MBK	1977
Harris, John A.	MTN	1955,56,57,58
Harris, John E.	MBK	1961,62,63
Harris, Melissa	WSW	1992,93

Harris, Mike	MBK	1990,91,92
Harris, Robert L.	MGY	1960,63
Harris, Robert L.	MTR	1946,47
Harris, Scott A.	MGY	1990,91,92
Harris, Selina	FH	1993,94,95,96
Harris, Stuart	FB	1978,79,81
Harris, Theodore L.	MTR	1986
Harris, Therlon G.	FB	1968
	WR	1969,70,71,72
Harris, William F.	FB	1984,85,86,87
Harris, William J.	FB	1968,69,70
Harris II, William J.	MSW	1989,90,91
Harris, Yvette	WBK	1979
Harrison, Gerald E.	MSW	1926
Harrison, Gregory W.	FB	1970
Harrison, Matthew G.	MGY	1989,90,91
Harrison, Richard D.	MGO	1953,54
Harrison, Richard D.	BB	1870,71
Harrison, Robert W.	MBK	1946,47,48,49
Harrod Jr., Jack	WR	1934,35
Hart, David	MBK	1969,71,72
Hart, Ray	BB	1894
Hart, Raymond	MTR	1925
Hart, Samuel D.	IHO	1928,29,30
Hart, Scott	MSW	1989
Hart, Terrill L.	MTR	1973,75,76
Hart, William J.	FB	1970,71,72
Hart, William N.	FB	1944
Harte, Peg	WBK	1982,83
Harte, K.D.	WBK	1981
Hartman, Gerald E.	FB	1966,67,68
	IHO	1967,68
Hartman, James O.	MD	1948,50,51
Hartman, Mary E.	WGO	1988,89,90
Harvey, Bradley P.	MGO	1974
Harvey, Gordon R.	MTR	1964,65,66,67,
Harvey, Karen	WCC	1991,92,93,94
	WTR	1992,93,94,95
Harvey, Roger S.	MBK	1990,91,90,91
Harvey, William S.	BB	1881,82
Haselby, Joseph W.	MSW	1954,55,56,57
Haskell, Michael	BB	1994,95,96
Haskins, Harold I.	BB	1911
Haskins, Paul A.	FB	1972
Haslerig, Clinton E.	FB	1970,71,72,73
Haslerig, Jacob W.	BB	1975,76
Haslett, William D.	FB	1969,72
Hassel, Richard A.	FB	1986,87,88
Hassel, Thomas J.	FB	1980,81,82,83
Hastings, Robert E.	MGO	1923,25
Hastings, Douglas D.	IHO	1970
Hatch, Diane	SB	1979,80,81,82
	WBK	1980,81
Hatch, Frank	MTR	1898,99
Hatch, M. Grove	BB	1905
Hatheway, E.	FB	1880
	MTR	1879
Hattendorf, William H.	MTR	1923,24
Haughey, Jennifer	FH	1979
Haughey, Louis W.	MD	1942,43
Haughey, Philip C.	MSW	1937
Haughn, Larry E.	WR	1980
Hauser, Leo W.	MGO	1948,49,50
Hauserman, A. John	WR	1932
Hausler, Richard C.	MSW	1960,60
Haven, Marjorie	SS	1974,75
Havran, Joseph G.	MSW	1977
Hawkins, Harry	FB	1923,24,25
	MTR	1925,26
Hawkins, John D.	IHO	1982
Hawkins, Maura	WGO	1992,93
Hawley, Arthur	IHO	1942
Hay, Thomas M.	MSW	1990,92,93,94
Hayden, Edward	FB	1929
Hayden Jr., Joseph	MTR	1948
Hayes, Andrew	MCC	1993
Hayes, Bobby	IHO	1996
Hayes, David B.	MTR	1961,62,63,64
Hayes, Douglas A.	MTR	1938,39
Hayes, Howard W.	MTR	1900,01
Hayes, J. Griffith	MBK	1909
Hayes, Mercury	FB	1992,93,94,95
Hayes, Patrick C.	MSW	1943
Hayes, Ralph	FB	1891
Hayes, Rebecca	WGO	1989,90,91
Hayes, Samuel	BB	1866,67,68,69
Hayes, Timothy A.	MBK	1968
Hayes, William T.	MD	1987,88,89,90
Hayman, Wayne	FB	1873
	BB	1871,72
Haynam, Bruce E.	BB	1950,51,52,53
Haynes, William S.	MTN	1945
Haynes, Gary E.	FB	1982
Haynes, Gregory A.	WR	1975
Haynie, Thomas G.	MSW	1937,38,39

Hays, N. Griffith	BB	1910,11
Hayslett, James R.	MGY	1956,57,58,59
Hayton, Barrie A.	IHO	1956,57,58,59
Hayward, Harry	MBK	1970,71
Hayward, Kenneth L.	BB	1982,83,84,85
Hazen, Francis C.	MTR	1932
Headrick, Jonathon S.	WR	1967
Headrick, W. Lane	WR	1967,69,70
Healy, Brian E.	FB	1967,68,69
Heard, Corydon	BB	1896,97
Heams, Stacey	SB	1989,90,91,92
Heaney, Robert C.	MTN	1928
Heaps, Douglas H.	WR	1992
Heater, Charles E.	FB	1972,73,74
Heath, Homer	MTR	1900,01
Heath, Milton	MTR	1923
Heath, William H.	FB	1926
Heathcott Jr., Robert V.	IHO	1949,50,51,52
Heavenrich, Walter	WR	1935,36
Hebert, Yves A.	IHO	1954,55
Heck, Maria	SB	1989,90,91
Hedding Kevin A.	FB	1991
Heddle, Frederick A.	IHO	1940,41
Hedke, Dave L.	FB	1969,72
Hedlund, Nevin N.	MGY	1981,82,83
Hedrick, J. Karl	MTN	1963,64,65,66
Heffelfinger, Jon P.	FB	1967
Hegarty, Kathleen	WSW	1991,92,94
Hegarty, Maureen A.	WSW	1988,89,90
Hegedorn, Duane	BB	1950,51
Heikkinen, Daniel R.	MCC	1976,78,79,80
	MTR	1977,78,79,80
Heikkinen, David W.	MCC	1977
Heikkinen, Douglas J.	MCC	1983
	MTR	1981,82,83
Heikkinen, Edwin A.	BB	1948
Heikkinen, Molly	WBK	1992,93
Heikkinen, Ralph	FB	1937,38
Heinle, Timothy M.	MTN	1961
Heintschel, Eric	BB	1991,92,93
Heinzman, David L.	MTR	1951,52,53
Helber, Michael A.	IHO	1989,90,91,92
Helber, Timothy A.	IHO	1988,89,90
Helliwell, Robert C.	WR	1932
Hellner, John C.	WR	1967,68
Helt, Peter W.	BB	1970,71,72,73
Helt, Robert B.	MSW	1974,75,76,77
Hench, Karla	SB	1979,80
Henchel, Jeffrey A.	IHO	1984,85,86,87
Hendershot, Fred	FB	1916,17,18
Henderson, Anthony	FB	1991,92,93,94
Henderson, C. Robert	IHO	1944,45
Henderson, Clayton	IHO	1923
Henderson, Dave	FB	1992,92
Henderson, Edward J.	IHO	1963,64,65,66
Henderson, Frederick A.	BB	1978,79
Henderson, John W.	FB	1963,64
	MTR	1962,64,65
Henderson, Kelli	WTR	1988
Henderson, Michael L.	MGY	1962,63,64,65
Henderson, Robert L.	MBK	1983,84,85,86
Henderson,William	FB	1919
Henderson, William P.	MBK	1920,23,24
Hendren, David W.	MGY	1979
Hendricks Jr., Thomas	FB	1954,55
	MTR	1953,54,55,56
Hendrix, Melissa	SS	1976,77,78
Heneveld, Lloyd A.	FB	1947,48,49
Heneveld, William R.	FB	1973,74,76
Henighan, Robert	MGO	1991,92,93,94
Hennessey, Michael S.	MTR	1989,90,91,92
Hennessy, John W.	FB	1974,75,76
Hennigar, Douglas R.	MTR	1975,76,77,78
Henning, Charles	FB	1877
Henninger, Fred	FB	1893,94,95,96
Henrie, Arthur C.	MTR	1948,49,50
Henry, Caren	WSW	1990
Henry, Carolayne	WBK	1983,84,85,86
Henry, James E.	MTR	1977,78,79,80
Henry, Mark W.	MBK	1967,68,69,70
	BB	1967,68
Henry, Preston	FB	1969,70
Henson, Geoffrey S.	WR	1967,68,69
Herbert, R. Beverley	MCC	1927
Heren, Dieter E.	FB	1983,84,85,86
Herhusky, Robert L.	MTN	1951
Herman, Harold B.	IHO	1965,66,67,68
Herner, Douglas A.	MBK	1961,62,63,64
Herr, Matt	IHO	1995,96
	BB	1995,96
Herrala, Scott W.	FB	1987
Herrala, Wallace R.	FB	1958,60
	MTR	1961
Herremans, Tamara J.	SB	1978,79
Herrick, David P.	FB	1985,87

Henry Hill (1968-70) was a walk-on who eventually became captain of Michigan's 1970 football team.

Herrmann, James M.	FB	1980,81,82
Herrmann, John H.	FB	1986,87,88
Hermann, William J.	MBK	1941
Herrnstein, A.E.	FB	1901,02
	MTR	1901,02
Herrnstein, John E.	BB	1957,58
	FB	1956,57,58
Herrnstein, William	FB	1923,24,25
	MTR	1925,26
Herron, Ross W.	MTN	1950
Hersh, Jack I.	MTN	1945,46,48
Hershberger, Donovan P.	FB	1945,46,47,48
Herter, Thomas J.	WR	1972,73,75
Hertzman, Jill	WTN	1980,81,82,83
Hescott, Jennifer	WGY	1987,88,89,90
Hess, John H.	FB	1949,50
	WR	1948,49
Hesse, Christopher J.	BB	1995,96
Hessler, David W.	MTR	1951,53,54,55
Hester, George B.	MTR	1926,27,28
Heston, John	FB	1931,32,33
Heston, LeRoy G.	FB	1926,27
Heston, William Jr.	FB	1929,30
Heston, Willie	FB	1901,02,03,04
	MTR	1903
Hetes, Michael J.	MTR	1977
Hetts, Charles	FB	1979
Hetzeck, Alexander T.	MTN	1949,50,51
Hetzler, Howard	FB	1885
Heuerman, Paul K.	MBK	1978,79,80,81
Hewitt, Andre	MTR	1992,93,94
Hewitt, Robert	WR	1928,29,30
Hewlett, Richard T.	FB	1979,80,82,83
Hewlett, Timothy Y.	MBK	1918,19
Hewitt, William	FB	1929,30,30
Heydanek, Jeffrey S.	MSW	1988
Heydnen, Dick	FB	1955,56,57
Heydt, Francis E.	MSW	1940,41
Heyl, Henry B.	MTR	1939,40
Heyliger, Donald T.	IHO	1967,69,70
Heyliger, Douglas J.	IHO	1967,69,70
Heyliger, Victor	BB	1935,36,37
	IHO	1935,36,37
Heynen, Richard B.	FB	1953,55,56,57
Hibbard, John D.	BB	1885,86,87
Hibbard, Mary	FH	1976,77,78,79
	SB	1978,79
Hickey, Edward L.	FB	1953,54,55
Hickman, G. Daniel	MTR	1950,51,52,53
Hickman, Jayne	VB	1984,85,86
Hickman, Jennifer	VB	1982,83,84,85
Hickman, William B.	MTR	1949,50,51,52
Hicks Jr., Jarvis S.	MGO	1930
Hicks, Dwight	FB	1974,75,76,77
Hicks, Gary A.	MTR	1977,78,79,80
Hicks, Grant T.	MTR	1925
Hicks, Ivan L.	FB	1984,85,86
Hicks, Justin	MGO	1995,97
Hicks, Robert S.	BB	1949,50
Higgins, Edward	MTR	1923,34
Higgins, Francis	FB	1885,86
Higgins, Kenneth E.	FB	1985,86
Higgins, Sean M.	MBK	1988,89,90
Higgins, Tara	WSW	1991,92,93,94
Higgins, Terry	WSW	1976,77,78
Higgs, Charles E.	MBK	1960,61,62
Highfield, Michael D.	MBK	1967,68
Higman, Gordon L.	MGY	1977,78,79,80
Hilberry, John D.	MTR	1954
Hildebrand, Willard H.	FB	1932,33,34
Hildebrand, Willard R.	FB	1958,59,60

Hildebrandt, Wilfried R.	WR	1958,59,60,61
Hilkene, Bruce	FB	1944,46,47
	MBK	1945
Hill, Conrad R.	IHO	1946,47,48,49
Hill, Danielle	WBK	1984,84
Hill, David J.	FB	1954,55
Hill, Donald P.	MSW	1951,52,53,54
Hill, Glenn R.	MGY	1989,90,91,92
Hill, Gyhandi	WR	1997
Hill, Henry W.	FB	1968,69,70
Hill, Kevin J.	WR	1982,84,85,86
Hill Jr., Michael	MGO	1992,94,95
Hill, Norman H.	BB	1909,10,11
Hill, Peter	MTR	1973
Hill, William S.	MCC	1931,32
	MTR	1932,33
Hill, Richard F.	FB	1954,55,56
	WR	1954
Hillberg, Leslie A.	IHO	1938,39
Hiller, Carl C.	MSW	1968,70
Hiller, Neil H.	FB	1969,69,70,70
Hillman, Douglas W.	IHO	1942
Hilton, Kevin R.	IHO	1993,94,95,96
Hilty, Bob D.	WR	1936
Hindes, Howard M.	MTR	1923
Hindle, Therese	FH	1975
Hinds, Selwyn G.	MTR	1990,91,92,93
Hines, Margaret	WSW	1987,88
Hinkle, Isaac	MGO	1994,95,96,97
Hinnegan, Kenneth A.	IHO	1959,60,61,62
Hinton, Gene	FB	1945,49
Hinton, Keith	MGO	1995,96
Hintz, Leon	FB	1947
Hippler, Charles H.	BB	1914
Hird, Urbane W.	FB	1935
	WR	1938
Hiremath, Satish I.	MTN	1983,84
Hirs, Gene	MTR	1942
Hirsch, Elroy L.	MBK	1944
	BB	1944
	FB	1943
	MTR	1944
Hirsch, Kirsten	WSW	1987,88,89
Hirsh, Nancy	FH	1981,82
Hirt, Frank C.	WR	1953,54,55,56
Hitchman Jr., Thomas N.	FB	1958
Hitt Jr., Richard D.	MSW	1982
Hoag, Robert F	MSW	1963,65,66
Hoag, William G.	MTN	1907,08
Hoagland, Edwin H.	MGO	1939
Hoard, Leroy	FB	1987,88,89
Hoban, Michael A.	FB	1971,72,73
Hoban, William P.	FB	1972,73,75
Hoddy, Jerry R.	WR	1968,69,70,71
Hodge, Starry	WTR	1986,87,88
Hodgen, John T.	MTR	1905,06
Hodges, Charles H.	BB	1879
Hodges, Maryanne	WTN	1981,84
Hodgman, Charles E.	MTN	1924
Hodgman, Willis E.	MTR	1893,94
Hodson, Christine	WSW	1981,82,83
Hoene, Daniel J.	IHO	1975,76,77,78
Hoey, George W.	FB	1967,68
	MTR	1966,67,68,69
Hoey, Marion C.	MTR	1964,65,66
Hoffman, Howard B.	MTR	1920,21,22
Hoffman, Leo W.	FB	1926,27
Hoffman, Mathew	MTN	1991
Hofmeister, Julie	WGY	1991,92,93
Hogan, Daniel D.	FB	1977
Hogan, Francis	MTR	1938,39,40
Hogan, Timothy	IHO	1992,93,94,95

Softball star Jody Humphries now serves as U-M's director of marketing and promotions.

Hogg, James	FB	1896,97
Holcomb Jr., Lyle D.	MGY	1950
Holcombe, Alan	WR	1950,51,52
Holcombe, W. Philip	WR	1945
Holden, George	FB	1890
Holdren, Nate	BB	1991,92,93
	FB	1991,92
Holdsworth, M.	MGO	1924,25
Holgate, James G.	FB	1943
Holiday Jr., Harry	MSW	1943,47,48
Holland Jr., Clay	MTR	1948,49
Holland, Bradley L.	MTN	1975,76,77,78
Holland, Joseph	FB	1974
Holland, Joseph H.	FB	1986,87,88
Holland, Thomas K.	FB	1947
Hollbacher, Katy	WCC	1992,93,94,95
	WTR	1993,94,96
Hollis, Peter J.	FB	1965
Hollis, Ronald	BB	1992,93,94
Hollister, John	FB	1893,95
	BB	1894,96
Holloway, Daniel	FB	1987
Holloway, Deborah D.	VB	1981,82
Holloway, Ernie	FB	1987
Hollway, Robert C.	FB	1947,48,49
Hollway, Robert K.	FB	1978
Holman, Bradford S.	WR	1975,76
Holman, Donald A.	MBK	1942
	BB	1940,41,42
Holman, James E.	MTN	1974,75,76
Holmboe, Laurence	MTN	1912,13
Holmes, William F.	MSW	1939,40,41
	BB	1895,96
Holmes, David F.	MSW	1938
Holmes, Daniel	FB	1928
Holmes, Elisabeth	VB	1976
Holmes, Kelly	SB	1994,95,96,97
Holmes, Michael G.	FB	1974,75
Holmquist, Peter C.	MD	1980,84
	MSW	1984
Holt, Charles	MTR	1892,93
Holt, Harold A.	WR	1950,51,53,54
Holt, Robert	MGO	1939
Holter, Anne	SS	1981,82
Holtry, Jeff	FB	1994
Holwerda, Bradley D.	MTR	1988,89,90,91
Holtz, James N.	IHO	1952
Holtzman, Joe L.	BB	1930
Honig, Amy E.	WSW	1987,88,89,90
Honig, Kerry L.	WSW	1987
Honig, Richard L.	BB	1960,61,62,63
Honnen, Susan	WSW	1977
Hood, Alexander M.	IHO	1963,64
Hood, E. Edward	BB	1959,60,61,62
	FB	1961,62
Hood, Edward J.	FB	1985
Hooiveld, Lara	WSW	1992,93,94
Hook Jr., R. Wallace	FB	1936,38
Hook, Robert M.	MTR	1939,40,41
Hool, Gerald K.	BB	1978,79,80,81
Hooper, James	FB	1895
Hooper, William	IHO	1925,262,7
Hoover, Donald E.	MTR	1948,49,50,51
Hoover, Nicole	FH	1990,91,92,93
	SB	1994
Hopkins, Cyrus C.	MSW	1956,57,58,59
Hopkins, Todd	WR	1990
Hopson, Dean J.	MBK	1981,82
Horlenko, Theodore	MSW	1941,42,43
Horn, Clarence	MSW	1927,28
Horn, Jason	FB	1992,93,94,95
Horn, Merrick L.	MGY	1981,82,84
Horn, Patricia	WTN	1984,85,86,87
Horn, T. Christopher	FB	1988
Hornbeck, William H.	FB	1958,60,61
	MTR	1961,62
Hornberger, Theodore	MCC	1925,27
Horner, Joseph	MTR	1909,10,11
Horning, Daniel D.	FB	1981,82
Horning, Douglas L.	WR	1962,64,65
Hornyak, John T.	BB	1969,70,71,72
Horrigan, Michelle	VB	1989,91,92,93
Horton, Bryson	MTR	1895
Horton, Walter	FB	1880,81
Horvath, Karen	SS	1980,81
Horwitch, Matthew W.	MTN	1978,79,80,81
Hose, Michel	FH	1990,91,92,93
Hose, Yael	FH	1990,91,92,93
Hosler, James J.	BB	1966,67,68,69
Hosmer, Rawson F.	MSW	1930
Houck, Lawrence B.	MBK	1955
Houser, Ralph L.	BB	1946
Houtman, John L.	FB	1960,61,63
Hovard, Peter J.	MSW	1985,86
How, Kenneth J.	MTR	1967,68,70

Howard, Christopher L.	FB	1994,95,96
Howard Jr., Edward N.	MGY	1969,70,71
Howard, Derek W.	FB	1974,75,76,77
Howard, Desmond K.	FB	1989,90,91
	MTR	1990,92
Howard, John C.	MGO	1930,31,32
Howard, Juwan	MBK	1992,93,94
Howard, Perry	BB	1912,13,14
Howard, Ronald J.	MSW	1988,89
Howe, Brandon	WR	1995,96
Howe, James E.	MTR	1972,74,75
Howe, Steven R.	BB	1977,78,79
Howell, Frank	BB	1951,52,53
	FB	1950,51,52
Howell, George W.	FB	1994,95
Howell, Richard S.	MSW	1949,50,51,52
Howell, Roderic B.	MCC	1933,34,45
Howes, Lorne D.	IHO	1953,55,56,57
Howland, George D.	IHO	1946,47
Howland, Glenn A. Sr.	BB	1917
Hoyles, Michael R.	WR	1957,58,59,60
Hoyne, Jeffrey B.	FB	1963,64,65
Hozer, Stan	FB	1928,30,31
Hribal, James F.	FB	1966
Hribar, Jeremy D.	BB	1962,63
Hribernik, Michael L.	BB	1995,96
Hubbard, Jarrett T.	WR	1971,72,73,74
Hubbard, Lyle	MSW	1923
Hubbard, Philip G.	MBK	1976,77,79
Hubbard, W. DeHart	MTR	1923,24,25
Hubbell, George E.	MSW	1927,28,29
Huber, Henry K.	BB	1919
Hubly, John D.	MSW	1930
Huckleby, Harlan C.	FB	1975,76,77,78
	MTR	1976
Hudas, Gregory L.	IHO	1984,85
Hudgins, William W.	MGY	1971
Hudson Jr., Lucius P.	WR	1967,68,69,70
Hudson, Rollie B.	MCC	1985,86
	MTR	1985,86,87,88
Hudson, Roy	FB	1929,30,31
	BB	1930,31
Huebel, Herbert	FB	1911,12
Hueber, Charles X.	BB	1883
Huff, Benjamin	FB	1994,95,96
Huff, R. Martin	FB	1968,69,70
	MTR	1970
Huffaker, Harry W.	MSW	1958,59,61
Huffman, Robert E.	BB	1984,85
Hughes, Byron O.	MSW	1930
Hughes, Daniel G.	MTR	1962,63,64,65
Hughes, Dawson	MSW	1996
Hughes, Hilary	FH	1988,89,90
Hughes, Lori	WSW	1977,78,79
Hughes, Mark A.	MBK	1986,87,88,89
Hughes, Patrick J.	IHO	1974,75,76
Hughitt, Ernest	FB	1912,13,14
	BB	1914,15
Huiskens, Thomas A.	FB	1970
Huizenga, Robert J.	WR	1971,74
Hulbert, Bruce	FB	1928
Hulke, Scott E.	FB	1971
Hull, G.M.	FB	1888
Hulse, Stewart H.	MTR	1925
Humbles, Matthew	BB	1992,93,94,95
Hume, H. Ross	MTR	1943,44,45,46
Hume, Malcolm J.	MTN	1931
Hume, Robert H.	MTR	1943,44,45,46
Hume, James	MSW	1990,91,92,93
Humenik, Edward F.	MGO	1978,80,81,82
Humphrey, Alecia	WSW	1992,93,94,95
Humphries, Derrick A.	FB	1966
Humphries, James N.	FB	1978
Humphries, Jody	SB	1981,82,83,84
Humphries, Stefan G.	FB	1980,81,82,83
Hunn, David S.	MTR	1934,35,37
Hunt II, Richard G.	MTR	1965,66,67,68
Hunt, Charis	WTN	1989
Hunt, Moreau C.	MTR	1933,34
Hunt, Reuben G.	MTN	1904
Hunt, Terry Schevers	WBK	1979
Hunter, Carla	VB	1986,87,88,89
Hunter, Daniel L.	MGO	1969,70,71,72
Hunter, Frederick D.	MBK	1991,92
Hunter, MacArthur	MTR	1961,62,63,64
Hunter, Marion	MTR	1922,23,24
Huntington, Edwin	MTR	1915,16,17
Huntzicker, George J.	MGY	1968,69,70
Hurd, Milton R.	MD	1952,53,54
Hurd, Scott E.	MTR	1977
Hurley, John J.	BB	1966,68
Hurley, Robert S.	FB	1952,53
	WR	1954
Hurley, William L.	FB	1941
Hurrell, Herbert G.	FB	1948

Hurst, Donald M.	MGY	1950,51,52,53
Husar, Michael A.	FB	1985,86,87,88
Huson, Margaret	WSW	1986,87,88,89
Hutchens, Edward J.	MSW	1938,39,40
Hutchings, Ralph L.	BB	1956,57,58
Hutchinson, Christopher H	FB	1989,90,91,92
Hutchinson, Loomis	FB	1897
	MTR	1897
Huttenga, Cory	MGY	1992,93,94,95
Hutton, John R.	IHO	1956,57,58,59
Hutzel, Raymond F.	MBK	1924,25
Hyde, Delance L.	MTR	1950,51
Hyde, George W.	MSW	1923
Hyde, Matthew	BB	1996
Hyduk, Vallery C.	WSW	1991,92,93,94
Hyman, Charles M.	IHO	1952
Hyman, Lewis A.	MGY	1961,62
Hynds, James E.	MGY	1960,61,62,63
Hynes, Michael	FB	1994,96

I

Iang, Theresa	SS	1979
Idalski, Brent	MGO	1994,95,96,97
Idomir, Jan E.	WGO	1983,84,85,86
Idoni, Matthew	BB	1991,92
Ignasiak, Michael J.	BB	1985,86,87,88
Ikola, Willard J.	BB	1951
	IHO	1951,52,53,54
Im, Jin Bin	MGY	1996
Imsland, Jerry L.	FB	1968,69
Ingalls, Don	FB	1939,40,41
Ingber, Gerald G.	BB	1949
Ingersoll, John L.	MTR	1942,43
Ingram, Jerald P.	FB	1979,80,81
Ippel, Arthur G.	BB	1918
Irons, Jarrett	FB	1993,94,95,96
Irvine, David E.	MTR	1986,87,88
Irvine, Nancy	FH	1992,93,94
Isaac, Jan	FH	1977,78
Isaac, Stuart A.	MSW	1971,72,73,74
Isbell, Egbert	MCC	1923
Iskenderian, Haig P.	MCC	1926,27
Ivans, Keith	FB	1986
Ives, Robin	FH	1985,86,87,88

J

Jabe Jr., John M.	FB	1959
Joblonski, John J.	MBK	1936
	BB	1936
Jackson Jr., Raymond	MBK	1992,93,94,95
Jackson, Allen M.	FB	1948,49,50
Jackson, Andrew	FB	1977
Jackson, Anthony M.	FB	1978,79,80,81
Jackson, Carlos A.	FB	1974
Jackson, Elizabeth	WSW	1993,94,95,96
Jackson, Eric E.	IHO	1971
Jackson, Gail	FH	1973
Jackson, Gretchen	WTR	1986
Jackson, Jeffery	FB	1980
Jackson, Jennifer	WSW	1989
Jackson, Keith A.	MBK	1976,77
Jackson, Kenneth	FB	1996
Jackson, Norman E.	FB	1950
Jackson, Richard R.	MBK	1950
Jackson, Sarah	VB	1994,95,96
Jackson, William I.	FB	1976
Jaco, J. Ronald	MD	1960,61,62
Jacob, Frederick E.	MTR	1920,21
Jacobi, George S.	MTR	1948,50,51,52
Jacobs, David A.	MGY	1966,67,68,69
Jacobs, Johnson	FB	1977
Jacobsen, Karen	VB	1992,93
Jacobson, Jeffrey L.	BB	1980,81,82,83
Jacobson, Marc	FB	1990
Jacobson, Tage	FB	1933,34
Jacoby, William T.	FB	1979
Jacoby, Mark J.	FB	1974
Jaconette, Michael L.	MBK	1984
Jacques, Sharon	WSW	1974
Jaeckin, John	FB	1992,93
Jaffe, Mark M.	MTN	1954,55,56,57
Jaffe, Matthew	MSW	1991,92
Jaffe, William	IHO	1988
Jagels, John C.	BB	1976
Jakob, Linda F.	WSW	1982
Jaksa, Christopher J.	BB	1981,82,83
James, Clifford W.	MGO	1941
James, Douglas R.	FB	1981,82,83,84
James, Efton	FB	1913
James, Eldon E.	IHO	1938,39,40
James, Gilbert	IHO	1936,37,38,39
James, Hugh	FB	1903
James, Jeffery A.	BB	1972,74,75
James, Joe P.	MBK	1980,81
James, John	FB	1903

Jameson, Laurie	WTN	1974
Janik, Joseph	MSW	1994,95,96
Janke, Fred C.	FB	1936,37,38
Jankovich, Bojana	WTN	1994,95
Jansen, Jon W.	FB	1995,96
Jansen, Philip	MTR	1913,14
Jarema, Robert H.	MTR	1963,64,65
Jaros, Stephen E.	MTR	1966,68
Jarry, Michael	IHO	1970,71,72,73
Jasper, David	MGO	1995,96,97
Jaycox, John	FB	1884,85,86
	BB	1885
	MTR	1883
Jayne, Trafford	MTN	1889
	BB	1888,89
Jefferies, Albert	BB	1892,93
Jefferis, A.W.	FB	1891,92
Jeffers, Robert H.	MTN	1940
Jefferson, Allen L.	FB	1987,88,89,90
Jeffrey, Julie	WD	1976,77,78,80
Jeffries, F. Wallace	MSW	1951,52,53
Jeffries, Janna	WGY	1987,88,89,90
Jelley, Duane J.	FB	1976
Jenkins, A.	WR	1922
Jenkins, Calvin W.	WR	1963,64,65,66
Jenkins, Dyan	WTR	1989,90
Jenkins, Trezelle	FB	1992,93,94
Jennett, Bernard P.	WR	1951,52
Jennings, Ferris	FB	1934
Jennings, Pamela	FH	1984,85
Jensen, Dale T.	MTN	1953,56,57
Jensen, Sidney A.	MGY	1967,68,69,70
Jensen, Thomas P.	FB	1973,74,75
Jenswold, John D.	MGO	1944,45,47
	IHO	1944,45
Jenny, Lee R.	BB	1906
Jerkins, Julie	WCC	1985
Jerman, Laura	WTR	1991,92,93,94
Jerome, Gilbert T.	MSW	1923
Jerome, Paul F.	MTN	1923,24
Jester, Thomas C.	MTR	1938,39,40
Jewell, John	IHO	1933,34,35
Jewett, George	FB	1890,92
Jilek, Daniel D.	FB	1973,74,75
Jobson, Tom E.	FB	1958,59,60
Johannesen, William A.	WR	1963,64,65,66
Johanning, Stan	MTR	1992,93,94,96
Johns, Brandon R.	FB	1986
Johns, James	FB	1920,21,22
Johns, William C.	BB	1865
Johnsen, Arnold W.	MBK	1974,75,74
Johnsen, Leisa	WD	1981
Johnson, Robert S.	FB	1958,59,60
Johnson Jr., Jesse	FB	1991,92
Johnson, Alden C.	MTN	1941,42,43, 44,45
Johnson, Alex	FB	1976
Johnson, Alison	FH	1981,82,83,84
Johnson, Amy	WBK	1994,95,96,97
	WTR	1996
Johnson, Andrew C.	MTR	1974,75,76,77
Johnson, Arnold W.	MBK	1974,75
Johnson, Arthur J.	MSW	1947,48
Johnson, Barbara	WBK	1974
Johnson, Carl E.	MTR	1918,19,20
Johnson, Deon	FB	1991,92,93,94
Johnson Jr., Earl	FB	1955
Johnson, Edgar H.	MTN	1972
Johnson, Edward	MTR	1946
Johnson, Ernest C.	FB	1935
Johnson, Ernest D.	MBK	1970,71,72,73
Johnson, Farnham J.	FB	1943
	MTN	1944
Johnson, Gene L.	FB	1975,76,77,78
Johnson, George H.	FB	1945,47
Johnson, Gilvanni M.	FB	1984,85
Johnson, Henry	MSW	1924,25
Johnson, Irvin	FB	1979
Johnson, James J.	BB	1921
Johnson, James W.	FB	1948
Johnson, Janice	SS	1980,81,82
Johnson, John J.	MBK	1978,79,80,81
Johnson, John M.	MTR	1955
Johnson, Joseph A.	MBK	1972,73,74,75
Johnson, Joyce	WSW	1978
Johnson, Keith A.	FB	1973,74,75
Johnson, Larry L.	FB	1973,74
Johnson, Leonard	MTR	1961,62
Johnson, Livetius H.	FB	1991
Johnson, Manly	WR	1942,43
Johnson, Mark A.	WR	1974,75,76,77
Johnson, Marvin J.E.	MGY	1951,52,53,54
Johnson, Oliver	FB	1980
Johnson, Orval	MTR	1945,46,47,48
Johnson, Paul J.	FB	1965,67
Johnson, Raymond J.	FB	1977
Johnson, Reginald B.	MTR	1971
Johnson, Robert J.	MGY	1971,72,73,74
Johnson, Ronald A.	FB	1966,67,68
Johnson, Roy	FB	1919
Johnson, Russell E.	MGO	1951,52
Johnson, Shelby D.	MTR	1979,80,81,82
Johnson, Shelly	FH	1996
Johnson, Stacy A.	FB	1976
Johnson, Steven W.	FB	1982
	MTR	1984
Johnson, Tearza	WTR	1993,94,95,96
Johnson, Thomas	FB	1949,50,51
	MTR	1949,51,52
Johnson, Walter N.	FB	1956,57,58
Johnson, Wendy	VB	1985
Johnson, William C.	BB	1875
Johnson-de-Boneur, Orval	MTR	1945,46,47,48
Johnston, Collins	FB	1878,81
Johnston, Donald A.	MBK	1973,74,75
Johnston, J. Derland	MSW	1933,34,35,36
Johnston, James D.	FB	1972
Johnston, Robert	WR	1945,47,48
Jokisch, Daniel E.	FB	1988,89,90
Jokisch, Paul H.	MBK	1983,84
	FB	1984,85,86
Jokisch, Rhonda	WBK	1991
Jolly Jr., Alexander H.	MGO	1931,32,33
Jolly, Michael A.	BB	1979
	FB	1976,77,78,79
Jones, Burwell O.	MSW	1952,53,54,55
Jones, Bradley S.	IHO	1984,85,86,87
Jones, Brian E.	BB	1980
Jones, Candice	SS	1977,78
Jones, Darren K.	MTR	1989
Jones, David	MTR	1992,93
Jones, Deanna	FH	1979,80,81,82
Jones, Dennis B.	FB	1962
	MTR	1962
Jones, Dhani	FB	1996
Jones, Frederick F.	BB	1935
Jones, Hobart B.	MTR	1954,55
Jones, Jessica	WSOC	1995
Jones, Joseph C.	BB	1960,61,62,63
Jones, Joseph M.	FB	1969
Jones, Karen M.	WSOC	1994
Jones, LaTara	WBK	1991
Jones, Lawerance	FB	1979
Jones, Paul	FB	1902
Jones, Rick	FB	1980
Jones, Robert J.	MBK	1976,77
Jones, Stafford	MTR	1927,28
Jones, Stephen	IHO	1927,28,29
Jonseck, Gary L.	WR	1975,76
Jordan, Forrest	FB	1939
	WR	1939,40
Jordan, John	FB	1936
Jorgensen, Thomas A.	MBK	1953,54,55,56
Joseph, Gabriel	IHO	1928,29,30
Joseph, Louis G.	WR	1977,79,80
Joseph, Matthew N.	MCC	1989
Joseph, Roger A.	FB	1980,83
Joslin, Richard S.	MBK	1934,35
Joubert, Antoine C.	MBK	1984,85,86,87
Joyce, Michael L.	BB	1960,61
Joyce, Thomas H.	BB	1972,73,74,75
Joyner, Nelson	MTR	1920,22,23
Jozwiak, Jeffrey	MD	1990,91,92,93
Julian, Alfred J.	FB	1956,57,58,59
Judd, Stacey	SB	1997
Julier, David	BB	1990
Jung, Charles C.	MTR	1925,26
Juttner, Charles	FB	1897,99
Juzysta, Lisa	SB	1984,85,86,87

K

Kadela, David A.	FB	1977,78
Kahl, James C.	WR	1969
Kahn, Howard P.	MTN	1933,34,35,36
Kahn, Bernard M.	MSW	1948,49,50,51
Kahn, Edgar	IHO	1923,24
Kailes, William	WR	1925
Kaiser, Douglas A.	BB	1986,87,88,89
Kakazu, Kendrick	WR	1994
Kalahar, Cathy A.	WTN	1974
Kalahar, Maurice	BB	1995,96,97
Kalczynski, Brian	BB	1996
Kamhout, Carl R.	FB	1955
Kamieniecki, Scott A.	BB	1983,84,85,86
Kamienski, Henry C.	MSW	1932,33,34
Kaminski, Richard D.	FB	1971
Kamman, James M.	WR	1964,65,66,67
Kampe Jr., Kurt	FB	1947
Kampe III, Kurt W.	FB	1974,75
Kampen, Kathryn	WTR	1979,80,81,82
Kampfe, Anne	WSW	1994,95,96,97
Kane, Gary F.	MBK	1958,59
	FB	1958,59
Kanitz, Tharel T.	MBK	1929,30
Kantor, Morton S.	MTN	1952
Kapenstein, James M.	WR	1984
Kaplan, Lisa	FH	1977
Karasinski, David F.	BB	1984,85,86
Karazim, Timothy D.	BB	1980,82,83
Karbel, S.J.	WR	1925
Kardos, Gary W.	IHO	1972,73,74,75
Karfonta, Nicholas	MTR	1992,93,94,95
Karmazin, Theodore	FB	1948
Karpinka, Jerry O.	IHO	1954,55,56,57
Karpinski, Alfred J.	MGO	1936,37,38
Karpus, Arthur	FB	1918
	MBK	1919,20,21
	BB	1919,20,21
Karras, Michelle	WGY	1982
Karsten, Henery M.	BB	1903
Kartusch, Wayne M.	IHO	1961,62,63
Karwales, John J.	FB	1941,42
Karzen, Jan	WTN	1975,76,77
Karzen, Jerry R.	MTN	1972,73,74,75
Karzen, John E.	MTN	1988,89,90,91
Karzen, Katherine	WTN	1977,78,79,80
Kasley, Jack H.	MSW	1935,36,37
Kasparek, Edward J.	FB	1978
Kass, David	MTN	1989,91,92
Katcavage, Karen	SB	1989
Katlin, Stacey K.	BB	1987,88,89,90
Kattus, J. Eric	FB	1981,83,84,85
Katz, Jay T.	IHO	1956,5758,59
Katz, Paul A.	MSW	1970,71
Kauffman, Ralph R.	MBK	1953
Kaufman, Lee A.	IHO	1951
Kaufman, Merrill L.	BB	1955
Kaufman, Mitchell H.	MBK	1976,77,78
Kaufmann III, Frederick	MGY	1980,81,82,83
Kaul, Andrew	WR	1952,53,54,55
Kautz, John W.	MTR	1940,41,42
Kawa, Ben	BB	1976
	IHO	1975,76,77,78
Kayner, Howard	FB	1911
Kazinec, Brenda	WTR	1980,81,82,83
Kaziny, Richard B.	MGY	1970,7172
Kazmierski, Michael R.	BB	1980
Kean, Daniel G.	MTN	1934
Keane, Christopher M.	MGY	1970
Keane, Dennis J.	MCC	1982,83
	MTR	1919,83
Kearney, Thomas F.	MTR	1966,67,68
Kearns, John E.	BB	1901
Kearns, John W.	MSW	1924
Keathley, Lisa	SS	1974,75
Keating, Thomas A.	FB	1961,62,63
Keating, William L.	FB	1964,65
Kee, Thomas G.	FB	1970,71,72
Keefe, Patrick C.	MGO	1956,57,58,59
Keefer, Colby	FB	1996
Keefer, Jackson	FB	1922
Keeler, Paul J.	MSW	1935,36
Keeler, Ralph W.	MTR	1904,05
Keen, James C.	WR	1962,63
Keena, Leo	FB	1897,99
Keenan, Richard T.	MSW	1959
Keenan, Daniel P.	FB	1975
Keeshin, Bruce M.	MGY	1972,73,7475
Keeshin, David L.	MGY	1975
Keilstrup, Geert G.	MTR	1955,56,57,58
Keith, Albert H.	BB	1898
Keitz, Dale T.	FB	1977,78,79
Kell, Walter G.	MBK	1945,46
	BB	1944,45,46
Keller, Clarence L.	MTR	1904
Keller, Frank R.	MSW	1948,49,50,51
Keller, John K.	WR	1949
Keller, Michael F.	FB	1969,70,71
Keller, Thomas J.	FB	1979
Kellermann, Fredrick E.	WR	1959,60,61,62
Kelley, Barry N.	FB	1992
Kelley, George M.	WR	1974,75,76,77
Kelley, John H.	BB	1891
Kelley, Lisa	SB	1996,97
Kelley, Ryan	BB	1996
Kelley, Stanley G.	MTR	1938,39,40
Kellman, Edward E.	WR	1933,37
Kellogg, Nelson A.	MTR	1901,02,03,04
Kelly, Brian J.	MTR	1964,65,66
Kelly, Earl A.	MTR	1925,26
Kelly, George A.	BB	1905,06,07,08
Kelly, James O.	WR	1929,30
Kelly, John N.	MBK	1933
Kelly, Max E.	MTR	1944

David Kass (1989-92) twice made the NCAA singles quarterfinals and was a three-time All American.

Kelly Jr., Paul R.	MTR	1988,89
Kelly, Peter W.	IHO	1957,58
Kelly, Theodore E.	MTR	1962,63,64
Kelly, William J.	IHO	1959,61,62
Kelsey, R. Thomas	FB	1949,50,51
Kelsie, Anthony	FB	1981
Kelto, Reuben W.	FB	1939,40,41
Kemp, Cass W.	MTR	1933,34
Kemp, Robert	IHO	1942,43
Kemp, Stan	FB	1964,65,66
Kempner, Ralph	MTN	1928
Kempthorn, Dana	WGY	1980
Kempthorn, Eric	FB	1983
Kempthorn, Richard J.	MBK	1948
	FB	1947,48,49
Kenaga, Raymond K.	MBK	1953
	FB	1953
	MTR	1951
Kendall, Linda	WSW	1978,79
Keniston, Kerri	VB	1979,80,81
Kenn, Michael L.	FB	1975,76,77
Kennedy, Carolynn	WD	1986,87,88,89
Kennedy, Charles	FB	1942
Kennedy, Donald G.	IHO	1955
Kennedy, Frank D.	MSW	1931,32,33
Kennedy, Robert	FB	1943
Kennedy Jr., Ted	FB	1940,41
Kennedy, William R.	MSW	1970,71
	FB	1968,69
Kenney, Richard F.	MGY	1966,67,68,69
Kenney, Stephen G.	FB	1967
Kenson, George W.	MTR	1892,93,94
Kent, Paul	MSW	1984
Kent, Steven A.	MTR	1988,89
Keough, James F.	IHO	1966,67,68,69
Keough, Kelly P.	FB	1980
Keough, Timothy J.	IHO	1989,90
Kercher, Ann	WTN	1977,78,79,80
Kern, Frank I.	FB	1943
Kerr, Derek J.	BB	1984,85,86
Kerr, James L.	MSW	1959,60,62
Kerr, John E.	MBK	1958
	BB	1959,60,61,62
Kerr, Joseph E.	BB	1964,65,66,67
Kerr, Thomas G.	FB	1960
Kerr, William W.	MSW	1924,25
Kerska, David A.	MSW	1984,85,86,87
Kessler, Heinrich B.	MSW	1944,45,46
Kessler, Roger H.	MGO	1946,47,48,49
	MTR	1947
Ketteman, Richard L.	FB	1957
Ketterer, Charles E.	MBK	1944
	BB	1943,44,47
	FB	1947,48
Kettinger, Thomas G.	BB	1970,71,72,73
Ketz, Wilford H.	MTR	1927,28,29
Key, David R.	FB	1987,88,89,90
Keyes, D. Earl	IHO	1950,51,52,53
Khan, Gulam A.	FB	1989
Khouri, George R.	MCC	1972
	MTR	1972
Kiani-Aslani, John	MSW	1993,94
Kibble, John E.	MGY	1987
Kiddon, Gene R.	FB	1947
Kidston, James A.	BB	1936
Kidston, R.H.	MGO	1902,03,05
Kidwell, John R.	MTN	1938,39
Kiefer, Jennifer	WBK	1994,9697
Kiegler, Augustus J.	BB	1930,31
Kiel, Jeffrey D.	BB	1985,86
Kiesel, George	FB	1947

Kiester, Fred	FB	1947
Kieta, Robert J.	FB	1968
Killian, Dan A.	BB	1902
Killian, Timothy J.	FB	1968,69,70
Killilea, Henry	FB	1884
Kilpelainen, Matti V.J.	MTR	1965,67,68
Kim, Eliot	MGY	1990
Kim, Joseph P.	MTN	1991
Kimball, Bruce D.	MD	1983,84,85
	MSW	1983,84,85
Kimball, Richard J.	MGY	1956,57,58,59
	MD	1956,57,58,59
Kimball, Victoria	WD	1980,81,82,83
Kimble, Keith D.	MSW	1982,83
Kimerer, Perry E.	MTR	1941
Kimmey, Byron R.	MTR	1988,89
Kinaia, Tiffany	WGY	1990,91
Kines, Charles G.	FB	1964,65
King, Harold J.	WR	1976,77
King, Jimmy	MBK	1992,93,94,95
King, John W.	WR	1972,73,75
King, Kevin J.	FB	1976,77
King, Kyle R.	MBK	1976,77
King, Mark H.	WR	1969,70,71,72
King, R. Steven	FB	1973,74,75
King, Robert D.	MTR	1939
King, Sean	MTN	1992
King, Sherrie	WTR,	1978,79,80,81
King, Stephen D.	WR	1993,94
King, Steven	FB	1993,94,95,96
King, Thomas V.	MBK	1944
King, Wayne F.	WR	1957,58
Kingery Jr., Russell F.	MSW	1964,65,66,67
Kingsbury, Dale H.	MBK	1957,59
Kingsley, James E.	MTR	1937,38
Kinkead, Gary L.	MSW	1967,68,69,70
Kinnel, R. Jackson	MTR	1952,53
Kinney Sr., Richard R.	MTR	1928
Kinon, Jen	WCR	1997
Kinyon, Peter C.	FB	1950,51
Kipke, Harry	FB	1921,22,23
	MBK	1922,23,24
	BB	1922,23,24
Kirar, Edward M.	MSW	1937,38
Kirby, Craig W.	MBK	1963
	FB	1963,64,65
Kircher Jr., Robert E.	MSW	1967,68,69
Kirchgessner, William E.	BB	1920
Kirk, Bernard	FB	1921,22
Kirkendall, Jimmie G.	MTR	1949,50
Kiss, Scott A.	IHO	1987,88
Kiskadden, Alex	FB	1886
Kitchen, Eric D.	MD	1988
Kivi, Louis P.	MSW	1942,43
Klann, Michael D.	MGY	1976
Klarreich, Betsy	SS	1976
Klass, Alexandra	WGY	1986,87
Klasson, Eric C.	WR	1980,81,82
Klein, Deborah E.	WTN	1980
Klein, Abraham A.	BB	1921,22
Klein, Adolph	BB	1921,22,23
Klein, John A.	FB	1971,74
Kleinschmidt, Owen H.	MSW	1961
Klepek, Jannette	WGY	1986,87,88,89
Kligis, Michael J.	FB	1979
Kline, Edward L.	MTN	1923
Kline, James D.	FB	1942,43
Klinger, Kristofer	MGY	1993,94,95,96
Klintworth, Robert E.	MSW	1931
Klomparens, Carol	WBK	1974,75,76,77
Kloote, Pamela	WSW	1974
Klotz, Jeffrey	MSW	1991

Brent Lang (1987-90) captured four individual NCAA swimming titles.

Klove, Ingrid	SS	1980,81
Kluge, Jessica	WCC	1991,92,93,94
	WTR	1991,92,93,94
Kluge, Keith S.	MTR	1989,92
Knapp, Charles D.	BB	1941
Knapp, Everett	FB	1948
Knickerbocker, Gary S.	MTR	1966,67,68,69
Knickerbocker, Stan	FB	1952,54,55
Knickerbocker, Steven G.	FB	1974
Knight, David M.	FB	1989
Knight, Fred G.	MGY	1949,50,51
Knight, Marcus	FB	1996
Kniivila, John L.	MBK	1947
Knipper, Kathleen	WSW	1994
Knode, Ken	FB	1918,19
	BB	1918,19,20
Knode, Robert T.	BB	1922
	FB	1921
Knoebel, Thomas	FB	1984
Knoepp, Louis F.	MTR	1928
Knoll, Scott	MBK	1991,92,93
Knox, Katherine	WSW	1974,75,76
Knox, Robert A.	MSW	1954,55,56
Knuble, Michael	IHO	1992,93,94,95
Knuth, Erik C.	FB	1990
Knutson, Gene P.	FB	1951,52,53
Kobane, Dean C.	MGO	1991,92
Kobrin, Theodore	BB	1948,49
Kobylarz, Paul M.	IHO	1982,83,84,85
Kocan, Ronald R.	FB	1962
Koceski, Leo R.	BB	1949,50,51
	FB	1948,49,50
Koch, Allan J.	BB	1957,58,59,60
Koch, David W.	MGO	1980
Kochanski, Mark G.	FB	1976
Kocoloski, James D.	BB	1970,71,72,73
Kocsis, Charles	MGO	1934,35,36
Kodros, Archie J.	FB	1937,38,39
Koehn, Frederick W.	FB	1948
Koeller, Donald M.	FB	1962
	WR	1965
Koenig, Marc A.	MBK	1989,90
Koepke, Scott P.	MTR	1979,80,81
Koepke, Sheryl	WSW	1979
Kogen, Clark C.	MSW	1975
Kogen, Max B.	FB	1946
Kogen, William E.	MSW	1944,48,49
Kohl, Harry E.	FB	1940
	MTN	1940
Kohl, Ralph A.	FB	1947,48
Kohler, Arthur W.	MTR	1913,14
Kohn, Robert I.	FB	1968,68,69
Kohns, Norman C.	MTR	1964
Kohut, Dawn	FH	1976,77
Kolb, Gerald P.	IHO	1959,60,62
Kolesar, John C.	FB	1985,86,87,88
Kolesar, Robert C.	FB	1940,41,42
Kolesar, William P.	FB	1953,54,55
Konovsky, William J.	WR	1978,79,80
Konrad, William E.	MTR	1949,50,51,52
Konuszewski, Dennis	BB	1990,91,92
Koo, Belinda	WCR	1997
Koontz, Bradley J.	MTN	1985,86,87,88
Kooser, Kathryn	WSW	1980,81
Kooy, Donald	MBK	1977
Kopas, Brice	MSW	1991,92,93,94
Kopas, William J.	MSW	1986,87,88,89
Kopcke, John L.	FB	1974,75
Kopcke, William R.	BB	1943,44
Kopel, Richard M.	WR	1942,43
Kopf, David L.	BB	1981,82,83
Koplin, Stephen A.	BB	1956
Kopmeyer, Peggy J.	WBK	1977
Koppelman, Craig	MBK	1989,90,90
Koppin, Lawrence L.	MSW	1944
Koreishi, Aaleya	FH	1992,93,94,95
Korol, George	MTN	1956,57,58
Korowin, James F.	FB	195961
Korowin, Michael J.	FB	1979
Korschewitz, Edwin	MTR	1985,86
Korson, Brian D.	BB	1990
Kosanke, Pam	SB	1997
Koschalk, Richard A.	FB	1974,75
Koschalk, Robin J.	FB	1979
Kosik, Joseph F.	WR	1951
Kositchek, Robert J.	MBK	1933
	MTR	1934,35
Koskinen, Erik K.	MCC	1986,87
Koss, Gregory A.	FB	1972,73
Kostantacos, Charles	MBK	1974,75,76
Koutonen, Erkki	MTR	1949,50
Kovac, Michael	FB	1987
Kovacevich, David A.	FB	1962,63
Kovach, Kelly	SB	1993,94,95,96
Kovacs, Louis S.	FB	1982

Koval, Louann	SS	1978,79,80
Koviak, Bruce R.	IHO	1965,66,67,68
Kowal, Elizabeth	WSW	1987,88,89
Kowalik, John	FB	1931,32,33
Kowalik Jr., John F.	FB	1962
Kozolowski, Jim	FB	1979
Kracht, W. Stanley	BB	1931
Kraeger, George W.	FB	1943,46
	MTR	1943,44
Kraft, John A.	BB	1966,67,68,69
Kramer, Brad	MTN	1994,95,96
Kramer, Jack H.	MBK	1987
Kramer, Jon E.	FB	1966,67
Kramer, Melvin	FB	1935
Kramer, Ronald J.	MBK	1955,56,57
	FB	1954,55,56
	MTR	1955,56,57
Kramer, Ted H.	IHO	1989,90,91,92
Kranz, Patricia	WTN	1974
Kratus, Patrick	FB	1996
Krause, Thomas S.	WR	1955
Krauss, Michael G.	FB	1985
	MTR	1985,86,87
Kreager, Carl A.	FB	1949,50
	MBK	1949
Krejsa, Bob	FB	1940
Kremer, Marian	WTN	1981,82,83,84
Kremer, Merle W.	BB	1936,37,38
Kress, Edward S. (Ted)	FB	1952,53
	MTR	1950
Krickstein, Kathryn	WTN	1978,79
Kring, Mark S.	MTR	1986,87
Krok, Joe	MBK	1992
Kromer, Paul S.	FB	1938,39,40
Kropschot, Bruce E.	BB	1962
Krpan, Tony	MTR	1981,83,84,85
Krueger, Frederick L.	FB	1957
Krueger, Karl F.	MTR	1968,70
Krumbholz, Leon R.	MGY	1952,54
Krussman, Donald A.	IHO	1981,82,83
Kruthers, James M.	MSW	1953,54,55,56
Kubicek, Louis A.	BB	1926,27,29
Kucher, Robert S.	BB	1958,59,60
Kuebbeler, Andrea	FH	1985,86,87
Kuenzel, Walter A.	MBK	1924,25
Kuhlman, Erich R.	MGO	1988,89
Kuhlmann, Karen	WSW	1983,84,86
Kuick, Don D.	FB	1947
Kulka, Edward L.	MTR	1973,75
Kulpinski, John J.	BB	1947
Kundtz, Margaret	FH	1987,88,89
Kunnen, Kari	SB	1990,91,92,93
Kunnen, Karla	SB	1990,91,92,93
Kunow, Walter	FB	1923,24
Kunsa, Joseph J.	FB	1968
Kunzelman, Karyn	VB	1982,83,84,85
Kupec Jr., Charles J.	MBK	1972,73,74,75
	FB	1972
Kurkland, Nancy	WGY	1976
Kurtz, David W.	FB	1961,62,63
Kutsche, John D.	MTR	1938,39
Kutschinski, Ronald C.	MTR	1966,67,68,69
Kuziak, Douglas P.	WR	1961,62
Kuzma, Tim L.	MBK	1973,74,75
Kuzma, Tom	FB	1941,42
Kuzniar, Chester	IHO	1946
Kwasiborski Jr., Stanley	MGO	1955,56,57,58
Kwiatkowski, Daniel S.	FB	1980
Kwok, Hugh W.	MTN	1983,84,85,86
Kwong, Randall	IHO	1987,88,89,90

L

LaFountaine, Sean	FB	1987,88
LaJeunesse, Omer J.	FB	1930,31
LaJeunesse, Terrance	IHO	1973
LaKritz, Dana	SB	1994,95
LaRue, Joseph W.	MTR	1950,51,53
Laatsch, Linda	WGY	1976,77
Laatsch, Sandra	WGY	1976
Labadie, George B.	BB	1914,15,16
Labadie, Lisa	WCR	1997
Labun, Nicholas M.	FB	1977
Lacher, Simone	WTN	1993,94,95
Lacure, Bill	WR	1995,96,97
Ladd, Robert B.	MSW	1930,31,32
Laffey, Andrea	WTN	1974,75
Laidley, Clive A.	MTR	1965,66
Laine, John T.	FB	1941
Laird, Linda	WBK	1974
Lake, David W.	MGY	1948,49
Lamb, Frederick D.	MGO	1940
Lamb, Robert H.	MTR	1934
Lambert, Bradley	MD	1990,91,92,93
Lambert, Frederick W.	MTR	1962,63,64,65
Lambert, Oscar P.	FB	1917

Lambros, Constantine H.	WR	1963,64,65,66
Lamey, Lorraine	WTN	1984
Lamm, Carol	WCC	1980,81,82,83
	WTR	1981,82
Lamm, Marla	WTN	1985,87
Lamont, Allen C.	MTR	1927,28,29
Lamont, Lawrence M.	MTR	1927
Lanard, Bruce J.	MBK	1961
	BB	1958
Lancaster, Christopher	MTR	1992,93,94,95
Lancaster, Jason	MSW	1995,96
Landis, Catherine	WSW	1978
Landman, Richard E.	MGY	1983
Landowski, John S.	MTR	1922
Landre, Joseph H.	MBK	1925
Landrum, R. James	WR	1932,33,34
Landsittel, Thomas A.	FB	1966
Landstrom, Eeles E.	MTR	1955,56,59
Lane, Gregory R.	BB	1975,76,77
Lang, Brent D.	MSW	1987,88,89,90
Lang, Jessica	SB	1994,95,96,97
Lang, Kristen	VB	1988,89
Lang, Robert J.	FB	1974,75,76
Lange, Edward W.	BB	1926, 28
Langen, Wilho	IHO	1930
	BB	1930
Langenham, Eric	BB	1919,20
Langguth, Elmer	WR	1925
Lanphier, Dominic A.	MGY	1985,86,87,88
Lantry, Michael W.	FB	1972,73,74
	MTR	1972,73,74
Lapham, John W.	MTR	1910
Lappo, Karmen	SB	1997
Larkin, Barry L.	BB	1983,84,85
Larose, Gilbert L.	MGY	1960,61,62,63
Larsen, Robert L.	BB	1948,50,51
Larsen, Lisa	WSW	1980
	WCC	1980,81,82
	WTR	1981,82,83
Larson, Berger	BB	1935,36
Larson, Dana W.	MGY	1958
Larson, John L.	MTR	1945
Larson, Jarl E.	MTR	1920
Larson, Roberts B.	IHO	1927
Lascari, Arno T.	MGY	1961,62,63,64
Laser, Ross S.	MTN	1981,82,83,84
Laskey, William G.	FB	1962,63,64
Laskowski, Chris	MSW	1995,96
Lasky, Byron H.	WR	1948,49
Laslo, Thomas J.	BB	1961,64
Lasser, Harold A.	MTR	1925,26,27
Lata, Timothy P.	BB	1987,88,89
Later, Curtis	MTR	1917,18,20
Lathers, Charles T.	MBK	1909
	BB	1909
Latora, Anthony C.	WR	1984,85,86,87
Lattany, Michael K.	MTR	1978,79,80
Lauring, Tim	MGY	1995,96
Lauritsen, Charles H.	MTR	1945,46
Lauterbach, Ronald L.	BB	1962
Lavan, John	BB	1913,14
Lavery, Gregory B.	WR	1977
Lavine, Louis	FB	1936,37,38
Law, John U.	MGO	1956,57
Law, Tajuan	FB	1992,93,94
Lawley, Jeffrey E.	FB	1975,8
Lawrence, Douglas J.	MBK	1951,52,53
Lawrence, James	FB	1902
Lawrence, Robert	MSW	1934
Lawson, Charles F.	BB	1888
Lawson, Gene	FB	1986
Lawton, George	FB	1910
Lawton Jr., Thomas S.	MSW	1966,67
Lawton Sr., Thomas S.	MTR	1940,41
Lazar, Robert J.	MSW	1980
Lazetich, Milan	FB	1944
LeClair, Keith C.	MGO	1949,50
LeClair, Lowell V.	MGO	1950,51,52,53
LeClaire, Laurence E.	FB	1950,51,52
LeClerc, Pierre	MGY	1973,74,75,76
LeFebvre, Jerry P.	IHO	1970,71,72
LeGalley, Kenneth E.	MBK	1921
LeRoux, Arthur N.	FB	1944
Leach, Larry H.	MGO	1956,58
Leach, Michael E.	MTN	1979,80,81,82
Leach Jr., Richard M.	MBK	1976
	BB	1976,77,78,79
	FB	1975,76,77,78
Leach Sr., Richard M.	BB	1952,53,54
Leach, Robert N.	BB	1951,52,53,54
Leake, Herbert T.	MTR	1941
Lease, Elizabeth	WSW	1977,78,79
Leddy, John T.	MBK	1944
Ledgard. Edwin	MGY	1996
Lee, Gary	FB	1981

Lee, George C.	MBK	1956,57,58,59
Lee, Louis R.	FB	1964,65,66
Lee, Miles D.	WR	1951,52,53
Lee IV, Robert E.	MCC	1991,92,93,94
	MTR	1992
Lee, Walter C.	MTN	1903,04
Leengran, Wayne	MSW	1950,51,52,53
Legacki, David T.	MTR	1966
Legacki, Frank L.	MSW	1958,59,60,61
Leger, Eugene F.	MTR	1909
Legette, Burnie A.	FB	1989,90,91,92
Legg, Michael	IHO	1994,95,96,97
Lehman, Paige E.	MGO	1925
Lehr, John J.	FB	1961
Lehrke, Fritz M.	WR	1989,90,91
Leible, Clark M.	MTR	1901
Leidy, Paul A.	MTN	1907,08,09
Liebner, Stefanie	WSW	1988,89,90
Leith, Jerry C.	FB	1959
	WR	1957
Leith, Thomas C.	FB	1955
	WR	1958
Leland, Robert C.	MBK	1928
Lelich, William M.	MBK	1975,76,77
Lemak, Louis	MSW	1932,33
Lemen, W. Edward	MTR	1932,33,34
Lemirande, Michael J.	FB	1979,80,81,82
Lence, Robert J.	WR	1978,80
Leney, Janet	SS	1978
Lenfestey, John R.	GO	1930,31,32
Lengemann, Alex	MTR	1996
Lentz Jr., Charles W.	FB	1948,49
Leonard, Ellen	FH	1974
Leonard, Frederick W.	BB	1987,89,90
Leonard, H.B.	FB	1892,93,94
Leonard, Noble D.	MTR	1928
Leonardi, Ernest L.	MTR	1942,43
Leoni, Michael C.	FB	1978,79
Leoni, Patrick A.	FB	1976,78,79
Leoni, Tony	FB	1978,79
Lepley, Paul M.	BB	1952,53,54
Leps, Ergas	MTR	1959,60,61,62
Leps, Taimo	MTR	1966,67,68,69
Lerg, Daniel F.	IHO	1977,78,79,80
Lerner, George J.	BB	1934,35,36
Lesser, Eric	MD	1991,92,93,94
Lessner, Donald G.	FB	1987
Lester, Kenneth L.	WR	1985
Leuchtman, Stephen N.	MTR	1964,65,66
Leung, Li Li	WGY	1992,93,94,95
Leung, May May	WGY	1992,95
Leutritz, Jack C.	MTR	1939,40,41
Lev, Jennifer	WTN	1989,90,91,92
Levi, Waldeck	IHO	1925
Levenson, Gordon E.	MGY	1948,49,50
Levenson, Neil T.	MTN	1936,37,38
Levine, Edward D.	MBK	1925
Levine, John C.	FB	1971,72,72
Levine, Louis	FB	1936,37,38
Levitt, Jack	MBK	1951,52
Levy, Allan B.	BB	1953,54,55
Levy, Paul A.	MGY	1961,62,63,64
Lewandowski, Phillip J.	FB	1984
Lewid, Robert E.	BB	1888,89
Lewis, Charles W.	MTR	1921,22
Lewis, David M.	MCC	1977,78,79,80
	MTR	1978,79,80,81
Lewis, Deborah	FH	1973,74,75
Lewis, Eric	MBK	1992
Lewis, Jack H.	MBK	1956,57,58
	BB	1956,57
Lewis, James	MGO	1929
Lewis, Jared	MTR	1996
Lewis, Kevin	BB	1990
Lewis, Kirk J.	FB	1973,74,76
Lewis, Michael	FB	1992
Lewis, Roger S.	MTN	1943,44,45
Lewis, Vanessa	WSOC	1995
Liakonis, Nicholas A.	BB	1957,58,59,60
Libby, Keely	FH	1990,91,92,93
Lichtman, Kurt S.	MTN	1983,84,85
Liedy, John B.	MGO	1940,41,42,43
Lieneck, John B.	BB	1973
Lightfoot, Robert W.	MGY	1969
Lightner, Henry	FB	1913
Lightvoet, Stephanie	WTN	1983
Likert, George H.	MTR	1925
Lilienfield, Robert	IHO	1945
Lilja, George V.	FB	1977,78,79,80
Lillard IV, Leonard H.	MBK	1976,77
Lilly, Orethia	WBK	1983,84,85,86
Limauro, Jessica	WSOC	1995
Linclau, Ronald L.	MTN	1961,62,63
Lincoln, James H.	FB	1935,36
	WR	1937
Lincoln, Richard M.	MTN	1947,48,49,50
Lind, Dean W.	MGO	1949,50,51,52
Lindemuler, Caroline	WSW	1984
Lindgren, Robert D.	MBK	1939
Lindquist, Donald H.	MBK	1945
Lindquist, John A.	MTR	1949
Lindsay, Rock D.	FB	1978
Lindskog, Douglas P.	IHO	1974,75,76
Lindskog, Thomas N.	IHO	1973,74,75,76
Lindstrom, Carlton	IHO	1924,25
Lindstrom, L.O.B.	MTR	1919
Lindstrom, Maren	WGY	1981,83,84
Line, Edward D.	MBK	1925
Lingenberg, Kathy	WSW	1976
Lingle, Milton F.	MBK	1954,55,56
Lingon, John	MTN	1991,92
Lingon, John G.	MTR	1951
Linthicum, Frank	FB	1908,09,10
	BB	1908,09,10
Linton, John	FB	1944,45,46
Lipa, Larry D.	BB	1976
Lipp, Stephen J.	FB	1983
Lisagor, Irvin	BB	1937,38,39
Litchman, Kurt S.	MTN	1985
Liu, Kimberly	FH	1982,83
Liverance, Howard H.	MTR	1952,55
Liverance, Howard J.	BB	1921,22,23
Livingston, Jasen	BB	1992,93,94,95
Livingston, Richard J.	MGO	1929,30,31
Lloyd, Laurie	WSW	1982
Loar, James E.	MGO	1938,39
Lockard, Harold	FB	1940,41
Lockard, John C.	MBK	1970,72,73
Locke, Raymond S.	MTR	1958,60,61
Locker, John H.	BB	1987,88,89
Lockwood, Joseph P.	IHO	1985,86,87,88
Lodeserto, Frank	WR	1996,97
Loeb, Henry S.	MGO	1954,55,56
Loeher, Barbara	WBK	1988,89,90,91
Loell, John L.	FB	1906,07
	BB	1906,07
Loesche, Dana E.	WTR	1980
	WCC	1982
Logan, Randolph	FB	1971,72
Logas, Philip L.	FB	1986
Loges, Alfred H.	IHO	1993,94,95
Logue, Holly	WCC	1995,96
Logue, W. Benson	FB	1983,84
Lonchar, John A.	MBK	1971
	BB	1971,72,73,74
London, Terrence	MTN	1992
Longe, Kevin T.	FB	1977,78,79
Longjohn, Julia	SB	1986
Longjohn, Mindy	WSOC	1994,95
Longman, Frank	FB	1903,04,05
Longs, Curtis O.	MBK	1977
	FB	1978
Lonstorf, George	BB	1876
Longstreth, Jeffrey G.	MSW	1961,62,63,64
Lonner, Mark S.	MTR	1975,76,77,78
Loomis, Halbert M.	MTR	1924
Loos, Carl M.	BB	1926,27,28
Lopez, Victor O.	MSW	1982
Lord, William M.	IHO	1965,66,67,68
Lorden, Gary E.	IHO	1985,88
Lorenzen, Hayley	VB	1989,90,91,92
Lori, Molly	WCC	1992,93,94
	WTR	1993,94
Losch, Richard D.	MTR	1919,20,21
Lothrop, Thompson	BB	1909,10
Lott, John	FB	1980,81,82,83
Loucks, Alvin	FB	1919
Loud, Henry C.	IHO	1941,42,43
Lounsberry, Fred L.	IHO	1945
Lousma, Jack R.	FB	1956
Louthen, Ray A.	BB	1945
Love, James G.	MTR	1952,53,54,55
Love, Jennifer	WSW	1989,90,91,92
Lovell Jr., Frank R.	MGO	1956,57,58,59
Lovell, Erik	FB	1992,94
Lovett, James	IHO	1939,40,41

Kay McCarthy (1980-83) holds Michigan field hockey career bests in goals and points.

Lovette, John	FB	1925,26
	MTR	1927
Low, Albert E.	MTR	1947,43,44
Low, Charles S.	MTR	1947
Low, E. Reed	IHO	1936
Lowe, Hal B.	MTN	1962,63,64,65
Lowe, John C.	IHO	1957
Lowe, John M.	MTR	1969,70
Lowe, Ronald	FB	1982
Lowell, William O.	WR	1933,36
Lowney, Dionysius	BB	1896
Loy, Katy	WGO	1996
Lozier, J. Mark	MBK	1977,78,79,80
Lozon, Alfred A.	WR	1973,75
Lubell, Richard A.	MSW	1975,76,77
Luby, Earle	FB	1935,36,37
Lubina, Allan F.	MTR	1952,54,55
Lucadam, Andrea	VB	1990
Luce, Josh L.	MSW	1976,77,78
Luchs, Harry A.	MGY	1952
Lucier, Dean W.	IHO	1964,65,66,67
Lucier, William G.	IHO	1952,53,54,55
Lucius, Edward B.	MTN	1906,07
Ludka, Benjamim	MTR	1994,95
Ludlow, Oliver A.	BB	1897
Ludolph, William T.	MGO	1943,47
Ludwig II, Frederick	WR	1958,60,61
Ludwig, H. Thomas	MBK	1962,63,64,65
Ludwig, Stephen J.	MGO	1984
Lugin, David A.	MTR	1981,82,83,84
Luhning, Warren	IHO	1994,95,96,97
Lukasik, Kelly	WSOC	1995
Lukins, Lester S.	MTR	1921
Lukz, Joseph E.	FB	1969
Lund, Donald A.	MBK	1943,44,45
	BB	1943,44,45
	FB	1942,43,44
Lundbeck, Laura L.	WGY	1989,90,91,92
Lundberg, Brian F.	IHO	1979,80,81,82
Lundin, Jon W.	MSW	1961,64
Lundquist, C. David	FB	1956
Lundquist, John	MTN	1996
Lundstedt, Thomas R.	BB	1968,69,70
Lundy, Katherine	WSW	1983,84,85
Lunghamer, Joseph E.	IHO	1959,60,61
Lunn, Ernest	BB	1897,88,89
Lunsford, Lisa	WSW	1984,85,86,87
Luoma, Kevin	MTR	1995
Luongo, Stephen P.	IHO	1978
Lupinski, Jennifer	FH	1992,93,94,95
Lutomski, Karl F.	WR	1956,57,58
Lutz, Christopher T.	BB	1986,87,88
Luxton, Thomas J.	FB	1980,81
Luze, Shareen	VB	1993,94,95,96
Lyall, James M.	FB	1973
Lybrook, Joan	WGY	1986
Lyijynen, James J.	BB	1964,65,66,67
Lyke, Heather R.	SB	1989,90,91,92
Lyle III, William C.	MGO	1992,93,94,95
Lyle Jr., William C.	MBK	1969,70
	MGO	1970
Lyles, Rodney K.	FB	1982,83,84
Lynch, George F.	MTR	1952,53,54
Lynch, John A.	FB	1968
Lyons, John	FB	1913,14
Lytle, Robert W.	FB	1974,75,76
	MTR	1975,76

M

MacBride, Owen E.	MCC	1968,69,70,71
	MTR	1969,70,71
MacCallum, Charles E.	MGO	1948,49,50
MacCollum, Donald	IHO	1934,35
MacConnachie, William M.	MBK	1942
MacDonald, A. Byron	MSW	1969,70,71,72
MacDonald, Bruce G.	MTN	1958,59,60,61
MacDonald, J. Barry	IHO	1963,64,65,66
MacDonald, Jason	MGY	1994,95,96
MacDonald, K. Scott	MCC	1992
	MTR	1993,94,95,96
MacDonald, Kirsten	WTR	1990
MacDonald, L. Dale	FB	1957
	IHO	1958,59,60,61
MacDuff, Harry	IHO	1925,26
MacDuff, Kunle	IHO	1923
MacFarland, William H.	IHO	1953,54,55,56
MacIntyre, M. Neil	MTR	1941
MacKay, Barry B.	MTN	1954,55,56,57
MacKay, Donald	MTN	1948,49,50
MacKay, Shawn	MCC	1990,91,92,93
	MTR	1991,93,94
MacKenzie, Douglas A.	FB	1970,71,72
MacKenzie, Kate	WCR	1997
MacKenzie, Martha	WSW	1982,83
MacLellan, Alexander D.	IHO	1950,51,52,53
MacMaster, Christine M.	WSW	1985
MacMichael, Robert J.	MGO	1955,56,57
MacMillan, Lincoln	BB	1883,84,88
MacPhee, William D.	BB	1957,58
	FB	1958
MacPherran, Ed	FB	1887,88,89
	MTR	1887
	BB	1893
Mace, William	FB	1882
Machemer, Kevin S.	MD	1980,81
Mack, Charles S.	MSW	1944
Mack, Christian N.	MTN	1915,16
Mack, Edward E. Jr.	MSW	1938,39
Mack Jr., Hugh R.	FB	1943
	WR	1947,48
Mack, Thomas L.	FB	1964,65
Mackall, Rex A.	FB	1975,76
Mackevich, Marietta	WGY	1977
Mackey, Leslie	WTN	1985,86,87,88
Mackey, Thomas F.	MTN	1937
Mackie, John W.	MGY	1969,70
Macmanus, F.A.C.	BB	1866
Macnab, Bruce J.	IHO	1984,85,86,87
Mactaggart, Mary	WTN	1981,82,83,84
Maddalena, Stephen J.	MGO	1979,80,81,82
Madar, Elmer	FB	1941,42,46
Madden, John	IHO	1994,95,96,97
Maddock, James A.	FB	1954,55,56
Maddock, Joseph	FB	1902,03
	MTR	1093
Maddox, Elliott R.	BB	1967,68
Mader, Gerald H.	FB	1962,63,64
Madill, Valerie E.	WGO	1983,84,85,86
Madison, Jacqueline	VB	1976,77,78,80
Madsen, Edgar	FB	1924
Maentz, D. Scott	MBK	1959,61
	FB	1959,60,61
	MTN	1959,61
Maentz, Thomas S.	FB	1954,55,56
Magarity, Charles J.	BB	1907
Magidsohn, Joe	FB	1909,10
Magnuson, John G.	MTR	1957
Magoffin, Paul	FB	1905,06,07
Mahan, Theodore R.	BB	1974,75,76,77
Mahler, Jay J.	MSW	1966,67,68,69
Mahler, Michael	MCC	1994,95,96
Mahoney, Winom J.	BB	1992
Mahony, William V.	MSW	1968,69,70,71
Maier, Ryan	BB	1991
Mains, John	MGY	1989,90
Mair, Peter K.	FB	1966,67
Maistros, Robert P.	MTR	1976
Major, Bethany	VB	1977,78
Makoski, Robert J.	BB	1970
Makris, Timothy J.	IHO	1985,86
Malaby, Robert C.	MBK	1974
Malchow, Tom	MSW	1996
Malcomson, Craig	IHO	1968,69
Malik, Amy	WTN	1989,90,91,92
Malicke, Gregg	IHO	1996
Malinak, Timothy A.	FB	1978
Mallard, Laurette	WTR	1984,85,86,87
Mallette, Richard Y.	IHO	1970,71,72,73
Mallory, Curtis S.	FB	1989
Mallory, Douglas S.	FB	1984,85,86,87
Mallory, Michael W.	FB	1982,83,84,85
Malloy, Woodrow W.	MGO	1934,35,36
Malone, Tait L.	MTR	1961,62
Maloney, Cindy	VB	1987
Maloney, Frank M.	FB	1961
Maloney, James W.	MTR	1906,07
Maloney, Patrick M.	BB	1990,91,92,93
	FB	1990,91,92
Malveaux Jr., Felman	FB	1991,92
	MTR	1994,95,96
Mandel, David M.	FB	1987
Mandel, Scott H.	FB	1987
Mandeville, Dick C.	FB	1947
Mandich, James M.	FB	1967,68,69
Mandich, John D.	FB	1975
Mandler, James E.	MBK	1941,42,43
Manery, Kris F.	IHO	1974,75,76,77
Manko, Dennis	BB	1944
Mann, Alexander W.	MTN	1952,53,54,55
Mann, John R.	MTR	1969,70,71,72
Mann III, Matt	MSW	1946,48,49,50
Mann, Rachel	WCC	1991,92
Mann, Robert	FB	1946,47
	MTR	1945
Mannard, Enn	MSW	1962
Manning, Paul	FB	1991,92
Manning, Timothy J.	IHO	1978,79,80,81
Manns, Kari	WTR	1983
Mans, Deborah	WTR	1991,93,94
Mans, George W.	FB	1959,60,61
Mans, James S.	IHO	1983,84
Manson, Tanya	WCC	1994,95,96
Manuel, Kenneth G.	BB	1932,33
Manuel, Warde J.	FB	1987,88
	MTR	1990
Manus, Dean A.	MGY	1982,83
Mapes, E.J.	BB	1865
Mapes, Pam	VB	1973
Maran, Patricia L.	FH	1987,88,89,90
Marcellus, Phillip B.	MGO	1942,43,44,45
Marcereau, Robert H.	BB	1958,59,60,61
March, Ron M.	WR	1986
Marchello, John L.	FB	1954
	WR	1955,56,57,58
Marchiano, Julie A.	WTR	1987,88
Marciniak, Gerald P.	FB	1956,57,58
Marcoux, William J.	MTR	1945,47,48,49
Marcovski, Abraham	FB	1932
Marcum, John F.	FB	1962,63,64
Marcus, Brian J.	MTN	1967,68,69
Marcus, Daniel L.	MSW	1931,32,33
Margolin, Robert M.	BB	1953
Margulies, Janice	VB	1979,80,81
Mariani, Paul	MGY	1992
Marich, David M.	IHO	1981,82,83,84
Marijonavick, Kathy	WBK	1974
Marinaro, Joseph	FB	1992,93,94,95
Marion, Nino A.	MGY	1957,58,59
Marion, Phillip	FB	1923,24
Marion, Robert L.	FB	1954,55
Marion, Todd	BB	1990,91,92,93
Marker, John J.	BB	1888
Marker, Stuart F.	MTR	1906
Markham, Clarence	MGO	1933, 34,35
Markman, Lawrence D.	MGO	1957,59,60
Markray, Triando	FB	1983,84
Marks, Ashley	WSOC	1995
Marks, Harold S.	IHO	1929
Marks, Tom	FB	1900
Marlin, Lloyd W.	BB	1910,11
Marmo, Joseph F.	IHO	1949,50,51
Marotti, Sandra	FH	1988,89,90,91
Marra, Thomas F.	IHO	1968,69,70,71
Mars, Jeffrey J.	IHO	1978,79,80,81
Marsh, Douglas W.	FB	1977,78,79
Marsh, Edward P.	MTR	1896
Marshall, Alex C.	FB	1988,89,90,91
Marshall, Barry H.	BB	1958,59,60,61
Marshall, Charles L.	MTR	1943
Marshall, James R.	MGO	1976,77,78,79
Marshall, John A.	IHO	1927,28
Marshall, Julie	VB	1986,87,88
Marshall, Karen A.	VB	1986,87,88,89
Marshall, Ross D.	FB	1947
Marshall, Wendy	WGY	1993,94,95,96
Marsicano, Mitchell B.	WR	1975,77
Marsich, Matthew M.	MGY	1991,93
Martay, Peter W.	BB	1996
Martens, Albert	FB	1916
Martin Jr., Alexander M.	MBK	1950
Martin, Alva C.	BB	1907
Martin, Carmel	BB	1905,06,07
Martin, Christopher J.	MSW	1987
Martin, Clarence	MTR	1966,67,68
Martin, Daisy A.	WTN	1980,81
Martin, David M.	MTR	1958,59,60,61
Martin, David W.	FB	1947
Martin, Frank H.	MTR	1923
Martin, Frederick	MTR	1937,38
Martin, George	WR	1929
Martin, Jack R.	MTR	1943,44
Martin, Harvey	MTR	1891,93,95
Martin, LeClair	MTR	1893,95
Martin, Mary Beth	SS	1981,82
Martin, Richard G.	MSW	1949,50,51,52
Martin, Shawn	MGY	1988,89,90
Martin, Strother D. Jr.	MSW	1940,42
Martin, Theodore W.	MGY	1969,70,71,72
Martin, Tinamarie	SB	1991,92
Martin, Wilfred A.	IHO	1963,64,65
Martino, Erin	SB	1993,94,95,96
Martins, Flavio	MGY	1994,95,96,97
Martinson, Ronald M.	IHO	1951,52,53
Marttila, C. Lee	IHO	1966,67,68
Marttila, Michael J.	IHO	1964,65,66,67
Martucci, Chris A.	BB	1976,77
Marubashi, Naomi	WSW	1983
Marvin, Stuart E.	MSW	1985
Marzonie, George	FB	1936,37
Mascarin, Telly A.	IHO	1952,53
Mason, A. Scott	MBK	1974
Mason, Bruce H.	BB	1942,44
Mason, Dale R.	BB	1978,79
Mason, Ira J.	MTR	1925
Mason, Joseph G.	MTR	1961,63,64
Mason, Peter J.	IHO	1979,81,82
Mason, Stevens T.	MTR	1936,37,38
Masters, Mary E.	FH	1973
Matchefts, John P.	IHO	1950,51,53
Mateka, Edward	IHO	1959,60
Maten, M. Allen	MSW	1957,58,59
Matheny, Michael S.	BB	1989,90,91
Matheson, Donald S.	MTR	1956,57,58
Matheson, Lisa	WSW	1978
Matheson, Robert K.	FB	1951,52
	MTR	1950
Mathias, James S.	WR	1978,79,80,81
Mathison, Derek	BB	1990
Matney Jr., William C.	MTR	1943
Matsumoto, Shuichi	MSW	1993,94,95,96
Matters, Robert J.	MSW	1946
Matteson, David	BB	1898,99,00
Matthews, David O.	MTR	1941,42,43
Matthews, Roy D.	BB	1902
Matthews, Trevor L.	MTR	1970
Matton, Douglas M.	FB	1988
Mattson, Gary	IHO	1958,59,60
Maturo, John E.	FB	1946,47,48
Matz, Jennifer	WGY	1984
Maugh, Martha A.	FH	1979,80,81,82
Maugh, Roger E.	FB	1950
	MTR	1951,52,53,54
Maulbetsch, John	FB	1914,15,16
Maundrell, Michael E.	MBK	1966,67
	BB	1966
	FB	1966
Maurer, Clifford A.	IHO	1975,76,77,78
Maves, Earl	FB	1943
Maxey, Kenneth E.	MBK	1966,67,68,69
Maxon, Bradley J.	FB	1980
Maxwell, D. Wallace	IHO	1955,57
May, Dennis F.	IHO	1979,80,81,82
May, Donald C.	MTR	1908,09,10
May, Douglas H.	IHO	1982,83,84,85
May, Edward A.	IHO	1949,50,51,52
Mayberry, Shelia	WTR	1980
Mayer, Albert Jr.	MSW	1926,27
Mayes, Eric T.	FB	1995,96
Mayhew, Catherine	FH	1983
Maynard, Fred A.	BB	1871,72,73
Maynard, T.J.	WR	1925
Maynard, Thomas R.	MTR	1920
Mayne, John D.	MBK	1958
Mazer Jr., William M.	BB	1952
Mazure, Ann	WTN	1983,84
Mazzetta, Dea	FH	1978
McAfee, William F.	BB	1928,29
McAlvey, Robert D.	MSW	1978
	WR	1978
McArdel, Owen	IHO	1948,49
McArthur, George H.	MTR	1929
McBride, John R. (Jack)	FB	1970
McBride, Paul T.	MGY	1975,78
McCaffree, Charles F.	MSW	1930
McCaffree, Floyd E.	MTR	1927
McCahill, John W.	IHO	1975,76,77,78
McCahill, Marita	VB	1990,91,92,93
McCain, George L.	MTN	1939
McCall, Stacie	WBK	1990,91,92,93
McCarren, Kenneth G.	MGO	1939
McCarthy, Frank C.	MTR	1941,42
McCarthy, Jean	FH	1976,77,78
McCarthy, John F.	MSW	1943,44,48,49

McCarthy, Kathleen	FH	1980,81,82,83
McCarthy, Marquis I. Jr.	MSW	1936
McCarthy, Stephen M.	MSW	1970,71,72,73
McCarthy, Vere L.	BB	1912,13
McCaslin IV, Thomas A.	WR	1968,69
McCaslin, Boyd L.	MBK	1947,48,49
McCaughey, Bradley J.	IHO	1985,86,87,88
McCauley, James A.	IHO	1981,82,83,84
McClain, Ebony	WTR	1995,96
McClatchey, Alan	MSW	1976
McCleary Jr., John F.	MTR	1984,85
McCleery, Alexander H.	MTN	1962
McClellan, David E.	MBK	1966,67,68,69
McClelland, Don	FB	1947,48,49
McClelland, Randall S.	MGO	1976
McClimon, Molly	WCC	1989,90,92,93
	WTR	1990,93,94
McClintock, James I.	MBK	1918,19
McClusky, Dean K.	MTN	1946
McColl, James D.	MTN	1986,88,89
McCollum, Jeff	WR	1990
McConkey, James G.	MTR	1896
McConnell Jr., William C.	MTR	1945
McCorkel, Tegan	WGO	1993,94
McCorkel, Tiffany	WGO	1994
McCormick, Amy	WTR	1989,90,91,92
McCormick, Janet	VB	1979
McCormick, Robert E.	FB	1947
McCormick, Timothy D.	MBK	1981,83,84
McCoy, C. Richard	FB	1968,69,70
McCoy, Ernest B.	MBK	1927,28,29
	BB	1928,29
McCoy, Ernest H.	FB	1957
McCoy, Matthew S.	FB	1989
McCracken, Marisa	WSW	1990,91,92,93
McCrimmon, Kelly J.	IHO	1981,82,83,84
McCrory, Bradley L.	WR	1972,73,75
McCubbrey, Doris	FH	1983,84,85,86
McCullough, Ray T.	MSW	1970,71,72,73
McCully, Kathleen	WSW	1976,77,78,9
McCurdy, Frederick B.	MGY	1968,69,70,71
McDivitt, Ann	WD	1977,78,79,80
	WSW	1977,78,79
McDonald, Alexander L.	MTR	1965,66,67,68
McDonald, Andrea	WGY	1994,95,96,97
McDonald, Bonnie	WCC	1982,83,84,85
McDonald, Charles	FB	1898,99
McDonald, Duncan B.	FB	1951,52,53,54
McDonald, Jason	MGY	1994,95,96,97
McDonald, John A.	BB	1948,49
	IHO	1947,48,49,50
McDonald, K. Scott	MCC	1996
McDonald, Neil W.	BB	1955,58
	IHO	1955,56,57,58
McDonald, Shannon F.	WGO	1994,95,96
McDonald, William F.	MSW	1929
McEldowney, John P.	BB	1977,78
McEwen, Donald S.	MTR	1949,50,51,52
McFarland, Lt. Robert	MBK	1983
McFarland, Joseph P.	WR	1981,82,84,85
McFee, Bruce C.	MCC	1976,77,78
	MTR	1976,77,78
McGee, Anthony L.	FB	1989,90,91,92
McGee, Harry S.	BB	1897,1902
McGee, Mike R.	MBK	1978,79,80,81
McGilliard, Stanley	WR	1929
McGinley, Dale R.	MSW	1956,57,58,59
McGinn, Dennis M.	BB	1958,59,60,61
McGinnis, Craig S.	BB	1975,76,77,78
McGinnis, Dan	MTR	1989
McGinnis, Edwin	BB	1898,99,00,01
McGonigal, John K.	IHO	1960,61,62,63
McGovern, Erin	VB	1993,94,95,96
McGowan, Shawn M.	BB	1976
McGraw, Rozanne	SS	1974
McGugin, Dan	FB	1901,02
McGuire, John J.	MSW	1959,61
McGuire, Michael S.	MCC	1974,75,76,77
	MTR	1975,76,78
McGuire, Paul K.	MD	1967,69,70
McHale, Frank	FB	1913,14
McIndoe, Charles	BB	1889
McIntosh, Donald B.	MBK	1948,50
McIntosh, Donald W.	IHO	1955,56,58
McIntosh, Paul M.	MGO	1972
McIntyre, Andree	FB	1984,85,86,87
McIntyre, David M.	IHO	1982,83,84
McIntyre, George W.	WR	1944
McIntyre, Kent	FB	1926
McIver, Richmond	MBK	1991,92
McKay, David C.	MCC	1987
	MTR	1988
McKay, Patrick T.	WR	1978,81,82
McKeachie, Karen	VB	1973
McKean, John B.	MTR	1942

McKean, Tom	FB	1890
McKee, Bradshaw C.	FB	1947
McKee, James L.	MD	1967,69
McKee, John C.	MTN	1980
McKee, Kevin P.	MGY	1980,81,82,83
McKee, Michael S.	MGY	1980,81,82,83
McKeithen, Dana	WTR	1986,87,88,89
McKennell, John H.	IHO	1951,52
McKenzie, Reginald	FB	1969,70,71
McKenzie, William D.	BB	1895,96
McKillen, James G.	BB	1928
McKim, Michelle	VB	1989
McKinney, Don C.	BB	1896
McKinney Jr., E. Kirk	FB	1947,47
McKittrick, Jennifer	SB	1995,96,97
McKown, Joseph A.	MCC	1987,89,91
	MTR	1990,91,92
McLaughlin, Daniel G.	MTN	1969,70
McLaughlin, Donald	MTR	1995,96
McLaughlin, F. Daniel	MTN	1980,81
McLaughlin, James C.	BB	1881
McLaury, Douglas P.	MTN	1968,70,71
McLean, Diane	WGY	1980,81,83
McLean, John	FB	1898,99
	MTR	1896,97,99,00
McLean, Melissa	WSW	1992,93,94,95
McLean, Randy	MBK	1974
McLenna, Bruce	FB	1961
McLeod, Jeffrey R.	MTR	1974,75,76,77
McLogan, Jennifer A.	WBK	1974
McMahon, John D.	WR	1953,54,55,56
McMahon, Michael J.	MTR	1975
McManaman, Bruce M.	MD	1967,69,70
McMann, Mark J.	MD	1981,82
McManus, Richard H.	MTR	1934
McMaster, John D.	MTR	1940,41
McMasters, Robert L.	MGO	1953,54,55,56
McMillan, Gordon	IHO	1946,47,48,49
McMillan, Neil	FB	1910,11
	BB	1910,11
McMurdy, Robert	BB	1877
McMurray, Francis	BB	1897
McMurtry, Gregory W.	BB	1987,88,89
	FB	1986,87,88,89
McNab, John A.	MTR	1945
McNamara, Mary Cathleen	WBK	1979,80
McNeal, Harley	BB	1931,32
McNear, David R.	MSW	1987
McNeil, Tom	FB	1883,84,85
McNeil, Trey	FB	1987
McNeill, Edward D.	FB	1945,46,47,48
McNelis, Michael P.	MGY	1980,84
McNitt, Gary D.	FB	1958,59,60
McParlan, Thomas J.	MBK	1972
	MGO	1973,74,75
McPeck, Jennifer	WCC	1986,87,88,89
	WTR	1989,90
McPhee, Riley	FB	1984
McPherson, James N.	FB	1959
McQuaid, Michelle	WSOC	1994
McQueen, Edmond P.	BB	1913,14,15
McRae, Benjamin P.	FB	1959,60,61
	MTR	1959,60,61,62
McRae, Patrick M.	WR	1985
McThomas, Greg	FB	1991,92
McVeigh, David H.	FB	1985
McWilliams, Richard H.	FB	1949,50
McWood, Arthur B.	MBK	1923,24
Mcginnis, Daniel E.	MTR	1989
Mead, Milton E.	MBK	1951,52,53,54
	MTR	1951,52,53,54
Meaden III, John A.	MD	1966,67,68,69
Meaden, Thomas F.	MD	1964,67
Meadows, Ilene	FH	1986,87,88-
Meads, G. Edgar	FB	1953,54,55
Medd, W. Bruce	MGY	1972,73,74,75
Meek, Richard	FB	1911
Meeker, M.	WR	1922
Mees, Mark A.	MTN	1980,81,82,83
Meese, William R.	MTR	1919,20,21
Mehaffey, Howard	FB	1938,44
Mehall, Joanna M.	WTR	1980,81,82,83
Mehihop, Fred W.	BB	1886,87,88
Mehl, Richard A.	MSW	1956,57
Meigs, Richard H.	MSW	1931
Meilziner, Alfred	MSW	1924
Meining, Henry C.	MTR	1896
Meislin, Barry H.	MBK	1975
Meissner, Ernest	MD	1959,60
Melchiori, Wayne F.	FB	1952
Meldman, Louis W.	MGO	1971,74
Melgaard, Paul J.	WR	1954,55
Melita, Thomas S.	FB	1977
Mellon, Ralph R.	BB	1907,08,09
Melnyk, Michael J.	FB	1984

Melnyk, Ronald M.	MSW	1987,88
Melvin, Laura	VB	1986,87
Meltzer, Milton	BB	1933,35
Meltzer, Stuart T.	BB	1987
Melzow, William	FB	1939,40,41
Mendrygal, Mitchell B.	WR	1970,71,72,73
Menees Jr., J. Stanley	MTR	1955,56
Menefee, Charles C.	MGO	1934
Menegay, Jonathan K.	MD	1979
Meno, Harlow B.	MTR	1985,86
Mercer, Brian V.	FB	1982,83
Mercer, James W.	MTR	1964,65,66
Mercer, William	WR	1993
Meredith, David M.	FB	1982,83,84
Merical, Burton W.	WR	1964,65,66,67
Mericka, James	WR	1938,39
Merkel, Charles C.	MTN	1921,22,23
Merrill, Jack R.	IHO	1933,36,37
Merriott, Ronald M.	MD	1980,81,82
Merritt, William E.	MTN	1950
Mertz, Richard C.	MSW	1929
Mertz, Thomas J.	MSW	1967,68,69
Merullo, Joseph R.	BB	1959,60,61,62
Messinger, Thomas F.	MGO	1944
	IHO	1944
Messner, Daniel K.	MTR	1918
Messner, Mark W.	FB	1985,86,87,88
Metcalf, Willard A.	MSW	1946
Meter, Gerard A.	FB	1976,77,78
Metnick, Larry H.	MGY	1965,67
Metz, David F.	FB	1972,73,74
Meyer, Amy	WGY	1986,87,88,89
Meyer, David S.	MCC	1983,84
	MTR	1983,84,85
Meyer, Gregory A.	MCC	1973,74,75,76
	MTR	1974,75,76,77
Meyer, Jack O.	FB	1938
Meyer, William H.	BB	1973
Meyerowitz, Gavin P.	MGY	1984,85,86
Meyers, David F.	MSW	1955,56,57
Myers, Earl	FB	1935
	MBK	1935
Meyers Jr., Earl J.	BB	1964,65
Meyers, John	FB	1989
Meyers, Ronda	WTR	1993,94
Michaels, William B.	MTR	1953,54
Michalek, Christopher J.	BB	1990,91,92
Michaud, Jeanne	SS	1977,78,79
Michaud, Lee C.	MD	1986,87,88,89
Mick, Cheryl	FH	1986,86,87,87
Micklow, Frederick A.	MGO	1955,56,57
Middlebrook, John F.	FB	1971
Middleton, Jerene	WBK	1984
Midlam, Larry D.	MTR	1966,67,68,69
Miele, Anthony M.	MGY	1954,55,56
Mielke, Robert W.	FB	1964,65,66
Miesel, Laurie	WGY	1979,80,81,82
Mihalic, Michael	WR	1993
Mihic, John H.	FB	1985
Mika, Tammy	SB	1996,97
Mike, Kenneth J.	MTN	1959,60
Miklos, Gerald W.	FB	1966,67,68
Mikulich, William H.	MBK	1947,48,49
Milani, Luigi A.	WR	1980,82
Milanowski, Paul G.	IHO	1948,49,50
Milburn, Joe H.	IHO	1980,81,82,83
Milczarski, Karen	WTN	1982,83,84
Mildner, Eric C.	MSW	1924
Miles, Les E.	FB	1974,75
Milia, Marc J.	FB	1991,92,93
Miller, Albert E.	BB	1882,83
Miller, Alison	WTN	1984,85,87
Miller, Aubrey L.	FB	1974,75,76
Miller, Charles I.	MTR	1936,37,38
Miller, Charles T.	BB	1885,86,87,88
Miller, David C.	MGY	1980,81,82,83
Miller, Donald C.	BB	1925,26,27
Miller, Douglas E.	BB	1931
Miller, F. Clayton	FB	1981,82,83,
		84,85
Miller, Glenwood I.	MSW	1952,53,54,55
Miller, Guy A.	BB	1896,97,98,99
Miller, Hugh D.	MBK	1943,44
Miller, James J.	FB	1907,09
Miller Jr., James K.	FB	1923,24
Miller, James R.	FB	1925,26,27
Miller, Jeffrey S.	MTN	1972,73,74,75
Miller, Mark A.	IHO	1976,77,78,79
Miller, Mitzi	WGY	1978
Miller, Morris B.	BB	1936
Miller, Paul S.	MTR	1903,04
Miller, Robert	MSW	1930,31,32
Miller, Robert L.	MGY	1952
Miller, Shawn C.	FB	1991,92,93
Miller, Terry O.	MBK	1958,59,60

Miller, Thomas A.	WR	1948,49
Miller, Timothy L.	BB	1979,80,81
Miller, Wallace B.	FB	1930
Miller, Wayne H.	WR	1962,63,64
Miller, Wayne L.	MGY	1965,66,67,68
Miller, William G.	MBK	1921,22
Millett, David	MTR	1993,96
Millett, Jon	WR	1990
Milligan, John D.	FB	1987,88,89,90
Mills, David B.	MTN	1953
Mills, John G.	MGY	1950,51
Mills, Joseph E.	MTN	1931
Mills, Robert W.	MTR	1972,73,74
Mills, Terry R.	MBK	1988,89,90
Mills, William J.	MTN	1937
Milnor, Robert C.	BB	1945
Milobinski, Marc	MSW	1990,91
Miner, Maureen	WTR	1981
Minick, Jeffrey T.	BB	1982,83,84
Miniuk, Collen	VB	1994,95
Minko, John P.	FB	1960,61,62
Mirageas, Debbie J.	SB	1979,80,81
Miranda, Christina	WGY	1993,94,95,96
Mistor, Paul G.	MCC	1983,84,85,
		86,87
Mitchell, Alan B.	FB	1978,79,80
Mitchell, Alistair W.	MTN	1933
Mitchell, Anthony L.	FB	1987,88
Mitchell, Charles	FB	1878,79
Mitchell, Elmer D.	BB	1910,11,12
Mitchell, James F.	MTR	1948,49,50,51
Mitchell, Keith A.	FB	1987,88
Mitchell, Robert C.	MTN	1951,54,55
Mitchell II, Robert I.	MTR	1971,72
Mitchell, Samuel A.	MBK	1991
Mitchell, William H.	MTN	1946,47,48,49
Mitchell, William J.	MBK	1982,83
Mitvalsky, Richard	MSW	1990,91
Mixer, Richard A.	IHO	1944
Moeller, Andrew G.	FB	1982,84,85,86
Moes, Michael A.	IHO	1987,88,89,90
Mogk, John E.	BB	1957,58,59,60
Mogk, William C.	BB	1950,51,52,53
Mogle, Glenn	FB	1986
Mogulich, Robert G.	FB	1969,72
Mohan, W. Keith	MGO	1967,68,69,70
Moiser, Arthur H.	WR	1932,33,34
Moisio, Konrad W.	MTR	1932,33,35
Mokris, Philip C.	MGO	1977,79,80
Molenda, John J.	FB	1925,26
Molina, Jorge	MGY	1992,93,94,95
Molla, Theodore	MCC	1992,93,94,95
	MTR	1993
Momsen Jr., Anton	FB	1945,46,49,50
Mondul, Patricia	FH	1985,86,87
Monroe, Randolph B.	MCC	1928
Monroe, Victoria	WGY	1977
Montague, Andrew R.	MSW	1984
Montague, Richard W.	BB	1930
Montgomery, Henry E.	BB	1883
Montgomery, Lorenzo	MTR	1968,69,70,71
Monthei, Dennis B.	FB	1967
Montour, Frederick O.	MTR	1958,59,60
Montpetit, Richard	MGY	1958,59,60,61
Montross, Steven P.	MTN	1972
Moodle, Frank B.	BB	1931
Moody, Eugene G.	MTR	1943,44,48
Moody, Linda L.	WBK	1974,75
Moon, Randall J.	BB	1979
Mooney, Joseph	BB	1990,91
Moons, Patrick J.	FB	1985,86

Shannon McDonald (1993-96) became the first Michigan women's golfer to earn All-Big Ten honors.

Moore, Albert	FB	1883
	MTR	1883
Moore, Ed	FB	1968,69,70
Moore II, Emerson	MBK	1994
Moore III, Warfield	MBK	1976,77
Moore, Angela	WTR	1991
Moore, Edward M.	FB	1967,68,69,70
Moore, Emerson	MBK	1994
Moore, Evan A.	MCC	1981
	MTR	1982
Moore, Jeffrey B.	MSW	1961,62,63,64
Moore, John T.	WR	1987,89
Moore, Kathy	VB	1973
Moore, Kingsley G.	MTN	1927,28,29
Moore, Pamela	WTR	1978,79
Moore, Patrick	MGO	1990
Moore, Paul A.	FB	1974
Moore, Rickey K.	WR	1985,86
Moore, Robert D.	IHO	1973,74,75,76
Moore, Scott T.	MGY	1985,86,87,88
Moore, Warfield	MBK	1976,77
Moore, Winston C.	MTR	1935
Moorhead, Donald W.	FB	1968,69,70
Morales, Elmo H.	MTR	1965,66,67
Morales, James R.	WR	1991
Moran, Martin T.	MSW	1986,87,88,89
Moran, William F.	FB	1969,72
Moretto, Angelo J.	IHO	1973,74,75,76
Morey, Edwin E.	FB	1947,48
Morey, Kenneth	MGO	1945
Morgan, Dennis	FB	1965,66,67
Morgan, Frank R.	WR	1937,39
Morgan, John L.	MGO	1977,78
Morgan, Kevin A.	MSW	1977,78,79,80
Morgan, Robert	FB	1930
Morgan, Ronald G.	MTN	1953,54
Morgan, W. Morris	MTR	1936
Morgaridge, Kenneth E.	MBK	1923,24,25
Moriartey, Gregory R.	FB	1983,84
Morley, Buel	MTR	1942
Morrill, Harold J.	MBK	1948,49,50
	BB	1948,49,50
Morris, Alexander I.	MTR	1947,48
Morris, Edward	MTN	1938,39
Morris, James W.	FB	1984,85,86,87
Morris, Jonathan A.	MTN	1985,86,87,88
Morris, William H.	BB	1984,85,86
Morrison, Arnold W.	IHO	1986
Morrison, Brendan	IHO	1994,95,96,97
Morrison, Chester	FB	1917,18
Morrison, Chester C.	BB	1981
Morrison, Gary L.	IHO	1974,75,76,77
Morrison, Maynard D.	FB	1929,30,31
Morrison, Ralph E.	BB	1947,48,49,50
Morrison, Ross G.	IHO	1961,62
Morrison, Steven C.	FB	1990,91,92,93,94
Morrissey, Mary	SS	1976,77,78,79
Morrissey, Shawn J.	WR	1977,78
Morrow, Andrew B.	MSW	1958,59,60
Morrow, Gordon H.	MBK	1955
	FB	1957
Morrow Jr., John M.	FB	1953,54,55
Morrow, Vicki	SB	1984,85,86,87
Morrow, William	FB	1885,86
	MTR	1885,86
Morse, Clair E.	MSW	1941
Morse Jr., John H.	MCC	1924
Morse, John P.	MGO	1980,81
Morse, Newell O.	BB	1927
Morse, Matthew V.	BB	1988,89,90
Morse, Wayne H.	MBK	1948,49
	FB	1948
Mortimer, John	MTR	1996
Morton, Charles F.	MTR	1955,57
Morton, Gregory A.	FB	1974,75,76
Morton, Leon	FB	1990
Morton, Neal	MBK	1995,96
Mosby Jr., James R.	MBK	1959
Mosketti, Joseph S.	FB	1980,82
Moskwa, Allison	WCR	1997
Moss Jr., Charles J.	MSW	1946,49,50
Moss, Nancy	WSW	1977
Moss Jr., Thomas E.	FB	1976,79
Motley, Frederick L.	FB	1979,80
Mott, Michael	MGY	1991,92,93,94
Moule, John W.	MTR	1952,53,54,55
Mouton, Kenneth L.	FB	1986
Mouw, Garrett C.	MGO	1961,62,63,64
Mowerson, G. Robert	MSW	1935,36,37,45
Mowrey Jr., Fred H.	MSW	1956,57
Mowrey, Harry	FB	1891
Mraz, Edward G.	BB	1918,20
Mroz, Vincent P.	FB	1943
Mrozinski, Sally	VB	1988
Muckalt, Bill	IHO	1995,96
Muehlmann, Autumn	FH	1974,76,77
Muelder, Wesley	FB	1945
Mueller, Beth	SB	1986,87,88,89
Mueller, Foorman	MTR	1925,26
Mueller, Ralph	MTR	1930,31
Mueller, Thomas D.	WR	1943
Muhich, Anthony L.	IHO	1978
Muir, David B.	FB	1965,66,67
Muir, Neil	BB	1941
Muir, William H.	BB	1887
Muir, William T.	FB	1962,64
Muirhead, Stan	FB	1921,22,23
Mullaney, Gerald L.	MBK	1943
Mullaney, John M.	MBK	1945,46
Mulvihill, Daniel V.	BB	1969,70,71
Mumby, Alan C.	MSW	1969,71
Munger, Inman L.	MTR	1926,28
Munich, Anthony	IHO	1978
Munson, Emery J.	BB	1911,12
Munson, James R.	MSW	1945
Munson, Stephanie	WSW	1991,92,93,94
Munz, Charles J.	MTR	1925,26
Munz, Lewis E.	MTN	1920
Muransky Jr., Edward W.	FB	1979,80,81
Murdoch, Michael R.	WR	1987
Murdock, Guy B.	FB	1969,70,71
Murphy, Daniel E.	BB	1996
Murphy, Frank W.	FB	1948
Murphy, George I.	MTR	1916,17
Murphy, John W.	MSW	1956,57
Murphy, Kim	SS	1978
Murphy, Michael J.	MTR	1981,82
Murphy, Robert E.	MBK	1980,81
Murphy, Susan T.	SS	1979,81,82
Murray, Charles A.	MBK	1948,49,50,51
Murray III, Robert F.	MSW	1978,79,80,81
Murray, Christopher D.	MTR	1961,62,63,64
Murray, Daniel A.	FB	1976,78
Murray, Godfrey E.	MTR	1970,71,72
Murray, Heath R.	BB	1992,93,94
Murray, James C.	MTR	1931
Murray, Laurence H.	WR	1956,57,58,59
Murray, Lisa	FH	1983,84,85,86
Murray, Robert L.	WR	1974
Murray, Vada D.	FB	1988,89,90
Murtaugh, Eileen	WGY	1987,89
Mussato, Natalie	SB	1988,90,90
Musser, James	FB	1912,13
Mutch, Craig A.	FB	1972,73
Muthart, Patricia	WBK	1978,79
Myers, Bradley J.	FB	1957,58,59
Myers, D. Fritz	MSW	1954,55,56,57
Myers, David J.	WR	1973,74,75,76
Myers, Earnest G.	BB	1954,55,57,58
Myers, James L.	MBK	1963,64,65,66
Myers, Jesse L.	MTR	1974,76
Myers, John L.	FB	1990
Myers, Kenneth E.	MGO	1954,55
Myll, Clifton O.	FB	1943
Myron, Harold G.	BB	1919,20

N

Naab, Fred W.	FB	1943
Nachman, Cathy	FH	1973
Nader, David	MGY	1991,92
Nadhir, Nemir R.	WR	1979,80,81,82
Nadler, Amy	WGY	1985,86
Nadlicki, Michael	FB	1992
Naft, Juliet	WTN	1981,82,83,84
Nagel, Ed P.	MTN	1987,88
Nagle, John N.	BB	1904
Nahrgang, David M.	MGY	1961
Nalan, Norvard N.	WR	1952,53,54
Namesnik, Eric	MSW	1989,90,91,93
Narcy, John	MD	1954,55,56,57
Natale, Gregory H.	IHO	1974,75,76,77
Natali Jr., Daniel E.	MSW	1967,68
Nate, Jeff B.	FB	1980,83
Natelson, Michael	MSW	1958,59,61
Naugle, Gordon P.	MTN	1945,47,48,49
Nauta, Steven B.	FB	1975,76,78
Navta, Jodi	WSW	1994,95,96,97
Naylor, Gordon C.	IHO	1950,51
Naylor, William C.	MTR	1922
Ndiaye, Makhtar	MBK	1994,95
Neafus, Ralph	WR	1934
Neahusan, James K.	MTR	1962,63
Neal, Randall A.	IHO	1972,73,74,75
Neal, Thomas F.	FB	1981
Neary, Glen H.	IHO	1987,88
Neaton, Patrick	IHO	1990,91,92,93
Nebelung, Raymond	BB	1927,28,29
Nedell, Tamara	WSW	1987,88,89
Nederlander, Robert E.	MTN	1953,54,55
Nedomansky, Vaclav	IHO	1990,92
Needham, Bennett L.	FB	1978,79,81
Neely, Sarah	WTR	1989
Neer, Penny	WBK	1979,80,81
	WTR	1979,80,81,82
	SB	1983
Neering, Ellen	WSW	1976
Neff III, Richmond B.	WR	1971,72,74
Neff, Glenn C.	MGY	1948
Neff, Michael D.	IHO	1982,83,84,85
Negus Sr., Fred W.	FB	1943
	MTR	1944
Nei, Julie	WGY	1986
Neidhardt, Jane	WGY	1978
Neilsen, Johnny K.	MTR	1983
Neinken, Jack T.	MTN	1977,78,79,80
Neira, Betsy	SS	1980,81,82
Neisch Sr., David L.	MSW	1949,50,51
Neisch, LeRoy	FB	1921,22,23
	MTR	1922
Neiswender, Edward C.	WR	1974,75,76,77
Nelson, Andrea	SB	1988,89,90,91
Nelson, Cleland K.	FB	1947
Nelson, David	FB	1940,41
Nelson, Douglas F.	BB	1966,67,68
	FB	1967
Nelson, Gregory P.	MGY	1983,85,86
Nelson, Lawrence	WR	1949,50,51,52
Nelson, Paul R.	MGY	1933
Nelson, Richard F.	MSW	1960,61,62,63
Nelson, Sim M.	FB	1982,83,84
Nelson, Viggo	FB	1920
Nelson, William A.	BB	1945
Nemacheck, Fred	FB	1960
Neu, Susan	SS	1976,77,78,79
Neubrecht, Franz	BB	1926
Neuenswander, Joe W.	MGY	1973,74,75,76
Neukom, Lawrence	MGY	1994
Neuman, F. Herbert	MTR	1951
Neville, William F.	BB	1926
Newby, John W.	MGO	1989
Newell, James F.	BB	1916,17,20
Newcomb, William K.	MBK	1959
	MGO	1960,61,62
Newcomer, Christian E.	MD	1970,73
Newell, Peter J.	FB	1968,69,70
Newingham, Jeffrey A	MCC	1982
Newman, Frank J.	MGY	1957,58,59
Newman Jr., Harry L.	FB	1958,59
Newman Sr., Harry L.	FB	1930,31,32
Newman, James H.	BB	1960,61,62,63
Newman, Karl R.	MTR	1950,51
Newman, Neal F.	MTR	1988,89,90,91
Newman, Robert	MGO	1926
Newsom, Jon	WR	1996
Newton, William G.	MGO	1963,64,65,66
Newton, Charles	MGO	1960,61,62,63
Newton, Christopher	BB	1991,92,93,94
Newton, David J.	IHO	1963,64,65
Newton, Fred	FB	1906
Nichols, Carl	MTR	1944
Nichols, Donald H.	WR	1938,39,40
Nichols, Harold J.	WR	1937,38,39
Nicholson, John	FB	1937,38,39
	MBK	1939
Nicksic, Timothy G.	MBK	1968,71
Nicol, Frank D.	MTR	1904
Nicolau, David W.	FB	1979,80
Nieberg, Michael	IHO	1989
Niedermeier, Norman A.	FB	1952,53,54
	MGY	1953,55,56
Nielsen, Bernard L.	IHO	1958,59,60,61
Nielsen, Johnny K.	MTR	1981,82,83,84
Nielsen, Paul	FB	1939
Nieman, Thomas S.	FB	1970
Niemann, Thomas A.	BB	1976
Niemann, Walter	FB	1915,16
Niemann, Walter W.	MGY	1948,49,51
Niemann, William K.	BB	1915,16,17
Niemiec, Scott	BB	1992,93,94,95
Niles, Douglas O.	MTR	1960,61,62
Nilsson, Fritz R.	MTR	1951,52,53,54
Ninde, Daniel	FB	1894
Nisen, Charles M.	MTN	1933
Nisivaco, Richard G.	MGY	1977,78
Nixon, Jane	FH	1983,84,86
Nixon, Julian S.	IHO	1971,72,73,74
Noble, Alison	VB	1980,81,82,83
Noble, Duncan	MGO	1944
Noble, Tyrone L.	FB	1994
Noel, Robert F.	WR	1966,67,68
Noetzel, Mark A.	MSW	1981,82,83,84
Noferi, Lisa	WTN	1982
Nolan, David C.	MGO	1983
Nolan, Delbert L.	FB	1961

Russ Osterman was a football and track standout for Michigan from 1949-51.

Nolan, John D.	MGO	1983
Nold, Michael F.	MTN	1992,93,94
Noonan, Roy T.	BB	1923
Norcross, Fred	FB	1903,04,05
	MTR	1903,04,05
Nordberg, Mary M.	WSW	1986,87
Norde, Cecil J.	MTR	1963,64,65,66
Norlen, Timothy R.	MSW	1970,71,72
Norman, Siobhan	WSOC	1994
Norrington, Ralph M.	MTN	1910
Norris, Edwin J.	MBK	1945
Norris, Mari	WSW	1986,87
Northrop, Philip M.	MTR	1925,26,27
Norton, Jeffrey T.	IHO	1985,86,87
Norton, John	FB	1915
Nortz, Megan J.	WTR	1989,90,91
	WCC	1989,90,91
Noskin, Stanton C.	FB	1957,58,59
Novak, Richard S.	FB	1976
Nowacki, Daniel M.	MTR	1973
Noyes, John R.	MTR	1930,31
Nuanes, Jennifer	WBK	1990,91,92,93
Nufer, Danile C.	MTR	1923
Nufer, Julius I.	MTR	1901,02
Nulf, Terry N.	FB	1949,50
	MTR	1950,51,52,53
Nunley, Frank H.	BB	1965
	FB	1964,65,66
Nuss, David M.	BB	1980,81
Nussbaumer, Robert J.	BB	1943,44,46
	FB	1943,44,45
	MTR	1944
Nuttall, Clifford R.	MTR	1961,63,64
Nye, Gerald F.	MBK	1918
Nygord, Albert	IHO	1928,30
Nygren, Mats O.	MSW	1986,87,88,89
Nyland Jr., Herman Z.	FB	1926,27
Nyren, Marvin R.	FB	1955,56,57

O

O'Brien, Cathleen	SS	1980,81,82
O'Brien, Falconer	BB	1904,05,06
O'Brien, Harold E.	MTR	1916,17
O'Brien, Isabel	WTN	1983
O'Brien, Rupert D.	WR	1956
O'Connell, Donald R.	WR	1950
O'Connell, Harry E.	MTR	1935,36
O'Connor, Erin	WSW	1994
O'Connor, Gerald A.	FB	1969,71
O'Connor, Kelly A.	SB	1988,89,90
O'Connor, John T.	IHO	1985
O'Connor, Michael J.	MSW	1966,67,68,69
O'Connor, Myles A.	IHO	1986,87,88,89
O'Dell, John	IHO	1934
O'Donnell, James A.	MSW	1987,88,89
O'Donnell, Joseph R.	FB	1960,62,63
O'Donnell, Stephen R.	FB	1979
O'Donnell, Susanna	VB	1992,93,94,95
O'Hara, Paul R.	MGO	1944,45,47
O'Malley, Thomas F.	MSW	1964,65,66
O'Neal, Calvin	FB	1974,75,76
O'Neill, Thomas P.	MD	1946
O'Reilly, Brendan M.	MTR	1955,56,57,58
O'Reilly, John P.	MSW	1953,54,55,56
O'Reilly, William C.	MCC	1980,81,82
	MTR	1980,81,82,83
O'Shaughnessy, Erin	SS	1982
O'Shaughnessy, Richard E.	FB	1951,52,53
	WR	1951,52,53,54
O'Toole, Timothy E.	MBK	1976,77
Oade, James	FB	1925

Oakley, Joseph R.	WR	1932,33,34
Oberly, Lowell H.	WR	1944
Oden, Daniel J.	MCC	1989,90,91
	MTR	1990,91,92
Odioso, Michael	FB	1984
Ogle, Jere	FB	1947
Ohlenroth, William G.	FB	1948,49,50
Ohlheiser, Harold R.	MTR	1925,26,27
Ohlmacher, Albert	BB	1916,18
Ojala, Kirt S.	BB	1988,89,90
Oksuyana, Taiwo	MTR	1996
Olabisi, Olanrewaju	WR	1994,96
Olcott, William	FB	1881
Oldham, Donald L.	FB	1950,51,52
Oldham, Michael	FB	1969,70,71
Olian, Irwin A.	MTN	1925,26,27
Olds, Fredric C.	FB	1937,38,39
Oliver, David	IHO	1991,92,93,94
Oliver, Ron	MBK	1996
Oliver, Russ	FB	1932,33,34
	MBK	1933,34,35
	BB	1933,34,35
Olm, Fred L.	FB	1956,57,58
	WR	1957,58,59,60
Olmsted, Sherman R.	MTR	1938,39
Olsen, Heather S.	VB	1984,85,86,87
Olsen, Jan-Erick	MSW	1985,86,87,88
Olsen, Jeffrey R.	BB	1996
Olsen, William E.	IHO	1937
Olshanski, Henry S.	FB	1943
Olson, James E.	BB	1951,52,53,54
Olson, John P.	FB	1947
Olson, Otto	WR	1997
Olson, Robert H.	MBK	1950,51
	MGO	1949,51
Olson, Sylvan L.	BB	1909
Olszewski, Patrick J.	FB	1988
Olver, John A.	IHO	1978,79
Ontiveros, Steven	BB	1980,81,82
Onuska, Christopher	MGY	1993,94,95,96
Oom, Wayne	MCC	1988
Oosterbaan, Bennie	FB	1925,26,27
	MBK	1926,27,28
	BB	1926,27,28
Oosterbaan, John	MBK	1961,62,63
Oosterbaan, John P.	MBK	1986,87,88,89
Oppman, Douglas K.	FB	1958
Orland, Rees M.	MSW	1963,64,65,66
Orr, Jennifer	WSW	1975
Orr, Richard L.	BB	1968,69
Ortmann, Chuck	FB	1948,49,50
Orwig, Brock W.	MGY	1984,86,87,88
Orwig, James	MBK	1928,29,30
Orwig, Jim	FB	1955,56,57
Osborn, Carol	FH	1975,76
Osbun, Tony	FB	1980,81
Osgood, Manley	MSW	1936
Osgood, Robert D.	MTR	1935,36,37
Osgood, William H.	MTR	1947
Osler, David A.	MGO	1940,41,42
Osler, Peter	MTN	1978,79
Osman, Todd J.	FB	1987,88,89,90
Ossman, Timothy G.	MTR	1974
Osterland, Thomas N.	MGY	1960,61,62
Osterman, Russ	FB	1950,51
	MTR	1949,51
Ostrander, Robert A.	MCC	1931,32
Ostroot, George	MTR	1940,42,43,46
Ostrovich, Edward	MCC	1979
Ott, Timothy L.	MTN	1970,71,72,73
Otto, Frederick A.	MTN	1947,48,49

Will Perry (1953-55) not only lettered three times for the Woverine baseball team, he later served as U-M's Sports Information Director.

Otto, Jeanne	WBK	1977,78
Otto, Roland L.	WR	1931
Ouimet, Mark	IHO	1993
Overton, Stephen B.	MTR	1960,61,62,63
Oviatt, Jill	WSW	1987,88,89
Ovitz, John W.	BB	1907
Owen, David G.	FB	1954,55
	MTR	1954,55,56,57
Owen, Kevin	FB	1990
Owens, Kamell T.	FB	1976,77,79,80
Owens, Mel	FB	1977,79,80
Owens, Oliver E.	MTN	1976,77,78
Owens, Raymond L.	MBK	1977,78
Owens, Thomas M.	BB	1976,77,78
P		
Pace, Jim	FB	1955,56,57
	MTR	1956,57
Pacholec, Frank	BB	1976
Pacholke, Paula	VB	1975
Pacholzuk, Rodney C.	IHO	1977,78,79
Paciorek, James J.	BB	1979,80,81,82
	FB	1979,81
Packard, Arthur T.	MTR	1881,82,83
	BB	1881,82m83
Paddy, Arthur	FB	1937
	WR	1941
Padjen Jr., John	FB	1950
Pafford, Rodney W.	MGO	1976,78,79
Page, Craig A.	FB	1978
Page, Gregory K.	IHO	1964,65,66,67
Painter, Lincoln R.	BB	1950,51
Palardy, Gregory J.	MTR	1986
Palenstein, John W.	IHO	1959,60,61
Paley, Robert J.	MTN	1952,53,54,55
Palinski, Ambrose	IHO	1938
Palko, Marie	WSW	1979,80,81,82
Palmaroli, John	FB	1926,27
Palmer, Deborah R.	WCC	1986,87,88
	WTR	1987
Palmer, Joe	MSW	1996
Palmer, Lowell M.	MTR	1926
Palmer, Paul D.	FB	1959
Palmer, Peter N.	MBK	1949
	BB	1949,50,51
	FB	1947,48,50
Palmer, Richard F.	IHO	1975,76,77,78
Palmer, Robert A.	MGO	1938,39,40
Palmer, Robert R.	IHO	1974,75,76,77
Palmisano, Michael R.	WR	1961,64
Palomaki, David J.	FB	1960
Pancratz, Stephen F.	MSW	1988,89
Panetta, Lisa	SB	1982,83,84,85
Pankopf, Bonnie	WD	1985,86,87,88
Pantaleo, Joseph A.	WR	1986,87,88,89
Pantlind, J. Boyd	MTR	1933
Paolatto, Louis B.	IHO	1950,53
Papa, Raymond	MSW	1995,96
Paparella, Gerald J.	BB	1979
Papenguth, Richard	MSW	1923,25
Paper, Meyer	MBK	1922,23
		1922,23
Papows, Nancy	WGY	1982
Papp, John A.	BB	1996
Papp, Robert A.	MGO	1986,87,88,89
Paradzik, David	MTN	1995,96
Parcells, Gretchen	WGY	1977
Pardoski, Ryan E.	IHO	1987,88,89,90
Parenteau, Gary L.	MCC	1977,78,80
	MTR	1978,82
Parini, Sean	FB	1994,95
Paris, Paul-Andre	IHO	1972,73,74,75
Paris, Scott G.	MGY	1965,66,67
Paris, William H.	FB	1978,79,80,81
Park, Laurel	WCC	1984
	WTR	1985
Parker, Amy	WCC	1992
	WTR	1993
Parker, Charles W.	BB	1935
Parker, Fred	FB	1924,25
Parker, Joseph E.	MSW	1984,85,86,87
Parker, Kevin L.	BB	1982
Parker, Louis A.	WR	1933,34
Parker, Michael J.	BB	1975,77,78
Parker, Noah	FB	1995,96
Parker, Peter M.	MTR	1957,58
Parker, Ray	FB	1929
	WR	1929,30
Parker, W. Oren	MGY	1931,32,33
Parkhill, Thomas H.	FB	1965
Parks, Dan	FB	1968,69
Parks, Douglas H.	MTR	1948,50,51
Parks, Marshall L.	FB	1980
	MTR	1979,80,81
Parks, Vernon H.	BB	1919,20

Parks, Lawana S.	VB	1975
Parris, Earl B.	MTR	1985,86,87
Parrish, David N.	MSW	1988
Parrish, James T.	IHO	1976,77,78,79
Parrish, Marc C.	MSW	1983,84,85,86
Parshall, Byron V.	FB	1947
Parsons, Archie J.	MTR	1945,46
Partchenko, John	FB	1994,95,96
Parvin, Charles F.	MTR	1934,34
Pascal, Charles E.	BB	1963,64,65
Pashak, Bernard H.	IHO	1967,68,69,70
Passenger, Donald H.	MCC	1982
	MTR	1983
Passink, Peter	MGO	1962,63,64,65
Patanelli, Matthew L.	FB	1934,45,36
	MBK	1935,36,37
	BB	1936,37
Patchen, Brian P.	FB	1963,64
Patchin, Arthur B.	BB	1933,34,35
Patek, Robert M.	FB	1975,76,77
Patel, Hersh D.	MGO	1986,87,88,89
Paterson, George	FB	1911,12,13
Patlovich, Susan	WTN	1985,86,87
Paton Jr., William A.	MTN	1947,48,49
Paton, Thomas C.	MTR	1944
Paton, Thomas E.	MGO	1987,88,89,90
Patrick, Carol	SB	1983,84
Patrick, Harry	FB	1905,06
Patt, Felicia	WGY	1989
Patten, John R.	MSW	1941,42,43
Pattengill, Vic	FB	1909,10
Patterson, Bruce J.	MGO	1975,76,79
Patterson, William H.	BB	1906,07,08
Patton, Harvey W.	MTR	1934,35,36
Paul, Louis	FB	1892,93
Paulson, Clayton H.	MBK	1933
	BB	1933,34,35
	FB	1932
Paulson, Jennifer	VB	1989,90
Paulus, Peter J.	FB	1951
	MTN	1952,53,54,55
Paumier, Kim	WSW	1980
Paumier, Tami	WSW	1982
Paup, John P.	WR	1940,41
Pavichevich, Raymond	MBK	1952,53,54
	BB	1951,52,53,54
Pavloff, Louis	FB	1959,62
Paxton, Bruce R.	WR	1948,49
Payne, David H.	FB	1979
Payne, Nanette	SB	1986,87,88,89
Payne, Reginald	FB	1993,94,95,96
Payne, Sonya	WTR	1987,88,89
Peacock, Wayne B.	MTN	1957,58,59,61
Peach, Willard	FB	1916,19
Pearcy, Cheryl	SB	1993,94,95,96
Peare, Robert S.	MBK	1920
Pearlman, Gregory Y.	FB	1980,81,82
Pearman, Charles L.	MBK	1922
Pearson, Mark E.	WR	1979,80,81,83
Pearson, Maxwell E.	WR	1954,55,57,58
Pearson, William	FB	1891,92,93
	BB	1891,92,93
Pease-Montoya, Dwight	WR	1989
Peck, Charles A.	BB	1981
Peck, Dennis W.	MTR	1981,82
Peck, Douglas E.	BB	1949,50,51,52
Peckham, H. John	FB	1953,54,55
	MTR	1953
Peckinpaugh, Walter S.	BB	1937,38,39
	FB	1935
Peddy, Jack E.	BB	1945
Pederson II, Bernhardt L.	FB	1975,78
Pederson Sr., Bernhard	FB	1951,52
	MTR	1950
Pederson, Chip	FB	1978
Pederson, Elise	WSW	1974
Pederson, Ernest A.	FB	1935,37
Pederson, Thomas W.	MSW	1978,79,80,81
Pelekoudas, Daniel L.	MBK	1981,82,83,84
Pelinka, Robert T.	MBK	1989,91,92,93
Pella, G. Roy	FB	1950,51,52
	MTR	1951,52,53,54
Pelow, Paul E.	IHO	1949,50,52
Pelto, Maurice S.	MTN	1953
Peltz Jr., Charles S.	MTR	1960,61,62
Pemberton, Marlin H.	BB	1963,64,65
Penberthy, Francisco	MTR	1922
Pendell Jr., W. Henry	MTN	1932
Pendlebury, Thomas S.	MGO	1962,63
	IHO	1960,61,62,63
Pendleton, Winston K.	MSW	1959,60,61,62
Penilo, Annette	WCC	1979,80
Penksa, Robert A.	FB	1967,68
Pennington, Karel	VB	1975,76,77,78
Pentaleri, Diane	FH	1988

Peoples, Shonte	FB	1991,92,93
Peper, Eric A.	MSW	1976,77,78
Pepple, Worth	BB	1892,93
Peralta, David	BB	1987,88,89
Percival, Don R.	MTN	1937,38,39
Percy, John A.	MTR	1893
Peristeris, Paul	FB	1995,96
Perkins, Bryan L.	WR	1993
Perkins, Kenneth L.	FB	1982,83,84
Perkins, Patrick	FB	1987
Perlinger, Jeffrey L.	FB	1973,74,75
Perrin, David C.	IHO	1967,68,69,70
Perrin, John	FB	1920
	BB	1920,21
Perry, Lowell W.	FB	1950,51,52
	MTR	1950,52
Perry, Mark R.	IHO	1979,80,81,82
Perry, Shay	FH	1990,91,92,93
Perry, Stephen G.	MBK	1976
	BB	1976,77,78,79
Perry, Walter B.	MTR	1901,02,03,04
Perry, Will A.	BB	1953,54,55
Perryman, Robert L.	FB	1983,84,85,86
Persinger, Eric V.	BB	1989,90,91,92
Person Jr., Isaac	MBK	1980,81,82,83
Peterjohn, Richard C.	MBK	1954,55,56
	BB	1954,55,56
Petermann, Daniel	IHO	1923,24,25
Peters, Alana	WSOC	1995
Peters, Mary	FH	1989,90
Petersen, Jennifer	WTR	1994,95,96
Peterson, Donald W.	FB	1949,50,51
Peterson Jr., Donald B.	MSW	1970,71,72,73
Peterson, Thomas R.	FB	1944,47,48,49
Peterson, Ward D.	WR	1946,47
Petoskey Sr., Fred L.	MBK	1933,34
	BB	1932,33,34
	FB	1931,32,33
Petoskey, E. Jack	FB	1943
Petoskey, William E.	WR	1977,78,79,80
Petrick, Denise	WTN	1974
Petrie, Robert G.	MBK	1931,32,33
Petrie, W. Richard	FB	1953
Petrie, Wilbur E.	MBK	1926,27
Petro, Charles	FB	1921
Petroff, Frank L.	FB	1988
Petsch, Michael	FB	1981
Petsche, Timothy S.	MSW	1987,88,89
Pettersen, George A.	MTR	1942
Petterson, Chad M.	FB	1993,94
Pettinger, John D.	MSW	1959,61
Pettitt, Lynn	SS	1977
Pettitt, William	MSW	1992,93
Peugeot, George L.	IHO	1947
Pfaff, Jason E.	BB	1989,90,91
Pfrender, Michael E.	MGY	1979,81
Phelps, Keith A.	BB	1944
Phelps, A. Eric	FB	1975
Phillips, Ed	FB	1936,38
Phillips, John R.	MBK	1963,64,65,66
Phillips, Kim	WSOC	1994,95
Phillips, Raymond	FB	1965,66,67
Philpott, Douglas M.	IHO	1951,52,53,54
Picard, Frank	FB	1910,11
Picard, John A.	FB	1948
Pickard, Frederick P.	FB	1949,50,51
Pickens, James E.	FB	1975,76,77
Pickett, Ruth	SS	1978,79,80
Pickus, Albert	IHO	1953
Pickus, Miriam I.	FH	1980
Piel, Alfred H.	MTR	1940,41,42
Pieper, Gillian	FH	1986,87,88
Pierce, David	MTN	1990
Pierce, F. Michael	MCC	1971
	MTR	1971,72
Pierce, James E.	MTR	1944
Pierce, Russell L.	MGY	1970,71
Pierce, Stephen B.	WR	1981
Pieri, Laura	FH	1976,77,78,79
Piersma, John	MSW	1994,95,96
Pierson, Barry F.	FB	1967,68,69
Pighee Jr., John A.	FB	1972
Piilo, Shelly	SB	1978
Pike, Jeff	MBK	1993,93
Pinch, Claude O.	MTR	1906
Pincham Jr., Robert E.	MTR	1970
Pink, Charles A.	MBK	1938,39,40
	BB	1938,39,40
Pinkerton, Paul W.	MTR	1935
Pinkowski, David J.	BB	1987,88
Pinney, Charles T.	MTR	1942,43
Piper, James R.	BB	1983
Piper, William J.	MBK	1922,23
Pitts, James A.	MBK	1965,66,67,68
Pitts, Robert W.	IHO	1954,55,56,57

Pizzutello, Michael P.	MTN	1986,87,88,89
Place, Ira	MTN	1991,92
Plagenhoef, Stanley C.	MTR	1948
Planck, Joseph H.	WR	1949,50,51
Plate, S. Troy	FB	1992
Plate, W. Todd	FB	1988,89,90
Ploeger, James P.	MBK	1965,69
Plotkin, Murray B.	MGY	1968,70,71,72
Plummer, Alfred H.	MBK	1933,34,35
Poch, Andrea S.	MTR	1978,79
Poe, Howard	FB	1927,28,29
Poelman, Mark A.	MTR	1979,80,81,82
Poglits, Anne	VB	1996
Polakowski, Alex J.	MTR	1986,87
Polanic, Thomas J.	IHO	1963,64,65
Polasky, David	MTN	1915
Polhamus, John R.	MTR	1924
Pollard, Karen A.	SB	1980,81,82,83
Pollick, Marissa W.	WTN	1975,76,77,78
Poloskey, Donald L.	BB	1954,55,56,57
Polston, Bryan	MBK	1991,92
Pomey Jr., George J.	MBK	1963,64,65
Pommerening, Otto P.	FB	1927,28
Pond, Christopher A.	MGO	1989,90
Pond, Irving	FB	1879
Pong, Theodore	MSW	1955,57,58
Pongracz, Edward R.	MSW	1958,59,60
Ponsetto, Joseph L.	FB	1943,44,45
Pontius, Miller	FB	1911,12,13
	BB	1912,13
Ponto, Hilton A.	WR	1934
	MGY	1932,33
Ponto, Scott W.	MGY	1974,75,76,77
Poorman, Edwin	FB	1928,29
	MTR	1928,29,30
Popek, Angela	WTN	1993,94,95,96
Poplawski, Thomas	FB	1971,72
Popowski, Robert L.	FB	1984
Popp, Herb	FB	1949,50
Porretta, Angela	WD	1983,84,85
Porte, Thomas	IHO	1932
Porter, Dave S.	FB	1966,67
	WR	1965,66,67,68
Porter, Donald J.	BB	1921
Porter, Jack E.	WR	1953,56
Porter, James G.	MTN	1939,41,42
Portnoy, Joel	MBK	1988,89,90
Porvin, Terry	MGO	1984
Posner, Debora	WGO	1978
Post, David B.	MTN	1944,45
Post, A. Richard	BB	1962,63
Post, David M.	WR	1962,64,65
Postma, Dean A.	MSW	1986
Potokar, Robert C.	WR	1987,88,89
Potter, Donald E.	MSW	1952,53,54,55
Potter, Earl F.	BB	1904
Potter, Joan	VB	1982,83,84
Potter, Nathan S.	MTR	1929
Potter, Richard S.	MTN	1955,56,57
Potter, Robert	MGO	1923
Potter, Russell F.	MSW	1945
Potter, Sandy	WCC	1988
Pottle, John L.	MTR	1930,31
Potts, Andy	MSW	1996
Poulin, Ruth	WSOC	1994,95
Poulos, Paul K.	FB	1958,59,60
	WR	1956
Povilaitis, Carrie	WSOC	1994
Powell, Gregory D.	FB	1980,83
Powell, Ross J.	BB	1987,88,89
Powell, Tanya	WBK	1987,88,89,90
Powers, Bobby T.	FB	1991,92,93,94
Powers, Hiram	FB	1891,92,93
Powers, John E.	FB	1947,48,49,50
	WR	1948,49,50
Powers, John J.	FB	1977,78,80
Powers, Richard	FB	1990,91,92,93
Powers, William M.	IHO	1988,95,96
Poynton, Jerome V.	MGY	1973,74,75,76
Pozza Jr., Clarence L.	MGO	1967,68,69,71
Prael, William M.	MBK	1978
Prahst, Gary K.	MBK	1956,57
	FB	1956,57,58
Prashaw, Milton	FB	1945
Pratl, Ronald E.	FB	1976,79
Pratt, Kimberly	WTN	1991,92
Precious, Robert W.	IHO	1945
Pregulman, Mervin	FB	1941,42,43
Pregulman, Robert	MBK	1982
Prentice, Geoffrey	MTN	1993,94,95,96
Prepolec, John	FB	1980
Prescott, Wilbur	WR	1928
Preston, Karen	WTR	1978
Preston, R.J.	WR	1925
Prettyman, Horace	FB	1882,83,85, 86,88,89,90
Price, David L.	MSW	1977,79,80
Price, Gerald P.	MSW	1959
Price II, Jimmie W.	BB	1982
Price, John H.	MTN	1908,09,10
Price, Laurence A.	MTR	1922
Price, Phillip S.	BB	1987,88,89,90
Prichard, Tom	FB	1961,62,63
Pritchard, Pamela	WTR	1986
Pritula, Robert V.	MTN	1965,67,68
Pritula, William	FB	1942,46,47
Pritz, Linda	SS	1982
Prokurat, Lisa	WGY	1976
Promack, Mark W.	MGO	1974,75
Propson, Thomas P.	MBK	1953
Prosser, William R.	MTR	1923
Prouse, Thomas	IHO	1931
Prout, Percy	MTR	1926,27,28
Pruente, Mark P.	MTR	1979,80,81
Prunk, Thomas W.	MSW	1954,55,56,58
Prusa, Ronald M.	FB	1980,83
Pryce, Trevor N.	FB	1993,94
Pryor Jr., Cecil L.	FB	1968,69
Przygodski, George M.	FB	1973,74,75
	MTR	1973,74,75
Ptacek, Robert J.	FB	1956,57,58
Puce, George	MTR	1961,63
Puckelwartz, Bill	FB	1925,27
	BB	1925,26,27
Pugsley, Richard E.	MSW	1971,72
Puhl, Diane A.	SB	1981
Pulford, Gordon S.	MSW	1944,45
Pullen, Drew	WR	1995,96
Pullen, Thomas R.	FB	1965
Purdue, John C.	MTR	1941,44
Purdum, Claire	FB	1930
Purdy, Harry D.	MTR	1924
Purdy, Kathy	SS	1979
Pursel, Thomas S.	MGO	1978,79,80,81
Purucker, Norman B.	FB	1937,38
	MTR	1938
Pusztai, Peter	MTN	1993,94,95,96
Putich, William	MBK	1949,50
	FB	1949,50,51
Putz, Joseph J.	BB	1996
Pyatt, Phillip R.	MTR	1968,70,71,72
Pyle, Nicholas J.	MTR	1983,84
Pyszynski, Ralph P.	MSW	1939

Q

Quaerna, Jerold O.	FB	1985,86
Quaintance, Cregar	BB	1913,14
Qualls, Sylvia	WTR	1984
Quebbeman, Charles W.	FB	1971,71
Queller, Donald E.	MTR	1947
Quinn, Candice	WSW	1986,87,88
Quinn, Clement	FB	1910,11,12
Quinn, Cyril	FB	1912,13
Quinn, Garrett M.	FB	1979
Quinn, Terrence G.	FB	1995,96
Quinn, Thomas L.	WR	1968,69,70,71
Quint, Richard M.	MD	1972,73,74
Quirk, Dan	MGO	1924
	IHO	1923,24
Quitmeyer, Gretal M.	VB	1973,74

R

Raber, Fenton	MBK	1927,28
Raber, Wendy	VB	1986,87
Rabiah, Susan	WSW	1986,87,88,89
Rabinovitch, Stephen D.	MSW	1963,64
Racht, Erin	WSW	1995,96
Raczak, Kelly	WCR	1997
Radakovic, Nik	BB	1965,66
Rademaker, Donald J.	FB	1978,79,80
Radigan, Timothy J.	FB	1965
Rae, James W.	MBK	1938,39,40
	MTR	1938,40
Raeder, J. Paul	FB	1959,60,61
Rafferty, Michael J.	MBK	1968
	BB	1968,69,70,71
Raftery, Mary Jo	WTN	1984,85,86,87
Raftery, Sheila	WSW	1982
Raiford, Frank K.	FB	1979
Raimey, David E.	FB	1960,61,62
	MTR	1960
Raisor, Thomas L.	MBK	1954,55,56,57
Raiss, James	MBK	1909
Raiton, Jake	MTN	1996
Rake, Sidney R.	MSW	1930,31,32
Ralston, Harris P.	MTR	1903
Ramey, Horace P.	MTR	1905,06,07
Ramirez, Marcelino	FB	1988,89
Ramsey, William S.	MGO	1946
Ramthun, Lana	VB	1982,83,84,85
Ranck, Wilson M.	MTN	1931
Rand, Warren	BB	1876,77
Randall, C. C.	BB	1954,56
Randall, Gregory G.	FB	1984,85
Randolph, Charles D.	FB	1975
Randolph, Robert L.	BB	1951,51
Rane, John W.	IHO	1940
Ranelli, Dianna	WGY	1993,94,95,96
Rankin, T. Allen	MTR	1951,52,53
Rankin, Walter	BB	1946,47,48,49
Ranney, Leroy	FB	1908,09
Rapper, Ronald J.	MGY	1967,68,69,70
Rasdale, Thomas J.	FB	1973,74
Rashap, Brian A.	MCC	1987
Rasnick, Nathan N.	MBK	1925,26
Rather, David E.	FB	1970,71,72
Ratnick, Diane	VB	1981
Ratterman, L. Fred	BB	1933,34
Ratza, Carol A.	VB	1977,78,79,80
Ravreby, Richard R.	MTN	1970,71,72,73
Rawak, Christine	WSW	1989,90,91,92
Rawls Jr., Jesse	WR	1992,94,95,96
Rawls Sr., Jesse	WR	1969,70
Rawls, James	WR	1990,91,92,93
Ray, Marcus K.	FB	1995,96
Ray, Victor A.	BB	1978,79,81
Rayford, Frank	FB	1982
Raymond, Harold R.	BB	1947,48,49
Raymond, Philip	FB	1916
Raynsford, Jim	FB	1912,13,14
Rea, Walter B.	MBK	1920,21,22
Read, G. Martin	IHO	1962,64,65
Read, George M.	MTR	1903,04,05
Read, Robyn	VB	1991,93
Rearick, Glenn O.	MCC	1923,24
Reason, Rex G.	MBK	1924,25
Rebstock, Arthur	MTR	1902,03,04
Rechsteiner, Robert L.	WR	1981,83,84
Rechsteiner, Scott C.	WR	1982,83,85,86
Reck, Benjamin H.	MTR	1912
Recker, Darlene	VB	1994,95,96
Reddan, Daniel	MTR	1990,91,92,93
Redden, Curtis	FB	1901,02,03
	BB	1902,03
Redmon, Glen V.	BB	1966,67,68,69
Redmond, Rudy C.	MTR	1988,89,90,91
Redner, Arthur	FB	1900,01
Reece, Edward T.	MBK	1925,26
Reed Jr., Robert E.	BB	1964,65,66
Reed, Catherine	SS	1982
Reed, Frank	FB	1878,79
	BB	1879
Reed, Laura	SB	1979,80,81,82
Reed, Orville W.	BB	1925
Reed, Victor R	MTR	1926
Reem, Guy A.	BB	1916,17
Reese, Carter C.	MTR	1960,61,62,63
Reeves, Jeffrey B.	FB	1979,80,81
Reeves, Melvin C.	MTR	1971,72,73
Regeczi, John M.	MBK	1933,34
	BB	1933,34,35
	FB	1932,33,34
Rehbein, Tracy	SS	1982
Rehberger, Dean A.	WR	1978,81
Rehor, Fred	FB	1915,16
Reich, John	MSW	1996
Reichert, Paula	WTN	1983,84,85,86
Reichert, R.E.	IHO	1942,43
Reichert, Robert J.	WR	1944
Reichman, Gerson	BB	1927,28,29
Reid, Brian	FB	1988
Reid, Dorie E.	FB	1962
	MTR	1963,64,65
Reid, Emerson	IHO	1931,32,33
Reid, Lawrence P.	FB	1978,79
Reid, Robert S.	FB	1981,82,83
Reid, William D.	IHO	1980,81,82,83
Reigel Jr., Thomas J.	MSW	1949,50,51
Reif, Albert	WR	1931,32
Reif, Ernest C.	MSW	1928,29
Reilly, Charles A.	WR	1966,67,68,69
	MSW	1968,69
Reilly, Steven	FB	1981
Reimann, Lewis	FB	1914,15
Rein, Russell R.	FB	1984
Reindel, George Jr.	MTN	1921,22
Reindel, Ira H.	MTN	1913,14,15
Reindel, John D.	MTN	1931,32
Reinhold, Michael W.	FB	1983,85
Reinke, Charles A.	MCC	1923,24,25
Reinke, Miles C.	MCC	1924
Reising, Richard P.	MSW	1988
Reissing, Michael G.	MSW	1962,63
Reissing, Theodore C.	MSW	1957,58
Rekowski, Stephen	FB	1990,91,92,93
Rellford, Richard A.	MBK	1983,84,85,86
Rembiesfa, Donald F.	BB	1956
	FB	1954,55,56
Rembisz, Amy	WBK	1983,84,85
Remias, Stephen	BB	1933
	FB	1934,35
Renaldi, Brian	MTR	1993,94,95,96
Renda, Hercules	FB	1937,38,39
Rendall, Thomas W.	IHO	1954,55,56,57
Renfrew, Allan M.	IHO	1946
Renke, David J.	BB	1967,68
Rennebohm, Robert B.	FB	1943
Renner, Arthur W.	FB	1943,44,45,46
Renner, Robert J.	MSW	1933,34,35
Renner, William	FB	1933,35
Rentschler, David F.	FB	1955,56
Rentschler, Debbie	WTN	1979
Renwick, Donald J.	MTR	1931,32
Reppert, D. Lantz	MSW	1962,63,64,65
Rescarla, Russell G.	FB	1951,52
Revere, Mary	SS	1974,75,76,77
Reyman, Dominica	SB	1982,83,84,85
Reynick, Charles	FB	1877,78
Reynolds, Ceroy	MBK	1974,75
Reynolds, Irving	IHO	1924,25,26
Reynolds, John C.	FB	1966
Reynolds, John K.	MTR	1966,67,68
Reynolds, Lisa	WBK	1987,88
Reynolds, Susan	WGY	1976
Rheinschild, Walter	FB	1905,07
Rhode, Dennis W.	IHO	1959,61
Rhodes, Carl F.	WR	1961,62,63
Rice, Daniel J.	FB	1982
Rice, Glen A.	MBK	1986,87,88,89
Rice, William J.	MBK	1923
Rich, Dawn	WTR	1982,83,84,85
Rich, George	BB	1893
Rich Sr., George E.	FB	1926,27,28
	WR	1926
Richard, Daniel J.	WR	1978
Richards, Harry S.	BB	1877
Richards, J.D.	FB	1894,95,96,97
Richards, Jerry W.	MBK	1956
Richards, Kathryn	VB	1991,92
Richards, Mayrie	WCC	1992,94,95
	WTR	1996
Richards, Melanie	WCC	1985
Richards, Richard S.	MGY	1966,67,68,69
Richards, Steven T.	WR	1984,85,86
Richards, Todd	MTR	1993,94,95
	FB	1993,94,95
Richardson, A.E.	FB	1899
Richardson, Airron	WR	1995,96,97
Richardson, Dennis J.	FB	1974,77
Richardson, James C.	WSW	1995,96
Richardson, Max C.	FB	1974,75,76,77
Richardson, Robert C.	WR	1943
Richart, Betsy	WGO	1978
Richart, John D.	MGO	1965,66,67
Richelew, Josh	IHO	1994,96,96
Richmond, Steven L.	IHO	1979,80,81,82
Richter, David E.	IHO	1979,80,81,82
Richter, James H.	FB	1948
Ricken, Raymond	BB	1993,94
Ricketts, Girard P.	MBK	1932
Ricketts, Ronda	WTR	1990
Ricketts, Whitney	WSOC	1994,95
Ricks, Lawrence T.	FB	1979,80,81,82
Riddle, Rhonda	VB	1973
Ridgley, Jennifer	WTR	1992
Rieckhoff, John W.	MGY	1979,80,81
Riedl, Richard J.	MSW	1940,41,42
Rieger, Joan	WBK	1987,88,89,90
Riegler, Andy	FB	1992,93
Rieke, Harry A.	MSW	1936,38
Riemersma, A. Jay	FB	1992,93,94,95
Ries, John L.	MSW	1950,51,52,53
Ries, Joseph	FB	1995,96
Ries, Richard G.	FB	1963
Riess, Lynn	MGO	1938,39,40
Rife, Jonathan J.	MGO	1985
Rifenburg, Dick	FB	1946,47,48
Riley, Eric	MBK	1989,90,91, 92,93
Riley, Tom	FB	1908
Rinaldi, Joe	FB	1935,36,37
Rinck, Robert T.	MTR	1988,89,90
Rinckey, Gordon R.	BB	1957,58,59,60
Rindfuss, Richard M.	FB	1962,63,64
Rinek, Lorenz W.	MBK	1940
Ring, Marianne	WTN	1982,83
Rio, Tony	FB	1957,59
Rioux, Jennifer	WCC	1983
	WTR	1984

Ripley, Clarence	MTN	1896,98,99,00
Risdon, Roberta	WTN	1980,81,82
Rish, Mary	WSW	1978,79,81
Risk, John F.	MTR	1978
Ritchie, C. Stark	FB	1935,36,37
Ritchie, Jon D.	FB	1993
Ritchlin, Sean	IHO	1996
Ritley, Robert M.	FB	1969
Ritter, Charles A.	FB	1954
Ritter, David R.	FB	1988,89,90,91
Ritter, Jack L.	BB	1953,54
Ritter, John G.	BB	1968,69
Ritzman, Roger A.	WR	1970,71,72,73
Riutta, James R.	MSW	1962
Rivers, Garland A.	FB	1983,84,85,86
Rizzo, Gary J.	MCC	1973
Roach, Bernard J.	IHO	1925,26,27
Roach, Michael J.	MSW	1957
Roach, Thomas G.	FB	1929
Roadhouse, David R.	MSW	1963,64
Robbins, Dammond R.	FB	1984,85,86,87
Robbins, J.E.	BB	1916
Robbins, Kevin F.	MTR	1979,80
Roberts, Daniel J.	MGO	1982,83,84,85
Roberts, David	IHO	1990,91,92,93
Roberts, J. Alex	IHO	1987,88,89,90
Roberts, Leon K.	BB	1970,71,72
Roberts, Samuel M.	MGY	1975
Roberts, Scott D.	FB	1982
Roberts, William C.	MBK	1947,48,49
Roberts, Willis	FB	1876
	BB	1874,75,76
	MTR	1876
Robertson, John T.	MSW	1966,67,68,69
Robertson, Julian (Tex)	MSW	1933,34,35
Robertson, Stephanie	WCC	1984
	WTR	1985,86,87
Robey, Virginia	WGY	1976,77,78
Robie III, Carl J.	MSW	1964,65,66,67
Robins, Richard K.	MBK	1958,59
Robinson, Don W.	BB	1942,46
	FB	1941,42,46
Robinson, John J.	MBK	1975,76,77
Robinson, John S.	MTR	1901,02,03
Robinson, Joseph	WR	1940
Robinson, K. Michael	MBK	1978
Robinson, Milton J.	MTr	1957
Robinson, Rumeal J.	MBK	1988,89,90
Robinson, Ryan R.	MCC	1987,88
	MTR	1988,89
Robinson, Thomas A.	MTR	1958,59,60,61
Robinson, Thomas E.	BB	1891,92
Robson, James J.	MGO	1968,71
Roby, Doug	FB	1921,22
	BB	1921,22
Roche, Andrew	BB	1902,03
Rockwell, Ferdinand A.	FB	1923,24
Rockymore, Leslie L.	MBK	1982,83,84,85
Rodgers, Donald N.	IHO	1960,61,62,63
Rodgers, Nathaniel	FB	1980,82,83,84
Rodgers, Robert B.	FB	1947
Rodney, Frederick E.	MGY	1966,67,68,69
Rodriguez, Mike	FB	1955
	WR	1953,55,56,57
Rodriguez, Sigfredo	MBK	1976
Rodriquez, John	MTN	1935,36
Roebuck, David M.	BB	1961,62,63
Roeder, Steven W.	MSW	1983,84
Roehm, Laurence	FB	1915
	BB	1916
Roek, Katie	WSOC	1994,95
Roesser, William D.	MTR	1923,24
Rogers, Charles T.	MBK	1973,74
	BB	1973,74,75
Rogers, Goodloe H.	BB	1912,13
Rogers, Gordon P.	MBK	1957,58,59
Rogers, Jacqueline	FH	1982,83,84, 85
Rogers, Jeffrey	MTR	1996
Rogers, Joe	FB	1939,40,41
Rogers, Martha	SB	1984,85,86,87
Rogers, Peter A.	MGY	1969,71
Rogers, Richard (Rick)	FB	1981,82,83,84
Rogers, Susan	VB	1980,81,82,83
Roland, Susan	WTR	1989
Rollins, J.H.	BB	1881
Rollins, Laura L.	WSW	1987,88,89,90
Rollins, Richard B.	MSW	1965,68,69
Romain, David L.	MTR	1961,63,64
Roman, William A.	BB	1957,58,59,60
Romas, John E.	MBK	1976,77
Rominiski, Dale	IHO	1996
Ronan, Franklin D.	BB	1953,54,55,56
Rood, Anne	WSW	1988
Rooney, Heather	FH	1992
Roos, Thomas R.	MSW	1975

Root, Edgar	FB	1874
	BB	1872,73,74
Root, John H.	MGO	1932
Root, Robert A.	MBK	1975
Root, Willard L.	WR	1956,57,60,61
Rorich, Johann	MTN	1921,22,23
Rosatti Jr., Edward J.	FB	1947
Rosatti, Rudy	FB	1922
Rose, Carleton S.	FB	1980,81,82,83
Rose, Daniel P.	MBK	1928,29
Rose, Hugh H.	WR	1925
Rose, Jack W.	MTR	1952
Rose, Jalen	MBK	1992,93,94
Rose, Mitchell D.	MGY	1984,85,86,87
Rose, Ralph W.	MTR	1904
Rosema, Robert J.	FB	1971
Rosema, Roger W. (Rocky)	FB	1965,66,67
Rosema, Thomas J.	BB	1945,46
Roseman, Neil D.	FB	1985
Rosen, Steven S.	MTR	1968,71
Rosen, Adam	BB	1992
Rosenbaum, Mark R.	MTR	1970,71,72,73
Rosenberg, Herb N.	FB	1947
Rosenberg, Marjorie A.	WBK	1974,75
Rosenberg, Meyer	MSW	1928
Rosencrans, Gordon W.	MBK	1946
	MBK	1946
Roska, John M.	MGO	1968,69,70,71
Rosloniec, Michael	MBK	1991
Rosowski, Mary	WBK	1988,89
Ross, Charles R.	FB	1937
	IHO	1939,40,41
Ross, Frederick R.	MTR	1911
Ross, Harold B.	MGY	1932
Ross, Heather	WSW	1991
Ross, Jaime	WSOC	1994,95
Ross, Joel N.	MTN	1969,70,71,72
Ross, John B.	MTR	1951,52,53,54
Ross, Jonathan E.	MGY	1983,85,86
Ross, Laura	WGY	1976
Ross, Mekisha	WBK	1994,95,96,97
Ross, Peter H.	BB	1973,74,75
Ross, William A.	FB	1968,69,71
Ross, Willie J.	MTR	1979,80,81
Rossi, Michael A.	IHO	1986,87
Rossi, Paul W.	IHO	1985,86
Rothwell, Nigel M.	MGY	1976,77,78,79
Rott, James E.	FB	1986
Rottmann, Vern C.	MTR	1973,81
Rotundo, Jennifer	WSW	1993
Rotunno, Michael J.	FB	1954,55,56
Round, James R.	MGY	1989,90,91,92
Roussel, Jean-Remy	MTN	1988,89
Rowand, Melinda	WCC	1986,87,88,89
	WTR	1988,89,90
Rowe, Denise	VB	1979
Rowe, Floyd A.	MTR	1905,06,07,08
Rowe, Kim A.	MTR	1971,72,73,74
Rowland, Charles	FB	1981
Rowland, Monroe K.	MGY	1950,51,52
Rowser, John F.	MBK	1963
	FB	1963,65,66
	MTR	1964
Roxborough, John W.	MTR	1942,43,44
Royce, Jon	MTR	1993,94,95,96
Royer, John W.	MTN	1984,85,86,87
Royston, J.R. Jr.	MGO	1929,30,31
Rubenstein, Mitchell	MTN	1991,92
Rubin, Allan A.	WR	1933,35
Rubin, Michael D.	WR	1969
Rubin, Seth	MGY	1991,92,93,94
Rubin, Seymour J.	WR	1933,34,35
Rubin, Steven L.	WR	1968,69
Rucinski, Michael A.	BB	1976
Rudesill, Robert P.	MTR	1952,54,56
Rudman, Jill	FH	1985
Rudness, George	MBK	1935,36
	BB	1935,36
Rudy, Gerard A.	MBK	1982,83,84,85
Ruehle Jr., George I.	MBK	1940,41
	BB	1940,41
Ruetz, Earl D.	BB	1927
Ruf, David W.	MCC	1986
	MTR	1987
Ruff, Daniel W.	BB	1988,89,90,91
Ruggles, Gregory G.	MBK	1978,79,80,81
Ruitta, James R.	MSW	1951,52,53
Rumley, Christopher	MSW	1994,95,96
Rumney, Mason	FB	1906,07
Rumsey, Bronson C.	FB	1950
	WR	1952,53,54
Rundell, Warren	FB	1893,94
Runnels, Herbert W.	MTR	1897
Running, Peter J.	MTR	1976,79
Runyan, Jon	FB	1993,94,95

Ruschiensky, Kristen	VB	1994,95,96
Ruskin, Herbert B.	BB	1948
Russ, J. Carlton	FB	1972,73,74
Russell Jr., Cazzie L.	MBK	1964,65,66
Russell, Edwin F.	MTR	1930,31,32
Russell, George E.	MTN	1962,64,65
Russell, Ira T.	MTR	1967,68,69,70
Russell, M. Campy	MBK	1972,73,74
Russler, Doren W.	MTN	1950
Rutledge, Regan	WR	1995
Rutsch, Nancy	WSW	1983
Ruzicho, Andrew	MCC	1989
Ruzicka, Charles W.	FB	1963,65
Ruzicka, Edward E.	MBK	1918
	BB	1981
Ryan, D. Scott	MSW	1988,89,90
Ryan, Desmond P.	MTR	1962,63,64
Ryan, Edmond C.	MTN	1930,31,32
Ryan Jr., John P.	WR	1972,73,74,75
Ryan, Prentice U.	FB	1947
Rychener, Ralph	MBK	1918,19,20
Rydland, Karen	WSW	1977,78,79
Rydze, Richard A.	MD	1968,69,70,71
Rye, Harold	FB	1917,19
Ryrholm, John N.	BB	1925

S

Saachuck, John J.	FB	1931
Saari, Jennifer	WCC	1986
	WTR	1987
Sabo, Christopher A.	BB	1981,82,83
Sabuco, Gil V.	BB	1950,51,52,53
Sachsel, Arthur J.	WR	1945
Sacka, Ronald	IHO	1992,93,94,95
Safford, Brian H.	MBK	1975
Safley, Ben	FB	1872,76
	MTR	1872,76
Saint-Jean, Olivier	MBK	1994
Sakai, James T.	FB	1947,48
Sakala, Mark	IHO	1993,94,95,96
Sakamoto, Randall F.	MGY	1973,74,75,76
Salaam, Shareef	MTR	1995
Salassa, John R.	MSW	1965,66,67,68
Salay, Roberta	VB	1976,77,78
Sale, Michael J.	MGY	1969,70,71,72
Salmon, Jack E.	MTN	1934
Sample, Frederick	FB	1968
Samplinski, Richard E.	BB	1987,88
Sampson, Jay A.	MTR	1961,62,64
Samson, Paul C.	MSW	1925,26,27
Samuels, Tom C.	FB	1930,31
Samuelson, Amanda	WGY	1991
Samuelson, Dayna	WGY	1982,83,84,85
Samuelson, Gilbert	IHO	1939,40,41
Sanborn, Phillip D.	MCC	1989
Sanchez y Escribano, F.	MTN	1922,23
Sanchez, Abel	MSW	1992,93,94,95
Sanders, Eric A.	BB	1983,84,85
Sanders, Ernest	FB	1994,95
Sanders, Fred B.	MGY	1962,63,64,65
Sanders, Tammie L.	SB	1979,80,81,82
	WBK	1979,80,81
Sanderson, Ed	FB	1892,93
Sanderson, Francis D.	MTR	1929,30
Sandler, Scott M.	MBK	1993,94,95
Sandmann, Lynn	SS	1974
Sanduski, Clinton D.	MTN	1933,34
Sanford, Jay P.	MSW	1947,48,49
Sanger, Frank E.	BB	1905,06
Sanger, James R.	WR	1967,68,69,70
Sansom, Elijah T.	FB	1968
Santana, Jose F.	MSW	1981
Santo, Bryan	BB	1990,91,92,93
Saponic, Melanie	SS	1980
Sarafian, Alexander M.	MTR	1990,91
Sarantos, Peter A.	FB	1969
Sarazin, Pierre	IHO	1973
Sargent, Charles	MTR	1921,22
Sargent, John A.	FB	1947
Sargent, Warren E.	MTR	1912,13
Sasich, Milan	MGY	1966,67,68,69
Sassone, Robert L.	MTN	1953,54,58,59
Satterthwaite, Lance	FB	1992,93
Satyshure, Elaine	WGO	1979,80,81
Sauer, Robert F.	MSW	1937,38
Sauer, Russell	WR	1927
Sauls IV, Reginald G.	MBK	1949
	FB	1948,49
Saunders, Allen	MGO	1935,36,37
Saunders, Harold J.	BB	1918,20
Savage, Carl	FB	1932,33
Savage, Colette	WTR	1992,93,94
Savage, Michael S.	FB	1933,34,35
	MTR	1935
Savage, Nicole	WSOC	1995

Savage, Richard E.	BB	1942,43,46
Savarino, Peter J.	MGO	1983,84,85,86
Savilla, Roland	FB	1937,38,39
	WR	1938,39
Sawyer, Dale B.	MTR	1959,60
Sawyer, Theron M.	BB	1897
Saxon, Charles S.	MTN	1960
Sayers, Kerry	SB	1992
Scales II, Bobby L.	BB	1996
Scandura, Joseph M.	WR	1950,51,52,53
Scarcelli, James J.	FB	1983,84,85
Schanski, Tate	FB	1996
Schaefer, Abbie	WTR	1993,94
Schafer, Kenneth C.	MTN	1927,28,29
Schafer, Walter E.	MTR	1959,60,61
Schaflander, Gerald M.	MTN	1941,42
Schalon, Edward I.	MGO	1946,47,48,49
Scharl, Matthew	MTR	1990
Scheer, Lawrence E.	MTR	1945
Scheerer, Paul J.	MSW	1964,65,66,67
Scheff, Monika	WSW	1978,79,80
Scheffler, Lance G.	FB	1968,69,70
Scheidler, Nicholas	BB	1918,20
Scheiner, Brad R.	BB	1996
Scheinman, Stephen B.	MGY	1981,83,85
Schell, Clark G.	MTR	1933,34
Schemanske, Jay K.	MCC	1993
	MTR	1994
Schembechler, Glenn E.	FB	1969,71
Schenthal, Stephen J.	MD	1972,73,74
Scheper, Robert S.	MCC	1974,75,76,77
	MTR	1976,77,78
Scherer, John O.	MCC	1985,86,87,88
	MTR	1986,87,88,89
Scherer, Julie	VB	1991,92,93,94
Scherer, Whitney	WD	1988,89,90,91
Schett, John L.	BB	1951
Schiappacasse, Joseph	BB	1902
Schick, Gary J.	FB	1965
Schiller, Robert P.	BB	1954
	IHO	1954,55,56,57
Schiller, Thomas D.	IHO	1964,65,66
Schinnerer, Lloyd C.	MBK	1973,74,75,76
Schissler, Helen	SS	1974,75
Schlanderer, Arthur	IHO	1930,31
Schlicht, Leo R.	MBK	1953
	FB	1951
	MTR	1952
Schlonsky, Allison	WTN	1992,93,94
Schlopy, R. Todd	FB	1983,84
Schloss, Milton J.	MGO	1934
Schmeidel, Christine	WTN	1990,91
Schmeidler, Laurence M.	FB	1947
Schmeltzer, Hope	WGY	1986
Schmerge, Mark J.	FB	1975,76,77,78
Schmerge, Paul L.	FB	1984,85
Schmidt, Carl J.	MTR	1922,23
Schmidt, Catherine	WTN	1987,88,89,90
Schmidt, Catherine M.	WCC	1983,84,85
	WTR	1985,86
Schmidt, Charles R.	BB	1966,67,68,69
Schmidt, James A.	MCC	1981,82,83,84
	MTR	1983,85
Schmidt, Joseph W.	MCC	1984,85,86,87
	MTR	1984,85,86,87
Schmidt, Paul R.	FB	1961
Schmidt, Stephen C.	BB	1960,61
Schmidtke, Richard A.	BB	1944,47
Schmieler, John A.	MSW	1931,32,33
Schmitt, Roger H.	FB	1961
	MTR	1961,62,63,64

Chris Sabo (1981-83) went from the Michigan baseball team to an outstanding major league career.

Schmitz, James E.	FB	1968,69,70,71
Schmitz, William E.	MTR	1922
Schneider, Brigid	SS	1981,82
Schneider, Todd M.	WR	1975,76,77,78
Schnorberger, Julie	WSW	1988,89,90,91
Schock, Harold	IHO	1994,95,96
Schoelch, Andrew	MTR	1993,94,95,96
Schoenfeld, John	FB	1926,27
Schoenherr, Steven R.	MBK	1960,61,62
Schoenlaub, Paul W.	MTN	1946
Schoetz, Max C.	WR	1939
Schofield, Lisa	FH	1981,82,83,84
Schopf, Jon B.	FB	1959,60,61
Schorer, Scott	BB	1990
Schork, Anna	WTN	1988,89,90
Schott, Richard R.	MCC	1971,72
	MTR	1971,73
Schrager, Alan	MBK	1989,90
Schram, Richard G.	FB	1962
Schravesande, John B.	MTR	1925,27
Schreiber, Rodd W.	MTN	1981,82,83,84
Schriefer, Paul C.	MSW	1986
Schroeder, J. Lance	MSW	1983
Schroeder, John L.	MGO	1965,66,67,68
Schroeder, Lawrence G.	MSW	1976,77,78
Schroeder, Matthew C.	MCC	1989,90,91,93
	MTR	1991,92,94
Schroeder, Susan	WCC	1982,83
	WTR	1983,84,85,86
Schroeder, Wayne	MBK	1926,27
Schrot, Christopher A.	MBK	1985,86,87
Schryer, Richard D.	BB	1964,65,66
Schubeck Jr., John	MGO	1954,55,56,57
Schuchard, Bruce G.	MGY	1977,78,79,80
Schuck, William F.	WR	1972,73,74,75
Schueler, David F.	FB	1990
Schuldt, Paul W.	MBK	1962
	BB	1962,64
Schule, Frederick W.	MTR	1904
Schulte, Greg J.	BB	1980,81,82
Schulte, Henry	FB	1903,04,05
Schulte, Timothy M.	FB	1984,85,86
Schulte, Todd M.	FB	1985,86
Schulz, Adolph	MTR	1907
Schulze, Adolf (Germany)	FB	1904,05,07,08
Schultz, Alfred L.	BB	1921,22
Schultz, Karl A.	MBK	1978
Schulwitz, Gustav W.	FB	1963
Schumacher, Gerald F.	FB	1970,71,72
Schuman, Stanton J.	FB	1935
	MTR	1934
	WR	1937
Schwan, Bonnie	VB	1977
Schwarten, Thomas E.	MSW	1964,65,66
Schwartz, Christine H.	WGY	1982,83,84,85
Schwartz, Michael D.	MTN	1951,52
Schwartz, Richard K.	MTR	1958,59,60
Schwartz, Stephen B.	MBK	1971,72
Schwarze, Fred H.	MGO	1938
Schwarzkopf, Ralph H.	MTR	1938,39,40
Scofield, Leland N.	MTR	1917
Scott, Rodney E.	BB	1965,68
Scott, Spencer	FB	1913
Scott, Wallace D.	BB	1896,98
Scruggs, Grant M.	MTR	1952,53,54,55
Scully, Andrea	WGY	1983,84,85
Scully, Francis J.	BB	1910,12
Scully, James L.	MGY	1969,70,71,72
Seabron, Thomas H.	FB	1975,76,77,78
Seager, J.B. Allan	MSW	1927,28,29
Seal, Paul N.	FB	1971,72,73
Sealby, Robert L.	BB	1955,56,57,58
Searle, John	FB	1921
Searle, William L.	FB	1950
Sears, Harold	FB	1934
Sears, James D.	MTR	1943
Sedgwick, Sherwald W.	MCC	1918,19
Seegert, Alicia	SB	1984,85,86,87
Seekell, Michael T.	MGO	1987
Seeley, Dana P.	MGO	1934,35
Seeman, Scott D.	MTN	1977
Seestedt, Michael P.	BB	1996
Seewer, Barbara	WTR	1985
Segula, Robert L.	MTR	1941,42,43,44
Seid, Richard S.	BB	1972
Seidenstein, Charles E.	MGO	1938
Seidler, Katherine	SS	1978,79
Seidman, Albert G.	MSW	1925
Selbo, Glen	MBK	1946
Selden, Barbara	WTN	1976,77
Sellman, Jeanne	VB	1976,77,78,79
Semchyshen, Norman	MSW	1974,75,76
Semegen, Ann	VB	1976
Senich, Kevin J.	MTN	1971,72,73,74
Senkowski, Raymond D.	MTN	1961,62,63

Senter, Henry	FB	1893
Serakos, Anthony L.	MTR	1934
Sergeson, Robert	MTR	1948,49
Sessa, Michael J.	FB	1984
Seter, Christopher E.	MBK	1989,90,91,92
Seth, Anthony O.	MTR	1958,59,60
Settle, David L.	BB	1948,49,50
Seufert, Chris	WSW	1977,78
Severin, Linda	WBK	1974,75
Seward, Howard H.	MTR	1913,14
Sexton, Frank J.	BB	1895
Sexton, Robert E.	MTR	1950,51
Sexton, Walter E.	FB	1971,72
Seychel, Christopher A.	IHO	1983,84,85,86
Seyferth, Fritz	FB	1969,70,71
Seyferth, Stephen Y.	BB	1976,77
Seymour, Dale A.	MTR	1929,30
Seymour, Dalton G.	MTR	1928,29,30
Seymour, Paul C.	FB	1970,71,72
Seymour, Philip H.	FB	1967,68,70
Seymour III, William	MBK	1944
Shackleford, John	BB	1921,22,23
Shafer, Mark A.	MCC	1985
	MTR	1987
Shafroth, Morrison	MTN	1909,10,11
Shaiper, Kristin	FH	1989,90,91
Shand, David A.	IHO	1974
Shank, Elmer S.	MTR	1903
Shannon Jr., David T.	MTR	1987
Shannon Jr., Edward J.	FB	1954,55,56
Shapiro, Eli E.	MGY	1975
Shapiro, Betsy	WTN	1981,82
Sharemet, C. Gus	MSW	1940,41,42
Sharemet, John J.	MSW	1940,41,42
Sharik, Stanley D.	MTR	1991,92,93
Sharp, J. Royce	MSW	1993
Sharpe, Catherine O.	WTR	1979,80,81,82
Sharpe, Ernest M.	FB	1965,66,67
Sharpe, Philip E.	FB	1941,42
Sharples, Warren J.	IHO	1987,88,89,90
Sharton, James F.	MTN	1983,84,85,86
Shatusky, Michael R.	FB	1956,57
Shaufler, Judson W.	MTN	1977,78,79,80
Shave, Reginald E.	IHO	1951,52,53
Shaver, Verne C.	IHO	1977,78
Shaw, Alex J.	MBK	1931,32
Shaw, Jeff R.	FB	1980
Shaw, Lawrence M.	FB	1947,48
Shaw, Murray M.	IHO	1970
Shaw, Russell	FB	1996
Shaw, Victoria	WBK	1989,90,91
Shaw, Vincent K.	FB	1979,80
Shaw, Walter	FB	1900
Shea, Aaron	FB	1996
Shea, Brian M.	MTR	1989
Shea, Christopher M.	BB	1980
Shea, Daniel	MCC	1993
Shea, Francis	IHO	1928
Shea, Michael J.	MTR	1979,80,81,82
Shea, Sylvester C.	FB	1930,32
Shearon, Cynthia	WGY	1979,80,81,82
Shearon, James C.	MBK	1954,55,56,57
Sheehan, Cecilia M.	WSW	1983,84,85,86
Sheehy, Frank W.	BB	1913,14,15
Sheldon, Douglas M.	MTR	1982
Shellman, Silver	WBK	1994,95,96,97
Shelton, James H.	MCC	1931
Shemky, Robert W.	MBK	1942
	FB	1940
Shepard, Nathan	MSW	1996
Shepardson, Oscar P.	BB	1874
Shepherd, George W.	MTR	1945,47,48
Shepherd, Terri	WGY	1983,84,85,86
Sherf, John	IHO	1933,34,35
Sheridan, Timothy P.	MSW	1984,85,86
Sherman Jr., Samuel S.	FB	1889-1890
Sherman, Ralph L.	FB	1947
Sherman, Roger	FB	1891,93
Sherrill, John C.	MSW	1939
Sherwood, Horace	MTN	1914,15
Shevrin, Marc J.	FB	1985
Shields, Edmund	FB	1895
	BB	1892,93,94,95,96
Shields, Megan M.	WGY	1990,91,92
Shields, Steven	IHO	1991,92,93,94
Shimko, Martin J.	FB	1985
Shingle, Stacy	WGY	1991
Shivel, Ralph B.	BB	1915
Shively, Emily	WCC	1993,94,96
Shoemaker, Clayton S.	MBK	1920
Shokes, C. Doug	MGY	1975,76
Shorr, Maurice J.	MSW	1926,27
Short, Hugh J.	MTR	1946

Shorts, Bruce C.	FB	1900,02
	MTR	1901
Shortt, Ronald J.	MTR	1967,68,69,70
Shrider, Richard G.	MBK	1944
Shultz, Jill	SS	1982
Shuster, Stephen M.	WR	1973,74,76
Shuta, William M.	BB	1981,82,83,84
Shuttlesworth, E. Ed	FB	1971,72,73
Siar, Robert M.	WR	1980
Sibilsky, George A.	IHO	1926,27
Sichta, John C.	BB	1973
Sickels, Quentin B.	FB	1944,46,47,48
Sickon, Bridget	FH	1982,83
Siddiqui, Nazema	WCR	1997
Siebers, Carolyn A.	VB	1974,75
Siegel, Don	FB	1936,37,38
Siegel, Seymour S.	MTN	1933,34,35
Siegmund, Rudolph	FB	1899
	MTR	1900
Sieler, Sue	SB	1990,91,92
Siemons, Adam	MTR	1923
Sigerfoos, Edward	WR	1930
	MSW	1930
Sigler, William K.	FB	1943
Sigman, Lionel A.	FB	1955,56
	BB	1956
Sigwart, Dallas	WR	1931
Sikkenga, Jay	FB	1931
Sikkila, Dennis	MGO	1990,91,92
Silfen, Jane	WTN	1982,83,84
Silver, Michelle	SB	1992,93,94,95
Silverman, Robert S.	MD	1988,89,90,92
Silvester, Kirsten	WSW	1992,93
Simkus, Arnold	FB	1962,64
Simmons, Brian	BB	1993,94,95
Simmons, Rasheed C.	FB	1995
Simmons, Victor H.	MTR	1915,16,17
Simmons, Walter H.	MTR	1921,22
Simms, Ernest L.	MTR	1957,58
Simon, Carol	SB	1985,86
Simon, David L.	FB	1984
Simonds, Chandler D.	MGO	1942
Simonds Jr., Chandler D.	BB	1963,64,65,66
Simpkins, Ronald B.	FB	1976,77,78,79
Simpson, Cornelius	FB	1987,89,90,91
Simpson, David A.	FB	1974
Simpson, James D.	MTR	1957,58
Simpson, James R.	MCC	1973,74
	MTR	1975
Simpson, Nicole A.	WGY	1991,92,93,94
Simpson, Ronald J.	MTR	1983,84,85
Simpson, W.A.	WR	1925
Simrall, James H.	FB	1928,29,30
Sims, Frank M.	MGO	1976,77,78,79
Sims, Lydia F.	WBK	1974,76,77
Sincich, Alan C.	FB	1981,82,83,84
Sinclair, Alan	IHO	1992,93,94,95
Sinclair, Harry M.	WR	1925
Sinclair, Jack P.	MCC	1975
	MTR	1976,77,79
Sinclair, Karen	WD	1989,90,91,92
Sindles, Harold	IHO	1934
Singer, Oscar	FB	1932,33
Singletary, Chris	FB	1996
Sipp, George T.	FB	1947,48
Sipp, Warren D.	FB	1966,67,68
Sippola, Alvin	IHO	1930
Sirosky, Dennis S.	FB	1968
Sisinyak, Eugene T.	FB	1956,57,58
Sisler, George H.	BB	1913,14,15
Skidmore, Stanley L.	BB	1926
Sittler, Ryan	IHO	1993,94
Siuda, Matthew	BB	1984,85
Sizemore, Ted C.	BB	1963,64,65,66
Skaff, George J.	BB	1962,63,64,65
Skala, James G.	MBK	1948,50,51,52
	FB	1949,50
Skene, Douglas C.	FB	1989,90,91,92
Skilling, William C.	FB	1979
Skillman Jr., Newton	WR	1945
Skimming, Thomas	MTR	1954,55
Skinner, James L.	FB	1885
	MTR	1885
Skinner, James W.	MSW	1941,42,43
Skinner, Brian H.	IHO	1969,70,71,72
Skinner, William L.	MGY	1957,58,59,60
Sklar, Dale W.	BB	1983
Skoglund, Scott	MSW	1991
Skorput, Ante	FB	1993,94
Skrepenak, Gregory A.	FB	1988,89,90,91
Slack, Brian D.	IHO	1968,69,70,71
Slade, Thomas A.	FB	1971,72,73
Slade, Ann	SB	1978
Slagle, George W.	BB	1928
Slater, Jill	WGY	1976

Slattery, Thomas G.	MTN	1938
Slaughter, E.R.	FB	1922,23,24
Slaughter, Marion	MTR	1920
Slavens, Jane	SS	1981
Slavin, Manuel	MBK	1938
Sleator, Frederick B.	MTN	1943
Slezak, David R.	FB	1961
Sloan, Blake	IHO	1994,95,96,97
Sloan, Laird L.	MTR	1954,55,56,57
Slusher, Wayne C.	BB	1961,62,63,64
Sly, Cheryl	WCC	1985,86,87
	WTR	1986,87,88
Slykhouse, John E.	MSW	1979,80,81
Small, Irwin A.	FB	1946,47,48
	WR	1945
Smart Jr., Jackson W.	MTN	1951
Smeja, Rudy	FB	1941,42,43
Smeltzer, Charles	BB	1892,93,94
Smick, Dan	FB	1936,37,38
	MBK	1937,38,39
	BB	1937,38,39
Smith, Aimee	VB	1991,92,93,94
Smith, Alan H.	MTR	1937,39,40
Smith, Alicia	WSOC	1994,95
Smith, Alison	WTR	1989,90,91
Smith, Alison V.	WGO	1978,79,80
Smith, Andrew	FB	1909
Smith, Benjamin S.	MGO	1941,42,43
Smith, Brian	MTR	1992,93,94,95
Smith, C. Lysle	MBK	1951
Smith, Cedric C. (Pat)	FB	1915,16,17
	MTR	1916,17,19
Smith, Cedric N.	FB	1980
Smith, Charles L.	MBK	1950,51
Smith, Charles M.	MTR	1912,13
Smith, Christina	WTR	1978,79,80,81
Smith, Christopher T.	FB	1989,90
Smith, Colleen	WD	1987,88
Smith, D. Ross	IHO	1946,48,50
Smith, Daniel T.	MTR	1984,85,86
Smith, Donald M.	BB	1943
Smith, Donna	WGO	1978,79,80
Smith Jr., Earl J.	BB	1939
Smith, Edwin J.	MTR	1954
Smith, Francis L.	MSW	1923
Smith, Frederic	FB	1888,89
Smith, G. Michael	FB	1974,75,76,77
Smith, Garrett	FB	1986
Smith, Gerald	FB	1958,59,60
Smith, Gordon H.	FB	1948
Smith, Harold E.	MTR	1916
Smith, Harlond L.	MTR	1914,15
Smith, Harvey H.	MCC	1932
	MTR	1933,34,35
Smith, Howard R.	BB	1909
Smith, Hugh	MGO	1923,24
Smith, James A.	FB	1973,74,75,76
Smith, James B.	BB	1937,38
	IHO	1937,38
Smith, James F.	FB	1950
	WR	1947,48,49,50
Smith, Jeffrey A.	FB	1958,60,61
Smith, Jennifer	SB	1994,95,96,97
Smith, Jodi	WGO	1997
Smith, John C.	BB	1920
Smith, John C.	MSW	1957,58,59,60
Smith, John E.	FB	1945
Smith, Keith R.	MBK	1979,80
Smith, Kerry D.	FB	1980,82,83
Smith, Kevin R.	FB	1980,81
Smith, Leon W.	WR	1946
Smith, Lewis D.	FB	1978
	WR	1977,78
Smith, Marcie	SB	1982,83,84,85
Smith, Matthew B.	MSW	1987
Smith, Matthew S.	MCC	1989,90,91,92
	MTR	1990,91,92,93
Smith, Maurice D.	WR	1946,47,48
Smith, Melanie M.	WBK	1984,85
Smith, Michael C.	FB	1968,69,70,71
Smith, Mike	FB	1977
Smith, Ray W.	MTR	1923
Smith, Richard S.	BB	1949
Smith, Roosevelt D.	FB	1977,78,79
Smith, Seth A.	FB	1994
Smith, Sampson	IHO	1935
Smith, Sandra	WSW	1990,91
Smith, Scott J.	MGY	1988,89,90
Smith, Scott T.	FB	1974
Smith, Sherene	FH	1992,93,94,95
Smith, Stephen B.	FB	1980,81,82,83
Smith, Stephen C.	MBK	1963,64
	FB	1963,64,65
Smith, Thomas E.	MSW	1948,49
Smith, Tony L.	FB	1970,71,72

Smith, Walter	FB	1991,92,93,94
Smith, William	FB	1937,38,39
Smith, Willie	FB	1956,57,58
Smithers, John A.	BB	1937
	FB	1935,36
Smolenski, Sara Jo	WBK	1978
Smoot, Clement E.	MGO	1902,03,05
Smulders, Michelle	FH	1993,94,95,96
Smykowski, Scott A.	FB	1989
Smyth, Charley J.	MTR	1930
Snadjr, Robert I.	BB	1912
Snell, Lawrence W.	MTR	1923
Snell, Richard E.	MTN	1932,33
Snider, Eugene M.	BB	1955,56,57
	FB	1954,56,57
Snover, Edward	FB	1876
Snow, Muir	FB	1896,97
	BB	1899
Snow, Neil W.	FB	1898,99,00,01
	MTR	1901,02
	BB	1899,00,01,02
Snow, Shirley	BB	1908,09
Snyder, Gerald	FB	1978
Snyder, Stuart A.	WR	1946
Snyder, Todd	MTR	1996
Sobkow, Cheryl	WBK	1982
Soble, Ronald N.	MTR	1950,51
Soboleski, Joseph R.	BB	1945
	FB	1945,46,47,48
Sobotta, Robin	WGO	1979
Sobsey, Solomon	FB	1935
Sofiak, Michael J.	MBK	1939,40,41
	BB	1939,40,41
Sohl, Robert R.	MSW	1946,47,48,49
Solik, John B.	MTN	1985,86
Sollom, Kenneth H.	FB	1988,89,90,91
Solomon, Alisa	FH	1974,75,76,77
Solomon, Edward	WR	1926,27
Soltero, Susan	VB	1979
Sommerville, Sharon	WTN	1976
Sonntag, Sharon	WBK	1986,87
Soodik, Eli	FB	1932
Soodik, J. Norman	MTN	1938
Sorensen, Lary A.	BB	1974,75,76
Sorensen, Mark A.	IHO	1988,89,90,91
Sorensen, T.C.	FB	1929
Sosinski, Bryan	WR	1994
Soudek, Ernst H.	MTR	1961,62,63,64
Soullier, Therese	WBK	1981,82,83
Space, David L.	WR	1949,50,51,52
Space, David S.	WR	1972,73,74,75
Space, Thomas L.	WR	1973,74,75
Spacht, Ronald L.	FB	1961
Spada, Anthony J.	MTR	1943
Spademan, C. Fred	FB	1979,80,81
Spahn, J. Jeffrey	FB	1974
Spaid, John L.	MSW	1979,80
Spalla, Dennis J.	BB	1960,61,62,63
Spaly, Robert F.	WR	1962,63,64,65
Spann, William C.	MSW	1963,64
Spannagel, Michele	WCC	1993,95
Sparkman, Wayne	FB	1962,63
Sparks, Cliff	FB	1916,17,19
Spearman, Clinton	FB	1970,71,72
Speek, Peter V.	WR	1943
Speers, Theodore R.	IHO	1980,81,82,83
Speicher, John S.	WR	1936,37,38
Spencer, Craig W.	MBK	1974
Spencer, James H.	MTN	1929
Spencer, Marc C.	FB	1988,89
Spencer, Royce E.	FB	1967
Spewock, Justin W.	WR	1988
Spicer, Keith L.	BB	1965,66,67
Spicer, Leslie	WBK	1987,88,89,90
Spicer, R. Barry	MGY	1960,61,62,63
Spidel, John W.	MBK	1956
	FB	1956,57,58
Spierling, Debra	WTR	1985,86
Spindle, Richard S.	MSW	1927,28,29
Spitalny, Neil H.	MGO	1971,72,73
Spitalny, Jack	MTR	1941
Spitalny, Peter J.	MGO	1973
Spitzberg, Eric H.	IHO	1976,77,78,79
Spitzer, Sherman C.	BB	1891,92,93,94
Splawn, Laurence	FB	1914
Spoden, John F.	WR	1933,34
Spoerl, Stephanie	VB	1974
Spohn, Jamie	VB	1975,76,77
Sprague, Ernest	FB	1887,88
Spring, Paul M.	IHO	1983,84,85
Springer, Jeffrey M.	FB	1994,95,96
Sproat, Harry J.	MTR	1898,99
Spurney, Edward F.	BB	1892,93
Squier, George	FB	1926,28
St. John, Raymond G.	MTN	1902,03
St. Peter, William G.	BB	1986,87,88
Staatz, Karl	FB	1914,15
Stabb, Chester C.	FB	1932,33,36
Stabile Jr., T. Andrew	MSW	1990,91
Stabovitz, Chester C.	FB	1936
Stabrylla, Robert G.	BB	1957,58,59
Stace, Rory A.	MTR	1988,89
Staehle, William C.	MTR	1936,37
Staelin, Carl G.	MSW	1931
Stager Jr., Augustus P.	MSW	1947,48,49,50
Stamman, Carl	FB	1924,25
Stamos, John E.	FB	1959,60,61
Standen, W. Scott	FB	1983
Standish, Stuart	MTR	1992
Stanford, Thad C.	MGO	1951,52,53
Stanger, Peter R.	MTR	1955,58,59
Stanley Jr., Sylvester	FB	1989,91,92,93
Stanley, Lisa A.	FH	1978
Stanley, Sherell	WBK	1991,92,93
Stanovich, Milan A.	MGY	1980,81,82,83
Stanton, Edward C.	FB	1936,37
Stanton, Suzanne	WGY	1976,77,78
Stanwood, Marion	WSW	1979,80,81
Stapleton, Christopher J.	FB	1989,91,92,93
Stapp, William B.	WR	1949,50,51
	FB	1949,50
Stark Jr., James W.	WR	1946
Stark, Randolph W.	FB	1990,91
Starmack, John R.	MTR	1984,85,86,87
Starne, Maurice	BB	1870
Staroba, Paul L.	FB	1968,69,70
Starr, Ben	MCC	1932
	MTR	1933,36,37
Starr, Chris P.	BB	1987
Starr, Gary J.	BB	1956
	IHO	1956,57,58
Starrak, Richard B.	IHO	1946,47,48,49
State, Rory A.	MTR	1988
Staton, Thomas D.	MBK	1976,77,78,79
Staub, Robert	IHO	1970,71,72
Stavale, David J.	MBK	1976
	FB	1975
Staveren, Howard M.	FB	1970,71,72
Stawski, Jeannette	WCR	1997
Stawski, Willard S.	MBK	1959,60
	FB	1961
Stearnes, Frederick K.	BB	1874
Steckle, Allen	FB	1897,98,99
Steckley, James R.	BB	1960,61,62,63
Stedman, Sam	IHO	1946,47,48,49
Steele, Harold	FB	1922,23,24
Steele Jr., James	FB	1994,95,96
Steele, Ronald G.	MTR	1978,79
Steen, Sidney T.	BB	1916
Stefan, Terrence G.	FB	1975
Steffes, Jackson T.	MTR	1958,59,60
Steger, Geoffrey C.	FB	1971,73,74
Steger, Herbert F.	FB	1922,23,24
	BB	1924,25
Stehman, Frederick B.	WR	1965,66,67,68
Stein, Joyce	FH	1973
Steinacker, Kyle	WR	1994
Steinbach, Brian	BB	1995,96
Steinberg, Abraham	MGY	1931,32
Steinberg, Harry	MGY	1932
Steinke, Alfred	FB	1928,29
	WR	1930
Steinmetz, Lara	WTR	1985
Steketee, Frank	FB	1918,20,21
Steketee, Tyler S.	BB	1995,96
Steketee, Paul F.	BB	1930
Stellwagen, Augustus	BB	1874
Stenberg, Robert E.	BB	1942,43
	FB	1942,43
	IHO	1943
Stenger, Donald	MTR	1996
Stennett, William E.	BB	1975,76,77,78
Stenson, Sherman D.	BB	1980
Stephens, David	MSW	1996
Stephens, James C.	MTN	1951,52
Stephens, Leighton	MTN	1925,26,27

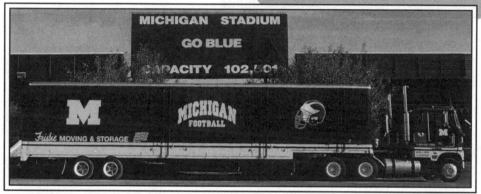

Stephenson, Curtis J.	FB	1975,76,77
Stephenson, H. Howard	IHO	1950
Steppon, William J.	BB	1939,40,41
Sterling, Gale O.	MTN	1935
Stern, Jerome	MBK	1955,56
Sternberg, Robert	IHO	1943
Sternisha, Donald J.	MTR	1943
Stetten, Maynard L.	FB	1958
Steuk, William R.	FB	1992
Stevens, Cheryl	WBK	1990,91
Stevens, Jane	VB	1995,96
Stevens, Margaret G.	WSW	1974
Stevens, Matthew C.	BB	1976
Stevens, Melvin M.	MGO	1953
Stevens, Patrick E.	MSW	1973,74
Stevenson, Robert E.	BB	1944,45
Steverson, G. Todd	MTR	1983,84,85,86
Stewart, Cameron G.	IHO	1991,92,93
Stewart, Carrie	WBK	1992,93
	WTR	1992,93,94,95
Stewart, Dennis E.	MBK	1966,67,68,69
Stewart, James A.	MSW	1976
Stewart, James Y.	MBK	1975
Stewart, Jerry B.	MTN	1964,65,66
Stewart, Raymond G.	MTR	1903,04,06,07
Stewart, Thomas	IHO	1934
Stewart, Walter S.	BB	1915
Stewart, Walter V.	MSW	1942,43,47
Stewart, William C.	MGO	1942
Stiegel, Sidney J.	WR	1937
Stieler, Stephen O.	FB	1959
Stielstra, C. J.	MBK	1954
	MTR	1952,53,54,55
Stiles, Frederick C.	MTR	1935,36
Stiles, Thomas W.	IHO	1983,84,85,86
Stille, Wayne W.	MTN	1940,41,42
Stillerman, Charles	MGY	1974,75,76,77
Stincic, Thomas D.	FB	1966,67,68
Stine, William R.	FB	1958,59,60
Stinson, David J.	FB	1950
	MTR	1951,53
Stinson, Derick R.	MTR	1983,84
Stipe, Clarence G.	MTR	1920,21,22
Stites, Richard L.	FB	1987
Stites, Robert W.	FB	1987
Stiver, Daniel	IHO	1990,91,92,93
Stober, David M.	BB	1981,82
Stock, Leon M.	FB	1951
Stoddard, Clifford	WR	1930,31,32
Stoddard, Maynard G.	BB	1940,41
Stodden, Richard	IHO	1939,40,41
Stodghill, Marion	WTN	1978,79
Stokes, James D.	MTR	1975,76,77,78
Stoliker, Frederick N.	MTR	1944
Stoll, Charles W.	MTR	1918,19
Stoll, Margaret	WD	1990,91,92,93
Stoll, Richard J.	BB	1981,82,83
Stoller, Sam	MTR	1935,36,37
Stollsteimer, Dale	MGY	1949
Stone, Bradford	WR	1948,50
Stone, Cynthia Lawson	FH	1974,75
Stone, Daniel B.	WR	1985
Stone, Donald J.	IHO	1988,89,90,91
Stone, Edward A.	FB	1932
	MTR	1933,34,35,36
Stone, Irving K.	MTR	1903,04,05
Stone, Kathy	WCR	1997
Stone, Melisa	WSW	1994,95,96,97
Stone, Michael	IHO	1991,92,93,94
Stone, Walter D.	MTR	1935,36,38

Lary Sorensen lettered for U-M baseball from 1974-76 and now serves as an analyst on Detroit Tiger radio broadcasts.

Stonehill, Dolph P.	WR	1931
Storey, Kent G.	MBK	1974,75
Storrey, Richard S.	MTR	1968,69,70,71
Stotesbury, Julie	VB	1978,79,80,81
Stottlebower, Joseph C.	MBK	1948
Stout, Matthew	WR	1992,94,95
Stowell, Christopher E.	WR	1962,63,64,65
Stoyko, Steven A.	MBK	1985,86,87,88
Strabley, Michael D.	FB	1975
Strack, David H.	MBK	1943,44,46
Strader, Richard B.	WR	1977
Straffon, Ralph A.	FB	1949,50
Strasburg, James	BB	1901
Straub, Harvey	FB	1928
	BB	1928,29,30
Straub Jr., Robert A.	IHO	1969,70,71,72
Strauss, Noel	MSW	1990,91,92,93
Strauss, Richard L.	FB	1946,47
Street, Charles	FB	1898,99
Street Jr., Meldon D.	WR	1995,96
Streets, Tai	FB	1995,96
Strefling, Nathalie	FH	1973
Strem, Mark	MTN	1982
Strenger, Richard G.	FB	1980,81,82
Strews, Eugene F.	BB	1958,59
Stribe, Ralph C.	FB	1950,51,52
Strinko, Gregory D.	FB	1975
Strinko, Stephen D.	FB	1972,73,74
Stripp, Albert E.	BB	1902
Striz, Barbara	SB	1981
Strobel, John A.	FB	1960,61,62
Stroia, Livius N.	MTR	1943
Strom, Jody	WTN	1976,77
Strong Jr., George J.	FB	1947
Strong, David A.	FB	1938,39
Stross, Wendy	WTN	1988,89
Stroud, Lawrence C.	MBK	1974
Strozewski, Richard J.	FB	1950,52,53
Stryker, Homer H.	BB	1924
Stuart, Duane R.	MTR	1896
Stuart, Theodore M.	FB	1904,05
	MTN	1905
Stuck, Linda	WTR	1993,94
Stuck, Richard W.	FB	1971,72,73
Studwell, Aaron M.	FB	1984,85,87
Stuhldreher, Harry A.	IHO	1950,51
Stuht, Jennifer	WCC	1992,95
	WTR	1996
Stumpfig, John L.	MGO	1950,51,53,54
Stuntzner, Denise	WSW	1981,82,83
Sturm, Julia	VB	1987,88,89,90
Stutzman, Tina	WCR	1997
Suckup, David	FB	1969,72
	MBK	1970
Sudarkasa, Michael E.	MTR	1982,83,84
Sukup, Milo	FB	1938,39,40
Sulentich, Karl F.	IHO	1945
Sullivan, Elizabeth A.	VB	1973,74,75
Sullivan, James M.	FB	1989
Sullivan, John T.	FB	1907,08
	BB	1906,07,08,09
Sullivan, Kevin	MCC	1993,94,95
	MTR	1994,95,96
Sullivan, Melissa	WSW	1994,95,96,97
Sullivan, Michael	FB	1993,94,95
Sullivan, Patrick J.	BB	1970,71,72,73
Sullivan, Robert C.	MBK	1955,56
Sullivan, Robert C.	MBK	1967,68,69
Sullivan, Timothy G.	MSW	1967,69
Sullivan, Will E.	BB	1897,98
Summers, Dorothy	WGY	1976,77
Sumpter, Rodney J.	MGO	1967,68,69
Superko, Arthur S.	BB	1930,31,32
Suprunowicz, Mack	MBK	1947,48,49,50
Surabian, Margaret	SS	1974,75,76,77
Sutherland, C.J.	FB	1889,90
Sutherland, George S.	FB	1947,49
Sutkiewicz, Rick A.	FB	1985,86,87
Sutton, Jennifer	WSW	1990,91,92
Sutton, John	FB	1889
Sutton, Robert J.	IHO	1979,80,81
Sutton, Walter J. (Pete)	MTR	1953,54
Svoboda, Sandra N.	WBK	1983,84,85,86
Swan, Arvid	MTN	1995,96
Swan, Don	FB	1921,24
Swan, Ryan	MTR	1996
Swanson, J. Elmer	BB	1953,54,56
	MTR	1953,54,56
	FB	1957,58
Swanson, Jeffrey M.	MTR	1975
Swanson, Jill	SS	1980,81,82
Swanson, Steven J.	MTN	1976
Swanson, Vernon L.	BB	1923
Swearengin, Julian	FB	1992

Sweat, Sean L.	MCC	1989,90,91,92
	MTR	1990,91,93,94
Sweazey, Douglas S.	MCC	1976,77,78
	MTR	1977,78,79
Sweeley, Everett	FB	1899,00,01,02
Sweeney, Lawrence M.	FB	1980,81,82,83
Sweeney, Thomas F.	MTR	1962,63,64,65
Sweet, Arthur G.	IHO	1954
Sweet, Carroll F. Jr.	MGO	1933,34,35
Sweet, Cedric	FB	1934,35,36
Swenson, Martha	WSW	1974
Swett, Robert	FB	1994,95,96
Swift, James E.	MTN	1963,64,65,66
Swift, LeRoy E.	MTR	1921
Swift, Thomas P.	FB	1944
Swilley, Ricky B.	MTR	1984,85,86
Swincicki, Renee	SB	1993,94
Switzer, Edward W.	BB	1955
	IHO	1955,56,57,58
Switzer, James D.	IHO	1984
Switzer, John S.	MTN	1915,16
Swix, Michelle	WSW	1989,90,91,92
Sword, Sam	FB	1995,96
Sygar, Daniel W.	BB	1980,81,82,83
Sygar, Richard S.	BB	1965,66,67
	FB	1964,65,66
Sylvester, Howland L.	MBK	1944
Syphax, Gregory C.	MTR	1970,71,72,73
Syring, Richard E.	BB	1958,59,60,61
	FB	1958,60
Syron, Bridget	WGO	1983,84
Sytek, James H.	FB	1958
Szabo, Christine	WTR	1991,92,93,94
	WCC	1990,91,92,93
Szabo, Lidia	WSW	1994,95,96,97
Szady, Sheryl M.	FH	1974
	WBK	1974
Szafranski, Roger A.	FB	1976
Szalwinski, Frank W.	BB	1955
Szara, Gerald R.	FB	1975,76,77
Szczechowski, Carol	WBK	1988,89,90,91
Szczesniak, Jeanine	VB	1995,96
Szenderski, Shaun R.	FB	1974
Szuba, Thomas D.	MSW	1973,74,75,76
Szydlowski, Ronald E.	FB	1973
Szymanski, Richard P.	FB	1961,62,63
Szyndlar, Erik	MBK	1996

T

Tabachino, Robert S.	FB	1984,85
Tack, Jeffrey B.	FB	1989
Tadian, Garabed	BB	1950,52,53,54
Tafel, Gretchen	WGY	1982
Taft, Henry C.	BB	1905,06,07,08
Taft, Jason	MGY	1993,94,95,96
Taft, William A.	BB	1948,49
Taggart, Herb M.	FB	1947
Tait, Charles R.	MBK	1987,88
Takach, Thomas J.	FB	1969
Talcott, William	FB	1898
Talley, Michael	MBK	1990,91,92,93
Tamagno, Chelso P.	MBK	1933,34,35,36
	FB	1932
Tamer, Christopher	IHO	1990,91,92,93
Tanderys, Jeffrey J.	BB	1988,89,90,91
Tanona, Leslie A.	BB	1964,65,66,67
Taraschuk, Katherine	WTN	1984
Tarbill, John W.	MTR	1929
Tarpley, Roy J.	MBK	1983,84,85,86
Tarrier, Randolph B.	MBK	1955,56,57,58
Tasch, Richard E.	WR	1937,38
Tashnick Jr., Anthony	MSW	1957,58,59
Tate, Kellyn	SB	1995,96,97
Tate, Ronald C.	BB	1962,63,64
	FB	1960
Taylor, Carrie	WSOC	1994
Taylor, Daydrion	FB	1995,96
Taylor, Gregory L.	MBK	1986,87,88
Taylor, Jennifer	WSOC	1995
Taylor, Joan	FH	1983,84,85,86
Taylor, LeVerne H. (Kip)	FB	1927
Taylor, Lonnie J.	FB	1971,74
Taylor, M. Kirk	MBK	1988,89,91,92
Taylor, Maurice	MBK	1995,96
Taylor, Michael	FB	1969,70,71
Taylor, Michael A.	FB	1987,88,89
Taylor, Michael E.	MCC	1971,72
	MTR	1972
Taylor, Robert J.	FB	1976
	WR	1977
Taylor, Ronald L.	FB	1973
Taylor, Tracy	SB	1994,95,96,97
Taylor, William L. (Billy)	FB	1969,70,71
Taylor, Sandra	SB	1980,81,82,83
Tebeau, Wesley B.	WR	1948

Tech, Karl E.	FB	1981
Tedesco, Dominic J.	FB	1976,77
Teeguarden, Ronald G.	MTN	1965,66,67,68
Teeter, Michael L.	FB	1986,87,88,89
Teeters, Randy	MSW	1993,94
Teetzel, Clayton T.	FB	1897
	MTR	1898,99,00
Teitelbaum, G.L.	IHO	1963,64
Teitelbaum, Jack	MBK	1933
	BB	1933,35
Telfer, William	WR	1945
Tellier, Tineke J.	WGY	1977
Temple, Mark A.	BB	1993,94,95,96
Templin, Lee F.	WR	1981
Teninga, Walter H.	FB	1945,47,48,49
Tenney, James C.	MTN	1959,60,61,62
Tennis, Chereena	VB	1994,95
Teppo, Jon A.	MSW	1986,87
Terris, Bradley	MGY	1996
Terry, Jonnie	FH	1981,82,83,84
Tessier, Jeff G.	IHO	1979,80,81,82
Tessmer, Estel	FB	1930,31,33
	MBK	1931,32,33,34
Teuscher, Charles G.	MBK	1957
	FB	1957
	MTR	1957
Tews, John	MGO	1944,45
Tharp, Kim	WSW	1976,77
Tharp, Randall J.	FB	1979,80,81
Thaxter, Joseph B.	MSW	1939,40,41
Thayer, William R.	IHO	1976,77,78
Theisen, Brian	MTR	1996
Thelwell, Richard M.	MTR	1960,61
Thibert, Steven J.	FB	1984,85,86,87
Thisted, Carl	FB	1925
Tholl, Bonita L. (Bonnie)	SB	1988,89,90,91
Thomas, Alfred S.	FB	1938
	MTR	1941,42
Thomas, Blair W.	WR	1928,32,33
Thomas, C.L.	MTR	1896,97,98
Thomas, Charles	FB	1891,92
Thomas, Earl C.	WR	1936,37,38
Thomas, Edmund J.	MBK	1937,38,39
Thomas, Glenn P.	BB	1916
Thomas, Gregory J.	MTR	1977,78,79,80
Thomas, James E.	WR	1969,70
Thomas, John E.	FB	1973
Thomas, John R.	FB	1968
Thomas, Joseph	FB	1896
Thomas, Katharine	FH	1990,91,92
Thomas, Lawrason D.	MSW	1953,54,55,56
Thomas, Marianne	VB	1977,78
Thomas, Melissa A.	SB	1981,82,83,84
Thomas, Michael A.	BB	1978,79
Thomas, Robert W.	MTR	1965,67,68
Thomas, Timothy P.	MTR	1977,78,79,80
Thomason, Robert A.	MTR	1945,46,48,49
Thompsen, Daniel	MTR	1994
Thompson, Clarence O.	FB	1993,94,95
Thompson, Janice	VB	1979
Thompson, Joel D.	MBK	1975,76,77,78
Thompson, Fredrick L.	MGY	1951
Thompson, Garde K.	MBK	1984,85,86,87
Thompson, George	FB	1910,11,12
Thompson, J.J.	MSW	1928,29
Thompson, John W.	MBK	1963,64,65,66
Thompson, Kourtney S.	BB	1986,87,88,89
Thompson, Mark C.	IHO	1964,65,66,67
Thompson, Melissa A.	WCC	1983,84,85,86
	WTR	1985,86,87,88
Thompson, Michael W.	BB	1980
Thompson Jr., Robert C.	FB	1979,80,81,82
Thompson, Tarnisha	VB	1989,90,91,92
Thompson, Wayne H.	MBK	1944
Thompson, William	BB	1955,56
Thompson, Yvonne	WBK	1987,88
Thomson, Waldemar A.	MSW	1937,38,39
Thornbladh, Robert N.	FB	1971,72,73
Thornton, John K.	MTR	1968,69,70,71
Thornton, Lorri	WTR	1980,81,82,83
Thorward, Benjamin F.	MTN	1910,12
Thorward, Theodore T.	MTN	1933,35,36
Thrasher, Steven D.	MSW	1960,61,63
Thrun, Thomas M.	IHO	1974
Thurlow, James P.	MSW	1954,55,56
Thurston, William E.	BB	1954,55,56
Thweatt, Suzette	WTR	1989,90,91,92
Tibbetts, Chad	MCC	1993
Tickman, Ronald J.	MGY	1977,79
Tidwell II, John W.	MBK	1958,59,60,61
Tiernan, Thomas L.	MBK	1949,50,51
Tiller, Claude J.	MTR	1986,87,88,89
Tillman, Marc L.	MTR	1989
Tillman, Thomas N.	MGY	1948,49,50
Tillotson, Peter S.	MBK	1955,56,57,58

Tillotson, Van W.	MBK	1963,65,66
Tilotson, Harry T.	BB	1933,34
Timberlake, Robert W.	FB	1962,63,64
Timm, Robert F.	FB	1950,51,52
Timmerman, Scott	BB	1990,91,92,93
Tincknell, Robert J.	FB	1973
Tinker, Horace	FB	1938,39
Tinkham, Bradley	BB	1994,95
Tinkham, David J.	FB	1950,51,52
Tinsley, Valerie	WTN	1976
Tippery, Kenneth A.	BB	1954,55,56,57
	FB	1953
Tippett, Bradley G.	IHO	1980,81,82,83
Tishman, John L.	FB	1946
Titas, Francis G.	FB	1967,68,69
Titone, Peter M.	BB	1968,69
Tittle, David S.	MSW	1946,48,49,50
Tobin, James E.	IHO	1939
	MTN	1939,40,41
Todd, Douglas W.	IHO	1977,78,79,80
Todd, John	IHO	1923,24
Todd, John H.	BB	1889,90
Todd, Karen	WSW	1992,93,94,95
Toepfer, A.K.	WR	1925
Toig, Randall M.	MTN	1969,70,71,72
Tolan, T. Edward	MTR	1929,30,31
Tolbert, Anthony	MBK	1990,91
Tomasi, Dom	FB	1945,46,47,48
	BB	1945,46,47,48
Tomasic, Andrew J.	MTR	1989,90,91,92
Tomek, Phillip C.	WR	1989,90,91,92
Tominac, Sheryl	SB	1978,79
Tomjanovich, Rudy	MBK	1968,69,70
Tomko, Kathleen	WTR	1991,93,94
Tommelein, Howard C.	BB	1953,54,55,56
Tompkins, Jack	IHO	1930,31,32
Tompkins, John A.	BB	1930,31,32
Toni, Royce	MGY	1991,93,94,95
Toole, Richard	MBK	1991,92
Tooman, Kathleen	SS	1974,75
Toomer, Amani	FB	1992,93,94,95
Topor, Ted P.	FB	1950,51,52
Topp, E. Robert	MBK	1951,52,53
	BB	1952
	FB	1950,51,52,53
Topp, Gene	FB	1952,53
Torbet, Roy	FB	1911,12,13
Torres, Alyson	WCR	1997
Torzy, Mark F.	FB	1978
Toth, Aaron	BB	1991,92,94,95
Totzke, John	FB	1928
Tower, Glenn L.	MTR	1908,09
Townsend, Brian L.	FB	1988,89,90,91
Townsend, Earl	MBK	1936
Townsend, Frederic	FB	1881
Townsend, John F.	MBK	1936,37,38
	MTR	1936,37,38
Townsend, Trinity	MTR	1993,94,95,96
Traber, Peter G.	FB	1973
Trainer, David	FB	1889,90
Trammell, Clara D.	WD	1986,87,88,89
Traphagan, Roice A.	FB	1913
Trapp, Deborah	SS	1977,78,79,80
Traupe, Eric H.	FB	1989,90
Travis, Jeff	MBK	1990
Treadway, Alicia	WSOC	1994
Tregoning Jr., Lawrence W.	MBK	1963,64,65
Trevarthen, Terry L.	MTR	1959,60
Trgovac, Michael J.	FB	1977,78,79,80
Trimborn, Ralph G.	MD	1946,47,48,49
Triplehorn, Howard	FB	1934

Roger Zatkoff (1950-52) is the namesake for the U-M Club of Detroit's top linebacker award.

Triplett, Todd E.	FB	1982
Trosko, Fred	BB	1938,39,40
	FB	1937,38,39
Trost, Kirk F.	WRR	1983,84,85,86
Troszak, Douglas A.	FB	1971,72,73
Trouhill, Thomas F.	BB	1901
Trout, Charles E.	FB	1920
Trowbridge, Ronald L.	MTR	1957,58,59,60
Trowbridge, W.R.	FB	1886
Trudeau, W. Randall	IHO	1972,73,74,75
Trueblood, B.C.	MGO	1902,03,05
Truitt, Brenda	WSW	1975,76,77
Truitt, Darrell F.	FB	1973,74,75
Trump, Jack	FB	1943
Truske, Joseph E.	BB	1929,30
Truskowski, Joe	FB	1926,28,29
Tryon, Charles T.	MTR	1898
Tryon, Fred M.	MTR	1898,99,01
Trytten, J. Perry	MSW	1942
Tschannen, Kent	MSW	1991,92,93,94
Tuerk, Christine	WBK	1984
	WTR	1985,86,87
Tucker, Curtis J.	FB	1971,72,73
Tucker, James E.	MBK	1976
Tudor, Connie L.	WBK	1983,84
Tuman, Jerame D.	FB	1995,96
Tummala, Srinivas	MTN	1989
Tumpane, Patrick W.	FB	1973,74
Tunnicliff, William H.	FB	1959,60,61
Tupper, Virgil	FB	1892
Turco, Marty	IHO	1995,96
Tureaud, Ken	FB	1959,60,61
Turek, Edward A.	BB	1989
Turetsky, Eric B.	MTN	1971,72
Turner, Bradley J.	IHO	1988,89,90
Turner, Dean C.	IHO	1977,78
Turner, Edwin T.	MTR	1931,32,33
Turner, Eric C.	MBK	1982,83,84
Turner, Immanuel	MTR	1994
Turner, Leigh C.	BB	1904
Turner, Leigh M.	MTR	1897,98,00
Turner, Tony A.	MD	1956,58,59
Turner, Valerie	WBK	1992,93
Turner, Renee	WTR	1979,80,81,82
Tussing, Thomas C.	MGO	1939,40
Twomey, John A.	MTR	1957,58,60
Tyler, Christine	WTR	1987,88,90
	WCC	1989,90
Tymko, Brenna	WSW	1987,88,89
Tyng, Alexander	FB	1870

U

Udell, Jon R.	MGY	1975
Udell, Louis N.	MTR	1901,02
Udvadia, Ava J.	WCC	1985,86,87,88
Ufer, Clarence E.	MTR	1915,16
Ufer, Robert P.	MTR	1941,42,43,44
Uhler, Warren G.	MSW	1961,62,63
Uhlmann, Richard O.	BB	1964,67
	FB	1963
Uhring, Heather	WCR	1997
Ulevitch, Herman	FB	1937
Ullyot, Ronald K.	IHO	1965,66,67,68
Ulvestad, Edward A.	MTR	1947,48,49,50
Unsworth, Gary T.	IHO	1957,58
Unsworth, Herbert H.	IHO	1931
Upthegrove, William R.	MSW	1947,48,49,50
Upton Jr., Herbert H.	IHO	1944,45,47
Upton, Arthur C.	MTR	1943
Urban, Diane	SS	1976,77
Urban, Jeffrey C.	IHO	1986,87,88,89
Urbanchek, Jon C.	MSW	1958,59,60
Uriah, Nicholas J.	FB	1975,76,77,78
Urick, Steve J.	BB	1936,37
Usher, Edward T.	FB	1918,20,21
Uteritz, Irwin	FB	1921,22,23
Utley, Jerome A.	BB	1900,01,02,03
Uttal, Lisa	WGY	1979,80
Utz, Irwin C.	BB	1921,22,23
Uzelac, Stevan	MGO	1954,55,56,57

V

Vahi, Lisa	VB	1984,85,86,87
Vainisi, Mark E.	FB	1992
Valek, Vincent	FB	1938
Valentine, Irving R.	MSW	1930,31
Valley, Richard L.	WR	1973,74,75,76
Vallortigara, John R.	MTR	1952,53,54,55
Valpey, Arthur L.	FB	1935,36,37
Van Appledorn, Scott	MSW	1988,89,90,91
Van Biesbrouck, Julian F.	IHO	1980
Van Boven, Leonard C.	BB	1923
Van Boven, Peter J.	BB	1919,20,21
Van Dyne, Yale F.	FB	1989,90,91
Van Mierlo, Chris	MGY	1978,79,80,82
Van Oeveren, Ryan C.	BB	1992,93,94,95
Van Orden, William J.	MTR	1921,23
Van Pelt Jr., James S.	FB	1955,56,57
Van Pelt, Toby	MTR	1991,93,94
Van Stee, Jill	WBK	1987,88,90,91
Van Summern, Robert W.	FB	1948,49
Van Tassell, Rodney	MSW	1991,92,93,94
Van Tongeren, Tim P.	MGO	1976,77
VanDervoort, Ed	FB	1922,23
VanDeWege Jr., Edwin J.	MBK	1977,78,79,80
VanDeWege, Len J.	MBK	1975
VanDyne, Rudd D.	FB	1956,59,60
VanOrden, Bill	FB	1920,21,22
VanVoorhis, Thomas C.	MTR	1949
Vance, John R.	BB	1976
Vance, Kimberly	SB	1979
VandeWater, Clarence H.	FB	1936,37
Vanden Broek, C.J.	MGY	1965,66,67
Vandenbark, Molly	WGO	1994,95,96,97
Vandenberg, Kris	FH	1974
Vandenberg, Kristy	SS	1974,75
Vandenberg, Robert W.	MCC	1984,85
	MTR	1984
Vander, Deb	VB	1973,74
	WBK	1974
Vander Kuy, Leo	MBK	1948,49,50,51
Vander Leest Jr., Robert	FB	1993,94,95
Vander Voort, Gary M.	MGY	1964,65,66,67
VanderPloeg, Melody	WTR	1982,83,84
VanderVelde, Edward J.	MSW	1935
Vanderbeek, Michael	FB	1993,94,96
Vandersluis, Kirstan A.	MSW	1982,83,84
Varian, Robin R.	MTR	1955,56,57,58
Varilke, James A.	MGY	1977,78,79,80
Varner, Cyrus B.	MBK	1972
Varner, Gregory B.	MSW	1986,87,88,89
Varvari, Rudy F.	IHO	1978,79,80,81
Vaughan, Michael W.	BB	1972
Vaughn, Jonathan S.	FB	1989,90
Vaughn, Rodney D.	FB	1977,78,79
Vaught, Loy S.	MBK	1987,88,89,90
Vaupre, Louis A.	MSW	1924
Vawter, Paul E.	MBK	1954
Veber, Christopher	MSW	1994,95
Vedejs, Christi	WSW	1985,86,87
Veigel, Lester L.	BB	1941
Vela, Jaime	BB	1980
Venhuizen, Brenda	WBK	1978,79,80,81
Ventura, Charles V.	MGY	1974,75,76,77
Ventura, Patricia	WGY	1982,83,84,85
Venturi, Bridget	SB	1985,86,87,88
	WBK	1989
Verburg, Myron	BB	1902
	MTR	1903
Vercel, Jovan	FB	1973
Verheyen, Alfred	BB	1910,11
Vernier, Robert W.	FB	1942,46
Vernor, Paul H.	MTR	1895,96,97
Verrall, Ben	MGY	1991,92,93,94
Veselenak, John J.	FB	1953,54
Vetter, George M.	MTR	1944,45,48
Vezina, John H.	MGO	1947
Vibert, Brady	WR	1995,96
Vick, Ernie	FB	1918,19,20,21
Vick, Henry A.	BB	1921,22
Vick, Richard	FB	1923
Victor, Julie	WTR	1990,91,92,93
Vidmer, Richard F.	FB	1965,66,67
Vieira, Claudia	WSW	1990,91,92
Viergever, John D.	FB	1933,34,35
	IHO	1933
	MTR	1933
Vieth, Paul W.	BB	1947,48
Vigiletti, Kenneth J.	MD	1979,80
Vigiletti, Kimberly	WD	1981
Vignevic, Catherine	FH	1989,90,91,92
Villa, Giovanni	FB	1893,94,95,96
Villarreal, Julian	BB	1976
Viola, Chris	WR	1996,97
Virgil, Bryan L.	FB	1978,79
Virgona, Alfred S.	BB	1949,50,51
Vismara, Lynn	SB	1987
Visser, Robin	VB	1980
Vitacco, Elly	SB	1991
Vitale, John S.	FB	1985,86,87,88
Voegtlen, Herbert D.	MTR	1946
Voelker, Emil J.	MTR	1925
Vogele, Jerry M.	FB	1974,75,76
Vogt, William F.	MTN	1957,58,60,61
Volk, Richard R.	BB	1965
	FB	1964,65,66
Volstad, Berit	VB	1994
von Richter, Owen	MSW	1995,96
Von Siegel, Donald J.	FB	1936,37,38
	MTR	1936
VonVoigtlander, Josephine	WCC	1980
Vose, James P.	MTN	1924,25,26
Voskuil, James T.	MBK	1989,91,92,93
Vreeland, V. Bruce	MTR	1948,49
Vry, John L.	MSW	1964,65,66
Vukovich, James M.	BB	1954,55,57
Vuocolo, Michael M.	FB	1960,61
	WR	1961,62
Vyse, Albert	MGO	1927,28

W

Wade, Andrew	BB	1994,95
Wade, George A.	MTR	1961,62,63,64
Wade Jr., Mark M.	MBK	1983,84,85,86
Wade, Mulford	FB	1887
Wadhams, Timothy	FB	1966,69
Wager, Adam	MTN	1992,93,94,95
Wagner Jr., Charles R.	BB	1979,80
Wagner, George M.	IHO	1974
Wagner, Robert B.	MGY	1968,69
Wagner, Robert W.	MSW	1927,28
Wagner, Steven R.	BB	1979
Wahl Jr., William C.	BB	1962,64,65
Wahl, Charles F.	FB	1944
Wahl, R. Allen	FB	1948,49,50
Wainess, P. Steven	MSW	1967,69
Waite, G.L.	MTR	1902,03
Waits, Edward A.	MTN	1966,67
Wakabayashi, Melvin H.	BB	1966
	IHO	1963,64,65,66
Wakefield, Richard	BB	1941
Walaitis, Frank W.	MSW	1928,29,30
Walch, John J.	BB	1909,10
Walchuck, Kenneth J.	MGO	1974,75,76,77
Waldo, Charles M.	MTR	1927,28
Waldron, Sherwood	IHO	1928
Walk, Raymond C.	MTR	1925
Walker, Alan G.	FB	1971
Walker, Allen	FB	1972
Walker, Art	FB	1952,53,54
Walker, Derrick N.	FB	1986,87,88,89
Walker, Fernando A.	BB	1883
Walker III, George W.	FB	1990
Walker, Harlan	FB	1918
Walker Jr., Jack C.	FB	1986
Walker, Jesse P.	MTR	1921,22
Walker, John C.	FB	1958,60,61
Walker, Joseph	BB	1990
Walker, M.F.	BB	1882
Walker, Marcus	FB	1991,92,93
Walker, Mary Ann	WSW	1977
Walker, Weldy W.	BB	1883,84
Wallace, Brian E.	FB	1990,91
Wallace, Coleman	FB	1989,90,91,92
Walker, Robert P.	MSW	1928,29,30
Wallace, Robert T.	MBK	1942
Wallace, Zeke	FB	1980
Wallingford, Anthony A.	MSW	1983,84,85,86
Wallingford, Ronald R.	MTR	1953,54,55,56
Walls Jr., Grant W.	FB	1960
Walls, Janet	FH	1976
Walls, Richard G.	MSW	1963,64,65,66
Walmroth, David J.	MTR	1980,81,82,83
Walmsley, Robert B.	MD	1966,67
Walsh, Mary Jane	VB	1973
Walter, Daniel L.	MTR	1953,54,55
Walter, Daniel R.	IHO	1964,65,66,67
Walter, Harland G.	BB	1925,26
Walters, Frank L.	MTR	1916
Walterhouse, David O.	MD	1977
Walterhouse, George	BB	1916,17
Walterhouse Jr., Richard	BB	1973,74,75,76
Walterhouse, Richard G.	BB	1943
Walters, James H.	MD	1952,53,54,55
Walters, Scott W.	MTR	1977,78,79
Waltner, Wilfred	BB	1910,11
Walton, William M.	MBK	1946
Waltz, Ralph M.	BB	1914,15
Wandersleben, Thomas C.	FB	1980
Wang, Patricia	VB	1984,85
Wangler, John T.	FB	1979,80
Ward, Aaron C.	IHO	1991,92,93
Ward, Carl D.	FB	1964,65,66
	MTR	1964,65,66
Ward, Dave	MGO	1929
Ward, Gilbert J.	MGO	1934
Ward, James A.	FB	1960,61,62
Ward, Jerod	MBK	1995,96,97
Ward, Willis	FB	1932,33,34
	MTR	1933,34,35
Wardley, Frank L.	FB	1942
Wardrop, John C.	MSW	1953,54,55
Wardrop, Robert	MSW	1953,54,55
Ware, Kenneth D.	MSW	1959,60,61

Ware, Dwayne K.	FB	1989,90,91,92
	MTR	1992
Ware, Margery	WBK	1986,87
Ware, Michael C.	MTN	1970,71,72,73
Ware, Stanton J.	BB	1933
Warland, Bjorn	MSW	1986,87,88
Warner, Donald R.	FB	1973
Warner, Edward L.	MSW	1929
Warner, Katrina	FH	1984,85,86,87
Warner, Matthew	WR	1997
Warren, Joe	WR	1996
Warren, Roderick E.	MTR	1949,50
Warren, Wayne A.	MGY	1954,55,56,57
Warren, William L.	MGO	1937
Warrick Jr., Woodward A.	WR	1944
Warshawsky, Albert	MTR	1956,57,58
Warth, Mark D.	FB	1979
Washburn, Carol	SB	1991
Washington, Brent	FB	1996
Washington III, Martin I.	FB	1968
Washington Jr., Sanford	FB	1981
Washington, Dennis	FB	1990
Washington, Gregory	FB	1984
Washington, MaliVai O.	MTN	1988,89
Wasilewski, Robert H.	BB	1975,76,77,78
Wasmund, William	FB	1907,08,09
Waterbor, E. Stanley	BB	1932,33,34
Waterman, Whitney	BB	1893,94
Waterman, William M.	WR	1964,66,67,68
Waters, Jean	SB	1986,87
Waters, William T.	WR	1984,85,86,88
Watkins, Carl J.	MTR	1966,67
Watkins, Charles F.	BB	1895,96
Watkins, James	FB	1907,09
Watkins, Kraig A.	MTR	1988,89,90
Watson, Alfred	WR	1926,27,28
Watson, Jeffrey J.M.	MTR	1986,87,88,89
Watson, Linda	WGY	1977,78
Watson, Nicholas	MCC	1994,95,96
	MTR	1996
Watson, Royal L.	BB	1901
Watson, Shawn	FB	1990
Watson, Thomas Y.	MSW	1927,28,29
Watson, W. Lee	MBK	1917
Watson, William	FB	1914,15
Watson, William D.	MTR	1937,38,39
Watt, Robert J.	IHO	1957,58,59,60
Watters, Michael R.	BB	1983,84,85
Watts, Harold	FB	1943,44,45,46
Watts, Jeffrey A	MSW	1969,71
Wayburn, Barrett S.	MSW	1951,52,53,54
Waymann, John R.	IHO	1976,77,78,79
Wayne, Gary A.	BB	1981,83,84
Weadcock, Arthur	BB	1920
Weathers, Andre L.	FB	1995,96
Weatherwax, Clyde B.	BB	1883,84
Weaver, Melanie	WCC	1979,80,81,82
	WTR	1980,81,82,83
Weaver, Scott	BB	1993,94,95
Webb, John M.	MTN	1951,52
Webb, Philip C.	MBK	1952
Webb, Phillip A.	FB	1985,86,87
	MTR	1984,87
Webb, Richelle	WTR	1991,92,93,94
Webber, Charles	BB	1901
Webber, Edward E.	BB	1913
Webber, M. Chris	MBK	1992,93
Weber, Gary	FB	1978,79
Weber, Mark D.	BB	1973,74,75,76
Weber, Susan	WTN	1978,79,80,81
Weber, Wally	FB	1925,26
Webster, John P.	MTN	1911
Webster, Keith R.	FB	1984,85
Webster, Louise H.	WSW	1983
Webster, McKenzie	WSOC	1994,95
Webster, Robert D.	MD	1958,60,61
Weckler, Jeanne	VB	1980,81,82,83
Wedenoja, Wilbert J.	MTR	1941
Wedge, Robert E.	FB	1966,67,68
	MTR	1968,69
Weeks, Alanson	FB	1898
Weeks, David M.	MTR	1924,25
Weeks, Edward C.	BB	1895
Weeks, Gordon A.	WR	1964,65,66,67
Weeks, Harold	FB	1907
Weeks, Harrison	FB	1899,00,01,02
Weemhoff, George A.	BB	1956,58,59
Wegener, C. Robert	MSW	1950
Wehner Jr., Harrison G.	MSW	1954,55,56,57
Weidenbach, William J.	MCC	1978,79,80
	MTR	1978,79,80,81
Weidig, Thomas A.	WR	1939,40,41
Weil, David C.	FB	1987,88
Weinberg, Richard E.	MSW	1946,47,48,49
Weingarten, Jill	FH	1973

Weinmann, Thomas R.	FB	1967
Weinstein, Barb	WD	1979,80
Weinthaler, Stacey	WSW	1987
Weintraub, Louis	BB	1927,28,29
Weir, D. Scott	MSW	1977,78,79,80
Weise, Rebecca	SS	1981
Weisenburger Jr., John E.	FB	1975
	BB	1976
Weisenburger Sr., John E.	BB	1945,46,47,48
	FB	1944,45,46,47
Weiskopf, Michael G.	FB	1992,93,93
Weiss, Benjamin	MBK	1920,21
Weiss, Henry	MBK	1930,31,32
Weitzel, George	IHO	1924,25,26
Welborne, Sullivan A.	FB	1987,88,89,90
Welch, Carl	BB	1963,64
Welchans, Jori	WSOC	1994,95,96
Welke, Karen	WCC	1987,88,89
	WTR	1989
Welke, Karl F.	MTR	1988,89,90
Welker, Karl F.	MCC	1988,89
Wellington, Frederick C.	MTN	1942,43,46
Wells, Charles	MCC	1927
Wells, Heather	VB	1989,90
Wells, Philip J.	MTR	1980,81,82,83
Wells, Rex C.	MBK	1944
	FB	1943
Wells, Richard C.	FB	1963,64,65
	MTR	1964,65
Wells, Russell C.	MTN	1957
Wells, Stanfield	FB	1909,10,11
Welsh, James E.	MSW	1939,40,41
Welton, Arthur D.	FB	1886
	BB	1885,86
Wendell, Roswell	BB	1904,05,06
Wendt, Eric W.	FB	1994
Wendt, John A.	MTR	1988
Wendt, Roy L.	MBK	1954
Wengrofsky, Nicole	WSW	1988
Wenrich, Wesley W.	MGY	1952,54
Wenson, Paul F.	BB	1985,86
Wentworth, Deborah L.	VB	1975
Wentworth, Lloyd J.	BB	1894
Wentworth, Peter A.	FB	1986
Wentz, Wayne A.	FB	1964
	WR	1965,66,68,69
Wenzel, Jan O.	MSW	1993,94,95,96
Wenzel, Martha	WD	1991,92,93,94
Wenzell, Peter J.	IHO	1977
Werner, Frank J.	IHO	1972,73,74,75
Werner, Mark W.	FB	1968,69
Wesbrook, Walter K.	MTR	1919,20
	MTN	1919
Weske, Dick	FB	1915,16,17
West, Charles R.	MGO	1964,65,66
West, Frank C.	MTR	1909
	MBK	1909
West, Robert G.	MSW	1941,42,43
West, Steven	MSW	1992,93,94,95
Westerberg, M. Harold	MSW	1945
Westerby, Kristine	WTR	1992,94
	WCC	1993
Westerman, Harold S.	MBK	1941,46
Westfall, Bob	FB	1939,40,41
Westfall, Christopher M.	MGO	1983,84,85,86
Westfall, Wendy	WGO	1994,95,96,97
Westfall, William A.	MTR	1898,99,00
Weston, Archie	FB	1917,19
Westover, Louis W.	FB	1931,32,33
Westrate, Jackie	WSW	1982
Wettlaufer, Lori	WSW	1977
Wetzel, Calvin G.	MTR	1920
Weyers, John W.	FB	1944
Weygandt, J. Allan	BB	1951
Weyl, George J.	MTR	1931
Whalen, Jim	FB	1915
Wheatley, Tyrone	FB	1991,92,93,94
	MTR	1993,94,95
Wheeler, Bradner D.	MTR	1920,21
Wheeler, Clare	FB	1928,29,30
Wheeler, Donald A.	MTR	1976,77,78,79
Wheeler, George B.	BB	1906,07,08
Wheeler, William E.	IHO	1976,77,78,79
Wherry, Henry P.	MTN	1900,01,02
Whitaker, Michael D.	MSW	1970,71,72,73
White, Albert	MBK	1996
White, Brent D.	FB	1986,87,88,89
White, Christine	VB	1990,91,92
White, Gerald E.	FB	1984,85,86
White, Gibson A.	MD	1953,54,55
White, Howell	FB	1922,23
White, Hugh	FB	1898,00,01
White, James A.	MSW	1949,50,51,52
White, James B.	IHO	1986,87,88,89
White, Jeanne	WBK	1979,80,81

White, John T.	FB	1946,47
White, Paul G.	FB	1941,42,43,46
	BB	1942,43,47
White, Richard A.	MBK	1974,75
	FB	1976,77
White, Robert C.	IHO	1957,58,59,60
White, Robert E.	FB	1969
White, William C.	IHO	1959,60,61,62
White, William T.	BB	1924
Whiteaker, Charles C.	MTR	1950,51
Whiteford, David W.	FB	1975
Whitehead, Philip A.	FB	1977,78,79
Whitehouse Jr., Frank	FB	1947,48
Whitledge, John R.	FB	1986
Whitley, Robert J.	WR	1973
Whitlock, Robert C.	MBK	1921
Whitney, Herbert P.	BB	1900
Whitney, Robert P.	MTN	1949
Whitridge, Bradford	MSW	1994
Whitten, John P.	MBK	1971,72,73,74
Whittingham, Manfred G.	MSW	1924,25,26
Whittle, John D.	MBK	1929
	FB	1927
Wicks, Douglas H.	FB	1947
Widman, Charles	FB	1898
Widmann, Frederick C.	MTN	1930
Wiebeck, Kenneth A.	MSW	1965,66,67,68
Wieman, Elton (Tad)	FB	1916,17,20
Wiemer, Jeanne	WSW	1987,88,89
Wierda, Gerrit J.	MBK	1947,48
Wiese, Bob	FB	1942,43,44,46
	MBK	1943,44
	BB	1943,44,47
Wiese, Nicholas	MGY	1954,55,56,57
Wiezycki, Ryan J.	MGO	1982
Wigglesworth, Sharon	WCC	1979
Wikel, Howard L.	BB	1943,47,48
	FB	1943,47
Wilbanks, Ambrose S.	WR	1958,60
Wilcher, Thomas	FB	1985,86
	MTR	1984,85,86,87
Wilcox, Andrea L.	WBK	1982,82,83
Wilcox, Gary G.	WR	1961,62,63,64
Wilcox, John H.	FB	1946,47
	MTR	1951
Wildfong, Brian	MTR	1994,95,96
Wiley, John M.	MBK	1957
	MTN	1957,58,59,60
Wiley, Diana	WBN	1982,83,84
	WTR	1984
Wilhite, Clayton E.	FB	1964,65,66
Wilhite, James R.	FB	1967,68
Wilkening, Richard K.	MSW	1987,88,89,90
Wilkie, Gordon J.	IHO	1961,62,63,64
Wilkins, F. Stuart	FB	1945,46,47,48
Wilkinson, Alfred E.	BB	1865,66,67, 68,69
Wilkinson, Thomas L.	BB	1886,87,91
	MTR	1888,89,90
Wilkinson, Wendy	WGY	1991,93,94
Willard, Ross P.	MTR	1945
Williams, Craig B.	MBK	1978
Williams Sr., Thomas V.	MSW	1940,41
Williams, Andrea R.	VB	1984,85
Williams, Angela	WGY	1985,86,87,88
Williams, Anthony C.	FB	1994,95
Williams, Ashley	WGO	1994,95,96,97
Williams, Bryan	FB	1995,96
Williams, Calvin J.	MTR	1977,78,79,80
Williams, Clarence	FB	1995,96
Williams, Cornel	MBK	1977,78
Williams, David S.	MTR	1974,75,76
Williams, Debra E.	WTR	1979,80,81,82
Williams, Derek	FB	1979
Williams, Gerald H.	FB	1952,53,54
Williams, Guy R.	MSW	1987
Williams, Harvey A.	MBK	1954,55,56
Williams, J. Otis	FB	1988,89,90,91
Williams, Jack G.	MBK	1919,20,21
Williams, Jerry	FB	1953,54
Williams, Josh	FB	1996
Williams, Justin C.	MTR	1948,49,50
Williams, Kenneth L.	MGY	1964,65,66
Williams, Kevin	WR	1991,94
Williams, Kyron K.	FB	1976,78
Williams, Louis	MTR	1957,58,59
Williams, Lyle K.	BB	1935,37
Williams, Michael E.	MBK	1977
Williams, Phillip B.	MTR	1960,61
Williams, R. Jamison	FB	1928
Williams, Richard G.	MBK	1949,51
Williams, Ronald M.	FB	1952,53
Williams, Stephen M.	MTR	1959,60,62
Williams, Steven	MSW	1995,96
Williams, Timothy L.	FB	1987,88,89

Williams, Tracy	FB	1988
Williams, Virgil	FB	1979
Williams, William A.	IHO	1931,32
Williamson, Ivan	FB	1930,31,32
	MBK	1931,32
Williamson, Kevin V.	MSW	1978,79,82
Williamson, Nicole	WSW	1991,92,93,94
Williamson, Richard P.	FB	1966,67
Williamson Jr., Walter L.	FB	1972,73
Willingham, John R.	FB	1986,87
Willington, Frederick C.	MTN	1942,43,46
Willis Jr., Richard	IHO	1992,93,94,95
Willmer, Frederick R.	MTR	1950
Willner, Gregg F.	FB	1977,78
Willoughby, Robert J.	MGY	1948,49
Wills, Warren M.	IHO	1957,58
Wilmore, Henry A.	MBK	1970,71,72,73
Wilmot, Brett	MSW	1996
Wilmot, Francis	IHO	1927
Wilpon, Fred	BB	1956
Wilson, C. Wilford	MBK	1919,20
Wilson, Curtis G.	MSW	1975
Wilson, Don	FB	1929
Wilson, Ebin	FB	1901
Wilson, Edwin C.	MTN	1913
Wilson, Hugh	FB	1920,21
Wilson III, Hugh	WR	1944
Wilson, Christine	WCC	1993
Wilson, Edward A.	BB	1934
Wilson, Hugh E.	BB	1922
Wilson, Janet	WTN	1974,75,76,77
Wilson, Joseph	MBK	1909
Wilson, Michael	FB	1983
Wilson, Steven F.	BB	1924,25,26
Wilson, Thomas A.	MGO	1960
	MTR	1959
Wilson, Thomas H.	IHO	1958,59,61
Wilson, Walter E.	WR	1931,32,33
Wimbles, Clark M.	BB	1922
Wine, Raymond L.	FB	1956,57
Wingrove, T.C.	IHO	1994
Wink, Jack S.	FB	1943
Wink, Kristi	WCC	1990,91,92,93
	WTR	1991
Winkel, Kathy	WSW	1991
Winkler Jr., William	MGY	1952,53,54,55
Winkler, Brian	MGY	1992,93,94,95
Winkley, Alan	MTR	1965,68
Winski, Allison L.	WGY	1990,91,92,93
Winslow, George H.	BB	1873
Winston, Todd B.	BB	1989,90,91
Winter, Jarret R.	MSW	1988,89,90,91
Winterlee, Scott	BB	1990,91,92,93
Winters, Charles	FB	1993,94,95,96
	BB	1995
Wise, Clifford C.	BB	1941,46,47
	FB	1940,42
Wise Jr., Eric W.	MSW	1988,89,90
Wise, H.A.	BB	1865
Wise, John R.	MTR	1941
Wise, Lynne	WTN	1985,86,87
Wise, Martha	WSW	1993,94,95
Wiseman, Brian A.	IHO	1991,92,93,94
Wisner, Harry K.	MTR	1939,40,41
Wisniewski, Irvin C.	MBK	1947,48,49,50
	FB	1947,48,49
Wisniewski, Marvin J.	BB	1952,53,54,55
Wisniewski, Renee	WGY	1987
Wissing, Joseph R.	BB	1979,80
Wistert, Albert A.	FB	1940,41,42
	WR	1942
Wistert, Alvin L.	FB	1947,48,49
Wistert, Francis	FB	1931,32,33
	BB	1932,33,34
Witherspoon, Julian	MTR	1944,45
Witherspoon, Thomas W.	FB	1950,51,52
Witter, Emily	VB	1975,76,77
Wittman, Leslie G.	MTR	1923,25
Wohl, Terri	WGO	1985,86,87,88
Wojcikiewicz, Kimberle J.	WGO	1988
Wolbert, Michelle	WCR	1997
Wolf, Andrea	WSW	1981,82,84
Wolf, Frank	MCC	1989
Wolf, Frederick D.	MSW	1959,60,61,62
Wolf, Mary Lou	FH	1977,78,79
Wolf, Ronald G.	BB	1986
Wolf, William J.	BB	1897,98
Wolfe, Harmon A.	MCC	1930,31,32
Wolfe, Larry A.	MTR	1969,70,72
Wolfe, Randy J.	BB	1984,85
Wolff, Robert F.	BB	1948,49,50
Wolin, Jack R.	MSW	1938,40,41
Wolter, James R.	FB	1949,50,51
Wombacher, John	FB	1895,96
Wong, Pia	WD	1982

Wood, Charles R.	MTR	1930
Wood, Beverly	SS	1980
Wood, David D.	MBK	1940
Wood, F.N.	BB	1872
Wood, George	FB	1887
Wood, Jeff	MTR	1994,95,96
Wood, Junius B.	MTR	1896,97,98,
		99,1900
Wood, Lisa B.	WTN	1978,79
Wood, Robert L.	FB	1975,76
Wood, Rodney	FB	1987
Woodard, Joseph	WR	1930,31
Woodbury, Colleen	WBK	1975
Woodford, Anthony B.	FB	1975
Woodlock III, John S.	FB	1991
Woodmore, Derek	FB	1985
Woodruff, Dawn	WCC	1979,80,81,82
	WTR	1979,80,81,82
Woodruff, P.G.	FB	1881
Woods, Cinnamon	WD	1991,92,93,94
Woods, James J.	MTR	1986,87,88
Woods, Joshua	BB	1990
Woods, Terry	BB	1990,91,92
Woodson, Charles	FB	1995
Woodton, Roy D.	MTR	1963,64,65,66
Woodward, Paul W.	FB	1962,63
Woodworth, Paul	FB	1891,92
Wooldridge, Leah	WBN	1989,90,91,92
Woolfolk, Harold E. "Butch"	FB	1978,79,80,81
	MTR	1979,80,81,82
Woolley, Carl T.	MSW	1956,58,59,60
Woolley, David K.	MTR	1982,83,84
Woolley, Edwin L.	FB	1968
Woolsey, William S.	MTN	1937,38,39
Woolwine, Edward J.	BB	1985,86,87,88
Workman, Harry	FB	1906
Wormwood, Frank	FB	1881,82
Worrell, Lionel R.	MBK	1974
Worzniak, Lisa	WTN	1990,91
Woschitz, Robert	BB	1951,52,53,54
Wouda, Marcel	MSW	1993,94,95
Wozniak, Alexander R.	BB	1996
Wreford Jr., William B.	MSW	1937
Wreford, Charles R.	IHO	1961
Wright, Charles D.	FB	1885,86,87
	MTR	1885,86
Wright, David	IHO	1991
Wright, Delman H.	WR	1953
Wright, Elizabeth	WD	1980,82,83
Wright, Gregory C.	WR	1983
Wright, Harry T.	FB	1933,35
	WR	1933,36
Wright, Hugh M.	MGO	1950,51,52,53
Wright, Kenneth J.	FB	1965,66
Wright, Laurel	WSW	1981,82
Wright, Marlon C.	BB	1996
Wright, Pamela	SB	1986
Wright, Ralph E.	MBK	1924
Wright, Timothy L.	MGY	1968,69,70
Wright, William D.	MBK	1955,56,57,58
Wriston, Jeffrey P.	MSW	1983
Wroten, Randal M.	BB	1978,79,80,81
Wuerfel, Joshua C.	FB	1992
Wuerfel, Ted C.	MCC	1928
Wunderli, Gregory P.	FB	1979
Wunderlich, Eric A.	MSW	1989,90,91,93
Wurfel, Mark M.	MGY	1988,89
Wyatt, Christopher	MTN	1993,94,95
Wyckoff, Mary	WTR	1986,87,88
Wyckoff, Teresa	WBN	1978
Wyland, Douglas J.	WR	1986,87
Wylie, Brian D.	MSW	1975,77
Wyman, James P.	MTR	1957,60,61
Wymer, Elizabeth	WGY	1993,94,95,96
Wyngarden, Geoffrey	BB	1991,92
Wynn, William	FB	1947
Wyrybkowski, Christi	SB	1995

Y

Yaffai, Salem	WR	1988,89,90,91
Yaffe, James S.	MGO	1980,81,82
Yahn, Marc F.	MGO	1962,63,64,65
Yani, Andy	MTN	1994,95
Yanz, John A.	FB	1962,64
Yanz, Richard C.	FB	1967
Yarano, Daniel A.	FB	1983
Yates, Carrie	WTR	1989,90,91,92
	WCC	1991
Yawger, Frederick H.	MSW	1974,75,76,77
Yearby, William M.	MBK	1963
	FB	1963,64,65
	MTR	1964,65
Yearnd, William H.	MGO	1937,38
Yee, Darrell A.	MGY	1978,79,80,81
Yee, Geary Y.	MTR	1974
Yerges, Howard F.	FB	1944,45,46,47
Yerkes, Raymond F.	WR	1987
Yirkosky, Richard N.	BB	1950,51,52,53
	FB	1950
Yoanides, George L.	MTR	1981,82,83,84
Yockey, Jeanne	WBK	1980
Yont, J.G.	FB	1894,95
York, Bert S.	MTR	1897
Yost, Fielding	FB	1931
Young, Douglas M.	MBK	1990
Young, Jacob	WR	1994,95,96
Young, Jeffrey L.	FB	1973,74,75
Young, John	MGY	1993,94
Young IV, John	MGY	1993,94
Young, John R.	BB	1979,80,81,82
Young, Josh	WR	1996
Young, Kathryn	WBK	1976,77
Young, Kim	SS	1974,75,76
Young, Thomas C.	MGO	1973
Young, William H.	BB	1933
Youngberg, Richard S.	MGO	1958,59,60
Yoxheimer, Steven R.	IHO	1981,82
Yuan, Steven	MGY	1986,87,88
Yuhn, Colleen A.	WCC	1989
	WTR	1990
Yuhn, Judy	WCC	1981,82,83,84
	WTR	1982,85

Z

Zacharias, Steven T.	FB	1989
Zachary, Jack	FB	1958
Zadel, Michael A.	MGY	1966,67
Zaharoff, Annette	WTN	1974,75
Zahn, Geoffrey C.	BB	1965,66,67
Zahour, Douglas L.	MGY	1977,79,80
Zaitzeff, Lawrence P.	MTN	1958,59
Zakrajsek, Jennifer	WSW	1990,91,92,93
Zald, Roberta L.	FH	1974,75,76,77
	SB	1978
	WBK	1974
ZanFagna, Donald M.	FB	1951
	IHO	1949
Zann, Robert B.	MSW	1968,69,70,71
Zann, Gregory J.	MSW	1968,69,71
Zatkoff, Roger	FB	1950,51,52
Zauner, John C.	WR	1960,61
Zausmer, Mark J.	MTN	1976
Zdravkovich, Dimitrije M.	FB	1978,78
Zelna, Patricia	WGY	1977
Zemon, Julian L.	MTN	1923
Zenkel, Gary B.	MGO	1982,83
Zenkewicz,Trent	FB	1992,93,94,95
Zepp Jr., William C.	BB	1964,65,66,67
Zervas, Stephen J.	FB	1954,55,57,55
	WR	1956,57
Zieger, Harold	FB	1916
Ziegler, David P.	MBK	1975
Zielinski, Ronald	FB	1990
Ziem Sr., Frederick C.	FB	1936
Ziemann, Chris	FB	1996
Ziemann, Frederick S.	MTN	1947
Zimmerman, Bob	FB	1939
Zimmerman, Eric L.	WR	1995
Zimmerman, Frank E.	IHO	1975,76,77,78
Zimmerman, Jennifer	WGO	1992,93,94,95
Zimmerman, Kurt D.	BB	1983,84,85,86
Zingales, John S.	FB	1985,86
Ziots, Paul M.	FB	1982
Ziskie, Daniel A.	MTR	1963,66
Zobler, Kate	WGY	1978
Zoellin, Frederick J.	MTR	1918
Zonder, Erica J.	WGO	1989,90,91,92
Zubkus, E. James	FB	1959,61
Zuccarelli, David C.	FB	1968,69,71,72
Zuganelis, George M.	FB	1969
Zurbrugg, Christopher M.	FB	1984,85,86
Zuver, Jerry L.	FB	1974,75,76
Zyjewski, Julianne	SB	1979,80,81